Drugs and the American Dream

Edited by
PATRICIA A. ADLER, PETER ADLER, and PATRICK K. O'BRIEN

DRUGS AND THE AMERICAN DREAM

AN ANTHOLOGY

WILEY-BLACKWELL

A John Wiley & Sons, Ltd., Publication

This edition first published 2012
© 2012 John Wiley & Sons, Inc.

Wiley-Blackwell is an imprint of John Wiley & Sons, formed by the merger of Wiley's global
Scientific, Technical and Medical business with Blackwell Publishing.

Registered Office

John Wiley & Sons, Ltd, The Atrium, Southern Gate, Chichester, West Sussex, PO19 8SQ, UK

Editorial Offices

350 Main Street, Malden, MA 02148-5020, USA

9600 Garsington Road, Oxford, OX4 2DQ, UK

The Atrium, Southern Gate, Chichester, West Sussex, PO19 8SQ, UK

For details of our global editorial offices, for customer services, and for information about how
to apply for permission to reuse the copyright material in this book please see our website at
www.wiley.com/wiley-blackwell.

The right of Patricia A. Adler, Peter Adler, and Patrick K. O'Brien to be identified as the authors
of the editorial material in this work has been asserted in accordance with the UK Copyright,
Designs and Patents Act 1988.

Library of Congress Cataloging-in-Publication Data

Drugs and the American dream : an anthology / edited by Patricia A. Adler, Peter Adler,
and Patrick K. O'Brien.
     p.   cm.
   Includes bibliographical references and index.
   ISBN 978-0-470-67027-9 (pbk. : alk. paper)
1. Drug abuse–Social aspects–United States.   2. Drug abuse–United States.
3. Drug control–United States.   4. Alcoholism–Social aspects–United States.
I. Adler, Patricia A.   II. Adler, Peter, 1951–   III. O'Brien, Patrick K.
   HV5825.D7898 2012
   362.290973–dc23

                                                    2011044221

A catalogue record for this book is available from the British Library.

Set in 10/12pt Bembo by SPi Publisher Services, Pondicherry, India
Printed and bound in Singapore by Markono Print Media Pte Ltd

1   2012

TO DRUG USERS: Do So Safely and With Moderation
TO DRUG ABUSERS: Don't
and
TO DRUG ABSTAINERS: It's a Choice

Contents

Part I: Perspectives on Drug Use   **1**

History and Theory

Drug Scares and Moral Panics

Part II: Social Correlates of Drug Use 61

Part III: Drug Lifestyles   213

Managing Drug Use

The Economics of Drugs

Crime and Violence

Part IV: Societal Response to Drug Use   313

Education

Figures and Tables

Figures

Tables

Preface and Acknowledgments

Paraphrasing Dickens, drugs may represent the best of times, and/or the worst of times. For some people, drugs may enhance their sociability, happiness, ecstasy, intimacy, dis-inhibition, and serve as a social lubricant. Other drugs help people increase their concentration, improve their work, enhance their focus, and control difficult parts of their intellect and emotion. Still more may aid people in gaining relief from uncontrollable mood swings, depression, and anguish, providing what were considered, a decade or two ago, "miracle cures." That's why they call it "getting high."

For others, drugs may lead to despair and trouble, spiraling them downward into cycles of depression, addiction, loss of self-control (and the accompanying loss of relationships, jobs, housing, and self-respect), poverty, anxiety, pain, desolation, hopelessness, anguish, gloom, despondency, dejection, physical debilitation, and overdosing/death. That's why they call it "down and out."

The ingestion of chemical substances for purposes of consciousness alteration has been practiced in virtually all human cultures and in all epochs of history. Sometimes this leads to problems, sometimes it does not. How a society defines and deals with drug use has a major impact upon whether drug use will result in abuse and problems. Even how we come to understand the concept of abuse is related to societal definitions. Contrary to popular wisdom, the mere existence of drug-related social harm or human suffering is not enough to constitute a "drug problem." The total social costs of the harm done by a single licit drug such as alcohol or tobacco dwarf the total costs and suffering related to *all* illicit drugs combined. Yet, we tend to think of alcohol and tobacco use as "normal" (though, interestingly, decreasingly less so in an era of "new sobriety") while the use of illicit drugs is automatically stigmatized as "deviant." We accept doctors' orders as "medically prescribed," but sometimes don't consider the effects of these medications on us because they are defined as "legitimate." Many of these drugs, such as Vioxx, which were approved by the Federal Drug Administration (FDA) were on the market for years, only to find out later that they have deleterious long-term effects and needed to be recalled. Thus, even drugs that undergo the most stringent trials before they are allowed to be introduced for human consumption can later turn out to be dangerous. Such conceptions are almost never based upon "objective" evidence, but rather reflect society's conflicts and express the fears and interests of dominant groups − conflicts, fears, and interests that are rarely related directly to the chemical substances themselves.

The vicissitudes of drug use range in the American dream throughout the entire socioeconomic spectrum of society, among all race/ethnicities and ages, and in all genders. Although the public stereotypically associates certain drugs and behaviors with specific demographic groups, sociological studies reveal that these are sometimes true and sometimes false. Our society, as the late drug historian David Musto pointed out, has gone through phases of extreme cycles regarding attitudes toward drug use, swinging from repression to embracement and back. Among other first-world countries, the United States is regarded as a bastion of prohibitionism with an unbalanced (and unsuccessful) emphasis on deterrence, interdiction, and punishment to the detriment of treatment, education, public health, and harm reduction. Drugs periodically spike in and out of the news, arousing public interest with the latest "scares" and developments. During the 1992 campaigns of George Bush, Sr and Bill Clinton, for example, drugs were a top policy concern (invoking Clinton's now infamous "I did not inhale" comment), yet during the Barack Obama vs. John McCain election of 2008 hardly a peep was heard about illicit substances, with the exception of some policy issues concerning drug dealing based violence on the Mexican–American border. Enormous amounts of money and political calculation continue to be fueled into America's global "war on drugs."

Our national attention is drawn to these waxes and wanes in drug usage and the changing moral meanings accompanying them. New drugs burst upon the scene, become wildly popular, are attacked by law enforcement, draw moral panics, and fade, only to be replaced by others or to be recycled in new incarnations. People of different ages hold vastly different attitudes toward various drugs and the potential dangers they represent.

College students are one of the age groups most interested in drugs. On their own for the first time, they are at a stage of life where they question their parents' lifestyles and values, explore new identities, and are highly immersed in their peer culture. Drugs are a prominent aspect of the college experience, and norms encouraging drug use (especially alcohol) are widely prevalent. Today's college students may be particularly interested in enrolling in courses on "Drugs and Society" (which can be under a sociology, criminology, or criminal justice curriculum) and these classes usually fill to capacity. These students run the gamut from those who do drugs and want to find out more about them, to those who have had previous problems and have gone through treatment for abusing drugs, to those who desire to go into law enforcement and want to punish people who use illicit drugs. This course may be established for majors only, but where it is not, it draws enormous interest as an elective. Students' attitudes toward drugs are likely to be affected by a number of sociological trends our society is currently experiencing.

First, in July 2008, a consortium of chancellors and presidents of universities and colleges across the United States launched the "Amethyst Initiative." These higher education leaders signed a public statement asserting that the problem of irresponsible drinking by young people continues despite the minimum legal drinking age of 21, and there is a culture of dangerous binge drinking on many campuses. The Amethyst Initiative supports informed and unimpeded debate on the 21-year-old drinking age, suggesting that lowering it to 18 might diminish young people's binge drinking before going out to bars and parties. Thus, the legalization of alcohol for college-age students is being debated.

Second, these young people have grown up during an era in which the stigma of some prescription drugs has greatly diminished. Although taking antidepressants and medications for controlling ADD was once regarded as a psychological deficit and shamefully hidden, these are now widely prescribed and used. The availability of such drugs on college campuses is rife, with many students accepting their non-prescribed use for studying. Even steroids, which are still broadly condemned, are becoming recognized as pervading certain segments of prestigious American sectors. This rise in prescription drug abuse is one of the emerging trends on the national scene.

Finally, marijuana is once again undergoing a decriminalization movement. Fourteen states and DC have now enacted laws that legalize medical marijuana use. New legislation or ballot measures are pending in eight more states. These trends may serve to legitimate drug use in the eyes of college students. In fact, in 2010, California had on its ballot an initiative that would legalize the use of marijuana for all citizens (of age), and although it lost by a margin of 55% to 45%, many argued that it was the unclear wording on the ballot, as much as any moral problems, that accounted for this defeat. Nevertheless, this vote shows significant interest in the legalization of marijuana, and it would not be hyperbole to suppose that its legality is not that far off into the future. In 2011, President Obama indicated that he was opposed to legalization, but thought that marijuana and other drugs were more of a public health issue, rather than a legal, moral, or medical one.

At the same time, drugs remain a scare for many sectors of the American public. Parents who send their children off to college worry about binge drinking and the rampant use of recreational drugs such as marijuana, cocaine, ecstasy, and psychedelics. Businesses report declining productivity, worker absenteeism, lack of care, and health problems by their employees due to the use of drugs (including alcohol and tobacco). The hegemonic psycho-medical community continues to demonize almost all illicit drugs, stigmatizing their detrimental effects and the life-long problems that they can engender. There are very few politicians who dare to run on a pro-drugs platform, as that would be one of the easiest ways to lose an election.

Thus, drugs still symbolically represent the best of times and the worst of times to many segments of the population, and interest rides high. It is our hope that this book presents a balanced approach to drugs, one that neither calls for their total legalization and liberation nor suggests that all drugs should be banned and prohibited in society. It should also be noted that this book is based on a "harm reduction" model, indicating that we do not believe that the altering of consciousness among our citizenry can be stopped altogether (the government's "Partnership for a Drug-Free America" is an impossible goal), but that if drugs will be part of the American landscape then people should have honest, truthful, and accurate knowledge of their effects, benefits, and detriments ("Just Say Know").

Our Book

Our book undertakes an examination of the relationship between drugs and social contexts. Understanding the nature of this relationship is critical for gaining insight into why, despite the risks, people find consciousness alteration meaningful, what kinds of experiences and problems arise from their use, and what types of social policies emerge in attempts to control use. We begin by exploring various sociological themes as they relate to the use of drugs in American society. Specific areas of interest will include: (1) the shifting perspectives and definitions on drug usage in society; (2) the emergence of drug crusades, moral panics, and drug legislation in America; and (3) the differences between "licit" and "illicit" drugs and why they become defined as such. The middle section of the book employs a sociological conceptualization, organizing selections around the themes of race/ethnicity, class, gender, and age. These are the current "hot topics" in sociology and criminology, and are the core building blocks that characterize these disciplines. This more original treatment will find resonance with many faculty and students. We conclude with a comprehensive examination and critical analysis of the drug treatment, rehabilitation, and education industries that have surfaced to reduce the level of drug-related problems, as well as with a section on drug policy informed by the harm reduction approach.

Drugs and the American Dream offers the most contemporary readings, with most selections (except classic historical and theoretical treatises) drawn from the twenty-first century. Our book is also noteworthy in its selection of entirely ethnographic empirical pieces, eschewing the demographic articulation of drug use that bores students (these are available in most of the texts on the market), and stimulating them with richly descriptive portrayals that place readers directly into the perspective of drug users, through their own voices.

We want this book to pull students into its chapters, giving them a compelling sense of some worlds that are exotic and different from theirs as well as some that are more experience near, which arouse their interest for the opposite reason. Endnotes that do not contribute to the empirical data have been cut, as have all citations not specifically discussed by the authors in the text. Our experience, and the more than 25,000 students we have taught in our combined total of 65 years of teaching (see the About the Editors section, below), have taught us that students like readings that are short, readable, rich with subjects' own words and descriptions of their settings and lives, and easy to understand (as jargon-free as possible). Our goal in editing articles is to make them student-friendly, while at the same time retaining important theoretical, historical, and policy selections vital to the course.

Drugs and the American Dream, with its distinct emphasis on sociological contexts and the way they affect users' "set and setting" (drawing on the classic Zinberg approach), stands in contrast to the psychological, biological, and pharmacological orientation taken by some other readers, making it much more compatible with some of the leading textbooks in the Drugs field, such as Goode's *Drugs in American Society*, Faupel/Horowitz/ Weaver's *The Sociology of American Drug Use*, and Mosher and Akins' *Drugs and Drug Policy*. Although the section organization of this book does not follow a strictly empirical drug-oriented approach, instructors will appreciate our full coverage of all current and important drugs (marijuana, alcohol, tobacco, cocaine, crack, heroin, steroids, psychedelics, and prescription drugs are all represented). Finally, students will appreciate our non-judgmental, reasoned, harm reduction approach to drugs that neither demonizes nor champions them. It is our goal to offer engaging, descriptive selections that can be analyzed and interpreted differently, depending on the perspective of the instructor and student.

Overview of the Book

It is our goal to integrate a combination of critical and classical pieces with new, fresh works that address contemporary drug issues. Let us outline these here.

History and Theory

We lead off the book with this section in which we present the main theoretical approach to the book and cover the history of specific drug trends and drug use in general. Selections will include the disease model, the set and setting concept, and historical treatments of alcohol, cocaine, prescription drugs, and social control.

Drug Scares and Moral Panics

This section presents the social constructionist approach to understanding drug use, interpretation, and control, the dominant theme used in "Drugs and Society" courses. We include a classic piece by Joseph Gusfield on "symbolic crusades," usually taught in these courses but not incorporated as a reading, and some other classics and new pieces on the underlying forces and struggles that operate behind-the-scenes to make drugs demonized or legitimated. We analyze the common pathways taken by drug scares, showing the trajectory followed as drugs are introduced, popularized, demonized, and discouraged. At the same time, students will gain a better understanding of the actors and forces that operate to engage in the conflicts over drug use and drug policy that ultimately influence how the effects of some drugs are perceived and interpreted, leading to different patterns of drug usage. A new selection by Dale Chitwood, Sheigla Murphy, and Marsha Rosenbaum reflects on the problematic and political nature of defining a drug epidemic.

Race/Ethnicity

This important section includes selections on how people's race/ethnicity affects their drug use. It looks at the drugs of choice for various groups, and the way the cultural norms and values of these groups lead them to interact with drugs and experience drug addiction. Separate selections focus on Whites, Latinos, Blacks, Asians, and American Indians. This section is sociologically embedded, with a wide appeal for people interested in the cultural factors influencing drugs of choice among different groups and the way they are used.

Social Class

Also critical to understanding how drugs are used and how their users are treated is the concept of socioeconomic status. We include selections on the poor, the blue collar/ middle class, professionals, and the rich. We examine, through these pieces, how class privilege enables some users to control their usage better than others, how different groups get introduced to various drugs, and how they interact with the American system of bureaucracy.

Gender

In this section we look at ways that women and men are situated within and affected by different gender norms. We examine male-dominated drug and alcohol scenes, a new piece, written for this volume, on the intersection between drugs and eating disorders for college women, and how gender roles and expectations shape women's drug use.

Youth and Aging

In this section we offer selections on how people use different drugs over the course of the lifespan. We begin by seeing how drugs are introduced to some very young children, look at the way young adults use drugs, and discuss the career patterns of aging drug users.

Managing Drug Use

This section is another way that our reader is unique. No other book draws attention to the ways that drug users engage their drugs of choice and the strategies that they use to manage these in their daily lives. Critically, it draws the important distinction between drug use and abuse. Students will appreciate some myth-busting selections showing the systems of logic and safety used by members of different class groups and the rationalizations they employ to legitimate their drug use and lifestyles. This section incorporates some diversity in sexual orientation with a selection on gay Latinos, found nowhere else, and some of the logic and rationales for medical marijuana that go beyond the traditional rhetoric of pain and nausea alleviation. We include a classic selection on the "fast life" of upper-level cocaine and marijuana dealers.

The Economics of Drugs

In this section, we also include pieces on the economics of illicit drug markets, particularly at the street level. One selection goes into detail about the structural opportunities available to women in the drug world, looking at the types of work that they do and showing how they are "ghettoized" into a small and non-lucrative part of the market that exploits their gender role and their bodies. The next selection offers a contrast to this by considering the opportunities for men in the street level selling market, economically dissecting the financial activities of a drug dealing gang and showing the extreme reward disparities between the leaders, the officers, and the foot soldiers. Foot soldiers, the most numerous positions, work, it appears, more for the lure of future riches rather than current wages.

Crime and Violence

A section on the nexus between crime, violence, and drugs addresses a theme that has been central to drug researchers for at least the past fifty years. Here we look at a spectrum of what happens from the micro level, in our communities, to the most macro, political, and international level, as represented by the horrendous amount of violence created by Mexican drug cartels along the United States–Mexican border. Thus, we include a classic piece on the three different types of crime engendered by drug use and dealing, a fascinating article on people who make their living robbing drug dealers, a highly current piece on the Mexican drug cartels and the violence pervading our Southern border, and a reasoned, counter-intuitive piece on the isolation of violence to within distinctly limited aspects of the drug dealing and using scenes.

Education

Our section on education examines the history and problems of drug education programs, particularly DARE. It also includes more recent approaches to educating young people about the difference between addiction/abuse and responsible drug use.

Treatment

We have included four selections in this section that address therapeutic communities, methadone maintenance, desistance without treatment, and drug courts.

Policy

We conclude with a section on policy that starts out by addressing an issue close to students' experience: how to reduce the dangers associated with the culture of binge drinking so prevalent on many college campuses today. It follows with an analysis of the history of drug policy, and a piece by Ethan Nadelmann, arguably the most visible and influential person arguing for more balanced drug legislation in the United States. We close with a piece by Harry Levine clarifying the underlying benefits of harsh global drug policies for various governments, showing the political motivations for the US-led war on drugs, and which addresses some of the current changes in drug policy that are being quietly pursued in the areas of treatment, decriminalization, and harm reduction.

Acknowledgments

Two of us, Peter and Patrick, have been teaching the course "Sociology of Drugs" for many years. Patti has been teaching her award-winning course, "Deviance in US Society," to five hundred students a semester for over twenty years, and many of the theories, ideas, and concepts in that class are relevant to the "Drugs" class as well. During these years, we have continually been frustrated by the lack of a reader in which the major issues of drugs in society coalesced in a sociological fashion. Instead, we found a number of texts and anthologies, with rare exceptions, organized around chapters that discussed the variety of drugs prevalent today, but without emphasis on the crucial sociological variables that drive, hinder, or deter drug use. Also, some of these volumes took an approach that drugs, by definition, were bad for people and illustrated all of the social ills that have been engendered by the rampant use of drugs in recent, as well as ancient, history. We were never satisfied with the books we ordered for our students to read, but there was not much out there to provide the more sociological and balanced approach we desired.

In the early summer of 2010, we were approached by Julia Teweles, now working for Wiley-Blackwell, who came to us with the idea of putting together our own drugs anthology. We had known Julia from our previous work with her while she was the President of Roxbury Publishing, and we were always impressed with their quality of texts, especially for a small publishing company during a time that these types of businesses were being gobbled up by the major conglomerates and big-time publishing houses. As was so common, Roxbury was eventually sold to Oxford University Press, and Julia faded into the woodwork, only to emerge again at Wiley-Blackwell about three years later. We were not ready, however, to take on another book, despite our disgruntlements with what was on the market. However, Julia can be very persuasive, and she politely waited, came back to us, and pitched the project and why she thought we could do a good job with it. Swayed by her graciousness, piqued by the intellectual challenge of the project, and armed with a sensible marketing program, in June of 2010 we agreed to dive fully into coordinating the production of *Drugs and the American Dream*.

At that same time, we asked Patrick O'Brien, an advanced graduate student at the University of Colorado with whom we had worked, to join us. Patrick had written his Master's thesis at Ohio University on the party scene and alcohol use among college students under the tutelage of Tom Vander Ven. Later, under our direction, he has been hard at work on continuing this project as part of his PhD dissertation, as well as beginning a new project on the emerging medical marijuana industry in Colorado, and the use of dispensaries for doling out the drug. Further, Patrick was a veteran of the "Drugs and Society" class, having already taught it six times by the time we conceived this book. It should be noted that Patrick is a full partner in this endeavor, and the order of names is alphabetical, not indicative of who did more work or contributed a greater amount to the division of labor.

As we spent much of the summer and fall of 2010 searching for the most contemporary and relevant research in the sociology of drug use, the volume came together in remarkably quick fashion. We knew what we did not want, we had a fairly certain idea about what we did want, and once we were able to conceive and organize the Table of Contents the book came into focus. We are pleased to have had this time to work together, and hope that you, our readers, agree with us that this collection of writings is fascinating, relevant, and teaches you things you heretofore did not know.

There was one other person on our "team" that was central to the production of the book, Nicole Benevenia, Editorial Assistant for Psychology and the Social Sciences for Wiley-Blackwell Publishing. Nicole was always there to answer our questions, to provide feedback, to make sure that reviewers were getting their comments to us in a timely fashion, and to oversee the entire production of the book. She even braved the horrible winter storms in Boston during January 2011, and was consistently at the other end of the phone or computer, despite the weather. Graeme Leonard did a masterful job of coordinating the editorial process and making sure that this book reflects the professionalism that has been the hallmark of the Wiley imprimatur for centuries. We also owe a thanks to Jackie Newman who coordinated the payment of permission fees to the various authors and publishers who were kind enough to allow us to reprint their work in this book. Finally, we are grateful to the many reviewers that Julia and Nicole contacted and who gave us excellent feedback on our prospectus and then on the completed manuscript. These people include: Brian Kelly, Charles Faupel, Erik Fritsvold, James Orcutt, Ralph A. Weisheit, A. Rafik Mohamed, Cynthia Robbins, Dina Perrone, Susan P. Robbins, Sheila Katz, and Angela P. Taylor.

Peter and Patti have been involved in researching the sociology of drug use since 1972, when we were part of a grant from the Sloan Foundation to estimate the number of heroin users in the metropolitan St Louis area. Since that time, we have been influenced, directly and indirectly, by myriad scholars of drugs who would have affected our thinking about the vagaries of drugs, licit and illicit, and the policies toward them in the United States and beyond. These people include: Elijah Anderson, Jerome Beck, Howard Becker, Philippe Bourgois, the late David Brown, Marvin Cummins, Jack Douglas, Troy Duster,

Jeffrey Fagan, Chuck Faupel, Chuck Gallmeier, Paul Goldstein, Bob Granfield, Joe Gusfield, the late John Irwin, Katy Irwin, the late Bruce Johnson, David Karp, Steve Koester, Harry Levine, Peter Manning, Jody Miller, Sheigla Murphy, the late David Musto, Ethan Nadelmann, the late David Pittman, Craig Reinarman, Marsha Rosenbaum, Claire Sterk, the late Dan Waldorf, Wayne Weibel, and Jackie Wiseman.

In the end, all decisions were made jointly by the three of us. We hope that you agree that these selections show the full panoply of issues that are inherent to the sociological study of drugs, and that you learn about how drugs, licit and illicit, have come to their place in society in the second decade of the twenty-first century. Enjoy!

Source Acknowledgments

The editors and publisher gratefully acknowledge the permission granted to reproduce the copyright material in this book:

Chapter 1
From Harvey A. Siegal and James A. Inciardi, "A Brief History of Alcohol," *The American Drug Scene: An Anthology*, Oxford University Press, USA; 6th edition. Reprinted with permission of Oxford University Press

Chapter 2
From David F. Musto, *The American Disease: Origins of Narcotic Control*, Oxford University Press, USA; 3rd edition, 1999. Reprinted with permission of Oxford University Press

Chapter 3
From James A. Inciardi and Theodore J. Cicero, "Black Beauties, Gorilla Pills, Footballs, and Hillbilly Heroin: Some Reflections on Prescription Drug Abuse and Diversion Research over the Past 40 Years," *Journal of Drug Issues*, Fall 2009, 101–14. Reprinted with permission of Florida State University, School of Criminology & Criminal Justice

Chapter 4
From Norman E. Zinberg and Wayne M. Harding, "Control and Intoxicant Use: A Theoretical and Practical Overview," *Journal of Drug Issues*, 9, 1979, 121–43. Publisher: Florida State University, College of Criminology and Criminal Justice. Reprinted with permission of Florida State University, School of Criminology & Criminal Justice

Chapter 5
From Joseph R. Gusfield, *Symbolic Crusade: Status Politics and the American Temperance Movement*, University of Illinois Press; 2nd edition (1986). Reprinted with permission of University of Illinois Press

Chapter 6
Craig Reinarman: "The Social Construction of Drug Scares." By permission of the author. Department of Sociology, University of California, Santa Cruz

Chapter 7
From Justin L. Tuggle and Malcolm D. Holmes, "Blowing Smoke: Status Politics and the Smoking Ban," *Deviant Behavior*, 18, 1997, 77–93. Publisher: Taylor & Francis. Reprinted with permission of Taylor & Francis

Chapter 8

From Dale D. Chitwood, Sheigla Murphy, and Marsha Rosenbaum, "Reflections on the Meaning of Drug Epidemics," *Journal of Drug Issues*, Fall 2009, 29–40. Publisher: Florida State University, College of Criminology and Criminal Justice. Reprinted with permission of Florida State University, School of Criminology & Criminal Justice

Chapter 9

From Todd G. Pierce, "Gen-X Junkie: Ethnographic Research with Young White Heroin Users in Washington, DC," *Substance Use & Misuse*, 34(14), 1999, from pp. 2097–8, 2099–104, 2106–10. Publisher: Informa Healthcare. Reprinted with permission of Taylor & Francis Inc

Chapter 10

Avelardo Valdez, Kathryn Nowotny, and Alice Cepeda, "The Intersection of Drug Use and Crime over the Life Course of Mexican American Former Gang Members"

Chapter 11

From Philippe Bourgois and Jeff Schonberg (excerpts from) *Righteous Dopefiend* 2009, University of California Press. Reprinted with permission of University of California Press. Reprinted with permission of the authors

Chapter 12

From Karen A. Joe Laidler, "The Lives and Times of Asian-Pacific American Women Drug Users: An Ethnographic Study of their Methamphetamine Use," *Journal of Drug Issues*, Winter 1996, 26(1), 199–218. Publisher: Florida State University, College of Criminology and Criminal Justice. Reprinted with permission of Florida State University, School of Criminology & Criminal Justice

Chapter 13

From Paul Spicer, "Toward a (Dys)functional Anthropology of Drinking: Ambivalence and the American Indian Experience with Alcohol," *Medical Anthropology Quarterly*, 11(3), 1997, 306–23. Publisher: Wiley-Blackwell for the American Anthropological Association. Reprinted with permission of American Anthropological Association

Chapter 14

From Eloise Dunlap, Andrew Golub, and Bruce D. Johnson, "The Severely-Distressed African American Family in the Crack Era: Empowerment is Not Enough," *Journal of Sociology and Social Welfare*, 33(1), 2006, 115–39. Publisher: Western Michigan School of Social Work. Reprinted with permission of The Journal of Sociology and Social Welfare

Chapter 15

From Matthew Petrocelli, Trish Oberweis, and Josesph Pertocelli, "Getting Huge, Getting Ripped: A Qualitative Exploration of Recreational Steroid Use," *Journal of Drug Issues*, Fall 2008, 1087–1206. Publisher: Florida State University, College of Criminology and Criminal Justice. Reprinted with permission of Florida State University, School of Criminology & Criminal Justice

Chapter 16

From Dean A. Dabney and Richard C. Hollinger, "Drugged Druggists: The Convergence of Two Criminal Career Trajectories," *Justice Quarterly*, 19(1), 2002, 181–213. Publisher:

Routledge in partnership with the Academy of Criminal Justice Sciences (ACJS). Reprinted with permission of Taylor & Francis UK

Chapter 17
From *Dorm Room Dealers: Drugs and the Privileges of Race and Class* by A. Rafik Mohamed and Erik D. Fritsvold. Copyright © 2010 by Lynne Rienner Publishers Inc. Used with permission of the publisher

Chapter 18
Katherine Sirles Vecitis, "Drugs and Eating Disorders: College Students' Instrumental Drug Use for Weight Control." Reprinted with permission of the author

Chapter 19
From Robert L. Peralta: "College Alcohol Use and the Embodiment of Hegemonic Masculinity among European American Men," *Sex Roles*, 56, 2007, pp. 741–56. Publisher: Springer. Reprinted with permission of Springer

Chapter 20
From Monica Hardesty and Timothy Black, "Mothering Through Addiction: A Survival Strategy among Puerto Rican Addicts," *Qualitative Health Research*, 9(5), 1999, 602–19. Publisher: Sage. Reprinted with permission of SAGE

Chapter 21
From Patricia A. Adler and Peter Adler, "Tinydopers: A Case Study of Deviant Socialization," *Symbolic Interaction*, 1(2) 1978, 90–105. Publisher: University of California Press. Reprinted with permission of University of California Press

Chapter 22
From Meika Loe and Leigh Cuttino, "Grappling with the Medicated Self: The Case of ADHD College Students," *Symbolic Interaction*, 31(3), 2008, 303–23. Publisher: University of California Press. Reprinted with permission of University of California Press

Chapter 23
From Tammy L. Anderson and Judith A. Levy, "Marginality among Older Injectors in Today's Illicit Drug Culture: Assessing the Impact of Ageing," *Addiction*, 98, 2003, 761–70. Publisher: Society for the Study of Alcohol and Other Drugs. Reprinted with permission of Wiley-Blackwell

Chapter 24
From Miriam Williams Boeri, Claire E. Sterk, and Kirk W. Elifson, "Baby Boomer Drug Users: Career Phases, Identity, Self-Concept, and Social Control," *Sociological Inquiry*, 76(2), 2006, 265–91. Publisher: Wiley-Blackwell for Alpha Kappa Delta, the International Sociology Honors Society. Reprinted with permission of Wiley-Blackwell

Chapter 25
From Brian Kelly, "Club Drug Use and Risk Management among 'Bridge and Tunnel' Youth," *Journal of Drug Issues*, 37(2), 2007, 425–44. Publisher: Florida State University, College of Criminology & Criminal Justice. Reprinted with permission of Florida State University, School of Criminology & Criminal Justice

Chapter 26
From René D. Drumm, Duane C. McBride, Lisa Metsch, Melodie Neufeld, and Alex Sawatsky, "'I'm a Health Nut!' Street Drug User's Accounts of Self-Care Strategies," *Journal of Drug Issues* 35(3), 2005, 607–30. Publisher: Florida State University, College of Criminology and Criminal Justice. Reprinted with permission of Florida State University, School of Criminology & Criminal Justice

Chapter 27
From Jose A. Bauermeister, "Latino Gay Men's Drug Functionality," *Journal of Ethnicity in Substance Abuse*, 7(1), 2008, 41–65. Publisher: Routledge. Reprinted with permission of Taylor & Francis

Chapter 28
From Wendy Chapkis, "Cannabis, Consciousness, and Healing," *Contemporary Justice Review*, 10(4), 2007, 443–60. Publisher: Routledge. Reprinted with permission of Taylor & Francis UK

Chapter 29
From *Wheeling and Dealing* by Patricia A. Adler. Copyright © 1993 Columbia University Press. Reprinted with permission of the publisher

Chapter 30
From Lisa Maher and Kathleen Daly, "Women in the Street-Level Drug Economy: Continuity or Change?," *Criminology*, 34(4), 1996, 465–91. Publisher: Wiley-Blackwell. Reprinted with permission of American Society of Criminology

Chapter 31
From Steven D. Levitt and Sudhir Alladi Venkatesh, "An Economic Analysis of a Drug-Selling Gang's Finances," *The Quarterly Journal of Economics*, 115(3), 2000, 755–89. Publisher: Oxford University Press. Reprinted with permission of Oxford University Press

Chapter 32
From Paul Goldstein, "The Drugs/Violence Nexus: A Tripartite Conceptual Framework," *Journal of Drug Issues*, Fall 1985, V. 39, 143–74. Publisher: Florida State University, College of Criminal Justice and Criminology. Reprinted with permission of Florida State University, School of Criminology & Criminal Justice

Chapter 33
Bruce A. Jacobs, Volkan Topalli, and Richard Wright, "Managing Retaliation: Drug Robbery and Informal Sanction Threats," *Criminology*, 38(1), 2000, 171–97. Publisher: Wiley-Blackwell. Reprinted with permission of American Society of Criminology

Chapter 34
From Stephanie Brophy, "Mexico: Cartels, Corruption, and Cocaine: A Profile of the Gulf Cartel," *Global Crime*, 9(3), 2008, 248–61. Publisher: Routledge. Reprinted with permission of Taylor & Francis

Chapter 35
Peter Reuter, "Systemic Violence in Drug Markets," *Crime, Law, and Social Change*, 52, 2009, 275–84. Publisher: Springer (footnotes removed). Reprinted with permission of Springer

Chapter 36

From Earl Wysong and David W. Wright, "A Decade of DARE: Efficacy, Politics, and Drug Education," *Sociological Focus*, 28(3), 1995, 283–311. Reprinted with permission of Sociological Focus

Chapter 37

Marsha Rosenbaum, "Safety First: A Reality-Based Approach to Teens, Drugs, and Drug Education." Reprinted with the kind permission of the author

Chapter 38

From George De Leon, "The Therapeutic Community and Substance Abuse: Perspectives and Approach," *Therapeutic Communities for Addictions*, edited by George De Leon and James T. Ziegenfuss. Springfield, IL: Charles Thomas, 1986, pp. 5–18. Reprinted with permission of Charles C. Thomas, Publisher Ltd

Chapter 39

From Lee Garth Vigilant, "'I Don't Have Another Run Left With It': Ontological Security in Illness Narratives of Recovering on Methadone Maintenance," *Deviant Behavior*, 26, 2005, 399–416. Publisher: Taylor & Francis. Reprinted with permission of Taylor & Francis Inc

Chapter 40

From Robert Granfield and William Cloud, "The Elephant that No One Sees: Natural Recovery among Middle-Class Addicts," *Journal of Drug Issues*, 26(1), 1996, 45–61. Publisher: Florida State University, College of Criminology and Criminal Justice. Reprinted with permission of Florida State University, School of Criminology & Criminal Justice

Chapter 41

From James L. Nolan, Jr, "Drug Treatment Courts and the Disease Paradigm," *Substance Use and Misuse*, 37(12 & 13), 2002, 1723–50. Publisher: Informa Healthcare. Reprinted with permission of Taylor & Francis Inc

Chapter 42

From Stanton Peele, "Reducing Harms from Youth Drinking," *Journal of Alcohol and Drug Education*, December 2006, 67–87. Publisher: Alcohol and Drug Problems Association; American Alcohol and Drug Information Foundation. Reprinted with permission of American Alcohol and Drug Information Foundation

Hope, A., and Byrne, S. (2002) ECAS findings: Policy implications from an EU perspective. In T. Norström (ed.), *Alcohol in Postwar Europe: Consumption, Drinking Patterns, Consequences and Policy Responses in 15 European Countries* (pp. 206–12). Stockholm: National Institute of Public Health. Reprinted with permission

Quote from Hingson, R., Heeren, T., Winter, M., & Wechsler, H. (2005) Magnitude of alcohol-related mortality and morbidity among U.S. college students ages 18–24: Changes from 1998–2001. *Annual Review of Public Health*, 26, 259–79. Reprinted with permission of Annual Reviews, Inc

Chapter 43

From Duane C. McBride, Yvonne Terry-McElrath, Henrick Harwood, James A. Inciardi, and Carl Leukefeld, "Reflections on Drug Policy," *Journal of Drug Issues*, Fall 2009, 71–88.

Publisher: Florida State University, College of Criminology and Criminal Justice. Reprinted with permission of Florida State University, School of Criminology & Criminal Justice

Chapter 44
From Ethan Nadelmann, "Think Again: Drugs," *Foreign Policy*, No. 162, 2007, pp. 24–30. Reprinted with permission of Carnegie Endowment for International Peace

Chapter 45
Harry Levine, "The Secret of Global Drug Prohibition: Its Uses and Crises." Reprinted with permission of the author

Every effort has been made to trace copyright holders and to obtain their permission for the use of copyright material. The publisher apologizes for any errors or omissions in the above list and would be grateful if notified of any corrections that should be incorporated in future reprints or editions of this book.

About the Editors

Peter and **Patti Adler** have been writing together for more than 35 years. Their original interest in sociology was founded in the sociology of drugs. In 1972, as undergraduates at Washington University in St Louis, they were part of a research team on a Sloan Foundation grant, under the directorship of Marvin Cummins (PI), "Report of the Student Task Force on Heroin Use in Metropolitan St Louis," and presented the findings of this research at the Kennedy School at Harvard University. Their first publication, "Tinydopers" (*Symbolic Interaction*, 1978) was in the area of drug research, and they are well-known for their study of upper-level drug dealers and smugglers, *Wheeling and Dealing* (1985; revised edition, 1993).

Both of the Adlers received their PhDs from the University of California, San Diego. Patti has worked at Oklahoma State University, Washington University in St Louis, and she is currently Professor of Sociology at the University of Colorado, where she teaches her award-winning "Deviance in US Society" course. Peter has worked at the University of Tulsa, Washington University in St Louis, and he is currently Professor of Sociology and Criminology at the University of Denver, where he teaches a "Sociology of Drugs" course.

Together, the Adlers are the co-authors and co-editors of numerous books, including *Momentum* (Sage, 1981), *Wheeling and Dealing* (1985; revised edition, 1993), *Membership Roles in Field Research* (1987), *Backboard & Blackboards* (1991), *Peer Power* (1998), *Paradise Laborers* (2004), and *The Tender Cut* (2011). They have edited *Constructions of Deviance* (7th edition, 2012), *Sociological Odyssey* (4th edition, 2013), *Encyclopedia of Criminology and Deviant Behavior* (vol. 1, with Jay Corzine), and *The Social Dynamics of Financial Markets* (1984). They have published over 100 articles and book chapters, and their various works have been reprinted more than 100 times in anthologies and readers. From 1986 to 1994, they served as Editors of the *Journal of Contemporary Ethnography*, and they were the Founding Editors of *Sociological Studies of Child Development*. Their work has been translated into Dutch, French, Italian, German, and Japanese.

Peter and Patti have been the recipients of numerous academic honors. Patti was honored with the Outstanding Junior Scholar Award from the Drinking and Drugs Division of the Society for the Study of Social Problems in 1994. At the University of Colorado, Patti has received the Excellence in Teaching Award and the Award for Excellence in Research, Scholarship, and Creative Work. At the University of Denver, Peter was the University Lecturer and the Scholar/Teacher of the Year. Both Adlers, in separate years, were given the Mentor Excellence Award by the Society for the Study of Symbolic Interaction. Their book, *Paradise Laborers*, won the Scholarly Achievement Award from the North Central Sociological Society. From 2006 to 2007, they served as Co-Presidents of the Midwest Sociological Society. In 2010, the Society for the Study of Symbolic Interaction bestowed upon them the George Herbert Mead Award for Lifetime Achievement.

Patrick K. O'Brien received his BA and MA degrees from Ohio University where he graduated as a distinguished alumnus in 2006. He is currently a fifth-year advanced graduate student in Sociology at the University of Colorado, Boulder. His abiding interest in sociology and criminology has been drug and alcohol research. His masters thesis, entitled, "The Intoxicated Self: An Exploratory Study of a University Student Sample," explored the role of alcohol use in university students' self-awareness and their techniques of neutralization. He is now at work on his dissertation focusing on undergraduate drug use, social control, and socialization, and his research on the burgeoning medical marijuana industry in Colorado. He has taught the course, "Drugs and Society," six times at the University of Colorado and has earned teaching awards at both Ohio University and the University of Colorado. In 2010, he won the Outstanding Graduate Student Paper from the Drinking and Drugs Division of the Society for the Study of Social Problems for his paper, "Masculinized Femininity: College Women Drink like Men, Act like Ladies."

About the Contributors

Tammy L. Anderson is a Professor of Sociology and Criminal Justice at the University of Delaware. Her areas of expertise include culture, deviance, music scenes, drug abuse, medicalization, social problems, gender, and ethnography. She has published many articles in these areas as well as three books: *Neither Villain Nor Victim: Empowerment and Agency among Women Substance Abusers* (2008), *Rave Culture: The Alteration and Decline of a Philadelphia Music Scene* (2009 – winner of the 2010 Charles Horton Cooley Award), and *Sex, Drugs and Death: Addressing Youth Problems in American Society* (2010).

José A. Bauermeister is Assistant Professor in the Department of Health Behavior and Health Education at the University of Michigan School of Public Health. Originally from San Juan, Puerto Rico, Dr Bauermeister completed his MPh and PhD in Public Health from the University of Michigan, followed by an NIH postdoctoral fellowship at Columbia University. Dr Bauermeister oversees the Sexuality & Health Research Lab (SexLab) at the School of Public Health. His primary research interests focus on sexuality and health, and interpersonal prevention and health promotion strategies for high-risk adolescents and young adults. He is Principal Investigator of several projects examining HIV/AIDS risk among young men who have sex with men (YMSM), and is co-investigator on several studies examining substance use among young adults. He is a member of the National Hispanic Science Network on Drug Abuse.

Timothy Black is Associate Professor of Sociology and Director of the Center for Social Research at the University of Hartford. He is the author of the award-winning book, *When a Heart Turns Rock Solid: The Lives of Three Puerto Rican Brothers On and Off the Streets* (2009, 2010). He is currently co-authoring a book with Mary Patrice Erdmans on adolescent mothers in Connecticut.

Miriam Williams Boeri is an Associate Professor of Sociology at Kennesaw State University in Georgia. She holds a PhD in Sociology from Georgia State University. Her paper "Hell I'm an Addict, But I Ain't No Junkie" published in *Human Organization* won the Peter K. New Award from the Society for Applied Anthropology in 2002. Her current research on older drug users and ongoing studies on methamphetamine use in the suburbs are supported by funding from the National Institute on Drug Abuse and the National Institutes of Health. The goals of these studies are to add to our understanding of the life course of drug users, their environments, and their relationships. Her long-term aim is to reduce the adverse health effects associated with drug use, such as the transmission of HIV/AIDS, hepatitis C, and sexually transmitted diseases, and the harmful social effects of drug use, such as incarceration, social isolation, unemployment, and violence.

Philippe Bourgois is the Richard Perry University Professor of Anthropology and Family & Community Medicine at the University of Pennsylvania. He is the author of over 150 articles on drugs, violence, labor migration, ethnic conflict, and urban poverty, as well as several books, including the multiple award-winning *In Search of Respect: Selling Crack in El Barrio* and also *Righteous Dopefiend*. He is currently conducting participant-observation fieldwork on inner city poverty and segregation in Puerto Rican North Philadelphia.

Stephanie Brophy was a student at the University of Maryland School of Law in Baltimore at the time this research was conducted.

Alice Cepeda is Assistant Professor in the Department of Sociology at the University of Houston where she is also Associate Director of the Center for Drug and Social Policy Research (CDSPR). Dr Cepeda received her PhD in Sociology from the City University of New York, Graduate Center. Her experience and research interest has been in examining the social and health risks associated with substance use and related risk behaviors among urban Latino populations including sex workers, injecting heroin users, and young adult males with a history of gang membership.

Wendy Chapkis received her PhD from the University of California at Santa Cruz and is Professor of Sociology and Director of Women and Gender Studies at the University of Southern Maine. Her publications include three books: *Beauty Secrets: Women and the Politics of Appearance*, *Live Sex Acts: Women Performing Erotic Labor*, and *Dying to Get High: Marijuana as Medicine* (co-authored with Richard J. Webb). In 2010, she was elected Vice-President of the Society for the Study of Social Problems.

Dale D. Chitwood is Professor Emeritus of Social Epidemiology at the University of Miami with appointments in the Departments of Sociology and Epidemiology & Public Health. He has conducted research on alcohol and drug misuse and related health issues and health care utilization for the past 35 years. A Principal Investigator of multiple NIH grants, he is published extensively in journals such as the *American Journal of Public Health* and *Journal of Drug Issues*.

Theodore J. Cicero is Professor in the Departments of Psychiatry and Anatomy and Neurobiology at Washington University in St Louis, School of Medicine. He was also Vice Chancellor for Research from 1996 to 2006.

William Cloud is Professor at the Graduate School of Social Work, University of Denver where he teaches courses in drug dependency treatment, drug dependency and mental health policy, and research methods. His research and writings have primarily been in the areas of substance abuse treatment, prevention, and policy. Central to this work has been an examination of "natural recovery from substance dependence" and theoretical constructs that explain the phenomenon, which is the subject of several books he has coauthored and numerous journal articles he has published.

Leigh Cuttino is currently pursuing a Master of Business Administration at the University of North Carolina's Kenan-Flagler Business School. Prior to beginning her graduate degree, Leigh worked for Bloomberg, L.P. in New York City, where she held a variety of roles including management, sales, and analytical support. Leigh graduated Magna Cum Laude from Colgate University, where she received a Bachelor of Arts in Sociology and Anthropology.

Dean A. Dabney is Associate Professor in the Department of Criminal Justice at Georgia State University. He received his doctorate in sociology from the University of Florida in 1997. Since 2007, he has served as the editor of the *Criminal Justice Review* and *International Criminal Justice Review*. His scholarly interests include the organizational culture within law enforcement agencies, forms of deviance and/or criminal behaviors that occur in organizational settings, and qualitative research methods. He has published two books and several dozen articles appearing in such outlets as *Criminal Justice & Behavior*, *International Journal of Offender Therapy & Comparative Criminology*, *Prison Journal*, *Journal of Drug Issues*, and *Justice Quarterly*.

Kathleen Daly is Professor of Criminology and Criminal Justice, Griffith University (Brisbane). She writes on gender, race, crime, and justice; and on restorative, Indigenous, and international criminal justice. Her book *Gender, Crime, and Punishment* (1994) received the Michael Hindelang Award from the American Society of Criminology. With Lisa Maher, she co-edited *Criminology at the Crossroads: Feminist Readings in Crime and Justice* (Oxford University Press, 1998); and with Andrew Goldsmith and Mark Israel, *Crime and Justice: A Guide to Criminology* (2006). In addition to books and edited volumes, she has published over 70 articles in journals, law reviews, and books. She is an elected Fellow of the Academy of the Social Sciences in Australia, and past President of the Australian and New Zealand Society of Criminology (2005–9).

George De Leon is an internationally recognized expert in the treatment of substance abuse, and acknowledged as the leading authority on treatment and research in therapeutic communities. He is senior scientist and former Director of the Center for Therapeutic Community Research and currently Science Director of the Behavior Science Training program at National Development and Research Institutes, Inc. (NDRI). He is Clinical Professor of Psychiatry, Division of Alcoholism and Drug Abuse, at New York University Medical School.

René D. Drumm is Professor and Dean of the School of Social Work at Southern Adventist University. Dr Drumm holds a doctorate degree in Sociology with an emphasis in Family Studies from Texas Women's University and a masters degree in Social Work from Michigan State University.

Eloise Dunlap is a sociologist and graduate of the University of California, Berkeley. She has extensive qualitative experience in research and analysis with African-American families, crack users, crack dealers, drug markets, and with drug-abusing families and households. Her work is rooted in an attempt to understand male-female and family relations and whether and how these relationships contribute to African-American family instability. She is now Director of the Institute for Special Population Research (ISPR) at the National Development and Research Institute (NDRI) and Principal Investigator of a study that builds upon findings from the grant entitled "Disruption and Reformulation of Illicit Drug Markets among New Orleans Evacuees."

Kirk W. Elifson is a Research Professor at the Rollins School of Public Health, Emory University. He is a sociologist who focuses on the determinants and consequences of sexual and drug use behaviors. More specifically, his areas of research include medical sociology, drug abuse, social stratification, and community-based prevention interventions. His recent publications have appeared in the *Journal of Sex Research*, *AIDS and Behavior*, *Social and Preventive Medicine*, *Justice Quarterly*, *Women's Health*, and the *Journal of Drug Issues*.

Erik D. Fritsvold is Assistant Professor of Sociology at the University of San Diego. He earned a PhD from the Criminology, Law & Society Department at the University of California at Irvine. Professor Fritsvold's research interests travel two major substantive arteries, affluent criminality (drug crime in particular) and the radical environmentalist movement. Ongoing projects include "The Bird Rock Bandits," a piece on subjectivity and gang labels derived from a 2007 gang-related murder in affluent La Jolla, CA.

Paul J. Goldstein is Professor Emeritus of Epidemiology at the University of Illinois at Chicago School of Public Health. He was formerly Deputy Director of Narcotic and Drug Research, Inc., and also worked for the New York State Division of Substance Abuse Services. Dr Goldstein has been a frequent consultant to various federal agencies, including the National Institute on Drug Abuse, National Institute of Justice, and Centers for Disease Control.

Andrew Golub is a Principal Investigator in the Institute for Special Populations Research at the National Development and Research Institute (NDRI). He received his PhD in public policy analysis from Carnegie Mellon University. His work has examined drug epidemics, the gateway theory, quality-of-life policing in New York City, the lived experience of inner-city drug users, cohabitation, and issues associated with violence, crime, poverty, and families.

Robert Granfield is Professor and Chair in the Department of Sociology at the State University of New York at Buffalo and is director of the Institute for the Study of Law and Urban Justice. He is also the co-founder of the Initiative on Civic Engagement and Public Policy at the University at Buffalo. He is the author of 5 books and over 70 scholarly articles, reports, and reviews in journals including *Social Problems*, *Law and Society Review*, the *Sociological Quarterly*, *Substance Use and Misuse*, the *Journal of Contemporary Ethnography*, and *Sociological Forum*. He has two major research interests: (1) the study of law and legal institutions with a particular emphasis on the legal profession, and (2) the sociology of alcohol and drug use with an emphasis on natural recovery from addiction. He is currently conducting research on global pro bono legal work, residential foreclosures in Buffalo, and community re-integration of formerly incarcerated drug offenders.

Joseph R. Gusfield is Emeritus Professor of Sociology at the University of California, San Diego. The founding Chair of the Department, Professor Gusfield is widely known for his work on sociology of law, social movements, and the rhetoric of social science. His many books include *Symbolic Crusade, Contested Meanings*, and *The Culture of Public Problems*.

Monica Hardesty earned her PhD from the University of Iowa where she studied under Carl Couch and specialized in Symbolic Interaction Theory. She is Full Professor in the Department of Sociology at the University of Hartford. Her publications have focused on authority relationships, the development of the self, and issues in health care delivery.

Wayne M. Harding, EdM, was a research associate at the Cambridge Hospital, Cambridge, Massachusetts.

Henrick Harwood is Vice-President with the Lewin Group and has studied the economics and policy of alcohol and drug abuse since 1976. Previously he served in the Office of National Drug Control Policy/Executive Office of the President. He has been on staff at the Institute of Medicine/National Academy of Sciences and at the Research Triangle Institute, where he directed Economic Costs of Alcohol and Drug Abuse and Mental Illness. Mr Harwood is currently conducting a new study of the costs of drug abuse for NIDA and NIAAA.

Richard C. Hollinger is Professor of Sociology, Criminology and Law at the University of Florida in Gainesville. Dr Hollinger is also the Director of the Security Research Project – an academic research institute that focuses exclusively on retail loss prevention and security issues. He received his PhD from the University of Minnesota. In addition to numerous articles published in scholarly and professional journals, Dr Hollinger is the author of three books, *Theft by Employees* (with John P. Clark, 1983), *Dishonesty in the Workplace: A Manager's Guide to Preventing Employee Theft* (1989), and *Crime, Deviance and the Computer* (1997).

Malcolm D. Holmes is Professor of Sociology at the University of Wyoming. He has published widely on various aspects of deviant behavior, including a recent book on the causes of police brutality (*Race and Police Brutality: Roots of an Urban Dilemma*, 2008). One focus of his work is the social construction and etiology of drug problems, including tobacco, alcohol, and methamphetamine.

James A. Inciardi was Co-Director of the Center for Drug and Alcohol Studies and Professor of Sociology and Criminal Justice at the time of his death in 2009. During his lifetime, he had 21 funded studies by the National Institute on Drug Abuse. During his scholarly career of over 40 years, Dr Inciardi published over 500 articles, chapters, books, and monographs in the areas of substance abuse, criminology, criminal justice, history, folklore, public policy, AIDS, medicine, and law. His scholarly publications included several seminal papers on the epidemiology of crack cocaine use, as well as the effectiveness of prison-based substance abuse treatment for drug-involved offenders.

Bruce A. Jacobs is Professor of Criminology at the University of Texas, Dallas. He studies offender decision-making. He received his PhD in Sociology, with a specialization in Criminology, from the University of Southern California (USC) and his Bachelor's degree from Duke University.

Karen A. Joe Laidler is Head and Professor of Sociology at the University of Hong Kong. Her research in the United States includes studies on drug use patterns and violence associated with youth gangs in California, the relationship between alcohol and drug use and violence among female gang members, and alcohol and drug cessation during adolescent pregnancy. In addition to her work on the sex work industry in Hong Kong, she is also involved in a number of drug related studies there, including the rise and problems associated with psychotropic drugs, the drug market, the relationship between violence and drug use, and Buddhist interventions with heroin users.

Bruce D. Johnson directed the Institute for Special Populations Research (ISPR) at NDRI (National Development and Research Institutes) at the time of his death in 2009. He earned his PhD in Sociology from Columbia University in 1971. He was affiliated with the National Institute of Justice's Arrestee Drug Abuse Monitoring program from its inception in 1987 to its close in 2003. His five books and more than 150 articles are based on findings emerging from over 20 federally funded research projects supported by the National Institute on Drug Abuse, National Institutes of Justice, Center for Substance Abuse Treatment, Substance Abuse and Mental Health Services Administration, and the Robert Wood Johnson Foundation.

Brian C. Kelly received his PhD from Columbia University and was educated as an undergraduate at Fordham University. He is currently Associate Professor of Sociology at Purdue University. His topical areas of research interest include drug use, sexual health, HIV/AIDS, and comparative youth cultures. The foci of his current research projects include work on prescription drug abuse among NYC-area youth, methamphetamine abuse and HIV risk in China, club drug use among young adults, and the health and well-being of adolescents in age discordant relationships.

Carl Leukefeld is Professor and Chair of the Department of Behavioral Science and Bell Alcohol and Addictions Chair at the University of Kentucky. His research interests include treatment outcomes, HIV, criminal justice, health services, and rural populations.

Harry G. Levine is Professor of Sociology at Queens College and the Graduate Center, City University of New York. For more than 25 years he has researched the history, sociology, and anthropology of drug policy and use. He has won awards for his writing about addiction, alcohol regulation, crack cocaine, the war on drugs, and global drug prohibition. With Craig Reinarman and others he wrote *Crack in America: Demon Drugs and Social Justice*. His most recent work has focused on why, since 1997, New York City has been arresting more people for possessing small amounts of marijuana than any city in the world, mostly young Blacks and Latinos who use marijuana at lower rates than young Whites.

Steven D. Levitt is the William B. Ogden Distinguished Service Professor of Economics at the University of Chicago, where he directs the Becker Center on Chicago Price Theory. In 2004, Levitt was awarded the John Bates Clark Medal, awarded to the most influential economist under the age of 40. Dr Levitt is the co-author of *Freakonomics*. He received his PhD in Economics from MIT.

Judith A. Levy is Associate Professor of Health Policy and Administration in the School of Public Health at the University of Illinois at Chicago. She also directs the NIH-funded Fogarty AIDS International Training and Research Program that collaborates with academic institutions and researchers in Chile, China, Malawi, and Indonesia. In addition, she directs the Social and Behavioral Science Core of the Chicago Developmental Center for AIDS Research. As a medical sociologist, Dr Levy's current research includes a study of traditional male circumcision as a rite of passage into manhood among the Yao of Malawi, HIV prevention among street children in Jakarta, and HIV couple counseling in Indonesia.

Meika Loe is Associate Professor of Sociology and Women's Studies at Colgate University. She is the author of *The Rise of Viagra: How the Little Blue Pill Changed Sex in America* (2004) and co-editor (with Kelly Joyce) of *Technogenarians: Studying Health and Illness through an Aging, Science, and Technology Lens* (2010). Her critical scholarship on culture, age, medicine, sexuality, and gender has appeared in a range of academic journals including *Contexts, Gender & Society, Feminism and Psychology, Symbolic Interaction, Sexualities, Sociological Inquiry,* and *Sociology of Health and Illness.* Loe's most recent book is an ethnography of aging tentatively titled *Doing it My Way: Lessons for Living from the Oldest Old* (2011).

Lisa Maher is Professor in the Faculty of Medicine at the University of New South Wales in Sydney, Program Head at the National Centre in HIV Epidemiology and Clinical Research, and NHMRC Senior Research Fellow. She has extensive experience in research, program development, and service delivery with drug users, sex workers, and people living with HIV in North America, South East Asia, Australia, and the Pacific. Her research focuses on the prevention of infectious disease in vulnerable populations and she currently leads a randomized controlled trial of hepatitis B vaccine completion in people who inject drugs and a program of HCV vaccine preparedness studies.

Duane C. McBride is Professor and Chair of the Behavioral Sciences Department at Andrews University as well as Director of the University's Institute for Prevention of Addictions. Dr McBride holds a PhD from the University of Kentucky. His research interests include drug policy, health services, and risk behavior prevention. Dr McBride has published over 100 papers in these areas of research. Currently he serves as the Principal Investigator on a drug policy project supported by the Robert Wood Johnson Foundation and serves as the Chair of a local Board of Health.

Lisa Metsch is Professor of Epidemiology and Public Health at the University of Miami Miller School of Medicine, Associate Director of the Comprehensive Drug Research Center, and is Director of the Behavioral, Social Sciences and Community Outreach Core of the NIAID-funded Developmental Center for AIDS Research. Her research interests include HIV prevention, behavioral interventions, women's health, oral health, substance abuse policy research, and access and use of health care services for vulnerable populations. Dr Metsch is Co-PI of the Florida Node Alliance of the NIDA-funded Drug Abuse Clinic Trials Network and is currently leading several NIDA-funded clinical trials focusing on HIV testing and strategies to address the prevention and care needs of drug users living with HIV. She is also working on NIDCR-funded studies related to oral health and HIV.

A. Rafik Mohamed earned his bachelor's degree from the George Washington University. Dr Mohamed went on to gain a masters degree in Social Ecology and PhD in Criminology, Law and Society from the University of California, Irvine. His masters research focused on racial disparities in domestic drug policy and his doctoral work explored issues of race, masculinity, and resistance in urban America. From 1999 to 2009, Mohamed was a professor in the Department of Sociology at the University of San Diego, where he ultimately served as the department chairperson. He currently resides in Atlanta, GA and is the Chairperson of Social Sciences at Clayton State University in Morrow, GA.

Sheigla Murphy, Director, Center for Substance Abuse Studies at the Institute for Scientific Analysis, is a medical sociologist who has been researching various types of licit and illicit drug use, pregnancy and drug use, violence, medical and drug treatment, and drug sales for more than thirty years. Dr Murphy has published numerous articles in *Addiction Research*, the *Journal of Psychoactive Drugs*, the *Journal of Drug Issues*, *Contemporary Drug Problems*, *Qualitative Sociology*, and *Social Science and Medicine* concerning heroin use, methadone maintenance, needle sharing, needle exchange, cocaine selling, natural recovery from drug use, drug users in health care systems and women's drug use, pregnancy and violence, drug sales, and nonmedical use of prescription drugs. She is the coauthor (with Dan Waldorf and Craig Reinarman) of *Cocaine Changes: The Experience of Using and Quitting* (1991). Her second book (with coauthor Marsha Rosenbaum) is *Pregnant Women on Drugs: Combating Stereotypes and Stigma* (1999).

David F. Musto was Professor of Child Psychiatry in the Child Study Center at the Yale School of Medicine and Professor of the History of Medicine when he passed away in 2010. His groundbreaking book, *The American Disease: Origins of Narcotic Control* (1973), was one of the first treatises that showed a close correlation, historically, between public outrage over certain drugs and their use by feared or hated minorities.

Ethan Nadelmann is the founder and executive director of the Drug Policy Alliance, the leading organization in the United States advocating for drug policies grounded in science, compassion, health, and human rights. Nadelmann was born in New York City, received his BA, JD, and PhD from Harvard, as well as an MSc in International Relations from the London School of Economics, and then taught politics and public affairs at Princeton University from 1987 to 1994. He has authored two books on international criminal law enforcement – *Cops Across Borders* and (with Peter Andreas) *Policing the Globe* – as well as many dozens of articles on drug policy in publications such as *Foreign Affairs*, *Foreign Policy*, *Science*, *International Organization*, *National Review*, and *The Nation*. Described by *Rolling Stone* as "the point man" for drug policy reform efforts, Ethan Nadelmann is widely regarded as the outstanding proponent of drug policy reform both in the United States and abroad.

Melodie Neufeld is pastor of Community Ministry at Seattle Mennonite Church (a position shared with her husband Jonathan), working with people experiencing homelessness in Lake City, a neighborhood of Seattle. She leads a congregational and broader neighborhood effort to end homelessness through the Lake City Taskforce on Homelessness. Melanie has graduate degrees in Social Work and Divinity. She is committed to community organizing, working with people on the margins, mothering, yoga practice, Interplay (the practice of bringing more playfulness into one's life), and spiritual direction group process.

James L. Nolan, Jr is Professor of Sociology and Chair of the Department of Anthropology and Sociology at Williams College. His new book, *Legal Accents, Legal Borrowing: The International Problem-Solving Court Movement* (2009), is a comparative analysis of the emergence of problem-solving courts in England, Ireland, Scotland, Australia, Canada, and the United States. Nolan is also the author of *Reinventing Justice: The American Drug Court Movement* (2001) and *The Therapeutic State: Justifying Government at Century's End* (1998). He is editor of *Drug Courts: In Theory and in Practice* (2002) and *The American Culture Wars: Current Contests and Future Prospects* (1996). His work has been published in the *Sociological Forum*, *Society*, *The Sociological Quarterly*, and the *American Criminal Law Review*. He is currently serving as the W. Ford Schumann Faculty Fellow in Democratic Studies at Williams College.

Kathryn Nowotny received her MA in Sociology from the University of Houston. She is currently the research coordinator at the Center for Drug & Social Policy Research at the University of Houston where she coordinates multiple NIDA-funded projects with a focus on the social and health consequences of drug use. She is also the project director for the NIDA-funded study entitled, "At Risk Hispanic Gangs: Long-term Consequences for HIV, Hepatitis, and other STI," which provided the data for our contribution to this book.

Trish Oberweis is Associate Professor of Criminal Justice at Southern Illinois University Edwardsville. Her current research interests involve marijuana use, civil asset forfeiture, and police attitudes about our nation's drug policies. She earned her PhD at Arizona State University in the School of Justice Studies.

Stanton Peele is a psychologist, attorney, and psychotherapist who has written extensively on drugs and alcohol. During his 40-year career, he has published nine books, including *Love and Addiction*, *The Meaning of Addiction*, *Diseasing of America*, and *The Truth about Addiction and Recovery*. He is widely known for his debunking of America's drug rehabilitation industry.

Robert L. Peralta is Associate Professor of Sociology at the University of Akron. He holds a BA in Psychology from the University of New Mexico and an MA and PhD in Sociology from the University of Delaware. His areas of interest and expertise include alcohol and other drug use, deviance, gender, social inequality, and interpersonal violence. Some of his publications appear in the *Journal of Health and Social Behavior*, the *Journal of Drug Issues*, *Violence Against Women*, *Gender Issues*, the *Journal of the American Board of Family Practice*, *Deviant Behavior*, *Substance Use and Misuse*, and *Violence and Victims*. Qualitative inquiries on the process of labeling across four areas (HIV/AIDS, interpersonal violence, sexualities, and substance abuse) are the focus of his current research.

Joseph Petrocelli (Detective) has spent over two decades in New Jersey law enforcement. His career has concentrated on drug interdiction on both interstates and in inner cities. He is recognized by the Federal Law Enforcement Training Center as a Subject Matter Expert in drug interdiction. He has earned two Master's degrees, including one from the Rutgers School of Criminal Justice in Criminal Justice. He has authored 2 books and written over 75 professional articles.

Matthew Petrocelli is Associate Professor of Criminal Justice Studies at Southern Illinois University (Edwardsville). His academic credentials include a BS from the United States Military Academy (West Point), an MCJ from the Graduate School of Public Affairs at the University of Colorado, and a PhD in Justice Studies from Arizona State University. A former Army Officer and Airborne Ranger, his research interests include drug policy and law enforcement. His most recent publication appears in the *Journal of Gang Research*.

Todd G. Pierce is a medical anthropologist and ethnographer who has published in the areas of drug abuse and HIV risk behaviors.

Craig Reinarman is Professor of Sociology and Legal Studies at the University of California, Santa Cruz. He has been a Visiting Scholar at the Center for Drug Research at the University of Amsterdam (1994–2003); a member of the Board of Directors of the College on Problems of Drug Dependence (1990–4); a consultant to the World Health Organization's Program on Substance Abuse; and a principal investigator on research grants from the National Institute on Drug Abuse and the National Institute of Justice. Dr Reinarman is the author of *American States of Mind* (1987) and co-author of *Cocaine Changes* (1991) and *Crack in America* (1997). He has published numerous articles on drug use, law, and policy in such journals as *Theory and Society*, the *British Journal of Addiction*, the *International Journal of Drug Policy*, the *American Journal of Public Health*, and *Addiction Research and Theory*.

Peter Reuter is Professor in the School of Public Policy and in the Department of Criminology at the University of Maryland. He is Director of the Program on the Economics of Crime and Justice Policy at the University and also Senior Economist at RAND. His research is primarily on policies toward illegal drugs, most recently on the consequences of international control efforts for drug markets. Currently he is completing a study for the World Bank, entitled *Draining Development: The Sources, Consequences and Control of Flows of Illicit Funds from Developing Countries*. Dr Reuter earned his PhD in Economics at Yale University. From 2007 to 2011 he served as the founding president of the International Society for the Study of Drug Policy.

Marsha Rosenbaum is a sociologist, former National Institute on Drug Abuse-funded researcher, and founder of the Safety First Project at the Drug Policy Alliance (www.drugpolicy.org). She is the author of *Women on Heroin* (1981), *Pursuit of Ecstasy: The MDMA Experience* (with Jerome Beck, 1994), *Pregnant Women on Drugs: Combating Stereotypes and Stigma* (with Sheigla Murphy, 1999), *Safety First: A Reality-Based Approach to Teens and Drugs*, and numerous scholarly articles and opinion pieces about drug use, abuse, treatment, and drug education. Dr Rosenbaum is the mother of two young adults who have helped to shape her perspective on teenagers and drugs. Her son, Johnny Irwin, a teacher in San Francisco, wrote the "Dear Mom" letter contained in *Safety First*.

Alex Sawatsky is Assistant Professor of Social Work at Booth University College in Winnipeg, Manitoba, Canada. He holds a BA in Psychology from Goshen College in Goshen, Indiana and a masters in Social Work from Andrews University in Berrien Springs, Michigan. He is currently engaged in mental health research as a doctoral student in Social Work at the University of Manitoba, Winnipeg, Canada.

Jeff Schonberg is a photographer and ethnographer in the joint Medical Anthropology program at the University of California, San Francisco and Berkeley. He has worked on projects in the United States on homelessness, gangs and inner-city violence, the drug economy, and HIV; in Latin America on social upheaval and street youth. He is interested in issues of photography, the representation of suffering, globalization, and neoliberalism. He is currently working on the subject of murder in his West Oakland community. *Righteous Dopefiend* is his first book.

Harvey A. Siegel was a sociologist, ethnographer, and professor and director of Substance Abuse Intervention Programs at Wright State University School of Medicine in Dayton, Ohio when he died in 2004.

Paul Spicer is a cultural anthropologist and Professor of Anthropology at the University of Oklahoma's Center for Applied Social Research. He conducts ethnographic research on substance abuse, mental health, and child development in American Indian communities, with an emphasis on intergenerational dynamics, life history, and discourse analysis. His recent work centers on the experiences of American Indian children.

Claire E. Sterk is Charles Howard Candler Professor of Public Health at Emory University. She is a sociologist with research in social stratification, deviance, and health disparities. Her monographs include *Tricking and Tripping: Prostitution during the AIDS Era* (2000) and *Fast Lives: Women and Crack Cocaine* (1999). Her articles have appeared in the *International Journal of Drug Policy*, the *Journal of Drug Issues*, *AIDS and Behavior*, and *Justice Quarterly*.

Yvonne Terry-McElrath is a research associate at the Institute for Social Research at the University of Michigan, and received her MSA from the University of Notre Dame in 1999. Her research and publication experience has focused on trends and correlates of tobacco and illicit drug use in adolescent populations, anti-tobacco and drug use media campaigns, drug policy, drug treatment provision within juvenile justice populations, the drug–crime cycle, HIV/AIDS prevention services among high-risk groups, and adolescent obesity.

Volkan Topalli received his PhD in Social Psychology from Tulane University and was an NSF Research Fellow with the National Consortium on Violence Research. He is currently an Associate Professor in the Department of Criminal Justice & Criminology at the Andrew Young School of Policy Studies, Georgia State University (GSU). His current research interests are in the areas of drug markets and crime, offender decision-making, and ethnographic approaches to studying noninstitutionalized (active) street criminals.

He chairs the Crime & Violence Prevention Policy Initiative at GSU, and has received funding from the National Science Foundation, the National Institute of Justice, and the Harry Frank Guggenheim Foundation for his research on hardcore offenders.

Justin L. Tuggle received his BA from Humboldt State University and his MA from the University of Wyoming. He teaches third grade at Grant Elementary School in Redding, California. He is married with two children.

Avelardo Valdez is Professor at the Graduate College of Social Work at the University of Houston and Director of the Center for Drug & Social Policy Research. His research focuses on drugs, violence, crime, and health. His current NIH funded grant examines the long-term consequences of adolescent gang membership among Mexican Americans. His most recent book is entitled *Mexican American Girls and Gang Violence: Beyond Risk.*

Katherine Sirles Vecitis has a PhD in Sociology from the University of Colorado at Boulder, and currently teaches at Tufts University. Her research interests include sociology of drugs, deviant behavior, and gender.

Sudhir Alladhi Venkatesh is William B. Ransford Professor of Sociology at Columbia University and Director of the Institute for Social and Economic Research and Policy, and Director of the Charles H. Revson Fellowship Program. His books include *Gang Leader for a Day*, *Off the Books: The Underground Economy of the Urban Poor*, and *American Project: The Rise and Fall of the Modern Ghetto*. He received his PhD in Sociology from the University of Chicago.

Lee Garth Vigilant received his PhD in Sociology from Boston College and is currently Associate Professor of Sociology at Minnesota State University Moorhead. He is a past recipient of the Donald J. White Teaching Excellence Award for Sociology at Boston College (2000) and the TCU Senate Professor of the Year Award for Tufts University (2001). His publications in the area of addiction treatment and recovery appear in the journals *Sociological Spectrum* (2008), *Deviant Behavior* (2005), and *Humanity and Society* (2004). Dr Vigilant is currently undertaking a study of the father's role in home-schooling families. He is co-editor (with Dr Joel Charon) of *Social Problems: Readings with Four Questions* (2012).

David W. Wright earned his doctorate at Purdue University and is Professor of Sociology at Wichita State University. His numerous publications and presentations address topics on drug-education, labor markets, class mobility, and income inequality. His current research includes economic trends related to class mobility, income, and employment.

Richard Wright is Curators' Professor of Criminology and Criminal Justice at the University of Missouri–St Louis and Editor-in-Chief of the *British Journal of Sociology*. Currently, he is collaborating with Rick Rosenfeld and Scott Jacques on research examining the influence of respectability on predation and social control among drug dealers in Amsterdam's red light district.

Earl Wysong is Professor of Sociology at Indiana University Kokomo. His current research is focused on class analysis, organizations, inequality, intergenerational mobility, and the American Dream. He is currently working, with co-authors Robert Perrucci and David W. Wright, on *The New Class Society: Goodbye American Dream!*, 4th edition, 2012.

Norman E. Zinberg was Clinical Professor of Psychiatry at the Harvard Medical School and a psychiatrist at Cambridge Hospital at the time of his death in 1989. He has long been recognized as a pioneer in studying the ways in which marijuana, heroin, and other drugs affect human behavior. He served for many years as a consultant to government agencies dealing with drug problems and testified frequently on legislation seeking to curb illicit drugs.

Matrix of Drugs Addressed

Alcohol

Harvey A. Siegal and James A. Inciardi: A Brief History of Alcohol

Norman E. Zinberg and Wayne M. Harding: Control and Intoxicant Use: A Theoretical and Practical Overview

Joseph R. Gusfield: Symbolic Crusade: Status Politics and the American Temperance Movement

Avelardo Valdez, Kathryn Nowotny, and Alice Cepeda: The Intersection of Drug Use and Crime over the Life Course of Mexican American Former Gang Members

Philippe Bourgois and Jeff Schonberg: Righteous Dopefiend

Paul Spicer: Toward a (Dys)functional Anthropology of Drinking: Ambivalence and the American Indian Experience with Alcohol

Robert L. Peralta: College Alcohol Use and the Embodiment of Hegemonic Masculinity among European American Men

Stanton Peele: Reducing Harms from Youth Drinking

All Drugs

Craig Reinarman: The Social Construction of Drug Scares

Earl Wysong and David W. Wright: A Decade of DARE: Efficacy, Politics and Drug Education

Marsha Rosenbaum: Safety First: A Reality-Based Approach to Teens, Drugs, and Drug Education

George De Leon: The Therapeutic Community: Perspective and Approach

Robert Granfield and William Cloud: The Elephant that No One Sees: Natural Recovery among Middle-Class Addicts

James L. Nolan, Jr: Drug Treatment Courts and the Disease Paradigm

Duane C. McBride, Yvonne Terry-McElrath, Henrick Harwood, James A. Inciardi, and Carl Leukefeld: Reflections on Drug Policy

Ethan Nadelmann: Think Again: Drugs

Harry G. Levine: The Secret of Global Drug Prohibition: Its Uses and Crises

Club Drugs

Brian C. Kelly: Club Drug Use and Risk Management among "Bridge and Tunnel" Youth

José A. Bauermeister: Latino Gay Men's Drug Functionality

Cocaine and Crack Cocaine

Heroin

Paul J. Goldstein, The Drugs/Violence Nexus: A Tripartite Conceptual Framework
Bruce A. Jacobs, Volkan Topalli, and Richard Wright: Managing Retaliation: Drug Robbery and Informal Sanction Threats
Peter Reuter: Systemic Violence in Drug Markets

Marijuana

Patricia A. Adler and Peter Adler: Tinydopers: A Case Study of Deviant Socialization
Avelardo Valdez, Kathryn Nowotny, and Alice Cepeda: The Intersection of Drug Use and Crime over the Life Course of Mexican American Former Gang Members
A. Rafik Mohamed and Erik D. Fritsvold: Why Rich Kids Sell Street Drugs: Wankstaz, Wannabes, and Capitalists in Training
José A. Bauermeister: Latino Gay Men's Drug Functionality
Wendy Chapkis: Cannabis, Consciousness, and Healing
Patricia A. Adler: The Dealing Lifestyle

Methamphetamines

Dale D. Chitwood, Sheigla Murphy, and Marsha Rosenbaum: Reflections on the Meaning of Drug Epidemics
Miriam Williams Boeri, Claire E. Sterk, and Kirk W. Elifson: Baby Boomer Drug Users: Career Phases, Identity, Self-Concept, and Social Control
Karen A. Joe Laidler: The Lives and Times of Asian-Pacific American Women Drug Users
René D. Drumm, Duane C. McBride, Lisa Metsch, Melodie Neufeld, and Alex Sawatsky: "I'm a Health Nut!" Street Drug Users' Accounts of Self-Care Strategies
José A. Bauermeister: Latino Gay Men's Drug Functionality

Opiates

David F. Musto: The American Disease: Narcotics in Nineteenth-Century America
Lee Garth Vigilant: "I Don't Have Another Run Left With It": Ontological Security in Illness Narratives of Recovering on Methadone Maintenance

Prescription Drugs and Steroids

James A. Inciardi and Theodore J. Cicero: Black Beauties, Gorilla Pills, Footballs, and Hillbilly Heroin: Prescription Drug Abuse and Diversion Research over the Past 40 Years
Meika Loe and Leigh Cuttino: Grappling with the Medicated Self: The Case of ADHD College Students
Avelardo Valdez, Kathryn Nowotny, and Alice Cepeda: The Intersection of Drug Use and Crime over the Life Course of Mexican American Former Gang Members
Matthew Petrocelli, Trish Oberweis, and Joseph Petrocelli: Getting Huge, Getting Ripped: An Exploration of Recreational Steroid Use
Dean A. Dabney and Richard C. Hollinger: Drugged Druggists: The Convergence of Two Criminal Career Trajectories

Psychedelics

Tobacco

Part I

Perspectives on Drug Use

To paraphrase Karl Marx, the history of all hitherto existing societies is the history of mind alteration through drug use. In virtually all societies that have existed since the start of civilization, people have been using drugs for consciousness altering purposes, medicinal reasons, and recreation. Whether it is alcohol, tobacco, peyote, opium, cocaine, marijuana, heroin, designer drugs, pharmaceuticals, or whatever the next fad will be, drugs have always been a part of human behavior. Therefore, to even consider a "drug-free" society is absurd, as people will always find some substance to ingest, digest, snort, shoot, or smoke to get high. In short, drugs have been around a long time and they are not going away.

People's perceptions of the effect of drugs, whether these are licit or illicit, are too often filtered through a pharmacological lens. Biochemists, neurologists, and psycho-pharmacologists offer a simple, determinist story about drugs that views their use as the result of endorphin pleasure stimulators, their addiction as physiologically generated, and their "cure" as related to neural blockages or sensory inhibitors. These biological, chemical, and physiological dimensions do offer some insight into how and why people take drugs or stop taking them, but they miss the sociological reasons that motivate people to use, abuse, or abstain from using various substances; they miss people's desires to be happy, less depressed, to escape from the horrors or mundanity of everyday life, or to ignore the problems they face. If, as Marx suggested, religion is the opiate of the masses, then drugs may offer the kind of replacement or "false consciousness" that parallels that of religion and sport. Or perhaps drugs are merely a scapegoat for the deleterious effects of modernity, and as we try to cope with the complexity of life in mass society. In reality, however, it is not drugs, but poverty, discrimination, prejudice, and crime that lie at the bedrock of our problems. Seen this way, drugs are only an artifact of much larger issues that cannot be so easily identified, scapegoated, or cured.

The same drugs used by different groups of people in different historical settings and contexts can have markedly different usage patterns. For example, two drinks of alcohol in a bar or party setting may make the consumer tipsy and happy, while the same amount of alcohol that is drunk at a wake might ordinarily make the user feel somber or serious. Or, tobacco, which was once hailed as the "cool" drug and used by movie stars and the

Drugs and the American Dream: An Anthology, First Edition. Edited by Patricia A. Adler, Peter Adler, and Patrick K. O'Brien.
© 2012 John Wiley & Sons, Inc. Published 2012 by John Wiley & Sons, Inc.

characters they portrayed, is now demonized so much that its use has been banned from practically all indoor and many outdoor settings. Drugs may be used to escape or to engage reality. In the 1960s, some users of LSD were thought to be "dropping out," while others were portrayed as expanding and broadening their consciousness. Drugs may be carefully controlled or they may lead users to lose their sense of self and self-dignity. Thus, although a majority of people use drugs such as alcohol and cocaine with few or no negative effects, others who experiment with these may stray down a pathway to addiction. Often the factors that influence the different patterns of drug usage are sociological ones, relating to the characteristics of the users, the meanings they attach to the drugs, and the settings in which they consume them. Subjectively, does a marijuana joint smoked for medicinal purposes have different effects than one smoked purely for pleasurable reasons? In this book we will explore these kinds of questions.

This first part of the book sets the stage for our broader understanding of how drugs have been perceived and interpreted over various eras by looking at the historical rise of drugs, the groups of people associated with using them, and the contexts that frame the way people understand them. The selections in Part I (a general overview) show how various drugs, such as alcohol, the opiates, cocaine, meth, crack, and pharmaceuticals have been viewed differently in various historical epochs. Most current illicit drugs were at one time legal, easily obtainable, thought to have curative powers, used as part of religious ceremonies, or ignored until powerful groups in society (what sociologists call "moral entrepreneurs") decided to attack these substances and legislate against them. In addition, in this part, we will also look at a variety of moral panics and scares that have surrounded almost every drug. Because our society is so fear-driven, with the media sensationalizing anything that might cause pain or damage, drugs have become one of the central topics that fear-mongering groups use to capture the public and catapult people into hysterical outrage. Thus, the selections in this section of the book show how powerful groups have created terror in the minds of many Americans. We hope that these chapters show that sometimes it is not the drugs that we have to fear (though it may be), but the people who decide to ban them.

History and Theory

A Brief History of Alcohol

Harvey A. Siegal and James A. Inciardi

Our media tend to make us believe that we are currently in the midst of a "drug craze" worse than any ever known. Harvey Siegal and James Inciardi point out that people have used drugs distilled from various plants and foods since the beginning of known history. Focusing on alcohol, the most widely used drug on the planet, they look at the way it first developed and then evolved over centuries. Readers will be interested to learn some basic facts about what differentiates assorted kinds of alcohol, what substances have been added to it to modify its color and effects, and how it influences our bodies and our health.

The desire to temporarily alter how our minds process the information brought by our senses is perhaps one of the oldest and most pervasive of humanity's wishes. In fact, some researchers have suggested that the need to do so is as powerful and permanent as the in-born drives of self-preservation, hunger, and security. In its pursuit, people have, at various times and in various places, subjected their bodies to beatings and mutilation, starvation and sensory deprivation; they have focused their minds solely on a single object, or let consciousness expand without direction; and they have often pursued a more direct route, changing the brain's chemistry by ingesting a chemical substance. Of all of these,

the chemical that has probably been used by more of the earth's people in more places and times is one of the by-products of a simple organism's conversion of sugar and water into energy. It is ethanol, or beverage alcohol. Each year, countless millions of people experience, both positively and negatively, the effects of this domesticated drug we call alcohol.

More is known about alcohol than any other drug; yet, how much more remains to be learned staggers the imagination. Our experiences with this most familiar and comfortable of drugs could readily constitute a social history of civilization. We've lauded and vilified it. We've brought it into our most important

Drugs and the American Dream: An Anthology, First Edition. Edited by Patricia A. Adler, Peter Adler, and Patrick K. O'Brien.
© 2012 John Wiley & Sons, Inc. Published 2012 by John Wiley & Sons, Inc.

religious rituals and have included it as part of our significant rites-of-passage. Conversely, we've discouraged its use, even prohibited its manufacture and sale by constitutional amendment. Wars have been fought over it, and underworld empires have been built on the proceeds from its sales. It's been acclaimed as having the power to comfort and cure and is held responsible for thousands of deaths each year, billions of dollars in losses, and an incalculable amount of human suffering. All of us, in some way, have been touched or influenced by this drug, so let's take a brief look at its history.

Early History

Like many significant inventions, the specifics of alcohol's discovery are not known. We conjecture that it likely occurred during the neolithic age. Perhaps someone left wild berries, fruit, or even grapes in a vessel for a few days. When they returned, airborne yeasts had already begun fermenting the mixture. The result – which we call "wine" – undoubtedly proved to be more interesting and enjoyable than the original fruit, and, like other innovations, it did not take people long to improve their invention.

As people settled into communities and began cultivating plants and domesticating animals instead of just simply hunting and gathering their food, they found that a surplus often ensued. Surplus grains could also be fermented once the starch in them – which by itself would not ferment – could be rendered into sugar. To accomplish this, as is still done in parts of the world today, these early agriculturists found that chewing the grain somehow changes it into a fermentable mixture. We know now that the chemical responsible for this transformation – ptyalin – is found naturally in saliva. Other societies discovered that by allowing the grain to germinate, then roasting the new shoots, the fermentation process could be initiated. In this way, the beverage we know as "beer" came into being. People discovered that not only fruits, berries, and grains could be used to produce alcohol, but leaves, tubers, flowers, cacti, and even honey could be fermented as well.

These early concoctions (roughly designated as wines or beers), however, were limited in their alcoholic strength. As yeasts metabolize the sugar, carbon dioxide (which is what makes bread rise, wine bubble, or gives beer a head) and alcohol are released as by-products. When the alcoholic content of the mixture exceeded 11 percent or 12 percent the process slowed markedly; as it approached 14 percent, the yeasts were rendered inactive (i.e., killed), and the process of fermentation stopped entirely. In addition to the limitation imposed by the biology of the yeasts, the alcoholic content could be affected by the producers themselves. For example, including more sugar (or fermentable material) would increase the amount of alcohol that would be produced. Whether the producers were willing to allow the yeasts the time necessary to complete the fermentation process or were too eager to consume the brew to wait, this influenced its alcohol content.

It was not until the time of the Crusades that Europeans were able to consume alcoholic beverages more potent than beer or wine. The Crusaders returned from the Holy Lands having learned a process known as "distillation." To distill wine, it first would be heated. Because alcohol has a lower boiling point than water, it would vaporize first. Then, as this vapor cooled, it condensed back into liquid form. This distillate made a considerably more potent beverage. In fact, beverages of quadruple potency now became possible. These were known as "distilled spirits" or "liquors," referring to the essence of the wine.

Aqua Vitae: The Water of Life

What is this drug which has been called by some the "water of life" – *aqua vitae*, in scholastic Latin, or *ambrosia*, the nectar of the gods – and "the corrupter of youth" and the "devil's own brew" by others? Ethyl alcohol or ethanol (whose chemical formula is C_2H_5OH) is a clear, colorless liquid with little odor but a powerful burning taste. Ethanol is just one of many alcohols such as methyl (wood) and isopropyl (rubbing) alcohol. All others are poisonous and cannot be metabolized by the body.

In addition to ethanol and water, alcoholic beverages generally contain minute amounts of substances referred to as "congeners." Many of these chemicals are important to the flavor, appearance, and aroma of the beverage. Brandy, for example, is relatively rich in congeners while vodka contains relatively few. Alcoholic beverages differ in strength. Beer generally has an alcoholic content of 5 percent; malt liquors are slightly higher. Natural wine varies in alcoholic content between 6 percent and 14 percent. Fortified wines – i.e., those that have had additional alcohol added – contain between 17 percent and 20 percent alcohol. Liquor or spirits contain approximately 40 percent ethanol. The common designation of "proof" originated centuries ago in Britain as a test for the potency of a beverage. To accomplish this test, if gun powder saturated with alcohol burned upon ignition, this was taken as "proof" that the liquor was more than half pure alcohol. In the United States, proof is calculated as being roughly twice the proportion of ethanol by unit volume of beverage; for example, an 86-proof Scotch is 43 percent alcohol.

Although the relative strengths of the beverages differ, current standard portions that are consumed actually provide the same amount of ethanol to the drinker. For example, the same quantity of alcohol is consumed if someone drinks either a 12-ounce can or bottle of beer, a three- to four-ounce glass of wine, or a mixed drink made with one and one-half ounces (i.e., one shot) of distilled spirits. Thus, the claim that "I don't drink much alcohol, but I do drink a lot of beer" is simply not true.

Alcohol's Effects

Unlike most other foods, alcohol is absorbed directly into the bloodstream without digestion. A small amount passes directly through the stomach lining itself; most, however, progresses on to the small intestine, where it is almost entirely absorbed. The feeling of warmth that one experiences after taking a drink results from the irritating effect that alcohol has on the tissues of the mouth, esophagus (food-tube), and stomach. Alcohol does not become intoxicating until the blood carrying it reaches the brain. The rapidity with which this occurs is in large measure determined by the condition of the stomach. An empty stomach will facilitate the absorption of the alcohol, while a full stomach retards it. To some degree, the type of beverage consumed has an effect on absorption, as well. Beer, for example, contains food substances which tend to retard this absorption.

Drinks which are noticeably carbonated – such as champagne – seem to "quickly go to one's head," since the carbon dioxide facilitates the passage of alcohol from the stomach to the small intestine.

Alcohol is held in the tissues of the body before it is broken down (i.e., metabolized), like any other food or chemical substance. The body metabolizes alcohol at a steady rate, with the individual being able to exercise virtually no control over the process. Therefore, a healthy man who weighs approximately 160 pounds, drinking no more than three-fourths of an ounce of distilled spirits every hour, could consume more than a pint in a day's time without experiencing any marked intoxication. If the same quantity was consumed over an hour or two, however, the person would be very drunk. Today, much research is directed at finding an "antidote" for alcohol: a chemical that would either break down the alcohol itself, or accelerate the body's metabolic process. Although several promising lines of research are under way, it will likely be many years before something is commercially available. Finally, the belief that black coffee (i.e., caffeine) is an "antidote" is without fact. What the caffeine does do, however, is to stimulate the drinker – the intoxicated person is still "drunk," but he or she may, after several cups of black coffee, feel more awake.

Ethanol is broken down (metabolized) by the liver. In experiments, animals have had their livers removed, and then were given ethyl alcohol. The alcohol remained, much like wood (methyl) alcohol, in their bodies without being metabolized and exhibited the toxic effects – such as nerve damage – brought on by unpotable alcohols. How does this process work? The liver produces and holds the enzymes responsible for alcohol metabolism. Once in the liver, alcohol combines with its enzymes. Alcohol is initially transformed into acetaldehyde, a chemical considerably more toxic than alcohol. Almost instantaneously, other enzymes convert the acetaldehyde into acetic acid (the same compound that constitutes vinegar), an essentially innocuous substance. The acetic acid is then further metabolized into carbon dioxide and water. Interestingly, one of the treatment strategies for managing alcoholism employs this metabolic process itself. In it, disulfiram (Antabuse), a chemical which compromises the body's capacity to convert acetaldehyde to acetic acid, is used as an adversive agent. By itself, disulfiram has little effect on a patient who takes a daily dose of it. If alcohol is consumed while disulfiram remains in the body, the produced acetaldehyde collects quickly, much to the great discomfort of the drinker. The patient is warned of this unpleasant effect, and the consequent fear of it can help increase his or her motivation to abstain from alcohol.

Alcohol does have some nutritional value. The primitive brews and concoctions were probably richer in nutritional value, especially carbohydrates, vitamins, and minerals, than the highly refined beverages we consume today. Alcohol itself is a rich source of calories which are converted into energy and heat. An ounce of whiskey, for example, provides approximately 75 calories, the equivalent of a potato, an ear of corn, a slice of dark bread, or a serving of pasta. The caloric content of mixed drinks is greater, since the sweeteners of the mixer provide additional calories. These extra calories are, of course, fattening, if the drinker does not reduce his or her intake of other foods.

The fact that alcohol provides sufficient calories for subsistence provides an additional health hazard. Many heavy drinkers express a preference to "drink their meals." While alcohol does provide calories, other nutrients, such as proteins, vitamins, and minerals vital to health and well-being, are entirely lacking. These heavy drinkers often suffer from chronic malnutrition and vitamin-deficiency diseases. In fact, adult malnutrition apart from heavy drinking is extremely rare in the United States.

Alcohol exerts its most profound effects on the brain. The observable behavior produced by drinking is as much a result of the social situation in which a person drinks as it is the drinker's mood and expectations about what the drinking will do and the actual quantity of alcohol consumed. For example, after drinking the identical quantity and type of beverage, one might experience euphoria or depression, while another may feel full of energy or simply wish to sleep; or a drink found initially stimulating might encourage sleep. Pharmacologically, alcohol is a central nervous system depressant drug. Currently, neuroscientists are studying the operation of specific biochemical mechanisms, but some research has suggested that alcohol acts most directly on those portions of the brain which control sleep and wakefulness.

The amount of alcohol within a person is conventionally described as Blood Alcohol Content (BAC). This measures the proportion of alcohol that might be found within an individual's bloodstream and can be assessed by analyzing body substances such as blood, breath, or urine. Although, as we mentioned, the effects vary by both drinking situation and the experience that the drinker has had, we can roughly expect to see some of the following occur. After two or three drinks in a short period of time, a person of about 160 lbs. will begin to feel the effects of the drug. These include feelings of euphoria, freeing of inhibitions, and perhaps impaired judgment. Such a person would have an approximate BAC of 0.04 percent.

If our subject has another three drinks in a short period, his or her BAC will elevate to around 0.1 percent. Now, besides affecting the higher centers of thought and judgment located in the cerebral cortex, the alcohol is beginning to act on the lower (more basic) motor areas of the brain. By law, in virtually all the states, this person would now be judged incapable of operating a motor vehicle and, if caught doing so, would be charged with Driving Under the Influence (DUI). The person would have some difficulty walking and appear to lurch somewhat; there would be noticeable decline in activities requiring fine hand–eye coordination; and one's speech would be somewhat slurred.

At higher concentrations of alcohol, from 0.2 percent BAC and up (resulting from the consumption of at least 10 ounces of spirits), more of the central nervous system is affected. The drinker has difficulty coordinating even the simplest of movements and may need assistance to even walk. Emotionally, he or she appears very unstable and readily changes from rage to tears and then back again. At 0.40 percent to 0.50 percent BAC alcohol depresses enough of the central nervous system's functions that the drinker may lapse into a coma. At concentrations of 0.60 percent BAC and above, the most basic centers of the brain – those that govern respiration – are so suppressed that death may occur.

Alcohol and Health

Abusive drinking has a profoundly negative influence on virtually every one of the body's organ systems. This negative impact occurs directly through the irritating and inflaming properties the drug has, and indirectly as an effect of alcohol's metabolism by the liver. Further, like many other drugs, tolerance (both physiologic and psychologic) to alcohol occurs. As such, one needs to drink more to achieve the desired effects. Naturally, the more one drinks, the greater the (potential and actual) damage caused by alcohol.

Alcohol irritates the lining of the stomach, which in turn causes an increase in the amount of gastric juices secreted. These irritate, inflame, and ultimately can chemically abrade the stomach's lining, causing ulcers. Alcohol can damage the small intestine itself, compromising the organ's ability to absorb nutrients, especially vitamins. Other organs that are involved in the digestive process, such as the pancreas, are damaged as well; adult-onset diabetes is typically linked to abusive drinking.

Because the liver is responsible for metabolizing the alcohol consumed, it is this organ which is most affected. Not only is the liver abused by the irritating and inflaming properties of alcohol, but, as it metabolizes the drug, proteins broadly described as "free fatty acids" are released. These settle throughout the liver and other internal organs, ultimately compromising their function by blocking blood and other vessels. The livers of alcohol abusers are characterized by fatty deposits, dead and dying tissues, and evidence of scarring. Ultimately, the organ may be so compromised that it fails entirely, and death follows.

Although there is support for the notion that very moderate alcoholic consumption – i.e., never more than two glasses of wine a day – has healthful benefits, heavy drinkers have increased rates of cardiovascular problems. Heart disease is more prevalent among this group – who are more likely to be heavy cigarette smokers as well – than the general population.

Chronic abuse of alcohol can have disastrous effects on the central nervous system. Alcohol is a tolerance-producing and ultimately addicting drug. For the addicted person, withdrawal distress can be life threatening. Longer term, permanent damage can include dementia, profound memory loss, the inability to learn, and impaired balance and coordination. Alcoholic people have higher rates of depression, suicide, and evidence of other mental illnesses.

Alcohol abuse is linked with automobile accidents, especially among adolescents. It is estimated that almost one-half of fatal crashes involve drinking. Other accidents, drownings, burns, and trauma are strongly associated with drinking. Drinking has been associated with violence, especially domestic violence and child abuse. Finally, when consumed by a pregnant woman, alcohol can cause profound damage to the fetus. Babies born suffering from fetal alcohol syndrome are less likely to survive, more likely to fail to thrive, and manifest both physiologic and psychologic developmental problems.

Alcohol, humanity's oldest domesticated drug, is also one of its greatest enemies. In the United States, we estimate that there are almost 10 million alcohol dependent or alcoholic people and perhaps twice that proportion of "problem drinkers." We estimate that each year alcohol abuse costs our nation well in excess of one hundred billion dollars in terms of loss, health care, and decreased productivity. We do pay a large personal and societal price for this chemical comfort.

Questions

1 If the need and desire to alter our consciousness is as powerful and permanent as the in-born drives of self-preservation, hunger, and security, what does this mean for the success of US prohibitionist drug policy?

2 Given the psychoactive properties and negative impacts of abusive drinking, if alcohol were introduced as a new drug today, would it be legal? Why or why not? Where might it be placed on the five schedules?

3 According to the article, alcohol abuse is linked with automobile accidents. What about our society's cultural and spatial landscape contribution to drinking and driving?

2

The American Disease
Narcotics in Nineteenth-Century America

David F. Musto

Moving from alcohol to narcotics, drug historian David Musto offers a highly informative account of the rise, cultivation, and legal transformations of opium and cocaine. You may be surprised to learn what some of the popularly taken medicines and soft drinks, readily available in years past, contained. In fact, the original formula for Coca-Cola contained tinctures of cocaine, and even to this day, the colors on a Coke can resemble the colors of the Peruvian flag (not a coincidence) that dates back to the beginning of the Coke product. These drugs were understood, in large part, through their associations with the groups of people who used them or endorsed them, either tainting them with their stigma or endorsing them with their celebrity. In fact, the pharmacology of these substances seems to have been a minor factor, compared to the populations associated with their use and the way the substances were delivered, in forging the connotations through which they were perceived.

Opium and cocaine were cast as alien to an American existence and tied to dangerous Asian and black groups. Marijuana was tied to Mexican-American groups in the Southwest. Other groups, such as law enforcement and moral crusaders, then moved into the fray, seeking to advance their collective interests and empower themselves by outlawing and prosecuting these drugs. The history of drugs in America can thus be viewed as a lens through which the struggles of various waves of immigrant versus "native" groups were played out and realized, much like other avenues such as sport and criminal activity.

Drugs and the American Dream: An Anthology, First Edition. Edited by Patricia A. Adler, Peter Adler, and Patrick K. O'Brien.
© 2012 John Wiley & Sons, Inc. Published 2012 by John Wiley & Sons, Inc.

Before 1800, opium was available in America in its crude form as an ingredient of multidrug prescriptions, or in such extracts as laudanum, containing alcohol, or "black drop," containing no alcohol. Valued for its calming and soporific effects, opium was also a specific treatment against symptoms of gastrointestinal illnesses such as cholera, food poisoning, and parasites. Its relatively mild psychological effect when taken by mouth or as part of a more complex prescription was enhanced by frequent use, and the drug was supplied freely by physicians. In addition, self-dosing with patent medicines and the ministrations of quacks contributed to narcotic intake. The medical profession's need for something that worked in a world of mysterious mortal diseases and infections cannot be overlooked as a major stimulus for the growth of the opium market. A drug that calmed was especially appealing since physicians could at least treat the patient's anxiety.

Technological advances in organic chemistry during the early nineteenth century led to plentiful supplies of potent habit-forming drugs. Alkaloids in crude opium were separated and crystallized to isolate active principles that give opium its physiological and psychic effects. Analysis of the coca leaf occurred in mid-century, and cocaine was finally isolated.

Opium and Its Derivatives

Morphine grew in popularity as its great power over pain became better appreciated. It was cheap, compact, and had a standard strength – unlike tinctures of other forms of opium extracted from the crude plant. When the hypodermic needle became popular in the middle of the century it permitted direct injection into the body of a powerful, purified substance. Of the many substances injected experimentally, morphine was found to be exceptionally effective as a pain-killer and calming agent, and it came into medical practice after the Civil War. Writers have remarked on the coincidence to explain the apparent frequency of addiction in the United States in the latter half of the century. Of course, this line of reasoning does not explain the relatively few addicts proportionally or absolutely in such nations as France, Germany, Great Britain, Russia, and Italy, which also fought wars

during the latter half of the nineteenth century and also used morphine as an analgesic.

Whatever the cause, a relatively high level of opium consumption was established in the United States during the nineteenth century. This appetite for narcotics calls for some examination if only because opiate addiction has been described in the United States as "un-American" and "non-Western."

Because opium has not been commercially grown to any great extent in America, the national supply was imported. Before 1915 (1909 for smoking opium) no restriction other than a tariff was placed upon importation, and except for opium for smoking, these tariffs were modest. Tariff records reveal the demand for opium and opiates during most of the nineteenth and early twentieth centuries. It is reasonable to assume that smuggling did not severely modify the overall trends of opium importation, because the period of free entry (1890–6) did not dramatically alter the importation curve. The imported opium was mostly crude, although it did include opium prepared for smoking. The United States exported almost no manufactured opiates before World War I because European drugs undersold them on the world market.

Crude opium contained an estimated 9 percent morphine content extractable by American pharmaceutical concerns. One of the largest morphine-producing firms in the nineteenth century, Rosengarten and Company of Philadelphia (later merged into what is now Merck, Sharpe and Dohme), began manufacturing morphine salts in 1832. The first statistics on the importation of opium date from 1840 and reveal a continual increase in consumption during the rest of the century. The per capita importation of crude opium reached its peak in 1896. The Civil War, far from initiating opiate use on a large scale in the United States, hardly makes a ripple in its constantly expanding consumption, but addicted Civil War veterans, a group of unknown size, may have spread addiction by recruiting other users. Although there is some reduction in crude opium imports during 1861–5, presumably due to the blockade of the South, the amounts imported within a few years before and after the war are very similar. The rapid rise in crude opium did not begin until the 1870s; then it quickly outstripped the annual increase in population. Morphine did not begin to be imported in great amounts until the late 1870s. Another cause of increased consumption was the widespread use of opiates by physicians and manufacturers of patent medicines during a period when there was little fear of their use. The unregulated patent medicine craze in the United States hit its peak in the late nineteenth century – a time when the opiate content in these medicines was probably also at its highest.

The characteristics of opium and its derivatives were ideal for the patent medicine manufacturers. There was no requirement that patent medicines containing opiates be so labeled in interstate commerce until the Pure Food and Drug Act of 1906. Many proprietary medicines that could be bought at any store or by mail order contained morphine, cocaine, laudanum, or (after 1898) heroin. Attempts at state regulation of sales were not successful during the last century. Even "cures" for the opium habit frequently contained large amounts of opiates. Hay fever remedies commonly contained cocaine as their active ingredient. Coca-Cola, until 1903, contained cocaine (and since then caffeine). Opiates and cocaine became popular – if unrecognized – items in the everyday life of Americans. The manufacturers were remarkably effective during the nineteenth century in preventing any congressional action to require even the disclosure of dangerous drugs in commercial preparations.

After 1896, the per capita importation of crude opium gradually began to decline and, just before prohibitive laws rendered the importation statistics valueless, had fallen to the level of the 1880s. That level was not low, but consumption did drop as agitation mounted for strict controls. One traditional opium import which did not decline after 1900 was smoking opium, in spite of its holding no special interest for prescribing physicians, patent medicine manufacturers, or wounded Civil War veterans. Smoking opium, solely a pastime, lacked any of the elaborate advertising campaigns which boosted morphine and cocaine preparations; it had had a slow but steady rise in per capita consumption since import statistics began in 1860. Suddenly in 1909 smoking opium was excluded from the United States. Weighing heavily against it was its symbolic association since mid-century with the Chinese, who were actively persecuted, especially on the West Coast. By then they were almost totally excluded from immigrating into the United States.

The prohibition of smoking opium also served notice to other nations that America was determined to rid itself of the evils of addiction. In 1909 the United States convened the first international meeting to consider opium traffic between nations, specifically that traffic into China which was so unwelcome to the Chinese government. Although motivation for American initiative in the Chinese problem was a mixture of moral leadership, protection of US domestic welfare, and a desire to soften up Chinese resistance to American financial investments, the United States was also led by the nature of the narcotic trade to seek control of international shipments of crude narcotics to manufacturing countries and thence to markets. But the United States, on the eve of entering an international conference it had called to help China with its opium problem, discovered it had no national opium restrictions. To save face, it quickly enacted one. American prejudice against the Chinese, and the association of smoking opium with aliens, was in effect an immense aid in securing legislation in the program to help China. Indeed, a prime reason for calling the International Opium Commission was to mollify China's resentment of treatment of Chinese in the United States.

What might explain the pattern of decline of opium importation for consumption in the United States before the Harrison Act in 1914? First would be a growing fear of opiates and especially of morphine addiction, which was marked by the quick spread of antimorphine laws in various states in the 1890s. That opium addiction was undesirable had long been common opinion in the United States. Oliver Wendell Holmes, Sr, in an address delivered just before the Civil War, blamed its prevalence on the ignorance of physicians. Holmes, then dean of Harvard Medical School, reported that in the western United States "the constant prescription of opiates by certain physicians ... has rendered the habitual use of that drug in that region very prevalent. ... A frightful endemic demoralization betrays itself in the frequency with which the haggard features and drooping shoulders of the opium drunkards are met with in the street."

As the century progressed and the hypodermic injection of opiates increased their physiological effect, the danger of morphine addiction was more widely broadcast. For this reason patent medicine makers resisted attempts to require the listing of ingredients on labels. The knowledge that such substances were in baby soothing syrups and other compounds would hurt sales. Nevertheless growing publicity disclosing the contents of patent medicines, early regulatory laws in the states, and public opinion all worked together as forces to curb this use of opiates and cocaine.

Another possible explanation, although untestable, is that the opiates had nearly saturated the market for such drugs: that is, those who were environmentally or biochemically disposed to opiates had been fairly well located by the marketers and the consumption curve leveled off as the demand was met. Such reasoning could apply also to a product like cigarettes, the use of which grew at a fantastic rate with the beginning of World War I but eventually leveled off in per capita consumption: although they are easily available not everyone desires to smoke them.

The numbers of those overusing opiates must have increased during the nineteenth century as the per capita importation of crude opium increased from less than 12 grains annually in the 1840s to more than 52 grains in the 1890s. Eventually the medical consensus was that morphine had been overused by the physician, addiction was a substantial possibility, and addition of narcotics to patent medicines should be minimized or stopped. There is reason to emphasize the gradual development of this medical opinion since physicians, as well as everyone else, had what now seems a very delayed realization that dangerously addicting substances were distributed with little worry for their effect. Cocaine and heroin were both introduced from excellent laboratories by men with considerable clinical experience who judged them to be relatively harmless, in fact, to be possible cures for morphine and alcohol addiction.

By 1900, America had developed a comparatively large addict population, perhaps 250,000, along with a fear of addiction and addicting drugs. This fear had certain elements which have been powerful enough to permit the most profoundly punitive methods to be employed in the fight against addicts and suppliers. For at least seventy years purveyors of these drugs for nonmedical uses have been branded "worse than murderers," in that destroying the personality is worse than simply killing the body. What is most human is what is destroyed in the drug habitués, the opponents of narcotics argued.

In the nineteenth century addicts were identified with foreign groups and internal minorities who were already actively feared and the objects of elaborate and massive social and legal restraints. Two repressed groups which were associated with the use of certain drugs were the Chinese and the Negroes. The Chinese and their custom of opium smoking were closely watched after their entry into the United States about 1870. At first, the Chinese represented only one more group brought in to help build railroads, but, particularly after economic depression made them a labor surplus and a threat to American citizens, many forms of antagonism arose to drive them out or at least to isolate them. Along with this prejudice came a fear of opium smoking as one of the ways in which the Chinese were supposed to undermine American society.

Cocaine was especially feared in the South by 1900 because of its euphoric and stimulating properties. The South feared that Negro cocaine users might become oblivious of their prescribed bounds and attack white society. Morphine did not become so closely associated with an ethnic minority, perhaps because from its inception it was considered a simple substitute for medicinal opium and suitable for all classes. When opiates began to be feared for their addictive properties, morphine was most closely attached to the "lower classes" or the "underworld," but without greater specificity.

The crusade for alcohol prohibition which culminated in the adoption of the 18th Amendment started in the South and West early in this century. Intrastate Prohibition weighed most heavily on the poor since, until the Webb–Kenyon Act of 1913, it was quite legal to purchase liquor in bulk from wet states for shipment into dry states. When poor southerners, and particularly Negroes, were alleged to turn to cola drinks laced with cocaine or to cocaine itself for excitement as a result of liquor scarcity, more laws against cocaine quickly followed. Here, however, the South was at a loss for comprehensive legal control since the goal was to prohibit interstate as well as intrastate shipment. This could be done only with a federal statute which would threaten the states' police and commerce powers. Consequently, the story of the Harrison Act's passage contains many examples of the

South's fear of the Negro as a ground for permitting a deviation from strict interpretation of the Constitution.

Cocaine

Cocaine is a good example of a drug whose dangers became widely accepted although at first it was immensely popular. It was pure, cheap, and widely distributed; its advocates distrusted not only the opinions of their opponents but also their motivation. Cocaine users were so impressed by its euphoric properties that they were unable to evaluate the drug objectively.

Cocaine achieved popularity in the United States as a general tonic, for sinusitis and hay fever, and as a cure for the opium, morphine, and alcohol habits. Learned journals published accounts which just avoided advising unlimited intake of cocaine. Medical entrepreneurs such as the neurologist William Hammond, former surgeon general of the army, swore by it and took a wineglass of it with each meal. He was also proud to announce cocaine as the official remedy of the Hay Fever Association, a solid endorsement for anyone. Sigmund Freud is perhaps the best-remembered proponent of cocaine as a general tonic and an addiction cure. He wrote several articles in the European medical press on the wonderful substance to which his attention had been drawn by American medical journals.

In the United States the exhilarating properties of cocaine made it a favorite ingredient of medicine, soda pop, wines, and so on. The Parke Davis Company, an exceptionally enthusiastic producer of cocaine, even sold coca-leaf cigarettes and coca cheroots to accompany their other products, which provided cocaine in a variety of media and routes such as a liqueurlike alcohol mixture called Coca Cordial, tablets, hypodermic injections, ointments, and sprays.

If cocaine was a spur to violence against whites in the South, as was generally believed by whites, then reaction against its users made sense. The fear of the cocainized black coincided with the peak of lynchings, legal segregation, and voting laws all designed to remove political and social power from him. Fear of cocaine might have contributed to the dread that the black would rise above "his place," as well as reflecting

the extent to which cocaine may have released defiance and retribution. So far, evidence does not suggest that cocaine caused a crime wave but rather that anticipation of black rebellion inspired white alarm. Anecdotes often told of super-human strength, cunning, and efficiency resulting from cocaine. One of the most terrifying beliefs about cocaine was that it actually improved pistol marksmanship. Another myth, that cocaine made blacks almost unaffected by mere .32 caliber bullets, is said to have caused southern police departments to switch to .38 caliber revolvers. These fantasies characterized white fear, not the reality of cocaine's effects, and gave one more reason for the repression of blacks.

The claim of widespread use of cocaine by Negroes is called into question by the report in 1914 of 2,100 consecutive Negro admissions to a Georgia asylum over the previous five years. The medical director acknowledged the newspaper reports of "cocain-omania" among Negroes but was surprised to discover that only two cocaine users – and these incidental to the admitting diagnosis – were hospitalized between 1909 and 1914. He offered an explanation for cocaine disuse among Negroes – that poverty prevented a drug problem equal to that among whites.

The most accepted medical use of cocaine was as a surface anesthetic, for example, on the eye to permit surgery on a conscious patient, or as an injection near a nerve to stop conduction of pain stimuli. When sniffed, cocaine crystals shrink mucous membranes and drain sinuses. Along with sinus drainage, the patient gets a "high." Eventually such substitutes or modifications of cocaine were developed as benzocaine and procaine, which do not have such euphoric effects but are still capable of preventing nerve conduction.

Since cocaine was by no means limited to physicians' prescriptions, the "lower classes," particularly in "dry" states, found they could get a jolt which took the place of hard liquor. Bars began putting a pinch of cocaine in a shot of whiskey and cocaine was peddled door to door. By 1900, state laws and municipal ordinances were being rapidly enacted against these activities. But law-abiding middle and upper-class employers also found practical uses for cocaine; it was reportedly distributed to construction and mine workers to keep them going at a high pitch and with little food. This value of cocaine had been first discovered by the Spanish in sixteenth-century Peru and was put to work among the native slaves who mined silver. Cocaine thus was economically valuable, but the fear of its overstimulating powers among social subgroups predominated, in the United States, and its provision to laborers waned.

State laws

State laws designed to curb the abuse of morphine and cocaine came mostly in the last decade of the nineteenth century. The realization of "abuse" and its seriousness gradually undermined confidence in simple regulatory laws and led to a determination that decisive action must be taken. Addiction became a challenge to medical and legal institutions. State and municipal laws generally required cocaine or morphine to be ordered on a physician's prescription, which then had to be retained for perhaps a year for inspection. The laws had one great loophole: the patent medicine manufacturers repeatedly obtained exemptions for certain quantities of narcotics in proprietary medicines. These loopholes permitted the narcotized patent medicines to be sold, but the laws lulled the public into believing that this abuse of narcotics was under control. To some extent these lacunary antinarcotic laws did alert the more wary, and manufacturers began to be cautious. But as curbs on the sale of narcotics for nonmedicinal use, the laws were not effective; they were not well enforced because, among other factors, the states did not have sufficient manpower to maintain surveillance.

Although a state might enact an antinarcotic law and even enforce it, bordering states without such laws often provided drugs for users and sellers. New York State reformers bitterly criticized New Jersey's lax narcotic regulations, which vitiated enforcement of New York's carefully framed legislation. Furthermore, although the law-abiding physician had more paper work, unethical physicians could circumvent state and local laws and the consequent paper work in various ways. The "dope doctors" could simply purchase drugs by mail from another state and then dispense them to their "patients," thereby bypassing laws which relied on prescriptions and pharmacies to monitor drug use. Generally, physicians resented the legal advantage of patent medicines which, by means of statutory

exemptions, contained narcotic dosages capable of producing addiction. These evasions were in painful contradiction to the intent of legislation and a distinct reminder of the political influence of those profiting from narcotic sales.

Federal control over narcotic use and the prescription practices of the medical profession were thought in 1900 to be unconstitutional. Gradually, federal commerce and tax powers were broadened by Supreme Court decisions, notably those upholding a federal tax on colored oleomargarine, federal prohibition against transportation of women across state lines for immoral purposes, the interstate transportation of lottery tickets, and carrying liquor into a state that prohibited liquor imports. But that congressional activity was still circumscribed by the Constitution was reflected in the Supreme Court ruling in *Hammer* v. *Dagenhart* (1918) wherein the court declared that congress could not regulate the interstate shipment of goods produced by child labor. The ruling clearly indicated that federal police powers under the guise of tax or interstate commerce powers had narrow application.

As a result of constitutional uncertainty over legislation enabling federal law to prevail in an area of morals, there was little effort until after 1900 to enact a federal law to control the sale and prescription of narcotics. After the passage of the Pure Food and Drug Act (1906), some elements of the pharmacy trade supported a regulatory antinarcotic law based on the interstate commerce clause, a movement seconded by Dr Harvey Wiley of the Agriculture Department. Finally, by 1912, when the State Department's campaign for a federal antinarcotic law was making substantial progress, proponents opted for basing it on government's revenue powers. Thus the framing of an antinarcotic law paralleled the widening possibilities open to Congress in the area of policing morals. Even so, the Harrison Act of 1914 had to survive a number of unfavorable or close court decisions until its broad police powers were upheld in 1919. And as late as 1937 the Marihuana Tax Act was carefully kept separate from the Harrison Act in order to discourage more court attacks. The Drug Abuse Act of 1970 scrapped the Harrison Act's foundation on revenue powers and rests on the interstate commerce powers of Congress, returning to the basis proposed more than sixty years before. In the last half century, the interstate commerce clause has been substantially broadened so that its powers can sustain strict regulation of drug use without the need to portray a police function as a revenue measure.

Reformers

Lay reformers took a vigorous and uncomplicated stand on narcotics. In general, two problems enflamed them: corporate disregard of public welfare and individual immorality. This dichotomy is artificial but it helps to identify the objects of the reformers' zeal and it made a difference in the kinds of laws proposed. Reformers like Samuel Hopkins Adams, whose "Great American Fraud" series in *Collier's* in 1905–7 revealed the danger of patent medicines, were of course concerned over the damage done to unsuspecting victims of such medicines. Adams directed his attack against pharmaceutical manufacturers whose expensive and inaccurate advertising promotions sold harmful nostrums to the public. In keeping with his exposés of crooked politicians and corporations, Adams argued that regulatory laws should be aimed at the suppliers. For other reformers, though, the addict evoked fears; their agitation resulted in legislation directed more at the user, who might be sent to jail for possession, than at the manufacturer who produced barrels of morphine and heroin. The Southerner's fear of the Negro and the Westerner's fear of the Chinese predominated in this approach to the drug problem. The origin of concern thus affected the aim and quality of the laws. Both classes of reformers looked to federal legislation as the most effective weapon, and both tended to measure progress in the reform campaign by the amount of legislation enacted.

The reformers can also be examined from another viewpoint. One group thought in moral abstractions while another was interested in a practical solution. The Right Reverend Charles Brent, who played an important role in the movement for narcotic control, was an abstract reformer who saw the narcotics problem, like any other social problem, to be a question which required first of all a moral approach to the decision. Did narcotics have a value other than as a medicine? No: unlike alcohol they had no beverage or caloric value. Should such substances be

permitted for casual use? No: there was no justification, since there was the possibility only of danger in narcotics for nonmedicinal uses. Therefore recreational use of narcotics should be prohibited, their traffic curtailed on a world scale, and a scourge eliminated from the earth. To compromise, to permit some (for instance the Chinese) to use narcotics would be inconsistent with morality, and therefore not permissible. Reformers like Brent were charitable but unwilling to compromise.

Other reformers sought a practical and partial solution which edged toward total narcotic restriction but was modified to allow for the cravings of addicts. These compromises often came from political divisions smaller than the federal government. In contrast to Bishop Brent's proposals, the compromise programs were based on the assumption that the supply of and the desire for narcotics could not be eliminated, and therefore any attempt at total prohibition would be a failure.

Narcotics, however, constituted only a small part of the American reform movement at the turn of the century. In the last decade of the nineteenth century, rising public interest in protecting the environment and health was evident in exposés, public education, and reform proposals in Congress for such things as a pure food law, but not until the presidential years of Theodore Roosevelt was this interest translated into substantial national legislation. Roosevelt's advocacy of ecology and conservation followed a popular revulsion against the excessive concentration of wealth and the manner in which it was amassed, and the disregard of general welfare by powerful private interest.

Upton Sinclair's bitterness led to *The Jungle*, in which the young Socialist portrayed the slaughterhouse owner's utter disregard for employee welfare. Often credited with giving the final push toward enactment of the Meat Inspection Act in 1906, Sinclair soon became disillusioned with his efforts at substantial reform through idealistic principles: the big meat packers benefited from the reforms enacted by Congress since small business firms could not afford the new inspection requirements nor meet the standards of foreign nations which had criticized the purity of American meat exports.

But if some reforms were actually an assistance to institutions reformers hated, other reforms were the nuisance or corrective their advocates desired.

An aggressive administrator of the new regulations restricting environmental and physiological damage was Dr. Harvey Washington Wiley, who developed the Agriculture Department's Bureau of Chemistry into an avid detector of unsavory manufacturing practices. He was condemned by industry because his criticisms and regulations often appeared to go beyond all reasonable limits. For example, he wanted to prohibit caffeine-containing drinks such as Coca-Cola as well as patent medicines containing narcotics. His particular attention to unlabeled additives resulted in an indictment of the Coca-Cola Company and the holding up of shipments of French wines not labeled to show sulfur dioxide as a preservative. These disputes required the attention of the President, the Supreme Court, or a Cabinet officer. Theodore Roosevelt's support of Wiley waned in 1908 as the criticisms grew, and he felt some personal evaluation was necessary. He called Wiley to the White House to confront industrial spokesmen. All went well until the conversation turned to the President's treasured sugar substitute, saccharin. Wiley at once declared saccharin a threat to health which should be prohibited in foods. Roosevelt angrily reacted: "Anybody who says saccharin is injurious is an idiot. Dr. Rixey gives it to me every day!" His doubt about Wiley strengthened by this encounter, Roosevelt established the Referee Board of Consulting Scientific Experts. By 1912 Wiley had been forced out of government service because of his aggressive and, some thought, unreasonable antagonism to food and drug impurities and false claims.

The health professions and narcotics

Medicine and pharmacy were in active stages of professional organization when they became involved with the issue of narcotic control. The status of both pharmacists and physicians was less than desirable, and both suffered from weak licensing laws, meager training requirements, and a surplus of practitioners. Their intense battles for professional advancement and unification had an effect on the progress and final form of antinarcotic legislation.

Although the state of medicine in the nineteenth century was improving, its only tangible progress lay in some ability to contain a few communicable diseases. Yet, if the physician could not effect cure, he could assuage pain and apprehension: opiates were preeminent for these functions and were apparently used with great frequency. Drugs are still overused in this casual, convenient way – penicillin, the sulfas, tetracycline, barbiturates, and so on – they carry a message of effective treatment to the patient, fulfilling his emotional needs even if sometimes risky and superfluous from an objective viewpoint.

The American Medical Association (founded in 1847), which now appears monolithic and powerful, was a weak institution at the close of the last century. The vast majority of doctors refrained from membership. The AMA's battle for higher standards of training, licensure, and practice was threatening to many within the profession and seemed to the public to be but a covert plea for special preferment by one of several schools of medical practice. While one may admit that the AMA reform program improved the political, economic, and social status of the medical profession, the public welfare was also to be improved. The Flexner Report, with its independent and corroborating analysis of the profession's weaknesses, was accepted by impartial critics. Meanwhile, however, the low standards of the nineteenth century predominated and were consistent with the great reliance on such symptomatic relief agents as the opiates.

Although the drive to organize pharmacy was contemporary with the AMA's efforts, it was not so successful. However fragmented medicine might appear, pharmacy was far more fundamentally split into special-interest groups, often divided on questions of legislation, ethics, and professional standards. The druggist operated a competitive retail business to which his prescription service usually contributed only a fraction of his profits. He had some difficulty adhering to the strict professional standards enunciated by the American Pharmaceutical Association (1852) – stressing the ancient science of pharmacy – as the highest priority in his business. He found that an ideal relationship with the physician was particularly difficult to attain since the oversupply of doctors led many of them to do their own dispensing. Similarly, pharmaceutical manufacturers, importers, exporters, and wholesalers were also engaged in businesses far removed from the archetypal pharmacist dispensing an intricate prescription. The various professional components often felt that their particular interests could not be adequately served by an association in which all elements of pharmacy had an equal voice. Dissatisfaction with the APhA led to many trade associations with specific membership criteria.

Physicians and pharmacists were vocal and effective in their lobbying efforts. Each saw that in addition to aiding the public welfare, strict narcotic laws could be a distinct advantage for institutional development if great care was exercised in their framing. Knowledge of this rivalry and ambition clarifies legislative history; it also reminds us that in the competition to find a convenient law it was rather easy to lose sight of the victim of drug abuse. The public's fear of addicts and minority-group drug users might supply the powerful motive force for legislation, but the law's final form would await the approval of the institutional interests affected.

Questions

1 What were the factors that influenced the passage of the Harrison Act in 1914? What do you think happened to cocaine and opiate users once they were declared illegal? Where did the drugs move?

2 According to the article, two problems enflamed reformers: corporate disregard of public welfare and individual immorality. How might these two claims apply to the pharmaceutical industry and/or illegal drugs today? Who has the social power to fight these claims?

3 In the article, how might the pharmaceutical and medical professions use carefully framed narcotic legislation to enhance their institutional and social power? How has the alcohol industry benefited from prohibitionist drug legislation over the years?

3

Black Beauties, Gorilla Pills, Footballs, and Hillbilly Heroin
Prescription Drug Abuse over the Past 40 Years

James A. Inciardi and Theodore J. Cicero

If opium and cocaine were delegitimized through being labeled as foreign, imported, and alien, we turn next in James Inciardi and Theodore Cicero's selection to the realm of a more distinctly native form of drug. The twentieth and twenty-first centuries have witnessed the dramatic rise of pharmaceuticals, a class of drugs coming out of the heart of American innovation and technology. Here, scientists working in the prestigious fields of research and development pushed the frontiers to bring us wave after wave of new drugs designed to alleviate our ills and make us feel good.

The history of pharmaceutical popularity reveals several repeated trends. Beginning in the early decades of the 1900s a pattern developed where one class of drugs after another burst upon the scene. "Uppers" in the 1930s (Benzedrine, Dexedrine, and Methedrine) were followed by "downers" in the 1940s and 1950s (Darvon®, Dilaudid, Demerol, Fentanyl, and OxyContin®), by "barbies" in the 1960s (Deconal, Pentothal, Fiorinal, and Luminal, also known as "reds," or "yellow jackets"), and by Quaaludes® and upper–downer "speedball" combinations (such as Dexamyl and Amytal), which rose in the 1970s and fell in the 1980s. Millions of these pills were prescribed by physicians who were supported and rewarded by the drug companies. Distribution of these substances through doctors and hospitals was robustly defended by the American Medical Association and the AMA's Council on Pharmacy and Chemistry. At the same time as the Harrison and Jones–Miller Acts were establishing prohibition against cocaine and the opiates, one class after another of pharmaceuticals were sanctioned as "medical treatment." Recreational use of these substances soon followed, as they spiraled into populations such as subcultural youth, middle-class housewives, and young, urban professionals.

Each successive wave of drugs was pronounced as beneficial and safely non-habit-forming by their medical and pharmaceutical sponsors, only to be revealed a decade or more later as similar to already outlawed illicit substances. By 1970, many of these substances became classified by the federal government as having a similar abuse potential to cocaine and the opiates. But once they became entrenched in the scene they were hard to dislodge. New restrictions might have taken them out of pharmacy shelves, but they became readily available in the black street markets. In the meanwhile, millions of dollars were made by the pharmaceutical industry.

These drug cocktails surged through the twentieth century in popularity, enjoying the legitimacy afforded them by their domestic origin, their heavily white, middle-class population of users, their endorsement by prestigious occupational professions, and their promotion through advertising. This history and enormous vested interest supporting the rise of pharmaceutical drugs sets the stage for the movement of these drugs into the black market subcultures described in this selection by Inciardi and Cicero. As you read this selection, you may want to reflect on the availability and patterns of abuse related to the pharmaceutical drugs in your surrounding social environment.

Introduction

If anything has been learned about the drug problem in the United States, it is that patterns of drug-taking and drug-seeking are continually shifting and changing. Fads and fashions in the drugs of abuse seem to come and go. Drugs of choice emerge and then disappear from the American drug scene. Still others are rediscovered, reinvented, revitalized, repackaged, recycled, and become permanent parts of the landscape. As new drugs of abuse become visible, concomitant media and political feeding frenzies call for a strengthening of the "war on drugs." There was heroin in the 1950s; marijuana, amphetamines (black beauties), and LSD in the 1960s; Quaaludes®, barbiturates (gorilla pills), and PCP in the 1970s; and crack and other forms of cocaine in the 1980s and 1990s. And then came Vicodin®, OxyContin® (hillbilly heroin), and Xanax® (footballs), which gained attention during the latter 1990s and the opening years of the twenty-first century. But where did it all begin?

With the prescription drugs, perhaps it goes back to the early part of the eighteenth century with Thomas Dover, a student of British physician Thomas Sydenham, considered the "father" of clinical medicine, and strong advocate of the use of opium for the treatment of disease. Following in the path of his mentor, Dover developed a form of medicinal opium. Known as Dover's Powder, it contained one ounce each of opium, ipecac (the dried roots of a tropical creeping plant), and licorice, combined with saltpeter, tartar, and wine. Dover's Powder was introduced in 1709 and soon made its way to America, where it remained one of the most widely used opium preparations for almost two centuries.

Although opium had been a popular narcotic for thousands of years, the attraction of Dover's Powder was in the euphoric and anesthetic properties of opium. The introduction of Dover's Powder apparently started a trend. By the latter part of the eighteenth century, similar patent medicines containing opium were readily available throughout urban and rural America. They were sold in pharmacies, grocery and general stores, at traveling medicine shows, and through the mail. This patent medicine industry eventually provided the backdrop for the abuse of prescription drugs and other pharmaceuticals.

The Early Days

Our introduction to the study of prescription drug abuse and diversion emerged during the late 1960s and early 1970s, with much of it coming from the work of the late Carl D. Chambers, who at the time was Director of Research for the New York State Narcotic Addiction Control Commission. [...] Years before the first National Household Survey on Drug Abuse was launched, for example, Chambers designed and fielded the first general population survey of drug abuse. It was done in New York, and it paved the way for National Institute on Drug Abuse's (NIDA) National Household and Monitoring the Future studies. Chambers' New York general population survey was the first to empirically document that prescription drug abuse and diversion were problems that needed to be addressed.

Chambers' subsequent work focused on the abuse and diversion of prescription drugs: pentazocine (Talwin®), propoxyphene (Darvon®), amphetamines, barbiturate-sedatives, and methadone. [...]

During the 1980s and much of the 1990s, however, prescription drug abuse took a back seat to other more pressing concerns. "Freebase" and powder cocaine were major concerns, with the attendant cocaine wars in Florida, Latin America, and the Caribbean instigated by Colombia's Medellín and Cali cartels. In inner-city crack houses across the nation, crack and the sex-for-crack exchanges appeared. Rates of drug-related street crime rose as did the violence associated with drug gang wars over control of emerging crack markets. The occurrence of HIV/AIDS among injection drug and crack users became a concern and was followed by early attempts to understand the phenomenon and develop effective science-based interventions. During those years, little attention could be focused on prescription drug abuse.

Recent Trends and Accomplishments

In 1994, with little fanfare and for the most part unknown to researchers in the drug field, Ortho-McNeil Pharmaceutical funded what turned out to be the longest and most expensive drug abuse research study to date (excluding, of course, the annual National Household and Monitoring the Future surveys). The focus was Ultram® (tramadol HCl), an opioid-like analgesic, which had just been approved by the Food and Drug Administration (FDA) as a nonscheduled drug under the Controlled Substances Act. [...]

Not long after the [...] surveillance study of Ultram® had been implemented, researchers, clinicians, and government observers began noticing that prescription drugs were being more widely prescribed and abused. A study conducted by the National Center on Addiction and Substance Abuse at Columbia University, for example, found that from 1992 to 2002, opioid prescriptions increased by 222%, codeine prescriptions increased by 12%, fentanyl by 1,106%, hydrocodone by 376%, meperidine by 66%, hydromorphone by 107%, methadone by 1,597%, morphine by 279%, and oxycodone by 380%. For the period 1995 through 1997, the Drug Enforcement Administration's Automation of Reports and Consolidated Orders System (ARCOS), which measures the retail distribution of pain medications in grams, found substantial increases in the medicinal use of morphine (up 59%), fentanyl (1,168%), oxycodone (23%), and hydromorphone (19%). Subsequently, the period of 1997 to 2001 demonstrated increases in the retail distribution of oxycodone (up 348%), morphine (49%), and fentanyl (151%). One could argue that these increases served as a catalyst for the increasing abuse, dependence, and diversion of prescription opioids.

At the same time, national data suggested that the abuse of many different prescription drugs had been escalating since the early to mid-1990s. The National Survey of Drug Use and Health found that the numbers of new nonmedical users of prescription opioids (primarily products containing codeine, hydrocodone, and oxycodone) increased from 600,000 in 1990 to over 2.4 million in 2004, marking it as the drug category with the largest number of new users in 2004. In addition, reports from the Drug Abuse Warning Network indicated that abuse-related emergency department (ED) visits involving narcotic analgesics increased by 153% from 1995 through 2002, and during the same period abuse-related ED visits involving benzodiazepines increased by 41%. Similar increases were reflected in data on drug abuse treatment admissions.

Although the abuse and diversion of prescription drugs was clearly an evolving problem, OxyContin® galvanized the attention of the media, the government, and the public at large. When the drug was first introduced in 1996, it was hailed as a breakthrough in pain management. The medication is unique in that its time-release formula allows patients to enjoy continuous, long-term relief from moderate to severe pain, but the honeymoon period for the drug turned out to be quite brief. Abuse of OxyContin® first surfaced in rural Maine, soon spreading along the east coast and Ohio Valley, and then into rural Appalachia. Communities in western Virginia, eastern Kentucky, West Virginia, and southern Ohio were especially hard hit, and a number of factors characteristic of these areas seemed to correlate with the apparent high rates of abuse. Aspects of the culture in northern Maine and rural Appalachia are markedly different from those in other parts of the country. Many of the communities are quite small and isolated, often situated in the mountains and "hollers" (small crevice-like mountain dens and valleys), a considerable distance from major towns and highways. As a result, many of the usual street drugs are simply not available. Instead, locals make do with resources already on hand, like prescription drugs. Isolation limits options for amenities and entertainment, a major contrast to the distractions of metropolitan areas. Many substance abuse treatment patients in these rural areas have told their counselors that they started using drugs because of boredom. Many start abusing drugs quite young, as well.

In addition, many adults in these rural areas tend to suffer from chronic illnesses and pain syndromes, born out of hard lives of manual labor in perilous professions: coal mining, logging, fishing, and other blue-collar industries that often result in debilitating injuries. As a result, a disproportionately high segment of the population lives on strong painkillers. Use of pain pills evolves into a kind of coping mechanism, and the practice of self-medication becomes a way of life for many. As such, the use of narcotic analgesics has become normalized and integrated into the local culture.

Media outlets in Maine began reporting on OxyContin® abuse in early 2000. The Bangor Daily News ran several features, which included information not only about the properties of the drug, but also about: (a) how to compromise its time-release mechanism, (b) the tactics of diversion that people were using to obtain the drug (including Medicaid fraud), and (c) the concerns of the medical profession about the potential for abusing the drug. In addition, numerous examples of alleged OxyContin®-related crimes were described in detail. A smattering of news articles followed in other parts of the nation, and in

May, 2000, the Boston Globe became the first major daily to focus on OxyContin®. After that, OxyContin® became a national media event, and the escalating rates of prescription drug abuse and diversion were more fully recognized.

[...]

Reflections on Prescription Drug Abuse

[...] [T]here is no question that the problems of prescription drug abuse and diversion continue to grow. The most recent National Survey on Drug Use and Health documented that US household residents are more likely to report the nonmedical use of prescription opioids than any illicit drug, other than marijuana. The 2006 Monitoring the Future survey reached the same conclusion. Moreover, ED visits involving the abuse or misuse of prescription drugs increased by 21% from 2004 to 2005. There were about 600,000 cases in 2005 – almost as many as for heroin and cocaine combined.

Although the reasons behind this are open to speculation, two things are indeed apparent. First, the number and variety of prescription drugs have increased significantly in recent years, which is a positive trend for patients in legitimate need of care. At the same time, however, it has been repeatedly documented that availability seems to invariably create demand for drugs with a high potential for abuse. Second, prescription drugs are popular among abusers because they are considered to be more acceptable, less dangerous, easier to rationalize, and less subject to legal consequences than are illicit drugs. These phenomena tend to support the contention that fads and fashions in both the preferences in, and patterns of, drug abuse appear to be continually shifting and changing. The current trend would appear to be prescription drugs.

One of the big mysteries about the prescription drug problem appears to be where the drugs are coming from, that is, "diversion." Specifically, diversion involves the unlawful channeling of regulated pharmaceuticals from legal sources to the illicit marketplace, and this can occur along all points in the drug delivery process: from the original manufacturing site, the wholesale distributor, the physician's office, the retail pharmacy, or the patient. Diversion, however, has been the focus of only minimal study, and ideas on the sources of illegal supplies of prescription drugs vary. Federal agencies maintain that diverted drugs enter the illegal market primarily through "doctor shoppers," inappropriate prescribing practices by physicians, and improper dispensing by pharmacists. Given this belief, the major solution suggested has been the creation of prescription monitoring programs, which enable pharmacists and drug control agencies to detect "script docs" who write prescriptions for a fee, as well as "doctor shoppers" who go from physician to physician and from pharmacy to pharmacy to obtain multiple supplies of prescription drugs. Federal authorities have also identified Internet sales as a major source of diversion. Correspondingly, in 2005 the authors surveyed diversion investigators in 300 police and regulatory agencies across the nation as to their perceptions of the primary sources of diversion. Interestingly, almost three-fourths of the survey participants considered drug abusers posing as patients to be the major source of diversion through doctor shopping and prescription theft and forgery. At the same time, only 3% considered the Internet to be a significant source of prescription drugs. By contrast, the 2005 National Survey on Drug Use and Health found that among individuals ages 12 and older who reported abusing prescription opioids in the last year, 72.3% had obtained the drugs from friends or relatives, 18.5% had obtained them from a physician, and less than 1% reported that they were getting the drugs from the Internet. One of the questions that these findings suggest is: Where are the friends and relatives getting the drugs? Are they sharing their legitimate supplies, or are they giving away pills that should have been discarded? Are the friends or relatives the doctor shoppers who are visiting multiple physicians, or forging prescriptions? Are they getting the drugs from street dealers, and if so, where are the dealers obtaining their supplies? Moreover, our research suggests that dealers are a major source of prescription drugs. There seems to be a "black box" that warrants some investigation.

One might begin by looking at losses of prescription drugs from pharmacies, distributors, hospitals and clinics, treatment programs, or any other business or organization where controlled substances are stored.

When losses occur through robberies, burglaries, shoplifting, or employee theft, the Drug Enforcement Administration (DEA) requires that its Form 106 (Report of Theft or Loss of Controlled Substances) be filed. Although the Form 106 data are not routinely tabulated and published, what has been released suggests the potential magnitude of losses. From 2001 to 2003, some 563,677 "standard dosage units" of methadone (1 methadone dosage unit in DEA terminology = 10 mg) were reported as lost or stolen, and almost all were through illegal means. From January 2000 to June 2003, the DEA reported that almost 1.4 million tablets of OxyContin® were lost or stolen through 2,494 separate incidents. Moreover, a request by the University of Wisconsin under the Freedom of Information Act found a total of 12,894 theft and loss incidents reported to the DEA from 2000 to 2003 in 22 Eastern states, involving some 28 million dosage units of controlled substances. These data suggest that massive quantities of prescription opioids are being stolen prior to being prescribed.

Residential burglary also should be studied. Millions of residential burglaries occur in the United States each year, and evidence suggests that prescription drugs are a major target in a significant portion of these crimes. In scores of focus groups and in-depth interviews conducted with hundreds of drug-involved offenders, active street drug users, and recovering addicts over the past decade, participants agreed that the four items typically sought in residential burglaries are cash, jewelry, guns, and prescription drugs. Studies conducted by the Department of Justice and by independent researchers as well as newspaper reports support this contention.

Are residential burglaries and pharmacy losses the major sources of supply for street dealers? Perhaps, but our research with prescription drug abusers also points to script doctors, illegal sales in small pharmacies, acquaintances who sell their personal prescriptions, sex workers' clients, disability patients, Medicaid recipients, and personal prescriptions intended for the treatment of drug dependence or mental illness. All of this suggests that focused research is needed targeting the "black box" of diversion. This also suggests that prescription monitoring programs are likely intercepting only a segment of those individuals diverting prescription drugs.

Questions

1   According to the article, the abuse of OxyContin® in rural Appalachian areas was a result of what intersecting sociocultural variables? How might sociocultural factors influence different forms of drug abuse in other locations in the United States?

2   What is meant by the "diversion" of pharmaceutical drugs? What is "doctor shopping?" What are the most popular pharmaceutical drugs on campuses today? How are students acquiring these drugs?

3   Why is the pharmaceutical industry exempt under the "Just Say No" discourse and policies?

Control and Intoxicant Use
A Theoretical and Practical Overview

Norman E. Zinberg and Wayne M. Harding

Norman Zinberg and Wayne Harding's classic piece on set and setting closes this sub-section of the book. It provides the theoretical underpinning of the way most sociologists approach the study of drugs and society. Avoiding a unilateral approach, they acknowledge the role of biochemistry (the pharmacology of the drug) and psychology (the personality characteristics of the user) in affecting the choice of drugs used, the way people use or abuse them, and the effects they have. But Zinberg and Harding focus primarily on the third variable: setting, or the social environment surrounding and framing the use of drugs. This is the sociological factor, the one that introduces the influence of larger historical, cultural, socioeconomic, political, and other abstract features of the world. Biological factors shape us as organisms, influencing the way we react to drugs physiologically as human beings. Psychological factors shape us as individuals, influencing the way we live in the world and are driven and constrained by a variety of personality factors. But neither of these dimensions brings the role of subculture or society into the equation. The sociological, demographic, and situational characteristics of people have an enormous influence over the way individuals learn about drugs, the role modeling they internalize, the meanings they encounter and adopt, the culture that surrounds them, and the history of their people with regard to various drugs, all of which play a significant role in shaping their drug usage patterns.

In reading this chapter, pay particular attention to the parts of society and social life on which Zinberg and Harding focus. How do these factors represent the sociological perspective and how is it different from the psychological and biological ones? Thinking back, ask yourself how the claims they make about the role of set and setting are reflected in the selections you have already read.

Drugs and the American Dream: An Anthology, First Edition. Edited by Patricia A. Adler, Peter Adler, and Patrick K. O'Brien.
© 2012 John Wiley & Sons, Inc. Published 2012 by John Wiley & Sons, Inc.

[…]

The Social Setting and Control

In the last decade (1970s) it has become increasingly commonplace for investigators to divide the variables that are presumed to influence drug-taking behavior into three groups: (1) drug variables (the pharmacological properties of the drug being used); (2) set variables (the attitudes and personality of the user); and (3) setting variables (the social and physical environment in which use occurs). Underlying this model – which corresponds to the public-health model of agent, host, and environment – is the premise that at any one time variables from each of the three groups interact in complex ways to determine who uses an intoxicant, how it is used, and what its effects are.

Our primary theoretical and research interest has been the impact of setting variables on control. We will begin by defining the two aspects of setting with which we are most concerned, rituals and social sanctions. Next, the importance of setting variables will be illustrated by considering how control over alcohol use has developed in American culture and how it operates today, and then by describing how today's social setting is influencing the development of control over illicit drug use. Finally, examples will be given of the interaction of the drug, set, and setting variables in shaping the use of illicit drugs.

Rituals and social sanctions. As used here, the term rituals refers to the stylized, prescribed behavior patterns surrounding the use of a drug. This behavior may include methods of procuring and administering the drug, selection of a physical and social setting for use, activities undertaken after the drug has been administered, and methods of preventing untoward drug effects. For example, two familiar alcohol-using rituals are having cocktails before dinner and drinking beer at ball games.

Social sanctions are the norms regarding whether and how a particular drug should be used. They include both the informal (and often unspoken) values and rules of conduct shared by a group and the formal laws and policies regulating drug use. Two of the informal sanctions or basic rules of conduct that

regulate the use of alcohol are "Know your limit" and "Don't drive when you're drunk." Although laws and regulations are clearly social sanctions, we will emphasize informal social sanctions, which frequently are internalized and actually may exert greater influence over use than do formal rules. For instance, most Americans avoid drunkenness more because they feel it is unseemly – and drunken driving more because they have learned it is unsafe – than because of the possible legal consequences.

Rituals and social sanctions operate in different social contexts that range all the way from small discrete clusters of users (drinks at a weekly poker game with friends) through larger collections of people (cocktail parties, or drugs at rock concerts) to entire classes or segments of society (morning coffee, or wine with meals in Italian households). Different segments of society may develop complementary, or even opposing, rituals and social sanctions, and usually each segment is cognizant of the alternatives and to some degree is influenced by them. Rituals and social sanctions can operate either for or against control. Drinking muscatel from a bag-wrapped bottle while squatting in a doorway is not a controlling ritual nor is the soliciting of psychedelics from strangers on the street. According positive status to the ability to withstand extraordinarily high doses of LSD or to the sizableness of one's heroin habit is not a controlling sanction. We are chiefly concerned with the rituals and sanctions that promote moderate use, as exemplified by the evolution of control over alcohol consumption.

Social setting and alcohol use

The history of alcohol consumption in America reveals striking variations in patterns of use from one era to another. Sometimes a period of control, or lack of control, has coincided with a major historical epoch. The following five social prescriptions defining controlled or moderate use of alcohol, which have been derived from studies of use in many different cultures, will serve as a standard for assessing control in the major periods of American history:

1 Group drinking is clearly differentiated from drunkenness and is associated with ritualistic or religious celebrations.

2   Drinking is associated with eating or ritualistic feasting.

3   Both sexes, as well as two or more generations, are included in the drinking situation, whether they drink or not.

4   Drinking is divorced from the individual effort to escape personal anxiety or difficult (even intolerable) social situations. Further, alcohol is not considered medicinally valuable.

5   Inappropriate behavior when drinking (violence, aggression, overt sexuality) is absolutely disapproved, and protection against such behavior is offered by the sober or the less intoxicated. This general acceptance of a concept of restraint usually indicates that drinking is only one of many activities and thus carries a low level of emotionalism. It also shows that drinking is not associated with a male or female rite de passage or sense of superiority.

The importance of these social prescriptions in controlling alcohol use is evident in the changing patterns of consumption through the colonial period, the Revolutionary War and nineteenth century, the Prohibition era, and the period that has followed repeal of the Volstead Act.

Pre-Revolutionary America (1620–1775), though veritably steeped in alcohol, strongly and effectively prohibited drunkenness. Families drank and ate together in taverns, and drinking was associated with celebrations and rituals. Tavern-keepers were people of status; keeping the peace and preventing excesses stemming from drunkenness were grave duties. Manliness or strength was not measured by the extent of consumption or by violent acts resulting from it. Pre-Revolutionary society, however, did not abide by all the prescriptions, for certain alcoholic beverages were viewed as medicines. For example, "groaning beer," a very potent alcoholic beverage, was consumed in large quantities by pregnant and lactating women. Even though alcohol was viewed as medicinally valuable, alcohol-related problems remained at a low level, due in part to the strict standards that limited consumption and dictated deportment when drinking.

Beginning with the Revolutionary War and continuing with the Industrial Revolution and expansion of the frontier through the nineteenth century, an era of excess dawned. Men were separated from their families, which left them to drink together and with prostitutes. Alcohol was served without food and was not limited to special occasions. Violence resulting from drunkenness became more common. In the face of increasing drunkenness and alcoholism, people began to believe (as in the case with some illicit drugs today) that it was the powerful pharmacological properties of the intoxicant itself that made more controlled use difficult or impossible. By the latter part of the nineteenth century the West was won, and the family and personal disruptions brought on by the Industrial Revolution were moderated. In both the West and the East, families became more closely integrated. There was a change in the character of the neighborhood saloon or bar. Customers partook of free lunches with their beverages and tended once again to represent a mix of generations and sexes who frowned on violence, overt sexuality, and excessive consumption of alcoholic beverages. This moderation, however, was interrupted in the early twentieth century by the passage of the Volstead Act, which ushered in another era of excess. In the speakeasy ambience of the Prohibition era, men again drank together and with prostitutes, food was replaced by alcohol, and the drinking experience was colored with illicitness and potential violence.

Although Repeal provided relief from excessive and unpopular legal control, years passed before regular but moderate alcohol use emerged as normative behavior. Today, however, the vast majority of drinkers manage to control their use. Of an estimated 105 million drinkers fewer than eight million are alcoholics (Harding and Zinberg, 1977). While alcoholism is still a major public health problem, the extent of noncompulsive use of such a powerful, addictive, and easily available intoxicant is remarkable. This can only be fully understood in terms of the rituals and sanctions that pattern the way alcohol is used.

Alcohol-using rituals define appropriate use and limit consumption to specific occasions: a drink with a business luncheon, wine with dinner, or perhaps beer with the boys. Positive social sanctions permit and even encourage alcohol use, but there are also negative sanctions that condemn promiscuous use and drunkenness; for example, "Don't mix drinks," "Don't drink before sundown," and "Know your limit."

This is not to say that users never break these rules, but when they do they are aware of making a special exception. They know, for instance, that having a Bloody Mary with breakfast is acceptable behavior for an occasional Sunday brunch, but that drinking vodka with breakfast every morning would violate accepted social standards.

The internalization of rituals and social sanctions begins in early childhood. Children see their parents and other adults drink. They are exposed to acceptable and unacceptable models of alcohol use in magazines and movies and on television. Some may sip their parent's drink or be served wine with meals or on religious occasions. So, by the time they reach adolescence they have already absorbed an enormous amount of information about how to drink. When the adolescent tests – as most do – the limits he has learned and gets drunk and nauseated, there is little need to fear that this excess will become habitual. As he matures the adolescent has numerous examples of adult use at hand and can easily find friends who share both his interest in drinking and his commitment to becoming a controlled drinker. Support for control continues throughout adult life.

Obviously the influence of social learning on the alcohol user is not always so straightforward. Social sanctions and rituals promoting control are not uniformly distributed throughout the culture. Some ethnic groups, such as the Irish, lack strong sanctions against drunkenness and have a correspondingly higher rate of alcoholism. Alcohol socialization within the family may break down as a result of divorce, death, or some other disruptive event. In some instances the influence of other variables – personality, genetic differences, as well as other setting variables – may outweigh the influence of social learning. Nonetheless, controlling rituals and social sanctions exert a crucial and distinct influence on the way most Americans use alcohol (Harding and Zinberg, 1977).

Social setting and illicit drug use

In contrast to the situation with alcohol, the opportunities for learning how to control illicit drug consumption, although changing, are still extremely limited. Neither the family nor the culture regularly provides long-term education or models of use.

The worst propaganda of the 1960s against illicit drug use has faded, but the chief educational message from media and the schools is still that reasonable, controlled use of illicit drugs is impossible. Certainly, no official advice is given on how to use these drugs safely. Compounding these disadvantages are the possible problems of variable dosage and purity of drugs on the black market, and the very real threat of arrest and incarceration. Ironically, the efforts to eliminate any and all uses of illicit drugs work against the development of control by those who decide to use drugs anyway.

Despite these difficulties, our DAC and NIDA studies and the work of other investigators have shown that it is possible to attain a high level of control over illicit drugs. Furthermore, there is some indication that occasional rather than intensive patterns of consumption predominate in the use of most if not all illicit drugs. Our research comparing controlled and compulsive users of marihuana, psychedelics, and opiates suggests that rituals and social sanctions promote this control in four basic and overlapping ways:

1 Sanctions define moderate use and condemn compulsive use. Controlled opiate users have sanctions limiting frequency of use to levels far below that required for addiction. Many have special sanctions, such as "Don't use every day." A complementary ritual would be to restrict the use of an opiate to weekends.

2 Sanctions limit use to physical and social settings that are conducive to a positive or "safe" drug experience. The maxim for psychedelics is "Use in a good place at a good time with good people." Rituals consonant with such sanctions are the selection of a pleasant rural setting for psychedelic use, or the timing of use to avoid driving while "tripping."

3 Sanctions identify potentially untoward drug effects. Rituals embody the relevant precautions to be taken before and during use. Opiate users may minimize the risk of overdose by using only a portion of the drug and waiting to gauge its effect before using more. Marihuana users similarly titrate their dosage to avoid becoming too high (dysphoric).

4   Sanctions and rituals operate to compartmentalize drug use and support the users' non-drug-related obligations and relationships. Users may budget the amount of money they spend on drugs, as they do for entertainment. Drugs may be used only in the evenings and on weekends to avoid interfering with work performance.

The process by which controlling rituals and sanctions are acquired varies from subject to subject. Most individuals come by them gradually during the course of their drug-using careers. But the most important source of precepts and practices for control seems to be peer-using groups. Virtually all of our subjects required the assistance of other noncompulsive users to construct appropriate rituals and sanctions out of the folklore and practices circulating in the diverse drug-using subcultures. The peer group provides instruction in and reinforces proper use; despite the popular image of peer pressure as a corrupting force pushing weak individuals toward drug misuse, many segments of the drug subculture stand firmly against misuse of drugs.

This does not imply that all illicit drug use, even among controlled users, is altogether safe or decorous. As with alcohol consumption, there are occasions when less than decorous behavior occurs. Obviously the only way to completely eliminate the attendant risks is to remain abstinent. We should never condone excessive use of any intoxicant, but we must recognize that if occasional lapses of control occur, they do not signify a breakdown of overall control. Drunkenness at a wedding reception is not a reliable indicator of alcoholism. Unfortunately, occasions of impropriety following the use of illicit drugs are likely to be taken (by abstainers, usually) as proof of the prevailing mythology that with these drugs the only possibilities are abstinence or compulsive use.

Despite occasional lapses by some subjects, the bulk of the controlled users we have studied demonstrate as much responsibility, caution, and control over their illicit drug use as does the average social drinker.

Interactions among drug, set, and setting

As stated earlier, in order to understand drug use, drug, set, and setting variables must all be taken into account. The use of opiates during the Vietnam War and psychedelic use during the past decade and a half illustrate how these variables can interact and also how control of an illicit drug can evolve.

Recent estimates indicate that during the Vietnam War as many as 35 percent of enlisted men used heroin. Of these, 54 percent became addicted to it, and 73 percent of all those who used at least five times became addicted. When the extent of heroin use in Vietnam was first realized, officials of the armed forces and government assumed that the commonly believed maxim, "Once an addict always an addict," would operate, and that returning veterans would contribute to a major heroin epidemic in the United States. Treatment and rehabilitation centers were set up in Vietnam, and the Army's claim that heroin addiction stopped "at the shore of the South China Sea" was heard everywhere. As virtually all observers agreed, however, those programs were largely failures. Often people in the rehabilitation centers used more heroin than when they were on active duty, and recidivism rates in Vietnam approached 90 percent.

Although pessimism was warranted at the time, most addiction did indeed stop at the South China Sea. As Lee Robins has shown, only 50 percent of the men who had been addicted in Vietnam used heroin at all after their return to the United States; and, what is more surprising, only 12 percent became readdicted (Robins et al., 1977). In order to account for the fact that so many veterans used heroin in Vietnam and that their rate of addiction dropped dramatically after they returned to the United States, set, drug, and particularly setting variables must be considered.

Undoubtedly some personality configurations are such that dependence on almost any available intoxicating substance is likely. But even the most generous estimate of the number of such individuals is not large enough to explain the extraordinarily high rate of use in Vietnam. And since the military screens out the worst psychological problems at enlistment, the number of addiction-prone personalities might even have been lower than in a normal population. Robins found that a youthful liability scale correlated well with heroin use in Vietnam. The scale included some items that could be indicative of personality difficulties (truancy, dropout or explusion from school, fighting, arrests, and so on), but it also included many non-personality-related items, such as race or living in the inner city. And it accounted for only a portion of the variance in heroin use.

It should be noted here that the bulk of research evidence linking personality with drug use has been riddled with serious methodological problems. Perhaps the most frequent problem in attempting to assess the importance of the user's personality is the difficulty of drawing sound conclusions when interviewing those who have become dependent on intoxicating substances. In the American cultural setting these users tend to sound and look like a group that is extremely vulnerable to dependence, and in a retrospective study it is easy to make a case for their original vulnerability. Until recently, studies of drug consumption have reinforced this tendency by centering on the most severe cases of misuse.

Another reasonable explanation for the high rate of heroin use and of addiction in Vietnam might be the availability of the drug. Robins notes that 85 percent of veterans had been offered heroin in Vietnam, and that it was remarkably inexpensive (Robins et al., 1977). Another drug variable, the route of administration, must also have contributed to widespread use in Vietnam. Heroin was so potent and inexpensive that smoking was an effective and economic method of use, and this no doubt made it more attractive than if injection had been the primary mode of administration. These two drug variables also seem to explain the decrease in heroin use and addiction among veterans following their return to the United States. The decreased availability of heroin in the United States (reflected in high price) and its decreased potency (which made smoking it wholly impractical) made it more difficult for the returning veterans to continue to use the drug as they had in Vietnam.

In the case of Vietnam, the drug variable may carry more explanatory power than the various personality variables, but like them it has limits. Ready availability of heroin seems to account for the high prevalence of use, but it alone does not explain why some individuals became addicted and others did not, any more than availability of alcohol is sufficient to explain the difference between the alcoholic and the social drinker. (Our current NIDA study, too, indicates that opiates are just as available to controlled users as to compulsive users.) Availability is inextricably intertwined with the social and psychological factors

that create demand for an intoxicant. Once a reasonably large number of users decide that a substance is attractive and desirable, it is surprising how quickly that substance can become more plentiful. (Cocaine is a current example.) When the morale of US troops in Germany declined in 1972, large quantities of various drugs, including heroin, became much more available than they had been before, even though Germany is much farther from opium-growing areas than Vietnam.

The social setting of Vietnam was both alien and extremely stressful. This abhorrent environment must have been a significant factor, if not the primary factor, in leading men who ordinarily would not have considered using heroin to use it and sometimes to become addicted. Their low rate of addiction after returning home suggests that the veterans themselves associated heroin use with Vietnam, much as hospital patients who are receiving large amounts of opiates for a painful medical condition associate the drug with the condition and do not crave it after they have left the hospital.

The importance of the three variables – drug, set, and setting – becomes even clearer when we attempt to account for the changes in psychedelic use that have taken place during the last ten or fifteen years. Whereas the Vietnam data primarily illustrate how the prevalence of use is affected by these variables, psychedelic use illustrates how a more specific aspect of control – control over adverse effects – is influenced by drug, set, and setting.

About 1963, the use of psychedelics became a subject of national hysteria – the so-called "drug revolution" – epitomized by Timothy Leary's "Tune In, Turn On, and Drop Out" slogan. These drugs, known then as psychotomimetics (imitators of psychosis), were widely believed to cause psychosis, suicide, and even murder. Equally well publicized were the contentions that they could bring about spiritual rebirth or a sense of mystical oneness with the universe. Certainly there were numerous cases of not merely transient but prolonged psychosis following the use of psychedelics. In the mid-1960s such psychiatric hospitals as the Massachusetts Mental Health Center and Bellevue were reporting that as many as one-third of their emergency admissions resulted from the ingestion of these drugs. By the late 60s, however, the rate of admissions had dropped dramatically. Initially, many observers concluded that this drop was due to a decline in use brought about by fear tactics – the warnings about various health hazards, the chromosome breaks and birth defects, reported in the newspapers. In fact, although psychedelic use continued to be the fastest growing drug use in America through 1973, the dysfunctional sequelae virtually disappeared. What then had changed?

Neither the drugs themselves nor the personalities of the users were the major factor in cases of psychotic reactions to psychedelics. A retrospective study of the way such drugs had been used before the early 60s has revealed that although responses to the drugs varied widely, they included few of the horrible, highly publicized consequences of the mid-60s. In another study conducted before the drug revolution, typologies of response to the drugs were found, but not a one-to-one relationship between untoward reactions and emotional disturbance. It appears therefore that the hysteria and conflict over psychedelic use that characterized the mid-60s created a climate in which bad trips occurred more often than they had before. Becker in his prophetic article of 1967 compared the then current anxiety about psychedelics to anxiety about marihuana in the late 1920s when several psychoses had been reported (Becker, 1967). He hypothesized that the psychoses of the 1920s had come not from reactions to the drug itself but from the secondary anxiety generated by the media, which had exaggerated the drug's effects. Suggesting that such unpleasant reactions had disappeared later because the actual effects of marihuana use had become more widely known, he correctly predicted that the same thing would happen in relation to the psychedelics.

Social learning about psychedelics also brought a change in the reactions of those who had expected to gain insight and enlightenment from their use. Interviews have shown that the user of the early 1960s who hoped for heaven, feared hell, and was unfamiliar with drug effects had a far more extreme experience than the user of the 1970s, who had been exposed to a decade of publicity about psychedelic colors, music, and sensations. The later user had been thoroughly prepared, albeit largely unconsciously, for the experience, and therefore his response was far less extreme.

Increased control over the psychedelics seems to be attributable to the subcultural development of controlling sanctions and rituals very like those regarding alcohol use in the larger culture. The rule "Use the first time only with a guru" counseled neophytes to team up with experienced users who could reduce their secondary anxiety about what was happening by interpreting it as a drug effect. "Only use at a good time, in a good place, with good people" gave users sound advice about taking drugs that would make them intensely sensitive to their inner and outer surroundings. In addition, it conveyed the message that the drug experience could be merely a pleasant consciousness change rather than a visit to the extreme of heaven or hell. The specific rituals that developed to express these sanctions – as to just when it was best to take the drug, how it was best to come down, and so on – varied from group to group, though some that were particularly effective spread from one group to another. Today (1979), controlling rituals and sanctions are widely available to those who use psychedelics.

The psychedelics also provide a good example of the role that pharmacology plays with regard to control of use. Since they produce a long period of well-defined consciousness change, they are more easily controlled than other drugs. The length of intoxication and its intensity make the psychedelics special-occasion drugs, requiring users to set aside a considerable period of time in which to deal with drug effects. And the process of defining a special occasion brings in a variety of controlling factors, including the development of sanctions and rituals. Although at the height of the drug revolution some users took psychedelics several times a week, reports from the Haight Ashbury Free Medical Clinic and from our own study show that no case of such use lasted longer than a year or two at the most. While that was, of course, a long time in which to make frequent use of such powerful substances, and the resulting psychological damage cannot be assessed, it is still hard to imagine anyone becoming habituated to the psychedelics. So, though the social setting variable explains the reduction and virtual elimination of severe emotional reactions to psychedelic drugs, the drug variable is most important in accounting for the low rate of dependence.

[...]

References

Becker, H. S. 1967. History, culture and subjective experience: an exploration of the social bases of drug-induced experiences, *Journal of Health and Social Behavior* 8:163–76.

Harding, W. M. and Zinberg, N. E. 1977. The effectiveness of the subculture in developing rituals and social sanctions for controlled use, *Drugs, Rituals and Altered States of Consciousness* (ed. B. M. du Toit). A. A. Balkema, Rotterdam, Netherlands.

Robins, L. N., Helzer, J. E., Hesselbrock, M. et al. 1977. Vietnam veterans three years after Vietnam: how our study changed our view of heroin, Problems of Drug Dependence, Proceedings of the Thirty-Ninth Annual Scientific Meeting, Committee on Problems of Drug Dependence, Boston, Massachusetts.

Questions

1   According to the article, what are rituals and social sanctions with regard to drug use? How do rituals and sanctions intersect to guide drug using behaviors? Provide examples from your own experiences.

2   According to the article, only a minority of drinkers are alcoholics, and while alcoholism is still a public health problem, the extent of noncompulsive use of such a powerful, addictive, and easily available intoxicant is remarkable. Do you think the similar use patterns would result from the regulation and control of currently illegal drugs? Why or why not?

3   What are some of the social sanctions and/or rituals that surround other forms of drug use? Do you think illegal drug users moderate and/or abstain due to forms of formal or informal sanctions? How might secondary anxiety influence set and setting with regard to illegal drug use today?

Drug Scares and Moral Panics

5

Symbolic Crusade
Status Politics and the American Temperance Movement

Joseph R. Gusfield

In another classic piece, Joseph Gusfield introduces the concepts of status and power into the struggles over the legitimacy of drug use in American society. Gusfield points out how the ability to define and enforce a group's definition of drug use as deviant fosters its status and power in society. The Temperance movement of the late 1800s and early 1900s empowered the existing American citizens to make rules aimed at the practices of other populations. More than just an ideological difference between the forces of abstinence and control against the forces of hedonism, Gusfield shows that Temperance pitted the political power of old-line WASPS against Catholic newcomers. Pitched to women's groups, it preyed on their fear of men hanging out in bars, which were heavily associated with unsavory Irish immigrant lifestyles. Alcohol became the symbolic wedge by which some groups showed that they had the muscle to restrict the behavior of others.

In reading this selection, you may want to think about what features of contemporary society currently play this role. What are some of the linchpin behaviors that differentiate different political and ideological parties in America? Much as we saw in Chapter 2 by Musto, how is the use of drugs tied to various groups and stigmatized or celebrated because of the power (or lack thereof) of these groups? How are moral and legal regulations of these behaviors and substances likely to rise and fall on the strength of their supporters? Today, we can see similar battles being waged over the legislation of medical marijuana, as political groups in society vie for the ability to define this drug's medical and/or recreational features.

Drugs and the American Dream: An Anthology, First Edition. Edited by Patricia A. Adler, Peter Adler, and Patrick K. O'Brien.
© 2012 John Wiley & Sons, Inc. Published 2012 by John Wiley & Sons, Inc.

For many observers of American life the Temperance movement is evidence for an excessive moral perfectionism and an overly legalistic bent to American culture. It seems to be the action of devoted sectarians who are unable to compromise with human impulse. The legal measures taken to enforce abstinence display the reputed American faith in the power of Law to correct all evils. This moralism and utopianism bring smiles to the cynical and fear to the sinners. Such a movement seems at once naive, intolerant, saintly, and silly.

Although controversies of morality, religion, and culture have been recognized as endemic elements of American politics, they have generally been viewed as minor themes in the interplay of economic and class conflicts. Only in recent years have American historians and social scientists de-emphasized economic issues as the major points of dissension in American society. We share this newer point of view, especially in its insistence on the significant role of cultural conflicts in American politics. Our social system has not experienced the sharp class organization and class conflict which have been so salient in European history. Under continuous conditions of relative affluence and without a feudal resistance to nineteenth-century commercialism and industry, American society has possessed a comparatively high degree of consensus on economic matters. In its bland attitude toward class issues, political controversy in the United States has given only a limited role to strong economic antagonisms. Controversies of personality, cultural difference, and the nuances of style and morality have occupied part of the political stage. Consensus about fundamentals of governmental form, free enterprise economy, and church power has left a political vacuum which moral issues have partially filled. Differences between ethnic groups, cultures, and religious organizations have been able to assume a greater importance than has been true of societies marked by deeper economic divisions. "… agreement on fundamentals will permit almost every kind of social conflict, tension and difference to find political expression."[1]

It is within an analytical context of concern with noneconomic issues that we have studied the Temperance movement. This is a study of moral reform as a political and social issue. We have chosen the Temperance movement because of its persistence

and power in the history of the United States. Typical of moral reform efforts, Temperance has usually been the attempt of the moral people, in this case the abstainers, to correct the behavior of the immoral people, in this case the drinkers. The issue has appeared as a moral one, divorced from any direct economic interests in abstinence or indulgence. This quality of "disinterested reform" is the analytical focus of our study.

[…]

The sociologist picks up where the historian closes. Put in another way, he delves into the assumptions with which the historian begins. The amount written about Temperance is monumentally staggering to someone who tries to read it all. Claims, counterclaims, factual histories, and proceedings of organizations overwhelm us in their immensity. Despite this plethora of documents and analyses, we are left with either partisan writings, histories which preach, or analyses which fail to go beyond general remarks about moral perfectionism, rural–urban conflict, or the Protestant envy of the sinner. It is here, in the analysis of the process, that the sociologist focuses his interest. He studies just that which is so often *ad hoc* to the interpretation of the historian.

We will describe the relation between Temperance attitudes, the organized Temperance movement, and the conflicts between divergent subcultures in American society. Issues of moral reform are analyzed as one way through which a cultural group acts to preserve, defend, or enhance the dominance and prestige of its own style of living within the total society. In the set of religious, ethnic, and cultural communities that have made up American society, drinking (and abstinence) has been one of the significant consumption habits distinguishing one subculture from another. It has been one of the major characteristics through which Americans have defined their own cultural commitments. The "drunken bum," "the sophisticated gourmet," or the "blue-nosed teetotaler" are all terms by which we express our approval or disapproval of cultures by reference to the moral position they accord drinking. Horace Greeley recognized this cultural base to political loyalties and animosities in the 1844 elections in New York state: "Upon those Working Men who stick to their business, hope to improve their circumstances by honest industry and *go on Sundays to church rather than to the grog-shop* [italics added] the appeals of Loco-Focoism fell comparatively harmless; while the opposite class were rallied with unprecedented unanimity against us."[2]

Precisely because drinking and nondrinking have been ways to identify the members of a subculture, drinking and abstinence became symbols of social status, identifying social levels of the society whose styles of life separated them culturally. They indicated to what culture the actor was committed and hence what social groups he took as his models of imitation and avoidance and his points of positive and negative reference for judging his behavior. The rural, native American Protestant of the nineteenth century respected Temperance ideals. He adhered to a culture in which self-control, industriousness, and impulse renunciation were both praised and made necessary. Any lapse was a serious threat to his system of respect. Sobriety was virtuous and, in a community dominated by middle-class Protestants, necessary to social acceptance and to self-esteem. In the twentieth century this is less often true. As Americans are less work-minded, more urban, and less theological, the same behavior which once brought rewards and self-assurance to the abstainer today more often brings contempt and rejection. The demands for self-control and individual industry count for less in an atmosphere of teamwork where tolerance, good interpersonal relations, and the ability to relax oneself and others are greatly prized. Abstinence has lost much of its utility to confer prestige and esteem.

Our attention to the significance of drink and abstinence as symbols of membership in status groups does not imply that religious and moral beliefs have not been important in the Temperance movement. We are not reducing moral reform to something else. Instead, we are adding something. Religious motives and moral fervor do not happen *in vacuo*, apart from a specific setting. We have examined the social conditions which made the facts of other people's drinking especially galling to the abstainer and the need for reformist action acutely pressing to him. These conditions are found in the development of threats to the socially dominant position of the Temperance adherent by those whose style of life differs from his. As his own claim to social respect and

honor are diminished, the sober, abstaining citizen seeks for public acts through which he may reaffirm the dominance and prestige of his style of life. Converting the sinner to virtue is one way; law is another. Even if the law is not enforced or enforceable, the symbolic import of its passage is important to the reformer. It settles the controversies between those who represent clashing cultures. The public support of one conception of morality at the expense of another enhances the prestige and self-esteem of the victors and degrades the culture of the losers.

In its earliest development, Temperance[3] was one way in which a declining social elite tried to retain some of its social power and leadership. The New England Federalist "aristocracy" was alarmed by the political defeats of the early nineteenth century and by the decreased deference shown to their clergy. The rural farmer, the evangelical Protestant, and the uneducated middle class appeared as a rising social group who rejected the social status, as well as political power, of the Federalist leadership. In the first quarter of the nineteenth century, the moral supremacy of the educated was under attack by the frontiersman, the artisan, and the independent farmer. The Federalist saw his own declining status in the increased power of the drinker, the ignorant, the secularist, and the religious revivalist. During the 1820s, the men who founded the Temperance movement sought to make Americans into a clean, sober, godly, and decorous people whose aspirations and style of living would reflect the moral leadership of New England Federalism. If they could not control the politics of the country, they reasoned that they might at least control its morals.

Spurred by religious revivalism, Temperance became more ultraist than its founders had intended. The settling of frontiers and the influx of non-Protestant cultures increased the symbolic importance of morality and religious behavior in distinguishing between the reputable and the disreputable. During the 1830s and 1840s, it became a large and influential movement, composed of several major organizations. Religious dedication and a sober life were becoming touchstones of middle-class respectability. Large numbers of men were attracted to Temperance organizations as a means of self-help. In the interests of social and economic mobility, they sought to preserve their abstinence or reform their own drinking habits. Abstinence was becoming a symbol of middle-class membership and a necessity for ambitious and aspiring young men. It was one of the ways society could distinguish the industrious from the ne'er-do-well; the steady worker from the unreliable drifter; the good credit risk from the bad gamble; the native American from the immigrant. In this process the movement lost its association with New England upper classes and became democratized.

The political role of Temperance emerged in the 1840s in its use as a symbol of native and immigrant, Protestant and Catholic, tensions. The "disinterested reformer" of the 1840s was likely to see the curtailment of alcohol sales as a way of solving the problems presented by an immigrant, urban poor whose culture clashed with American Protestantism. He sensed the rising power of these strange, alien peoples and used Temperance legislation as one means of impressing upon the immigrant the central power and dominance of native American Protestant morality. Along with Abolition and Nativism, Temperance formed one of a trio of major movements during the 1840s and 1850s.

Throughout its history, Temperance has revealed two diverse types of disinterested reform. By the last quarter of the nineteenth century, these had become clear and somewhat distinct elements within the movement. One was an *assimilative reform*. Here the reformer was sympathetic to the plight of the urban poor and critical of the conditions produced by industry and the factory system. This urban, progressivist impulse in Temperance reflected the fears of an older, established social group at the sight of rising industrialism. While commercial and professional men saw America changing from a country of small towns to one of cities, they were still socially dominant. The norm of abstinence had become the public morality after the Civil War. In the doctrines of abstinence they could still offer the poor and the immigrants a way of living which had the sanction of respect and success attached to it. Through reform of the drinker, the middle-class professional and businessman coped with urban problems in a way which affirmed his sense of cultural dominance. He could feel his own social position affirmed by a Temperance argument that invited the drinker (whom he largely identified with the poor, the alien, and the downtrodden) to follow the reformer's habits and lift himself to middle-class respect and income. He was even able to denounce the rich for their sumptuary sophistication. He could do this because he felt secure that abstinence was still the public morality. It was not yet somebody else's America.

A more hostile attitude to reform is found when the object of the reformer's efforts is no longer someone he can pity or help. *Coercive reform* emerges when the object of reform is seen as an intractable defender of another culture, someone who rejects the reformer's values and really doesn't want to change. The champion of assimilative reform viewed the drinker as part of a social system in which the reformer's culture was dominant. On this assumption, his invitation to the drinker to reform made sense. The champion of coercive reform cannot make this assumption. He sees the object of reform as someone who rejects the social dominance of the reformer and denies the legitimacy of his life style. Since the dominance of his culture and the social status of his group are denied, the coercive reformer turns to law and force as ways to affirm it.

In the last quarter of the nineteenth century, coercive reform was most evident in the Populist wing of the Temperance movement. As a phase of the rural distrust of the city, it was allied to an agrarian radicalism which fought the power of industrial and urban political and economic forces. Already convinced that the old, rural middle class was losing out in the sweep of history, the Populist as Temperance adherent could not assume that his way of life was still dominant in America. He had to fight it out by political action which would coerce the public definition of what is moral and respectable. He had to shore up his waning self-esteem by inflicting his morality on everybody.

As America became more urban, more secular, and more Catholic, the sense of declining status intensified the coercive, Populist elements in the Temperance movement. The political defeat of Populism in both North and South heightened the decline, so evident in the drama of William Jennings Bryan. With the development of the Anti-Saloon League in 1896, the Temperance movement began to separate itself from a complex of economic and social reforms and concentrate on the cultural struggle of the traditional rural Protestant society against the developing urban and industrial social system. Coercive reform became the dominating theme of Temperance. It culminated in the drive for national Prohibition. The Eighteenth Amendment was the high point of the struggle to assert the public dominance of old middle-class values. It established the victory of Protestant over Catholic, rural over urban, tradition over modernity, the middle class over both the lower and the upper strata.

The significance of Prohibition is in the fact that it happened. The establishment of Prohibition laws was a battle in the struggle for status between two divergent styles of life. It marked the public affirmation of the abstemious, ascetic qualities of American Protestantism. In this sense, it was an act of ceremonial deference toward old middle-class culture. If the law was often disobeyed and not enforced, the respectability of its adherents was honored in the breach. After all, it was *their* law that drinkers had to avoid.

If Prohibition was the high point of old middle-class defense, Repeal was the nadir. As the Prohibition period lengthened and resistance solidified, Temperance forces grew more hostile, coercive, and nativist. The more assimilative, progressivist adherents were alienated from a movement of such soured Populism. In 1928, anti-Catholic and anti-urban forces led the movement with a "knockout punch" thrown at Al Smith in an open ring. By 1933, they had lost their power and their fight. In the Great Depression both the old order of nineteenth-century economics and the culture of the Temperance ethic were cruelly discredited.

The repeal of the Eighteenth Amendment gave the final push to the decline of old middle-class values in American culture. Since 1933, the Temperance movement has seen itself fighting a losing battle against old enemies and new ones. In contemporary American society, even in his own local communities, it is the total abstainer who is the despised nonconformist. The Protestant churches and the public schools are no longer his allies. The respectable, upper middle-class citizen can no longer be safely counted upon to support abstinence.

What underlie the tragic dilemmas of the Temperance movement are basic changes in the American social system and culture during the past half-century. As we have changed from a commercial society to an industrial one, we have developed a new set of values in which self-control, impulse renunciation, discipline, and sobriety are no longer such hallowed virtues. Thorstein Veblen, himself the epitome of the rural, middle-class Protestant, saw the new society of consumers coming into being. In his satirical fashion, he depicted a society in which leisure and consumption fixed men's status and took precedence over the work-mindedness and efficiency concerns of his own Swedish-American farm communities. More recently, David Riesman has brilliantly depicted the major outlines of this society by pointing to the intensity with which modern Americans are replacing an interest in work and morality with an interest in interpersonal relations and styles of consuming leisure.

For the "other-directed" man neither the intolerance nor the seriousness of the abstainer is acceptable. Nor is the intense rebelliousness and social isolation of the hard drinker acceptable. Analysis of American alcohol consumption is consistent with this. The contemporary American is less likely than his nineteenth-century ancestor to be either a total abstainer or a hard drinker. Moderation is his drinking watchword. One must get along with others and liquor has proven to be a necessary and effective facilitator to sociability. It relaxes reserve and permits fellowship at the same time that it displays the drinker's tolerance for some moral lapse in himself and others.

For those who have grown up to believe in the validity of the Temperance ethic, American culture today seems a strange system in which Truth is condemned as Falsehood and Vice as Virtue. The total abstainer finds himself the exponent of a point of view which is rejected in the centers of urban and national society and among their followers at all levels of American communities. Self-control and foresight made sense in a scarcity, production-minded economy. In an easygoing, affluent society, the credit mechanism has made the Ant a fool and the Grasshopper a hero of the counter-cyclical maintenance of consumer demand. In a consumption-centered society, people must learn to have fun and be good mixers if they are to achieve respect. Not Horatio Alger but *Playboy* magazine is the instructor of the college boy who wants to learn the skills of social ascent. Though they have their noses to the grindstone, their feet must tap to the sound of the dance.

It is at this point that the study of Temperance assumes significance for a general understanding of contemporary American politics and social tensions. Social systems and cultures die slowly, leaving their rear guards behind to fight delaying action. Even after they have ceased to be relevant economic groups, the old middle classes of America are still searching for some way to restore a sense of lost respect. The dishonoring of their values is a part of the process of cultural and social change. A heightened stress on the importance of tradition is a major response of such "doomed classes."

This fundamentalist defense is a primary motif in the current phase of Temperance. To different degrees and within different areas, the contemporary Temperance adherent is part of the rear guard with which small-town America and commercial capitalism fight their losing battle against a nationalized culture and an industrial economy of mass organizations. Increasingly, he fights alone. Churches, schools, and public officials are disdainful of "rigid" attitudes and doctrines. Within the American middle class, in almost all communities, there is a sharp split between two stylistic components. In one the abstainer can feel at home. Here the local community of neighbors and townsmen is the point of reference for behavior. In the other, the more cosmopolitan centers of urban institutions are mediated to the town through national institutions, communications media, and the two-way geographical mobility which brings in newcomers and sends out college students for training elsewhere. The clash between the drinker and the abstainer reflects these diverse references. The localistic culture clings to the traditional while the easier, relaxed, modern ways are the province of the national culture. It is this national culture which becomes the more prestigeful and powerful as America becomes more homogeneous.

The anger and bitterness of the "doomed class" is by no means an "irrational" reaction. There *has* been a decline in the social status of the old middle class and in the dominance of his values. This sense of anger at the loss of status and bitterness about lowered self-esteem pervades the entire Temperance movement today. It takes a number of forms. At one extreme and within certain Temperance elements, it is expressed as a general, diffuse criticism of modern political and social doctrines and a defense of tradition in almost all areas of American life. At the other extreme, within other parts of the Temperance movement, it is part of the intense nationalism, economic conservatism, and social stagnation of the radical right. (This latter is especially true of the Prohibition Party.)

The study of the American Temperance movement is a phase of the process by which, as Richard Hofstadter expressed it, "a large part of the Populist-Progressive tradition has turned sour, become ill-liberal and ill-tempered."[4] The values and the economic position of the native American Protestant, old middle class of individual enterprisers have been losing out in the shuffle of time and social change. The efforts of the old middle class and of those who have built their self-conceptions on their values to defend and restore their lost prestige have taken a number of forms. In fluoridation, domestic Communism, school curricula, and the United Nations, they have found issues which range tradition against modernity. Temperance has been one of the classic issues on which divergent cultures have faced each other in America. Such issues of style have been significant because they have been ways through which groups have tried to handle the problems which have been important to them.

It is this conception of political acts as symbolic acts that is, for us, the most valuable part of this chapter and the most significant fruit of studying Temperance. We consider Temperance as one form which the politics of status goals has taken in the United States. Far from being a pointless interruption of the American political system, it has exemplified one of its characteristic processes. Since governmental actions symbolize the position of groups in the status structure, seemingly ceremonial or ritual acts of government are often of great importance to many social groups. Issues which seem foolish or impractical items are often important for what they symbolize about the style or culture which is being recognized or derogated. Being acts of deference or degradation, the individual finds in governmental action that his own perceptions of his status in the society are confirmed or rejected.

These considerations take us a long way toward understanding why and how social status has been a provocative and frequent source of political tensions in the United States. Issues like fluoridation or domestic Communism or Temperance may seem to generate "irrational" emotions and excessive zeal if we fail to recognize them as symbolic rather than instrumental, pragmatic issues. If we conceive of status as somehow an unfit issue for political controversy, we are simply ignoring a clash of interests which generate a high order of emotion and political action in the United States. When a society experiences profound changes, the fortunes and the respect of people undergo loss or gain. We have always understood the desire to defend fortune. We should also understand the desire to defend respect. It is less clear because it is symbolic in nature but it is not less significant.

Notes

1 Lee Benson, *The Concept of Jacksonian Democracy* (Princeton, NJ: Princeton University Press, 1961), p. 275.
2 Quoted in Benson, p. 199.
3 The term "Temperance" is an inadequate name for a movement which preaches total abstinence rather than "temperate" use of alcohol. The word was affixed to the movement in its early years (1820s) when its doctrine was not yet as extreme as it later came to be.
4 Richard Hofstadter, *The Age of Reform* (New York: A. A. Knopf, 1955), pp. 19–20.

Questions

1 According to the article, the moral reform efforts of the Temperance movement attempted to correct the behavior of immoral people (i.e., drinkers). Do we see moral issues presented as justification for our current prohibitionist policies? Why or why not?

2 How does the idea of the "other-directed" man apply to other forms of drug use in our society today? With regard to illegal drug use, what is the norm, abstention, or dysfunction? What policies do you think would encourage moderate drug use, assimilative or coercive? Why?

3 How have social status and/or social power influenced the drug policies we have in place today? Is our drug policy influenced by the golden rule: "Whoever has the gold, makes the rules?"

6

The Social Construction of Drug Scares

Craig Reinarman

Craig Reinarman offers us an insightful glimpse into the way drug morality is socially constructed in this now-classic selection that dissects the elements necessary to develop a moral panic. You will find his analysis of the groups of different players, the elements that empower them, the role of other parties, and the way they all act to pursue their own interests particularly compelling. Although this article is about drugs, it could equally well be about anything that could be blown up into a moral scare. Given the fear culture in which we live, if the media and other moral entrepreneurial groups can convince a significant portion of the public that a behavior will destroy society, filter down to young children, or spread across society, then the likelihood of demonizing it increases. Scares make it easier to convince the lay public that agents of social control need to more severely punish people who engage in these behaviors. After you have read this article, pay particular attention to the news around you and the actions and pronouncements of the various groups being reported. Instead of taking news at face value, ask yourself what the bias is that comes from the media, what each party to a crusade is looking to gain, and how the social and historical context of the people affected by the behavior also shapes the debate.

Then ask yourself if you agree with Reinarman's contention that there is something in American culture that makes us more prone to drug scares than other societies. Do you agree with his model of conflicting forces that pull Americans between the opposing poles of moderation and excess? What is the nature of how our society analyzes the cause of various social problems such as drugs? Is this manufactured? Who benefits from this kind of definition and who suffers?

Drug "wars," anti-drug crusades, and other periods of marked public concern about drugs are never merely reactions to the various troubles people can have with drugs. These drug scares are recurring cultural and political phenomena *in their own right* and must, therefore, be understood sociologically on their own terms. It is important to understand why people ingest drugs and why some of them develop problems that have something to do with having ingested them. But the premise of this chapter is that it is equally

Drugs and the American Dream: An Anthology, First Edition. Edited by Patricia A. Adler, Peter Adler, and Patrick K. O'Brien.
© 2012 John Wiley & Sons, Inc. Published 2012 by John Wiley & Sons, Inc.

important to understand patterns of acute societal concern about drug use and drug problems. This seems especially so for US society, which has had *recurring* anti-drug crusades and a *history* of repressive anti-drug laws.

Many well-intentioned drug policy reform efforts in the US have come face to face with staid and stubborn sentiments against consciousness-altering substances. The repeated failures of such reform efforts cannot be explained solely in terms of ill-informed or manipulative leaders. Something deeper is involved, something woven into the very fabric of American culture, something which explains why claims that some drug is the cause of much of what is wrong with the world are *believed* so often by so many. The origins and nature of the *appeal* of anti-drug claims must be confronted if we are ever to understand how "drug problems" are constructed in the US such that more enlightened and effective drug policies have been so difficult to achieve.

In this chapter I take a step in this direction. First, I summarize briefly some of the major periods of anti-drug sentiment in the US. Second, I draw from them the basic ingredients of which drug scares and drug laws are made. Third, I offer a beginning interpretation of these scares and laws based on those broad features of American culture that make *self-control* continuously problematic.

Drug Scares and Drug Laws

What I have called drug scares have been a recurring feature of US society for 200 years. They are relatively autonomous from whatever drug-related problems exist or are said to exist.[1] I call them "scares" because, like Red Scares, they are a form of moral panic ideologically constructed so as to construe one or another chemical bogeyman, à la "communists," as the core cause of a wide array of preexisting public problems.

The first and most significant drug scare was over drink. Temperance movement leaders constructed this scare beginning in the late 18th and early 19th century. It reached its formal end with the passage of Prohibition in 1919.[2] As Gusfield showed in his classic book *Symbolic Crusade* (1963), there was far more to the battle against booze than long-standing drinking problems. Temperance crusaders tended to be native born, middle-class, non-urban Protestants who felt threatened by the working-class, Catholic immigrants who were filling up America's cities during industrialization. The latter were what Gusfield termed "unrepentant deviants" in that they continued their long-standing drinking practices despite middle-class WASP norms against them. The battle over booze was the terrain on which was fought a cornucopia of cultural conflicts, particularly over whose morality would be the dominant morality in America.

In the course of this century-long struggle, the often wild claims of Temperance leaders appealed to millions of middle-class people seeking explanations for the pressing social and economic problems of industrializing America. Many corporate supporters of Prohibition threw their financial and ideological weight behind the Anti-Saloon League and other Temperance and Prohibitionist groups because they felt that traditional working-class drinking practices interfered with the new rhythms of the factory, and thus with productivity and profits. To the Temperance crusaders' fear of the bar room as a breeding ground of all sorts of tragic immorality, Prohibitionists added the idea of the saloon as an alien, subversive place where unionists organized and where leftists and anarchists found recruits.

This convergence of claims and interests rendered alcohol a scapegoat for most of the nation's poverty, crime, moral degeneracy, "broken" families, illegitimacy, unemployment, and personal and business failure – problems whose sources lay in broader economic and political forces. This scare climaxed in the first two decades of this century, a tumultuous period rife with class, racial, cultural, and political conflict brought on by the wrenching changes of industrialization, immigration, and urbanization.

America's first real drug law was San Francisco's anti–opium den ordinance of 1875. The context of the campaign for this law shared many features with the context of the Temperance movement. Opiates had long been widely and legally available without a prescription in hundreds of medicines, so neither opiate use nor addiction was really the issue. This campaign focused almost exclusively on what was called the "Mongolian vice" of opium *smoking* by Chinese immigrants (and white "fellow travelers") in dens. Chinese immigrants came to California as "coolie" labor to build the railroad and dig the gold mines. A small minority of them brought along the practice of smoking opium – a practice originally brought to China by British and American traders in the 19th century. When the railroad was completed and the gold dried up, a decade-long depression ensued. In a tight labor market, Chinese immigrants were a target. The white Workingman's Party fomented racial hatred of the low-wage "coolies" with whom they now had to compete for work. The first law against opium smoking was only one of many laws enacted to harass and control Chinese workers.

By calling attention to this broader political–economic context I do not wish to slight the specifics of the local political–economic context. In addition to the Workingman's Party, downtown businessmen formed merchant associations and urban families formed improvement associations, both of which fought for more than two decades to reduce the impact of San Francisco's vice districts on the order and health of the central business district and on family neighborhoods.

In this sense, the anti–opium den ordinance was not the clear and direct result of a sudden drug scare alone. The law was passed against a specific form of drug use engaged in by a disreputable group that had come to be seen as threatening in lean economic times. But it passed easily because this new threat was understood against the broader historical backdrop of long-standing local concerns about various vices as threats to public health, public morals, and public order. Moreover, the focus of attention were dens where it was suspected that whites came into intimate contact with "filthy, idolatrous" Chinese. Some local law enforcement leaders, for example, complained that Chinese men were using this vice to seduce white women into sexual slavery. Whatever the hazards of opium smoking, its initial criminalization in San Francisco had to do with both a general context of recession, class conflict, and racism, and with specific local interests in the control of vice and the prevention of miscegenation.

A nationwide scare focusing on opiates and cocaine began in the early 20th century. These drugs had been widely used for years, but were first criminalized when the addict population began to shift from predominantly white, middle-class, middle-aged women to young, working-class males, African-Americans in particular. This scare led to the Harrison Narcotics Act of 1914, the first federal anti-drug law.

Many different moral entrepreneurs guided its passage over a six-year campaign: State Department diplomats seeking a drug treaty as a means of expanding trade with China, trade which they felt was crucial for pulling the economy out of recession; the medical and pharmaceutical professions whose interests were threatened by self-medication with unregulated proprietary tonics, many of which contained cocaine or opiates; reformers seeking to control what they saw as the deviance of immigrants and Southern blacks who were migrating off the farms; and a pliant press which routinely linked drug use with prostitutes, criminals, transient workers (e.g., the Wobblies), and African-Americans. In order to gain the support of Southern Congressmen for a new federal law that might infringe on "states' rights," State Department officials and other crusaders repeatedly spread unsubstantiated suspicions, repeated in the press, that, e.g., cocaine induced African-American men to rape white women (Musto, 1973: 6–10, 67). In short, there was more to this drug scare, too, than mere drug problems.

In the Great Depression, Harry Anslinger of the Federal Narcotics Bureau pushed Congress for a federal law against marijuana. He claimed it was a "killer weed" and he spread stories to the press suggesting that it induced violence – especially among Mexican-Americans. Although there was no evidence that marijuana was widely used, much less that it had any untoward effects, his crusade resulted in its criminalization in 1937 – and not incidentally a turnaround in his Bureau's fiscal fortunes. In this case, a new drug law was put in place by a militant moral-bureaucratic entrepreneur who played on racial fears and manipulated a press willing to repeat even his most absurd claims in a context of class conflict during the Depression. While there was not a marked scare at the time, Anslinger's claims were never contested in Congress because they played upon racial fears and widely held Victorian values against taking drugs solely for pleasure.

In the drug scare of the 1960s, political and moral leaders somehow reconceptualized this same "killer weed" as the "drop out drug" that was leading America's youth to rebellion and ruin. Bio-medical scientists also published uncontrolled, retrospective studies of very small numbers of cases suggesting that, in addition to poisoning the minds and morals of youth, LSD produced broken chromosomes and thus genetic damage. These studies were soon shown to be seriously misleading if not meaningless, but not before the press, politicians, the medical profession, and the National Institute of Mental Health used them to promote a scare.

I suggest that the reason even supposedly hard-headed scientists were drawn into such propaganda was that dominant groups felt the country was at war – and not merely with Vietnam. In this scare, there was not so much a "dangerous class" or threatening racial group as multi-faceted political and cultural conflict, particularly between generations, which gave rise to the perception that middle-class youth who rejected conventional values were a dangerous threat.[3] This scare resulted in the Comprehensive Drug Abuse Control Act of 1970, which criminalized more forms of drug use and subjected users to harsher penalties.

Most recently we have seen the crack scare, which began in earnest *not* when the prevalence of cocaine use quadrupled in the late 1970s, nor even when thousands of users began to smoke it in the more potent and dangerous form of freebase. Indeed, when this scare was launched, crack was unknown outside of a few neighborhoods in a handful of major cities and the prevalence of illicit drug use had been dropping for several years. Rather, this most recent scare began in 1986 when freebase cocaine was renamed crack (or "rock") and sold in precooked, inexpensive units on ghetto streetcorners. Once politicians and the media linked this new form of cocaine use to the inner-city, minority poor, a new drug scare was underway and the solution became more prison cells rather than more treatment slots.

The same sorts of wild claims and Draconian policy proposals of Temperance and Prohibition leaders resurfaced in the crack scare. Politicians have so outdone each other in getting "tough on drugs" that each year since crack came on the scene in 1986 they have passed more repressive laws providing billions more for law enforcement, longer sentences, and more drug offenses punishable by death. One result is that the US now has

more people in prison than any industrialized nation in the world – about half of them for drug offenses, the majority of whom are racial minorities.

In each of these periods more repressive drug laws were passed on the grounds that they would reduce drug use and drug problems. I have found no evidence that any scare actually accomplished those ends, but they did greatly expand the quantity and quality of social control, particularly over subordinate groups perceived as dangerous or threatening. Reading across these historical episodes one can abstract a recipe for drug scares and repressive drug laws that contains the following *seven ingredients:*

1 **A kernel of truth** Humans have ingested fermented beverages at least since human civilization moved from hunting and gathering to primitive agriculture thousands of years ago. The pharmacopoeia has expanded exponentially since then. So, in virtually all cultures and historical epochs, there has been sufficient ingestion of consciousness-altering chemicals to provide some basis for some people to claim that it is a problem.

2 **Media magnification** In each of the episodes I have summarized and many others, the mass media has engaged in what I call the *routinization of caricature* – rhetorically recrafting worst cases into typical cases and the episodic into the epidemic. The media dramatize drug problems, as they do other problems, in the course of their routine news-generating and sales-promoting procedures.

3 **Politico-moral entrepreneurs** I have added the prefix "politico" to Becker's (1963) seminal concept of moral entrepreneur in order to emphasize the fact that the most prominent and powerful moral entrepreneurs in drug scares are often political elites. Otherwise, I employ the term just as he intended: to denote the *enterprise*, the work, of those who create (or enforce) a rule against what they see as a social evil.[4]

In the history of drug problems in the US, these entrepreneurs call attention to drug using behavior and define it as a threat about which "something must be done." They also serve as the media's primary source of sound bites on the dangers of this or that drug. In all the scares I have noted, these entrepreneurs had interests of their own (often financial) which had little to do with drugs. Political elites typically find drugs a functional demon in that (like "outside agitators") drugs allow them to deflect attention from other, more systemic sources of public problems for which they would otherwise have to take some responsibility. Unlike almost every other political issue, however, to be "tough on drugs" in American political culture allows a leader to take a firm stand without risking votes or campaign contributions.

4 **Professional interest groups** In each drug scare and during the passage of each drug law, various professional interests contended over what Gusfield (1981: 10–15) calls the "ownership" of drug problems – "the ability to create and influence the public definition of a problem" (1981: 10), and thus to define what should be done about it. These groups have included industrialists, churches, the American Medical Association, the American Pharmaceutical Association, various law enforcement agencies, scientists, and most recently the treatment industry and groups of those former addicts converted to disease ideology.[5] These groups claim for themselves, by virtue of their specialized forms of knowledge, the legitimacy and authority to name what is wrong and to prescribe the solution, usually garnering resources as a result.

5 **Historical context of conflict** This trinity of the media, moral entrepreneurs, and professional interests typically interact in such a way as to inflate the extant "kernel of truth" about drug use. But this interaction does not by itself give rise to drug scares or drug laws without underlying conflicts which make drugs into functional villains. Although Temperance crusaders persuaded millions to pledge abstinence, they campaigned for years without achieving alcohol control laws. However, in the tumultuous period leading up to Prohibition, there were revolutions in Russia and Mexico, World War I, massive immigration and impoverishment, and socialist, anarchist, and labor movements, to say nothing of increases in routine problems such as crime. I submit that all this conflict made for a level of cultural anxiety that provided fertile ideological soil for Prohibition. In each of the other scares, similar conflicts – economic, political, cultural, class, racial, or a combination – provided a context in which claims makers could viably construe certain classes of drug users as a threat.

6 **Linking a form of drug use to a "dangerous class"** Drug scares are never about drugs *per se*, because drugs are inanimate objects without social consequence until they are ingested by humans. Rather, drug scares are about the use of a drug by particular groups of people who are, typically, *already* perceived by powerful groups as some kind of threat. It was not so much alcohol problems *per se* that most animated the drive for Prohibition but the behavior and morality of what dominant groups saw as the "dangerous class" of urban, immigrant, Catholic, working-class drinkers. It was *Chinese* opium smoking dens, not the more widespread use of other opiates, that prompted California's first drug law in the 1870s. It was only when smokable cocaine found its way to the African-American and Latino underclass that it made headlines and prompted calls for a drug war. In each case, politico-moral entrepreneurs were able to construct a "drug problem" by linking a substance to a group of users perceived by the powerful as disreputable, dangerous, or otherwise threatening.

7 **Scapegoating a drug for a wide array of public problems** The final ingredient is scapegoating, i.e., blaming a drug or its alleged effects on a group of its users for a variety of preexisting social ills that are typically only indirectly associated with it. Scapegoating may be the most crucial element because it gives great explanatory power and thus broader resonance to claims about the horrors of drugs (particularly in the conflictual historical contexts in which drug scares tend to occur).

Scapegoating was abundant in each of the cases noted previously. To listen to Temperance crusaders, for example, one might have believed that without alcohol use America would be a land of infinite economic progress with no poverty, crime, mental illness, or even sex outside marriage. To listen to leaders of organized medicine and the government in the 1960s, one might have surmised that without marijuana and LSD there would have been neither conflict between youth and their parents nor opposition to the Vietnam War. And to believe politicians and the media in the past six years is to believe that without the scourge of crack the inner cities and the so-called underclass would, if not disappear, at least be far less scarred by poverty, violence, and crime. There is no historical evidence supporting any of this.

In short, drugs are richly functional scapegoats. They provide elites with fig leaves to place over unsightly social ills that are endemic to the social system over which they preside. And they provide the public with a restricted aperture of attribution in which only a chemical bogeyman or the lone deviants who ingest it are seen as the cause of a cornucopia of complex problems.

Toward a Culturally Specific Theory of Drug Scares

Various forms of drug use have been and are widespread in almost all societies comparable to ours. A few of them have experienced limited drug scares, usually around alcohol decades ago. However, drug scares have been *far* less common in other societies, and never as virulent as they have been in the US. There has never been a time or place in human history without drunkenness, for example, but in *most* times and places drunkenness has not been nearly as problematic as it has been in the US since the late 18th century. Moreover, in comparable industrial democracies, drug laws are generally less repressive. Why then do claims about the horrors of this or that consciousness-altering chemical have such unusual power in American culture?

Drug scares and other periods of acute public concern about drug use are not just discrete, unrelated episodes. There is a historical pattern in the US that cannot be understood in terms of the moral values and perceptions of individual anti-drug crusaders alone. I have suggested that these crusaders have benefited in various ways from their crusades. For example, making claims about how a drug is damaging society can help elites increase the social control of groups perceived as threatening, establish one class's moral code as dominant, bolster a bureaucracy's sagging fiscal fortunes, or mobilize voter support. However, the recurring character of pharmaco-phobia in US history suggests that there is something about our *culture* which makes citizens more vulnerable to anti-drug crusaders' attempts to demonize drugs. Thus, an answer to the question of America's unusual vulnerability to drug scares must address why the scapegoating of consciousness-altering substances regularly *resonates* with or appeals to substantial portions of the population.

There are three basic parts to my answer. The first is that claims about the evils of drugs are especially viable in American culture in part because they provide a welcome *vocabulary of attribution* (cf. Mills, 1940). Armed with "DRUGS" as a generic scapegoat, citizens gain the cognitive satisfaction of having a folk devil on which to blame a range of bizarre behaviors or other conditions they find troubling but difficult to explain in other terms. This much may be true of a number of other societies, but I hypothesize that this is particularly so in the US because in our political culture individualistic explanations for problems are so much more common than social explanations.

Second, claims about the evils of drugs provide an especially serviceable vocabulary of attribution in the US in part because our society developed from a *temperance culture* (Levine, 1992). American society was forged in the fires of ascetic Protestantism and industrial capitalism, both of which demand *self-control*. US society has long been characterized as the land of the individual "self-made man." In such a land, self-control has had extraordinary importance. For the middle-class Protestants who settled, defined, and still dominate the US, self-control was both central to religious world views and a characterological necessity for economic survival and success in the capitalist market. With Levine (1992), I hypothesize that in a culture in which self-control is inordinately important, drug-induced altered states of consciousness are especially likely to be experienced as "loss of control," and thus to be inordinately feared.

Drunkenness and other forms of drug use have, of course, been present everywhere in the industrialized world. But temperance cultures tend to arise only when industrial capitalism unfolds upon a cultural terrain deeply imbued with the Protestant ethic.[6] This means that only the US, England, Canada, and parts of Scandinavia have Temperance cultures, the US being the most extreme case.

It may be objected that the influence of such a Temperance culture was strongest in the 19th and early 20th century and that its grip on the American *Zeitgeist* has been loosened by the forces of modernity and now, many say, post-modernity. The third part of my answer, however, is that on the foundation of a Temperance culture, advanced capitalism has built a *postmodern, mass consumption culture* that exacerbates the problem of self-control in new ways.

Early in the 20th century, Henry Ford pioneered the idea that by raising wages he could simultaneously quell worker protests and increase market demand for mass-produced goods. This mass consumption strategy became central to modern American society and one of the reasons for our economic success. Our economy is now so fundamentally predicated upon mass consumption that theorists as diverse as Daniel Bell and Herbert Marcuse have observed that we live in a mass consumption culture. Bell (1978), for example, notes that while the Protestant work ethic and deferred gratification may still hold sway in the workplace, Madison Avenue, the media, and malls have inculcated a new indulgence ethic in the leisure sphere in which pleasure-seeking and immediate gratification reign.

Thus, our economy and society have come to depend upon the constant cultivation of new "needs," the production of new desires. Not only the hardware of social life such as food, clothing, and shelter but also the software of the self – excitement, entertainment, even eroticism – have become mass consumption commodities. This means that our society offers an increasing number of incentives for indulgence – more ways to lose self-control – and a decreasing number of countervailing reasons for retaining it.

In short, drug scares continue to occur in American society in part because people must constantly manage the contradiction between a Temperance culture that insists on self-control and a mass consumption culture which renders self-control continuously problematic. In addition to helping explain the recurrence of drug scares, I think this contradiction helps account for why in the last dozen years millions of Americans have joined 12-Step groups, more than 100 of which have nothing whatsoever to do with ingesting a drug (Reinarman, 1995). "Addiction," or the generalized loss of self-control, has become the meta-metaphor for a staggering array of human troubles. And, of course, we also seem to have a staggering array of politicians and other moral entrepreneurs who take advantage of such cultural contradictions to blame new chemical bogeymen for our society's ills.

Notes

1 In this regard, for example, Robin Room wisely observes "that we are living at a historic moment when the rate of (alcohol) dependence as a cognitive and existential experience is rising, although the rate of alcohol consumption and of heavy drinking is falling." He draws from this a more general hypothesis about "long waves" of drinking and societal reactions to them: "[I]n periods of increased questioning of drinking and heavy drinking, the trends in the two forms of dependence, psychological and physical, will tend to run in opposite directions. Conversely, in periods of a 'wettening' of sentiments, with the curve of alcohol consumption beginning to rise, we may expect the rate of physical dependence … to rise while the rate of dependence as a cognitive experience falls" (1991: 154).

2 I say "formal end" because Temperance ideology is not merely alive and well in the War on Drugs but is being applied to all manner of human troubles in the burgeoning 12-Step Movement (Reinarman, 1995).

3 This historical sketch of drug scares is obviously not exhaustive. Readers interested in other scares should see, e.g., Brecher's encyclopedic work *Licit and Illicit Drugs* (1972), especially the chapter on glue sniffing, which illustrates how the media actually created a new drug problem by writing hysterical stories about it. There was also a PCP scare in the 1970s in which law enforcement officials claimed that the growing use of this horse tranquilizer was a severe threat because it made users so violent and gave them such super-human strength that stun guns were necessary. This, too, turned out to be unfounded and the "angel dust" scare was short-lived (see Feldman et al., 1979). The best analysis of how new drugs themselves can lead to panic reactions among users is Becker (1967).

4 Becker wisely warns against the "one-sided view" that sees such crusaders as merely imposing their morality on others. Moral entrepreneurs, he notes, do operate "with an absolute ethic," are "fervent and righteous," and will use "any means" necessary to "do away with" what they see as "totally evil." However, they also "typically believe that their mission is a holy one," that if people do what they want it "will be good for them." Thus, as in the case of abolitionists, the crusades of moral entrepreneurs often "have strong humanitarian overtones" (1963: 147–8). This is no less true for those whose moral enterprise promotes drug scares. My analysis, however, concerns the character and consequences of their efforts, not their motives.

5 As Gusfield notes, such ownership sometimes shifts over time, e.g., with alcohol problems, from religion to criminal law to medical science. With other drug problems, the shift in ownership has been away from medical science toward criminal law. The most insightful treatment of the medicalization of alcohol/drug problems is Peele (1989).

6 The third central feature of Temperance cultures identified by Levine (1992), which I will not dwell on, is predominance of spirit drinking, i.e., more concentrated alcohol than wine or beer and thus greater likelihood of drunkenness.

References

Becker, Howard S. 1963. *Outsiders: Studies in the Sociology of Deviance*. Glencoe, IL: Free Press.

Becker, Howard S. 1967. "History, Culture, and Subjective Experience: An Exploration of the Social Bases of Drug-Induced Experiences." *Journal of Health and Social Behavior* 8: 162–76.

Bell, Daniel. 1978. *The Cultural Contradictions of Capitalism*. New York: Basic Books.

Brecher, Edward M. 1972. *Licit and Illicit Drugs*. Boston: Little Brown.

Feldman, Harvey W., Michael H. Agar, and George M. Beschner. 1979. *Augel Dust*. Lexington, MA: Lexington Books.

Gusfield, Joseph R. 1963. *Symbolic Crusade: Status Politics and the American Temperance Movement*. Urbana: University of Illinois Press.

Gusfield, Joseph R. 1981. *The Culture of Public Problems: Drinking-Driving and the Symbolic Order*. Chicago: University of Chicago Press.

Levine, Harry Gene. 1992. "Temperance Cultures: Concern About Alcohol Problems in Nordic and English-Speaking Cultures." In G. Edwards et al., eds., *The Nature of Alcohol and Drug Related Problems*. New York: Oxford University Press.

Mills, C. Wright. 1940. "Situated Actions and Vocabularies of Motive." *American Sociological Review* 5: 904–13.

Musto, David. 1973. *The American Disease: Origins of Narcotic Control*. New Haven, CT: Yale University Press.

Peele, Stanton. 1989. *The Diseasing of America: Addiction Treatment Out of Control*. Lexington, MA: Lexington Books.

Reinarman, Craig. 1995. "The 12-Step Movement and Advanced Capitalist Culture: Notes on the Politics of Self-Control in Postmodernity." In B. Epstein, R Flacks, and M. Darnovsky, eds., *Contemporary Social Movements and Cultural Politics*. New York: Oxford University Press.

Room, Robin G. W. 1991. "Cultural Changes in Drinking and Trends in Alcohol Problems Indicators: Recent U.S. Experience." In Walter B. Clark and Michael E. Hilton, eds., *Alcohol in America: Drinking Practices and Problems*, pp. 149–62. Albany: State University of New York Press.

Questions

1 According to the article, drug scares are often attributed to "disreputable groups" or linked to a "dangerous class." How have drugs been linked to minority populations in the past? What are more current examples of drugs, such as MDMA, Salvia Divinorum, or Medical Marijuana, being linked to less socially powerful groups to create fear and direct policy?

2 How does the media depict drugs in our society? Who represent the majority of drug users in the United States, experimental, moderate, or dysfunctional users? Where does the media place its focus? Why? Why are dysfunctional users overrepresented in the media, while moderate/controlled users are largely ignored? How might this representation impact broader conceptions about drug use across the United States?

3 Why do drug scares resonate so well within the United States? How do these factors inform Gusfield's piece on the Temperance movement? What elements do you think are the most crucial in perpetuating a drug scare? Why?

7

Blowing Smoke
Status Politics and the Smoking Ban

Justin L. Tuggle and Malcolm D. Holmes

Justin Tuggle and Malcolm Holmes extend Gusfield's and Reinarman's analyses of the status and power struggles in American society that use drugs as an instrument for domination and control. Although they analyze the conflict between smoking and nonsmoking groups in Shasta County, California at the turn of the twenty-first century, battles over smoking continue to rage. College campuses are one of the locations where these discussions are currently occurring, with some schools outlawing smoking on campus and others voting against such measures.

They build on several of Reinarman's elements of a drug scare in discussing the various elements in the fight over smoking rights. Which of these do they echo, and which of them do they keep but modify in some way? With which analysis do you agree, or do they converge? What elements give some groups greater social power in society to enforce their will on others? And does this answer the question of why groups seek to legislate the behavior and morality of others in our society? Just like homosexual marriage, gambling, or prostitution, what drives people to compel others to abstain from certain voluntary behavior, especially those representing people's lifestyle choices and their roots in specific social groups?

How do Tuggle and Holmes build on the concepts advanced in the Gusfield selection? How do the two styles of reform represent the nature of the groups choosing them? Does this analysis of the dynamics of the struggle between social groups reflect your view of society or do you believe things are more harmonious and consensual? Finally, do you agree that American society is characterized by a persistent conflict between interest groups that use drugs as the vehicle to empower some while disempowering others? Are drugs unique in filling this role?

Drugs and the American Dream: An Anthology, First Edition. Edited by Patricia A. Adler, Peter Adler, and Patrick K. O'Brien.
© 2012 John Wiley & Sons, Inc. Published 2012 by John Wiley & Sons, Inc.

Over the past half century, perceptions of tobacco and its users have changed dramatically. In the 1940s and 1950s, cigarette smoking was socially accepted and commonly presumed to lack deleterious effects. Survey data from the early 1950s showed that a minority believed cigarette smoking caused lung cancer. By the late 1970s, however, estimates from survey data revealed that more than 90% of the population thought that this link existed. This and other harms associated with tobacco consumption have provided the impetus for an antismoking crusade that aims to normatively redefine smoking as deviant behavior.

There seems to be little question that tobacco is a damaging psychoactive substance characterized by highly adverse chronic health effects. In this regard, the social control movement probably makes considerable sense in terms of public policy. At the same time, much as ethnicity and religion played a significant role in the prohibition of alcohol, social status may well play a part in this latest crusade.

Historically, attempts to control psychoactive substances have linked their use to categories of relatively powerless people. Marijuana use was associated with Mexican Americans, cocaine with African Americans, opiates with Asians, and alcohol with immigrant Catholics. During the heyday of cigarette smoking, it was thought that

> Tobacco's the one blessing that nature has left for all humans to enjoy. It can be consumed by both the "haves" and "have nots" as a common leveler, one that brings all humans together from all walks of life regardless of class, race, or creed. (Ram, 1941, p. 125)

But in contrast to this earlier view, recent evidence has shown that occupational status, education, and family income are related negatively to current smoking. Further, the relationships of occupation and education to cigarette smoking have become stronger in later age cohorts. Thus we ask, *is the association of tobacco with lower-status persons a factor in the crusade against smoking in public facilities?* Here we examine that question in a case study of a smoking ban implemented in Shasta County, California.

Status Politics and the Creation of Deviance

Deviance is socially constructed. Complex pluralistic societies have multiple, competing symbolic-moral universes that clash and negotiate (Ben-Yehuda 1990). Deviance is relative, and social morality is continually restructured. Moral, power, and stigma contests are ongoing, with competing symbolic-moral universes striving to legitimize particular lifestyles while making others deviant (Schur 1980; Ben-Yehuda 1990).

The ability to define and construct reality is closely connected to the power structure of society (Gusfield 1963). Inevitably, then, the distribution of deviance is associated with the system of stratification. The higher one's social position, the greater one's moral value (Ben-Yehuda 1990). Differences in lifestyles and moral beliefs are corollaries of social stratification. Accordingly, even though grounded in the system of stratification, status conflicts need not be instrumental; they may also be symbolic. Social stigma may, for instance, attach to behavior thought indicative of a weak will (Goffman 1963). Such moral anomalies occasion status degradation ceremonies, public denunciations expressing indignation not at a behavior per se, but rather against the individual motivational type that produced it (Garfinkel 1956). The denouncers act as public figures, drawing upon communally shared experience and speaking in the name of ultimate values. In this respect, status degradation involves a reciprocal element: Status conflicts and the resultant condemnation of a behavior characteristic of a particular status category symbolically enhance the status of the abstinent through the degradation of the participatory (Garfinkel 1956; Gusfield 1963).

Deviance creation involves political competition in which moral entrepreneurs originate moral crusades aimed at generating reform (Becker 1963; Schur 1980; Ben-Yehuda 1990). The alleged deficiencies of a specific social group are revealed and reviled by those crusading to define their behavior as deviant. As might be expected, successful moral crusades are generally dominated by those in the upper social strata of society (Becker 1963). Research on the anti-abortion and antipornography crusades has shown that activists in these movements are of lower socioeconomic status than their opponents, helping explain the limited success of efforts to redefine abortion and pornography as deviance.

Moral entrepreneurs' goals may be either assimilative or coercive reform (Gusfield 1963). In the former instance, sympathy to the deviants' plight engenders integrative efforts aimed at lifting the repentant to the superior moral plane allegedly held by those of higher social status. The latter strategy emerges when deviants are viewed as intractably denying the moral and status superiority of the reformers' symbolic-moral universe. Thus, whereas assimilative reform may employ educative strategies, coercive reform turns to law and force for affirmation.

Regardless of aim, the moral entrepreneur cannot succeed alone. Success in establishing a moral crusade is dependent on acquiring broader public support. To that end, the moral entrepreneur must mobilize power, create a perceived threat potential for the moral issue in question, generate public awareness of the issue, propose a clear and acceptable solution to the problem, and overcome resistance to the crusade (Becker 1963; Ben-Yehuda 1990).

The Status Politics of Cigarette Smoking

The political dynamics underlying the definition of deviant behaviors may be seen clearly in efforts to end smoking in public facilities. Cigarettes were an insignificant product of the tobacco industry until the end of the 19th century, after which they evolved into its staple. Around the turn of the century, 14 states banned cigarette smoking and all but one other regulated sales to and possession by minors. Yet by its heyday in the 1940s and 1950s, cigarette smoking was almost universally accepted, even considered socially desirable. Per capita cigarette consumption in the United States peaked at approximately 4,300 cigarettes per year in the early 1960s, after which it declined to about 2,800 per year by the early 1990s. The beginning of the marked decline in cigarette consumption corresponded to the publication of the report to the surgeon general on the health risks of smoking. Two decades later, the hazards of passive smoking were being publicized.

Increasingly, the recognition of the apparent relationship of smoking to health risks has socially demarcated the lifestyles of the smoker and nonsmoker, from widespread acceptance of the habit to polarized symbolic-moral universes. Attitudes about smoking are informed partly by medical issues, but perhaps even more critical are normative considerations; more people have come to see smoking as socially reprehensible and deviant, and smokers as social misfits. Psychological assessments have attributed an array of negative evaluative characteristics to smokers. Their habit is increasingly thought unclean and intrusive.

Abstinence and bodily purity are the cornerstones of the nonsmoker's purported moral superiority. At the center of their symbolic-moral universe, then, is the idea that people have a right to breathe clean air in public spaces. Smokers, on the other hand, stake their claim to legitimacy in a precept of Anglo-Saxon political culture – the right to do whatever one wants unless it harms others. Those sympathetic to smoking deny that environmental tobacco smoke poses a significant health hazard to the nonsmoker. Yet such arguments have held little sway in the face of counterclaims from authoritative governmental agencies and high status moral entrepreneurs.

The development of the antismoking movement has targeted a lifestyle particularly characteristic of the working classes. Not only has there been an overall decline in cigarette smoking, but, as mentioned above, the negative relationships of occupation and education to cigarette smoking have become more pronounced in later age cohorts. Moreover, moral entrepreneurs crusading against smoking are representatives of a relatively powerful "knowledge class," comprising people employed in areas such as education and the therapeutic and counseling agencies.

Early remedial efforts focused on publicizing the perils of cigarette smokers, reflecting a strategy of assimilative reform. Even many smokers expressed opposition to cigarettes and a generally repentant attitude. Early educative efforts were thus successful in decreasing cigarette consumption, despite resistance from the tobacco industry. Then, recognition of the adverse effects of smoking on nonusers helped precipitate a turn to coercive reform measures during the mid 1970s. Rather than a repentant friend in need of help, a new definition of the smoker as enemy emerged.

Legal abolition of smoking in pubic facilities became one locus of social control efforts, and smoking bans in public spaces have been widely adopted in recent years.

The success of the antismoking crusade has been grounded in moral entrepreneurs' proficiency at mobilizing power, a mobilization made possible by highly visible governmental campaigns, the widely publicized health risks of smoking, and the proposal of workable and generally acceptable policies to ameliorate the problem. The success of this moral crusade has been further facilitated by the association of deviant characteristics with those in lower social strata, whose stigmatization reinforces existing relations of power and prestige. Despite the formidable resources and staunch opposition of the tobacco industry, the tide of public opinion and policy continues to move toward an antismoking stance.

Research Problem

The study presented below is an exploratory examination of the link between social status and support for a smoking ban in public facilities. Based on theorizing about status politics, as well as evidence about patterns of cigarette use, it was predicted that supporters of the smoking ban would be of higher status than those who opposed it. Further, it was anticipated that supporters of the ban would be more likely to make negative normative claims denouncing the allegedly deviant qualities of smoking, symbolically enhancing their own status while lowering that of their opponents.

The site of this research was Shasta County, California. The population of Shasta County is 147,036, of whom 66,462 reside in its only city, Redding. This county became the setting for the implementation of a hotly contested ban on smoking in public buildings.

In 1988, California voters passed Proposition 99, increasing cigarette taxes by 25 cents per pack. The purpose of the tax was to fund smoking prevention and treatment programs. Toward that end, Shasta County created the Shasta County Tobacco Education Program. The director of the program formed a coalition with officials of the Shasta County chapters of the American Cancer Society and American Lung Association to propose a smoking ban in all public buildings. The three groups formed an organization to promote that cause, Smoke-Free Air For Everyone (SAFE). Unlike other bans then in effect in California, the proposed ban included restaurants and bars, because its proponents considered these to be places in which people encountered significant amounts of secondhand smoke. They procured sufficient signatures on a petition to place the measure on the county's general ballot in November 1992.

The referendum passed with a 56% majority in an election that saw an 82% turnout. Subsequently, the Shasta County Hospitality and Business Alliance, an antiban coalition, obtained sufficient signatures to force a special election to annul the smoking ban. The special election was held in April 1993. Although the turnout was much lower (48%), again a sizable majority (58.4%) supported the ban. The ordinance went into effect on July 1, 1993.

Analytic Strategy

Data were analyzed in our effort to ascertain the moral and status conflicts underlying the Shasta County smoking ban: interviews with five leading moral entrepreneurs and five prominent status quo defenders.[1] These individuals were selected through a snowball sample, with the original respondents identified through interviews with business owners or political advertisements in the local mass media. The selected respondents repeatedly surfaced as the leading figures in their respective coalitions. Semistructured interviews were conducted to determine the reasons underlying their involvement. These data were critical to understanding how the proposed ban was framed by small groups of influential proponents and opponents; it was expected that their concerns would be reflected in the larger public debate about the ban.

[...]

Findings

Moral entrepreneur/status quo defender interviews

The moral entrepreneurs and status quo defenders interviewed represented clearly different interests. The former group included three high-level administrators in the county's chapters of the

American Cancer Society and American Lung Association. A fourth was an administrator for the Shasta County Tobacco Education Project. The last member of this group was a pulmonary physician affiliated with a local hospital. The latter group included four bar and/or restaurant owners and an attorney who had been hired to represent their interests. Thus the status quo defenders were small business owners who might see their economic interests affected adversely by the ban. Importantly, they were representatives of a less prestigious social stratum than the moral entrepreneurs.

The primary concern of the moral entrepreneurs was health. As one stated,

I supported the initiative to get the smoking ban on the ballot because of all the health implications that secondhand smoke can create. Smoking and secondhand smoke are the most preventable causes of death in this nation.

Another offered that

On average, secondhand smoke kills 53,000 Americans each year. And think about those that it kills in other countries! It contains 43 cancer-causing chemical agents that have been verified by the Environmental Protection Agency. It is now listed as a Type A carcinogen, which is in the same category as asbestos.

Every one of the moral entrepreneurs expressed concern about health issues during the interviews. This was not the only point they raised, however. Three of the five made negative normative evaluations of smoking, thereby implicitly degrading the status of smokers. They commented that "smoking is no longer an acceptable action," that "smoke stinks," or that "it is just a dirty and annoying habit." Thus, whereas health was their primary concern, such comments revealed the moral entrepreneurs' negative view of smoking irrespective of any medical issues. Smokers were seen as engaging in unclean and objectionable behavior – stigmatized qualities defining their deviant social status.

The stance of the status quo defenders was also grounded in two arguments. All of them expressed concern about individual rights. As one put it,

I opposed that smoking ban because I personally smoke and feel that it is an infringement of my rights to tell me where I can and cannot smoke. Smoking is a legal activity, and therefore it is unconstitutional to take that right away from me.

Another argued that

Many people have died for us to have these rights in foreign wars and those also fought on American soil. Hundreds of thousands of people thought that these rights were worth dying for, and now some small group of people believe that they can just vote away these rights.

Such symbolism implies that smoking is virtually a patriotic calling, a venerable habit for which people have been willing to forfeit their lives in time of war. In the status quo defenders' view, smoking is a constitutionally protected right.

At the same time, each of the status quo defenders was concerned about more practical matters, namely business profits. As one stated, "my income was going to be greatly affected." Another argued,

If these people owned some of the businesses that they are including in this ban, they would not like it either. By taking away the customers that smoke, they are taking away the mainstay of people from a lot of businesses.

The competing viewpoints of the moral entrepreneurs and status quo defenders revealed the moral issues – health versus individual rights – at the heart of political conflict over the smoking ban. Yet it appears that status issues also fueled the conflict. On the one hand, the moral entrepreneurs denigrated smoking, emphasizing the socially unacceptable qualities of the behavior and symbolically degrading smokers' status. On the other hand, status quo defenders were concerned that their livelihood would be affected by the ban. Interestingly, the occupational status of the two groups differed, with the moral entrepreneurs representing the new knowledge class, and the status quo defenders a lower stratum of small business owners. Those in the latter group may not have been accorded the prestige and trust granted those in the former. Moreover, the status quo defenders' concern about business was likely seen as self-aggrandizing.

[...]

Summary and Discussion

This research has examined the moral and status politics underlying the implementation of a smoking ban in Shasta County, California. Moral entrepreneurs crusading for the ban argued that secondhand smoke damages health, implicitly grounding their argument in the principle that people have a right to a smoke-free environmemt. Status quo defenders countered that smokers have a constitutional right to indulge wherever and whenever they see fit. Public discourse echoed these themes, as seen in the letters to the editor of the local newspaper. Thus debate about the smoking ban focused especially on health versus smokers' rights; yet evidence of social status differences between the competing symbolic-moral universes also surfaced. Competing symbolic-moral universes are defined not only by different ethical viewpoints on a behavior, but also by differences in social power – disparities inevitably linked to the system of stratification (Ben-Yehuda 1990). Those prevailing in moral and stigma contests typically represent the higher socioeconomic echelons of society.

The moral entrepreneurs who engineered the smoking ban campaign were representatives of the prestigious knowledge class, including among their members officials from the local chapters of respected organizations at the forefront of the national antismoking crusade. In contrast, the small business owners who were at the core of the opposing coalition, of status quo defenders, represented the traditional middle class. Clearly, there was an instrumental quality to the restaurant and bar owners' stance, because they saw the ban as potentially damaging to their business interests. But they were unable to shape the public debate, as demonstrated by the letters to the editor.

[...]

In many respects, the status conflicts involved in the passage of the Shasta County smoking ban were symbolic. The moral entrepreneurs focused attention on the normatively undesirable qualities of cigarette smoking, and their negative normative evaluations of smoking were reflected in public debate about the ban. Those who wrote in support of the ban more frequently offered negative normative evaluations than antiban writers; their comments degraded smoking and, implicitly, smokers. Since the advent of the antismoking crusade in the United States, smoking has come to be seen as socially reprehensible, and smokers as social misfits characterized by negative psychological characteristics (Markle and Troyer 1979).

Ultimately, a lifestyle associated with the less educated, less affluent, lower occupational strata was stigmatized as a public health hazard and targeted for coercive reform. Its deviant status was codified in the ordinance banning smoking in public facilities, including restaurants and bars. The ban symbolized the deviant status of cigarette smokers, the prohibition visibly demonstrating the community's condemnation of their behavior. Further, the smoking ban symbolically amplified the purported virtues of the abstinent lifestyle. A political victory such as the passage of a law is a prestige-enhancing symbolic triumph that is perhaps even more rewarding than its end result (Gusfield 1963). The symbolic nature of the ban serendipitously surfaced in another way during one author's unstructured observations in 42 restaurants and 21 bars in the area: Whereas smoking was not observed in a single restaurant, it occurred without sanction in all but one of the bars. Although not deterring smoking in one of its traditional bastions, the ban called attention to its deviant quality and, instrumentally, effectively halted it in areas more commonly frequented by the abstemious.

Although more systematic research is needed, the findings of this exploratory case study offer a better understanding of the dynamics underlying opposition to smoking and further support to theorizing about the role of status politics in the creation of deviant types. Denunciation of smoking in Shasta County involved not only legitimate allegations about public health, but negative normative evaluations of those engaged in the behavior. In the latter regard, the ban constituted a status degradation ceremony, symbolically differentiating the pure and abstinent from the unclean and intrusive. Not coincidentally, the stigmatized were more likely found among society's lower socioeconomic strata, and their denouncers among its higher echelons.

Certainly the class and ethnic antipathies underlying attacks on cocaine and opiate users earlier in the century were more manifest than those revealed in the crusade against cigarette smoking. But neither are there manifest status conflicts in the present crusades against abortion and pornography; yet the underlying differences of status between opponents in those movements are reflected in their markedly different symbolic-moral universes, as was the case in the present study.

This is not to suggest that smoking should be an approved behavior. The medical evidence seems compelling: Cigarette smoking is harmful to the individual smoker and to those exposed to secondhand smoke. However, the objective harms of the psychoactive substance in question are irrelevant to the validity of our analysis, just as they were to Gusfield's (1963) analysis of the temperance movement's crusade against alcohol use. Moreover, it is not our intention to imply that the proban supporters consciously intended to degrade those of lower social status. No doubt they were motivated primarily by a sincere belief that smoking constitutes a public health hazard. In the end, however, moral indignation and social control flowed down the social hierarchy. Thus we must ask: Would cigarette smoking be defined as deviant if there were a positive correlation between smoking and socioeconomic status?

Note

1   Although the term moral entrepreneur is well established in the literature on deviance, there seems to be little attention to or consistency in a corresponding term for

the interest group(s) opposing them. Those that have been employed, such as "forces for the status quo" (Markle and Troyer 1979), tend to be awkward. "Status quo defenders" is used here for lack of a simpler or more common term.

References

Becker, Howard S. 1963. *Outsiders: Studies in the Sociology of Deviance*. New York: Free Press.

Ben-Yehuda, Nachman. 1990. *The Politics and Morality of Deviance: Moral Panics, Drug Abuse, Deviant Science, and Reversed Stigmatization*. Albany, NY: State University of New York Press.

Garfinkel, Harold. 1956. "Conditions of Successful Degradation Ceremonies." *American Journal of Sociology* 61: 402–24.

Goffman, Erving. 1963. *Stigma: Notes on the Management of Spoiled Identity*. Englewood Cliffs, NJ: Prentice-Hall.

Gusfield, Joseph R. 1963. *Symbolic Crusade: Status Politics and the American Temperance Movement*. Urbana, IL: University of Illinois Press.

Markle, Gerald E. and Ronald J. Troyer. 1979. "Smoke Gets in Your Eyes: Cigarette Smoking as Deviant Behavior." *Social Problems* 26: 611–25.

Ram, Sidney P. 1941. *How to Get More Fun Out of Smoking*. Chicago: Cuneo.

Schur, Edwin M. 1980. *The Politics of Deviance: Stigma Contests and the Uses of Power*. New York: Random House.

Questions

1   What factors do you think have contributed to the significant decline in cigarette smoking over the last few decades? What can we learn from these strategies? Do you think prohibiting/criminalizing smoking, similar to our current illicit drug policies, would have been more effective?

2   What strategy do you think would better reduce the harms associated with certain forms of illicit drug use in our society today, educational or coercive? Why?

3   What demographic characteristics separated the "proban" supporters from the "antiban" supporters? Who had the upper hand in the anti-smoking debate? Why? Do you see any similarities between the anti-smoking campaign and the anti-drinking campaign discussed by Gusfield?

Reflections on the Meaning of Drug Epidemics

Dale D. Chitwood, Sheigla Murphy, and Marsha Rosenbaum

Rounding out our introduction to the major drugs in current and historical popular use, Dale Chitwood, Sheigla Murphy, and Marsha Rosenbaum use the cases of methamphetamine and crack cocaine to ponder the rise and nature of the drug scares that develop into social fears of an "epidemic." Although this word is bandied around by the media, whose bias is to create sensationalism, these authors analyze and differentiate ordinary and high levels of drug use from its epidemic form. The dividing line, they find, can be rather subjective. Once again, we find that strictly objective factors may not necessarily be the ones that propel this label, but rather elements of set and setting, as well as factors associated with the social power of the drug users.

Since this selection concludes this part of the book, see if you can apply the concepts presented in earlier selections, such as Reinarman's elements of a drug scare, Gusfield's and Tuggle and Holmes' ideas about status politics, and other historical accounts that link the rise and fall of drug legislation to the groups associated with various drugs to this discussion of drug epidemics. How would you build a model, using the sociological tools you have learned thus far, to explain why some drugs are hailed as attaining "epidemic" proportions? What individuals or groups in society benefit from the social construction of such labels? Who is harmed by them, and do groups gain at, or only at, the expense of others? What is the currency of winning and losing in the war to declare a drug epidemic? Think about other drugs in society, as well as other social behaviors, and see if you can come up with any ideas of behaviors or substances that are ripe for being defined as epidemics.

Drugs and the American Dream: An Anthology, First Edition. Edited by Patricia A. Adler, Peter Adler, and Patrick K. O'Brien.
© 2012 John Wiley & Sons, Inc. Published 2012 by John Wiley & Sons, Inc.

Introduction

Since the 1960s, the measurement of psychoactive substance use in the United States has expanded extensively. Today governmental and other cooperative organizations routinely generate official statistics about drug use and produce data through such systematic programs as the Drug Abuse Warning Network (DAWN) and the Drug and Alcohol Services Information System (DASIS). Other statistics are gathered to estimate the incidence and prevalence of drug use through annual national surveys, such as the National Survey on Drug Use and Health (NSDUH) and Monitoring the Future (MTF), as well as from complementary research endeavors such as the Community Epidemiology Work Group (CEWG). Such longitudinal data sets have enhanced the ability of researchers to identify and characterize fluctuations in patterns of use over time.

These data systems have allowed researchers to monitor increases and decreases in the patterns of drug use in the United States during the last 40 years. We know, for example, that per capita cigarette consumption has declined substantially since 1960, as has the prevalence of smoking among men and women. Hard liquor consumption increased in the 1960s and 1970s, but has declined over recent decades. The use of these licit drugs considerably exceeds the use of illicit substances. The incidence of marijuana use peaked around 1979–1980, declined through the 1980s, increased once again in the 1990s, and has fluctuated since that time. The incidence of cocaine use peaked in the early 1980s and then declined, even as crack cocaine emerged in that decade.

The cumulative data from the last four decades permit us to describe fluctuations in use, but our ability to explain the reasons beyond these variations is far less certain. The evolution in both street and commercial pharmacology continues to introduce new formulations into the street pharmacopeia that adds complexity to these patterns of drug use. The emergence of crack cocaine two decades ago illustrates the influence that street pharmacology can have on patterns of use, and synthetic formulations of the early and late twentieth century, such as methamphetamine and oxycodone, continue to expand the list of illicit substances that should be systematically monitored.

The Phenomenon of Drug Epidemics

Although our ability to anticipate increases and decreases in the patterns of drug use is quite limited, we know that most of the illicit drugs monitored in this era have one thing in common. At one time or another, the media, public officials, and/or the research community have characterized these fluctuations as drug epidemics. Investigators involved in drug-related research can recall how the attachment of the term "epidemic" to individual drugs has uniquely linked substances to specific decades: heroin in the late 1960s and early 1970s, LSD in the 1960s, PCP in the late 1970s, marijuana at the close of the 1970s, crack in the 1980s, MDMA in the 1990s, and methamphetamine in the 1980s and again in this decade. Sometimes, as in the case of heroin use in the late 1960s, data support the observation that the incidence and prevalence of heroin use was higher during that era. At other times, as in the case of LSD use in the 1960s, data indicate that the use of LSD was lower in that decade than it was in the 1970s, even though the perception that LSD use peaked in the 1960s persists in common lore. The emergence of a new drug on the street or a new formulation of an existing drug, as in the case of crack cocaine, is almost inevitably heralded as an epidemic.

The Case of Methamphetamine

Many view methamphetamine as a new drug, even though it has been around since the 1930s. It was identified as a drug of abuse in the 1960s and was considered a drug used and sold primarily by motorcycle gangs and by gay men who used it for marathon sex parties. Methamphetamine, however, also has been associated with night and swing shift workers, particularly truck drivers who need to stay awake for long hours. The use of methamphetamine grew steadily throughout the 1990s in the West and Midwest. By the turn of this century, it had appeared in many areas of the Midwest and South and had surfaced to a lesser degree in the Northeast and Mid-Atlantic. As reported in NSDUH, methamphetamine use rose from just under 2% of the adult population in 1994 to just over 5% in 2003. Unlike prior outbreaks of other drugs that were generally identified with minorities and people living in inner city communities, methamphetamine abuse has spread from the biker and trucker communities of California to the Pacific Northwest, mountain states, and the rural heartland. In February 1998, General Barry R. McCaffrey, Director of the Office of National Drug Control Policy, stated: "Methamphetamine has 'exploded' from 'a west coast biker drug' into America's heartland and could replace cocaine as the nation's primary drug threat" (Copley News Service, 1998).

Although the use of methamphetamine has increased, this stimulant still accounts for a relatively small percentage of the people affected by drug and alcohol problems in the United States. In 2003, alcohol accounted for 42% of people admitted for drug treatment in the United States; heroin and other opiates accounted for 18%; marijuana, 15%; cocaine, 14%; and methamphetamine and other stimulants, just 7%. Nevertheless, rural communities that previously had little experience with illicit drug addiction or drug-related crime have seen an increase in several direct and collateral consequences of addiction.

What is interesting about this progressive increase in methamphetamine use is the nature of media coverage. Media reports around the United States have virtually created the idea that methamphetamine abuse has reached rampant proportions. These reports often include depictions of a scourge raging across the country and enveloping communities in chaos. The media feeds a sense of growing alarm by continuously circulating the dire reports delivered by officials from the reported epicenters of use. The spirit of these images is reflected in newspaper headlines like these: "Spread of meth near epidemic, Czar says" (Ruff, 1997); "Governor warns meth epidemic growing like kudzu" (Bluestein, 2004); "Officials brace for meth epidemic; labs on the rise in New England" (Valencia, 2005); "Attorney General calls meth an epidemic in Illinois" (Nauman, 2005); and "Meth epidemic forcing grandparents to raise grandchildren" (Dillon, 2006).

The parallels between the coverage of crack in the 1980s, where it was described as a "plague" and an "epidemic," and the reporting on methamphetamine are so striking one could swap the word "meth" for "crack." Some media stories seem to have done exactly that: "Methamphetamine sinks its teeth into Arkansas; like crack's epidemic rise in '80s, police say" (Waite, 1999).

The depiction of a pattern of drug use as an epidemic, as is the case with methamphetamine in this decade, is certainly a proven mechanism for communicating that a problem exists, but are such depictions wise? We need to question our national tendency to use the term "drug epidemic" to describe such patterns of drug misuse: When is it methodologically accurate to call a pattern of drug use an epidemic? And what are the consequences of doing so?

Our response to these questions should be informed by an understanding of the concept of epidemic central to the field of epidemiology. Epidemiology originally referred almost exclusively to the study of the outbreak of life-threatening infectious diseases, as in the classic investigation by John Snow of cholera in London during the mid-1850s. Early investigations of epidemics were prompted by elevated mortality rates associated with dangerous infectious diseases. The concept of epidemic originally referred to infectious diseases (such as cholera) that occurred so frequently they clearly exceeded normal expectations.

Changes in the distribution of disease during the 20th century extended the concept of epidemic to include chronic as well as infectious diseases. Epidemic is defined quite broadly today and can refer to any kind of illness or injury. There is no universally applicable minimal number of cases that constitutes an epidemic. An epidemic can be said to exist whenever the number of cases exceeds that which is considered normal or expected based upon past experience for a given population. The level of normal expectation varies for different diseases and in different circumstances. An epidemic may span any time period and may last a few hours (bacterial food poisoning), a few weeks (influenza), or many years (HIV/AIDS). An epidemic may exist within a census tract, a city, or a nation, or may be worldwide as is true in pandemics of influenza. Endemic occurrence, in contrast to epidemic occurrence, refers to periods of the habitual presence or the usual prevalence of a given disease within a geographic area. Epidemiology today encompasses a comprehensive perspective of the dynamics of disease and is concerned not only with epidemic occurrences but also with inter-epidemic periods and endemic occurrences of disease.

From a strictly epidemiological perspective, a pattern of drug use becomes an epidemic occurrence when the incidence and/or prevalence of use exceed normal expectations. But who determines that threshold for any given drug? When a new drug appears in society, how many must initiate its use before it becomes an epidemic occurrence? The answer is elusive. In a society with strong prohibitionist perspectives, many would say that it refers to any use that exceeds what is normal and expected. In that scenario, all use is epidemic use, and the concept loses meaning. Others, who believe that psychoactive drug use is an established reality in American society, would say that some level of use is expected, and a benchmark of endemic use should be established against which the actual incidence of use is compared. No mechanism has been advanced that definitely answers this question.

Even if society could agree on an endemic threshold of use against which an outbreak could be compared, and even if we had universally accepted criteria for when to apply the term "drug epidemic" to an elevated level of drug use, the public characterization of drug use as a drug epidemic remains saddled with additional problems. The concept of epidemic, as it is commonly applied to drug use, represents more than its epidemiological meaning of unusually elevated occurrence. When epidemic is used to characterize illicit drug use, the term also communicates elements of the fear and panic that traditionally accompanied life-threatening infectious diseases like cholera and the plague to which the term was first applied. Drug outbreaks have been likened to plague, and the media at times has fed that sense of alarm by continuously circulating the dire reports delivered by officials who are reacting to a sense of crisis.

This association of drug epidemic, and at times the equation of drug epidemic with the plague, creates significant obstacles to the appropriate investigation of the outbreak, to understanding its causes, and to the reduction of harm associated with heightened misuse of a drug. Again we can turn to the epidemiologic perspective to help frame the nature of these obstacles.

A declaration that the frequency of drug misuse has become an epidemic occurrence ideally should be the first step in a reasoned approach to protect the user and others who are at risk or otherwise affected. Three closely interrelated components embrace all descriptive and analytic epidemiologic principles and methods: frequency, distribution, and determinants of disease. The first component, frequency, involves the quantification of the occurrence of disease (i.e., the incidence and prevalence of disease). Unusually elevated occurrence is epidemic occurrence. Determining that the frequency or prevalence of drug use has reached an unacceptable level is only the first step in the process. The second epidemiologic component – distribution of disease – considers the who, where, and when of the epidemic occurrence of drug use. The third factor, determinants of disease, derives from the first two, because knowledge of frequency and distribution of disease is essential to test an epidemiologic hypothesis about the risk factors for use, which in turn can inform us about strategies for the reduction of drug misuse. From this perspective, the determination that an outbreak of drug misuse is an epidemic occurrence of use becomes the starting point for exploring the nature of the distribution of that use. This information should then be used to test hypotheses and to design appropriate responses to the elevated use so that the level of misuse can be reduced and any harm associated with use can be mitigated. If the concept of drug epidemic could be used within this ideal of epidemiologic inquiry, the term would serve a positive function in resolving drug-related problems. Nevertheless, when the term drug epidemic is invoked, the process can become distorted.

Unfortunately, the use of the term drug epidemic has other social roots and political ramifications that frequently impede and misdirect the investigative process. When drug use is declared to be a drug epidemic, panic often is substituted for reasoned action. The declaration of a drug epidemic is at least as likely to truncate an epidemiological investigation as it is to announce the initiation of one. When any drug is characterized this way and simultaneously portrayed as the most dangerous drug in existence, fear rather than reasoned action is usually generated, leading to reactive and punitive measures meant to stem the advance of the "deadly menace" that infects society and threatens its survival.

Veterans of the last three decades of the war on drugs are keenly aware of how good intentions can lead to poor policies. In the 1980s, congress enacted mandatory minimum drug sentencing laws that mandated long prison terms for persons convicted of nonviolent drug offenses. Federal laws imposed the harshest sentences on those convicted of offenses involving the drug epidemic of that decade: crack cocaine. We believe that the national media first mentioned crack by name on November 17, 1985 when an obscure article in *The New York Times* noted that three teenagers were in treatment for a new form of cocaine called crack. Less than 11 months later, major newspapers, wire services, and leading weekly magazines, such as *Newsweek* and *Time*, had produced more than 1,000 stories about crack. Some of these accounts compared the spread of crack throughout the United States with the plagues of medieval Europe, and some called crack the most addictive drug in existence. One product of the fear that developed around crack cocaine is reflected in differential federal sentencing guidelines that were established for powder cocaine and crack cocaine. The mandatory minimum drug sentences created a 100:1 differential in punishment for crack versus powder cocaine offenses. A person convicted of possessing five grams of crack cocaine would serve a minimum of five years in federal prison, while it would take 500 grams of powder cocaine to trigger the same sentence.

The decision to single out crack cocaine for more severe punishment was driven by sensationalist news coverage about the ravages of crack cocaine on inner-city communities and the violence it spawned. As a result of these laws, judges were forced to impose sentences that many jurists believed to be unjust. The severity of punishment was based in large part on the perception of crack as a "powerfully addictive" and "dangerous" drug that posed a significant threat to communities and society, language we are hearing again with methamphetamine. These laws have been criticized as ineffective, unnecessarily punitive, and racially discriminatory. It has taken 20 years for legislators to begin seeking redress to this problem.

During the rush to respond to the crack cocaine epidemic, little consideration was given to the impact of the new policies on women. The frightening reports that children born to women who used crack were radically different from other children are well-known. Researchers and media stories that associated crack cocaine with this concept of epidemic reported this information widely in the 1980s. This misconception about the children of women who used cocaine continued to be reported in the media even after research in the 1990s found that most of the perceived impact of prenatal cocaine use disappeared when one controlled for alcohol use, other drug use, and lifestyle factors.

One consequence of the panic-driven reaction to the depiction of crack cocaine as a drug epidemic has been that thousands of children have grown up without their mothers who have been incarcerated for extended periods of time. Laws imposing mandatory prison sentences, eliminating or severely restricting parole, and expanding the scope of conspiracy and civil asset forfeiture laws have all had a disproportionate impact on women. The sanctions for persons convicted of drug offenses renders them ineligible for public housing, welfare benefits, financial aid, and many civil service jobs, making it even more difficult for women to rebuild their lives and reclaim their families. Most tragically, the 1996 Adoption and Safe Families Act, designed to facilitate the adoption of children languishing in foster care, had the unintended effect of adding the possibility of termination of parental rights as an additional consequence of a woman's incarceration.

In each of these cases, policy makers failed to consider the impact of their proposed responses on women, and they did not acquire information about the prevalence and patterns of drug use among women. This created a perfect storm of punitive drug policies colliding with increasing drug use and drug involvement of women. The results have been shocking. Between 1986 and 1999, the number of women incarcerated for drug offenses in state facilities alone has increased by over 888%.

Over the past four decades, we have learned that naming specific patterns of use as drug epidemics influences the allocation of public monies and influences whether jail or treatment will be the intervention of choice for users who get in trouble with those drugs. Sometimes elevated levels of use have occurred before drug researchers have figured out what was happening. Sometimes so-called drug epidemics were more like what Craig Reinarman and Harry Levine (1989) named media-fueled "drug scares" that reinforced gender, race, and class intolerance. When the research community invokes the concept of epidemic to describe elevated levels of use, we must be aware that others may also use this phrase in ways that are inconsistent with a reasoned epidemiological approach. Many of those alternative interpretations are more likely to increase fear and unreasoned reaction than they are to facilitate appropriately balanced responses that address the real problems associated with drug misuse.

The message we need to take away is that the phrase "drug epidemic" should never be used lightly. Using alternative terminologies to describe increases in the incidence and prevalence of drug use may be more successful in directing both researchers and policy-makers toward effective techniques for reducing the problems associated with the misuse of drugs. We are not saying that researchers can control the media's quest for dramatic drug stories sprinkled liberally with words like "plague" and "epidemic" to sell publications or to generate viewership, but we can do a better job of making our careful and systematic examinations of drug users and drug use trends available to the media and the public. We have a professional and ethical responsibility to do our very best to use our knowledge, talents, and resources to suppress hysteria and support equitable and effective drug policy.

References

Bluestein, G. 2004. Governor warns meth epidemic growing like kudzu. *The Associated Press State & Local Wire* (Aug. 17).

Copley News Service 1998. Methamphetamine seen as next major threat. *San Diego Union-Tribune* (Feb. 12).

Dillon, J. 2006. Meth epidemic forcing grandparents to raise grandchildren. *The Associated Press State & Local Wire* (March 31).

Nauman, B. 2005. Attorney general calls meth an epidemic in Illinois. *The Pantagraph*, p. A3. (November 11).

Reinarman, C. and Levine, H. G. 1989. Crack in context: Politics and the media in the making of a drug scare. *Contemporary Drug Problems, 16,* 535–77.

Ruff, J. 1997. Spread of meth near epidemic, Czar says. *Lincoln Journal Star*, p. 2. (May 30).

Valencia, M. J. 2005. Officials brace for meth epidemic; labs on the rise in New England. *Sunday Telegram*, p. A1 (August 7).

Waite, M. 1999. Methamphetamine sinks its teeth into Arkansas; like crack's epidemic rise in '80s, police say. *Arkansas Democrat-Gazette*, p. A1 (March 21).

Questions

1   How can we account for the fact that actual rates of use generally do not support the fervor-created drug epidemics? How do we see Reinarman's drug scare stages represented in the methamphetamine "epidemic?"

2   What is the "normal" or "expected" use of a drug in our society? How might those with social power influence societal definitions of drug epidemics?

3   How might the declaration of some form of drug use as an epidemic, likened to the plague and cholera, impact policy and lawmaking decisions? What are some of the latent consequences of the punitive drug laws created within the context of a "drug epidemic?"

Part II

Social Correlates of Drug Use

We noted earlier, and several of our selections have indicated, the importance of the population of users in affecting the nature of how drugs are perceived, interpreted, and consumed. All sociological and criminological research places a great deal of emphasis on the culture or subculture of particular drug users and on their social position and power in affecting the nature of their usage patterns. These may be more important than the drugs consumed in influencing whether people seek out drugs to escape or engage, they control them or are overwhelmed by them, they maintain or cut legitimate ties to people and jobs in the midst of drug use, and they endanger or maintain their health, than the actual drugs used. Moreover, there are strong connections between groups of drug users and the drugs that are popular with them.

In this part of the book, we present readers with sections that are organized around some of the most important demographic factors characterizing drug users and people in society more generally: race/ethnicity, social class, gender, and youth/aging. These population variables serve to place people in their social positions, to organize them into pockets of advantage or disadvantage, to bring them together with others having similar characteristics, and to describe their sociological distinctions. We can see that some drugs, which are not evenly distributed throughout society, are more likely to be used by youth, with others preferred by the middle-aged or elderly. Youngsters may experiment with drugs that make their parents nervous, but these same adults may ingest pharmaceuticals, that may have more far-reaching negative side effects, because they were prescribed by a physician. Yet teen drug use may be not nearly as problematic as that of older people, as we see millions of middle-aged individuals who lightly dabble with pain pills despite their highly addictive nature. Similarly, racial and ethnic subcultures, while not having a monopoly on any single drug, often can be predicted to cleave toward some substances and away from others. These predilections for certain drugs can also be socioeconomically based, as the price of some substances may be too costly for lower-income groups. During the crack epidemic, most Blacks and other lower-income minority groups partook of this drug, although snortable (HCL) cocaine, a more expensive alternative, was the drug of choice for "yuppies" and other upper-middle-class professionals. We also know that gender operates to demark some people's desires. Thus, what might be central to masculine, macho culture may be anathematic to women. What might appeal to women, perhaps due to the great amount of pressure society puts on them to attain an idealized body image, may make them prefer some drugs and disdain others. For instance, women who desire to get high may turn down alcohol because of its caloric content, but accept amphetamines ("speed") because they suppress appetite. Within each section, we offer a range of people and the different appeal that some drugs have within these population groups.

—— Race/Ethnicity ——

Gen-X Junkie
Young White Heroin Users in Washington, DC

Todd G. Pierce

We begin the race/ethnicity section with a selection by Todd Pierce on Caucasians. Contrary to popular imagery, the drugs consumed by Whites are not always high-status or expensive substances; Whites use street drugs as well. Pierce's excellent participant-observation research with a group of heroin and cocaine snorters and injectors interweaves an analytic focus on the network dynamics of this young, urban group with a career analysis of how people are drawn into the behavior, manage the behavior through upheavals in their social lives, and transition away from using drugs. He offers an important comparative analysis between the drug using patterns of this White network and networks of Black street drug users he also encountered. This is the first, but not the last, selection that explicitly addresses differences in the drug-using patterns of Whites and Blacks.

Based on this research you may begin to formulate some ideas about the effect of race (skin color, physical attributes) and ethnicity (the culture – norms and values – of the group) on the things that are important to drug users and that influence a range of important elements such as affluence, opportunity, outlook, lifestyle, peer and family influences, and societal expectations. As with some of the previous selections, you should use this piece to begin formulating a set of ideas about how people live in society that go beyond the stereotypic and superficial portrayals of groups presented in the media.

Introduction: Research Objectives, Design, and Population

Historically, both ethnographic and epidemiologic research conducted with intravenous drug users (IDUs) focuses on people from poor socioeconomic situations. They are easier to access on the streets, monetary incentives for interview participation is very attractive, the ethnographer can be fit within the IDUs' world view (often as an HIV counselor, outreach worker, or case manager), and they are at the most risk for HIV because intravenous drug use or sex-for-crack exchanges are overrepresented in poorer populations.

Drugs and the American Dream: An Anthology, First Edition. Edited by Patricia A. Adler, Peter Adler, and Patrick K. O'Brien.
© 2012 John Wiley & Sons, Inc. Published 2012 by John Wiley & Sons, Inc.

Beyond the possible political implications, maintaining this exclusive and extended focus (fifteen some-odd years of HIV research with these populations) also limits our theoretical understanding of the nature of networks of IDUs and the gambit of risk behaviors. This project focuses on economically well-off White IDUs or those who grew up in that socioeconomic condition. "Studying up" or "sideways," meaning the study of people with either the same or greater levels of mainstream power (that of the researcher's), allows us to better understand the range of behaviors we are investigating while also allowing us to create a better cultural comparative model. As Murphy (1987) points out, IDUs can be found in every part of our society, not just the inner city.

[...]

The core sample for this study was drawn from a snowball sampling design and consisted of 12 White intravenous drug users (six male/six female) ranging in ages from 19 to 31. The snowball sample was achieved through the ethnographer's networking through the social networks of the IDUs first, and then introduced to the IDUs from their friends and other IDUs. The typical scenario would occur over a game of 8 ball (pool) where the ethnographer's opponent would ask what the ethnographer did for a living, and then when told that he studied heroin users, the opponent would say "Oh, I have a friend that you should meet. He's a junky." Then the ethnographer would give the opponent his business card and tell him to give it to the friend to arrange for a meeting.

In total, 12 egocentric networks were studied. The sample of networks contained two or three core or main members as well as periphery and outer periphery members. Primary analysis for each network was based on dyadic and triadic core relationships within each network. Each network had members that connected one network to the next (a "bridger"). Bridged networks contained White, Black, and Hispanic members. Most of the 12 IDUs in the main sample came from a White, suburban, middle- or upper-middle-class background. Several were from very "well-off" families. All had at least a high school education, while some had either a four-year college degree or some college time. Other individuals in the study included eight who were either heroin or cocaine snorters, cocaine injectors, or rehabilitated heroin

injectors. In addition to these eight, about 25 peripheral network members were included in the study. These members were part of the social environment of the 12 core IDUs and were either cocaine snorters or sexual conjugates (sex partners) of the core. [...] Almost all of the subjects for the study admitted to wanting to participate because of the money offered for the interviews, but later came to rather enjoy working with the ethnographer. After a time the ethnographer and the subjects became close friends and colleagues, working together in this ethnographer endeavor.

[...]

Network Attributes: Formation, Change, and Dissolution

Network formation

When studying the creation of an IDU network, you must first ask whether networks formed before or after drug use were put into the mix. In most cases the networks studied in DC turned to injecting drugs after network formation. This point is central for our understanding of risk networks because it helps us better understand the foundations of the network itself (thus a better understanding of the risk relations). In most cases the network members knew each other and had a relationship prior to drug use. Those who did not know their network before "using" acquired them after accessing key roles within their drug environment (i.e., drug running).

What was discovered in DC was that there were two general ways young White IDU networks formed. The first was a network relationship that stemmed from long-term friendships. The second was centered around IDUs that had an ability to cop dope successfully.

Cindy's network is a good example of a long-term friendship network. Her network had three main members who were IDUs, one of which was her boyfriend (her main sex partner). She also had a number of other sexual partners who were part of her network, but they were not IDUs. The main members of the network, Cindy (age 20), her boyfriend Jimmy (age 31), and her best friend Sandy (age 19), had had a relationship before shooting up together. Cindy and Sandy had known each other since the age of 13 or

14. They had literally grown up together and had been hanging out in the rock and roll "scene" since their early teenage years. Cindy had started injecting with one of her boyfriends when she was in her late teens. Sandy had acquired a snorting habit by using with several of her friends, but then asked Cindy to help her in administering her first injection. The ethnographer witnessed her first injection (Pierce, forthcoming:1), and interviewed Sandy the next day to discuss the event, and why she did it with Cindy:

> She's (Cindy) been an intravenous drug user for years, and she never wanted me to, she wouldn't, we hadn't done heroin together. We never have done heroin together until this [past] weekend, because she doesn't want me to get like her, she doesn't want me to shoot up heroin. She doesn't like this, but she saw that I was going to do it anyway. And she's lonely, really. She's very lonely. She's got her boyfriend, and he's not very nice to her, and she kind of didn't want me to do it, but she really like, I mean that's what she told me afterwards. She said "I really enjoy doing this with you, een though it's very bad." Then she's like "Okay, fine. Let's get the heroin, let's get the needles. We'll do this." She taught me how to do it. I've seen it done before, I just never went that step until this weekend. (Pierce Interview: WX: 14)

This scenario was common for most of the users in the study. In fact, all of the users "turned on" to injection through a friend who was using. In such cases the formation of both young White and Black injection networks came from much deeper sociocultural roots, i.e., neighborhood communities or schoolmates, than simply the need to inject. People are generally social beings, and form networks within their lives to satisfy different social needs they have (i.e., feeling accepted, belonging, loved). Different networks fulfill different needs. Some networks, like the family, may fulfill a need for stability or safety, others may be for advancement of knowledge, or adventure. Like many social activities, the first time one does something, it is usually done with somebody else who can experience it with you or show you how to do it.

[...]

With experimentation comes new experiences and the feelings and knowledge that come with them. The evolution of a person's drug addiction is a learning process that is often learned with their network, but also on their own through trial and error. Sandy explains for us the feelings she had about injecting heroin as opposed to just snorting it:

> I'm used to needles because I have a bad history with asthma, and I'm just used to needles from getting blood drawn, and whatever, and I find it kind of ... it's hard to explain, it's a lot more sexy, almost. It's a lot more, you're really getting into the whole feel of the high. It's part of ... the preparation's almost like, it's an anticipation ... you're not just spreading a few lines out and snorting it this time. You're now cooking it and you're putting a needle in your vein. It's, if you have time to kind of sit there and do it, like have the whole symbolism thing, it's, it makes it a lot more impressive in your mind. It's uh, I don't, it's hard to explain. It's almost a fun thing, but it's not fun. I mean the pain of the needle, or whatever, that's not fun, but it's, you've got these little toys to play with, and you've got all this stuff that you have, that's illegal. And if you get caught, you feel like shit with it, but when you have it, it's almost like it's, it's more ... almost like a toy ... drugs. To play with, I don't know, it's not a happy thing, if you really think about it, but it gets you really excited about the whole thing and it's fun. ... It's almost like a permanent thing in your mind. You're really going to get high. It's really happening, you're really getting prepared for this whole thing, things like that, it's just the whole anticipation of getting high. You've got to do all [these things], it's part of the whole process. (Pierce Interview: WX: 14)

How these new experiences are discussed and learned within a network and certain socioeconomic contexts is important for understanding the injection processes, the personal nature and the social nature of the drug-using rituals. Also, the behavior that is learned through trial and error as an individual IDU builds a habit is important because it illustrates how some behaviors are not taught or discussed. Many aspects of drug misuse were not discussed by network members, such as morning sickness from withdrawal symptoms. In one discussion with the ethnographer, early on in her addiction, Sandy had described having a headache all day long. The ethnographer asked her how much dope she was using. She replied "three or four bags a night." Essentially, she was binging on heroin, but only at night instead of a constant stream of use through-out the day. And she was unaware of the detox effects occurring in the morning. Nobody from her network had told her! Even though her network members were very experienced users. In fact, it was the ethnographer who had to educate her on her biophysical reactions to the drugs. "Man, you just don't know why you have these headaches all day do you? You're dope sick!" She was horrified upon learning this. It was as if the reality of her level of use had just set in. That's when her long uphill struggle to recovery started, after the fact. A few days after learning this she told the ethnographer her headaches were all better, now she "got off E" (see note[1]) in the morning with that coveted first shot of dope for the day.

This transference of cultural information (or lack of it) is important for understanding risk reduction in injection behaviors because it tells us how people learn (or do not learn) certain behavioral procedures for injecting drugs. And, to make matters more complicated, this transference of information happens differently for all subpopulations or microcultures.

The second type of network formation is centered around copping dope. Young, new, White IDUs generally have a lot of difficulty trying to cop dope off the street. They fall prey to more experienced IDUs who will "take" them for all they are worth. They are literally sitting ducks for a "hard-core" street junkie who knows the ropes. Also, dealers do not trust people whom they do not know well, and so will be reluctant to sell to them. Therefore, the young White user must earn his stripes on the streets by going through a series of rip-offs and takes, gaining access to a runner, and then establishing a steady relationship. Not all young White IDUs can or want to do this. It is a risky endeavor, and the stakes are high when playing the street game. Only a few users from this study were any good at copping their own dope; even fewer held the highly respected runner position.

What this meant was that users who were not very adept at copping for themselves sought out users who could do that for them (for a small fee, usually in the form of money or drugs). In the first type of network formation discussed earlier, the network members were forced to go through trial and error routines in order to cop. In most cases only one of the members would do the copping for the entire network. Some of these successful buyers would find routes to copping other than the streets, like a dealer at a night club or an acquaintance from another network who had access to the drug. If a trusting relationship could be established with that acquaintance, then maybe the buyer and his or her network would join up with the runner's network, thus expanding the network based on the need for drugs (on the seeker's side), the need for money (on the runner's side), and trust. The runner then becomes the bridger of the two networks (the runner's own network and that of the seeker).

A good example of such network formation was Ken's, a 25-year-old White male, with long brown hair and tattoos. He's a musician, works at different clubs as a doorman, and plays a good game of pool. He is the center of his network because he is a drug runner. He was taught how to deal drugs by an older Black man (Q) who had been running drugs for about 20 years, and who is also part of Ken's network. Ken has six network members, both male and female; all are White except for Q. His network members are not only customers for drugs, but they are also friends. He has known many of them for several years and socializes with them outside the context of injecting or scoring drugs. Although they pay him either in drugs or money for helping them score, the relationship doesn't stop there. They will often eat meals together, stay at each others apartments, go out on the town together, etc.

Ken is a bridger to Q's network which consists of about 30 people from different ethnic and socioeconomic backgrounds. Although Ken has injected with Q at Ken's apartment (which doubles as an exclusive shooting gallery), there is no risk of HIV infection between the two men or the two networks. This is because there is no direct or indirect sharing occurring during injection episodes. In networks that do directly or indirectly share drug-use equipment, bridgers can be a very high-risk agent for the network members because they can spread the virus from one network to the next. But because Ken's network is very safe in their drug-use behaviors, there is no (or extremely low) risk of infection.

There are other ways that networks form as well, most of which happen by the pure chance of being at the same place at the same time. A good example of this might be if one user sees another trying to cop some dope on the street and decides to approach the person to either aid in copping or to maybe ask if the person knows where they can get a good deal. They might even go as far as to pool their money in an attempt to cop a higher quantity of dope. This is rare, but it does happen.

[...]

A nice example of how networks are created can be drawn from the ethnographer's own experiences when meeting the respondents for this project. The ethnographer was not familiar with DC nor its drug scene. He did not know anybody when he moved into town, but found in-roads to one or two IDUs located within the alternative punk scene (from which the ethnographer himself hails). These in-roads occurred within the social networks of the IDUs and through participating in social activities (like pool, as described earlier). The ethnographer then had those IDUs introduce him to other IDUs in their network, or members of other networks. The chain of people made up the sample for the study: it is not much different for an IDU who moves into town and doesn't know anybody, let alone other IDUs. This sort of network begins with a superficial "weak link" or peripheral connection within a network (as opposed to long-term "core" connections like Cindy and Sandy's), but that changes over time as relationships are developed.

The differences found between the way younger White risk networks formed in comparison to older African American networks is revealing. Most of the Black IDUs studied had grown up in neighborhoods with a long history of drug economies. Many had relatives working within that economy as drug dealers, hustlers of some sort, and users. Their neighborhoods were inundated with drugs, and they quickly learned what it was all about at a young age. Many of the Black IDUs had histories of incarceration because of their dealings with the drug market. Many of the users (almost all of them) had grown up knowing each other, but had entered the drug scene at different points in their lives. Their networks were much larger than the Whites, yet they tended to have a small core network in which they created relationships based on either sexual relations or hustling schemes. The number of people they might inject with is much higher and changes more rapidly, but those people appear to be drawn from a limited number of people within their neighborhood.

The young White IDUs, in contrast, tend to come from suburban communities that do not have a visible active drug economy of nearly the scale that is found in poorer urban neighborhoods. They learn about drugs in their teenage years, and in many cases pass through a series of drugs before ending up on heroin.

Their networks are small, with only a few people at the core (close sexual relations and best friends), and those networks are usually formed around trying to cop dope. They do not cop in their home neighborhoods (dealers are hard to find in Bethesda, MD), they do not use there frequently, and they have very few run-ins with the law.

In sum, one critical difference between the Black low-income (or informal economy incomes only) networks and White middle-class networks was that the Black networks were focused on getting money to buy the dope (they knew exactly how to go about getting it, but couldn't afford it), while the Whites were focused on purchasing it (they had sufficient economic means to afford it, but were not good at getting it). Exact opposites in that respect, but both working for the same goal: dope.

[...]

Drug Use Behaviors: Needle Procurement, Needle Hygiene, and HIV Risk

Unlike most IDU subpopulations, the young White IDUs in this study were extremely safe users. As noted by many researchers, seropositivity levels will vary from population to population based on several factors. Actual seropositivity data for the sample networks were not gathered. Self-report data indicated that only one member of the study was HIV-positive, but he did not directly or indirectly share any of his drug-use paraphernalia. In fact, there was almost no direct or indirect sharing of syringes or drug-use equipment observed within any of the direct observations of injection events of the networks. Most of the IDUs studied have the resources to buy their own bags of dope, which decreases the chance of indirect sharing occurring. And because most come from a well-educated and well-off economic background, they have had access to a wealth of information about HIV, safe sex, safe drug use, and safe cleaning practices. Basic concepts of viral transmission were well known by all of the IDUs studied, which made them very conscious of their behaviors.

The young White subpopulation worked with might be considered sexually liberal due to the high rate of sexual partners they had. Several of the participants had an average of one new partner a month, in many cases they had co-occurring sexual relationships (affairs or multiple partners), and in some cases there was group sexual encounters (both two men and one woman, or two women and one man). These cases usually occurred when the participants were intoxicated (drunk), but were reportedly consensual events. New partners or new sexual adventures were always reported to the ethnographer as if they were telling stories of a great hunting expedition. One informant, Cindy, would even run up to the ethnographer with a smile and say, "I have a new one for my network plot!" And 9 times out of 10 she meant a new sexual partner. Although most are aware of and practice safe sex, there were many reports of unsafe sex, usually during sex when drunk.

Syringe procurement was usually done by buying the needles off the street or from a pharmacy. Although the latter is not legal in DC (you must have a prescription), it was easily done by a well-dressed young White person. The typical scenario was that the IDU cleaned themselves up, dressed up in their finest clothes, and came up with a line for why they needed the needles. One informant (Carol) said she needed them to inject vitamin B. In most cases the pharmacist took the line and made them sign a waiver, releasing the pharmacy of any legal responsibilities they might have for selling the works to someone without a prescription.

When purchasing on the street, young White IDUs have to trek into some pretty rough areas to find sellers. A large network of Black sellers (the network discussed above in the discussion on network formation) sold works as their hustle. Most of the works they sell are new and in sealed packages. But in some cases they will use the needles and then try to sell them as new, without cleaning them first. This is looked down upon by most sellers, and they will often yell at those who do. It is considered a very bad thing to do, even among other needle sellers. But it does happen, which puts the young White user at risk when purchasing a needle from the street.

Awareness of needle hygiene and hygienic drug use is well known among this population. It is enforced by many of them in conversation and in practice. One of the networks worked with had an HIV-positive member who had contracted HIV from sharing needles in the 1980s. He was an older IDU, but was very aware of his HIV status and so made sure he did not share liquids or syringes with anybody else. He did not disclose his status to anybody besides the ethnographer, but promoted safe use within his network "… because it's the right thing to do."

As discussed earlier, direct sharing was extremely rare within the White networks that were observed. In fact, the only direct sharing observed was between two core members of a network that had two outer periphery members within it as well. This core is made up of a 31-year-old man named Tim and his 22-year-old girlfriend Lucy. They keep their own sets of works, but they get them mixed up on occasion.

Because they divide their bags of dope in liquid (they are a live-in couple and pool all resources), they do partake in indirect sharing. They also have unprotected sex. This does not create any real risks for them or their network because it is a contained sharing of fluids. They do not indirectly or directly share with anybody else, nor do they routinely have sex with other people (Lucy does have sex with other women on occasion). This would place her at some small risk of HIV transmission, in which case, if infected, she could then infect Tim. This is a possible risk, but slim in comparison to other risky behaviors (such as unprotected vaginal or anal sex and sharing needles). In sum, young White IDUs were found to be at little risk for HIV in comparison to older Black IDU networks. This had a lot to do with socioeconomic and educational levels as well as the level of drug use. While indirect sharing (through the sharing of cookers, cottons, or rinse water) is almost nonexistent in this population, it is the norm within the older Black population. While direct sharing of syringes/needles is close to nil within the younger White population, it does happen on occasions within the older Black networks.

Level of drug use and economic resources are key to understanding the differences between different types of IDU risk networks. The young White users who began to build up substantial heroin habits began to use up more than their economic resources could support. This eventually made them have to rely on street hustles to get by. By that time, when they had used their other resources, they had potentially gained access to dealers for whom they could run drugs. This helped them carry their habits for a while longer. That, too, would only last so long before they exceeded that resource. Then they were left to the streets with virtually no knowledge of the cultures of the street economy, and so they became prey to those who are accustomed to it, i.e., those who are from a poorer socioeconomic condition and who are very familiar with the streets. When this happens to young White middle-class heroin users, it is usually time for them to kick.

Kicking the Dope: Economic Loss, Cultural Stresses, and Transitions

Heroin addiction has taken on many cultural symbols within the larger part of American society, both in the way it is imagined and in the ways we have treated it. These symbols are utilized by the user and the nonuser alike when discussing drug use and addiction. A young White heroin user's addiction is commonly couched within a context of personal trauma or depression. It is the saddened "rock star" or the depressed inner turmoil of the teenager. Their pain is imagined as being *inner* pain, with psychological issues that must be addressed. A poor Black user's addiction is often discussed in relation to larger *exterior* circumstances. He or she is often discussed in terms of systemic poverty and institutionalized racism. The "system" has gone wrong, not the addict. This is a terribly interesting and important fact, and must be kept in mind when studying these sorts of microcultures. The users at both ends of the economic spectrum will often use this discourse. The White users often referred to personal problems in their lives that led them to drug use. The Black users often referred to a lack of jobs and opportunities and to poverty as being causes of their drug addictions.

Also, the way in which heroin addiction is discussed and illustrated by the popular media and academia reflects the same discourse used by the addicts themselves. It is common to see writings on heroin addiction (or drug addiction in general) among minorities being represented with statistics and graphical charts. This is a depersonalized way of representing real people. On the other hand, young White addicts are often represented, especially in the media, through documentaries in a journalistic style – very personal, very tragic. [...].

Understanding how an addict perceives his or her addiction, how and why they became an addict, is important for trying to understand why they want to clean up, and how they do it.

Cleaning up off a heroin habit is an interesting topic because it relates to all the topics discussed above: the reasons why networks form, their changes, their dissolution, their risk behaviors, etc. What was discovered through watching several of the younger White IDUs enlarge their habit size was that they went through the phases of use and economic support discussed above, but they had also undergone stresses as they underwent transitions from the White suburban life they grew up with and knew so well to the urban ghetto and the street-based economies of the drug world. The users were quickly losing parts of their "selves" as the different cultural roles that created them, i.e., the student, the daughter or son, the champion horse rider, the hard worker, the brother or sister, etc., began to slip away as the drugs took over their lives (chemically, socially). They slowly but surely moved closer to the street environment, to the home of "the real junkies," the hardened street addict that researchers of today are so familiar with. They didn't realize that these street junkies were no different than themselves, just better at surviving within their own environment.

Beyond being traumatic to the young White user emotionally, heading to the street life can often be deadly as they do the wrong things in the street because they don't know the proper roles in that environment. Also, they must learn the street way of using, where you do NOT divide bags of dope in powder form because you might end up ripping someone else off of their 0.02 cc of dope or end up with less cut than them. Thus the users now find themselves in a world of higher risk for HIV and no way to get out, except to kick.

In most cases kicking came well before that point, but not because they couldn't afford the drugs. Rather, it was also personal stresses that caused the kick. The fear of losing friends, family, and social status was enough stress to force the IDUs to clean up. These cultural and social forces can be a powerful influence in a person's life, more powerful than dope. When these things are slowly being torn away, and the user sees him or herself changing both physically and culturally, it scares the living daylights out of them.

And when the next stop is some street corner or a shooting gallery, it's often enough to help them try to kick. Although many of the White IDUs had visited such locations, it was only because they were trying to cop. But they were not part of that scene, and they didn't know how to act or play the role when there.

Kicking dope happened a lot with the young White IDUs in the study. Many of them had attempted it numerous times with some success. They might stay clean for a few months, a half a year, maybe a few years. But then they'd end up using again, building a habit, losing cultural identities, money ran short, and then kicking completely or ending up on the streets. In most cases kicking was done informally, without knowledge of their habit or clean up being divulged to anyone outside their drug use and close social networks. This was either done through "chipping" one's way down to detox (meaning they used less and less each day), the straight kick (no drugs to help the pain of withdrawal), or they used drugs purchased on the street to ease the pain of the kick (drugs that help you sleep it off were preferable). The ethnographer aided several IDUs who asked him to help them kick. One stayed at his apartment during the initial kick.

Compared to the older Black IDUs, the younger White IDUs attempted kicking much more. The process of using, stresses, and kicking discussed above occurred rapidly and multiple times for most, while the older Black IDUs were able to maintain a consistent habit for up to 20 years. This is because they have a limited economic resource that is determined, by and large, by their particular hustle. For instance, a needle seller knows he can sell only so many needles in a day, and so he pretty much knows how much dope he will be able to shoot in a day. This amount may vary on "good" days, but it is pretty constant. The White user, on the other hand, will build a large habit quickly, and thus he or she will "crash and burn" quickly, which leads to the repeated kicks. Many of the older Black IDUs talk about wanting to kick, but because they are from the streets they do not feel the cultural stresses that might influence a kick attempt at the same level by the younger Whites. Many of the older Black IDUs kicked only when forced to do so by the law (either when locked up or forced into a rehab clinic for a 21-day detoxification).

[...]

Note

1 "Get off E" is to satisfy the "craving" for heroin. The term is allegorical to a car that has an empty gasoline tank.

Reference

Murphy, S. (1987, Fall). Intravenous drug use and AIDS: Notes on the social economy of needle sharing. *Contemp. Drug Probl.* pp. 373–95.

Questions

1 How were IDU networks formed? What are some other reasons drug-using networks may form? For problem solving reasons? Do you think the information from informal drug networks is always the most accurate and/or trustworthy? Why or why not? What is the alternative information source? What might cause these drug networks to splinter or dissolve?

2 What were the differences between White IDU networks and Black IDU networks? How did these differences account for health risks? How might these differences impact arrest, adjudication, and possible jail time?

3 What were some of the reasons IDU users decided to "kick" their dope habit? How do these reasons illustrate the power between the drug itself and sociocultural factors? How might socioeconomic status impact a user's ability to quit?

10

The Intersection of Drug Use and Crime over the Life Course of Mexican-American Former Gang Members

Avelardo Valdez, Kathryn Nowotny, and Alice Cepeda

Hispanics are another prominent drug-using population, and they comprise several sub-groups including those people born in Mexico (often called Mexican-Americans), those born in America (Chicano/as), and those from other Latin American or Spanish ancestry (broadly Latino or Hispanic), although these terms do not seem to be used consistently by authors. In this article Avelardo Valdez, Kathryn Nowotny, and Alice Cepeda address a common public perception: Mexican-American gangs and drug dealing. Following several people over the course of years, these authors were able to differentiate between four types of patterns of involvement with drugs and crime and to chart the career progressions they showed. Gangs are particularly interesting to study from a career perspective because individuals age through them so quickly.

As you read through this selection be sure to ask yourself about the relationship between working at crime versus working at legitimate jobs, about the effect of significant others and family members on drug use and crime, about the relation between gang membership, incarceration, and drug dealing, and about the types of drugs that these people often use. In what ways does this research affirm or challenge your prior conceptions about Mexican-American drug users and their lives? You may also want to ask yourself about how much their lives are influenced by the social structural (opportunity structure) factors framing them versus the norms and values inherent in their culture and the relationships they forge.

Drugs and the American Dream: An Anthology, First Edition. Edited by Patricia A. Adler, Peter Adler, and Patrick K. O'Brien.
© 2012 John Wiley & Sons, Inc. Published 2012 by John Wiley & Sons, Inc.

Introduction

Youth involved in street gangs are more associated with increased incidents of violence, drug use, and criminality including drug dealing than others. However, less is known about the long-term effects of gang membership as the individuals become young adults. Using a life-course perspective, this chapter qualitatively examines the influence of informal social control on the life-course trajectories of drug use, crime, gang membership, and other socially deviant behaviors among former Mexican-American gang members over a thirteen year period. The informal social control factors of peer influence, partner attachment, and labor force attachment along with incarceration history will be considered within the cultural context of an economically disadvantaged Mexican-American community. The association of juvenile delinquent behaviors and adult criminality and other negative behaviors such as drug abuse and violence through the life course has been well established in previous studies, but not among Hispanics, even though they are overrepresented among youth involved in street gang activities.

Mexican Americans and Street Gangs

Evidence indicates that youth street gangs have proliferated in the United States and have spread across the country in large and small cities, suburban and rural areas. Hispanics make up a disproportionately large proportion of existing street gangs due to the increasing numbers of Mexican, Central American, and other Latino young males living in geographically dispersed communities recently occupied by this population. These Hispanics often reside in neighborhoods in these communities characterized by unemployment, poverty, welfare dependency, single-headed households, and other socioeconomic characteristics that are traditionally associated with street gang formation.

Mexican Americans have a long gang tradition that is focused in Southern California (Moore, 1978; Vigil, 1988). Many of the "street gangs in Southern California have existed within particular localities as extended families or clans for three or more generations" (Spergel, 1995: 63). Some of these gangs

have evolved into highly organized criminal networks engaged in heroin distribution. Other gangs have evolved into adult prison gangs whose illegal activities now extend beyond correctional institutions. The majority, however, were territorially based gangs concerned with protecting their turfs from rival Mexican-American gangs. A distinguishing characteristic of early Mexican-American gangs was their connection to family networks and community based institutions.

During the 1990s, Mexican-American gangs began to exhibit characteristics that were different from those gangs of earlier periods. Although the gangs continued to be territorial and provide an identity, contemporary gangs have been associated with increased incidents of episodic and lethal violence such as drive-by shootings. Similar to earlier periods, these gangs are turf-oriented, and are known for using more lethal violence to protect their territory. Other Chicano gangs are involved in organized criminal activities such as drug dealing often in association with adult gangs. This growth in Mexican-American gangs coincided with increased US incarceration rates especially for minorities. During this period, Latinos and African Americans and other minorities accounted for approximately 70% of the new inmates admitted into the prison population. Most of these were for nonviolent drug related offenses for small amounts of illegal drugs. This has serious implications for youth that are involved in gangs as they transition to early adulthood since many are drug consumers and/or involved in the drug trade – more often as dealers than large traffickers.

Age-graded theory of informal social control

The life course has been defined as "pathways through the age-differentiated life span" and "the sequence of culturally defined age-graded roles and social transitions that are enacted over time" (Caspi, Elder, and Herbener, 1990: 15). Life-course theory is sensitive to the personal histories of individuals and the timing of their lives in history, as well as the social and cultural systems in which they are embedded. Two concepts central to the life course are *trajectories* and *transitions*. Trajectories are a pathway over the life span and refer to long-term patterns of behavior. These trajectories are marked by transitions. Transitions are life events that evolve over shorter time spans, some of which may be age-graded. Turning points are an alteration in a trajectory that can be abrupt or part of a process. These changes can be either positive or negative.

This chapter examines the intersections of crime and drug use among Mexican-American youth gang members as they transition into young adulthood. The focus will be on the turning points and transitions that lead to the desistence from crime and cessation from drug use or conversely persistent criminality and dependent drug use. We are interested in exploring the long-term consequences of youth gang membership. Does involvement in street gangs exact a toll on the later life course of the individual? Or is gang membership simply a transitory adolescent stage with few if any long-term consequences?

Methods

The data collected for this analysis is part of a larger NIH, NIDA funded study utilizing a multi-method longitudinal cohort design using a nested qualitative component to investigate long term health consequences of risk for infection with HIV, hepatitis B and C, STIs, and infection risks among Mexican-American young adults with a history of adolescent gang membership. We followed up a sample of 160 adolescents and recruited an additional 150 from the original sampling frame. This preliminary analysis includes a total of 90 respondents who successfully completed the follow-up interview.

Context: the Westside

The Westside neighborhood in San Antonio is comprised predominantly of Mexican-origin persons and is one of the poorest urban areas in the United States. The population in 2008 was estimated at 1.3 million with over 50% of Mexican descent. The city's economic base is centered on service and tourism and is sustained by one of the lowest wage structures in the United States. Compared to other cities, San Antonio has one of the largest populations of "working poor." Fifty-five percent of the Westside families have children living in poverty and only 23% of the families receive public assistance. It is also an area that has a high concentration of crime, violence, substance use, and some of the highest rates of teenage pregnancy in Texas (second highest in the nation).

The mean age of the follow-up sample was 31.14 years and ranged from 26 to 42 years. All were of Mexican descent with 98.9% being US-born and the majority (87.8%) being native to San Antonio. The mean number of years of school completed is 9.4 with 13.3% graduating from high school and 38.8% earning a GED. At the time of the interview, 44.4% were employed with 38.9% of respondents reported to be living with a parent or relative. The average number of incarceration episodes is 10.77 with 65% reporting having been convicted of a felony. When asked about gang membership, 18.9% reported that they were still affiliated with their street gang and 7.8% reported that they were now affiliated with a prison gang.

Current drug use

Current drug use was defined as self-reported use in the 30 days prior to the interview. Current prevalence rates for tobacco (78.9%) and alcohol (76.7%) were high. Marijuana (54.4%), cocaine (33.3%), and injecting heroin use (26.7%) were the most commonly endorsed substances followed by tranquilizers (13.3%), non-injecting heroin use (12.2%), methadone (11.1%), and other opiates (8.9%). Less than 5% reported current use of crack (4.4%), amphetamines (2.2%), hallucinogens (1.1%), or inhalants (0.0%).

Findings

All of the respondents were gang members in adolescence and were involved in an array of criminal activities and substance use patterns. Their level of substance use, particularly heroin, during this period and the type and length of early incarcerations seem to impact their life-course trajectories. A typology of trajectories is emerging based on patterns across respondents. These distinct types include the heroin dependent, the career gangbanger, the acceptable offender, and the non-offender, and are illustrated here in the form of case studies.

The heroin dependent

Joe joined his gang at age 14 and by age 16 he was smoking marijuana and sniffing heroin daily, using cocaine recreationally. He stored guns at his house for his gang and was involved in shootouts often with a rival gang, "To be honest, I used to like it when we used to always have shoot outs. Cause every time, or a lot of times we'd walk the tracks I mean it never failed we'd started having shoot outs, in broad day light and I mean it used to just be a rush, I mean it was like a rush, cause you could just shoot in day light and nobody would tell you nothing, cops don't even come, nothing I mean you could just shoot all you want." He sold heroin and cocaine for another dealer and this was his primary source of income.

In 1997 at age 17, Joe served a 12-month sentence in TYC for the unauthorized use of a vehicle. He stopped claiming his gang when he was incarcerated because, "It just got old, everybody just started going their separate ways and when we went to prison everybody got into different things in prison so, it just got old, like when you go to prison you can't do that gang stuff in there, it's a whole different world in there." Joe didn't use while he was incarcerated, but upon his release in 1998 he began injecting heroin. He maintained relationships with his gang friends, two of whom (Brandon and Marcos) used alcohol, marijuana, cocaine, and heroin regularly and were involved in drug dealing and other criminal activities. Joe was only out a month and a half before he was incarcerated again for parole violation. This began a series of incarcerations and releases where he was clean while in prison but relapsed upon release, injecting heroin daily.

In 2006, while Joe was incarcerated, his girlfriend Flora gave birth to their daughter, but CPS immediately took the child because of Flora's heroin use, leading to their breakup.

In 2007, Joe and Brandon went into business together dealing heroin and cocaine. Brandon also introduced him to speedballing (injecting heroin mixed with cocaine). He described this period as, "Just partying, living it up like nothing. Just didn't care for nothing." In addition to dealing, Joe got a job working in construction for 8 months. He worked 45 hours and earned $319.50 a week, but this was nothing compared to the $5,000 a week he reported making from dealing with Brandon. He continued to inject heroin and speedballs daily. By the time of the follow-up interview in 2009, Joe was 29 years old and was trying to slow down his drug use. Joe stopped using speedballs and only injected heroin 2 to 3 times a week. He was living at his father's house and selling drugs, stealing, and participating in other illegal activity for income. In reflecting on his gang participation Joe said:

> To be honest, it just made my life a living hell. It wasn't worth it at all. I don't think that if I would have never gotten involved I would have probably never been in prison and nothing, before the gang I always went to church, going to school, never cussing, nothing. I think I would have been something better than I am now. I wouldn't be doing drugs. Just the way my sister is, straight A student, I would have probably been on that road right now.

This life history is common among those that started using heroin regularly during adolescence. The heroin dependent maintains their heroin use and struggles with addiction throughout young adulthood. Their crime and drug use trajectories are intertwined and characterized by multiple incarceration episodes. These respondents experience low levels of informal social control since they continue to maintain relationships with negative peers and partners. Experience with the labor force is minimal and usually in the informal sector such as this example in which the respondent did construction jobs with friends.

The career gangbanger

Richard joined his gang in 1991 when he was 12 years old. He was introduced to the gang by a friend of his and was "rolled" (beaten) in by 3 older guys. That same year he began using tobacco, alcohol, and marijuana. He only lasted in school through the 8th grade. Beginning in middle school he became involved in gang-related fights, violence, and performing sex acts for gang initiations. When gangs would "claim" females these girls would often have to have sex with gang members as a form of initiation. Richard was also involved with other crimes such as burglaries, robberies, carrying a weapon, and selling drugs and was convicted of his first felony at age 13. He sold cocaine and heroin for his gang, but in 1993 at the age of 14 he worked part-time in construction for 18 months earning $105 a week. He also began using a variety of drugs including LSD, inhalants, PCP, cocaine, and prescription medication barbiturates.

In 1996, Richard had his first incarceration for assault with bodily injury. Upon his release he moved back with his mom, resumed association with his gang, and was using marijuana, cocaine, and heroin daily. Later that year he went back to state prison for 6.5 years for the intent to deliver heroin and burglary, during which he forged a strong association with a prison gang.

Released in June of 2003, Richard immediately picked up where he left off, selling heroin and cocaine for a friend and using cocaine heavily. In late 2004 the leader of his street gang was killed. As a consequence, his cocaine use increased and the street gang as he knew it broke up, although it re-formed with a new generation of members and leadership. So Richard decided to dedicate himself to the prison gang.

Between 2005 and 2009 Richard was in and out of prison for aggravated assault, armed robbery, and drug possession. While on release he used cocaine and sniffed heroin daily. Getting into fights frequently, he carried a gun and participated in home invasions, violent acts, extortion, and carjacking. But his sole source of income was from dealing heroin, which earned him about $2,000 a week. By age 31, Richard had 6 felony convictions, had been incarcerated 14 different times, and was about to begin serving a 10-year sentence. He stated that being in a gang, "really fucked myself up. I would have done better if I had taken more opportunities, honestly."

The career gangbanger is someone who either stays affiliated with their street gang or "graduates" to a prison gang. They are involved heavily in crime as a major source of income and drug use throughout young adulthood. However, their drug use does not prohibit them from making an income. Like Richard they have early felony convictions that prohibit them from obtaining any meaningful employment. The career gangbanger is heavily influence by the negative peers they continue to associate with; often times these individuals are also gang affiliated.

The acceptable offender

Sam started smoking marijuana when he was 9 years old, drinking alcohol at age 12, and using cocaine at age 15. He tried crack and heroin when he was 17 but never became a user. Even though he started using drugs at a young age, he didn't join his gang until the age of 17. During this time he was using alcohol, marijuana, and cocaine regularly. Sam reports growing up in a household where he was discouraged from joining a gang. It was a heavy "church going" family, even though Sam didn't attend very often, if ever. In his household, nobody else was gang affiliated or involved in drug use. Sam reported that his family never had a rough time with things like food, clothing, or housing.

In 1997, at the age of 19, he had already started disassociating with his gang because he was almost shot and had been jumped a few times by rival gang members and, "I was just tired of that shit." Sam was working full-time as a restaurant supervisor, a job that lasted almost 2 years. That same year, Sam got arrested and spent 2 months in county jail for marijuana possession. After getting out, Sam continued to smoke marijuana and drink alcohol daily, using cocaine only a couple of times a month. But he got busted for cocaine possession and went back to jail for six months in 1998. Upon release, he resumed his daily alcohol and marijuana use although his cocaine use dropped from 2 to 3 times a month to about once a month. He used only with friends: "'Yeah, [I use cocaine] like once a month. It's like whenever I go visit a friend and they have it."

From late 1998 to 1999, Sam began an intimate relationship with Rosa while still in a relationship with Alice, fathering his first child in August of 1999. But by the end of 1999 both Rosa and Alice had left him. He got a job as a full-time supervisor at a restaurant and was able to maintain steady employment at different restaurants while still drinking and smoking pot on a daily basis, but added sales of marijuana, cocaine, and LSD in small quantities to his income repertoire in 2000. For example, he would purchase an ounce and a half of cocaine and "flip it" by cutting it and selling small $10 bags. Sometimes he would "double it up" by making crack cocaine and selling rocks: "That's how I started with the 8-ball that's exactly what I did with it and I fucking bagged it up, sold some rock and then after that I started selling pot." Sam also stole cars and sold them to "chop shops" or took orders for car parts:

> Yeah, I had people that came up to me and they'd say "you have Mustangs or Escorts?" Back in the day they were kinda popular, and people would pick up the Escorts for the look put an exhaust on it and older people you know would come up to us and said like "I need this part or that these rims or I saw this car with these rims in this apartment complex go get it for me I'll give you some money."

At the time of the follow-up interview in 2008 Sam was living with his wife Crystal and their 3 children, and they both had stable legitimate jobs (Sam as an airport mechanic).

The acceptable offender is characterized by their consistent drug use and intermittent participation in criminal activities as a source of income. Like Sam, they may have early incarcerations but they are typically short sentences and most importantly they do not have a felony conviction. These former gang members are able to join the armed forces or obtain stable employment in the formal marketplace. They are able to maintain control of their drug use so that they can participate in both worlds: the conventional world including a steady partner, employment, and family, and the deviant world where they can consume alcohol and marijuana on a regular basis and even use "hard" drugs recreationally.

The non-offender

Albert began using drugs at a young age: alcohol and marijuana at age 9, cocaine at age 12, and heroin at age 14. Born in 1973, Albert only completed the 8th grade of school. He was the leader and founder of a gang:

> Well back in the day, there wasn't any gangs. The gangs were all in the north west side. There wasn't really any gangs on the west side back in '88–'89. So, I hung out with one of the gangs in the [north west side], I hung out with them. They were younger than the older guys, so I hung out with them and we were the younger guys in the summer. At that time, that summer we hung out with them and I brought that mentality back to the west

side and that's why I became the [the gang]. We categorized ourselves as a gang. We used the colors and we started the gang mentality. We were already a gang without even knowing it, because we were just homeboys,

He used to sell drugs and guns to other gangs and steal cars, motorcycles, rims, and stereos:

> [We'd sell] *soda*, yeah … coke or even pot yeah. But the majority was stolen stuff, radios, at the time it was alpine radios, base and rims and stuff, that's where the majority of our income came from. And it was more an individual deal, but we sold it and we got paid, or certain people got paid, it wasn't like where we all put it in a pot, and like "ok this is going to be for guns, this is gonna be for …" it wasn't like that. It was more like let's go do this or that.

At the time of the interview, Albert was already disassociating himself from the street gang. He left the gang because of his girlfriend and the birth of his first child. He explains how he wanted to start a family:

> Family man, moving out on my own really. You know having a kid, this is the first time I ever had a kid with my wife, having a kid live with me you know what I'm saying, you know with my first girl I never lived with her having a kid, so it's more the concern about my kids well being, you know just small stuff, going to the movies and not having to think about someone going to jack you from behind. At the time that was the thing to do, catch someone at the movies, you know the respect wasn't there, if someone had a family.

Albert has been in a relationship with his wife since 1990. She didn't do drugs, has never been arrested, and has had steady employment throughout this period.

Albert began working full-time at age 13 and maintained steady employment for 10 years working mostly in restaurants, with one construction and one office job. In 1996, when he was 23 years old, Albert was in a serious motorcycle accident and began receiving annuities from a settlement. This money enabled him to buy his family a house and pay his bills and expenses without the need of a job. He also made investments for long-term financial security. He has never been incarcerated and he was never really heavy into drug use. He stopped using marijuana and cocaine and just drank alcohol steadily several times a week. Albert stayed in contact with a couple of guys from his gang after it broke up in 1997. His friends all maintained steady employment and only drank alcohol. In 2001 Albert learned how to illegally program cable boxes and satellite cards for televisions. He begins selling these for extra money:

> I rather make my money doing a cable box and make more money, you know $200, $300. And then when I got into the satellite business, I would read the cards and I would make programs and write my programs on cards and for [a satellite provider], and I would like make $600 a pop. You know just having a couple of cards a month, maybe 10 cards every three months, $600 a pop, depending on who it was. So that's $100 maybe once every two weeks.

A couple of years later, he began to experience bouts of depression and anxiety that caused him to drink less: "The drinking came a little bit less. The drinking came less. I guess it was to about once a month, because I was always just depressed. I was just in my room."

In 2006 Albert's house was raided by the police. His cousin who sold *ice* was staying at his house and the cops raided the house to arrest his cousin. This incident led Albert to cut people out of his life and he began to disassociate with even his close gang friends: He explained, "Nah, James is not much around … well yeah … after … well after the raid happened, everybody just … actually I kinda' cut everybody off. I didn't want to talk to anybody anymore." Albert also stopped selling programmed satellite cards.

In 2008 he moved out of the Westside to another city in Texas. He got a job and began to hang out with office buddies. This interaction brought him out of his depression. At the time of the follow-up interview Albert was still married with 6 children, 3 of whom live with him. When asked about his involvement with gang life, he almost viewed his gang as a positive experience, stating that he learned:

> leadership skills. Being able to walk away. Being able to make a decision and being able to walk away, uh … always living by example, doing something, but not let anybody do it if I haven't done it myself … Just leading by example, just doing, leading by example, just doing stuff before passing the task to somebody else. Just like I

can say "Hey man I did it why can't you do it?" Always having that second nature, well it's really first nature you know, when you, your survival skills, in any way, physically or even financially. Always being able to go back to what you learned in the streets.

The non-offender is able to make the transition to a conventional lifestyle despite being involved with a gang as well as drug use and criminal activities during adolescence. His peer network of other gang members matured out with him and he is able to maintain stable employment because he does not have an incarceration record or a felony conviction.

Discussion

By following the subjects over time – during and after the period they were gang members – we are able to understand the ways in which gangs influence the lives of their members. What we see emerging here is a process whereby those who have early incarcerations and more importantly felony convictions are resocialized into accepting the criminal identity. Howard Becker (1963) famously stated, "the deviant is one to whom that label has successfully been applied; deviant behavior is behavior that people so label" (p. 9). Individuals who are labeled or dramatically stigmatized as deviant are likely to take on a deviant self-identity and become more, rather than less, deviant than if they had not been so labeled. Stigmatization renders participation in criminal groups and taking advantage of illegitimate opportunities more attractive which increases the likelihood of repeating criminal behavior. The informal social control in the form of partner attachment and labor force attachment seems to have moderate influence in this population. However, intimate peer groups seem to have some influence on the continuation of deviant behaviors.

This is confounded by systemic social factors and cultural processes such as poverty, discrimination, and a lack of steady partners. Within this community there may be a normalization of deviant lifestyles such as the *tecato* and the *cholo* family. This *tecato* subculture is characterized by heroin use, aggression, and a willing-ness to confront and dominate others, criminality, and incarceration. Quintero and Estrada (1998: 153) state that "for the *tecato*, machismo is simply 'being a man' – invulnerable and a social locus of power and influence … Those who control the supply of drugs, who use drugs to excess, and who engage in violence and intimidate others, are more macho than those who do not." It is further argued that, "the tecato subculture is reinforced by the social isolation of multigenerational cholo family networks" (Valdez, Neaigus, and Kaplan, 2008: 86). Among Mexican Americans, family-based networks are particularly important because of the strong cultural value that Mexican Americans place on family, identified as *familismo*. In her studies on Mexican-American addicts, Moore (1994) identified study participants as having come from "cholo" families. According to Valdez, Neigus, and Kaplan (2008) *cholo* families are characterized by generations of drug use, criminality, incarceration, and street connections among its members.

The present analysis begins to understand the processes that lead to persistent criminality as well as desistance among a sample of male Mexican-American young adults with a history of gang membership. This has implications for intervention efforts related to offender reentry and employment. This analysis also underlies the importance of the gang's role in perpetuating injecting heroin use from adolescence to young adulthood and the dominance of heroin and the *tecato* subculture in San Antonio. Future analysis should focus on further understanding the specific factors and social processes that may lead to the continuation of these deviant behaviors by Mexican-American young adults with a history of gang membership within this culture and context.

References

Becker, H. (1963). *Outsiders* (1st edn). New York: Free Press.

Caspi, A., Elder, J. G. H., and Herbener, E. S. (1990). Childhood personality and the prediction of life-course patterns. In L. Robins and M. Rutter (eds), *Straight and Devious Pathways from Childhood to Adulthood* (pp. 13–35). New York: Cambridge University Press.

Moore, J. W. (1978). *Homeboys: Gangs, Drugs, and Prison in the Barrios of Los Angeles*. Philadelphia: Temple University Press.

Moore, J. W. (1994). The chola life course: Chicana heroin users and the barrio gang. *International Journal of the Addictions*, 29(9), 1115–26.

Quintero, G. A. and Estrada, A. L. (1998). Cultural models of masculinity and drug use: "machismo," heroin, and street survival on the US-Mexico border. *Contemporary Drug Problems*, 25, 147–68.

Spergel, I. A. (1995). *The Youth Gang Problem: A Community Approach*. New York: Oxford University Press.

Valdez, A., Neaigus, A., and Kaplan, C. D. (2008). The influence of family and peer risk networks on drug use practices and other risks among Mexican American noninjecting heroin users. *Journal of Contemporary Ethnography*, 37(1), 79–107.

Vigil, J. D. (1988). *Barrio Gangs: Street Life and Identity in Southern California* (1st edn). Austin: University of Texas Press.

Questions

1   What sorts of life-course transitions unfolded for the respondents in the article? What sorts of life-course transitions and/or trajectories do we see unfold over the college career? How might socioeconomic status and/or social power impact life-course trajectories and transitions?

2   How does early incarceration affect life-course trajectories? How does early substance use affect life-course trajectories? What role did gang affiliation play in peer influence and informal social control?

3   How is the *Acceptable Offender* able to participate in "both worlds?" What seemed to be the most important factors that impacted the respondents' life-course trajectories? What sociocultural factors influenced behavior and life-course trajectories?

11

Righteous Dopefiend

Philippe Bourgois and Jeff Schonberg

Blacks are the group under examination in Philippe Bourgois and Jeff Schonberg's in-depth participant-observation study of urban homeless drug injectors in San Francisco. They show, up close and personal, what everyday life is like for people in this down-and-out situation. Bourgois and Schonberg reveal a portrait of their subjects through the thick descriptions of their behaviors and interactions, and they bring people to life in their own words. Again, the comparison is raised between the Black people and the Whites who make their "homes" in and around them, and who also fend on the street for survival. This research shows some of the choices individuals make in the situations they face, as well as how their lives are constrained by the lack of choices they can make. How would you assess the influence of both of these factors on the way they end up living?

Bourgois and Schonberg call them "righteous dopefiends." Why do you think they call them that? Do you think the picture they paint is sympathetic? How so, and how not? Do you agree with the members' presentations of themselves as righteous? Why and why not? As you read this article, you may want to reflect on ways that it fits versus challenges your prior conceptions of populations like these. In what ways do the policies of our government and the members of our political parties affect the lives of groups of people like these?

The Edgewater Homeless

From November 1994 through December 2006, we became part of the daily lives of several dozen homeless heroin injectors who sought shelter in the dead-end alleyways, storage lots, vacant factories, broken-down cars, and overgrown highway embankments surrounding Edgewater Boulevard (not its real name),

the main thoroughfare serving San Francisco's sprawling, semi-derelict warehouse and shipyard district.

The maze of on-ramps and off-ramps surrounding the shooting gallery nicknamed the hole is part of the commuter backbone servicing the dot-com and biotech economies of Silicon Valley and downtown San Francisco. These freeways connect some of the highest-paying jobs in the United States to some of the nation's

Drugs and the American Dream: An Anthology, First Edition. Edited by Patricia A. Adler, Peter Adler, and Patrick K. O'Brien.
© 2012 John Wiley & Sons, Inc. Published 2012 by John Wiley & Sons, Inc.

most expensive residential real estate. By building freeways all across the nation since the 1950s, granting generous mortgage tax breaks, and pursuing monetarist policies to stem inflation and lower interest rates, the US government has effectively subsidized wealthy, segregated suburban communities, draining wealthy and middle-class residents from inner cities. The hole was merely one of the many accidentally remaining nooks and crannies at the margins of this publicly funded freeway infrastructure where the homeless regularly sought refuge in the 1990s and 2000s. It was a classic inner-city no-man's-land of invisible public space, out of the eye of law enforcement.

Frank and Felix chose to inject in a filthy, difficult-to-access spot like the hole rather than in Max's nearby camp, where they were sleeping, not only out of fear of the police but also to avoid having to share a portion of their bag of heroin with Hogan, another one of their campmates, who had been complaining all day of being "dopesick." They did not mind treating Max to a "wet cotton shot" because they knew he would be receiving money from his moving job the next day and he was likely to reciprocate their gift should they need it some time in the future. Hogan, in contrast, had a reputation for being lazy and perennially broke.

At any given moment, the core social network we befriended usually consisted of some twenty individuals, of whom fewer than a half dozen were women. They usually divided themselves up into four or five encampments, which frequently shifted locations to escape the police. All but two of these injectors were over forty years old when we began our fieldwork, and several were pushing fifty. All but the youngest had begun injecting heroin on a daily basis during the late 1960s or early 1970s. In addition to the heroin they injected every day, several times a day, they also smoked crack and drank large quantities of alcohol – primarily inexpensive, twelve-ounce bottles of Cisco Berry fortified wine (each one equivalent, according to a denunciation by the surgeon general of the United States, to five shots of vodka). According to national epidemiological statistics, the age and gender profile of our social network of homeless men and women was roughly representative of the majority of street-based heroin injectors in the United States during the late 1990s and early 2000s.

A separate generational cohort of younger heroin or speed injectors also existed in most major U.S. cities, but they maintained themselves in entirely separate spaces from older heroin addicts. Most of these youthful injectors were whites fleeing distressed and impoverished families, and they represented a smaller proportion of their generation than those who had been attracted to heroin in the 1960s and 1970s. Hip-hop youth culture in the 2000s actively discouraged injection drug use or crack smoking despite its celebration of drug selling. Consequently, those African-American and Latino youth who used drugs primarily smoked marijuana and drank alcohol, even when they sold heroin or crack on the street.

Addiction is a slippery and problematic concept. The American Psychiatric Association's diagnostic manual does not have an entry under the word *addiction*, and its criteria for identifying substance abuse refer primarily to maladaptive social behaviors caused by "recurrent substance use," including, among others, the political-institutional category of "recurrent legal problems" (American Psychiatric Association 1994: 182–3). Nevertheless, there is no doubt that within a couple of weeks of daily use, heroin creates a strong physiological dependence operating at the level of basic cellular processes.

The Edgewater homeless embrace the popular terminology of addiction and, with ambivalent pride, refer to themselves as "righteous dopefiends." They have subordinated everything in their lives – shelter, sustenance, and family – to injecting heroin. They endure the chronic pain and anxiety of hunger, exposure, infectious disease, and social ostracism because of their commitment to heroin. Abscesses, skin rashes, cuts, bruises, broken bones, flus, colds, opiate withdrawal symptoms, and the potential for violent assault are constant features of their lives. But exhilaration is also just around the corner. Virtually every day on at least two or three occasions, and sometimes up to six or seven times, depending on the success of their income-generating strategies, they are able to flood their bloodstreams and jolt their synapses with instant relief, relaxation, and pleasure.

The central goal of this ethnography of indigent poverty, social exclusion, and drug use is to clarify the relationships between large-scale power forces and intimate ways of being in order to explain why the

United States, the wealthiest nation in the world, has emerged as a pressure cooker for producing destitute addicts embroiled in everyday violence. Our challenge is to portray the full details of the agony and the ecstasy of surviving on the street as a heroin injector without beatifying or making a spectacle of the individuals involved, and without reifying the larger forces enveloping them.

Hustled in the Moral Economy

Begging, working, scavenging, and stealing, the Edgewater homeless balance on a tightrope of mutual solidarity and betrayal as they scramble for their next shot of heroin, their next meal, their next place to sleep, and their sense of dignity – all the while keeping a wary eye out for the police. Following the insights of the early twentieth-century anthropologist Marcel Mauss on the way reciprocal gift-giving distributes prestige and scarce goods and services among people living in nonmarket economies (Mauss [1924] 1990), we can understand the Edgewater homeless as forming a community of addicted bodies that is held together by a moral economy of sharing. Most homeless heroin injectors cannot survive as solo operators on the street. They are constantly seeking one another out to exchange tastes of heroin, sips of fortified wine, and loans of spare change. This gift-giving envelops them in a web of mutual obligations and also establishes the boundaries of their community. Sharing enables their survival and allows for expressions of individual generosity, but gifts often go hand in hand with rip-offs.

[…]

Ethnic Hierarchies on the Street

[…]

On a typical warm summer evening, the main corner where the homeless spend a great deal of their time, in front of the A&C convenience store, attracted a half dozen very distinct groups of people. Most visible were the middle-aged African-American men who, on their way home from work, congregated and drank beer by a barbecue at the entrance to the alley behind the store. By nightfall, younger

African-American crack dealers arrived. They camouflaged their sales by mingling with the barbecue crowd and by circulating among the Latino and Asian commuters around the corner who were waiting at the bus stops. Cars pulled up to the sidewalk, pausing just long enough for a subtle exchange of dollar bills through the passenger-side window. In the doorway of the A&C, two or three Yemeni men chatted in Arabic with the cashiers. Sometimes they chewed qat, a psychoactive stimulant imported from Eritrea. On rare occasions, the wife of the store's owner, fully veiled in a black chador that revealed only her eyes, walked out from the back of the premises carrying a shopping bag and a baby. Young, new-immigrant Latino men crisscrossed the sidewalk running late errands for the primarily white- and Arab-owned construction-related businesses along the boulevard.

In this mix, two or three of the white homeless leaned against a wall at the edge of the African-American barbecue scene or inside one of the bus shelters nodding in deep heroin sedation. Latino and Filipino youths, mostly high school age, in the latest hip-hop outfits, passed by to ask the Edgewater homeless to buy beer, cigarettes, and cigars for them. They would hollow out the cigars to prepare "blunts" of marijuana, but they rarely stopped to smoke on the corner.

The homeless, middle-aged, white heroin injectors we befriended were at the bottom of the corner's social hierarchy and often displayed their low status by begging in tattered clothing. An early set of fieldnotes reveals how rapidly we had to learn the meaning of our skin color in this scene. Even though we looked healthy and dressed in clean clothes, we were lumped by default with the low-status "stanky white dopefiends."

[…]

The ethnic hierarchies of street culture in San Francisco are not exclusive to drug culture and homelessness. The hegemony of African-American style extends throughout the United States and through much of global popular culture. It is historically inscribed in slang (from jive to hip-hop), in music (from blues and jazz to rap), in clothing (from zoot suits to sagging jeans), and in body posture (from handshakes to gait and facial expressions).

But the "coolness" of African-American street culture does not translate into economic and political power in the United States. On the contrary, blackness and expressions of hip-hop or working-class street culture exclude individuals from access to upward mobility in the corporate economy. Despite their clear subordination within the local street-hustler hierarchy and their exclusion from mainstream white society, the durability of racism in the United States allowed the homeless whites on Edgewater Boulevard to hold on to an ideology of white supremacy. Among themselves, for example, they used the word *nigger* routinely. When African-Americans were in earshot, however, they practiced deference, fearing violence or humiliation. [...] They treated racialized distinctions as self-evident common sense and often used the clichés of middle-class society when we asked them about race relations.

[...]

Drug Consumption as Racialized Habitus

Heroin injectors often brag about the size of their habit, exaggerating how many "grams of dope" they inject per day. Like many of the identity and micropower relations along Edgewater Boulevard, competition over who had the biggest heroin habit often became racialized:

> FELIX: Man, none of these niggers is real dopefiends. They're crackheads. These guys can't shoot dope like I do. I don't have their kind of habit. They ain't even in my league. Give 'em a half a gram ... and they'll die. Carter would die for sure.

Polydrug preferences also followed ethnic patterns. The whites, for example, referred to crack as "a nigger drug," even though most of them also smoked crack themselves. With the notable exception of Al, however, they were ashamed to admit it. Even those whites who smoked large quantities of crack would pretend shamefacedly, as they lit their pipes, that they only smoked opportunistically: "I never buy it. But if someone has it – sure, I'll take a hit." A few of the whites, such as Nickie and Max, never smoked crack, even when it was offered to them, claiming that it ruined their heroin highs. Everyone on Edgewater Boulevard, black and white, agreed that "crack makes you sicker quicker."

Virtually all the African-Americans devoted significant effort to raising money to buy crack once they had satisfied their daily physical need for heroin. When successful, they often stayed up all night on binges. The whites generally hustled less money than the African-Americans, and when they did obtain a sudden windfall, they usually purchased fortified wine or extra heroin rather than more crack. As a result, many of the whites had larger heroin habits and tended to fall asleep at sunset, unless they were dopesick or belligerently drunk.

On special occasions, the African-Americans injected speedballs to propel themselves onto a roller-coaster high and mesh the sedative effects of heroin with the wide-awake exhilaration of cocaine. They would sometimes celebrate their speedball sessions by "booting-and-jacking" their injections – that is, repeatedly flushing blood in and out of their syringes to provide multiple rushes of pleasure. When we were filming a speedball session on one occasion, Sonny chuckled, "Lady in red give daddy some head," as a plume of red blood flooded into the barrel of his syringe, indicating that his needle tip was safely inside a vein. He then pushed the plunger halfway into the barrel, only to follow it with, "Come back, Little Sheba," as he pulled the plunger back to reflood the barrel with blood. On the final flush, he sang, "Hit the road, Jack, and don't come back." All of the whites dismissed booting-and-jacking as "a nigger thing." In all our years on Edgewater Boulevard, Al was the only white we saw inject a speedball on purpose.

The whole crack package – the rapid spending, the celebratory binges, and the stimulating physiological effect – meshed with the racialized late-twentieth-century persona of the enterprising black "outlaw," which, on Edgewater Boulevard, was mobilized in opposition to the persona of the broken-down white "bum." Most of the homeless in the scene, of course, fell somewhere in between these two stereotyped ways of being in the world, but the African-Americans in our social network strove more consistently to maintain the public appearance of being in control of their lives and having fun. In sustaining a sense of self-worth, they embraced an ecstatic commitment to getting high. Most of the whites, in contrast, considered themselves to be depressed and, indeed, most of the time looked and acted dejected.

Furthermore, even though we often observed Frank, Hank, Hogan, Max, Petey, and Scotty nodding after they injected, they usually claimed with stoic boredom that they no longer enjoyed shooting and that they were merely staving off withdrawal symptoms: "I get well. I don't nod no more."

Everyone in our scene had severely scarred the veins in their arms as a consequence of long careers of injection. It was difficult for them to "direct deposit" heroin into a vein. By the midpoint of our fieldwork, most of the whites had given up searching for operable veins and skin-popped. They sank their needles perfunctorily, often through their clothing, into their fatty tissue.

In contrast, the African-Americans, even in the final years of our fieldwork, rarely skin-popped their injections. Instead, they often spent up to forty-five minutes searching for a functional vein. This could become a bloody process as they made a half dozen or more punctures, pulling back on the plunger each time in order to register a vein. An intravenous injection, though difficult, provides an instantaneous rush of pleasure. Rejecting the aura of failure and depression associated with the whites, even the oldest African-Americans continued to pursue this kind of exhilarating high. They also expressed their pleasure openly in public sessions of deep nodding immediately after injecting. Some individuals, such as Carter, Sonny, and Vernon, performed their highs dramatically, collapsing into full-bodied relaxation and moaning with pleasure or jumping hyperenergetically to their feet. The white addicts, however, usually tried to nod discreetly, their chins slowly dipping onto their chests as if they were merely cat-napping. When energized, they might, at most, talk enthusiastically, scratch their noses compulsively, or clean up their camp.

These distinct injection methods and manners of experiencing and expressing the heroin high become physically inscribed on the body. The whites, for example, suffered from more abscesses, because skin-popping traps impurities in the soft tissue under the skin (picked up from dirty fingers, cookers, water, lint, or whatever adheres to a needle point when it is pushed through filthy clothing and unwashed skin). In an intravenous injection, these same impurities are usually safely filtered out by the body's vascular system. The disadvantage of an intravenous injection, however,

is that it increases the risks of fatal overdose and also of hepatitis C and HIV infection because of the greater potential for blood-to-blood contact when syringes are shared. Significantly, the Centers for Disease Control and Prevention documented that the rate of AIDS in the United States in 2005 was ten times higher among African-Americans than among whites. [...]

De Facto Apartheid in the Day Labor Market

The African-Americans tended to be more openly oppositional than the whites to the business owners along Edgewater Boulevard, who in turn often referred to them as "goddamn niggers." Relations with the Yemeni and Palestinian storekeepers were especially antagonistic. The African-Americans routinely called them "motherfuckin' A-rabs" and were frequently 86'ed for shoplifting, badgering customers for change, demanding free matches, or cursing over high prices. The whites adopted more subservient, dependent attitudes toward the storekeepers and were sometimes rewarded with odd jobs such as sweeping the sidewalk or stocking new deliveries. Some of the whites were also periodically 86'ed, but usually it was for being malodorous rather than for being oppositional. Nevertheless, out of earshot, they too engaged in xenophobic rants:

> FRANK: These fuckin' A-rabs don't know how to spend American money. They'll give you twenty dollars for a whole day's work if you're lucky.
> SPIDER-BITE LOU: All A-rabs are the same. They're worse than the Chinese. They think you're just a junkie – just shit! "Just give the man a Cisco; he'll do anything for it."

During our twelve years on Edgewater Boulevard, only two local businesses hired African-Americans from our social network, and they did so only at the height of California's dot-com boom, when no whites were available. Sammy, at the Crow's Nest liquor store, gave Carter "a chance" when Felix, his former steady worker, left to drive a taxi for six months. It was during the period when Frank and Max were selling heroin and when Andy, the mover, had enough jobs each week to keep Hank, Petey, and even Al busy most days. Ben was working at his unionized asbestos removal job under the Bay Bridge, and Spider-Bite Lou was shoveling sand at Macon's.

[...]

The only other local business to hire the homeless African-Americans on Edgewater Boulevard was a Christmas tree seller who arrived each year to set up shop on the first Friday after Thanksgiving in the empty lot across from the A&C corner store. He paid just above minimum wage but offered steady work for ten hours a day, plus tips – all tax-free cash. More than half his workers were heroin injectors, and he accommodated their multiple lapses and petty rip-offs. This enabled him to tap into an inexpensive, just-in-time, seasonal labor force in order to sell several thousand trees during the four-week Christmas rush. The Edgewater homeless eagerly anticipated this opportunity for full-time work, even though few lasted for the entire month. Those who did gained weight and improved their relationships with the surrounding businesses on the boulevard.

[...]

Panhandling

Passive begging was an income-generating option that the African-Americans actively shunned. Most of the white drug users on Edgewater Boulevard generated a large proportion of their resources (money, food, clothing) by flying signs at passing cars: WILL WORK FOR FOOD. VIETNAM VET. GOD BLESS. They often spent hours at a stretch, their eyes on the ground, with an empty fast-food soda cup held aloft. They usually raised enough money to "stay well." Although passersby were sometimes willing to contribute spare change to visibly needy whites on the street, they rarely spontaneously gave alms to even the oldest, feeblest African-Americans on the boulevard, because blacks were deemed intimidating or unworthy. The police also enforced public nuisance and panhandling laws more rigorously against blacks.

The African-Americans in our scene did not discuss their rejection of passive begging in terms of limited options resulting from racism. Instead, they referred to it as a function of their way of being in the world and of their natural sense of dignity. Furthermore, they reduced their opportunities for receiving charitable gifts and for avoiding police detection by engaging in flamboyant or oppositional behaviors such as conspicuously drinking alcohol in public and talking loudly on streetcorners. Once again, the outlaw habitus that offered them a sense of self-respect through asserting control of public space convinced those who interacted with them that they deserved their fate.

[...]

When the African-Americans did panhandle, they distinguished it from passive begging by engaging passersby actively, offering a service, a friendly quip, or a threat. [...] Passersby from all ethnic groups, including other African-Americans, gave more easily and more generously to whites than to blacks. Flying a sign was especially lucrative on national holidays.

[...]

Most of the homeless whites subsisted primarily on the food given to them when they panhandled in fast-food parking lots. They rarely visited soup kitchens because they found these institutional environments unwelcoming and excessively time-consuming. Sometimes private individuals came down to Edgewater Boulevard spontaneously to give the homeless clothes, blankets, or sleeping bags or to pay for haircuts and rounds of laundry at the laundromat. One of Petey's "regulars" took him to a San Francisco 49ers' football game. It was Petey's first time at a professional sports event, and the seats were on the forty-yard line. The African-Americans, however, rarely received free food, clothes, or random acts of kindness from people whom Carter called "good Samaritans." They resolutely refused to present themselves as pitiable, down-on-their-luck panhandlers. As a result, they often remained hungry and dopesick.

[...]

In contrast to the generosity of private citizens, public welfare entitlements were difficult to access. Rarely were more than two or three individuals in our network receiving public assistance checks or food stamps at any given time. The whites negotiated the complicated, and sometimes humiliating, bureaucratic hoops more frequently than did African-Americans. Few, however, managed to remain on welfare for longer than a few months. [...]

Honor among Thieves

The Edgewater homeless did not recognize the complex array of structural forces around ethnicity, gender, economy, public policy, law enforcement, and social stigma that shaped their subjectivities and habituses and constrained their survival options. Instead, as we have shown, they acted out socially structured roles through their everyday practices, confirming to themselves and to those around them that they deserved their fate. They also talked about race and culture in moral, essentialized terms. The whites condemned African-Americans for being thieves, and the African-Americans criticized the whites for "lacking initiative" and for "being too stupid and lazy to hit licks." Both groups, however, engaged in petty, opportunistic theft.

The whites pretended that they did not do so, whereas the African-Americans exaggerated their professional skills as criminals. They often reminisced about the dramatic criminal escapades of their youth, whereas the whites generally spoke in hyperbolic terms of past successes in the legal labor market.

[...]

References

American Psychiatric Association. 1994. *Diagnostic and Statistical Manual of Mental Disorders*. 4th edn. Washington, DC: American Psychiatric Association.

Mauss, Marcel. [1924] 1990. *The Gift: The Form and Reason for Exchange in Archaic Societies*. Translated by W. Halls. London: Routledge.

Questions

1 In the article, what forms of stratification appear among drug users? What accounts for this stratification and/or hierarchy? Was race a factor?

2 What forms of racism existed within these drug using subcultures? How did African-American men deal with instances of racism?

3 How did the behavior and demeanor of White users and Black users differ? Was this a factor in the way they were treated by others?

4 How might harm reduction strategies or policy changes improve the lives of these "righteous dopefiends?"

12

The Lives and Times of Asian-Pacific American Women Methamphetamine Users

Karen A. Joe Laidler

Culture is very much the focus in Karen Joe Laidler's study of Asian-Pacific Islanders on Hawaii's main island of Oahu. Ice, or methamphetamine, is omnipresent in the drug scene there, and this opportunity structure leads people toward its use where they might, in mainland locales, turn to crack cocaine or heroin. Joe Laidler offers us a look into the situations faced by the young women in her study and the way they are affected by the surroundings in which they are raised, the drugs being used around them, their economic strains, and the continuing role of their immediate and extended kinship networks ("ohana"). How do you think the importance of family, to these women, is affected by their gender? By their culture? By their opportunity structure? To what extent do their families provide them with a source of support versus a drain and obligation that makes their lives more difficult? Finally, as you read this, you may want to think about the interconnection between gender, culture, and family in affecting drug-using behavior.

Introduction

During the latter part of the 1800s, Asians represented a small proportion of the nation's immigrant population. Chinese, Japanese, Filipinos, and Asian-Indians were the primary Asian ethnic groups moving to the United States. [...] Since the passage of the 1965 United States immigration law reforms, Asian-Pacific Americans have become the most diverse minority population in the United States. At least 32 different Asian-Pacific American ethnic groups now reside in the United States. Asians are also the fastest growing group with an increase of 5 million during the last 20 years. In 1990, the Asian population climbed to 7.3 million, and by 2020 is expected to reach 20 million. [...]

This paper challenges the persistent stereotype of the passive yet exotic Asian-Pacific American woman, and is concerned with uncovering the complexities of the lives of a group of women drug users and their strategies for coping with and managing their problems. [...] I examine the ways in which the cultural claims in their lives interact with and shape their initiation into and continued use of

Drugs and the American Dream: An Anthology, First Edition. Edited by Patricia A. Adler, Peter Adler, and Patrick K. O'Brien.
© 2012 John Wiley & Sons, Inc. Published 2012 by John Wiley & Sons, Inc.

illicit substances based on an ethnography of female methamphetamine users in Hawaii.

[...]

The Ice and Other Methamphetamine Study

The setting

Health and law enforcement authorities grew increasingly concerned in the mid-to-late 1980s over the emergence of ice and other forms of methamphetamine. Many believed that ice, a smokable form of methamphetamine, had already reached "epidemic" proportions in Hawaii, and would become the drug of the 1990s. Hospital and emergency room reports indicated that this central nervous system stimulant had a highly addictive quality within a short period of use, and was also connected with several physical and psychological problems, including insomnia, hypertension, emaciation, irritability, and depression. Aside from the limited information available from clinical and treatment populations, little was known about the demographic, social, and cultural attributes of methamphetamine users. Clinical staff in Hawaii reported that the state's diverse ethnic population, including its Asian-Pacific American populations, were using ice. Moreover, they observed growing numbers of young women and housewives using ice as a diet suppressant.

The Research Design and Methods

The data are drawn from a cross-cultural community-based study of moderate-to-heavy methamphetamine users in Honolulu, San Francisco, and San Diego. These three sites were selected because each one was associated with the highest usage and problems in the United States. Also, the predominant mode of use differed in each of the sites. While San Francisco had a significant rate of intravenous use, San Diego had a high rate of nasal use. By contrast, Honolulu users primarily smoked ice. Interviews were conducted with 150 active users in each site. This analysis is based on Honolulu interviews with 37 women of Asian-Pacific American ethnicity.

[...]

Asian-Pacific American Women Ice Users and Their Family Ties

Who Are They?

Our female respondents represent the ethnic diversity of Hawaii. The majority of the sample, however, identified as Hawaiian (54%) and Filipina (30%). The Hawaiian, the Portuguese, and, to a slightly lesser extent, the Filipino women were of mixed ethnicity; this reflects the complexity of ethnicity in the state. Nearly all of the women were born in the United States, usually Hawaii, and only two of the Filipinas immigrated to the United States during early childhood. The Samoan and a few of the Filipinas report that their parents were immigrants.

Overall, the women's median age was 27 years. Over one-half of the women (57%) had never been married, but had at least one child (60%). Among those women with children, 68% of them were living with their offspring.

Overall, 40% had obtained a high-school diploma and another 30 had dropped out prior to completing the 12th grade. Because the state's major industry is tourism, the most readily accessible job opportunities are in the service sector, particularly in the hotel, restaurant, retail, and construction businesses. Overall, 38% of the women supported themselves during the last year through a job, and most of them worked in retail or clerical positions (19%). Others principally supported themselves through government assistance (30%), their family (22%), or illegal activities (11%). The majority of the women (54%) were living in poverty, with a yearly income of $10,000 or less.

Growing up in Chaos

Several themes emerged from the qualitative interviews which underscore the strained interplay between economic marginality and the cultural traditions and norms of Asian-Pacific American families. Many of our female respondents grew up, in various degrees, in an extended family network, known locally as the ohana system (Joe 1995). Ohana derives from Hawaiian culture, and historically referred to the family clan and its strong sense of solidarity, shared involvement, and interdependence. This kinship system has changed over the decades as Hawaii's culture has come to reflect the blending of its various Asian and Pacific Islander populations and their cultures. In contemporary Hawaii, ohana has retained the traits of cooperation and unity, but extends to persons who are not necessarily blood-related, but closely connected to the family and considered part of the social support system.

In Hawaii, today, where the cost of living is among the highest in the United States, this extended family arrangement acquires new meaning in the Western economic context. The extended family system offers financially strapped families a readily accessible and stable source of help and relief. Over 70% of all the women in this study came from working and lower working-class families where their fathers, when employed, worked principally in skilled and unskilled labor-intensive jobs. Seventy percent of their mothers worked in similar occupations. Overall, 18% of the women reported that they had lived principally with other relatives – grandparents, aunties, uncles, cousins – until adulthood. One-fourth of the Hawaiian women indicated that they had grown up primarily with relatives. Our respondents' life histories, however, suggest a more complex pattern whereby many lived between households, shifting constantly from various relatives to their parents.

The ohana system acts not only as a resource for economically strained families, but also as a source of relief for heated conflicts within the family. With only a few exceptions, women described growing up in tension-filled households. While the ohana system provides relief, it can also introduce intergenerational gaps.

[...]

Part of the tension in the family was due to financial worries, but also to the presence of alcohol and other drug use by one or both parents.

[...]

Joanne, a 44 year old homeless Hawaiian Filipina, states that her father consumed several cases of beer on the weekends, but was only a "recreational drinker" because he "never missed work due to his drinking" and, most importantly, provided for his family. She had her first drink at 22 years of age when her father

became seriously ill and died, and, "for the next ten years stayed in an unconscious drunken state by noontime everyday."

[...]

Parental alcohol or drug use was typically connected with violence. More than 40% of the females describe their home life as violent. In some cases, the intensity of the violence was extreme as Susan, a 19-year-old Hawaiian woman, recalls her "unhappy" childhood.

From about five years old, Susan remembers that her father would routinely beat up her mother to the point where she would be unable to walk. Subsequently her father would come looking for her or her mother would take out her own anger and hostility by beating on Susan and her siblings. Both parents were heavily involved in drugs, and her father was a dealer. She describes having a loose family structure as her father had several children by other women.

While growing up, she was exposed to many "adult" situations including drug deals and hanging out in bars. Her father was sent to prison for hanging a man on a fence and beating him to death while drunk. At 14, an unknown teenage male raped her at a family function. She tried to isolate herself, but when her mother learned of the incident she punished her for "promiscuity" by repeatedly hitting her on the head and sending her to a group home for troublesome teenagers.

In some cases, the violence was expressed through sexual assault.

Jacky is 20 years old, and of Hawaiian, Korean, and Filipino ancestry. She has one older brother who she has not seen since she was six when they were both placed in foster care. Her mother died when she was five. She and her brother lived with the stepfather who was an "abusive drinker" and sexually molested them repeatedly. This went on for one year at which point, six year old Jacky stabbed her stepfather for sexually abusing them. Although she does not have a clear recollection of the stabbing incident, she does remember having her arm broken by her stepfather while he was trying to sexually assault her.

Another important dimension of the family centers around the cultural expectations of Asian-Pacific American women. This was clearly felt by women who were living in chaotic family situations as well as those few who described their family life as "normal." In traditional Samoan families, gender relations are organized around Polynesian traditions of male dominance, separation, and obligation (Joe and Chesney Lind 1995). While Hawaiian customs were similar to the Polynesian model of separation, this was severely altered with the death of Kamehamehakunuiakea in 1819, and subsequent arrival of the missionaries (Nunes and Whitney 1994). Although the Hawaiian system retains some male domination features, it is the women who have "learned the ways of the malihini (strangers). Women adjusted to and became clever at cultural and economic transactions with the new world" (Nunes and Whitney 1994: 60). At the same time, however, Hawaiians, who are the most marginalized group in the state, have accommodated to poverty through normalizing early motherhood, high dropout rates, and welfare dependency for girls (Joe and Chesney Lind 1995). In modern Filipino families, girls and women have been socialized according to colonial cultural and religious, usually Catholic, norms that emphasize the secondary status of women, girl's responsibility to their families, and the control of female sexual experimentation.

Cultural expectations about "being a good girl" combined with economic marginality and heavy parental alcohol consumption erupts into violence. Helen, a 38-year-old Filipino, Hawaiian, Portuguese woman, recalls her childhood years:

> I come from a family of six children and I'm the fourth. We are all scattered. One brother is in prison and one passed away. When we was growing up we lived with both my parents. They stayed married until my dad passed away. Home was very strict. My dad was an alcoholic so he couldn't hold a job. He always had a strict hand on us. Discipline kind. He was either drunk or coming down from a hangover when he hit us. My mom was the one that went to work. Beatings were all the time from my dad. Severe kind with belt buckles.
>
> The last time my dad hit me was when I was 17 years old. He found out that I was smoking cigarettes. I was almost 18. My youngest brother was able to drink with him, smoke cigarettes, and pot with him! But not me. The boys could do what they wanted. My mom wasn't the one to discipline us. She really had no say in it.

Coping Strategies in Managing Family Chaos

The women's first response is to endure the turmoil in their families. Given the extended kinship network, some women stayed with relatives when the situation at home became unbearable. As Whitney (1986) points out, local cultural norms stress that "outsiders" not be brought into family problems, and children's respect for their elders should be shown through deference. In his clinical work with young adult Asian-Pacific American male alcoholics, those who were physically abused tended to retreat temporarily to a relative's house and were unable to negatively evaluate their parents' abusive behavior (Whitney 1986).

The majority of women, however, eventually, could no longer endure the chaos and family violence and sought refuge in one of two ways. Approximately one-half of them believed that the best strategy for dealing with the violence in their own home was by starting their own family and became pregnant in their teen years. Marty, a 34-year-old Hawaiian, Chinese woman, describes the process:

> My parents were working. Then in the fifth grade, we moved, and… my father got sick, mom had to go on welfare. Things started not working out for the family. My parents was fighting, my father used to give my mother lickings every time and put us down. They were strict. We pretty much rely on each other [the siblings].

[...]

Other women took a different path and escaped the violence by running away, living periodically with friends, relatives, or on the streets, and sometimes turning to prostitution for survival. Linda is 28 years old and of Hawaiian Caucasian ancestry. Her parents divorced after her birth, and she has never known her mother. She and her sister were raised principally by her grandmother. Her father raped her and her sister, in addition to constantly beating them. The sexual abuse started when she was nine and continued until she ran at 12 years of age by "hopping on a bus to Waikiki" and getting lost. She had been in and out of foster homes and on the streets, but this break was permanent. She hooked up with a girl in her 20s, "I watched her, she was a prostitute. I asked her how to do that cause she had a lot of money. She taught me the ropes and I went for it. I made my money and stayed away from home. I lived out of hotel rooms."

The problems these women confronted, usually from an early age – poverty, gendered expectations and obligations, parental alcohol and illicit drug use, violence, living on the streets—underscore the complexities of Asian-Pacific American families, and raise questions about their initiation into drug use, especially ice.

Initiation into Drug Use

[...] The majority of women have used alcohol, tobacco, marijuana, cocaine, and crack. [...] According to their life histories, the most common pattern in their initiation started with alcohol, tobacco, marijuana, cocaine, and then went into ice. Initial use of crack varied, with some women moving back and forth from ice to crack depending on availability. Their peer groups from school and the neighborhood, and/or family members usually introduced them to alcohol, tobacco, and marijuana during their early teen years. In some cases, the family member was a parent, usually the father, or an uncle. [...] One 32-year-old Hawaiian Chinese woman recalls her route into alcohol and illicit drugs, which paralleled the accounts described by other female respondents:

> Our next door neighbor was this mother who had seven kids. My two brothers were going with their two sisters. I was 13 at the time I started drinking. ... Pakololo [marijuana] I don't remember. ... My girlfriend asked me if I ever tried acid before. I said no. My sister was already taking it. ...
>
> I was 16 when I graduated. That's because I graduated a year early. When I was 17, I moved with my uncle because he was running this condominiums so I was like a maid. I was making $7 an hour! My cousin was a mason there. He was like maintenance on the grounds. That's when I first, I didn't know to, what to feel. We went into this place where my aunt and uncle would let us kick back in. He asked me if I wanted to try it [cocaine] ... I had a lot of friends that had coke or I'd be in the house and they'd be weighing their coke and I didn't want to do it ... He gave me a line and told me to stick the straw in the nose and he showed me. He did one first and told me to just do that. I did it and we went

back into my uncle's place ... I panicked and said I'll never do this shit again. And I didn't not until later. Later I was doing a lot, lines, mega lines.

[...] [T]he majority of women (62%) were first introduced to ice from 1988 to 1992. While nearly all of the Filipinas started during this period (82%), 45% of the Hawaiian women tried ice earlier, between 1984 and 1987. Given the broadening of their social networks from the use of other drugs, there were several sources by which women first encountered ice. Approximately 46% of the women first tried ice with a small group of their girlfriends. Another 16% were introduced to ice by a relative, typically a cousin or sister-in-law. The combination of curiosity, and camaraderie with and trust of a relative or their girlfriends, was often the reason for trying ice.

[...]

Thirty-eight percent of the Asian-Pacific American women first tried ice with their partner or spouse, and the experience often was associated with enhancing sex.

> That was my 23rd birthday. I wanted to go out and drink and come home and make love. I didn't want to stay home. He went to the store, bought drinks, came home and we had some drinks before we went out to a show. I got drunk, I was so ripped. ... We came home and he said, "Here's the pipe, just inhale!" I had five big hits. ... I was wide-eyed and ready. We smoked some more ... we watched t.v. and hung for a while. Then we fucked for hours! [laughs]

With continued use, however, our respondents' relationships to their partners, families, and friends begin to change.

Continuing Use and Family Ties

After the introduction to ice, most of the women began using regularly. Overall, the median number of grams used per month was 3.5. Filipinas tended to use slightly more ice than Hawaiian women, reporting a median of 4 grams per month. The median number of days of using ice in an average month was 15. Their longest period of use without sleeping was a median of 6 days. Filipinas reported a slightly longer binging episode compared to the other women, with a median of 6.9 days.

Women first rationalize their regular use of ice in very gendered ways (Joe 1995). The appetite suppressant quality of the drug allows them to keep thin, and in turn provides them with self-confidence. Also, the long-lasting speedy energy associated with ice allows them to clean up after their children and partners, and to transcend and enjoy the mundane tasks of domestic chores.

There were a number of ways in which they would obtain their supply, and this would vary depending on their existing financial situation. While approximately one-third principally bought their supplies, 46% received it free by "hanging around the dealers" or by running an array of errands for their supplier who was sometimes a relative:

> I started buying from one of my cousins. I used to always burn myself cause i was trying to learn how the hell to do this thing without wasting 'em. My cousin used to see me do that so she taught me. ... I caught on that night! That's when I really felt good! I was up all night long till the next day. ... I stayed with her for three months. They were big time dealers. They was selling big quantities. I help her clean up the house, a big big house. My auntie's house because I would help her clean and cook, she always used to give me free stash. ... Right now, the only one supply me is my husband [who does not use]. Then check in one hotel.

With prolonged use, however, they become increasingly isolated from others—their children, partners, friends, and families. When this occurs, ice becomes medicinal.

Their isolation, sometimes periodic, stems from several sources. First, they are growing increasingly irritable with long episodes of limited or no sleep and food. [...] [O]ver half of them have experienced anxiety, depression, hallucinations, and paranoia. Many respondents spoke of periods of paranoia. The paranoia usually involved their being watched and followed by the police and by other users wanting to steal their stash, and consequently, they tried to limit their interaction with others. Second, nearly all of them report weight loss (89%). Some have grown emaciated and exhibit facial sores from tweaking and dehydration. As such, they try to limit contact with their family and friends, hoping that they will not see their deterioration. Third,

if the partner is also using ice, they are both becoming more irritable as a result of lack of sleep and food, and money problems. The partner's irritability often is expressed through domestic violence (Joe 1995).

Although many of these women have become isolated and have a strained relationship with their family, because of the ohana family system and its traditions, they rely on various relatives—immediate family members as well as extended kin—to manage their everyday life. This includes financial support, temporary shelter for themselves, but especially the shelter and care of their own children. While this extended kinship system provides them with a stable resource, it has the paradoxical consequence of enabling their use, intensifying dependency, and further aggravating family tensions.

Stephanie is a 35-year-old Hawaiian Irish woman. While growing up, she recalls that her parents, both alcoholics, began physically beating her at five years of age with "extension cord wires, water hoses, punches, everything." She ran away, and after high school, married and became pregnant. Her husband died shortly after the son's birth in a work-related accident. She has been homeless for seven years, and sometimes stays with friends. Periodically she visits her mother and son, but adds that her ice use has "interfered" with her relationship with her mother. Her mother has been caring for her son since she has "no place for me and my boy." She regularly gives half of her welfare monies to her mother for her son's food and clothing.

Like other women in this study, Stephanie takes refuge in ice as she finds her options narrowing. As she states, "I can't get no help finding me and my boy a place. So because I'm homeless, that's why I do the drug, I get so depressed cause I don't have no roof over my head for me and my boy." Ironically, her family, which caused her to run away, is one of her few remaining resources.

Conclusion

[...]

Unlike mental health studies on Asian-Pacific Americans, this analysis suggests that stress from the family is not restricted to cultural and generational conflict. Social problems like drug use among

Asian-Pacific American women are quite complex. From their early childhood, these women lived in the midst of heated, sometimes violent, conflict, which was connected to economic marginality, parental problems with alcohol, and distinctive cultural norms of femininity. Neighborhood and school peers, and male relatives initially introduced them to alcohol and marijuana. Over time, their user networks widen and their introduction into cocaine and ice is through friends, extended kin (e.g., cousins), and partners. Despite the long standing tension in their family and their more recent isolation from others from using ice, the cultural traditions embedded in the extended kinship system allow many to "return home."

[...]

References

Joe, K. 1995. Ice is strong enough for a man but made for a woman. *Crime, Law and Social Change* 22: 269–89.

Joe, K., and M. Chesney Lind. 1995. Just every mother's angel: An analysis of gender and ethnic variations in youth gang membership. *Gender and Society* 9: 408–31.

Morgan, P., D. McDonnell, J. Beck, K. Joe, and R. Gutierrez. n.d. Uncharted communities: Preliminary findings from a study of methamphetamine users. In *Methamphetamines: An illicit drug with high abuse potential*, eds. B. Sowder and G. Beschner.

Nunes, K., and S. Whitney. 1994. The destruction of the Hawaiian male. *Honolulu Magazine* July: 58–61.

Whitney, S. 1986. Getting sober local style: Strategies for alcoholism counseling in Hawaii. *Alcoholism Treatment Quarterly* 3: 87–107.

Questions

1 How might a family network like the Ohana system contribute to drug problems? How might such a family network reduce drug problems? What are some examples from the chapter?

2 How did some Asian-Pacific women use gender expectations to rationalize their use of ice? How might gender mediate other forms of drug consumption in our society?

3 How did the increasing use of ice lead to increased social isolation for these Asian-Pacific women? What were the main elements that contributed to the cycle of drug use and domestic turbulence for these Asian-Pacific women?

Toward a (Dys)functional Anthropology of Drinking
Ambivalence and the American Indian Experience with Alcohol

Paul Spicer

Paul Spicer's study of American Indians also focuses on the role of culture in affecting an ethnic group. Although they do not live on the reservation, they are very much embedded in the norms and values of their community. To what extent do you suppose their drug use is affected by the factors of social class, opportunity structure, ethnic identity, or cultural ties? How would you assess the relative empowerment or disempowerment of the women versus the men compared to the women Joe Laidler portrays in the last selection? What is the influence of the family on the drinking patterns of this group?

How would you assess the influence of the patterns of social learning surrounding the use of alcohol for these American Indians? How are they steered towards a model of loss of control over their drinking as opposed to the model of moderation found in some other subcultural groups? Compared to Bourgois and Schonberg's righteous dopefiends, what kind of attitude do these drug abusers take toward themselves? What makes such a difference? How are their feelings of worth and self-control affected by their socioeconomic status, the culture in which they are embedded, their individual personalities, and/or the drug they are using? Why is alcohol the drug for them?

Finally, how does this portrayal reflect the image you have of American Indians in contemporary American society? What segment of the Indian population do you think is like this? How do their lives reflect the choices they have made from among the repertoire of choices they have? Concluding the section on race and ethnicity, how powerful an element do you think this factor is in the lives of drug users?

Drugs and the American Dream: An Anthology, First Edition. Edited by Patricia A. Adler, Peter Adler, and Patrick K. O'Brien.
© 2012 John Wiley & Sons, Inc. Published 2012 by John Wiley & Sons, Inc.

When anthropologists analyze American Indian drinking, they almost always argue for the important functions that it serves. Whether it be the articulation of social and cultural values, the assertion of an ethnic identity, or a means of escaping the feelings of inadequacy engendered by social and cultural changes, the impulse has nearly always been to delineate the reasons that Indian people drink as they do. This is clearly important information. Indeed, anthropologists have been at the forefront of our attempts to understand how alcohol fits in people's lives, and their analyses have been invaluable in helping us to see the social and cultural patterning of drinking and drunkenness throughout the world. But what is usually absent in such accounts is a serious engagement with the negative consequences of drinking. This has had the unfortunate effect of creating the impression that people are untroubled by their drinking, and in the cultural area of North America nothing could be further from the truth.

Rather than merely to instantiate the negative things that happen to Indian drinkers, however, I seek to present a more complex picture than has previously been offered. I argue that the American Indian experience with alcohol is profoundly ambiguous: drinking is at once recognized as a means of articulating core cultural values *and* vilified as an alien and degrading influence; it is simultaneously something to which people are drawn *and* by which they are repelled; and it is associated with some of the best *and* some of the worst in contemporary American Indian life. My goal is to develop a theory of American Indian drinking that is adequate to account for the complex and contradictory nature of the American Indian experience with alcohol – an approach that I call a "(dys)functional anthropology" to highlight the ways in which the functional and dysfunctional aspects of drinking work together to engender an often profound ambivalence on the part of the drinker.

Fieldwork in an Urban Indian Community

This article describes the way that drinking was talked about by a group of Indian people in Minneapolis in the early 1990s. [...]

When I began this research I was particularly interested in the diverse ways that people responded to alcohol. I knew from the literature that Indian people drank in different ways, and I wanted to explore how drinking style was related to a person's understanding of his or her ethnic identity. What I discovered when I sat down and listened to people's stories, however, was quite different from what I had in mind. People seldom talked about differences between their drinking and anyone else's. Instead, they emphasized the unity of all Indian drinkers. To my surprise, even people who seemed to be getting in little trouble because of their drinking emphasized that their use of alcohol was heavy, uncontrolled, and problematic. In fact, drinkers and nondrinkers alike went so far as to assert that there was no way that Indian people could use alcohol in a moderate or responsible way. The idea that someone could "maintain" or "drink like a Whiteman," as they put it in Los Angeles, struck the people I knew as a very bizarre notion. From their perspective, to drink was to get drunk, and those people who thought they were drinking moderately were only kidding themselves.

Discovering this, I had to modify my research strategy. I originally wanted to interview equal numbers of abstainers, moderate drinkers, and heavy drinkers – as indigenously recognized categories; but since moderate drinking was not salient in the context of the life of people at the Branch, I decided to focus on how *drinkers* understood and talked about their use. Nevertheless, I still tried to get a sample that represented a wide range of drinking styles. I deliberately selected people who were obviously drinking to excess as well as those who seemed to me to be getting along fairly well with their drinking, at least at the level of public behavior. It is important to remember, however, that these differences in consumption were minimized when people discussed their experiences with alcohol. All told, I did interviews with 48 self-defined problem drinkers, 13 of whom had been abstinent for at least a year before I interviewed them and 35 who were currently drinking. My strategy was to interview only those people I previously knew to ensure that I had some knowledge of them and their lives prior to the interview, but I also ended up accepting a few referrals from people to whom I was especially close. In terms of tribal affiliation, 28 of the people I interviewed were Ojibwe, 16 were Lakota, 3 were Winnebago, and I was Cree. The sample was evenly divided in terms of sex; I interviewed 24 men and 24 women.

The Complexities of American Indian Drinking

In my interviews I discovered that everyone had very negative things to say about their drinking, and this was as true for those people who were currently drinking as it was for those who had quit. While I obviously expected such comments from former drinkers, I was initially quite surprised when current drinkers said exactly the same things about their drinking. I will focus on those 35 men and women who have continued to drink despite having strong negative opinions about their alcohol use, as I try to understand how it is that individuals can engage in drinking at the same time that they condemn it.

My interviews with current drinkers revealed men and women who were deeply troubled by their drinking. Nevertheless, they continued to drink, and the obvious question is why. From a clinical perspective, at least, the quick answer is that these are people who have become dependent on alcohol, and there is ample evidence to support this. For example, complaints about the physical distress of withdrawal were quite common, and people in the midst of a binge would often greet others by announcing how sick they were. These comments were obvious, if implicit, appeals for money or something to drink, and they were sometimes accompanied by direct requests for such aid. Yet, we miss much that makes the American Indian case so culturally interesting if we focus simply on tolerance and withdrawal, for there is much more at work here. An overly narrow focus on the physiological dimensions of alcohol use obscures what makes the situation so troubling to the people involved, chiefly the way in which their drinking is implicated, for both good and bad, in their relationships with others. It is these connections that will be my focus in this analysis.

There are obviously two sides to this story. In order to understand people's ambivalence, we need to understand not only why they want to quit, but also why they want to continue drinking. I will begin with a consideration of the reasons that people have to drink – those positive and functional ways that

alcohol is implicated in their social lives. These are the dimensions that have received so much anthropological attention, and, as should be clear in my discussion, these have been crucial findings. In the next section, however, I will turn to a consideration of some of the equally powerful reasons that people have to quit. These are the negative and often devastating consequences that can result from people's use of alcohol. While clinicians have long focused on these, they have received considerably less attention in the anthropological literature, as Room (1984) has so forcefully documented. Rather than presenting these as diametrically opposed analyses, my goal is to try and reconcile these two very different perspectives on American Indian drinking, analyzing the ways in which these contradictory and conflicting opinions about alcohol can be, and often are, held by the same American Indian drinker.

The Pull: Drinking and Social Connectedness

When Indian people discussed their drinking with me, they always emphasized how it began in the context of peer relationships. Whether they were raised on the reservation or in foster homes and institutions, initial experiments with alcohol were thoroughly social affairs, imitative of the drinking of adults and a means of connecting with others of one's age. This dynamic was particularly pronounced for people who were trying to reestablish connections to Indian people after being raised apart from them. But even children raised by their parents on the reservation told me that drinking provided them with a means of acting like adults while socializing with their peers. As Brad, an Ojibwe man, put it, "We'd get all tore up, stumble around, y'know? (laughs) Thinking we were old because we were drinking, y'know?"

Furthermore, the excitement of drinking often provided relief from the boredom that was seen to characterize reservation life. Verna, an Ojibwe woman, told me, "I'd always be around drinking cause everybody drank up there, y'know? There's nothing else to do. I mean, that's just the way we were raised up there." In this regard, the social aspects of drinking are difficult to overestimate. Those with alcohol were never alone, procuring and consuming alcohol were quite common topics of conversation, and exchanges of drink were readily assimilated into more general patterns of reciprocity. Drinking resonated with several positive aspects of American Indian sociability, and it was remarkable to me to see the degree to which people would contribute their own precious resources to keep the party going. I found this out one day when I drove a Lakota man to a shop so that he could pawn his brand new TV. From there we went straight to the liquor store where he spent all the money he had received on alcohol, which we then brought back to the apartment to share with everyone there. Indeed, in all the time I spent with drinkers, I never saw anyone claim alcohol as his or her personal possession. As far as I could tell, it was always seen as communal property, available to anyone who wanted it, and drinks were usually offered as a way of welcoming people to the circle of those who had gathered on any particular day.

Thus sharing was clearly the norm, which also meant that people could not get by without contributing. There was an expectation of balanced reciprocity, and people were usually bothered if someone did not meet his or her obligations to the group [...]

These dimensions of the American Indian experience with alcohol go a long way toward helping us to understand the reasons people were drawn to drinking: it was congruent with crucial values such as hospitality, kinship, and reciprocity, and it provided a ready-made arena for articulating these values in the context of complementary social relationships. [...]

The Push: Drinking and the Destruction of Relationships

While the use of alcohol may well facilitate complementary relationships, it often has the opposite effect, making it more difficult, for example, to meet obligations to children and elders. Furthermore, there is always the possibility that conflicts may develop even within the complementarity and good feeling of the drinking circle. All of which suggests that the human experience with alcohol may be much more ambiguous than functional analyses would lead us to believe. Whatever the positive social functions served by their drinking, each of the 35 drinkers I interviewed

emphasized what was bad about their drinking, not what was good, and it is testimony like this that should give us pause when we discuss the culturally integrated nature of Indian drinking.

There is a profound contradiction between the social connectedness found in the drinking group and the social fragmentation that often accompanies drunkenness, and American Indian drinkers are often painfully aware of this dilemma. While anthropologists have generally avoided an explicit engagement with these aspects of drinking, there are nevertheless hints in the anthropological literature to suggest that such consequences weigh heavily on the minds of Indian people. [...] Furthermore, there is considerable historical evidence to indicate that Indian people have often seen alcohol as the source of their difficulties. One of the most consistent findings concerns the negative opinions that Indian leaders have had about alcohol, attitudes that are based on their direct experience with its effects. [...] Finally, there could be no clearer condemnation of the perceived effects of alcohol than in the efforts of local leaders to regulate the liquor trade in their communities. [...]

While we know that specific segments of the population – leaders, some wives, and abstainers – have had extremely negative things to say about drinking, it is by no means obvious how these attitudes impact those who use alcohol. Do drinkers reject the warnings of nondrinkers, reveling in the assertion that a drunken persona is a way of articulating their identity? Do they enjoy what Weibel-Orlando (1985) calls a "deviant solidarity" that is based on their deliberate flaunting of any attempt by others to regulate their drinking? Based on the analyses I presented earlier, the idea that drinkers may celebrate their drinking and drunkenness is certainly reasonable. After all, they say things that celebrate the solidarity that drinking promotes all the time. My data, however, provide compelling evidence that drinkers are much more conflicted than such pronouncements may suggest.

Indeed, it was the testimony of drinkers themselves, even more than that of the abstainers, that convinced me of the extent to which the consequences of greatest concern – family quarrels, mistreatment of children, lowered economic productivity, and mayhem and murder at drinking parties – remained vitally important issues in Minneapolis in the 1990s. Several drinkers, for example, described to me the way that alcohol had devastated their home communities, and they often provided extraordinary claims for the number of people who had been killed in drinking contexts. Reggie, a Dakota man, put it this way:

> REGGIE: Well, I wish I could take you back to the reservation, Paul. See how the people live over there. Oh, christ.
>
> PAUL: How is it living there?
>
> REGGIE: Well, I don't know, they're all drunkards, I know that, y'know? Yep.
>
> PAUL: You said there's just a really small town there?
>
> REGGIE: Yeah, it's only three thousand. But, town's here OK? Then they made these housing projects, OK? Like about ten miles out of town, and around there, and another one over here, around like that. Gee, they fight. Geez, every day somebody's getting killed.
>
> PAUL: What are the things people fight about?
>
> REGGIE: You know when you get drunk, when the argument starts, and then they don't know. What the hell you gonna do.
>
> PAUL: So that's how it happens?
>
> REGGIE: Yeah, that's how that happens, and shit, that's why I think I'm better off over here, y'know? Man, I would have been dead a long time ago.

Even in the urban environment, however, drunken violence remained a persistent fact in people's lives, and it affected not only their public relationships, but several of their most intimate ones as well. One day at the Branch, for example, I saw an obviously drunken man stand up and throw scalding hot coffee at the woman he was with as he began shouting obscenities at her. He was promptly escorted out of the agency, but the conflict did not end there. While he was being led to the door, he repeatedly demanded that his girlfriend come out on the street with him to settle the matter, and he remained on the sidewalk for several minutes, ragefully declaring his case to anyone who happened by. Several people, including some who were obviously inebriated, shook their heads after he left, indicating what I took to be their displeasure with the situation. And, while no one around knew why the fight had started, everyone was of the opinion that his drinking had contributed to the outburst.

[...]

While tensions between people certainly existed before the drinking began, and may well have been expressed whether or not people had been drinking, it was obvious to everybody I knew that conflicts surfaced more frequently after the use of alcohol. Whether or not these conclusions are statistically warranted is not the issue here. The point is that people clearly understood their own and others' drinking to be something that increased the chances for some kind of conflict within the community, and this was regarded negatively by each of the people with whom I talked.

Conflict was not the only concern that people had, however. Women were especially troubled by the effect their drinking had on their children, and they would often describe their remorse over how they had neglected their children when they were drinking. Bertha, an Ojibwe woman, had this to say about her regrets:

> BERTHA: My drinking, it caused a lot of pain, while I was drinking. Nobody's fault but my own. I mean I'm the one, y'know? I'm the one who caused myself to lose em. Cause of my drinking. And then I almost lost em again cause of my drinking, y'know? But they've grown up. And she's got her kids. And he's got his own life, his girlfriend. I worry about em. But nothing I can do, y'know? I told him I didn't drink as much as I used to. A lot of good that does.
>
> PAUL: Do you regret all of that stuff that's happened then? And the choices you've made when it comes to drinking?
>
> BERTHA: Yeah. If I could do it all over again I would stay home and take care of my kids like I was supposed to.

Despite (or, perhaps because of) these regrets, Bertha continued to drink, and while several women told me that they tried to change their drinking habits in order to protect their children, not all were able to do so. Therefore, statements such as "I didn't want my children to go through what I went through" indicated not only the powerful incentive that some women had to quit, but also how guilty many of them felt when they nevertheless continued to drink.

Men mentioned their children far less often, but at least one Ojibwe man, whom I'll call Ben, told me that his drinking had gotten really bad when his marriage broke up. He had been raised by drinking parents himself, and he had hoped to avoid the familial disorganization of his childhood. But when his wife left him, he resigned himself to the drinking life, discouraged by how he had repeated the very thing he had tried so hard to avoid. As he put it, "Growing up in all these foster homes, and my parents being what they were, y'know? I thought that well, hell, when I have kids, I'm gonna keep my kids, y'know? I'm gonna keep the family together. Well, so, in 1973, when we divorced, I lost my kids. I just gave in." Since that time, Ben has found himself on the streets, unable to escape the drinking life, but obviously feeling quite sad about what it has cost him.

Many other men devoted special attention to how their drinking prevented them from keeping jobs. The comments of Jeff, an Ojibwe man, were typical in this regard.

> JEFF: I lost quite a few jobs from the drinking too.
> PAUL: Um hm.
> JEFF: Jobs I could've had a good chance with. But drank little bit too much.
> PAUL: Called in sick too much?
> JEFF: Yeah really. I'd go to work Monday to Friday. But Mondays I wouldn't come in, cause I'd be drinking Friday, Saturday and Sunday, and I'd be hanging over on Monday. And well, they let it go by a few times, y'know? But, then that started getting kind of old to them, so they just told me that they no longer needed my services anymore. So I said OK.
> PAUL: That happened more than once then? Or –
> JEFF: Oh yeah. Many times. Right now. Even today.

While men like Jeff were obviously concerned about the financial consequences when they lost their jobs, there seemed to be more at issue than mere dollars. The ability to keep a job and to support or at least contribute to one's family were understood as marks of a mature man, and men who continued to drink saw themselves as failures in their communities and as weak or nonexistent members of their families. [...]

The Tensions of Quitting for an American Indian Drinker

The negative consequences associated with drinking often engender a strong desire to quit, and people were sometimes desperately frightened by what was

happening to them. This was dramatically reinforced to me one day, as I talked with Alphonso, a Lakota man, who had come up to me clasping both of my hands and speaking in a tremulous voice. He was at the point of tears when he told me how scared he was that his drinking might get him killed. He had almost lost his life once before in a violent altercation when he was drunk, and his brother's drunken girlfriend had just recently been killed. These events, combined with deteriorating health, made him desperate to quit, and he said that he had come to the conclusion that he would have to leave the neighborhood to do so. He told me that he wouldn't even be able to tell his brother where he was staying because, if he knew, he was sure to come by to encourage him to drink. At the time, I assumed that Alphonso was seriously committed to moving. But he was still drinking in town when I saw him a few days later, and he was in town throughout the rest of my fieldwork.

At this point in the analysis, it is probably clear why Alphonso did not leave. Although he desperately wanted a life without alcohol, he did not want to cut himself off from several of his most important relationships. He found himself deciding in favor of his family and friends, and this meant that he could not avoid the alcohol that so scared him. Similar dilemmas were confronted by most of the people I knew. While some sober people insisted that this was a false choice – they said that when they had quit drinking they had not lost anyone they would truly call a friend – drinkers nevertheless perceived it as a real predicament, one that was made all the more difficult because drinking associates were so often actual kin. Furthermore, there was at least some evidence that people who quit drinking actually did find themselves more isolated, protestations to the contrary notwithstanding. For example, Jim, a Winnebago man, told me the earliest days of his sobriety "were lonely. Real fucking lonely." He eventually did find sober people to replace the companionship of his drinking buddies, but his early sobriety was intensely difficult because it involved such a thorough change in his social life.

Given these dynamics, it is hardly surprising that so many people have found it difficult to maintain their abstinence. Each of the problem drinkers I interviewed had tried to quit at some point in their lives, but most of them (35 out of 48) were unable to stay sober.

Invariably, the social costs of abstinence were mentioned when these people talked about why they had gone back to drinking. Since the use of alcohol had become an integral aspect of proper social relationships, to quit drinking was often perceived as an attempt to elevate oneself above others. Several people mentioned that when they tried to quit drinking they had been chastised with comments such as, "Do you think you're better than us?" Furthermore, they found it difficult to quit because it seemed as though there were always people encouraging them to drink. As Reggie put it: "No matter what locality you go in, y'know? Your friends will be there, y'know? And I don't know. No matter where you go nowadays, somebody there you know, y'know? Just like that, you'd be [drinking] again. That's my excuse. I can't quit."

[...] Thus Indian drinkers in Minneapolis found themselves in the horns of a dilemma. Their drinking obviously caused them a host of difficulties in some of their relationships, but they were reluctant to quit because abstinence seemed to pose equally significant problems in other social contexts.

Ambivalence and the American Indian Experience with Alcohol

The tension created by people's conflicting impulses to continue and to quit drinking colors a good deal of the American Indian experience with alcohol in Minneapolis. There is simply no basis for arguing that the drinkers I knew were in denial about the effects of their drinking; they were fully cognizant of the negative consequences and often tremendously concerned about them. Nevertheless, there were powerful social incentives to continue drinking, and it is these contradictory tendencies that make alcohol such a complicated issue both for American Indian communities and individuals alike. Indian drinkers simply do not exemplify one opinion about drinking. Instead, their attitude is a product of the tension between two mutually incompatible positions: those that favor alcohol use and those that condemn it.

The testimony of Indian drinkers presented here demonstrates the often profound conflicts that people feel about their use of alcohol. They may continue to drink, but they do so with a good deal of regret, and this dynamic, this push and pull, is quite evident when they talk about their experiences. [...]

References

Room, Robin. 1984. Alcohol and Ethnography: A Case of Problem Deflation? *Current Anthropology* 25: 169–78.

Weibel-Orlando, Joan. 1985. Indians, Ethnicity, and Alcohol: Contrasting Perceptions of the Ethnic Self and Alcohol Use. In *The American Experience with Alcohol: Contrasting Cultural Perspectives*. L. Bennett and G. Ames, eds. pp. 201–26. New York: Plenum.

Questions

1   How were the American Indians in this article conflicted by their alcohol use?

2   How does this article illustrate the importance of peer relationships and social bonding with regard to drug use? How do friendship circles contribute to the persistence and/or desistance of substance use?

3   Were the American Indian drinkers in the article more influenced by physiological and/or social factors when trying to reduce their alcohol use? Why or why not?

The Severely Distressed African American Family in the Crack Era
Empowerment Is Not Enough

Eloise Dunlap, Andrew Golub, and Bruce D. Johnson

Eloise Dunlap, Andrew Golub, and Bruce Johnson take social class, or opportunity structure, as their primary focus in this study of urban African-American families in the crack cocaine era. They offer a powerful picture of how historical changes to the economic conditions of urban ghettos have affected their residents. How do their economic circumstances compare to some of the groups previously presented? They then interweave this with a thoughtful discussion of the way extended kinship networks have arisen in these Black communities. How might you compare these to the extended kinship network of the "ohana" system described by Joe Laidler? Why do you think that these kinds of arrangements are fostered? Do they apply to the American Indians Spicer described?

The rise of the crack era is described in this article. How would you compare the wax and wane of various street drugs compared to the vicissitudes of the pharmaceutical market? Why do you think crack cocaine became so popular with this group? To what extent is this grounded in the pharmacology of the drug compared to other factors?

How would you compare the role and influence of family in the lives of Ricochet and Island to the women in Joe Laidler's Asian-Pacific Islanders and the American Indians or Valdez, Nowotny, and Cepeda's Mexican Americans? What kind of gendered expectations do these African-American men and women face, both the older ones and the younger ones, compared to other populations?

Finally, where do these people stand in the hierarchy of American opportunity structure? Is there anything that can be done to help their situation? To what extent do they create their situations as opposed to having little choice? How do their "homed" lives compare to the homeless junkies described by Bourgois and Schonberg? Do they employ a similar set of standards, goals, and rationalizations? Why and why not?

Introduction

Poverty can be much more than a lack of money or work or even motivation. For many, it is the circumstances resulting from a trans-generational social history filled with struggle against harsh conditions, structural impediments, and limited opportunities as well as the continuation and evolution of cultural traditions, and the emergence of new subcultural norms in the face of these conditions. [...]

This paper looks at a recent chapter in the story of the African-American family, the devastation of crack cocaine on already distressed inner city families. As an analytic vehicle, this paper presents the experiences of two households that were identified and followed in the course of an extended ethnographic study of drug use and violence in the innercity. Their experiences are presented as sharing many characteristics common within the population of interest. Their stories provide detailed insights into the lived experience in context.

[...]

To illuminate the complex dynamics of the crack era on distressed African American families, this paper takes a life-course approach: This perspective explores how each family's experiences depend on prevailing conditions, social structures, and norms that are historically rooted; historical events; the family's position relative to these macro-phenomena; and the personal capacities and agency of family members. Thus, each family's narrative illustrates the nature of the times as well as the dynamics at work in their lives. The remainder of this introduction reviews the severely-distressed conditions faced by many African American families during the 1980s and 1990s, the historical tradition of extended family among African Americans, and the Crack Era as a defining historical event for many. The discussion examines the implications of the findings for both problems- and strengths-based social work practice and social policy development.

Severely-Distressed Conditions

Entering the 1980s, many African American families were facing tremendous structural challenges in poor inner-city areas. Massey and Denton (1993) provided a comprehensive analysis of the increasing hypersegregation of African Americans and the historical forces behind this phenomenon. After World War I and continuing into the 1960s, a massive wave of African Americans migrated to cities in pursuit of industrial jobs. They were forced into a few increasingly crowded, dilapidated neighborhoods through violence, restrictive covenants (from 1900 until a 1948 Supreme Court decision), and discriminatory practices by real estate agents. Meanwhile, white families were moving to segregated suburban areas, especially following World War II. Wilson (1987, 1996) contended the civil rights movement in the 1960s had a perverse unintended impact on the inner city. Successful African Americans moved their families to newly-integrated communities leaving an even higher concentration of poverty in the predominately African American inner city.

Based on an extensive literature review, Small and Newman (2001) identified the increasing concentration of poverty during the 1970s and into the 1980s, particularly among African Americans, as primarily the result of three phenomena: black middle-class flight, continued residential discrimination (especially against less wealthy African Americans), and the departure of low-skilled jobs from Northeast and Midwest cities. Economically, the 1970s was a particularly difficult period for inner-city families: there was a recession, manufacturing plants moved to the sunbelt and abroad, many of the employers that remained in the North moved to suburban areas placing them out of the range of public-transportation for inner-city residents, and the new economy emphasized advanced education and computer literacy. Many African Americans were left unemployed and unqualified for emerging opportunities.

Poverty and long-term joblessness have been associated with a constellation of other negative consequences: overcrowded housing, poor physical and mental health, despair, post-traumatic stress disorder, family dissolution, teen pregnancy, school dropout, interpersonal violence, crime, and drug and alcohol abuse, among others. These factors help perpetuate disadvantage across generations. Some of these factors are the direct consequences of structural disadvantage. Others involve personal volition, particularly those regarding sexuality, relationships, violence, and illicit drug use. Hence, there appears to be a clear cultural (or subcultural) basis to these behaviors.

The meaning and role of culture has been at the center of much controversy in research and public policy dialogues about the African American family. Dodson (1997) divided this contentious literature into two primary camps: ethnocentrism and cultural relativism. A number of prominent ethnocentric studies presumed the two-parent nuclear-family structure of white middle-class America represents a cultural ideal. Accordingly, this perspective maintains that female-headed households are central to a *tangle of pathology* that constrained African American families within a *culture of poverty*. Stevenson (1995) described how the civil rights movement and the larger sociopolitical sensitivities led to a revisionist perspective that celebrates the female-headed household, extended family, and fictive kin traditions as cultural adaptations indicating the strength of the African American family: Moreover, much of this cultural relativism holds that these family forms are rooted in African tribal beliefs and practices regarding the central importance of extended family.

This paper takes a less all-encompassing view of the nature of culture than either the ethnocentric or cultural relativism perspective. Rather, culture is viewed as a *toolkit* specifying a range of behaviors as well as values, symbols, and norms from which persons construct narratives that give meaning to their lives: This perspective dovetails with the life course approach by allowing that individuals select from a range of historically-situated cultural elements adopting or adapting them to their own purposes. For African American families these influences may include among other African traditions, conventional American (Eurocentric) expectations, popular culture movements, and subcultures of illicit drug use.

Several studies of impoverished communities have documented interconnected behaviors, norms, symbols, and values that differ from conventional expectations. We refer to these frameworks as non-conventional subcultures as opposed to various near synonyms that imply a value judgment including oppositional culture, cultural deviance, and code of the street. Non-conventional subcultures prescribe and attach significance to dress, musical preference, attitude, interpersonal interactions, carrying weapons, violence, childcare, sexuality, crime, and drug use. Adherence to non-conventional subcultures can hinder a person's ability to develop a healthy and prosperous lifestyle through the conventional paths of education and employment. Moreover, subcultural participants frequently indoctrinate their children and serve as possible role models to youths in the community. In this manner, non-conventional subcultures further isolate the inner city from conventional society beyond the effects of discrimination and other structural disadvantages, which in turn contributes to the spread and persistence of severely-distressed conditions.

Extended Family Tradition

Historically, African American children have been less likely to live in a two-parent household. Since emancipation and up until 1960, the percentage had been roughly stable at about 70%, continually below the steady 90% level recorded for white children. The cultural relativism camp maintains that these household structures are not by themselves necessarily problematic. Stack (1974, p. 122) contended that, "[C]ensus statistics on female-headed households ... do not accurately reveal patterns of residence or domestic organization." During the late 1960s, Stack (1974) embedded herself among poor African American families living in a midwestern city and observed their daily activities. She found single mothers employed mutual-support networks of relatives and close friends who came to be defined as kin (*fictive kin*) providing the basis to various survival techniques: single mothers often lived in multi-generational households; female kin frequently adopted the child of a young mother and served as the child's *mama*; non-resident fathers provided money, supplies, emotional support and child care to various degrees; current boyfriends provided similar support; single mothers continually traded goods and services (especially childcare); more fortunate network members shared monetary windfalls; more stable households performed child-keeping, raising children whose household dissolved from changing relationships, eviction, and economic circumstances; and, more stable households took in boarders and allowed families with nowhere else to go to double up.

Jarrett and Burton (1999) confirmed the use of extended kin networks among low-income African American households in the late 1980s. They found many single mothers had very active extended kin (and fictive kin) networks. They also found that many of the households were characterized by continual changes in family composition due to new relationships, births, and deaths. One child noted, "So many things keep happening all at one time. My mother gets married. My real father gets a divorce for the fifth time. My youngest sister (age 18) has her third baby. My oldest sister leaves to go live with her boyfriend. One of my brothers dies. My grandpop is dying. Another woman says she is having a baby by my father. ... Too many changes all the time. Who is my family anyway?" (p. 182).

Since 1960, the percentage of African American children living in two-parent households plummeted from two-thirds to a low of one-third in the mid-1990s. Conversely, the prevalence of African American children living with their mother only increased from 20% in 1960 to over 50% in the 1980s and 1990s. The prevalence of white children in mother-only households also increased from its historically steady level of 6%, but by 2002 still comprised less than 20%.

This decline of African American children in two-parent households reflects a general decline in marriage among African Americans. The percentage of African American women age 15 and above that were married declined from 62% in 1950 down to 36% in 1998. Tucker and Mitchell-Kernan (1995) reported that African American women where facing lower prospects for marriage due to an ever-declining ratio of eligible African American men to women, especially due to death and imprisonment. Additionally, the increasing economic marginality of black men rendered even more of them undesirable as long-term household partners. Social policy may have inadvertently contributed to the decline in marriage. During the 1960s, many States denied AFDC payments (Aid to Families with Dependent Children) to single mothers suspected of living with a man. These types of eligibility requirements were struck down by the Supreme Court in 1968. However, even under the revised welfare policy, poor couples had an incentive to cohabit instead of marry, in order to maintain welfare eligibility.

[...]

The Crack Era

The life course perspective maintains that persons are differently affected by major historical events depending on their social position at the time. Sweeping events like a major war or depression can define circumstances, shape attitudes, and effect behaviors. We contend the Crack Era had this type of an impact, especially in the inner city.

Various illegal drugs have tended to rise and fall in popularity over time. Heroin had been broadly popular in the inner city during the 1960s and early 1970s. Snorting cocaine became popular during the 1970s, but mostly among wealthier populations. During the early 1980s, some cocaine users (especially drug dealers) started to smoke freebase, a costly and challenging process involving mixing powder cocaine with ether over an open flame. Crack cocaine represented an innovation that allowed users to conveniently smoke cocaine vapors on a low cost-per-dose basis. During the mid-1980s, the use of crack spread widely, especially in inner-city New York. Use was quite common in other American cities, although the timing of the crack era and prevalence varied across locations.

For many, continual crack use became an obsession that dominated their lives. Many crack users organized their lives around their drug habits and their extended binges. Dedicated crack users sold drugs, committed various hustles, and stole from family members to support their habits. Crack markets emerged in the inner city to serve users 24/7. Wealthier customers would come to these markets bringing much needed cash into impoverished communities and providing illegal jobs for many inner-city residents as dealers and in other drug distribution roles. These growing crack markets were associated with increased levels of violence in the inner city. Unfortunately, most low-level dealers and operatives ended up consuming their profits through their own growing drug habits without having saved any of their money.

The subcultural behaviors associated with crack use also led to much interpersonal violence, duplicity in relationships, increased prostitution, child neglect and abuse, and family dissolution. Crack users placed a heavy burden on families of orientation, extended kin, and community members who sought to support these persons. Crack users also greatly disappointed their offspring who might otherwise have depended upon them, thereby placing additional burdens on family, kin, and community.

Since 1989, the crack era in New York City has been drawing to a close. All across the U.S., the prevalence of crack use has been declining, especially among youths. In a related shift, inner-city violence has also decreased dramatically. Moreover, this appears to be a conscious choice. Since the early 1990s, inner-city youths have been purposefully avoiding crack and heroin, having seen the devastation these drugs brought into the lives of older community members. Marijuana supplanted crack as the drug of choice among inner-city youths, especially when smoked as a blunt – an inexpensive cigar in which the tobacco has been replaced with marijuana. However, many existing crack users persisted with their habits throughout the 1990s and into the 2000s. Davis et al. (2003) estimated that as of 1998–99 10% of nearly 100,000 residents of one inner-city section of New York (Central Harlem) were still actively using crack.

Methods

Data for this project came from a series of intensive ethnographic projects on drug use and violence in poor inner-city households that spanned the 1990s and has continued into the 2000s. Field staff followed key informant procedures to recruit focal subjects from severely-distressed (predominately African American) households located in inner-city New York neighborhoods, primarily Central Harlem, South Bronx, and the Brownsville and East New York sections of Brooklyn. Focal subjects purposefully represented multiple social networks as well as a range of family compositions and experiences typical of the inner city. Parents were asked to give informed consent to participate and for researchers to talk to their children (who also assented to participation). The sample included 178 subjects of varying ages from approximately 72 households. A precise count of households was complicated by factors such as eviction, relationships ending, families splitting up, families broken up by child protection services, and persons moving out and moving back.

Staff regularly visited each household (and as of 2006 were still making visits) to interview subjects and make direct observations. Most households were followed for three to five years and interviewed at

least quarterly over that period. As many as ten years of field notes were available for some subjects who had participated in previous studies. With time, the interviewers developed personal empathic connections into subjects' lives. Staff also spent a great deal of time participating in the life of the neighborhood, learning about its peer groups, its informal organization, and its social structures. Staff members took careful measures to assure their safety in locations where violence was commonplace. Interviews were tape recorded, transcribed verbatim, and stored in an electronic database. Field notes of interpersonal interactions and conversations observed were also stored in the database.

This paper presents syntheses of the extensive qualitative data regarding Ricochet Strutter and Island Bersini's households. (All names used in this paper are pseudonyms chosen by the subjects.) Based on our field work and knowledge of the inner city, we present these experiences as typical of the inner city at the time. [...]

Findings

Ricochet's family

The interviewer reported, "I was introduced to Ricochet on one of those calm clear winter days when a bright sun mocks the bitter-cold temperature. She was very large, well over 300 pounds. She wore an oversized dress with spandex pants underneath and slip-on shoes. Her hair was short and brushed back. She had a slight scar on her lip. She came across as friendly and outgoing, but there was a clear undertone of despair."

Ricochet was born in 1961 in Brooklyn, New York, the last of 10 living children. Unlike most of the children, Ricochet knew her father, Tom, who lived with them while she was growing up. Ricochet's mother, Joyce, hated Tom's drinking. She took out her anger on Ricochet, because Ricochet resembled him. She would force Ricochet to eat excessively and then beat her for being fat. Joyce would often tell her, "Get off your fat stinking ass." Joyce generally left the care of her children to the oldest child living at home. Ricochet reported, "My mother was into parties and stuff.

Everything I ask her, 'Go ask your sister.' My father, he was like messing with everybody, everybody, [he was always at] somebody's mother's house. … So, he wasn't there either. … [My sister Denise] was more like my mother. You know, come to school with me and stuff."

At age 18, Ricochet dropped out of school. She started dating a man she met while he was installing new doorbells in her apartment building. They had a daughter together, Tushay, but the relationship did not last long. He had said that he was in his twenties. However, he was actually almost 40 and already married. Ricochet would leave care of the child to her mother.

Ricochet had emerged. At 19, she was in the prime of life. She had a large circle of friends. She knew what was happening. She attended parties, drank alcohol, smoked marijuana, and started to smoke cocaine freebase. It was 1980, and her life was fun and carefree. In contrast, Joyce was greatly displeased with this turn of events and would routinely fight with Ricochet, verbally and physically.

At 21, Ricochet became romantically involved with John, who had just returned from jail to live with his mother in the apartment above Joyce's. Ricochet and John had a daughter together, Fruitloops. John was a heroin addict and mostly hustled to support his habit. He was also very violent. To protect herself, Ricochet would call the police, "I kept him locked up. [To keep him] from beating me all the time. … So, he's back in there, [in prison,] doing another seven. So, he rather be in there. It's his second home. That's what his mother said."

Joyce got an apartment in a senior citizen building, which left Ricochet and her children homeless. They spent nine months in a shelter, until they were placed in one of Harlem's high-rise, low-income projects. Many homeless women with children turned to the shelter system for temporary housing. In conjunction with this emergency service, the New York Department of Housing attempted to place all homeless families in apartments. However, given housing shortages the demand for these placements out-stripped the supply. Families often waited for months and even years for run-down apartments, most often in housing projects. Given their lack of income and lack of discipline in paying rent and bills, many families did not remain in their units for long.

Once Ricochet set up her own household, there was a steady parade of boyfriends and other shorter-term relationships. Ricochet was spending even less time with her children and more time with her crack habit. Ricochet reported, "I used to smoke up all my money. I was getting like $311 cash in the projects. But the stamps, I used to always, you know, take the stamps and buy food. I always bought food." Tushay, who was effectively in charge, disagreed. Tushay recalled, "I call the BCW [Bureau of Child Welfare] on my mother, when she didn't buy me no school clothes.… She didn't even feed me. She didn't feed me for like two days." Indeed, Ricochet's mother, Joyce, as well as her two children Tushay and Fruitloops, all called BCW at different times to complain about Ricochet's inattentive parenting.

After a few years, Ricochet lost the apartment for not paying the rent and the family moved back in with Joyce. At the height of the Crack Era in 1988, Ricochet began to support her habit through prostitution. The father of her next daughter, Shena, was a one-night stand. Two years later, Ricochet obtained an apartment in the projects. There, she met Bill. He was a very violent man. Like Ricochet, he was heavily involved with crack. Bill was living with his mother at that time. When Bill came to the house, everyone was afraid. He stole money from Tushay and Fruitloops whenever he could. Bill and Ricochet had a son, Timothy. Then the housing cycle continued. Ricochet was evicted from her apartment again, moved her family into a shelter, and eventually obtained another apartment.

Tushay resented her mother's boyfriends continually invading her home and her private life. Some tried to act like a father. Many threatened her with violence. Some wanted to have sex with her. In response, Tushay learned to run away from home and stay with a friend for a while as a reprieve from her mother, the boyfriends, and school. Far from protecting her daughters from sexual advances, Ricochet would encourage her daughters to prostitute. Ricochet explained, "A lotta times my vic didn't come and I didn't wanna fuck 'em, and they [Tushay or Fruitloops] used to bust them off.… I'm sayin' I didn't make them prostitute. But when they did, I wanted some of the money for the drugs, and I know that. I had to talk about that [years later while in drug treatment]. I said that's how fucked

I was." At ages 14 and 12, Tushay and Fruitloops were hospitalized with a venereal disease. BCW removed them from the household and placed them in foster care. Ricochet was able to get them back by pleading that they were wild and she was trying to control them. However, she quickly lost custody of them again.

In 1995, Ricochet met George. Like so many of her previous boyfriends, George was intensely violent. As a young man, George had shot a man while robbing a supermarket, and served 13 years for the offense. Ricochet met him soon after he got out. Crack cocaine was their common interest and shared passion. Ricochet was soon pregnant, but George beat her so badly that she had a miscarriage. After another particularly violent domestic incident, George was arrested and returned to prison. Meanwhile, Ricochet was pregnant again. Ricochet said that one time while having sex early in their relationship, George told her, "Daddy die, mama die." This cryptic avowal seemed romantic at the time. Later, she realized that George had knowingly infected her with HIV. When the next baby, Zena, was born, she was HIV positive. The hospital would not release her into Ricochet's custody. Ricochet had Zena placed in kin foster care with one of her mother's nieces, Willie Mae. In 1998, Ricochet also placed her next son, Vernon Jr., with Willie Mae.

By the end of 1998, all of Ricochet's children had been removed from her household, including her two oldest daughters. However, Tushay and Fruitloops continually ran away from the foster homes and institutions in which they were placed. Eventually, BCW grew tired of continually searching for them, and they returned home to Ricochet's apartment. In due course, Ricochet was again evicted from her apartment. This time, however, she did not have any children in her care so she was not eligible for subsidized housing. Instead of living in one place, she shuttled between the apartments maintained by Tushay, Fruitloops, Joyce, and Victor, a senior citizen in Joyce's apartment building with whom she smoked crack.

As of 2003, Fruitloops was maintaining an apartment provided by welfare. This household served as the primary residence for 15 people: Fruitloops, her four children, her long-term boyfriend Patrick (who stayed about half the time and was legally married to someone else), Ricochet and her current boyfriend Brian, Tushay, and her five children.

During the 1980s and 1990s, Ricochet was primarily a crack-using sex worker. Most of the time, her family did not have an apartment of its own. According to Census Bureau definitions, her family would be variously categorized over time as a multi-generational single household (with varying household heads), as members of multiple households, or as members of no household. Ricochet's experiences illustrate the devastation that prevails when the responsible parent is caught up in her own personal concerns. Men regularly circulated through Ricochet's household between periods of jail and prison. Children attended school sporadically, if at all. Food was often not available. Lights and water went off regularly because of unpaid bills. In a sense, Ricochet's household can be viewed as caught in a whirlwind, moving about, bumping up against hard circumstances, and sending children off in various directions. In contrast, Willie Mae's household seemed like a relatively safe haven. In the inner city, however, stable residence does not alone ensure a wholesome environment for child development as illustrated by Island's story.

Island's family

Island Bersini chose her pseudonym because she was born in the Islands. This label also conveniently describes her family role, as an island, a possible haven in stormy times. Like Willie Mae, she accepted care of numerous children. As a kin foster care provider, she held legal and personal responsibility for them. Her home provided a constant address, food, and a place to sleep. However, it did not shield children from the hardships of poverty nor the broader ravages of the Crack Era. Crack-related problems had a wide reach in the inner city. Originally, field staff selected some poor households in inner-city neighborhoods as a comparison group because the household heads reported that no one in the family used drugs. However, in-depth interviewing eventually revealed significant drug use, especially crack, in virtually all the households included in the study.

It was a quiet day in the neighborhood. Usually, there were people hanging out near Island's apartment building day and night, mostly teenagers, most of them involved in some type of hustle. This activity flowed like a stream from the street into the lobby of the building. They used the lobby for dice games and drug selling. Young prostitutes used the scene as a convenient spot to turn a quick trick. Essentially, the activities of the park, street, and lobby continued its flow right into Island's apartment. Island tolerated high levels of drug use and violence in her household. It became a favorite place for drug-using family members to visit. Island's apartment usually teemed with people, their lives, and their noises. Today it was serene, eerily calm as if we were in the eye of a storm. Everyone was out except Island. Even still, the apartment felt crowded with boxes and furniture and everyone's things. Amidst the clutter, Island Bersini, age 62, sat cross-legged with a cup of tea in her hand.

Island reported that, "Growing up, I was always kind-hearted and loved to take care of other people's children and I guess that has followed me all my life." Island was born in 1930 in the Caribbean. Her biological parents were never married and their relationship didn't last. Island never knew her mother, never knew the circumstances of her birth, never knew why her mother abandoned her and disappeared from her life. Island's father had a common-law relationship with another woman who became Island's stepmother and the leading influence in her early life. The stepmother already had five children of her own. So, Island became the youngest of six. When she was four, her father died. Within a year, Island's stepmother decided to move the family to New York in search of a better life. As a temporary measure, they moved in with the stepmother's sister, who was raising five children of her own. The arrangement became permanent and the 11 kids grew up together. Island remembered how her stepmother worked long hours as a domestic. Island dutifully did most of the daily housework, washing clothes, washing dishes, and overall cleaning.

As a child, Island felt no one really cared for her and yearned for the day she would have her own family. At age 18, she was introduced to Jim, who had just gotten out of prison. After a short courtship, they married. In 1953, they had a daughter, Sonya, and in 1956, their son, Ross, was born. Jim worked hard delivering coal during the week. However, on the weekend he drank heavily, argued, and physically abused Island. No matter the strain, Island vowed, "I was willing to live with him because he was my husband and I wanted to stick by him." Until, one day she came home and found Jim

trying to have sex with Sonya, then age seven. She had Jim arrested and established her own household. Two years later, Jim was hit by a car and killed.

After Jim's death, Island took responsibility for everyone in the family who needed help. Many of Island's siblings or in-laws fell into criminal activity or drug addiction. As a result, their children needed to be raised by others, sometimes only temporarily but often permanently, as one thing led to another. In time, Island became the prominent caregiver of the children, grandchildren, and great-grandchildren of her generation, sometimes with foster care support and often without such support. Alas, Island's love of family, apartment space, and food were not enough. These children did not receive much of an education, and they failed to develop the type of social capital needed for participating in the modern economy. They did, however, receive a good introduction into street life and an education in the prevailing inner-city subcultures.

Sonya reached age 17 in 1970, during the peak years of the Heroin Era. After her initial introduction to the drug, Sonya quickly became addicted, as did many of her cousins, uncles, and aunts. She left high school and married a heroin addict and dealer. She and her husband lived in shooting galleries. Sonya raised additional money as a prostitute. After a few years, they separated and he moved to Florida. Soon afterward, Sonya was arrested and sent to prison for participating in the robbery of a jewelry store with a friend. After release, Sonya returned to live with Island. While imprisoned, she had gotten clean from heroin.

In the 1980s, Sonya started using crack and again quickly became dependent. Her life revolved around her habit. Whenever she had any money, she would smoke crack. Her main income came from prostitution. As soon as she would turn a trick and make a few dollars, she would find a dealer, buy some crack, and smoke. Sometimes she would directly exchange sex-for-crack, avoiding dealing with the money and having to find a dealer.

Island's second child, Ross, also became part of the street scene. As a child, he always hated being poor and felt stigmatized by public assistance. At age 16, he dropped out of school to try to support the family by selling PCP. Ross married at age 18. Soon afterwards, he was arrested for dealing and sent to prison for two years. Upon release, he returned to Island's household, rather than to his wife, and returned to selling marijuana and PCP. In 1975, he started selling heroin but hated the drug because of what had happened to his sister. Heroin had become known as one of the worst if not the worst drug on the street. When the police increased their pressure on dealers, Ross was arrested and sent to prison for another two years. After release, he was shot during a robbery. As a result, he was paralyzed and confined to a wheelchair for the rest of his life. His condition, however, did not stop him from dealing drugs. Even though he was still legally married, Ross began living with another woman, Gladys, who bore three children by him. Eventually, however, Ross moved back in with Island.

In the mid-1980s, Ross' business practice was well established. He had his territory, his client base, and his connections with dealers. He learned how to cook-up crack and set up a thriving business. Crack dealing evolved into the family business. When young men came to live in Island's household, they became involved in drug dealing through Ross. The family and extended family resident in the household lived in style, at least by Harlem standards. That money was never invested (no one in the family ever had a bank account) and the household returned to poverty in the 1990s as Ross' discipline gave way and he became his own best customer.

In 2003, Island's household was no longer as active as it had been in either drugs or childcare. Island had heart problems and received a pacemaker to keep her going. Sonya was hit by a car and spent several months in the hospital. Ross became progressively more sick from AIDS and passed away. Island reported, "[having] done raised 89 kids. Not one is employed at a legal job. They are all alcoholics, heroin and crack addicts, drug sellers, and what not." When asked if any came to see her, she was taken aback and replied quickly, "I don't want no drug addict around me. I'm tired of that."

Discussion

These life histories identify how the Crack Era added to the miseries facing many inner-city African American families in the 1980s and 1990s. Crack represented a major distraction contributing to child abuse, neglect, and abandonment of parental responsibilities. Children born to crack users like

Ricochet had a challenging home life. The African American tradition of extended family served as only a modest stopgap for Ricochet's family. The children received some support from their maternal grandmother and from Aunt Willie Mae, Ricochet's sister, who had stepped up as a member of a broader kin support network. Even stable inner-city households were greatly affected by the Crack Era. Island held onto her apartment and her children and provided refuge for a continual flow of children from kin who were unable to support them. However, children growing up in Island's household did not fare much better with the extensive crack use, sales, and other street activities taking place in their home.

[...] The challenges faced by distressed African American families as they emerge from the crack era are profound and complex. Children from households like these have been becoming the parents of the next generation of African Americans in the inner city. Many of these young adults inherited from their parents structural disadvantages, poor preparation for a conventional lifestyle, and counterproductive behaviors based in non-conventional subcultures: Moreover, the legacy of the Crack Era has left profound deficits in kin support networks. Many of the older relatives who might have otherwise helped are unavailable due to persistent drug use, poor health, imprisonment, and death stemming from crack use and sales. These young parents face major challenges in obtaining and maintaining jobs that could lift them and their families out of poverty. Welfare reform has set a goal of moving families from dependence on government aid to economic independence through employment at legitimate jobs. However, many African American families are still feeling the effects of a long history of structural disadvantages as well as the residual consequences of the Crack Era.

It will take a wealth of services and comprehensive case management to elevate a large percentage of the distressed African American families. Many parents and responsible adults do not have the human and social capital necessary to pull together a healthy and productive lifestyle for themselves and their dependent children, let alone other unfortunate children stranded by the collapse of inner-city households. Consequently, young children in these households are at great risk of never rising above the persistent poverty dogging their family histories. There are strengths in these families and communities. However, from the problems perspective, we conclude that it is hopelessly optimistic and even immoral to applaud the strengths of the African American family and leave these distressed households to struggle or more likely wallow in their problems. These families that are embedded within the larger American experience deserve and should be entitled to greater opportunity, especially the young children that have not yet become engulfed in self-destructive behaviors and who have all of their lives and potential ahead of them. We further contend that aggressive social service agencies should be established within distressed communities to assure that every child receives these opportunities. No child should go hungry, have medical needs untreated, endure physical or sexual abuse, or fail to receive an education because they are poor.

[...]

References

Davis W. R., Johnson B. D., Randolph D., and Liberty H. J. An enumeration method of determining the prevalence of users and operatives of cocaine and heroin in Central Harlem. *Drug and Alcohol Dependence* 2003; 72: 45–58. [PubMed: 14563542]

Dodson, J. E. Conceptualizations of African American families. In: McAdoo, H. P., ed. *Black families*. 3rd edn. Sage; Thousand Oaks, CA: 1997. pp. 67–82.

Jarrett R. L., and Burton L. M. Dynamic dimensions of family structure in low-income African American families: Emergent themes in qualitative research. *Journal of Comparative Family Studies* 1999; 30: 177–87.

Massey, D. S. and Denton, D. A. *American apartheid: Segregation and the making of the underclass*. Harvard; Cambridge, MA: 1993.

Small M. L. and Newman K. Urban poverty after the truly disadvantaged: The rediscovery of the family, the neighborhood, and culture. *Annual Review of Sociology* 2001; 27: 23–45.

Stack, C. B. *All our kin: Strategies for survival in the Black community*. Harper and Row; New York: 1974.

Stevenson, B. E. Black family structure in colonial and antebellum Virginia: Amending the revisionist perspective. In: Tucker, M. B.; Mitchell-Kernan, C., eds. *The decline in marriage among African American: Causes, consequences, and policy implications*. Russell Sage; New York: 1995.

Tucker, M. B. and Mitchell-Kernan, C., eds. *The decline in marriage among African American: Causes, consequences, and policy implications*. Russell Sage; New York: 1995.

Wilson, W. J. *The truly disadvantaged: The inner city, the underclass, and public policy*. University of Chicago; Chicago: 1987.

Wilson, W. J. *When work disappears: The world of the new urban poor*. Random House; New York: 1996.

Questions

1 How might the adherence to non-conventional subcultures hinder a person's ability to develop a healthy and prosperous lifestyle? How did poverty and drug use intersect to exacerbate the life conditions for Ricochet and Island? What practical social service solutions may have helped these two women?

2 According to the article, prominent ethnocentric studies presumed the two-parent nuclear-family structure of the White middle-class American represents the cultural ideal. What forms of drug use do we view as the cultural ideal? Do these forms of drug use also reflect a White, middle-class ideal? Is drug use associated with minority populations treated differently in our society? What does history tell us?

3 According to the article, many parents and responsible adults do not have the human and social capital necessary to pull together a healthy and productive lifestyle for themselves and their dependent children. What exactly do the authors mean by this? What other articles in this text exhibit a lack for social/human capital for those interviewed?

Getting Huge, Getting Ripped
An Exploration of Recreational Steroid Use

Matthew Petrocelli, Trish Oberweis, and Joseph Petrocelli

If Dunlap, Golub, and Johnson offer us a portrait of the family lives of the urban poor, Matthew Petrocelli, Trish Oberweis, and Joseph Petrocelli take us into the realm of blue-collar, middle-class drug users. Although steroids may not be the only drugs they use, we get a glimpse into how and why recreational bodybuilders turn to these in spite of the huge stigma associated with them. As we move slightly up the socioeconomic ladder, do we see a shift in the motivations for drug use along the escapist/engagement dimension or any others? How do these individuals' greater resources affect their drug use?

This is also a portrait of men and masculinity, as they chase the embodiment of strength and appearance. To what extent do the norms and values of their subculture influence the importance of these factors to them? How much are they able to compartmentalize their drug use into one dimension of their lives, rather than letting it spill over and drive them? What factors make them more likely to maintain this level of control? To what extent do they benefit from racial/ethnic, class, and gender privilege?

How would you compare the factors leading them into this kind of drug-using? How do their rationalizations compare to Bourgois and Schonberg's homeless junkies? Do they experience any of the pull and push factors Spicer describes for the American Indians, and if not, why not?

Finally, we have been offered portraits in the media of steroid use by professional athletes, yet few or none by recreational athletes. How do these groups compare in their motivations, their pull and push factors, and the risks they take? What are their perceptions of the long-range risks to their health from using these drugs, and how do these compare to other drug users? What factors account for this difference?

Drugs and the American Dream: An Anthology, First Edition. Edited by Patricia A. Adler, Peter Adler, and Patrick K. O'Brien.
© 2012 John Wiley & Sons, Inc. Published 2012 by John Wiley & Sons, Inc.

Introduction

Steroid use has exploded into our national consciousness. As a nation, we slowly began to realize that illegal supplementation had infiltrated athletics in the late 1980s, when Olympic sprinter Ben Johnson was stripped of his gold medal after testing positive for a banned steroid. Since then, it has been impossible to ignore the massive muscular gains and record shattering performances of men and women across the athletic spectrum. NFL players grew to gargantuan proportions, track and field athletes redefined the limits of human speed and endurance, and baseball players not only began to resemble bodybuilders but also started hitting tape measure home runs at a frenetic pace. Indeed, St. Louis Cardinal Mark McGuire captured the imagination of the sporting world and single-handedly rejuvenated interest in our "national pastime" in 1998 when he chased and eventually broke one of the most heralded records in baseball: the single season home run record. His 70 home runs, 9 more than the 1961 record held by Roger Maris, marked an astounding athletic accomplishment. Yet skeptics raised their eyebrows and questioned the validity of McGuire's accomplishment. It was impossible to ignore how his physical dimensions had changed in the twilight of his career. McGuire began his career as a tall, lanky infielder weighing about 200 lbs; by 1998, at the age of 35, he had added 50 lbs. of solid muscle to his frame. Like other athletes who exhibited such phenomenal growth, he scornfully denied using steroids, instead attributing his physique to scientific improvements in weight training and dietary regimes, along with legal nutritional supplements.

That explanation began to unravel on September 3, 2003 when agents from the Internal Revenue Service, the US Food and Drug Administration, and the San Mateo (CA) Narcotics Task Force raided the Burlingame Bay Area Laboratory Co-Operative (BALCO). Scientists at the Olympic drug-testing lab at UCLA had discovered new and powerful steroids in some athletes and forwarded that information to the Department of Justice, which tracked the new drugs to BALCO. Owned by Victor Conte (a former rock musician of some notoriety in the 1970s), BALCO's client list read like a veritable "Who's Who"

in American sports. Clients included members of the Miami Dolphins, All Pro NFL linebacker Bill Romanoski, track and field gold medalist and world record holder Marion Jones, baseball All Stars Jason Giambi, and, most notably, Barry Bonds (who broke McGuire's record in 2001 with 73 home runs and who, like McGuire, had added 40–50 lbs of muscle to his frame late in his career).

[...] Recent investigations and research into national steroid use has begun to demonstrate that these drugs are widely used by athletes of all ages and at all levels of competition. The present study explores the use of steroids by amateur bodybuilders.

Literature Review

Although we are only now recognizing the prevalence of steroid use in professional athletics, these drugs have been part of the American sporting culture since the 1950s when synthetic testosterone was first produced and marketed. Early academic research into the efficacy of anabolic steroids did much to damage the credibility of medical doctors and scientists as these "experts" made claims that steroids did little or nothing to improve athletic performance. Of course, steroid users learned from direct experience that steroids were effective at enhancing strength and muscle mass and thus began the entrenched belief that neither the government nor the scientific community could be trusted to reliably report the positive or negative effects of anabolic steroids.

Recent research has attempted to rectify past shortcomings and studies have concentrated on medical evidence of effectiveness, trends, and patterns of usage among adolescent and high school students, college athletes, and professional competitors. In terms of the medical literature, scientists are universal in their agreement that anabolic steroids can lead to a host of ill-effects including acute acne, hypertension, blood clotting, jaundice, tendon damage, reduced fertility, the development of breasts in male users (technically known as gynacomastia but crudely referred to as 'bitch tits' in the vernacular of steroid users), and a myriad of psychiatric and behavioral problems. More controversial studies have made the case that protracted steroid use is fatal.

Studies of adolescent and high school steroid users focus on their motivation to use the drugs and their intended and unintended consequences. Most studies are in agreement that 3–12% of American youths have experimented with steroids. Their inspiration of these steroid users largely stems from either a desire to better their athletic performance or improve their body image (termed the "Adonis complex") [...]. Increased rates of violent behavior have been noted among these users.

Additionally, some researchers conclude there is a "gateway effect" associated with adolescent steroid use. Namely, there is evidence to suggest that these steroid users are significantly more likely to use other illegal drugs (including inhalants, cannabis, hashish, PCP, sedatives, amphetamines, cocaine, heroin, and opiates), tobacco, and alcohol. [...]

Studies centering on collegiate and professional steroid use demonstrate similar findings. Along with verifying the litany of detrimental side effects noted in clinical trials, the same gateway effect has been found in mature steroid users. Specifically, adult use was significantly associated with higher rates of psychotropic drug use and overall substance dependence, particularly with opiates. Additionally, male bodybuilders exhibited an abnormal incidence of eating disorders and obsessive dietary tendencies [...].

It is clear that steroids pose risks to the users that have been identified by experts. Yet the black market for steroids is estimated to generate somewhere between $400–500 million a year. It seems unlikely that high school students, collegiate athletes, and competitive bodybuilders comprise the entirety of that marketplace. Thus, it is logical to assume that there is a group of steroid users that remains unidentified and unstudied by researchers. We hypothesize that a significant portion of this segment of the steroid using population are recreational weightlifters, or individuals who bodybuild as a hobby. [...]

The problem, then, is that there are no studies examining the motivations, knowledge, and attitudes of recreational steroid users. From a social scientific standpoint, we know little to nothing about this potentially large group of steroid users in the United States. Thus, the significance of the present study is apparent. It is much easier to understand why professional or Olympic athletes would take steroids – namely, to gain a competitive edge, for the glory of victory, and for the enormous monetary compensation tied to performance or endorsement deals. However, it is much more difficult to understand why someone who lifts weights as a hobby would risk arrest and felony conviction, along with a host of medically verified detrimental side effects. The need for social scientific analysis of recreational steroid users is crucial to round out our understanding of the entire spectrum of steroid users and thus to foster policies that address the entire problem of illegal steroid use, rather than just one subgroup or another.

Methods

This project entailed the use of semi-structured interviews and snowball sampling techniques in gyms in California, New Jersey, and Illinois. In order to tap into the steroid subculture, we trained at gyms rumored to have steroid access. These were not fitness clubs but rather more dingy structures that catered to the hardcore weightlifting crowd. There were massive amounts of free weights, very few (if any) women, blaring music, and larger than average men. Our access to our original research subjects was facilitated by the fact that two of the authors are lifelong weightlifters (Petrocelli, M. was a fairly successful collegiate powerlifter and Petrocelli, J. was a nationally recognized powerlifter); we could hold our own in the gym, knew the repartee, and gradually built a good rapport with most other lifters. Over time, as jocular insults and training tips were exchanged, we broached the subject of steroid use with likely research subjects (chosen for their noticeable strength, size, muscularity, and approachability). Despite our familiarity with both the subject matter and with the potential interviewees, developing a rapport with any individual interviewee took a long period of time.

Initial interviews took place in the gym, usually after a training session. By that time, most gym members knew we were academics. When we approached our initial subjects we further identified ourselves as researchers interested in discussing various aspects of steroid use, promising complete confidentiality.

[...]

Over the course of four years, from 2000–2004, we collected 37 interviews. Most interviews took place in a private area of the gym (out of earshot) or in the parking lot and lasted approximately one hour. Each interview was recorded (audio only) and later transcribed for analysis.

Our sample proved fairly homogeneous for key demographic variables. All the respondents were men. In terms of race, approximately 90% were white, and all were employed in essentially blue collar or public service related professions. Approximately 60% were married with children, 30% were divorced, and the remainder were unmarried. Ages ranged from 19 to 43 years old.

[...]

Analysis

Motivations for use

In stark contrast to the motivations espoused by adolescents, collegiate athletes, or professional steroid users, we found that frustration seems to be a primary motivator for the recreational steroid user. Essentially, these employed, adult men report having grown up reading muscle magazines their entire lives. They believed what they read and thought that a good diet and hard workouts would get them a "magazine look" (competitive bodybuilder appearance). Naturally, they were bewildered that years of weight training had not yielded that dividend. This quote is typical of their epiphany:

> I grew up idolizing Arnold (Schwarzenegger, former bodybuilding champion and Governor of California) and Lou (Ferrigno, another champion bodybuilder who starred in "The Incredible Hulk" television series). I used to train in my basement with my brother and friends all the time. Monster workouts. Dieted like crazy and everything the magazines said, and after five years my build wasn't even close. I couldn't understand it. Finally, I started going to a gym where muscle heads trained and learned what everyone on the inside knew: You gotta use if you want to get huge.

Nearly every research subject we interviewed mirrored this sentiment. [...] When dieting, training, and legal supplements all failed to produce the magazine-like results, respondents realized that they would need illegal supplements to achieve their goals. Now, as individuals who had insider knowledge, they reported feeling obligated and compelled to pass on the secret to aspiring weightlifters. As one subject put it:

> If I see a kid training hard, doing all the right things and asking questions about why he isn't making gains, I'm gonna tell him the truth. I spent too many years busting my ass in the gym like that. I don't tell anyone they should use, but I do tell them they can only get so far without using.

Another major motivation which surfaced in our interviews was the desire to "get huge." Although this is another motive that was almost universally asserted by our subjects, the meaning of "getting huge" varied from person to person. Some reported that they wanted to achieve, at least once in their lives, the kind of "comic book" size proportions they always dreamed of. A few reported having grown up small or being bullied and they wanted to build the type of size and strength that would forever alter those early perceptions or experiences. However, these were mostly men who were either naturally big or who had attained above average dimensions through years of weight training. Part of their desire to use steroids seems to stem from some sort of internal or external competitive obsession:

> It's addictive.... you can never be too big. There's always another guy with more size and you want to outdo him. And you think to yourself, "If I can get this big doing this cycle, I'll be huge if I do that cycle." So you up your cycles and train harder.

Another major motivation we found is the craving to "get ripped." This is a common term among weightlifters and bodybuilders, which has also become part of the popular lexicon. Being ripped means stripping away enough body fat so your muscles are clearly defined and vascular. Most of our research subjects reported the desire to get ripped but realized, like getting huge, they could only achieve their goal through steroid use:

> You can only go so far with diet and exercise. Yeah, there's a guy here or there that has great genetics and has a good build. But most of us don't.

Still others reported that being ripped increased and enhanced their confidence and love life, as they claimed having a defined, muscular physique allowed them to meet and have sexual relations with more partners. Quite simply, most believed that they had become either more attractive to their partner or more desirable in a singles setting, or both.

Lastly, many subjects reported an odd blend of psychological and physical power, or "feeling strong." It seems that for these individuals, the development of material strength via steroids had a profound impact on their psyche:

> When I'm on (steroids), I feel great. Unless you've been on, you don't know what I'm talking about. It just gives you a feeling that you can handle anything. You just feel so powerful and that makes you feel good about the rest of your life, like you can do anything.

This theme resounded among most of the users we interviewed, who claim a kind of raw, primitive strength and enthusiasm: "When I'm on, I feel like Superman."

Usage patterns

Most users in our study did two or three "cycles" a year. According to our subjects, cycles are tailored to achieve particular gains. For instance, a "bulking cycle," intended to build as much muscular mass as possible, entails using steroids designed for that purpose, lifting very heavy weights with low repetitions and eating tremendous amounts of food and protein supplements (as many as 6000 plus calories per day), whereas a "cutting cycle" is meant to achieve the ripped look. "Cutting up" involves using different types of steroids than would be used for "bulking up," as well as training with lighter weights and higher repetitions and eating a stringent, low fat, calorie conscious diet. Normally, a bulking cycle is followed by a cutting cycle. As mentioned, a cycle lasted approximately 12 weeks and our subjects were very quick to point out the importance of "cycling." This means doing a steroid cycle and then "cycling off," or refraining from steroid use for at least 12 weeks. The reasons for cycling were varied, but most subjects indicated that they had health concerns if

they did not take a break between use cycles (e.g., "It gives your body a rest"). However, most held the belief that the bodybuilders who appeared in magazines never cycled off: "Those guys are always 'on.' They might taper their cycles after a competition, but they're always on."

Another popular reason for cycling on and off was the expense of steroids. All of our subjects made less than $77,000 per year (range: 23–77k), so cost was an issue. Steroid cycles varied in cost, depending on type and amount of steroids. Users reported that the amount of money they had on hand for a given cycle would primarily dictate the ingestion method, as steroid users can take steroids via an oral pill or through injections. There are pros and cons to each technique. Using pills is obviously easier in terms of intake. It is also easier to conceal your use in that it does not require the ritual of injection or any subsequent marks, and oral steroids are generally cheaper than injectables. The downside is that they are widely viewed as not being nearly as effective as "the darts." Most users believe that injectable steroids are superior to orals because they make you stronger, bigger, or more cut. The reported negatives to injecting steroids include having to learn to inject yourself, which can be painful:

> Shooting yourself is tough at first. You have to learn the spot on your ass that is best for you, and then you have to learn not to shoot there too often. A lot of guys who start out keep shooting themselves in the same place and you can get like an abscess or something there. It feels like a hard, round golf ball. You can always tell the guys in the gym who have them, because they're always squirming when they sit down. It's pretty funny.

Interestingly, none of the users in our study mentioned any concerns about sharing needles. When queried about this, all those reporting injectable steroid use claimed that getting clean needles was the easiest part of the process, as they are normally sold in bulk by steroid dealers.

All users reported that if they had the money and resources, they would take both oral and injectable steroids in tandem, commonly known as "stacking." This is perceived to be the absolute best way to achieve maximum gains. But whether doing an oral cycle (at a cost of about $300–500), an injectable cycle (at a cost of about $600–800), or stacking (at a cost of about $1,200–1,500), the research subjects were unanimous in their approach to ingestion. Specifically, users employed a "pyramid" technique, in which small amounts are used in the preliminary weeks, increasing amounts in the middle weeks, maximum dosage at the midpoint, and then gradually decreasing portions until the final week where the amount is the same as the start of the cycle.

Access

Most subjects reported that it is fairly easy to get steroids. A typical response: You go to a gym where you know the muscle heads go. You start training and get to know some of the guys over time. After a while, you can start sniffing around. If everyone is sure you're not a cop or an asshole, then people will start talking to you. Usually, there are at least a few guys who are selling and they'll set you up.

Or, potential users would approach a friend who they know to be on steroids, who would then in turn make the appropriate introductions to his dealer and vouch for the new user. Interestingly, this dynamic mirrors some empirical findings concerning some market distribution systems for other illicit drugs.

[...]

Health concerns

Amazingly, the steroid users in our study were only minimally, if at all, concerned about any adverse health risks stemming from their drug use. Their lack of anxiety stemmed from both their experiential reality and a type of adulterated agreement reality. In terms of their own experience, none of our research subjects reported ever having an ill health effect. When asked about such side effects as hair loss, infertility, acne, "roid rage," or liver damage, they universally assailed such empirical findings as unbelievable and intentionally manipulative on the part of the medical community and government. For example:

> That's total bullshit. I've been taking steroids for eight years and I have three kids and a full head of hair. As long as you know what you're doing, they are only

going to help you, not hurt you. The government is just totally fucked when it comes to drugs, so I don't pay any attention to their hype.

[...]

Since none of our research subjects reported ever experiencing a significant negative side effect, coupled with the seemingly good health of well-known steroid users from the recent past, their fear was slight. They simply do not believe that steroids will hurt them. While hair loss, development of breasts, and other potential side effects of steroids might be readily identified by users, other potential effects may not be obvious. "Rage" may be present but not attributed to steroids. Kidney or liver damage may go unknown to users for long periods of time. This is not to suggest that the users in our study suffered from these ill effects, but rather to point out that the lack of side effects is the subjects' perception.

Illegality concerns

Anabolic steroids have been classified as Schedule III drugs in the Controlled Substances Act since 1991. According to the Drug Enforcement Administration: Simple possession of illicitly obtained anabolic steroids carries a maximum penalty of one year in prison and a minimum $1,000 fine if this is an individual's first drug offense. The maximum penalty for trafficking is five years in prison and a fine of $250,000 if this is the individual's first felony drug offense. For a second felony drug offense, the maximum period of imprisonment and the maximum fine are doubled. While the above listed penalties are for federal offenses, individual states have also implemented fines and penalties for illegal use of anabolic steroids.

Most users voiced at least some concern about getting caught, although it was clear that their apprehension was not enough to deter them. Users who were married were the most worried about getting caught, but almost all dismissed the possibility and repercussions:

> It would suck to get arrested, but it's not like you're going to do time. Talk about a victimless crime. Why is everyone so worried if I take steroids? Why would anyone want to put me in jail for it? It's just stupid.

Others believed that steroid enforcement was such a low law enforcement priority that only either the very stupid or the very brazen need to be concerned. In short, our research subjects exhibited disdain for the laws banning steroids, did not fear law enforcement efforts, and were not particularly worried about receiving a harsh or unmanageable punishment.

Discussion and Implications

There are several key findings in our research and other ideas that merit further thought and discussion. Our study identifies average men of average means who are long time and dedicated steroid users. First, we found that ... a [users'] ... frustration with their lack of results using natural bodybuilding techniques was critical in terms of understanding their motivation for use. The source of this frustration seems to stem from an earlier belief that competitive bodybuilders are truthful when they assert in muscle magazines that certain diet and training techniques are the keys to their success. Our respondents unanimously believe that they are not. Although our results stem from a nonprobability sample, hence negating generalizability, it is noteworthy that our subjects hail from three different states in distinct regions of America (i.e., the West, the Midwest, and the East Coast) and this finding was consistent across that geography.

Moreover, our respondents clearly articulated their disenchantment with the magazines' advertisements for legal supplements. These, our respondents insist, did not produce the effects promised in words and pictures, while anabolic steroids do. [...]

It was only with the use of anabolic supplements, our respondents suggest, that they were finally able to achieve their goals. They got huge. They got ripped. They got the added bonus of a sense of power that was part physical and part psychological, yet they did not report feeling the more well-known side effects of illegal steroids. No one reported uncontrollable anger, for example. Moreover, our respondents' accounts of their drug use did not include a concern over the health risks that may be associated with anabolic steroids. [...].

Financial concerns posed a larger issue, though these were overcome by use patterns in which users cycled on and off of a variety of substances to obtain maximum benefits at a minimal cost. "Off" time, or a resting period between cycles, helped to ease the financial burden without compromising results. Friends were a major source of steroids for new users, although the Internet was mentioned as a possibility as well. Already, some nonprofessional users have found a route to obtaining steroids legally through choosing medical doctors that specialize in "anti-aging" therapies. Essentially, these doctors measure testosterone levels in middle-aged men, and then provide anabolic supplementation and HGH to bring these levels up to those commonly found in much younger men. As one research subject put it, "It's the newest scam. If you have the cash to pay the doctors, then you can be 'on' legally."

Our research suggests that, like most street drugs in the US, steroids are easy to get and used by an array of individuals across the socioeconomic spectrum. It is hard to deny that they have become part of the American fabric. Competitive bodybuilding is obviously stacked with hardcore users who operate in the open. Professional sports teams are only now reluctantly acknowledging the rampant use that most fans and experts have suspected or known about for decades. Even the entertainment industry is under suspicion. While it is impossible to empirically verify Hollywood actors' use of steroids, strong suspicions, bordering on certainty, abound among recreational users:

> Ever see Will Smith? Tall, skinny guy most of the time. But then he decides to play Ali (Former Heavyweight boxing champ Muhammad Ali) and he slaps on 40 pounds of muscles almost immediately. C'mon. Look at the difference in Stallone's body (Sylvester Stallone) from the first "Rocky" until now. He's got a better build today than he did 30 years ago.[1]

Yet given all the national attention about steroid use, the subjects in our study were universally unfazed by the clamor; they are just getting huge and getting ripped.

Note

1   Stallone is 60 years old and in May, 2007 pled guilty to the illegal importation of Human Growth Hormone into Australia after a search by Australian law enforcement officials. Stallone, who was visiting the country to promote his new film "Rocky Balboa" called the event a "minor misunderstanding" and will pay approximately $10,000 in fines.

Questions

1   Is steroid use stigmatized in the same manner as other illicit drugs? Why or why not? How might social class, race, and gender factor into this question?

2   According to the article, anabolic steroids can have multiple side effects for the user. What are these ill effects? Do you think most people are aware of the deleterious side effects of anabolic steroids? Why do people, the vast majority men, take the risk?

3   How do the usage patterns, motivations, financial concerns, and health perceptions of the steroid users in the article compare and contrast with other forms of illicit drug use? Would you consider the weightlifters' steroid use instrumental or recreational use? Why?

Drugged Druggists
The Convergence of Two Criminal Career Trajectories

Dean A. Dabney and Richard C. Hollinger

Moving up another notch along the socioeconomic scale, we turn to professionals who use drugs. These are not individuals who need them for their careers, such as athletes, but who have occupational opportunity and use them either recreationally or medicinally. How would you compare the drug-using pharmacists with other groups along some of the lines previously suggested of motivation, control, and rationalization? How does their social learning of drug use compare to those who learn about drugs in their families, their communities, or their ethnic subcultures? Why are these people not embedded in these kinds of webs, as we have seen in other populations (Asian–Pacific Islanders, American Indians, poor urban Blacks, and Mexican Americans)?

Dean Dabney and Richard Hollinger divide their subjects into two distinct groups based on how individuals came to their drug abuse. Can you think of what factors led these groups to start out so different from each other? Do they wind up in the same place, or do their differences continue to remain meaningful? How do they compare to the other groups of pharmaceutical users discussed? Are they righteous dopefiends, like Bourgois and Schonberg's homeless junkies? How do their race and class advantages affect them here, compared to some of the other populations we have seen? Does their professional status, opportunity structure, subcultural background, and education give them any more control over their drug use?

Self-report studies have revealed that between 40 percent to 65 percent of all practicing pharmacists engage in some form of illicit drug use at least once during their professional careers. Approximately 20 percent of pharmacists in earlier studies reported using drugs regularly enough that they experienced negative life consequences, such as missing work, blackouts, health problems, or difficulties with interpersonal relationships, but only 5 percent to 10 percent considered themselves to be drug abusers.

Although scholars have generally agreed about the high incidence and prevalence of the illegal use of drugs by pharmacists, substantial knowledge gaps prevent us from fully understanding the complex

Drugs and the American Dream: An Anthology, First Edition. Edited by Patricia A. Adler, Peter Adler, and Patrick K. O'Brien.
© 2012 John Wiley & Sons, Inc. Published 2012 by John Wiley & Sons, Inc.

causal etiology of the problem. Most vexing is the limited understanding of how these individuals initially come to use and then abuse the prescription substances that they are entrusted to dispense. In this study, we attempt to fill this gap in knowledge by identifying the underlying causes of the illicit use of prescription drugs among practicing pharmacists.

[...]

Review of the Literature

Drug-using pharmacists

[...]

The explanations most commonly found in the scholarly literature regarding medical professionals' drug abuse can be divided into two generic conceptual categories: recreational abuse and therapeutic self-medication. Some of the first studies of the abuse of prescription drugs suggested that health care professionals steal and use prescription drugs primarily for recreational purposes, exacerbated by their nearly unlimited access to prescription medications and their belief in their invincibility to drug addiction. However, the momentum has turned away from recreational-abuse explanations toward a less judgmental model. Most scholars and practitioners alike have come to assume that the vast majority of health care professionals steal and use prescription drugs principally for therapeutic reasons. In the case of pharmacists, factors such as work-related stress, heightened access to drugs, and the physical and emotional demands of pharmacy practice are thought to be the impetus for early forays into illegal drug use. Driven by pitfalls of drug tolerance, levels of use escalate and the pharmacists draw on their vast clinical knowledge as a means of regulating their use and convincing themselves that they are in control of their ever-growing drug habits.

The principal objective of this research was to ascertain which of these two competing models – recreational or therapeutic – is the most accurate in explaining the illicit prescription drug use careers of practicing pharmacists. Despite the pervasiveness of both explanations in the literature, we quickly recognized that perhaps neither was entirely correct.

In fact, we ultimately concluded that both models were partially accurate. As will be seen, one can readily identify two different paths of entry to drug use. However, as the theft and use of drugs give way to drug abuse and eventually uncontrollable addiction, these two deviant career trajectories converge, so that the motivational and behavioral patterns of mature deviants appear very much the same.

[...]

Methodology

Procedure

We used structured personal interviews to examine the individual life histories of a group of pharmacists, all of whom had previously been in treatment and were now in recovery for the past illicit abuse of prescription drugs. Individuals were accessed through a "snowball" sampling technique. Each interview was conducted using a loosely structured guide. The guide was divided into 13 "topical areas" that allowed the interviewer to probe various aspects of the individual's pharmacy career, deviant drug use, and the intertwined nature of these two conflicting worlds. Interviews generally lasted 90–120 minutes.

[...]

The respondents were recruited with the active participation of three leaders in the state-level impaired pharmacists' recovery movement. A total of 50 interviews were completed in 1995 during four data collection trips to pharmacy conferences and recovery networks. Interviews were conducted in a wide variety of physical locations, such as hotel rooms, dormitory rooms, public parks, restaurants, respondents' homes, and private rooms in the respondents' workplaces. Each interview involved only two people, the first author and the pharmacist being interviewed. The snowball selection process allowed us to gain access to drug-impaired pharmacists in 24 states.

[...]

Our reliance on drug recovery networks produced a potential selection bias in our sample. Namely, we pursued access only to those pharmacists who had been apprehended or came forward for what they considered to be their serious drug problems. This recruitment strategy limited our access to occasional drug-using pharmacists, those who go undetected, or those who are particularly adept in their wrongdoings. The inclusion of these other varieties of drug-using pharmacists may well have altered the nature and dynamics of the data and conceptual frameworks that are detailed here.

The respondents

The pharmacists who were interviewed represented a variety of social and demographic backgrounds. For example, 78 percent were men and 22 percent were women. Of the 50, 48 were white, 1 was Hispanic, and 1 was African American. Furthermore, the respondents varied widely in age: 8 percent were 30 or younger, 38 percent were in their 30s, 36 percent were in their 40s, 12 percent were in their 50s, and 6 percent were over age 60.

[...]

Two Paths of Entry into a Deviant Career

Given our specific interest in the various career aspects of deviant behavior, a significant portion of each interview was focused on the pharmacist's entry into illicit drug use. An examination of the transcripts of the interviews quickly revealed that their initial deviant drug use took two distinct forms. One group (23 pharmacists) – classified as recreational abusers – began using prescription drugs recreationally to "get high." These individuals usually had a history of "street" drug use before they began the formal pharmacy education process. The other group (27 pharmacists) – classified as therapeutic self-medicators – described how they began using prescription drugs much later for therapeutic purposes when they were confronted with some physical malady while on the job.

Recreational abusers

One of the defining characteristics of recreational abusers is that they all began experimenting with street drugs, such as marijuana, cocaine, alcohol, and various psychedelics, while in high school and during their early college years. The motivation behind this use was

simple: they were adventurous and wanted to experience the euphoric, mind-altering effects that the drugs offered. Because of procurement problems, these individuals reported that they engaged in little, if any, prescription drug use before entering pharmacy school.

Initial use of prescription drugs

For the recreational abusers, the onset of their careers in the illicit use of prescription drugs usually began shortly after they entered pharmacy training. These respondents were quick to point to the recreational motivations behind their early prescription drug use. As one 42-year-old male pharmacist stated, "I just wanted the effect; I really just wanted the effect. I know what alcohol is. But what if you take a Quaalude and drink with it? What happens then?" [...].

Trends in the data indicate that pharmacy school provided these individuals with the requisite access to prescription drugs. The respondents recalled how they exploited their newly found access to prescription drugs in an effort to expand or surpass the euphoric effects that they received from weaker street drugs. For example, a 27-year-old male pharmacist said:

> It was a blast. It was fun. ... It was experimentation. We smoked a little pot. And then in the "model pharmacy" [a training facility in college], there was stuff [prescription drugs] all over the place. "Hey this is nice ... that is pretty nice." If it was a controlled substance, then I tried it. I had my favorites, but when that supply was exhausted, I'd move on to something else. I was a "garbage head!"[1] It was the euphoria. ... I used to watch Cheech and Chong [movies]. That's what it was like. I wasn't enslaved by them, [or so I thought]. They made the world go round.

Pharmacy as a drug-access career choice

It is important to note that the majority of the recreational abusers claimed that they specifically chose a career in pharmacy because it would offer them an opportunity to expand their drug-use behaviors. For example, a 37-year-old male pharmacist said: "That's one of main reasons I went to pharmacy school because I'd have access to medications if I needed them." Further evidence of this reasoning can be seen in the comments of a 41-year-old male pharmacist:

A lot of my friends after high school said, "Oh great, you're going into pharmacy school. You can wake up on uppers and go to bed on downers," all that stuff. At first, [I said] no. The first time I ever [used prescription drugs] I thought, "No, that's not why I'm doing it [enrolling in pharmacy school]. No, I'm doing it for the noble reasons." But then after a while I thought, "well, maybe they had a point there after all." I [had to] change my major. So I [based my choice] on nothing more than, "Well, it looks like fun and gee, all the pharmacy majors had drugs." The [pharmacy students] that I knew ... every weekend when they came back from home, they would unpack their bags and bags of pills would roll out. I thought, "Whoa, I got to figure out how to do this." [I would ask:] "How much did you pay for this?" [They would respond:] "I haven't paid a thing, I just stole them. Stealing is OK. I get shit wages, so I got to make it up somehow. So we just steal the shit." Well, I thought, "This is it; I want to be a pharmacist." So I went into pharmacy school.

[...]

Learning by experimentation

Once in pharmacy school, the recreational abusers consistently described how they adopted an applied approach to their studies. For example, if they read about a particularly interesting type of drug in pharmacy school, they often would indicate that they wanted to try it. Or if they were clerking or interning in a pharmacy that offered access to prescription medicines, they would describe how they stole drugs just to try them. If a teacher or employer told them about the unusual effects of a new drug, they would state that this piqued their interest. This pattern of application-oriented learning is exemplified in the comments of a 49-year-old male pharmacist:

> I began using [prescription drugs] to give myself the whole realm of healing experience ... to control my body, to control the ups and the downs. ... I thought I could chemically feel, do, and think whatever I wanted to if I learned enough about these drugs and used them. Actually, I sat in classes with a couple of classmates where they would be going through a group of drugs, like, say, a certain class of muscle relaxants, skeletal muscle relaxants, and they would talk about the mechanism of pharmacology and then they would start mentioning different side effects, like drowsiness, sedation, and some

patients report euphoria, and at a high enough dose hallucinations and everything. Well, hell, that got highlighted in yellow. And then that night, one of us would take some [from the pharmacy], and then we would meet in a bar at 10:00 or in somebody's house and we would do it together.

This quote is an example of how recreational abusers often superimposed an educational motive onto their progressive experimentation with prescription drugs in pharmacy school. The respondents explained that they wanted to experience the effects of the drugs that they read about in their pharmacy textbooks. They adeptly incorporated their scientific training and professional socialization in such a way that allowed them to excuse and redefine their recreational drug use. Many went as far as to convince themselves that their experimental drug use was actually beneficial to their future patients. This adaptation strategy is illustrated in the comments of a 59-year-old male recreational abuser:

> In a lot of ways, [college drug use] was pretty scientific. [I was] seeing how these things affected me in certain situations ... [just] testing the waters. I thought that I'll be able to counsel my patients better the more I know about the side effects of these drugs. "I'll be my own rat. I'll be my own lab rat. I can tell [patients] about the shakes and chills and the scratchy groin and your skin sloughing off. I can tell you all about that stuff."

Socially acceptable use of recreational drugs in pharmacy school

The recreational abusers unanimously agreed that there was no shortage of socially acceptable experimental drug use while in pharmacy school (both alcohol and street drugs). Moreover, all 23 claimed that it was not uncommon for students to use amphetamines to get through all-night study sessions once or twice each semester. Many of the recreational abusers recalled that they were not satisfied with this type of controlled drug use. They were more interested in expanding their usage. One 48-year-old male pharmacist described the makeup of his pharmacy school cohort as follows:

> There were a third of the pharmacy students in school because Mom and Dad or Grandfather or Uncle Bill

were pharmacists. They looked up to them and wanted to be one [too]. A [second] third had been in the [Vietnam] war. They were a pharmacy tech in the war or had worked in a pharmacy. They had the experiential effect of what pharmacy is and found a love for it or a desire to want it. Then you had the other third ... and we were just drug addicts. We didn't know what the practice was all about, but we did know that we got letters after our names, guaranteed income if we didn't lose our letters. And we had access to anything [prescription drugs] we needed.

Many of the recreational abusers claimed that they specifically sought out fellow pharmacy students who were willing to use prescription drugs. The most common locus of these peer associations was pharmacy-specific fraternities. The respondents said that there was usually ample drug use going on in these organizations to allow them the opportunity to search cautiously for and identify other drug users. Once they were connected with other drug users, the prescription drug use of all involved parties increased. This type of small-group drug use gave them access to an expanded variety of drugs, a broader pharmacological knowledge base, and even larger quantities of drugs. However, numerous respondents clearly stated that these drug-based associations were tenuous and temporary in nature. Over time, as the intensity of their drug use increased, the recreational abusers described how they became more reclusive and guarded and selective in their relationships, fearing that their heightened use of prescription drugs would come to be defined as a problem by their fellow pharmacy students. One 43-year-old male pharmacist said:

> You get the sense pretty quickly that you are operating [using] on a different level. Those of us [who] were busily stealing [prescription drugs] from our internship sites began to tighten our social circle. We might party a little bit with the others, but when it came to heavy use, we kept it hush, hush.

Unlike other pharmacy students who were genuinely experimenting with drugs on a short-term basis, these recreational abusers observed that there was an added intensity associated with their own use of prescription drugs. Although most of these recreational abusers

entered pharmacy school with some prior experiences in the recreational use of street drugs, these experiences were generally not extensive. It was not until they got into pharmacy school that they began to develop more pronounced street and prescription drug use-habits. A 38-year-old female pharmacist had this to say about her transition to increased usage:

> I went off to pharmacy school. That was a three-year program. I had tried a few things [before that], but I would back off because it was shaming for me not to get straight As. The descent to hell started when I got to pharmacy school. There were just so many things [prescription drugs] available and so many things that I thought I just had to try. It might be a different high; it might be a different feeling – anything to alter the way that I just felt. I was pretty much using on a daily basis by the time I got to my last year.

Pharmacy practice yields even more access and use of drugs

Pharmacy school was just the beginning of the steep career trajectory for the recreational abusers. School was followed by pharmacy practice, which offered even greater access to prescription medicines. Daily work experiences meant exposure to more new drugs. Introduction to a newly developed compound was followed by some quick research on the effects of the drug and then almost immediate experimentation, as is illustrated by a 37-year-old male pharmacist's description of his early work experience:

> I remember I came down here and applied for a job .... in May of '82. I remember even then, I went out to the satellite [pharmacy facility] and I heard about this one drug, Placidil. As soon as I got to the interview, they were showing me around. A friend took me around ... and I saw Placidil on the shelf there. ... I took a chance, kind of wandering around and I went back and took some off the shelf. So even then, I was [stealing and misusing]. You know, why would you do that in the middle of interviewing for a job? I took it even then. I just jumped at the chance.

Once the recreational abusers got into their permanent practice setting, most described how they quickly realized that they had free reign over the pharmacy stock. At first, they relied on other, more experienced pharmacists for guidance in gaining access to (or using) newly available prescription drugs. Later, their nearly unrestricted access meant that they could try any drugs that they pleased. And most did. More important, increased access allowed the pharmacists-in-training to secretly use the drugs that they most liked. No longer did they have to worry about others looking over their shoulders. Thus, it is not surprising that the level of their drug use usually skyrocketed shortly after they entered pharmacy practice. This trend is demonstrated in the comments of a 41-year-old male pharmacist:

> By the time I got to pharmacy school in 1971, I was smoking dope [marijuana] probably every day or every other day, and drinking with the same frequency, but not to the point of passing out. ... Then in 1971, that was also the year that I discovered barbs [barbiturates]. I had never had barbs up until I got to pharmacy school. So it was like '75 or '76 [when I got out of pharmacy school], I was using heavy Seconals and Quaaludes and Ambutols [all barbiturates]. I withdrew, and it [the heavy abuse] just took off.

At the start, the recreational abusers' drug use was openly displayed and took on an air of excitement, much like others' experimentation with street or prescription drugs. However, as it intensified over time, the majority described how they slowly shielded their use from others. They thought it important to appear as though they still had the situation under control. As physical tolerance and psychological dependence progressed, these individuals began to lose control. Virtually all the recreational abusers eventually developed severe prescription drug–use habits, using large quantities and sometimes even multiple types of drugs, and their prescription drug use careers were usually marked by a steep downward spiral. This trend was clearly evidenced in the time line that each respondent drew. What started out as manageable social experimentation with drugs persistently progressed to increasingly more secretive drug abuse. In almost all the cases, it took several years for the drug use to reach its peak addictive state. The intense physical and psychological effects of the drug use meant that the recreational abusers' criminal-deviant careers were punctuated by a "low bottom." Commonly identified signs of "bottoming out"

included life-threatening health problems, repeated dismissal from work, having actions taken against their pharmacy licenses, habitual lying, extensive cover-ups, divorce, and suicide attempts. By all accounts, these recreational abusers' personal and professional lives suffered heavily from the drug abuse. In the end, most were reclusive and paranoid – what started out as collective experimentation ended in a painful existence of solitary addiction.

Therapeutic self-medicators

The criminal-deviant career paths of the 27 (54 percent) therapeutic self-medicators fit a different substantive theme. One of the defining characteristics of this group was that they had little or no experience with street or prescription drugs before they entered pharmacy school. In fact, many of these individuals did not even use alcohol. What little drug involvement they did report was usually occasional experimentation with marijuana. If they had ever used prescription drugs, they had done so legitimately under the supervision of a physician. Members of this group did not begin their illicit use of prescription drugs until they were well into their formal pharmacy careers.

The onset of the therapeutic self-medicators' drug use was invariably attributed to a difficult life situation, accident, medical condition, or occupationally related pain. When faced with such problems, these pharmacists turned to familiar prescription medicines for immediate relief. Rather than a recreational, hedonistic, or pleasure motivation, they had simply decided to use readily available prescription drugs to treat their own medical maladies.

Therapeutic motives for using prescription drugs

The therapeutic self-medicators unanimously insisted that their drug use was never recreational – that they never used drugs just for the euphoric effects. Instead, their drug use was focused on specific therapeutic goals. This trend is illustrated in the comments of a 33-year-old male pharmacist:

> There was no recreation involved. I just wanted to press a button and be able to sleep during the day. I was really having a tough time with this sleeping during the day. I would say by the end of that week I was already on the road [to dependence]. The race had started.

Other pharmacists stated that they began using drugs as a way of treating insomnia, physical trauma (e.g., injury from a car accident, a sports injury, or a broken bone), or some chronic occupationally induced health problem (e.g., arthritis, migraine headaches, leg cramps, or back pain).

It is important to point out that during the earliest stages of their drug use, these individuals appeared to be "model pharmacists." Most claimed to have excelled in pharmacy school and continued to be successful after they entered full-time pharmacy practice. Personal appraisals, as well as annual supervisory evaluations, routinely described these individuals as hardworking and knowledgeable professionals.

Since they were usually treating the physical pain that resulted from the rigors of pharmacy work, all the therapeutic self-medicators described how their early use of prescription drugs began under seemingly innocent, even honorable, circumstances. Instead of taking time off from work to see a physician, they chose simply to self-medicate their own ailments. Many felt that they could not afford to take the time off to get a prescription from physicians who often knew less about the medications than they did. A 50-year-old male pharmacist described this situation as follows:

> When I got to [a job at a major pharmacy chain], the pace there was stressful. We were filling 300 to 400 scripts a day with minimal support staff and working 12- to 13-hour days. The physical part bothered me a lot. My feet and my back hurt. So, I just kept medicating myself until it got to the point where I was up to six to eight capsules of Fiorinol-3 [a narcotic analgesic] a day.

Peer introductions

Without exception, the therapeutic self-medicators described how there was always a solitary, secretive dimension to their drug use. Although they usually kept their drug use to themselves, many claimed that their initial drug use was shaped by their interactions with coworkers. That is, they got the idea to begin self-medicating from watching a coworker do or merely followed the suggestion of a concerned senior pharmacist who was helping them remedy a physical malady, such as a hangover, anxiety, or physical pain. For example, a 38-year-old male pharmacist described

an incident that occurred soon after he was introduced to his hospital pharmacy supervisor:

> I remember saying one time that I had a headache. [He said] "Go take some Tylenol-with-Codeine elixir [narcotic analgesic]." I would never have done that on my own. He was my supervisor at the time, and I said to myself, "If you think I should?" He said, "That's what I should do." I guess that started the ball rolling a little bit mentally.

Members of the therapeutic self-medicator group took notice of the drug-related behaviors and suggestions of their peers but never acted upon them in the company of others. Instead, they maintained a public front of condemning the illicit use of prescription drugs but quietly following through on the suggestive behaviors in private.

Perceived benefits of self-medication

Whereas the recreational abusers used drugs to get high, the therapeutic self-medicators saw the drug use as a means to a different end. Even as their drug use intensified, they were able to convince themselves that the drugs were actually having a positive effect on their work performance. This belief was not altogether inaccurate, since they began using the drugs to remedy health problems that were detracting from their work efficiency.

Some therapeutic self-medicators looked to their notion of professional obligation to justify their illegal drug use. For example, in describing his daily use of Talwin, a Schedule II narcotic analgesic, a 43-year-old male pharmacist maintained: "I thought I could work better. I thought I could talk better with the nurses and patients. I thought I could socialize better with it."

A slippery slope

At first, these pharmacists reported that their secretive and occasional therapeutic self-medication seemed to work well. The drugs remedied their problems (e.g., pain or insomnia) and thus allowed them to return to normal functioning. However, over time, they invariably began to develop a tolerance for the drugs and thus had to take larger quantities to achieve the same level of relief. In the end, each had to face the fact that the regular use of a seemingly harmless therapeutic medicine had resulted in a serious and addictive drug habit. The following comments of a 50-year-old male pharmacist offer a good overview of the life history of a therapeutic self-medicator:

> Well, I didn't have a big problem with that [early occasional self-medication behavior]. I wasn't taking that much. It was very much medicinal use. It was not an everyday thing. It really was used at that point for physical pain. But that's when I started tampering with other things and started trying other things. I would have trouble sleeping, so I would think, "You know, let's see what the Dalmane [benzodiazepine] is like?" When I was having weight problems …. "Let's give this Tenuate [amphetamine] a try." And I just started going down the line treating the things that I wanted to treat. And none of it got out of hand. It wasn't until I came down here [to Texas] … that things really started to go wild.

It generally took between 5 and 10 years for these pharmacists to progress to the later stages of drug abuse. Such a time frame suggests that the therapeutic self-medicators were able to prevent their drug abuse from interfering with their personal or professional lives for a considerable time. For example, consider the exchange that occurred between the interviewer (I) and a 42-year-old male pharmacist (P):

> P: Every time I [drank] even two martinis I [would] throw up. I [would] get diarrhea and [would be] … sick. So I took some Zantac [antacid]. I tried to cure my hangovers a little bit.
>
> I: These were just for medicinal purposes?
>
> P: Yeah, medicinal. Zantac [antacid], I mean how can that hurt? And I go to work, but I'm sick and I don't want to go in smelling like alcohol. Now I am deeply trying to just make it by. So now I begin to take pills to cure being sick so I can go to work. First, I'm taking things strictly to cure hangovers, which began happening with practically drinking nothing and it's scaring me to death…. So I start working and I start to take a few pills. I feel a little better. Now the [mood-altering] meds start to happen. I take a couple Vs [Valium, a benzodiazepine] now and then. I'm taking a few Xanax [benzodiazepine]. Next, I'm taking some Vicodin [narcotic analgesic]. It took years [for the usage pattern] to go anywhere. Then somebody comes in with drugs and says, "These are my mother-in-law's prescriptions, she passed away, she had cancer." I look at it, and it's all morphine. She says, "I don't know what to do. Will you please take it for me?" [P replies, laughing], "We'll destroy the drugs, don't worry."

With the exception of their unauthorized self-medication, most of these individuals continued to be "model pharmacists." Despite their progressive drug use, they usually continued to garner the respect and admiration of their peers and employers alike. It was not uncommon for them to be promoted to senior management positions even after they began using prescription drugs daily. The bulk of the self-medicator group experienced a slow, progressive transition from the occasional use of therapeutic drugs to a schedule of repeated daily doses. In retrospect, they attributed their increased usage to the body's tendency to develop a chemical tolerance to the medications. This situation necessitated larger and more frequent dosage units to achieve the desired therapeutic effects.

[…]

These 27 therapeutic self-medicators had entered their pharmacy careers admittedly as extremely naive about drug abuse. They were either counseled or had convinced themselves that there was no harm in the occasional therapeutic use of prescription medicines. In short, the normative and behavioral advances in their criminal and deviant behavior were largely the result of a well-intentioned exploitation of their professional position and knowledge. The justifications for their drug use were firmly entrenched in their desire to excel in their jobs and to care for their patients efficiently. The therapeutic self-medicators always used their drugs in private, carefully disguising their addiction from others. Over time, their false confidence and self-denial allowed their drug use to progress significantly into addiction. Once their façade was broken, these pharmacists awoke to the stark reality that they were now chemically dependent on one or more of the drugs that they so confidently had been "prescribing" for themselves.

Common Cognitive and Behavioral Themes

Although there were clearly two different modes of entry into drug abuse for the recreational abusers and therapeutic self-medicators, these two groups of offenders were *not* mutually exclusive categories; that is, these two categories were not completely dichotomous. Rather, we identified a number of cognitive and behavioral themes that were common to almost all the respondents, regardless of how they initially began their illicit drug abuse careers. The existence of these common themes suggests that pharmacy-specific occupational contingencies play a central role in the onset and progression of the illicit use of prescription medicines. The three most common of these cognitive and behavioral themes are discussed next.

"I'm a pharmacist, so I know what I am doing"

Intuitively, it should not be surprising that pharmacists would steal prescription medicines to treat their own physical ailments. After all, they have been exposed to years of pharmacy training that emphasized the beneficial, therapeutic potential of prescription medicines. Each pharmacist has dispensed medicines to hundreds of patients and then watched the drugs usually produce the predicted beneficial results. They have all read the literature detailing the chemical composition of drugs and studied the often-dramatic beneficial, curative effects of these chemical substances. Pharmacists, more so than any other members of the society, are keenly aware of how and why drugs work. There was strong evidence to suggest that both the therapeutic self-medicators and the recreational abusers actively used the years of pharmacological knowledge they had acquired. So, when they developed health or emotional problems, it made perfect sense to them that they should put their knowledge to work on themselves. This personal application of pharmaceutical information can be seen clearly in the comments of a 40-year-old female self-medicator:

> In 1986 I was sent to the psychologist. That was when I was forced to recognize that I had an alcohol problem. And I recognized that I had to do something. And in my brilliant analysis, I made a decision that since alcohol was a central nervous system depressant, the solution for me was to use a central nervous system stimulant. That would solve my alcohol problem. So I chose the best stimulant that I had access to, and that was [pharmaceutical grade] cocaine. I started using cocaine in 1986. I never thought that it would progress. I never thought it was going to get worse. I thought, "I'm just going to use it occasionally."

Similar trends were observed among the recreational abusers, but their applied use of drugs was based on more recreational motives.

Virtually all the therapeutic self-medicators and the recreational abusers described how they became masters of quickly diagnosing their own ailments or emotional needs and then identifying the appropriate pharmacological agent that would remedy the problem. Moreover, as professionals, they were confident that they would be able to limit or self-regulate their drug intake so they would never become addicted. All the respondents drew on their social status as pharmacists to convince themselves that their drug use would not progress into dependence. As a 40-year-old female self-medicator put it, "I'm a pharmacist; I know what I am doing." The respondents all agreed that a well-trained, professional pharmacist could not possibly fall prey to drug addiction. They recalled being even more adamant in their view that they were immune from such problems, believing that only stupid, naive people became addicted to drugs. [...]

No cautionary tales or warnings

Remarkably, the vast majority of both the recreational abusers and therapeutic self-medicators claimed that they had never been warned about the dangers of drug addiction. Rather, they insisted that their formal training had stressed only the beneficial side of prescription medicines. For example, a 48-year-old male recreational abuser stated:

> I never had anybody come right out and tell me that [prescription drug abuse] was probably unethical and illegal because they assumed that we knew that. But nobody ever said this is something that is not done.

Left without precise ethical guidance on the issue, some pharmacists assumed that their drug use was acceptable behavior. In explaining this point of view, a 39-year-old female self-medicator stated:

> It's [self-medication] ...just part of it [the pharmacy job]. It's just accepted because we know so much. I'm sure it's the same way when the doctors do it. It wasn't a big stretch to start [thinking], "You know, I got a headache here; maybe I should try one of these Percocets [narcotic analgesic]?"

In fact, many pharmacists spoke about their theft of prescription drugs as if the drugs were a fringe benefit that went along with the job. Much like a butcher who eats the best cuts of meat or a car dealer who drives a brand-new automobile, pharmacists always have access to free prescription drugs. This theme is illustrated in the comments of a 45-year-old, male pharmacist:

> Why take plain Aspirin or plain Tylenol when you've got this [Percocet – a narcotic analgesic]? It works better … [so] you don't even have to struggle with it. I really believed that I had license to do that … as a pharmacist. I mean with all that stuff sitting there, you know. Oh, my back was just killing me during that period … and this narcotic pain reliever [was] sitting right there. I thought, "Why should [I] suffer through back pain when I have this bottle of narcotics sitting here?"

Out-of-control addiction

The aforementioned themes involve cognitive dimensions of the pharmacists' drug abuse in that they speak to common motivational and justification themes that were present in all the interviews. Perhaps more important is the fact that there was a common behavioral characteristic that all 50 pharmacists shared. In every case, the occasional abuse of prescription drugs eventually gave way to an advanced addictive state that was marked by an enormous intake of drugs, unmistakable habituation, and the constant threat of physical withdrawal. Both the recreational abusers and therapeutic self-medicators routinely reported daily use levels exceeding 50–100 times the recommended daily dosage. One pharmacist noted that his drug-use regimen progressed to 150 Percocets [a strong narcotic analgesic] per day, another reported injecting up to 200 mg of morphine each day, and still another described a daily use pattern that, among other things, included 5 grams of cocaine.

[…]

The advanced stages of addiction almost always produced traumatic physical and psychological events, as in the following comments by a 39-year-old male pharmacist:

I was out of control for four years. I was just lucky that I never got caught. I don't know how I didn't get caught. I fell asleep twice coming home on Interstate 95. I fell asleep at the wheel doing 70 once, and then I scraped up the side of the car and blew out the tires. I also tried to kill myself with a shotgun. She [my wife] was going to leave me. My world was falling apart, but I couldn't do anything about it. I didn't know what to do.

These out-of-control drug-use patterns, along with the realization of their chemical dependence, left the pharmacists in a problematic mental state. It was at this point that all the respondents recalled coming to grips with their addiction. This realization was accompanied by a shift in the way they thought about their drug use. They no longer denied the situation by drawing on recreational or therapeutic explanations. Instead, they finally admitted the dire nature of their situation and became more and more reclusive. In short, all the respondents grew to realize that they had a drug problem, turning to fear and ignorance to foster the final weeks or months of their addiction.

[…]

Conclusions

[…]

Pharmacists are a highly sought-after commodity in this country. At the same time that we see a new hospital or retail pharmacy popping up on virtually every street corner, there is a severe shortage of licensed pharmacists. In light of this supply-and-demand squeeze, employers have been forced to be less selective about who they hire. Our conversations with corporate executives of major retail drug chains verify that "zero tolerance" policies have been relaxed, so that some companies now hire pharmacists who are known to have had past drug abuse problems. Increased surveillance and social control will undoubtedly be a by-product of these liberal personnel decisions, and security personnel must be sensitive to the ever-changing nature of these individuals' criminal careers and thus devise intervention and surveillance programs that are duly flexible.

Nationwide data collection efforts have established that the levels of the illicit use of prescription drugs are on the rise in the United States. Of particular concern are the disturbing increases among young people. With increasing regularity, adolescents are turning away from traditional street drugs and coming to rely more heavily on prescription drugs (i.e., narcotics, such as OxyContin, or stimulants, such as Ritalin or Meridia) to satisfy their urge to use drugs recreationally. This situation has produced a coordinated call to arms in which governmental agencies, such as the National Institute on Drug Abuse (NIDA), have begun to direct research dollars toward understanding the trends. Simultaneously, law enforcement agencies from the Drug Enforcement Administration (DEA) to local sheriffs' departments have begun to step up their interdiction efforts. Preliminary findings suggest that unethical or incompetent pharmacists play an important role in the proliferation of these drugs in the hands of street users. Moreover, in 2001, the flagship trade journal of the pharmacy industry published several commentaries on the topic of prescription drug abuse among pharmacists. Pressure continues to mount at the state and local levels to address prescription-dispensing errors that endanger patients. These trends suggest that it is only a matter of time until regulatory, private security, and criminal justice agents launch a concerted effort to be more stringent in regulating the pharmacy profession. When such an initiative gets under way, it is critical that the powers that be direct considerable attention toward the types of deviant pharmacists who were interviewed in this study. In doing so, it is critical that they consider: (1) the evolving nature of the drug abuse that affects some pharmacists, (2) whether the deviant drug-use careers documented in this article coincide with or exacerbate additional forms of professional wrongdoing, and (3) whether the career trajectories outlined here are applicable on a larger scale.

Note

1   The term *garbagehead* is commonly used among recovering drug-impaired pharmacists to refer to a polydrug user who is willing to experiment aggressively with any mind-altering substances that he or she can gain access to.

Questions

1   How does the recreational use of pharmaceutical drugs compare and contrast with other forms of illicit and/or licit drug use? What other professions might people pursue to simply have access to a steady drug supply? Do we see this occurrence in the illegal drug world?

2   Is the abuse of pharmaceutical drugs in the pharmacy setting dependent on social class? Why or why not? Do you think addicted pharmacists are treated similar to other addicts in our society? With which group of "drugged druggists" might people have more sympathy with? Why?

3   How did the pharmacists' expert knowledge and/or education contribute to their abuse of pharmaceutical drugs? Is such a knowledge base or educational opportunity available to illegal drug users? Would a different educational approach for pharmacists reduce the potential for abuse?

Why Rich Kids Sell Street Drugs
Wankstaz, Wannabes, and Capitalists in Training

A. Rafik Mohamed and Erik D. Fritsvold

We finish up the social class section by looking at the children of the rich and privileged, attending a high status and expensive private college but dealing drugs. Rafik Mohamed and Erik Fritsvold's portrait of rich kids selling street drugs focuses on the motivations and consequences of their involvement in the criminal world of drug dealing. At the top of the societal ladder, how do their motivations for entry into this lifestyle compare with less fortunate groups? Do they experience similar consequences? To what extent are they tied into the webs of their families, communities, and ethnic (White) subculture, compared to other groups of drug users? How can you compare and contrast the resources upon which they can draw with those of less fortunate populations? How do you feel about the level of social inequality between this group and some of the others we have seen here? Are they righteous dopefiends? To what extent do they defend the circumstances that afford them these benefits? Do their rationalizations seem more credible to you than those of the homeless street junkies or other groups? Why or why not?

How would you imagine the career trajectory of these college drug users and dealers compares to the Mexican-American gang users and dealers? To the poor, ghetto Blacks, the American Indians, or the Asian-Pacific women?

Finally, how would you compare the influence of race/ethnicity versus class on the lives of drug users more generally? Can these factors be separated? How or how not? What role does pharmacology play in the way these drug users interact with their drugs compared to other factors?

Criminology, as a social science, was built around attempts to explain the origins of criminal and deviant behavior. Based upon historic suppositions within the discipline, the discourse of US drug policy has been guided by the overwhelming assumption that drug dealers are motivated predominantly by profit. [...]

One of the most obvious, yet provocative, questions that guided this research was *why* – specifically, why do affluent college students, poised to embrace a series of legitimate avenues for upward mobility and success, choose to become drug dealers? With seemingly so much to lose, haphazardly delving into criminality

Drugs and the American Dream: An Anthology, First Edition. Edited by Patricia A. Adler, Peter Adler, and Patrick K. O'Brien.
© 2012 John Wiley & Sons, Inc. Published 2012 by John Wiley & Sons, Inc.

appears at the very least counterintuitive. Ultimately, what we found was that these affluent drug dealers contradict some longstanding criminological assumptions about crime, the public policy dialogue concerning the war on drugs, and the archetypical portrayal of drug dealers and users.

The approximately fifty subjects at the center of this study were all college students at various Southern California colleges and universities, but most attended one particular private university that served as the focal point of this research. With two exceptions, each of the dealers in our network was active (they had not yet walked away from drug dealing) when we were acquainted with them. During the primary period of interviews and observation, these subjects ranged in age from eighteen to twenty-four and all but three of the dealers we formally interviewed were men. We do not think that this reflects a selection bias; rather it reflects a gender imbalance among college students who choose to sell drugs. Regarding other demographic data, with the exception of two Hispanics, one African American, one Black/Caucasian person, one Persian/Caucasian-American, and one Asian/Caucasian person, all of the dealers in our network were Caucasian. Further, among the relatively few minorities listed above, most either white-identified and/or their nonwhite ethnic attributes were imperceptible. As was the case with gender, we did not choose to interview principally white dealers. We simply did not encounter many who were nonwhite. As is the case with most of the private universities in Southern California, the vast majority of the student body at our study's hub university is white.

After several years of observation and interviews with the dealers who formed this affluent college drug network, we were able to identify six primary motivations that we feel in many ways explain why affluent college students make the seemingly irrational choice to participate in drug crime. These material and nonmaterial motivations proved valuable enough to entice these dealers to risk the status, comfort, and privilege they already enjoyed and could count on [...] enjoying in the future provided they followed the socially proscribed pathway to success that accompanied their socioeconomic status. [...] [O]ur dealers were apparently motivated by a combination of tangible and identity-based rewards and, at different times and in response to varying

social circumstances, their reasons for selling drugs often drifted among the various motives.

Motive #1: Underwrite Costs of Personal Drug Use

While the affluent drug dealers in this study did not constitute an entirely homogeneous group, the vast majority of them consumed a considerable amount of marijuana, a finding that was as anticipatable as it was devastatingly obvious from an even cursory glance around their respective dwellings. [...] The majority of these dealers not only consumed large quantities of marijuana, but pot use was a routinized part of their daily existence and often coexisted with social, professional, and scholastic commitments. Indeed, marijuana was not reserved for weekend bingeing or celebratory occasions; rather, a regimen of marijuana use was seemingly a staple of daily life.

At the time of his first interview with us, Beefy was a twenty-year-old, white, middle-class college student with a 3.1 grade point average, and a campus drug dealer of several years. His statements exemplify the omnipresent role of marijuana in the everyday lives of many of these affluent drug dealers.

> [INTERVIEWER]: *Do you smoke everyday?*
> BEEFY: Yeah. I smoke before work. If I work all day I will come home on my lunch break and smoke. I smoke before most classes. Not usually tests, but sometimes. Yeah [laughs].
> [INTERVIEWER]: *What was your job?*
> BEEFY: I worked at Bank of America as a teller, still do.

Throughout this study, we found that many of these avid pot smokers were initially motivated to venture into drug dealing, in significant part, as a mechanism to underwrite the costs of their personal drug use. In fact, this was by far the most common explanation offered by dealers to explain why they initially became involved with drug dealing and the underground economy. Even the smaller-scale dealers that we spoke with were able to avoid paying "retail prices" for their own marijuana or made enough of a profit to offset the costs of their personal drug habit, a trade practice commonly dubbed "selling for head smoke." In fact, per their calculations, by cutting away three-eighths of an ounce for their personal use and putting the remaining five-eighths up for sale, heavy smokers turned roommate-dealers C-Money and The Rat only spent about $30 of their own money for every ounce of marijuana they purchased. In all, these affluent drug dealers seem to exemplify the "user–dealer" model that pervades the criminological literature. [...]

Cecilia, a biology student and native to our network's California hub city, eventually became the largest female dealer in our sample. Evidently, her initial foray into drug sales was a somewhat organic evolution and not a distinct, conscious decision. As an area native and veteran marijuana user, her experience and connections in the underground economy were an asset within the college community, an asset that helped her offset the costs of her personal drug use.

> [INTERVIEWER]: *What motivated you to get involved in the first place?*
> CECILIA: Um, what motivated me? Not having to buy it [pot] myself ultimately ... I had enough people calling and troubling me anyway when I was in college because they knew I smoked so they were certain I must know where to get some. And it ended up starting out as an "everybody pitch in altogether" movement. You know, it changed from that because it is not always convenient, so I will just front it for them. And so then you have your four or five friends that you are always sort of servicing, and then before you know it you are getting larger and larger sums to service more and more of your friends. It's not something that you sit ... or at least not something where I sat down and said "hmmm, I think I'll do this." You know, it just sort of started out and it was you know ... you were sort of rewarded by again not having to pay for it yourself. And that allowed you to be more generous with your friends.

In addition, Cecilia expressed that the expansion of her business was further facilitated by the increasingly large demands of her friends. These friends were not only looking to Cecilia to acquire quality marijuana, but to acquire quality marijuana within the familiarity and relative safety of the closed market "college umbrella."

[...]

Motive #2: Underwrite Other Incidental and Entertainment Expenses

The criminological literature archives a plethora of accounts of individuals reluctantly venturing into drug sales and other criminal behaviors out of necessity, social-structural marginality, and the scarcity of legitimate means for upward mobility. In stark contrast to this body of literature and most studies of drug dealing, the bulk of the dealers in this study had their living and scholastic expenses covered by their parents, and their college-related expenses were also sometimes supplemented by academic scholarships and other financial aid. In addition, many dealers had disposable income from sporadic part-time jobs and allowances and credit cards provided by their parents. Therefore, in all cases, our network's dealers were not strapped for cash or otherwise pushed into drug sales out of any kind of economic hardship or necessity.

For many dealers in the sample, beyond covering the costs of their personal drug use, drug sales became a mechanism to underwrite the other incidental and entertainment expenses typically associated with the college lifestyle. [...] Cecilia explained that her profits, while relatively modest, helped to underwrite her incidental and entertainment expenses and those of her roommates.

> [INTERVIEWER]: *What did you spend your profits on?*
> CECILIA: Profit? There wasn't a lot of profit for me because I was keeping up with the habits of my roommates at the time mostly. So I think that was the profit, was that everyone in the house got to not pay and enjoy you know that extra spending money for whatever that was worth. Um, any amount of extra money that I did make if there was any ... which wouldn't be a lot ... certainly was spent on holidays and small trips ... just generally like spending money ... oh I need twenty bucks to go out to have a happy hour drink and skim off the top kinda thing you didn't typically notice. I never really felt like I had a large sum of money and went and spent a large sum of money on anything.

[...] [T]rue to his form and in support of the idea that many of our network's dealers chose to sell drugs as a means to underwrite entertainment and other incidental expenses, an interview with LaCoste offered the following explanation (of many that he either gave or displayed) for his choice to become a student drug dealer.

> [INTERVIEWER]: *Do you ever save any of the money [that you make selling drugs]?*
> LACOSTE: Hell no! Hell no, I blow that shit! Strip clubs and fucking gambling, throwing money around [laughs] … I just get shit-faced and then I get all competitive and what not, and lose all my money.

LaCoste went on to explain that, as an eighteen year old, he also thought it necessary to spend a considerable sum of his ill-gotten profits to acquire top-of-the-line fake IDs to better facilitate his partying lifestyle. He even went so far as to spend top-dollar for a Mexican counterfeiter who specialized in making US identifications for undocumented Mexican immigrants.

> LACOSTE: I've got a couple of good ass [fake IDs]. I had one made in Mexico. That's like the best one, but I lost it when I was drunk. Ah man, it was so bomb, like police scanning, black light, hologram … it was like a real ID! I was like a citizen. I was a person in the DMV's shit! It was great. I'm such a drunk though. And I got this California one right here. [He shows us the ID.] And then I got this Texas one in the car … Those are essential for going gambling and stuff.

Motive #3: The Spirit of Capitalism

Ashcan's statements provide evidence that for some, the principal motivation to plunge into criminality was quite straightforward – disposable income. Typically, these initial profits were relatively modest, but the taste of the lifestyle they facilitated often ballooned into a gluttonous arbitrage opportunity. At the time of the study, these affluent drug dealers were disproportionately current or former business majors and some already owned and operated their own legitimate small businesses. They embodied the entrepreneurial spirit of capitalism and the corresponding centrality of the profit motive, a spirit that further motivated their venture into criminality. These well-heeled, well-trained, and rather pragmatic

capitalists often recognized the economic opportunity that becoming a drug dealer provided based on their initial sampling of the market. Early dabbling in the college drug market very quickly revealed ubiquitous demand and minimal market risks; a return on their investment was a virtual lock, and the perceptible risks of adverse social or criminal justice consequences were negligible.

[…]

Relative sensibility, tact, and a healthy dose of caution perhaps spawned by campus authorities forcing a few of his would-be peers to close up shop (again without formal law enforcement intervention) seemingly restrained the scope and financial yield of Ashcan's modest drug-dealing operation. However, many of the other dealers we encountered readily expanded their businesses upon realizing the potential for profit created by the ubiquitous demand for drugs on college campuses. Despite some substantial and profitable criminal enterprises, not a single subject in this study abandoned their legitimate pursuits entirely. However, fueled by the spirit of capitalism, many dealers nurtured their fledgling drug-dealing operations into more diverse drug-dealing enterprises. For example, LaCoste sold marijuana exclusively for only a few weeks. He quickly realized that product diversification and larger quantities of drugs would allow him to do far more than merely underwrite the costs of his own drug use and incidental social expenses. As for most of the dealers we interviewed, marijuana remained the staple of LaCoste's illegal business. However, he eventually offered a product line that also included ecstasy, hallucinogenic mushrooms, an assortment of prescription drugs, and cocaine, the real "moneymaker." According to LaCoste, aside from its markup, cocaine was so profitable because of its widespread popularity with "everybody" at the network's hub university.

> LACOSTE: Dude … [cocaine is] fifty dollars a gram. A hundred and fifty an eight ball [a quantity equivalent to an eighth of an ounce or 3.5 grams]. Ah, yeah, that's where the money's at. Pick up like a six hundred or seven hundred ounce of yey [cocaine]. Yeah, you make tons of money just 'cause it's so expensive.

According to LaCoste and the few other dealers who routinely sold both cocaine and marijuana, market dynamics artificially inflated the price – and thus profit potential – of the "white lady." Generally, in this market there were an insufficient number of drug dealers attempting to meet the massive drug-use demands of the student-user population. Beyond that, in its powder form, as LaCoste's aforementioned accounting breakdown shows, cocaine can prove cost prohibitive for many. However, given the relative affluence of the network's consumer base, powder cocaine was in relatively high demand and, perhaps because of perceived risk or distributor access factors, cocaine had even fewer suppliers than marijuana. For some, pragmatically choosing to take advantage of this market opportunity was nothing more than a simple economic calculation, a calculation that would further sharpen the teeth and claws of these emerging cubs of capitalism as they eventually graduated from the illicit college drug-dealing market to hopefully become lions in the larger world of legitimate capitalism.

Motive #4: Ego Gratification and the Pursuit of Status

When asked explicitly about their motivation to begin selling drugs, dealers almost universally offered pragmatic answers focused on financial benefits. It seemed that framing their own criminality as a rational business decision was, in part, an attempt to absolve them from self-identifying as criminals or at least to mitigate some of their seemingly irrational decision-making. The narratives offered by LaCoste, Ashcan, and Raoul D. typified the initial and explicit responses posed by many dealers that their goal in selling drugs was to offset personal drug, entertainment, and other incidental expenses. However, as the interviews progressed, elements of other implicit, less palatable justifications became apparent. We found that for many dealers ego gratification, the pursuit of status, peer recognition, and unadorned greed contributed significantly to their choice to enter and continue in the drug game.

While elements of this fourth motive were evident in interviews with nearly all of our dealers, many

seemed to deliberately talk around issues of gained status and none reveled in the social status afforded by their position as a drug dealer more than LaCoste. By self-declaration, LaCoste was "very popular" at his Midwest high school, where his wealth and family identity facilitated some degree of status. However, as an eighteen-year-old freshman in Southern California, his fashion-forward designer clothes and $50,000 SUV failed to distinguish him on a campus and in a region with a reputation for overt materialism. Consequently for LaCoste, heavy pot smoking and drug sales became a variable that he was able to manipulate in order to differentiate himself from his equally wealthy peers on campus and to quickly enhance his reputation and status. [...] With his characteristic swagger, LaCoste revealed the sense of importance and status that he derived from his reputation as a drug dealer,

> LACOSTE: If you said, where'd you get pot, where can I get pot? I'm sure my name would be mentioned at least 50 percent of the time. Just 'cause, from the minute I got here, I was like "does anybody need weed?" I was like, "Who needs weed? I got that shit ... come and get it!"

[...]

Since popular culture and advertising campaigns apparently teach young people to connect their lifestyle with illicit drug use, it seems commonsensical that young, affluent college students would derive status from immersing themselves in drug crime and otherwise flirting with the perceived dangers associated with being a drug dealer. Again, pursuing status through deviance seems particularly practical in social situations where the traditional trappings of material success are commonplace and an additional edge is needed to really stand out among one's peers.

Motive #5: Sneaky Thrills and Being a Gangsta

> RAOUL D.: I am almost as addicted to selling as I am to getting faded.

In addition to the previous tangible, material, and identity-based motivations, a critical mass of the dealers in our sample seemed motivated by the simple thrill of deviant behavior, the ecstasy of getting away with activities they knew to be criminal, and otherwise displaying the ornaments of pseudo gangstaism. [...] Specifically, the affluent, predominantly white drug dealers we interviewed and observed were, by virtue of their socioeconomic status alone, not motivated or driven into drug crime by economic necessity. Rather, the "sneaky thrills" of anti-authoritarianism and attempting to outwit formal agents of social control seemed to serve as an additional enticement into criminality. On the rare occasions when these dealers' illegal activities are detected by campus authorities or other formal agents of social control, they can rather easily mobilize the necessary symbolic and actual capital to avoid the full ire of the drug war hawks. Additionally, when it seemed socially or personally beneficial, some of these dealers would openly revel in their ability to voluntarily take risks and challenge traditional expectations.

LaCoste personifies the pseudo-gangstaism and sneaky thrills that apparently further motivated some of our dealers to immerse themselves in the drug game. He somewhat brazenly utilized both his dormitory room and SUV as the homebases for his illicit drug-dealing operation. In fact, LaCoste openly arranged a drug sale from his dorm room during one of our interviews with him. In the middle of answering a question about the quantities of marijuana he typically purchased, his cell phone rang.

LACOSTE: Hold on. Yeah, what do you want? ... Yeah, there's herb [marijuana] above the fucking refrigerator ... Yeah there is ... No there's not, it's in my car. I'm sorry, I was really drunk. Remember, we went out there and put it in there? ... But where's my car at? It's up at what? ... Do you need some? ... Send him here, I'll give him one ... What? Ah, I'll come down there ... I'll come down there in fucking twenty-five minutes, alright? Is that straight? ... Peace ... [He hangs up the phone] What else now were we talking about?

Among his many other flagrant statements of disregard for authority, LaCoste would also routinely illegally park his SUV in the loading or fire zones directly in front of his residence hall. And, per his statements, both locations would typically have stashes

of contraband sufficient to warrant his arrest. These actions seemed to suggest that he was not tremendously concerned with the campus police detecting his illegal activity, a suspicion he confirmed when asked about the danger posed by campus authorities.

LACOSTE: They can kiss my ass. They can't touch me. They can't do anything to me ... I'd rather get caught by [the campus police] than the [real] police.

We concluded that LaCoste's renegade attitude was nurtured by a belief that the status and resources of his family would ultimately mitigate any possible university or criminal justice consequences, a conclusion supported by several other off-the-cuff and flippant remarks made by LaCoste in regard to formal authority figures. Apparently, his pomposity was not totally unfounded. Indeed, discussions with several university officials revealed that the campus authorities were very much aware of LaCoste's drug-dealing endeavors. In addition, they suspected that he had perpetrated other crimes on campus, including a series of recent thefts from dormitory rooms. In the typical fashion of our hub university, however, officials tended to watch LaCoste and other prominent suspected dealers from afar, reluctant to formally confront him for fear that he would bring his parents' wrath down upon the university or that a major drug bust would bring unwanted attention to the campus. There were a couple of "meetings" with residence-life officials in which LaCoste was made aware that they felt some of his activities were suspicious. But beyond that, there was never any formal intervention on the part of university police or administrators. And, as we have already discussed, this negated any external authorities' investigation into his illegal activities as campus authorities served as the gatekeeper for outside law enforcement interests.

[...]

While, on the one hand, LaCoste's bravado and the kid gloves with which his drug and other illegal activities were handled might seem difficult to comprehend, it is important to understand them in the context of a tuition-dependent university located in a major US city that markets itself to its potential student-clients and their families as a place of safety in the broadest terms. In this light, a major drug bust is bad for business in two significant ways. First, in a competitive climate where reputation is everything, drug arrests and publicly acknowledging the existence of an on-campus flourishing drug market clearly would not do much for short-term new student recruitment. Further, if students like LaCoste who come from well-to-do families were treated by university officials like garden variety corner boys, any endowment growth or other capital development plans specific to their families would most certainly be dashed. Therefore, the prudent approach, as dictated from on-high, is to handle cases like LaCoste's as cautiously as possible. [...]

While this air of invincibility was not universally embraced by all dealers in our sample, many were motivated by the sneaky thrill of the game; apparently mimicking the renegade, thuggish images that are commonplace in popular culture, politics, and mainstream media's depictions of drug dealers. For our dealers, it apparently was desirable and socially beneficial to appear tough and for them to be able to, at least intermittently, embrace the trappings of gangstaism.

[...]

Motive #6: Warding off the Emasculating Force of Privilege

In "A New Vision of Masculinity," Cooper Thompson [1987: 63] writes, "Traditional definitions of masculinity include attributes such as independence, pride, resiliency, self-control, and physical strength. This is precisely the image of the Marlboro man and, to some extent, these are desirable attributes for boys and girls."

The expectations posed by the iconic US cowboy, an image conveying the ultimate rugged individualist, resonate in US culture. Not surprisingly, we also found that this image served as a motivating force within the network's group of affluent drug dealers. Dovetailing with sneaky thrills, embracing pseudo gangstaism and the pursuit of status, our network's dealers are also apparently motivated by a desire for independence. Like most college students, these affluent drug dealers were in a transitional phase in their lives. While they are not under the immediate supervision of their parents, most are still directly

dependent on their parents for tuition, room, board, and other expenses. On elite college campuses, with the necessities of life readily provided, they are far from the anti-authoritarian, independent US cowboy of cultural lore. Thus, drug dealing also becomes a mechanism to embrace traditional expectations of masculinity and to ward off the emasculating force of privilege.

By flamboyantly embracing the trappings of gangstaism and the often-displayed hyper-masculinity accompanying the role, our network's upper-middle-class male hustlers could use their drug-dealing activity as a means to publicly reject the perception of them as spoiled or coddled kids. Further, risk-taking behavior (although the risks were somewhat artificial) and bucking against the status quo and behavioral expectations imposed upon them helped these dealers carve out some degree of autonomy despite their lifestyle of dependence. In describing this connection between voluntary risk-taking behavior, resistance, and identity construction, Stephen Lyng [2004: 359] wrote "Criminal edgework represents a form of escape and resistance to the prevailing structures of political and economic power." These affluent drug dealers may be "crowding the edge" precisely because it helps to create a sense of individual identity that is distinct from the status of their parents. This criminal edgework may also allow these dealers to construct an identity of masculinity or ruggedness in what otherwise might be perceived as a pampered or emasculating existence. Indeed, visible and voluntary risk taking may serve the function of resisting the emasculating forces that stem from the wealth, privilege, and ascribed upper-class status that trickle down from their families. Economic self-sufficiency, or at least the demonstrated ability to make your own money, especially via the underground economy, is alluring to our network's male dealers precisely because it evokes the masculine, independent, anti-authoritarian, rugged individualism of the Marlboro Man. Recall Ashcan's statements regarding his motivation to become a drug dealer – for beer money and to avoid having to ask his parents to underwrite the cost of his parking tickets. Later in the interview, he speculates about his future as a drug dealer. Quite obviously, drug dealing facilitated his independence from his parents.

ASHCAN: Well, once I get into law school [which he ultimately did], then I might do it [sell drugs] if I need some money or something. 'Cause they do not let you work your first year of law school. So I might have to, even though my parents will probably give me money. I just don't like asking my parents for a lot of money.

While less explicit than some of the other motivations that we uncovered and outlined, we inferred that the ornamental and financial independence, or feelings thereof, produced by dealing drugs helped these dealers ward off the emasculating force of privilege.

Combinations and Permutations

As we noted at the beginning of this chapter, we do not believe that these six motivations that propelled "good kids" into drugs are mutually exclusive. On the contrary, while one or a handful of motivations might be prominent, we conclude there is no magic bullet or single dynamic that comprehensively captured why our network's dealers entered the illicit drug game. An afternoon conversation with Brice exemplified the ways these motivations intertwined in different combinations and permutations, enticing and then subsequently rewarding the dealers for their criminal behavior. Conspicuously absent in Brice's comments was any allusion to the ego gratification and pursuit of status that seemed to be powerful driving forces for some of our other dealers. Rather, it seems that he largely was motivated to become a drug dealer to underwrite the costs of his own indulgence in marijuana use, to underwrite other entertainment expenses, and by the spirit of capitalism.

BRICE: I don't know if anyone chose it as a career path you know. I mean, I mean it was something to do when you are young and allowed for a … for a … fun lifestyle. It allowed for … I would just say the lifestyle more or less ya' know … Um … And ya know, we were all in school or just out of school and primarily I mean I don't think anyone did that as their career path. I just think it was something that they were doing at that time.

[INTERVIEWER]: *Got it. Looking back on it, why do you think most people, including yourself, started selling drugs?*

BRICE: The original reason I did is simply because of the economics of it. Buy more at a [wholesale] price. And so I never could justify myself buying that much for myself, so I probably wouldn't have like the willpower or whatever … to make whatever last however long it was supposed to last until I would buy more. So what I would try to do is … when I was originally starting was try to sell ya know enough to either pay for it … or get my stuff at a … price.

[INTERVIEWER]: *What did you spend most of your profits on, looking back?*

BRICE: Well I would say the vast majority went right back in the pot. Ya know that vast majority. At a time it was profitable enough to make income off of it. Where I could say … umm … pay credit card bills, stuff like that. Monthly house bills, rent check, stuff like that. Well I would say ultimately, like life long term, because of everything that happened. Everything I ever made went right back into it.

These six interconnected motivations enticing affluent college students into the underground economy effectively debunk some prevailing popular culture and academic assumptions about deviant behavior. While financial motivations were significant within this population, it was not necessity that pushed these affluent young men and women into drug dealing. If fact, these dealers seemingly had the skill sets, social positioning, networking advantages, education, and desire to thrive in the larger legitimate economy. Their financial motivation was more about indulgence than necessity, more about convenience than desperation. This is a striking finding given one of the prevailing assumptions about the origins of criminal behavior and the policing of drug crime, specifically that acquisitive crimes are the byproduct of social-structural disadvantage and exclusion from the mainstream, legitimate economy. Moreover, the combination of material and identity-based motivations within this population further complicates rational-choice theories of crime and the accompanying deterrence-based models for criminal justice policy. Within this group, material rewards were seemingly no more important than the ability to appear as masculine, tough gangstas, at least when these appearances were deemed socially desirable and beneficial. Of course, when these traits were not advantageous, our network's dealers could conveniently morph back into their "good kid" personas without consequence. It seems that in certain circumstances privilege and luxury do not dissuade criminality, but rather encourage it. The interconnectedness of these six motivations suggests that for some the Katzian "seductions of crime" are too tasty to resist.

[…]

References

Lyng, S. "Crime, Edgework and Corporeal Transaction." *Theoretical Criminology* 8 (2004): 359–75.

Thompson, C. "A New Vision of Masculinity." In *New Men, New Minds*, edited by A. Franklin, pp. 630–6. Freedom, CA: Crossing Press, 1987.

Questions

1   What were the motivations behind dealing for the informants in the article? How did these motivations differ from the reasons for the informants in the previous article enrolled in pharmacy school? Do you think the entrance into drug dealing is an abrupt or gradual process? Why or why not?

2   Why do you think most drug dealers in the article were mostly men? Why were they mostly White? Is dealing in the university environment a sign of privilege? How might experiences of college drug dealers differ from lower-class dealers? What about risks and agents of control?

3   Did the informants in the article view themselves as criminals? Why or why not? How does the pursuit of masculinity for the drug dealers in the article compare to the pursuit of masculinity through heavy drinking practices? Do you think femininity can be accomplished through dealing illegal drugs? Why or why not?

Gender

18

Drugs and Eating Disorders
Women's Instrumental Drug Use for Weight Control

Katherine Sirles Vecitis

Katherine Vecitis keeps us in the world of White college students with her study of the intersection between drug use and eating disorders. Although the deviance of each of these behaviors may be rationalized as "righteous" by subcultural members, their combination offers the potential of dramatically increasing the stigma. Vecitis offers us a fascinating typology of how these instrumental drug users may be differentiated by their use of licit versus illicit drugs and their entry to this behavior through the route of recreational drugs versus eating disorders. How legitimate do you think the rationalizations of these drug users are compared to some of our other groups? To what extent are their drug use patterns influenced by their race/ethnicity and class? How do you imagine their career patterns are likely to be similarly influenced? In what ways do they differ from or resemble the pharmacists or the steroid users? The rural Oxycontin people? Why?

Is this a behavior that you think is common at your school? Why or why not? How are these young women affected by their gender role? How does their search for the ideal body image resemble the bodybuilders'? How do they reflect the norms and values of their dominant subculture? How do their routes of entry and legitimations compare? To what extent are pharmaceutical drug users tied more closely into conventional society than street drug users? How would you compare the instrumental nature of the bodybuilders' drug use compared to these college women's?

Finally, as women, are they as tied into the networks of family and community as some of the other groups of women we have seen? Why and why not? What does this tell us about the different effects of the factors separating them?

Sociological scholarship on substance use has focused on either recreational or medicinal manifestations. But as I approached college I read about someone who was taking amphetamines to moderate her eating. The use of drugs for weight control struck me as utilitarian, purposeful, and extreme, and I became interested in learning more about it. In addition, the use of substances in this manner was largely the pursuit of women, a population that I was most suited to research.

Drugs and the American Dream: An Anthology, First Edition. Edited by Patricia A. Adler, Peter Adler, and Patrick K. O'Brien.
© 2012 John Wiley & Sons, Inc. Published 2012 by John Wiley & Sons, Inc.

This research draws on in-depth life-history interviews I conducted with 57 college aged women at a large, public university. This was an appropriate place to study drug use and eating disorders because body image distortions and disturbances in eating were common among college women, and illicit drug use was widespread at university campuses. As women transitioned from high school to college, changes occurred socially, psychologically, and academically. Women's eating patterns, usually set by family in the past, were subject to change, and the pressures at college of academics, dating, and peer expectations were precursors to developing eating disorders. Finding subjects for this study was difficult, as this behavior is hidden by people, even from their closest friends. I gathered a convenience sample of anyone I could find to interview, culling research participants through the posters with which I blanketed the campus and from visits I conducted to many classes (upper and lower division), where I announced my intentions for this project. Participants contacted me via email or phone after my research solicitations, whether they heard about it directly or through others on campus. I pre-screened research candidates before scheduling an interview to insure that individuals currently or historically used drugs, either licit or illicit, for the primary purpose of weight management.

This chapter introduces the research population, describes and analyzes participants' reports of their drug use, restricted eating, and other related weight control practices. These two variables, restricted eating practices and drug use, went hand in hand for these young women, and my research aimed to understand this pattern: how drug use and disordered eating were related, dependent, or supported one another.

After a few dozen interviews it was apparent that while no experience was exactly like another, there were major patterns developing in the reports of these drug users collectively. In order to organize my data and effectively document these patterns, I formulated a typology of the drug users who participated in this research. Given the number of interviews I conducted, creating a typology allowed me to reduce numerous pieces of complicated information into a simple model based on patterns as they emerged from the data. Although no typology will ever perfectly fit an empirical data set, the better the model fits, the

stronger its utility as a descriptive and analytical tool will be.

Typology of Instrumental Users

Participants reported using two distinct types of substances: licit (pharmaceutical substances) and illicit (street) drugs. Overwhelmingly, women who used drugs to manage their weight preferred *stimulants*. The packaging and distribution of these substances varied, but they all shared the side effect of appetite control, and as such were sought for that purpose. Women's drug use was oriented towards accomplishing a specific goal and thus defined them as *instrumental* users. This concept denotes substance use that is motivated by a substance's specific effects. Their drug use was a *tool*, a mechanism to accomplish a goal. Instrumental drug use does not share all of the qualities commonly associated with other types of drug use, such as recreational or experimental. Participants did not cite mind expansion, hedonism, or novel experience as motivating factors for their behaviors. Not unlike body-builders who use steroids instrumentally, women in this research conceived of their drug use as essentially *performance-enhancing*. The use of stimulants helped women achieve their own personal goals of weight management. Differential motivations for drug use, such as having fun versus controlling weight, significantly affected women's behavioral patterns.

From these two main varieties, users of licit or illicit drugs, four specific categories of instrumental substance users emerged. Women who used prescriptions drugs versus women who used street drugs were distinguished from one another by the *temporal* nature of their disturbed eating and drug use. Some women reported disordered eating behaviors *before* the onset of their instrumental substance use. For these women, the discovery of drugs' instrumental utility followed months or years of experience with significant and deliberate weight management. Women with this history of extreme weight controlling behaviors reported methods of body modification that often crossed normative boundaries.

Many participants reported the development of non-normative weight managing behaviors *after* drug use. Generally, these women transformed their personal use patterns from recreational or medicinal,

Table 18.1   Types of instrumental drug use among women

	Licit drug users	Illicit drug users
Disordered eating foundation	Conventional over-conformists	Scroungers
Drug use foundation	Journeyers	Opportunists

into instrumental drug use. This usually followed positive social reinforcement and personal satisfaction concerning changes in the appearance of their bodies. Initially, weight loss was not necessarily intentional. Recreational users of licit and illicit stimulants commonly lost weight as a result of the appetite controlling side effects of their substances of choice. If their drug use was regular enough to produce noticeable changes in body weight, women often received feedback from others. While all this feedback may not have included comments that were intended to be *compliments*, women often perceived reactions from others as positive. Women who then identified drug use as a desirable means to maintain or continue weight loss, and perceived the results of their efforts as positive, were compelled to further develop their behaviors. Stages of this transformation varied among participants. However, during the time period of data collection, women described their drug using patterns instrumentally. To be clear, I termed the behaviors women engaged in first, whether it was drug use or problematic eating, as women's instrumental drug using *foundation*. Table 18.1 introduces the four types of instrumental drug users analyzed in this research.

The first group of women in my typology was the "conventional over-conformists." These women reported a history of disordered eating prior to their instrumental *prescription* drug use for weight loss. This term is descriptive in a number of ways. First, women were conventional in their choice to use the more socially accepted prescription drugs instead of consistently denounced street drugs. Second, although these women were instrumentally using drugs, which is arguably deviant behavior, the overall goal of the behaviors centered on achieving the cultural ideal of thinness, and were thus conforming. However, in most instances, women's weight management goals evolved from conforming to *over*-conforming, with an acute fixation on weight that tended to exceed average social expectations for personal body modification.

Participants' excessive adherence to ideals of beauty, along with their non-normative means used to accomplish this ideal, distinguished women as deviants. Although women may be described as deviant, it is a label based on behaviors that were largely unknown to others in everyday life. Women instrumentally using drugs for weight control often called attention to their weight socially, but their outward appearance generally fulfilled societal standards. By this I mean that women presented as thin, but not *too* thin. Conventional over-conformists represented the largest category in my typology of users.

The second largest category of instrumental drug users in this typology was the "scroungers." This group consisted of women who reported a history of disordered eating and later (after the onset of problematic weight control) instrumentally used *street* drugs for weight control. I termed them scroungers because their choice of street drugs represented a much less socially accepted form of substance use. In addition, many of the women conceived of these drugs as "dirty," "unacceptable," or "inappropriate." The term "scrounger" refers to their access to, and conception of, illicit drugs. Women's access to illicit substances was customarily not as consistent or reliable as it was for those using pharmaceuticals. At times women were forced to forage or *scrounge* for their supply. However, generally speaking, women reported no more difficulty in obtaining street drugs than is typically expected for illicit substances. My use of the term *scrounger* is not intended as a moral or judgmental label; it is merely descriptive.

Third, women who recreationally or medicinally used prescription drugs prior to their instrumental use for weight control made up the category of "journeyers". This term depicts the *journey*, or evolution, that drug use patterns went through. This process was a transformation from recreational or medicinal drug use into instrumental. While some women in this category reported using pharmaceuticals instrumentally for academic purposes, intentionally gearing drug use towards weight management shifted aspects of their deviant career in ways that were specific to goals of body modification. For example, journeyers tended to ration their supply of pharmaceuticals in a different manner once weight management was a priority.

The last, and smallest, category within this typology of instrumental drug users was the "opportunists". Opportunists were women who initially used street drugs recreationally, and later transformed their recreational drug use into instrumental for the purpose of weight control. I termed them opportunists for the way they recognized the positive social feedback regarding any weight loss resulting from drug use, and saw it as an *opportunity* for the transformation of self. As was the case of journeyers, opportunists reported experience using substances before their behaviors transformed into instrumental. Opportunists, like journeyers, shifted a wide array of behavioral practices in order to accommodate their instrumental drug use. Opportunists did not necessarily stop using drugs recreationally during periods of instrumental use. In fact many participants (not just journeyers or opportunists) reported recreational drug use, some on a fairly regular basis.

Structure of the Deviant Act

Women who used street drugs chose cocaine (by far the most popular), crystal methamphetamine, other street amphetamines, and rarely opiates, all of which are known to strongly control appetite. Those who used prescription drugs chose Adderall (the most popular), Ritalin, Concerta, Dexedrine, certain types of opiates (also rarely), Xenical, or Meridia. Of these, the anti-obesity drugs (which were not very popular) were specifically counter-indicated for those with a history of disordered eating. First, I discuss the structure of the deviant acts that were reported by women within the two main categories presented in this research: licit and illicit substance users. Second, I describe the restricted eating practices of participants in general. Last, I discuss the temporal nature of restricted eating practices and instrumental drug use, the variable that separated participants into these four categories.

Deviance among licit substance users

Approximately 61% of the women interviewed for this research used pharmaceutical substances in their efforts to manage weight. Most commonly, participants preferred prescription stimulants, which have been utilized in medicine since the early 1880s. Currently, physicians routinely prescribe stimulants for the treatment of Attention Deficit Hyperactivity Disorder

(ADHD), Attention Deficit Disorder (ADD), depression that has not responded to other treatments, narcolepsy, and in some cases short-term treatment of obesity. Van Vranken (2005) estimated that over a million and a half adults took prescription stimulants for ADHD, and that over two and a half million children were diagnosed with this disorder. These medications have also been prescribed in the past for the treatment of asthma and neurological disorders. Historically, the prescription of pharmaceutical stimulants was less regulated by the government. Physicians cited the addictive nature and the potential for abuse of these medications for the stricter policies utilized today. Although the medicinal indication guidelines have narrowed, prescription *rates* for stimulants have recently increased. Stimulants are prescribed for fewer ailments, but the number of prescriptions filled *overall* has grown.

This increase has led to public concern over the potential misuse of medical stimulants in general. The non-medical use of stimulants is most common among young people ages 12 to 25. The prevalence of non-medical use of pharmaceuticals among young people is greater than that for other illicit drugs, save marijuana. In addition, college students have higher rates of stimulant use than do their age peers not attending school. College students who used pharmaceutical stimulants non-medically were found to have higher rates of marijuana use, binge drinking, and episodes of drunk driving than their non-using peers. Non-medical pharmaceutical users were also found to have higher use rates of cocaine, ecstasy, and other types of amphetamines. Hall et al. (2005) reported that many recreational users of prescription stimulants mixed pharmaceuticals with other substances in order to amplify the drugs' effects. Accordingly, the non-medical use of stimulants is of particular concern among college students. This relationship may be due to the nature of these particular substances' utility within the college environment. College was unique in that the scholarly demands faced by students created a setting in which the non-medical use of pharmaceutical stimulants flourished.

Commonly, college students who used stimulants for non-medical purposes reported increased concentration, aid in studying, increased alertness, and getting high as motives for use. Many college students across the country use pharmaceutical stimulants instrumentally for academics. Prescription stimulants have a reputation for helping people focus, study, or pull all-nighters. In addition, college students at large often crushed and snorted these drugs recreationally, likening the feeling to that of cocaine or speed. Crushing pills was a practice that quickly released the active ingredients of substances into the bloodstream. However, researchers have found variance in terms of motivations for use along gender lines, with women being motivated to use stimulants for weight loss. Most college students taking prescription stimulants focused on academic achievement. In contrast, while women in this research often recognized the benefits of stimulants for academics, the majority of their drug using behaviors were oriented towards weight control.

Currently, the market is dominated by four stimulant medications: Adderall, Ritalin, Dexedrine, and Concerta. A small percentage of those whose disordered eating behaviors preceded prescription drug use choose medications other than those prescribed for ADHD or ADD. For example, a few chose Meridia, a medication specifically indicated for weight loss, and for those whose weight category is considered obese (never for people with a history of disordered eating). A handful of respondents preferred Wellbutrin, a speedy anti-depressant legitimately used to aid in smoking cessation and the treatment of depression. These substances were available as pills or tablets, either in fast-acting or extended-release doses. The long-acting stimulants are thought to have less potential for non-medical use and abuse than the fast-acting formulations. Among college students who diverted their prescription stimulant medications, 83% did so with fast-acting pills. In the short-term, prescription stimulants increase dopamine and norepinephrine in the brain. This increased respiration, heart rate, blood pressure, and constricted blood vessels. A person under the effects of these stimulants may feel more alert, with an increased attention span, energy, sense of euphoria, and loss of appetite. High doses of stimulants may cause depressive thoughts, hostility, paranoia, impulsive behavior, aggressiveness, loss of coordination, hallucinations, and disruptions in sleep patterns. Long-term effects of prescription stimulants include tolerance, weight loss, liver problems, and risk of physical and psychological dependence.

Women in this research predominantly used stimulants for the purpose of weight management. Although some physicians occasionally prescribed stimulant medications for weight loss over a short period of time, use of the medication for this purpose is considered "off-label." Stimulants were not approved by the Federal Drug and Food Administration for weight control. In the 1960s and 1970s however, Adderall, which was then known as Obetrol, was marketed as a diet-pill. During this period, prescription amphetamines such as Obetrol were FDA approved for weight loss. This indication was withdrawn by the FDA after abuse of the medication became apparent.

Despite increased governmental regulation, access to prescription stimulants among college students was rated third, behind alcohol and marijuana. Research participants reported three common modes for getting the medication. First, some women obtained prescriptions in their name. Second, participants were able to locate a black market drug dealer with access to the medication. Last, some participants had friends, family members, or roommates who were willing to supply them with the medication. A few women also reported obtaining pharmaceuticals from work associates. This was not surprising, as research into college students with a legitimate prescription for ADHD and ADD medications has shown that up to 45% had sold or given away their pills. Women who obtained prescription stimulants without consulting a doctor took risks, as often they were not properly informed about the drugs' effects, potential interactions, or side effects.

Many women in this research successfully obtained medical stimulants by persuading a physician to write a script in their name. A few women easily accomplished this by visiting their doctor at "home," often a childhood doctor. These doctors, who were usually general practitioners, had a relationship with the individual that developed over the course of a few years. This relationship may have instilled trust, on the part of the doctor, in the patient. Knowing the individual personally may have also made it more difficult for the physician to decline a woman's request. Two of the women in this research, who asked their hometown doctors for ADHD medication, were first put on non-stimulant prescriptions, such as Strattera. Both of these women were later successful at convincing their doctors to give them stimulants, citing the negative side-effects of non-stimulant medication for the requested switch. Cadence,[1] a 19-year-old sophomore and college athlete, explained:

> I knew I'd probably have to be patient to get it. Umm, I mean, doctors have to be careful ya know? So, uh, I tried to play it cool, I didn't just ask for it ... I said something about how I was having trouble paying attention at school and this and that about how it was so much easier for everybody else ... She said we should try Strattera for a couple months ... She said she wasn't *comfortable* giving me Adderall ... I went back and said that Strattera was making my mouth really, really dry and that I was embarrassed to talk in class. But she made me stay on it and I think like, like a month later and went back and she gave it [Adderall] to me.

However, most participants did not march into their doctor's office and ask for a prescription by name, even if they knew exactly which medication they wanted. Doctors may become suspicious of an individual asking for a controlled drug by name. They also may suspect ulterior motives from those who suddenly manifest new symptoms of ADHD or ADD, without the supporting medical history. However, women who obtained their prescription while at school generally did so at the university's health center, where their medical history was less relevant. Many students on campus, in general, felt that the health center was a relatively easy place to obtain pharmaceuticals. Cady, a freshman Adderall user, said:

> I think it's easier to get it at [the student health center] than maybe anywhere else, I mean, uh, they hand it out. I mean, *not really*, but it's not hard ...You're supposed to take all these tests to see if you have it but you can say that you had it when you were a kid and uh you took Ritalin or whatever ... So they might not make you go through all that. And even if you do, you can just fake not being able to pay attention.

Dr Robert A. Winfield, director of University Health Services at the University of Michigan, reported to the New York Times (Jacobs 2005) that he has seen a growing number of students falsely claiming to have ADHD in order to obtain prescription stimulants, and that "things have really gotten out of hand in the last four to five years." The high number of ADHD and ADD prescriptions written on college campuses may be due, in part, to the increased rates of the *diagnoses* of corresponding disorders in the late 1980s and 1990s. Many students currently in college, and those about to enter, are a part of this generation. Students of today are more likely to be diagnosed with ADHD, or know someone who is. They are also likely to know about the specific medications that are used to treat these conditions. This trend may have led to a university medical culture that is more willing to, and more comfortable with prescribing, stimulant medications.

> I googled "how to get Adderall," or something like that. It comes up with all sorts of stuff but mostly all of it says you just gotta pretend like you have no attention span. So I uh just figured out what sort of uh things go along with being all ADD ... I get distracted easy, I can't pay attention at school, things like that.

During our interview Cailyn laughed when she recounted her initial visit to the doctor for a prescription. When asked about her relationship with the doctor, she rolled her eyes and explained, "He totally believed me ... no way he thought I was faking." In fact, many women felt that they had successfully tricked their doctor, even those consulting psychiatrists, professionals who specialize in the diagnosis and treatment of mental disorders. Cindy, a college sophomore, conveyed surprise when she recalled obtaining her first prescription for stimulants:

> See the thing is, last year I came to [the campus health center] to talk to a person downstairs, um, I think he was a psychologist, about the nerves I was having over eating stuff, I mean, it was weird, I was obsessing about some weight I gained ...When I went in to talk about attention I was sure they would just look at my chart and be like no way am I gonna give this girl pills. But she totally did and didn't even ask anything about my weight ... It was pretty easy.

Success at acquiring a personal script for pharmaceuticals was the first step. Maintaining it, however, required continued engagement with the medical system. The fact that prescription stimulants are schedule II substances, in that they have accepted medical uses with the potential for abuse, meant that regulations on how they were to be prescribed were stricter than for other medical substances. Physicians and pharmacists were required to register with the Drug Enforcement Agency and received a DEA control number upon doing so. This number was present on all prescriptions written for a controlled substance. They were also required to follow all governmental written rules and regulations, including codes of recordkeeping, valid prescription directions, and security requirements.

One such government regulation stated that schedule II prescriptions were not to be refilled, which limited the pill count that individuals could fill at a time to one month's supply. This meant that every time a woman wanted to get more pills, she had to have a new prescription written. Thus, many women were required to visit the doctor once a month in order to keep a regular supply. However, a few women had doctors who were willing to post-date prescriptions, lowering the number of times they had to meet face-to-face. For example, Camilla told me:

> I think I am supposed to go in once a month but there is no way my doctor is making me do that … He just gives me three [prescriptions] for the next months and changes the date … I just hold onto them and wait until they are supposed to be filled … It's never been a problem.

The practice of post-dating, or writing "do-not-fill-until" orders, on prescriptions was prohibited prior to December 2007, during the time I conducted interviews. As a result, many research participants visited their doctors frequently. While this was an annoyance to many women, month after month most of the pharmaceutical users went back to the doctor for more medication.

The actual act of *doing* the medical stimulants was largely consistent among respondents. Women would take a pill first thing in the morning, usually before their normal routine. Claire, a college sophomore, reported:

> It's pretty much the first thing I think of when I wake up, I mean, um, I'm not like, crazy obsessive about it or anything, it's like thinking about getting up and making coffee. I just take it right away … At first it wakes me up and makes me really talkative … It's a good feeling.

During the day, women would sometimes take a few more pills, spacing them out over the course of a few hours. Almost all of the women in this research

though, when deciding what dose to take for the day, were careful to take into account their supply levels, tracking the number of days until they would run out of drugs against the amount of time until they were able to refill their prescription. This accounting allowed participants to ration out their supply so they would not have to go without pills between refills.

Some women visited multiple physicians in order to compensate for this limit on obtaining a legitimate supply of drugs. Generally, visiting other doctors (double-dipping) to obtain multiple prescriptions is a common practice of individuals diverting pharmaceuticals of all kinds. Other women went to street dealers to get more pills than they were prescribed. In addition, some women claimed to their primary physician that they lost their prescription or it was stolen, classic attempts to get more pills. Although citing a lost or stolen bottle of medication worked on occasion, it was not a tactic that could be used repeatedly. Carly took a different approach, utilizing deviant means for her supply:

> I am a college student so I guess they gave me the normal dose [20 mg extended release once daily]. But I'm super hooked on it. I take twice that 'cause I just went out and got another doctor. My doctor at home post dates prescriptions for me while I'm at school then I go to [student health services] and get another one. But it's a pain in the ass here 'cause I have to go in every month.

A few women supplemented their medical supply with extra pills here and there, buying medication from dealers, or receiving free pills from roommates, friends, or family. It was not uncommon among research participants to stock pile doses of stimulants, perhaps filling two prescriptions and taking only one each month, securing a future supply. Women were largely successful in obtaining their licit drugs consistently, as almost all pharmaceutical users reported daily use.

For many women in this research, the school year contained spans of time away from school, which may have affected their supply. Stock piling was a way to store up for these times. Most however, stayed within the confines of their medically prescribed daily dose, as did Carol:

> Well, I took one 30 mg one morning and I loved the feeling. It wasn't a high feeling it was just a feeling of

goodness. Anyways, the Adderall made me want to socialize more, made me more talkative, I was always in better moods, I had way more energy and time just seemed to go by so fast. The reason I liked it most was it made me not hungry. I loved that feeling instantly. I'm a person who is concerned about looks, weight, and appearance. I guess you can say I've always been like that. Taking one Adderall a day gave me so much energy, made me so much happier and decreased my appetite like, one hundred and ten percent.

The daily prescription stimulant dosage of women varied greatly, from conservative levels to relatively high daily intake. For reference, Adderall's manufacturer suggested that an adult initiating use should be prescribed as either 5 milligrams of the fast-acting pills up to three times a day, or 20 milligrams of the extended-release formulation once a day. This dosage may be increased as needed to adjust for individual tolerance and symptom control.

The lowest level of use reported in this research was 15 milligrams a day, well within the medically recommended limit. The highest daily dosage reported was one 120 milligrams daily, a high amount for any adult. This high dosage level was not usually maintained for long periods of time. Rather, some women would phase in and out of high and low dosages. One user explained to me that during the times when she took excessive amounts of Adderall and Ritalin, she felt "insane." Jackie said:

I get so shaky, see look, it's not that bad right now but sometimes I cannot control my hands at all ... It really makes me want to chain smoke too, I smoke way more. If you take too much you get this really awful taste in your mouth and it'll make my tongue tingle ... I have to remind myself to calm down when my friends are around, I'll just talk and interrupt, it definitely gets outta control and the problem is too that I end up not eating, like at all and that makes you feel loopy and cracked out.

Women reported that taking higher amounts of Adderall led to feeling jittery, sometimes nervous, and caused problems with sleep patterns. As a result, women who took very high doses of prescription stimulants daily, generally did so for a short phase, and then weaned themselves to lower doses. Many participants, not just licit drug users, reported periods of abstinence, ranging from a day or two, to months at a time.

Deviance among illicit substance users

Approximately 39% of women who participated in this research used illicit drugs in their efforts to control weight. Not only is the use of street drugs deviant, it is illegal. Thus participants using these substances differed from women using licit pharmaceuticals, in terms of the structure of their deviant acts. Most women using illicit drugs chose cocaine, while a few preferred illegal amphetamines (speed). Cocaine and speed can be snorted, injected, or smoked. These illegal stimulants were similar in their effects to the pharmaceutical substances that were previously described. They increased energy, alertness, talkativeness, caused a loss of appetite, and gave the user an overall sense of well-being. Street stimulants also increased respiration, heart rate, and raised blood pressure. High doses of street stimulants can lead to seizures, stroke, sudden cardiac death, or breathing failure. Repeated, chronic use can also lead to dependence, psychosis, and paranoia. While cocaine is sometimes used medically for legitimate procedures, it is rarely found in its pharmaceutical formulation (a solution in a glass vial) on the black market. Currently this substance, when sold on the street, is usually found in powdered or crack-cocaine forms. Women in this research almost exclusively used powdered cocaine, which may have been an expression of privilege among research participants.

Most women instrumentally using street drugs reported little to no problems accessing their supply. There was no need to research elaborate symptoms of a medical disorder in an attempt to fraudulently gain access to a given substance. Illicit users needed to find a person in possession of the type of substances they wanted, and persuade that person to sell them said drugs. Most women who used cocaine, for example, reported that the drug was very easily found on campus. Sadie, a young college student and habitual powder cocaine user, explained:

I was always hanging out with people that were drinking and doing drugs. You know, drugs would just be around. I remember my boyfriend did coke but I said I never would. But then later I was with one of my best girlfriends and I was sort of like, why not? ... About once a month I started doing it when I would go out, and then like, it got to the point with my friends, that we were getting it all the time, all the time.

While women tended to report easy access to this drug, many did not find their suppliers to be as altogether steady or reliable as women who used prescription stimulants. The conditions of the black market were not as stable as those of the medical industry and as a result, campus dealers were often less reliable. At times, campus dealers were likely to run low on, or out of, drugs. Some women also reported their street dealers to be unreliable professionally, in that they were difficult to get a hold of, unfair in pricing, or sold drugs excessively "cut" with unknown materials. These complaints aside, most research participants using illicit substances for weight control reported overall satisfaction in their access to drugs. While many voiced strain in dealing with the black market, it was generally understood that some difficulties were inherent, given their choice to use illicit substances.

The specific deviant behaviors reported by women using street drugs varied greatly from the behaviors of women who used pharmaceuticals. First and foremost, being an illicit drug user required breaking the law. Although pharmaceutical users may have lied or used manipulation to access their substances, they did not have to engage with the black market. Also important were the differential modes of administration of substances. Cocaine users generally inhaled, or "snorted," the substance through their nostrils, where it entered the bloodstream via nasal tissues. This method caused blood cocaine levels to quickly rise, reaching their peak around thirty minutes after snorting. This rise was followed by rapidly declining levels of cocaine in the blood, leaving the user ready for another dose in roughly forty minutes. Pharmaceuticals, on the other hand, even the fast-acting formulations, had effects that lasted for at least a few hours. Consequentially, women who snorted cocaine to curb their appetite did so a few or more times throughout the day. Sally, a college junior studying biology, explained her frequent daily use:

> Cause I just always had it. And I would do it before, it was so easy to hide from people, so I would do it in the bathroom, or in my car on the way to school. That's what this thing is for [she pulled out a small metal case that was attached to her keychain]. You can just stick a gram of coke in it, did you know that? I can take it to school no problem, it's not like someone is going to notice.

However, this act required a bit more discretion on the part of the participant, as snorting a drug versus popping a pill were two distinctly different actions.

The frequency of use and dosage levels of women who instrumentally used illicit substances for weight loss varied among respondents. The majority of instrumental cocaine users consumed their substances daily. Often, those who were not daily users at the time of data collection had gone through periods of using daily. A few daily users did cocaine in small amounts once or twice a day, while others used more repeatedly. For example, Sarah, a college junior who was noticeably fidgeting during our interview, said:

> I do it, like, a lot. Consistently, like totally consistently. When I was at school, I guess I never did a lot at school, but I would have my schedule so I'd be done at like twelve every day. So then I would leave and usually meet up with someone I could do it with. Or go to my dealer's house, but it got to the point where I was doing it so much, like people I used to do it with occasionally must have known I was doing it that much. So I was sort of on my own. Sometimes I would do it like every twenty minutes... I'd have days where I wouldn't eat at all... I'd try to make sure I got a lot of liquids.

The highest dosage reported by research participants was one gram of powdered cocaine a day. That translates to twenty 50-milligram "lines," a fairly standard amount. However, a few participants reported their *daily* use to be around 50 to 100 milligrams, or a line or two.

Generally, instrumental illicit drug users were most comfortable consuming their substances at home. Cocaine users were often wary of doing drugs in public, but many were still willing to do so. Many women felt at least slightly comfortable finding a private place to do drugs, either on campus or when out in town. However, unless women were out with friends celebrating the weekend or just partying in general, drug use was generally kept very private. Respondents each had personal methods for hiding their drug use: sneaking off to the bathroom or excusing themselves to make a phone call.

Restricted eating practices among instrumental drug users

Both the licit and illicit drug users described in this research focused attention and energy on controlling their body weight. Charlotte, an Adderall user, voiced a theme that was common among instrumental users when she said, "You don't understand, if I'm not skinny, then I feel like shit. I am always making sure that I don't get above one ten." While the substances utilized in this quest varied among these young women, the overall goal remained constant. The different drugs participants chose all had one major side effect in common: they curbed appetite. Oksana explained:

> So I still do it [coke] and yeah, I think it really does help with not, like, uh, like I just literally wanted to stop eating. It got to the point where my stomach shrank so much that if I ate, my stomach would get so bloated and I would just flip out, it would freak me out.

For women using street drugs such as cocaine, appetite was controlled in small bursts throughout the day. Most of these instrumental users reported a chronic dulling of their appetite in general, but this effect was most acute immediately following the consumption of the drug. As such, instrumental street drug users often habitually used small amounts of cocaine when they felt their hunger was growing. Consequentially, women reported ups and downs in both their moods and appetites on the days they were instrumentally using.

The ups and downs that were reported by illicit drug users were not as frequently cited among licit drug users. This difference may be largely attributed to the modes of administration for these substances, as well as the drugs' specific psychopharmacology. Women taking pharmaceuticals felt the effects over a longer period of time than did street drug users. This was especially true of participants taking extended-release formulations, which were *designed* to last a long time. Licit instrumental users were also more likely to describe the effects of their medications as smooth, versus the unstable effects that were reported by street drug users. While both licit and illicit users reported disruption in their sleep habits, insomnia was commonly most pronounced among illicit users.

Sammy, a 20-year-old student, complained about this particular side effect of cocaine use:

> I'd go days when I couldn't get any sleep at all which was awful. I had these horrible ugly bags under my eyes and I was really skinny. I know I'm skinny now, but I was *really* skinny … I'd force myself to lie in bed and shut my eyes. My body felt tired but I just couldn't sleep at all. It gets you all tight and completely wound up.

Licit and illicit stimulants alike proved to be extremely effective tools for weight management. Both groups of women reported significant and relatively easy weight loss. Over time, most participants gradually transformed their weight control methods. Many women in this research reported that they had a few means of losing and controlling weight before they started instrumentally using drugs. After the discovery of appetite controlling substances, women generally relied largely on drugs for weight management. The temporal nature of their drug use and restricted eating practices varied however, further distinguishing research participants from one another. Some participants reported practices commonly associated with eating disorders *prior* to adopting drug use as a tool for weight management. This was true among women who used licit or illicit substances.

The Temporal Nature of Weight Control and Substance Use

Women who instrumentally used drugs for weight management *after* a history of disordered eating made up the largest portion of participants. These were the conventional over-conformists and the scroungers. Regardless of whether women within this larger category chose to use street drugs or prescription drugs, they all shared many similar experiences. However, participants reported a few significant in-group differences. First, they diverged from one another in the length of their eating disordered behavior. This history ranged from one to twelve years. Second, women with a history of disordered eating also varied in the severity of their behaviors. Some women reported disordered eating symptoms that were relatively mild and short lived. Others' behaviors were more severe, sometimes resulting in a formal psychiatric diagnosis, and in one particular case, hospitalization.

One particular surprise finding of this research was discovering women who instrumentally used prescription or street drugs to control their weight not as a last extreme resort within the career of an eating disorder, but rather as the *result* of recreational (or medicinal) drug use. These women were the journeyers and the opportunists. The notion that women who lost weight as a result of a recreational or medicinal drug use would face the same level and strength of positive reinforcement from the social world as those with a history of disordered eating was unexpected. However, women consistently reported this pattern. Reportedly, the positive social reinforcement women received concerning weight loss was influential enough to bring weight control to the forefront of their lives. This force was enough to precipitate *disordered eating*. Many of the women with *no* history of disordered eating behaviors prior to their instrumental drug use insisted that before the positive reinforcement on weight loss, concerns over weight control or even dieting were not a large part of their daily lives. This suggested that while their weight loss was completely (or at least partially) accidental, reactions from family, friends, and the general public made them feel so positive about themselves that many chose to make weight management a priority. For some, the transformation from recreational or medicinal drug use into instrumental resulted from their personal evaluations of changes in their bodies. This was true even if their methods came at the cost of their physical and psychological health.

Note

1 Proper names of respondents are pseudonyms. As a rule, pseudonyms correspond with categories in the typology by the first letters in the women's *name* and user *type*.

References

Hall, Kristina M., Irwin, Melissa, Bowman, Krista A., Frankenberger, William, and Jewett, David C. (2005). Illicit use of prescribed stimulant medication among college students. *Journal of American College Health*, 53(4).

Jacobs, Andrew (2005). The Adderal advantage. Available online at www.nytimes.com/2005/07/31/education/edlife/jacobs31.html.

Van Vranken, Michele (2005). Why do some people abuse prescription drugs? *Heathology: ABC News Internet Ventures*. Accessed February 17.

Questions

1 How might the social context and demographics of the participants have informed their opportunities and willingness to use licit and/or illicit drugs? How might privilege and desired body image intersect to encourage drug use?

2 How do the differences in drug using careers among these participants challenge or reinforce stereotypes about drug users?

3 What role did formal regulations play in participants buying and using licit and illicit drugs? What role did informal regulation seem to play?

19

College Alcohol Use and the Embodiment of Hegemonic Masculinity among European American Men

Robert L. Peralta

Serving as an interesting contrast to Vecitis, Robert Peralta offers a portrait of college men and one of the ways they assert their masculinity: through drug consumption. Despite the wax and wane of various waves of drug popularity, alcohol remains the most widely consumed college intoxicant and the problem of binge drinking has drawn repeated attention from numerous groups. Yet Peralta discusses how and why it forms such a cornerstone of male college culture. Based on your own experiences, you may want to reflect on the relation between his portrayal and your impressions of the scene. You may also want to ask yourself about how this image of masculinity, as well as that depicted for the bodybuilders, stands in the pantheon of versions of how men enact masculinity. How, then, does the type of alcohol consumption described here stratify college men into different rungs on the hierarchy of prestige? What norms do you see in colleges that promote some kinds of drinking over others or over abstinence?

Comparing the gender roles portrayed in these last two pieces, how do you think the move into drug consumption beyond moderate levels is viewed differently for men and women? How are norms for drinking alcohol different for college men and women? What role do men generally have in obtaining and distributing drugs like alcohol and others (at frat parties, house parties, bars) and how does this affect their gender status and power? Finally, why do you think the binge drinking discussed by Peralta is so social compared to the instrumental drug use discussed by Vecitis?

The reduction of alcohol-related problems among college students remains a formidable task. "Alcohol-related problems among college students" may be a euphemism for "European American (EA) college students who are men" given that the vast majority of college students are EA and those students who experience alcohol related problems are disproportionately EA men. An important aspect in promoting social and behavioral change is to understand the racialized and gendered underpinnings that shape the desire to engage in heavy drinking in college. [...]

The literature suggests that alcohol use or abstention from alcohol has been used for gender construction purposes. Although college campuses have been described in the literature as settings where men and women "do gender" (West and Zimmerman 1987), alcohol use among college students has received relatively little gender accomplishment analysis.

[…]

A nationally representative study showed that 42.7% of students had been binge drinking in the 2 weeks before they were surveyed. Twenty percent of these students binged three times or more per month. Gender differences in alcohol consumption by college students continue to be reported routinely in the literature, although differences are dwindling. Nineteen percent of female students and 24% of male students in one nationally representative study reported frequent "binge drinking" (defined as imbibing five or more drinks in a single sitting for men and four for women) three or more times in a 2 week period. Twenty-three percent of those who drank three times per week drank ten or more drinks per week.

Although these studies provide important insight into college students' drinking, large nationally representative studies of college students overlook important sociological issues that pertain to gender. For instance, Wechsler et al.'s (1995) analysis of gender in college students' alcohol use is limited to only three gender-specific qualifications. The first is a gender-adjusted measurement for "binge drinking" (described above). Second, Wechsler reported prevalence differences between men and women where women had a slightly lower prevalence rate of abusive drinking. Third, Wechsler's data suggest that women face a disproportionately greater risk than men do for violent victimization.

Survey research has shown significant differences by gender, however the researchers have not satisfactorily interpreted the nuanced impact of gender on the epidemiological distribution of drinking. In other words, we stand to gain from a more sophisticated understanding of the way in which drinking is implicated in creating and sustaining variant forms of masculinity. Although we know that gender differences exist, we have not fully understood their origins, their meanings, or the ways in which men's drinking exists in relation to women's or subjugated men's drinking. Given the pronounced and routine differences reported in the scientific literature, it is important to investigate how gender accomplishment influences drinking

behavior among college students. This approach provides insight into the meaning of alcohol use that is not possible within the traditional epidemiological approaches used by Wechsler and others.

[…]

The Current Study

In the present study of alcohol use, I took an interactionist approach to view gender as (1) dynamic, (2) as emerging from situated interaction, and (3) as produced and reinforced through accomplishment. I interpret students' accounts of alcohol use as reflections of their conceptualization of gender and the alcohol-related behaviors as necessary to engage in doing masculinity. I argue that alcohol is used by EA male students to align with hegemonic standards of masculinity. I use accounts from EA men and subjugated men and women (e.g., African American [AA], gay) enrolled in an institution of higher education to illustrate this process.

The purpose of this research was to explore the process of local hegemonic masculinity construction (as opposed to regional or national constructions) via alcohol use among a diverse sample of college students. Is the process of drinking and, in particular, heavy drinking a form of masculinity construction? Are ideological assumptions about masculinity expressed through drinking behavior in a social location where such expressions are accepted, legitimized, and often expected? Does heavy alcohol use among men become a resource where presumed "essential" characteristics of manhood can be expressed? Juxtaposing the experiences of AA, EA, homosexual, and heterosexual men and women was a critical aspect of analyzing the local construction of this form of masculinity.

Method

Participants

Respondents were a volunteer sample of 78 undergraduate students at a medium sized state university in the mid-Atlantic region of the US.

Sixty-nine percent ($N = 55$) of the total sample was EA, and 27% ($N = 20$) was AA. Forty-four men and 34 women participated. Seventy-two percent ($N = 56$) self-identified as heterosexual, 22% ($N = 17$) self-identified as gay or lesbian, and the remaining 6% ($N = 5$) self-identified as bisexual. Two respondents were both Hispanic and gay. One respondent was self-identified as a gay Asian man. Two AA men identified as gay; the remaining gay participants were EA ($N = 17$; ten EA gay men; seven EA lesbians).

The respondents were evenly distributed across the college years; almost one-third were either freshmen ($N = 24$) or seniors ($N = 25$), 15% were sophomores ($N = 11$), and 22% were juniors ($N = 18$). The average age was at the median point of age of traditional college students: 20 years, 5 months. Fifteen percent ($N = 11$) of the sample reported that they were members of a fraternity or sorority. Nearly all (95%) respondents reported themselves as "middle" or "upper-middle" class.

[...]

A semi-structured, open-ended interview guide that consisted of 12 main questions was developed and pilot tested by the author of the present study. Demographic questions were asked in addition to questions about drinking quantity and frequency, attitudes toward drinking, reasons for drinking, expectations of alcohol use, and consequences of drinking such as blackouts, inability to stop using, injuries, and failure to meet responsibilities. Questions were expanded through the use of probes and projective questioning to reduce the response effect of sensitive questions (e.g., I asked questions about friends' use of alcohol in addition to questions about interviewees' own use of alcohol).

Results

The data presented here are based on over 100 hours of interview data. Three themes that emerged from the interviews are reported here. I grouped the findings into three distinct − yet interrelated − categories to demonstrate how masculinity operates and is understood within the context of alcohol use and heavy alcohol use. These three themes together exemplify the association between alcohol use and the embodiment of hegemonic masculinity construction for a specific group of men: EA college men.

Markers of embodied masculinity: Stories and trophies

Drinking and heavy drinking is understood to be a form of "macho" or masculine behavior. [...] Thus men and women alike believe that drinking, especially heavy drinking, is indicative of masculinity accomplishment for those who drink. Thus *evidence* of heavy drinking via stories and trophies (e.g., physical evidence of alcohol use) are used as markers of masculinity.

Because the majority of students in this sample asserted that alcohol use expresses a form of "macho" or masculine behavior (70%), these data suggest that drinking is within the repertoire of behaviors associated with "masculinity" as it is defined in this specific college environment. Although many students' associated drinking with (EA) masculinity, the tone of men's responses differed from that of women's responses. Men's stories about their own alcohol use and the use of alcohol by their peers were in reference to their own perceived power and strength as men. This power was evidenced by the extent to which their *bodies* could endure and withstand the effects of alcohol consumption. These qualities were demonstrated by their stated ability not only to withstand heavy alcohol use, but also to *enjoy* the act of drinking heavily. For example, [...] Keith, an EA heterosexual student, said:

> One night last semester we started drinking at 10 A.M. and didn't stop until 4 A.M. the next day! It was like 18 hours of drinking. That was straight beer. The hard alcohol part started out at a brewery...we had three beers there, then we bought a 6-pack at a liquor store, went to a micro brewery, had three big beers there, had dinner, went to a bar, and started doing shots, and then went to some other bar, and after that we don't remember. We just woke up. And this one time, I put down a whole bottle of vodka just straight down!

EA male undergraduates talked about their alcohol use as if "drinking" and "getting drunk" were badges of honor. It is perhaps not surprising that it was EA men who more often discussed alcohol as an approach to a local construction of hegemonic masculinity, as previous researchers have found that EA college men are among the heaviest of drinkers. EA men's drinking accounts often had the tone of battle stories told by war veterans. They were more likely to discuss their alcohol use and their male friends' alcohol use with awe and as symbols of essential masculine strength, ability, stamina, and, most important, power.

Drinking stories for men are important because they are expressions of a specific type of masculine identity – one that is wild, tough, popular, youthful, aggressive, competitive, confident, and anti-feminine. [...] The telling of drinking stories, particularly heavy drinking stories, is part of the imagery of gender accomplishment for this particular local setting. The reference group is specific: the college students' peers. This style of drinking did not take place in front of older adults. This is important and perhaps relevant to the tone of their accounts. Students may have exaggerated their drinking experiences. But regardless of the actual amount consumed, their efforts to convey a particular image reflect "doing gender" in general, and "doing masculinity" in particular. [...]

Men counted the number of bottles consumed as evidence of masculinity accomplishment. In the need to address masculine standards as defined by their reference group, empty alcohol containers were used as symbolic markers of achieving that goal. These men drew a sense of pride from the amount and frequency of alcohol use. Kristen (EA, heterosexual) substantiated this observation by saying: "Guys value that (drinking) more than girls. Guys pride themselves on that and they have to prove they can drink and hold their liquor." The types (e.g., beer versus wine coolers) of drinks appear to serve as trophies as well. Take Karen's statement (EA, heterosexual) as an example: "Girls are supposed to drink girly drinks, and guys are supposed to drink beer."

Many men interviewed were brimming with pride when they discussed their heavy alcohol use. If excessive alcohol use among men is perceived to be an expression of masculinity, power, and authority, what is the perception of women's alcohol use according to respondents? Women who openly drink heavily were regarded as infringing upon traditional masculine behavior according to both male and female respondents. Seth, an AA man, for example, said:

I think that if a female is tanked [drunk], like I don't think that she is at all attractive. I'm not being sexist, but there is something about a woman chugging back a beer that looks so masculine, you know what I mean? Just like why doesn't she just burp or fart in front of everybody or something? Men drink. They get violent, rape. When women drink, that is really masculine. It looks masculine.

It appears Seth, similar to other male respondents, does not approve of women drinking because it violates gender norms, which calls into question her gender status and also his.

Alcohol was often said to be the primary reason for men's get-togethers. Masculinities, however, were understood by women to be embodied in men's ability to tolerate heavy alcohol use. Respondents assumed that men's bodies can absorb more alcohol than women's and are more likely to withstand its effects. Succinctly put: Men reminisced proudly and boasted about their alcohol use in terms of masculinity accomplishment. The use of it in and of itself was meaningful. Heavy alcohol use demonstrated bodily power and superiority. Ironically, however, heavy and prolonged alcohol use in fact *weakens* one's body.

"Liquid courage," "beer muscles," and "case races": Alcohol induced risky behavior, aggression, and competition

Body practices such as risk-taking behavior in the context of alcohol use were evident in the present study. The gender and masculinities literatures illustrate how hegemonic masculinity emphasizes the representation and use of men's bodies as a process of social embodiment. Male students "do" a specific type of masculinity by reproducing hierarchical images of what a "real man" is thought capable of doing. Here, alcohol use is assumed to fuel strength, aggression, and confidence, creating contexts where risky behaviors are more apt. In this context, competitive activities surrounding alcohol use also emerge. [...]

Risk-taking behavior and feeling invincible are central to the construction and embodiment of local masculinities. With what is known about the deleterious effects of heavy and long term alcohol use, alcohol is a form of risk-taking in and of itself. [...]

The vast majority of students discussed the associations among alcohol use, risky behaviors, and the induced sense of courage or "invincibility" that occurred particularly among EA men. [...]

Being "courageous" and engaging in risk-taking behavior are indicative of local hegemonic masculinity. Courage is a sign of power and thus a potent ingredient of masculinity. "Liquid Courage" was defined by students as the courage that emerges because of alcohol use. [...] "Invincibility" was a term used frequently by both men and women to describe feelings that "men" express when binge drinking. Again, the male body is implicated in the embodiment of gender as illustrated in the accounts that follow. Consider Henry's (EA, heterosexual) account:

> I've done all kinds of stupid things [when drinking]. One of my friends was driving my jeep, and I tried to jump out of it and into my friend's pick up doing like 80 on the freeway. We used to do flips off my roof and into the pool back home. We used to do all kinds of stupid stuff.

Commitment to risk-taking practices as a means of establishing a masculine reputation in a peer group context was evident in students' accounts. These behaviors appeared to be expected, as evidenced by respondents' assumptions about the "natural" links between masculinity, alcohol use, and risk-taking. These assumptions are a product of negotiations between EA men, women, and other subordinated groups. The power of expectations should thus not be underestimated. There is no emphasized effort to curtail or prevent alcohol-related behaviors because so many expect it to occur as part of a "natural" byproduct of men's drinking. The statements below exemplify this. Jerry, an EA, heterosexual fraternity brother, stated:

> When you are wasted, that's when you have a head change. Alcohol brings out the mean side. It definitely causes problems…it definitely gives you beer muscles. People think that they can fight better, can be tougher. They can take a beating and they just feel invincible a lot of times. I mean it happens to me, it happens to everyone I know.

[...]

Drinking and driving is a criminal act predominantly committed by men and perhaps tied to the construction of gender. The alcohol-related act is rebellious, risky, and may serve as a sign of bravado signified by the willingness to overcome the effects of alcohol and or evade formal control agents such as police officers. Shana, an AA heterosexual female student, elaborated upon this theme while making connections among men's alcohol use, masculinity, power, and violence. The capacity for violence is a part of the masculine construct. The link between violence and substance use, particularly alcohol use, has been well documented. [...] Shana evoked this link as follows:

> … the *main* reason why I don't like dating guys who drink is because a lot of them do get aggressive…I know that if I was ever in a situation where (my intimate partner became intoxicated) they better not hit me for no other reason…I am not giving them that excuse, I'm not going for it either way. I don't care if you are in your right mind or not! I think that (alcohol and violence) is a bad combination. Especially when it is like a man against a woman. I think especially with guys… when they are drunk you know their drinking gives them this power I guess (laughter), and you know…they just start hitting everybody… I feel that they think they have this power or something when they drink.

[...]

Because the concept of hegemonic masculinity is based on a practice that permits men's collective dominance over "others" to continue, it is not surprising that, in some contexts, hegemonic masculinity refers to men's engagement in toxic practices including physical violence, which works to stabilize gender dominance in particular settings. Sexual violence and sexual risk-taking emerged as themes as well. Consider the following account that illustrates this from an EA, heterosexual women recruited from the Dean of students' office.

> FAYE: I know too much about what goes on with alcohol and sexual aggression at frat parties and alcohol contributes to that, like my guy friends act invincible when they drink…and with the sorority and fraternity stereotypes of girls are good and boys can be bad, I had a friend who was raped by a fraternity brother.

Many students discussed the centrality of drinking games in the culture of college drinking. Drinking games are contests where the ability to tolerate alcohol is instrumental in the social embodiment of masculinity. Students talked about the importance of drinking games in expressing power and control as evidenced by the male body's ability to withstand intoxication. [...] Competition and risk-taking are characteristics of local forms of masculinity expression, and alcohol appears to be used as a vehicle to approximate the local ideal of masculinity situated in the context of the college environment. Janice, an EA female student, said:

> Males go on longer (drink for longer periods), and they would take the drinking (game) more seriously. Who wins tells you who can hold their liquor better. I know for myself and a lot of my girlfriends, you kind of fake it, like you were full or you couldn't do it anymore you would fake it. And guys, they drink the beer till it is gone. I think it was more of a guy thing; they took the games more seriously than girls. It is all about winning for the guys. They think it is everything.

[...]

Drinking games illustrate how ideological hegemonies present dominant interests as everyone's interests. Drinking heavily is expected, as it is the point of the game in the local context of "the party." Sanctions are imposed upon those who do not participate in these games or align themselves with hegemonic standards in general. To avoid sanctions, many students discussed turning to alcohol as a means of compensating for the lack of fundamental components of hegemonic masculinity, such as heterosexual identity.

"Two-beer queers" versus "real drinkers": Exaltation and stigmatization of drinking and non-drinking behavior

Alcohol is a readily available and socially legitimized tool that is gendered in terms of how and when it is used. Its use (particularly its heavy use) was observed to be associated with demonstrations of power, whereas abstention or light use was associated with "weakness" or otherness. Who drinks, who drinks heavily, who drinks frequently, who can withstand heavy alcohol

use, and who can relationally distance themselves from drinking styles characterized as feminine are important components of the gender work discussed here.

Gough and Edwards (1998) found that men's bonding talk and/or talk about alcohol-related activity demonstrates the dependence of hegemonic masculinities on the discursive subordination of the "other," most notably women and gay men. Similarly, most students who engaged in the drinking culture marginalized those who do not drink by decrying the latter as outcasts. Students were relegated to, or relegated themselves to, less influential, less popular, less glorified, less powerful positions of college life (as defined by the students). If a student did drink, that is, if the student adopts the notion that drinking is and should be a dominant activity to be taken seriously, then he or she is rewarded with a prized social life, social outlets, networking opportunities, status, and positive reputation.

[...]

Gender theorists have called for theorizing about the embodiment involved in hegemony. For boys and young men, skilled bodily activity becomes a prime indicator of masculinity. This is instrumental in the linking of heterosexuality and masculinity in Western cultures and how prestige is conferred onto boys and young men (Connell and Messerschmidt 2005). Bodies are both agents in social practice and objects of social practice. Alcohol use is a conspicuous way to display endurance and strong bodies in young men's leisure practices. It is the practice of social embodiment involving institutions such as higher education and legitimized alcohol use on which their privilege as EA heterosexual men rests.

[...]

Sean, an EA gay man, reinforced how alcohol use is viewed as an important aspect of being the "standard" type of man. Consider his thought about what it is heterosexual "men" do:

> during the past 2 years, I have kind of stopped hanging out with straight men, and I'm not quite sure why. I think part of it is because they do nothing but drink. I don't mean to make stereotypes or anything, but the straight guys I used to hang with, their social life revolved around drinking. So lately I have been hanging out mostly with women.

It is important to note Sean's reference to "straight guys" and the behavior he believes to be associated with "straight guys" (i.e., heavy alcohol use). This differs from his perception of how women use alcohol, hence his conscious decision to socialize with those who are assumed to drink little or not at all – women. Sean relied on the stereotype that heterosexual men engage in drinking behavior and that this behavior is normative. Additional evidence that drinking heavily is indicative of youthful EA heterosexual masculinity was provided by James, a heterosexual EA man.

> JAMES: (A terrible drunk is when a person after using alcohol) can't walk, can't talk. (They) spill other people's beer (due to their intoxication). You spill it on yourself. You know, (when some one behaves like) the old "two-beer queer".
> INTERVIEWER: "Two-beer queer?"
> JAMES: You never heard that expression, the "two-beer queer?" (For instance, if I were to say) "That girl is a "two-beer queer" (it means) she can't hold her drink; she has no tolerance, um, that's what it is, having no tolerance.

"Two-beer queers" are a subset of the population who are less able to handle liquor in the prescribed masculine tradition. That is, those who literally cannot withstand a total of two beers are not in compliance with hegemonic expectations. This "lesser" group is linked with a pejorative (i.e., "two-beer queer"), not because it rhymes but because queers are an inferior class of people (i.e., males who are not really men). In the account, gay men (as understood by the term "queer") and all women are referred to with the derogatory "two-beer queer" as a way to distinguish collectively between those who can drink (i.e., hegemonic men) and those unable to "handle" excessive alcohol consumption. It is believed that heavy alcohol use and the concurrent maintenance of control thus "make the man" and simultaneously define those who do not meet the ideal hegemonic masculine standard. Consider Fran's statement (EA, heterosexual).

> FRAN: It is a good thing if you can hold your own with the guys. If you are taking too long to finish your beer, they will ask, "Do you need a nipple for that beer?" because you are taking too long to finish it.

[...]

Discussion

The present article expands upon the existing gender and alcohol research by integrating the study of drinking with the broader issue of gender construction, specifically the embodiment of masculinity. In the present study, I examined alcohol's role as a resource in the expression of hegemonic masculinity among men in comparison with subjugated masculinities and femininities. I discuss the role of alcohol, as both a substance and a symbol. This research follows the symbolic interactionist tradition where alcohol is viewed as a symbol through which meaning (hegemonic masculinity) is created in the privileged local context of the college campus.

Hegemonic masculinities do not exist in the statistical sense, yet their qualities are considered normative. Masculinity is defined as a configuration of practice organized in relation to the structure of gender relations. Masculinity needs to be reproduced actively in social settings. For youth, sport is among the most common means of masculinity reproduction. Among youth in college, the prevalence and centrality of drinking alcohol suggests that it is an area in which masculinity will be an issue. [...]

In the study of masculinity, it is useful to differentiate hegemonic masculinity from subordinated masculinities. The hierarchy of masculinities is a pattern of hegemony (i.e., unquestioned) and not a pattern of simple domination based on force. Hegemony works through the use of exemplars of masculinity – symbols have authority despite the fact most boys and men do not fully live up to them. "Cultural consent, discursive centrality, institutionalization, and the marginalization or delegitimation of alternatives are widely documented features of socially dominant masculinities" (Connell and Messerschmidt 2005, p. 846). This research highlights these inter-relationships through an analysis of accounts of alcohol use.

I argue that the process of drinking and, in particular, heavy drinking for EA college men is a form of embodied masculinity construction. Ideological assumptions about masculinity are expressed through drinking behavior in a social location where such expressions are accepted, legitimized, and often expected. Heavy alcohol use among men becomes a resource where presumed "essential" characteristics of "manhood" can be expressed. In addition, how men and women discuss drinking behaviors illustrates the nuanced nature of gender performance.

[...]

It is important to understand masculinity in terms of its supposed antithesis, the construction of femininity. In contrast to men's accounts, EA and AA women did not assert that women's heavy alcohol use was a way to express power. Their drinking stories did not symbolize strength or power as women. Women largely viewed heavy drinking among women as potentially problematic, shameful, and stigmatizing behavior unbecoming of women.[1] Some women had fond memories of the "party atmosphere" associated with drinking, but did not present alcohol use as symbols of femininity. Drinking was not the focus of their social events. For women, drinking was secondary to the primary goal, which was to socialize and/or meet potential romantic partners. During these interviews, the majority of women simply did not espouse gender pride through their drinking accounts as did the men. Women's accounts of alcohol use did not reflect feminine accomplishment; they did, however, reflect a form of masculinity.

For many women, the costs associated with drinking, both physical and educational, were often discussed. Thus, many women discussed controlling and managing drinking. It appears women do gender by limiting their alcohol intake so as not to appear as bad, promiscuous, or masculine women. The handicapping of women's alcohol intake in drinking games may also be a means of accomplishing femininity.

[...]

Research routinely suggests that marriage significantly reduces the quantity and frequency of drinking (known as the "marriage effect") across social strata (Leonard and Rothbard 1999). Note that this is a different local setting with different gender relations. In this setting, heterosexual intimate relationships and fathering children are prominent symbols of hegemonic masculinity. Indeed, marriage and family are not prominent features of collegiate lifestyles and are therefore not typically associated with masculinity accomplishment for this population. Perhaps marriage

and family replace alcohol as symbols of masculinity in a culture where if one's (masculine) gender is questioned, one's (masculine) identity is threatened.

These considerations are relevant to the sociology of alcohol use and gender. Drinking behaviors appear to have the potential to reinforce, create, or challenge existing dominant hierarchical systems of gender. How much alcohol is used and how often, for example, relays culturally understood messages about identity. By choosing to drink or not to drink, individuals position themselves in the larger context of dominant, subordinated, sexualized, and racialized categories. These behaviors thereby reemphasize and normalize the domination of men over women and other types of men.

[...]

The question of race and drinking is of relevance here. Studies suggest that young racial and ethnic minorities tend to drink less than their EA counterparts. Social structural conditions shape the understanding of what gender means and inform how gender work is carried out differently depending on demographic differences. Gender accomplishment depends upon cultural definitions of gender and the availability of resources necessary to meet those standards. Because socially acceptable resources, skills, and physiological assets needed to "do gender" are limited and/or unequally distributed, masculine and feminine definitions often differ across categories of race, class, and sexuality. This may be indicative of why minority students tend to drink less often than their EA counterparts. Models of gender that differ from those adopted by dominant members of society could help to explain the disparity.

[...]

Note

1 It is interesting to note here that the gender gap in drinking for young people in the US appears to be closing for this age group. This may be in line with research that suggests that it is more acceptable for women to adopt traditionally masculine activities than it is for men to adopt activities traditionally reserved for women. However, women in the present study were subject to social control from other women and men.

Although drinking was tolerated, women were likely to be stigmatized more readily for heavy drinking often referred to as "sloppy" drinking.

References

Connell, R. W. and Messerschmidt, J. W. (2005). Hegemonic masculinity: Rethinking the concept. *Gender and Society,* *19* (6), 829–59.

Gough, B. and Edwards, G. (1998). The beer talking: Four lads, a carry out, and the reproduction of masculinities. *Sociological Review, 46,* 409–35.

Leonard, K. E. and Rothbard, J. (1999). Alcohol and the marriage effect. *Journal of Studies on Alcohol, 13,* 139–46.

Wechsler, H., Dowdall, G. W., Davenport, A., and Rimm, E. B. (1995). A gender specific measure of binge drinking among college students. *American Journal of Public Health, 85* (7), 982–5.

West, C. and Zimmerman, D. H. (1987). Doing gender. *Gender and Society, 1,* 125–51.

Questions

1 How was hegemonic masculinity personified through heavy drinking practices for undergraduate men? Do you think undergraduate women drink in a similar manner, or do they develop distinct drinking practices?

2 Do you think men need to control and manage their alcohol intake to maintain masculinity? Do women need to control and manage their intoxication to maintain femininity? Why or why not?

3 How do the norms and informal rules of the college party scene influence drinking behavior? How is good and/or bad drinking learned in the college years?

20

Mothering Through Addiction
A Survival Strategy among Puerto Rican Addicts

Monica Hardesty and Timothy Black

Monica Hardesty and Timothy Black offer a different picture of how women's gender role enactment is affected by their use of drugs in this study of Hispanic drug addicts. This selection offers a view of women who have vastly different levels of resources compared to Vecitis' college students. It also shows a route into drugs that contrasts sharply with the individual choice model Vecitis observed. As you read it you may want to think about how this portrait compares to Joe Laidler's Asian-Pacific Islanders and Spicer's American Indians in the way users were embedded within their cultures and families. You may also want to think about how these women, who often are in charge of female-headed households, compare to Dunlap, Golum, and Johnson's ghetto crack addicts. How do the resources of these two groups compare socioeconomically, and how is the composition of the family different in these two cultures?

After you read Peralta's piece, we suggested that you think about the way men benefit from being resourced with drugs. Carrying this idea further, you may want to think about what gender relations are like for many of these women? How are they treated by their fathers, their boyfriends, their husbands? What is their status in the family and community?

How does their drug use affect their ability to perform their gender role? In this regard, a good base for comparison is between these Puerto Rican women and the Black women in Dunlap, Golub, and Johnson's study. Further, how do the gender roles for these women compare with Vecitis' college students and Joe Laidler's Asian-Pacific Islanders? What are the main priorities each group faces and how does their drug use impact on their gender role enactment, either positively or negatively?

Finally, how does their status as women affect their social resources and their ability to carry out both the roles and obligations demanded of them as well as to live their own lives as they like? What role do drugs play in this equation?

Drugs and the American Dream: An Anthology, First Edition. Edited by Patricia A. Adler, Peter Adler, and Patrick K. O'Brien.
© 2012 John Wiley & Sons, Inc. Published 2012 by John Wiley & Sons, Inc.

Often the public, policy makers, and academics are quick to judge female addicts, to question their ability to parent, and to penalize them for their drug use by taking away their children. Before rushing to judgments and enacting social policies based on these premises, the mothering life of the addict needs to be examined more carefully. Important questions need to be addressed empirically. What is the bond between the addicted mother and her children? Does female drug addiction involve the pursuit of self-interest at the neglect of children? How do female addicts feel about their ability to parent? In this article, we examine the importance of mothering among a group of Puerto Rican addicts.

Our research exposes some common misconceptions about these women. Contrary to popular belief, we found that motherhood is vital. It is a lifeline into, through, and out of addiction. Although seemingly contradictory, motherhood remains central to Puerto Rican addicts and provides an anchor in an embattled and disruptive life. Motherhood serves as a survival strategy to escape problem histories, to sustain the women through drug addiction, and to repair the damage drug abuse has caused their children. Female Puerto Rican addicts recognize that they do not conform to everyone's notions of what it means to be a good mother. Nevertheless, they struggle to bridge the chasm between being a drug user and a mother. Although most falter in this struggle, they embrace a cultural ideal of motherhood in their steps toward recovery.

Research Method

We adopt an interpretive framework that allows female addicts to be the experts of their experiences and understandings as mothers. We seek, rather than impose, an understanding of mothering by asking questions and allowing the women to construct the stories of their lives. Using a life history method for data collection, we gathered information about how they viewed themselves as mothers before, during, and after addiction. To get a more complete story, we conducted three consecutive interviews. The first interview was about family background, children, and drug history. The second interview included questions

about health care, pregnancies, and Latino family values and expectations. The final interview discussed relationships with partners, social service agencies, and drug recovery.

Our sample included 20 Latina women from the Hartford, Connecticut area. These women were addicted to either crack-cocaine or heroin. Because our interest was in recording a range of life histories, we interviewed a sample of women whose experiences varied. All of them had some contact with a treatment program for Latina addicts, but they were in varying stages of recovery and demonstrated varying commitments to their recovery. Some were still very active in drug use, whereas others had been in the process of recovery for several years and were "clean." All were mothers except one who miscarried and subsequently was unable to conceive. The ages of their children varied from newborns to grown children. The ages of the women ranged from 23 to 48, with a median age of 29. Most abused drugs during their pregnancies. All of the women were Puerto Rican, except for one woman who was from the Dominican Republic. Fourteen of the women were born in Puerto Rico, although the majority had spent most of their lives on the mainland. Half of the women began using drugs as teens; the remainder began using in their early 20s.

[...]

Mothering on Limited Resources: The Puerto Rican Community in Hartford

To understand Puerto Rican addicts as mothers, one must first understand the place of motherhood in the lives of Puerto Rican women as well as the larger Puerto Rican experience in Hartford, Connecticut. There are few small cities in the Northeast that illustrate the devastating effects of deindustrialization, racial segregation, and increasing concentrations of poverty among Puerto Ricans better than Hartford. Hartford has the highest concentration of Puerto Ricans of any city in the country, with 30% of the city's population claiming Puerto Rican ancestry. Five of the city's 18 neighborhoods have a majority Hispanic population, and all 5 of these neighborhoods are highly distressed communities. [...]

Industrial decline, the changing labor force, and increased poverty have created conditions that are extremely difficult for many Puerto Rican families. Unemployment and underemployment, substance abuse, AIDS, discrimination, crime, violence, sexual abuse, school dropout, homelessness, and the lack of culturally appropriate social services overwhelm the Puerto Rican community in Hartford. [...]

The traditional values of the Latino family have helped to form the backbone of resiliency among the impoverished Puerto Rican community. Extended family networks are life-saving resources in times of need. Because women perform the work of organizing these kin networks, it provides them with a special place in their community. The Latino family system and its creative adaptations and nurturing dispositions can help to facilitate family interests and routines or, as in areas of concentrated poverty, can place undue stresses and strains on family members. Families can provide a refuge from a cruel world; the resilience of any community riddled by the historic realities of scarcity and exploitation is almost always rooted in kin networks. Conversely, sustaining a nurturing and stimulating home environment can be undermined greatly in neighborhoods in which legitimate income-generating strategies are limited, educational facilities underfunded and overburdened, public services debt impaired, and venues for realizing self-value severely restricted.

The reliance on family creates a cultural contradiction for the Puerto Rican woman. For Puerto Rican women, home is an anchor. Through kin work and caring for others, women find rewarding opportunities for self-expression, satisfaction, and recognition. However, because they carry the disproportionate burden of family responsibilities, home can become exploitative and oppressive. If her core identity consists of family duty and motherhood, what happens to a Puerto Rican woman when poverty-beleaguered neighborhoods overwhelm her efforts to be a good mother? What happens when the chaos and disruption associated with economic and social marginality impede the cultural identity through which self-salvation depends? What happens when partners become abusive or "fail" in the breadwinner role? Home cannot always be a safe haven from race, class, and gender oppression; hence, the ability to live up to family responsibilities is jeopardized. Culture can act as a double-edged sword: The failure to live up to deeply held cultural convictions about family life can foster destructive tendencies, and yet the resources from which one draws to reorient or reconstitute one's life may be the very same deeply held convictions. As we will see, the failure to live up to the ideal of being a good mother for Puerto Rican addicts can further deepen addiction at the same time that the identity of mother can become the cultural resource for seeking and sustaining drug recovery.

Problem Histories

Latina addicts in our study share the painful consequences of economic and social marginalization. Although the majority of Puerto Ricans socially reproduce cultural strategies for adapting to and resisting these conditions, carving out dignity and respect and sustaining communities against the odds, our participants represent the fringe that spins off into self-destructive patterns of behavior. The disruptions that constitute their life journeys begin long before addiction. For the women in our study, problems go back to their earliest childhood experiences, back to memories of instability and mistreatment in their families.

Like other female addicts, they experienced early physical and sexual abuse involving parents and stepparents, brothers and stepbrothers, and family friends, and in a few instances family members condoned or denied these incidents. Others recalled the damage done by decades of drug and alcohol abuse by family members, and some were initiated into the drug culture by family members. Others told stories of alcoholic fathers and stepfathers who routinely beat their mothers. When talking about these early childhood experiences, the women see themselves as fulfilling a prophecy of instability. As one participant succinctly explained, "I am unstable; my mother was unstable."

Patterns of abusive relationships carry over into adulthood, particularly in relationships with men. Like other female addicts, partner abuse was common, even during pregnancy. Most had been abused by their partners, and about one third admitted they were in an abusive relationship at the time of the interview. One woman described abuse in every relationship with men. Abusive partners isolated them, dominated their everyday activities, and sometimes forced drugs on them when they struggled to quit.

The constant threats and episodes of domestic violence and the ever-increasing isolation of the victim not only deepened the trauma in the lives of these women but also served to further restrict their already narrowed life options. Of course, we do not know the cause and effect here, but the lifelong trauma of abuse created a situation in which the use of drugs may have fulfilled many needs: momentary pleasure, escape, endurance, or a respite from physical and emotional pain. Drug addiction, however, can further trap the victims in the viciousness of domestic violence. Because many of our study participants depended on their partners for drugs, to give up the abusive relationship with their partners meant taking on greater responsibilities for supporting their drug habits, which also meant reorganizing their mothering responsibilities, creating perhaps more problems than remaining in the violent situation.

Problem histories carry over and accelerate in full-blown addiction. To secure a regular supply of drugs to support their $300- to $500-a-day habits, many women sustained a relationship with a man who was a drug dealer or who had a steady supply of drugs. In this way, the women never had to leave their homes, a preferable situation for women caring for children. Our participants favored the cultural tradition of men working outside the home and women staying home to care for children. Despite the violence in the home, the women usually relied on the partner until he could no longer provide. This decision carries negative consequences because it increases one's dependency on addicted, abusive, and domineering men.

Sometimes partners were unable to meet the increasing demand for drugs, or they were caught and incarcerated. Then the women became more self-reliant and like other female addicts financed their drug habits by entering illegal labor markets. Some women began to deal drugs, an ever-increasing practice among female drug addicts. Stealing, bartering, conning, prostituting, and pimping were other illegal strategies they employed. Most did not rely on a single method for securing drugs but alternated in their reliance on male partners, drug trafficking, theft, and prostitution.

With increased time in the heroin and cocaine street life, women became more and more encumbered with problems, a stage characterized as "full-blown chaos." The career of the female street drug addict, with its roots in early childhood trauma and repeated physical and sexual abuse in adulthood, moved into a situation of full-blown chaos in which physical annihilation and a predatory street culture became their lives. In full-blown chaos, women become fatalistic; they express feelings of being "trapped in their situation, their histories, and eventually their drug habits" (Kearney, Murphy, and Rosenbaum, 1994, p. 147). They accept the elevated chaos and its painful consequences as normal; they adopt a belief in "the bizarre as the usual."

The addicts' fatalistic perceptions of their life courses have profound ramifications for their views of self. Female addicts internalize an identity as "loser," as having very little self-worth or self-value. They recognize a limited number of options for constructing new and different lives and often adopt a strategy of "settling for less." The narrowing of options that began in childhood and tightened in adulthood was squeezed in addiction. They accommodate this shrinking control over their lives by protecting the remaining options for selfhood and exert a kind of "motherhood control." Unlike male addicts, who organize their daily lives entirely around the drug – seeking money for drugs, copping, networking, rationing, and so on – female addicts' life organization includes children.

Their histories as victims of sexual abuse and domestic violence and their exposure to generations of substance abuse did not deter these women from valuing family and themselves as mothers, even though problem histories make it difficult to fulfill this role. Like other oppressed Puerto Rican women, they continued to construct home as a place of meaning. Motherhood became their symbolic anchor: a culturally reinforcing, self-sustaining identity that grounds them amidst the turmoil in their lives. Even at the point of full-blown chaos, even when women lost custody of their children, children remained central in their lives – in fantasies, yearnings, and plans – which, as we will see, results in a numbing surrender to self-destruction or becomes the seeds for recovery. By controlling motherhood, the addict sustained an identity not completely defined by her life with drugs. Such connections to children structure the experiences differently for women.

The Centrality of Motherhood and Mother Work

The centrality of motherhood in our participants' lives is rooted in the Latino culture. Latino families generally adhere to traditional gender roles. A woman's life revolves around the family and home. Latinas typically hold themselves responsible for the majority of household and child-rearing tasks and stress the importance of mothers in the parent–child relationship. It is the woman's responsibility to provide the day-to-day care and to transmit the cultural values to her children. Mothers occupy a special place within the Puerto Rican family and community. Cultural activities such as Mother's Day in Puerto Rico, a holiday only exceeded by Three Kings Day in gift giving and celebration, reinforce the normative standards surrounding the importance of motherhood for the Latina. Our participants described their central role of child rearing: "Fathers go away, but mothers stay," and "fathers are part time; mothers are full time."

In the Puerto Rican culture, woman and mother are inseparable. Raising children is the primary role of a Puerto Rican woman, valued above her responsibilities as wife. The ultimate measure of womanhood is being a mother. As with other low-income women, motherhood validates the Latina's womanhood. When discussing her children, one Puerto Rican addict explained the centrality of motherhood in her life: "I would do anything for them. I wouldn't allow anyone to harm them. It is as I told you, I am mother before woman." Failure as a mother is equated with failure as a woman. The death of a child brings unspeakable loss, a loss of self:

> My baby died, crib death, Sudden Infant Death Syndrome. I found her dead in her crib. It was too much for me. My addiction began then. I was frustrated. I was feeling lonely. … Crack was something really fantastic. It was like going out of this world, forgetting everything, and that was exactly what I was looking for, to forget

everything. It is a way to shut out your feelings. Not facing them. Back then, it was what I wanted to do. I saw those people "getting fixed," looking so happy, blind and deaf to everything around them. I wanted to be like them. I wanted to forget everything that was surrounding me. I was having nightmares where I saw my child. I saw her crying. I wanted to get out of this world. I wanted a hole in the ground and get in there, to get into my own world.

So central is motherhood to their female identity, Puerto Rican women have been described as being unable to make the choice not to have children; they opt to do it all rather than relinquish the role of mother.

When we asked our participants to describe Puerto Rican women, they too spoke about the importance of motherhood. They told us that a Puerto Rican woman is the caretaker of children. She cooks, cleans, and sacrifices for the children. Being there for her children gives her a sense of identity and a place within her community. Children come first in her thoughts and actions. Many described their children as more important than themselves. Through self-sacrifice, they derived a sense of self. Children became a way of marking the important events in their lives. Restricted by poverty, joblessness, and addiction, our participants indicated that motherhood is the only positive identity that they possess. Not unlike other low-income mothers, motherhood reveals the deeper meaning of the Latina's existence and provides a rite of passage into adulthood. Because a Puerto Rican mother is charged with the responsibility of maintaining ethnic values and social ties, motherhood grounds her within her community as well.

These cultural expectations for motherhood did not disappear when Puerto Rican women became addicted. Instead, the desire to mother intensified and became most important for defining oneself. While addicted, our participants could not, or would not, relinquish their mother identities. This maintenance of the mother identity entailed a considerable amount of work at defining oneself in a positive light in relation to one's increasingly illegal actions. The mother identity was constructed and reconstructed over the course of her addiction and recovery, an activity we call "mother work."

Doing it all

Maintaining a mother identity is not an easy task for the addict. In the beginning, she struggled to "do it all," to juggle the responsibilities of motherhood with her everyday drug activities. In a desire to preserve her connectedness to others, she guarded her mother identity. Our participants preserved their identities by claiming to meet four requirements of motherhood. First and foremost, a mother must continue to meet the physical needs of her children: food, clothing, and shelter. One addict described taking care of these physical needs during addiction: "I like the children to dress clean, to smell good, that they do not stink or be mucousy and that they eat." Second, she must continue to provide discipline to sustain the child's moral character. They claimed a need to use physical punishment to teach right from wrong: "I have to hit them a little bit so that they learn respect," and "good mothers know how to discipline her children. She doesn't wait until it is too late." Third, she must continue to meet the emotional needs of her child. One had to "be there for them when they need you," and no matter what they do, "you never turn your back on them." Finally, she must prevent the harm of unstable child-rearing practices. For those who experienced an abusive childhood, this meant "righting the wrongs" that happened to them as a child. It also meant preventing or repairing any harm that arose from their own actions as a drug addict.

A mother who can maintain a drug habit and take care of her children wins respect in the drug world. Being a good mother is an ongoing source of pride when mothering is maintained through the addiction. The maintenance of discipline and taking care of their children's needs for food, clothing, and shelter are essential elements of mother work. Although mother work involves taking care of children both physically and emotionally, it also involves identity management. Given the stigma placed on addicts, especially female ones, maintaining an "unspoiled" view of oneself as a good mother despite the addiction serves as a self-survival tool.

Many Puerto Rican addicts affirmed that they were good mothers during their addictions. They were able to stay on top of both their drug work and their mother work:

You can be a good mother and be using at the same time because the love for your kids is always there. I take care of my kids. I worry about them. I see that they don't go hungry. I see that they don't get hurt. Wherever I go I take them along.

In doing it all and balancing these two lines of work, an addict divided herself into two separate spheres of existence: her habits as an addict and her life as a mother.

I was a good mother to my child in spite of being, you know, an addict. … I never have taken addicts to my house! The one that used drugs in my house was me, and I kept it hidden. I did it in fear. I never dared disrespect my son by taking people to my house to get high, to drink or to smoke crack. I never dared! To me that is a lack of respect for my son. I always tried to have a house for him, a place for him to live where he could feel safe and sound. A safe home for him.

By creating a dual life, the addict attempted to maintain home as a safe haven and to minimize the effects of her addiction on her children.

This strategy of compartmentalizing one's life was accomplished more easily by some addicts than others. For one, the dual life was easier to maintain if she had enough money or a regular supply of drugs:

If she has enough for her vice, she can be a good mother and use drugs. She has to have enough [money] to meet her children's needs. Because the most important thing is her children, more than the drug. That is what I used to do. First I had my children's things bought, then [I bought] the drug.

Many described a regular drug supply as an aid to their work in the home. Some women stated that the daily use of drugs allowed them to perform their mother role more easily and more effectively. Drugs eased a depression that immobilized some of them. They described a new level of enthusiasm that allowed them to get out of bed in the morning, to cook, to complete housework, and in general to "be there" for their children. For some, drug use provided them with a lift, a more positive outlook on life. With a constant supply of drugs, they could do it all. Paradoxically, this ability to do it all was accomplished most often through active drug dealing.

For their identity management to be successful, addicts had to reject others' standards of mothering and to avoid facing the label of bad mother. The growing tension between their and others' evaluations of their performances as mothers increased the difficulty of their mother work. Like other female addicts, our participants routinely discounted the judgments of others about their negative performances as mothers. They insisted that they were good mothers, which required them to meet minimal expectations of the Puerto Rican culture and to compare favorably with the negative mothering they saw in others. Some claimed they did not abuse their children as others did: "During my addiction I never mistreated my child. I never did any [physical] harm to my child. Had I seen that I was not able to handle the child, I would have given him to DCF [Department of Children and Families]." Others claimed they adhered to the cultural norms of motherhood as defined by Puerto Ricans:

> [Do you believe that a woman that uses drugs can be a good mother?] Yes. If you take good care of your children. You have a roof over them to sleep, have their food and all their clothing, take them to the doctor. That nothing is missing, that is being a good mother. Because in spite of me using drugs, I always was there for my girls, and they always had what they needed.

Those who were able to perform their responsibilities successfully experienced it as a source of pride. Those who performed marginally interpreted their efforts as a sign that they were not bad mothers.

However, not every addict could fend off all challenges to her status as a good mother. There was widespread recognition that some addicts maintained the dual roles of mother and drug user better than others:

> There are two types of drug addicts: the responsible one and the irresponsible one. I was doing drugs since I was 16 years old, and no one knew I was doing drugs because I took care of my children. The same thing happens with some of my friends. They have their homes in order, and they take care of their children. And if there is money left and they want to waste it [on drugs], they do it. That is the responsible addict. The irresponsible addict is the one that thinks first about getting high and the children come next.

Maintaining a mother identity became problematic, especially when one experienced difficulty in fulfilling her responsibilities as a mother. Over time, the juggling of addict and mother roles became increasingly difficult, and strains developed between the two lines of work. Because more time was spent in support of the drug habit, less time was given to the children and home. Some began to sense impending failure and experienced profound doubts about their abilities. Our participants recognized that in the long run, most addicts could not maintain both lines of work and told stories of some who fell completely into life on the streets.

Falling through or failing as mothers

Having internalized the normative images of what it means to be a good mother, our participants lived between believing that they were good mothers and that they were bad mothers. Although proud of their achievements as mothers under duress, off and on they became exasperated with themselves as mothers. A time came when their attempts to compartmentalize their lives failed. They realized their mothering had suffered and was no longer "good enough."

As drug work competed more and more with mother work, the women in this study described themselves as less skillful in the performances of their mothering duties. When she had a reliable source of money or drugs, usually through her male partner, then she was able to stay home and be there for her children. However, when drug supplies became sporadic or when her addiction expenses skyrocketed to a $500-a-day habit, she spent most of her time and money on the drug. The search for drugs, or the money to finance them, became time-consuming and all engrossing.

Women often interpret thinking about others as caring for our participants, and not thinking about children was interpreted as not caring. When drug work became all engrossing, the addict forgot her children; she removed from her mind their physical needs, neglected to feed them, and failed to see that they had a safe place to sleep. They stopped thinking of their children first:

> [How did drugs help you to deal with that situation?] I did not think. When I was using, I did not think. I just

wanted to keep using. Worrying about getting it, I did not have time to think about my child.

I lived for the drug. If they [her children] woke up and were hungry, I said, "Wait a minute." Now [that I'm in recovery] when they wake up, I say, "Baby are you hungry? Do you want to eat?" Drugs were first then.

As the search for drug money took addicts into the streets to hustle or prostitute, they left their children unsupervised for greater periods of time. Even when addicts were able to meet the physical needs of their children, they still expressed an overriding fear of emotional damage to their children. In some cases, the illegal street work led to arrest and jail time, which further curtailed their abilities to be with and care for their children. As addiction escalated, children were overlooked, neglected, or discarded. At this point in their lives, the women claimed to have lost balance; their mothering had fallen through:

A bad mother is a woman who abandons her children. Someone that has put something else first, like me. I decided I preferred addiction over my own daughters. I put addiction first. Not being there when they take ill, not knowing if they eat or if they are fine.

A bad mother is someone that gives her children away, such as I did. I did not mean any harm. I meant to do good when I did it because I did not have a place to stay. I was not going to let them stay in the halls where the homeless sleep to catch pneumonia on my account, or that they may die.

While struggling to stay connected to their children throughout addiction, the women realized that they often lost touch.

We found these points of falling through happened at key junctures in their lives. Puerto Rican addicts recognized their inadequacies when they completely disregarded their child care responsibilities. They acknowledged deficiencies when they gave their children to family members. They admitted failing when the DCF forcibly removed the children from the home. Admitting deficiencies and anticipating the loss of children further eroded the cherished identity of mother; nevertheless, they maintained mother work. They made numerous efforts to minimize these damaging effects, emphasizing their efforts as evidence

of being a good mother and voluntarily transferring children into a family member's household.

[...]

The parenting bond between mother and daughter is particularly strong. Daughters experience themselves as an extension of their mothers and their mothers as an extension of themselves. It is not unusual for grandmothers in Puerto Rican families to provide care for their daughters' children in their homes at some time in their lives. The strength and vitality of the "grandmother–mother–child triad" enable Latinas to feel connected to one another and empowered within their communities and families. That is, in their shared parenting bonds, they affirm themselves as "Latinas," women with a unique way of relating to one another through close interaction with other women in their kin networks.

Because Puerto Ricans construct family differently, we need to understand their decisions about children differently. An addict's decision to place her children in the custody of a female relative was not a complete relinquishing of mothering responsibilities; rather, it was another way of doing mother work. It was an enactment of shared motherhood that is so vital among Latina women. They placed their children in the care of a companion parent, one who is obligated to act on their behalf with all the love and attention of a biological parent. The reliance on a companion parent is entirely normal in the culture, and it, therefore, did not produce the kind of "mother guilt" as might be expected among Anglo women. Among the mothers in this study, this custody arrangement was preferred. It was temporary and allowed them to maintain some control over mothering. In their eyes, they were not completely failing as mothers; instead, their own mothers were standing in for them.

Another point of falling through occurs when children are removed forcibly from their home by child welfare agents from the DCF. Various transfers of custody had occurred among our participants. Some children of Puerto Rican addicts were placed in homes of relatives, but in some cases, children were placed in foster homes, and in a few cases, parental rights were terminated. The DCF's actions had the most damaging effect on their mother identities. Some feared serious damage to the mother–child bond: "[What is the worst thing they could have done to you?] To take my children away. Because the children are very attached to me. If taken away they would suffer. They [foster parents] might mistreat them." Numerous mothers feared their children would be mistreated in foster homes:

It is dangerous for children because even foster homes have [sexually] violated girls. And DCF stays quiet and does not say anything. DCF helps some families, and it damages others for the rest of their lives. They do not understand that, the Whites.

Placement of children in foster homes violated the ethnic tradition of compadrazgo. The Puerto Rican extended family was undermined: "When they take the children away sometimes they don't place them with people from their own culture and the children suffer." The involuntary removal of children from the home produced great damage to the mother identity and, as a result, more mother guilt. The forced removal of their children was an undeniable sign of their failures as mothers. In addition to failing their children, they failed their communities as well. The placement of their children into the homes of strangers, people outside the extended family system or outside the ethnic community altogether, attacked the cultural foundation of community on which Puerto Rican motherhood, kin networks, and proper childcare are built.

Recovering the mother identity

The loss of children was devastating to these women. Many described it as the worst thing they could ever imagine happening in their lives. The loss of children often spiraled them further into addiction. A number stated that their drug use substantially increased when DCF became involved in their lives: "I was depressed because DCF told me that if my next baby was born positive to drugs they were going to take him away. That led me to use more drugs." Some feared that DCF would not ever return their children to them. For example, one mother feared that DCF would put her children up for a legal adoption:

I am trying to remake my life in a correct way. But I am afraid that when the time comes and I fight for my

children they [DCF] are going to say, "No!" That I can't take them back. I have that fear.

Despite numerous challenges to their mother identities, many put faith in their abilities to repair their relationships with their children and to have them returned to them. Rather than letting go of aspirations, hope became a new form of mother work. Although they had lost many things – stability, money, health, marriage, and a fulfilling sex life – they were determined not to lose their children. During the most traumatic times of their lives, they longed for their children, fantasized and dreamed about them. Like women in general, these thoughts of children were interpreted as signs of caring. Even when children were no longer present in the home, they continued to labor as mothers and discussed better ways of demonstrating to their children and others that they could be good mothers:

When they took the girl away, they [DCF] helped me to reflect. If they would not have taken the baby away I would still be a good mother, but not to the maximum of how it should be. They took my daughter away to make me react and calm down, and they accomplished that.

Good mothers do not give up hope and do not cease their mother work just because their children are gone: "If someone takes my children away I fight for them, to get them back. They [bad mothers] don't do anything." Some mothers focused on the temporariness of the physical separation and on the permanence of the emotional bond between mother and child. The return of the child, though distant and vague in its timetable, shaped her mother work during these periods of separation:

[Why did you want a child?] Because I need it in my life. [Why do you think you needed it in your life?] One always needs something in her life. It is good to have a child. [If you think you need a child, how come she is not living with you?] Because of the drugs. ... [What do you value most?] My daughter. [If you value her that much, why don't you fight to have your child with you?] It is as I told you. I do not want to fight yet. I just began recovery and I do not want to relapse, having her and relapsing.

For female addicts, recovery means more than "getting clean"; it is about "creating a new life." For our participants, it was about recreating their lives as mothers. For them, recovery involved recovering the role of mother. Reclaiming one's children was the primary motive for recovery, regardless of whether one had given away her children voluntarily or had them taken away by a state agency. As one woman explained, "I have enough reasons to get into treatment – these are my children. I was in addiction and my children pushed me into treatment. What thing could [give me more strength] than my children?"

When confronting their past failures, women relived their drug experiences from their children's perspectives:

> I can imagine that they felt bad because they use to tell me, "Mama, please stop using drugs, we want the sweet mother that you were before." And I didn't care, didn't care, didn't care about my children. Drugs were more important. I was having no feelings.
>
> It was the worst experience when my daughter realized that I was under the influence of drugs. I locked myself up in the bathroom [to use]. She was little, but even being little, she knew something was happening. She had a negative attitude. She didn't want to talk to me. [How old was she?] Seven years old. She would tell me, "Mama, you are doing something wrong. I know it."

For the recovering addict to reclaim her motherhood, however, she must confront her guilt, repair the damage inflicted on her children, and renegotiate her mother identity. This was a monumental task fraught with anxiety and guilt:

> In the beginning it was very difficult for me to explain all this to my children, especially the oldest one. He is the one I offended the most. Now I feel better because he understands that I have that disease. [Why did you say that you offended him?] Because many times I spoke ill to him and he answered me in the same way. He was mad at me. He probably noticed my problem and didn't say anything to me. I offended him a lot. Not long ago I asked him for his forgiveness.

While talking about her son's placement in a detention home, another mother was consumed with the grief of having been a bad mother:

> I feel guilty. Sometimes I tell myself, you know, that is the result of my using drugs. It created in him emotional problems. He was greatly affected when I was sent to jail, that and the fact that he saw me using drugs. He has become a very rebellious child. He has no interest in school. It is the pain of seeing me using drugs.

Our participants did not measure their success in recovery by counting the number of meetings attended or days of sobriety. They measured their success relationally; they watched for, kept track of, and felt joy in their children's loving actions toward them. A child's kindness meant more than another day of sobriety. Reconnecting with lost children was essential to their recovery. They experienced frustrations when these loving actions did not happen as often as they desired because it meant they were not progressing as planned:

> You see the damage you have caused them when you were in the addiction [and you want to repair it]. It is like when you try to straighten a bent stick little by little, then when you have the stick almost straight and the stick gets bent again. I would like to have more time with him [her son], but I cannot.

For the Puerto Rican addict, commitment to recovery involved commitment to one's children. For virtually all of the addicts, their motivations to succeed in recovery were to reconnect with their children and to recover the identity of a good mother. Yet, their successes largely depended on their children's willingness to participate in the process:

> [How is the boy with you? Does he trust you?] Now he does. He has been living with my daughter for a year. The first year, that was a war, war over power. You know, "I am the boss, you are not." I think his fears of me going back to drugs were great, but not now. Since we are in therapy, he has been able to bring out all of his rage against me. There is more communication and trust between he and I.

It was important to the addicts that their children noticed the positive changes in them and encouraged their rehabilitation efforts:

> They [used to] cry, "Mama, get out of that [drugs]. Look how ugly you are." When I finished the program, I came

home and they said, "Oh mom, how beautiful you look." They said this to my face, and they kissed me.

[Even though] they wanted me to quit, my oldest even offered me her things [shoes and coat] for me to sell in order to have money to get fixed. She used to tell me, "Mom, sell these things, you can buy another for me later." They knew when I was *enferma de droga* (drug sick, in need of a fix). [Now] they ask me every day, "Have you gone to get your methadone treatment today?"

The desire to have their children back and to reclaim their identity as mother was essential yet often idealistic. It was a very difficult task because repeated drug use was intertwined with the guilt of being neglectful mothers in the past. Of their mothering tasks, reclaiming children was the most challenging, one that takes years to accomplish:

> Social services in Puerto Rico have two of my children. I have lost all of my parental rights, so far. [Is that for good?] At least it will be this way till my kids grow up and become aware that I am a different mother now. Then they will have to decide if they want to come to live with me. That will be the only way. In court, there is nothing I can do to get my children back. I can fight for the one that is here in Hartford. Still I call my children. I look for them. On June 16, I sent a present for one of the kids. I called him up and I asked him, "Sonny, would you like to come with mama just for vacation," and he said, "No mama, I don't want to go with you." I can't force them, see. It has been 3 years since they were taken away. So many things can happen in 3 years. I did many wrong things. I was wrong. I regret that, and I begged for his forgiveness. It hurts, you know, because I see that my child doesn't want to stay with me. It is not easy. Maybe I want to see the result of my recovery too soon. But I am going to continue my struggle. I am going to keep trying. I know that one day my son is going to realize that his mother was sick, but at least she went ahead – it would be bad if they had to say, "My mother was an addict and never changed."

Mother work in the recovery stage can set into motion a cycle of great expectations, failure to meet those expectations, and then drug relapse. The grand expectations of motherhood were repeatedly dashed in the actual practice of parenting after drug addiction; the failed mother identity resurfaced, and recovering addicts fell back into old drug habits in response to

failure. Their abilities to embrace the possibilities of renewed relations, rather than succumb to past failures and to the obstacles to parenting, enhanced their success to recover motherhood. Puerto Rican addicts moved through this cycle of parental hope and despair several times before reaching a recovered status, a status that meant reclaiming one's place in the culture and reaffirming one's position in the family. The vacillation between the good mother and the bad mother identities fueled the movement between recovery and relapse.

Conclusion

Puerto Rican mothers in Hartford live on limited resources and with significantly reduced opportunities for achievement. Women confronted with limited opportunities very often seek the cultural ideal of motherhood to acquire self-value and personal identity. This identity provides a ray of hope, albeit dim, in the lives of women marked by oppression. Motherhood becomes a central way of staying connected and surviving in hard times.

Puerto Rican addicts cherished their role as mothers and performed a significant amount of mother work throughout their addiction and recovery. The nature of their mother work evolved over the course of the addiction. In the early stage of drug addiction, mothers juggled the responsibility of motherhood with their ever-enlarging drug activities. They constructed dual lives to shield and preserve the good mother identity. As their addictions progressed, the duality collapsed. They fell through and faltered as mothers. Their mother work correspondingly shifted; they confronted the bad mother in their past acts. Moving toward recovery, they walked the tightrope between the good mother and the bad mother identities – the bad mother image pushing them into relapse, and the good mother image pulling them out again. Finally, in recovery, they worked on their connections with their children to reclaim the good mother ideal.

The frustrations of parenting, especially in poverty environments in which resources for parenting are limited, may lead to feelings of failure, drug abuse, and neglect of children. We have found in the lives of Puerto Rican women a different story. Addicts, even in extreme circumstances, struggle to maintain their place as mothers. They juggle overwhelming and contradictory demands, fend off negative criticism, and find support in kin relations. Yes, we found that this crisis can accelerate self-destructive behavior and drug use, but it also can act as a wake-up call. Notwithstanding the devastation of poverty, marginalization, and other forms of oppression, women can and do mother. Despite the problem histories and abusive partners, despite the absorption into the anesthetizing world of drugs, and despite the damage caused to their children and other family members, these addicts moved into the frightening world of recovery where they confronted the consequences of their past failures. They did so because of their children. Motherhood is their lifeline; it provides continuity in a discontinuous life and sustains the Puerto Rican woman through the stages of addiction into recovery.

Reference

Kearney, M. H., Murphy, S., and Rosenbaum, M. (1994). Learning by losing: Sex and fertility on crack cocaine. *Qualitative Health Research, 4* (2), 142–62.

Questions

1 For the women in the article, how did the mother identity operate as justification or excuse for their drug use?

2 Do you think these women might be more likely to seek help if drug addiction was considered a medical problem rather than a criminal problem in our society? Why or why not?

3 How did having children impact the level of drug involvement for these Puerto Rican mothers? Were children beneficial in the recovery process? Why or why not?

Youth and Aging

Tinydopers
A Case Study of Deviant Socialization

Patricia A. Adler and Peter Adler

We include a piece in this anthology on young children smoking marijuana that we wrote in the 1970s, a vastly different time in history and in the drug landscape. Jimmy Carter was president, there were rather liberalized laws concerning marijuana that grew out of the "hippie" era, and decriminalization of the drug was becoming popularized, especially in the Western sections of North America, such as California, Oregon, British Columbia, and Alaska. However, shortly thereafter, in 1980, we saw the election of Ronald Reagan, the institution of Nancy Reagan's "Just Say No" and DARE programs as near-required subjects in most American school districts, and the establishment of the Partnership for a Drug-Free America. Once again marijuana became subjected to Draconian laws, paralleling the ones enacted in the 1930s under Henry Anslinger and the "Reefer Madness" campaigns. Marijuana remained on the forefront of drug policy and accounted for much of the imprisoned population throughout the rest of the twentieth century. Throughout the 1990s, marijuana remained illegal, demonized, and connected with crime, delinquency, the amotivational syndrome, and a growing problem among a youthful population. This attitude, in large part, continued through the administration of George H. W. Bush.

Under President Obama, in 2008, Attorney General Holder announced that marijuana would be a low priority item on this Administration's agenda of criminality. This time period was also characterized by a growing number of states (about 30% by 2011) passing "medical marijuana" laws, with many municipalities decriminalizing the possession of less than an ounce of the drug. Although epidemiological research finds that youth are routinely being exposed to marijuana as young as 10–12 years old, there is little indication that "tinydoping" has spread. In fact, media coverage suggests that parents of the flower child generation are more commonly hiding the facts about their former drug use from their kids, afraid of

Drugs and the American Dream: An Anthology, First Edition. Edited by Patricia A. Adler, Peter Adler, and Patrick K. O'Brien.
© 2012 John Wiley & Sons, Inc. Published 2012 by John Wiley & Sons, Inc.

being turned in or of encouraging them to participate in a behavior that has become more demonized than it was in its efflorescence.

This article may represent merely an artifact of a particular moment in history or it may still be practiced among some parents, but hidden because it is still an obvious stigmatizing phenomenon, no matter the political winds. Nevertheless, we believe, the issues about drug use, parents, and children that are highlighted in this article are still salient. For example, to what extent is drug use learned in families and passed down from parents to children? How does this compare to the way drugs were shown within the families of Joe Laidler's Asian-Pacific Islanders, Dunlap, Golub, and Johnson's ghetto crack addicts, or any drug scene where the family is a significant location for the social learning of drug use? How does intra-family learning compare with the community-based learning of the American Indians? Finally, how does society regard the use of drugs by children, especially given the rise in prescriptions of pharmaceutical drugs among this very young population for ADHD and other psychological disorders?

Marijuana smoking has now filtered down to our youngest generation; a number of children from 0–8 years old are participating in this practice under the influence and supervision of their parents. This phenomenon, *tinydoping*, raises interesting questions about changes in societal mores and patterns of socialization. We are not concerned here with the desirability or morality of the activity. Instead, we will discuss the phenomenon, elucidating the diverse range of attitudes, strategems, and procedures held and exercised by parents and children.

An examination of the history and cultural evolution of marijuana over the last several decades illuminates the atmosphere in which tinydoping arose. Marijuana use, first located chiefly among jazz musicians and ghetto communities, eventually expanded to "the highly alienated young in flight from families, schools and conventional communities" (Simon and Gagnon, 1968: 60). Blossoming in the mid-1960s, this youth scene formed an estranged and deviant subculture offsetting the dominant culture's work ethic and instrumental success orientation. Society reacted as an angry parent, enforcing legal, social and moral penalties against its rebellious children. Today, however, the pothead subculture has eroded and the population of smokers has broadened to include large numbers of middle-class and establishment-oriented people.

Marijuana, then, may soon take its place with alcohol, its "prohibition" a thing of the past. These two changes can be considered movements of moral passage:

> Movements to redefine behavior may eventuate in a moral passage, a transition of the behavior from one moral status to another…What is attacked as criminal today may be seen as sick next year and fought over as possibly legitimate by the next generation. (Gusfield, 1967: 187)

Profound metamorphoses testify to this redefinition; frequency and severity of arrest is proportionately down from a decade ago; the stigma of a marijuana-related arrest is no longer as personally and occupationally ostracizing; and the fear that using grass will press the individual into close contact with hardened criminals and cause him to adopt a deviant self-identity or take up criminal ways has also largely passed.

The transformation in marijuana's social and legal status is not intrinsic to its own characteristics or those of mood-altering drugs in general. Rather, it illustrates a process of becoming socially accepted that many deviant activities or substances may go through. This research suggests a more generic model of social change, a sequential development characteristic of the diffusion and legitimation of a formerly unconventional practice. Five stages identify the spread of such activities from small isolated outgroups, through increasing levels of mainstream society, and finally to such sacred groups as children. Often, however, as with the case of pornography, the appearance of this quasi-sanctioned conduct among juveniles elicits moral outrage and a social backlash designed to prevent such behavior in the sacred population, while leaving it more open to the remainder of society.

[…]

Methods

Collected over the course of 18 months, our data include observations of two dozen youngsters between the ages of birth and eight, and a similar number of parents, aged 21 to 32, all in middle-class households. To obtain a complete image of this practice we talked with parents, kids, and other involved observers (the "multiperspectival" approach, Douglas, 1976). Many of our conversations with adults were taped but our discussions with the children took the form of informal, extemporaneous dialogue, since the tape recorder distracts and diverts their attention. Finally, our study is exploratory and suggestive; we make no claim to all-inclusiveness in the cases or categories below.

The Kids

The following four individuals, each uniquely interesting, represent many common characteristics of other children and adults we observed.

"Big Ed": The diaperdoper

Big Ed derives his name from his miniature size. Born three months prematurely, now three years old, he resembles a toy human being. Beneath his near-white wispy hair and toddling diapered bottom, he packs a punch of childish energy. Big Ed's mother and older siblings take care of him although he often sees his father who lives in a neighboring California town.

Laxity and permissiveness characterize his upbringing, as he freely roams the neighborhood under his own and other children's supervision. Exposure to marijuana has prevailed since birth and in the last year he advanced from passive inhalation (smoke blown in his direction) to active puffing on joints. Still in the learning stage, most of his power is expended blowing air into the reefer instead of inhaling. He prefers to suck on a "bong" (a specially designed waterpipe), delighting on the gurgling sound the water makes. A breast fed baby, he will go to the bong for oral satisfaction, whether it is filled or not. He does not actively seek joints, but Big Ed never refuses one when offered. After a few puffs, however, he usually winds up with smoke in his eyes and tearfully retreats to a glass of water. Actual marijuana inhalation is minimal; his size renders it potent. Big Ed has not absorbed any social restrictions related to pot use or any awareness of its illegality, but is still too young to make a blooper as his speech is limited.

Stephanie: The social smoker

Stephie is a dreamy four-year-old with quite good manners, calm assurance, sweet disposition and a ladylike personality and appearance. Although her brothers are rough and tumble, Stephanie can play with the boys or amuse herself sedately alone or in the company of adults. Attendance at a progressive school for the last two years has developed her natural curiosity and intelligence. Stephanie's mother and father both work, but still find enough recreational time to raise their children with love and care and to engage in frequent marijuana smoking. Accordingly, Stephanie has seen grass since infancy and accepted it as a natural part of life. Unlike the diaperdoper, she has mastered the art of inhalation and can breathe the smoke out through her nose. Never grasping or grubbing for pot, she has advanced from a preference for bongs or pipes and now enjoys joints when offered. She revels in being part of a crowd of smokers and passes the reefer immediately after each puff, never holding it for an unsociable amount of time. Her treasure box contains a handful of roaches (marijuana butts) and seeds (she delights in munching them as snacks) that she keeps as mementos of social occasions with (adult) "friends." After smoking, Stephanie becomes more bubbly and outgoing. Dancing to records, she turns in circles as she jogs from one foot to the other, releasing her body to the rhythm. She then eats everything in sight and falls asleep – roughly the same cycle as adults, but faster.

When interviewed, Stephanie clearly recognized the difference between a cigarette and a joint (both parents use tobacco), defining the effects of the latter as good but still being unsure of what the former did and how the contents of each varied. She also responded with some confusion about social boundaries separating pot users from non-users, speculating that perhaps her grandmother did smoke it but her grandfather certainly did not (neither do). In the words of her father: "She knows not to tell people about it but she just probably wouldn't anyway."

Josh: The self-gratifier

Everyone in the neighborhood knows Josh. Vociferous and outgoing, at age five he has a decidedly Dennis-the-Menace quality in both looks and personality. Neither timid nor reserved, he boasts to total strangers of his fantastic exploits and talents. Yet behind his bravado swagger lies a seeming insecurity and need for acceptance, coupled with a difficulty in accepting authority, which has led him into squabbles with peers, teachers, siblings and parents.

Josh's home shows the traditional division of labor. His mother stays home to cook and care for the children while his father works long hours. The mother is always calm and tolerant about her youngster's smart-alec ways, but his escapades may provoke an explosive tirade from the father. Yet this male parent is clearly the dominating force in Josh's life. Singling Josh out from his younger sister and brother, the father has chosen him as his successor in the male tradition. The parent had himself begun drinking and smoking cigarettes in his early formative years, commencing pot use as a teenager, and now has a favorable attitude toward the early use of stimulants which he is actively passing on to Josh.

According to his parents, his smoking has had several beneficial effects. Considering Josh a "hyper" child, they claim that it calms him down to a more normal speed, often permitting him to engage in activities which would otherwise be too difficult for his powers of concentration. He also appears to become more

sedate and less prone to temper tantrums, sleeping longer and more deeply. But Josh's smoking patterns differ significantly from our last two subjects. He does not enjoy social smoking, preferring for his father to roll him "pinners" (thin joints) to smoke by himself. Unlike many other tinydopers, Josh frequently refuses the offer of a joint saying, "Oh that! I gave up smoking that stuff." At age five he claims to have already quit and gone back several times. His mother backs this assertion as valid; his father brushes it off as merely a ploy to shock and gain attention. Here, the especially close male parent recognizes the behavior as imitative and accepts it as normal. To others, however, it appears strange and suggests surprising sophistication.

Josh's perception of social boundaries is also mature. Only a year older than Stephanie, Josh has made some mistakes but his awareness of the necessity for secrecy is complete; he differentiates those people with whom he may and may not discuss the subject by the experience of actually smoking with them. He knows individuals but cannot yet socially categorize the boundaries. Josh also realizes the contrast between joints and cigarettes down to the marijuana and tobacco they contain. Interestingly, he is aggressively opposed to tobacco while favoring pot use (this may be the result of anti-tobacco cancer propaganda from kindergarten).

Kyra: The bohemian

A worldly but curiously childlike girl is seven-year-old Kyra. Her wavy brown hair falls to her shoulders and her sun-tanned body testifies to many hours at the beach in winter and summer. Of average height for her age, she dresses with a maturity beyond her years. Friendly and sociable, she has few reservations about what she says to people. Kyra lives with her youthful mother and whatever boyfriend her mother fancies at the moment. Their basic family unit consists of two (mother and daughter), and they have travelled together living a free life all along the West Coast and Hawaii. While Josh's family was male dominated, this is clearly female centered, all of Kyra's close relatives being women. They are a bohemian group, generation after generation following a hip, up-to-the-moment, unshackled lifestyle. The house is often filled with people, but when the visitors clear out, a youthful, thrillseeking mother remains, who raises this daughter by treating her like a sister or friend. This demand on Kyra to behave as an adult may produce some internal strain, but she seems to have grown accustomed to it. Placed in situations others might find awkward, she handles them with precocity. Like her mother, she is being reared for a life of independence and freedom.

Pot smoking is an integral part of this picture. To Kyra it is another symbol of her adulthood; she enjoys it and wants to do it a lot. At seven she is an accomplished smoker; her challenge right now lies in the mastery of rolling joints. Of our four examples, social boundaries are clearest to Kyra. Not only is she aware of the necessary secrecy surrounding pot use, but she is able to socially categorize types of people into marijuana smokers and straights. She may err in her judgement occasionally, but no more so than any adult.

Stages of Development

These four and other cases suggest a continuum of reactions to marijuana that is loosely followed by most tinydopers.

From birth to around 18 months a child's involvement is passive. Most parents keep their infants nearby at all times and if pot is smoked the room becomes filled with potent clouds. At this age just a little marijuana smoke can be very powerful and these infants, the youngest diaperdopers, manifest noticeable effects. The drug usually has a calming influence, putting the infant into a less cranky mood and extending the depth and duration of sleep.

After the first one and a half years, the children are more attuned to what is going on around them: they begin to desire participation in a "monkey see, monkey do" fashion. During the second year, a fascination with paraphernalia generally develops, as they play with it and try to figure it out. Eager to smoke with the adults and older children, they are soon discouraged after a toke (puff) or two. They find smoking difficult and painful (particularly to the eyes and throat) – after all, it is not easy to inhale burning hot air and hold it in your lungs.

But continual practice eventually produces results, and inhalation seems to be achieved somewhere during the third or fourth year. This brings considerable pride and makes the kids feel they have attained semi-adult status. Now they can put the paraphernalia to work. Most tinydopers of this age are wild about "roachclips," itching to put their joints into them as soon as possible after lighting.

Ages four and five bring the first social sense of the nature of pot and who should know about it. This begins as a vague idea, becoming further refined with age and sophistication. Finally, by age seven or eight kids have a clear concept of where the lines can be drawn between those who are and aren't "cool," and can make these distinctions on their own. No child we interviewed, however, could verbalize about any specific effects felt after smoking marijuana. Ironically, although they participate in smoking and actually manifest clear physical symptoms of the effects, tinydopers are rationally and intellectually unaware of how the drug is acting upon them. They are too young to notice a change in their behavior or to make the symbolic leap and associate this transformation with having smoked pot previously. The effects of marijuana must be socially and consensually delineated from non-high sensations for the user to fully appreciate the often subtle perceptual and physiological changes that have occurred. To the youngster the benefits of pot smoking are not at all subtle: he is permitted to imitate his elders by engaging in a social ritual they view as pleasurable and important; the status of adulthood is partially conferred on him by allowing this act, and his desire for acceptance is fulfilled through inclusion in his parents' peer group. This constitutes the major difference in appreciation between the child and adult smoker.

Parents' Strategies

The youth of the sixties made some forceful statements through their actions about how they evaluated the Establishment and the conventional American lifestyle. While their political activism has faded, many former members of this group still feel a strong commitment to smoking pot and attach a measure of symbolic significance to it. When they had children the question then arose of how to handle the drug vis-à-vis their offspring. The continuum of responses they developed ranges from total openness and permissiveness to various measures of secrecy.

Smoking regularly permitted

Some parents give their children marijuana whenever it is requested. They may wait until the child reaches a certain age, but most parents in this category started their kids on pot from infancy. These parents may be "worried" or "unconcerned."

Worried

Ken and Deedy are moderate pot smokers, getting high a few times a week. Both had been regular users for several years prior to having children. When Deedy was pregnant she absolutely refused to continue her smoking pattern. [...]

This abstinence satisfied them and once the child was born they resumed getting high as before. Frequently smoking in the same room as the baby, they began to worry about the possible harmful effects this exposure might have on his physical, psychological, and mental development. After some discussion, they consulted the family pediatrician, a prominent doctor in the city.

> I was really embarrassed, but I said, "Doctor, we get high, we smoke pot, and sometimes the kid's in the room. If he's in the room can this hurt him? I don't want him to be mentally retarded." He said, "Don't worry about it, they're going to be legalizing it any day now – this was three years ago – it's harmless and a great sedative."

This reassured them on two counts: they no longer were fearful in their own minds, and they had a legitimate answer when questioned by their friends. Ken and Deedy were particularly sensitive about peer reactions:

> Some people say, "You let your children get high?!" They really react with disgust. Or they'll say, "Oh you let your kids get high," and then they kind of look at you like, "That's neat, I think." And it's just nice to be able to back it up.

Ken and Deedy were further nonplussed about the problem of teaching their children boundary maintenance. Recognizing the need to prevent their offspring from saying things to the wrong people, they were unsure how to approach this subject properly.

How can you tell a kid, how can you go up to him and say, "Well you want to get high, but don't tell anybody you're doing it"? You can't. We didn't really know how to tell them. You don't want to bring the attention, you don't want to tell your children not to say anything about it because that's a sure way to get them to do it. We just never said anything about it.

They hope this philosophy of openness and permissiveness will forestall the need to limit their children's marijuana consumption. Limits, for them, resemble prohibitions and interdictions against discussing grass: they make transgressions attractive. Both parents believe strongly in presenting marijuana as an everyday occurrence, definitely not as an undercover affair. When asked how they thought this upbringing might affect their kids, Deedy offered a fearful but doubtful speculation that her children might one day reject the drug.

> I don't imagine they'd try to abuse it. Maybe they won't even smoke pot when they get older. That's a big possibility. I doubt it, but hopefully they won't be that way. They've got potheads for parents.

Unconcerned

Alan and Anna make use of a variety of stimulants – pot, alcohol, cocaine – to enrich their lives. Considered heavy users, they consume marijuana and alcohol daily. Alan became acquainted with drugs, particularly alcohol, at a very early age and Anna first tried them in her teens. When they decided to have children the question of whether they would permit the youngsters to partake in their mood-altering experiences never arose. Anna didn't curtail her drug intake during pregnancy; her offspring were conceived, formed, and weaned on this steady diet. When queried about their motivations, Alan volunteered:

> What the hell! It grows in the ground, it's a weed. I can't see anything wrong with doing anything, inducing any part of it into your body any way that you possibly could eat it, smoke it, intravenously, or whatever, that it would ever harm you because it grows in the ground. It's a natural thing. It's one of God's treats.

All of their children have been surrounded by marijuana's aromatic vapor since the day they returned from the hospital. Alan and Anna were pleased with the effect pot had on their infants; the relaxed, sleepy and happy qualities achieved after inhaling pot smoke made child-rearing an easier task. As the little ones grew older they naturally wanted to share in their parents' activities. Alan viewed this as the children's desire to imitate rather than true enjoyment of any effects:

> Emily used to drink Jack Daniels straight and like it. I don't think it was taste, I think it was more of an acceptance thing because that's what I was drinking. She was also puffing on joints at six months.

This mimicking, coupled with a craving for acceptance, although recognized by Alan in his kids, was not repeated in his own feelings toward friends or relatives. At no time during the course of our interview or acquaintance did he show any concern with what others thought of his behavior; rather, his convictions dominated, and his wife passively followed his lead.

In contrast to the last couple, Alan was not reluctant to address the problem of boundary maintenance. A situation arose when Emily was three, where she was forced to learn rapidly:

> One time we were stopped by the police while driving drunk. I said to Emily – we haven't been smoking marijuana. We all acted quiet and Emily realized there was something going on and she delved into it. I explained that some people are stupid and they'll harm you very badly if you smoke marijuana. To this day I haven't heard her mention it to anyone she hasn't smoked with.

As each new child came along, Alan saw to it that they learned the essential facts of life.

Neither Alan nor Anna saw any moral distinction between marijuana smoking and other, more accepted pastimes. They heartily endorsed marijuana as something to indulge in like "tobacco, alcohol, sex, breathing or anything else that brings pleasure to the senses." Alan and Anna hope their children will continue to smoke grass in their later lives. It has had beneficial effects for them and they believe it can do the same for their kids:

> I smoked marijuana for a long time, stopped and developed two ulcers; and smoked again and the two ulcers went away. It has great medicinal value.

Smoking occasionally permitted

In contrast to uninterrupted permissiveness, other parents restrict marijuana use among their children to specific occasions. A plethora of reasons and rationalizations lie behind this behavior, some openly avowed by parents and others not. Several people believe it is okay to let the kids get high as long as it isn't done too often. Many other people do not have any carefully thought-out notion of what they want, tending to make spur-of-the-moment decisions. As a result, they allow occasional but largely undefined smoking in a sporadic and irregular manner. Particular reasons for this inconsistency can be illustrated by three examples from our research:

1   **Conflicts between parents** can confuse the situation. While Stella had always planned to bring her children up with pot, Burt did not like the idea. Consequently, the household rule on this matter varied according to the unpredictable moods of the adults and which parent was in the house.
2   Mike and Gwen had trouble **making up their minds.** At one time they thought it probably couldn't harm the child, only to decide the next day they shouldn't take chances and to rescind that decision.
3   Lois and David didn't waver hourly but had **changing ideas over time.** At first they were against it, but then met a group of friends who liked to party and approved of tinydoping. After a few years they moved to a new neighborhood and changed their lifestyle, again prohibiting pot smoking for the kids.

These are just a few of the many situations in which parents allow children an occasional opportunity to smoke grass. They use various criteria to decide when those permissible instances ought to be, most families subscribing to several of the following patterns:

Reward

The child receives pot as a bonus for good behavior in the past, present or future. This may serve as an incentive: "If you're a good boy today, Johnny,

I may let you smoke with us tonight," or to celebrate an achievement already completed like "going potty" or reciting the alphabet.

Guilt

Marijuana can be another way of compensating children for what they aren't getting. Historically, parents have tried to buy their kids off or make themselves loved through gifts of money or toys but pot can also be suitable here. This is utilized both by couples with busy schedules who don't have time for the children ("We're going out again tonight so we'll give you this special treat to make it up to you") and by separated parents who are trying to compete with the former spouse for the child's love ("I know Mommy doesn't let you do this but you can do special things when you're with me").

Cuteness

To please themselves parents may occasionally let the child smoke pot because it's cute. Younger children look especially funny because they cannot inhale, yet in their eagerness to be like Mommy and Daddy they make a hilarious effort and still have a good time themselves. Often this will originate as amusement for the parents and then spread to include cuteness in front of friends. Carrying this trend further, friends may roll joints for the little ones or turn them on when the parents are away. This still precludes regular use.

Purposive

Giving marijuana to kids often carries a specific anticipated goal for the parents. The known effects of pot are occasionally desired and actively sought. They may want to calm the child down because of the necessities of a special setting or company. Sleep is another pursued end, as in "Thank you for taking Billy for the night; if he gives you any trouble just let him smoke this and he'll go right to bed." They may also give it to the children medicinally. Users believe marijuana soothes the upset stomach and alleviates the symptoms of the common cold better than any other drug. As a mood elevator, many parents have given pot to alleviate the crankiness young children

develop from a general illness, specific pain or injury. One couple used it experimentally as a treatment for hyperactivity (see Josh).

Abstention

Our last category of marijuana smoking parents contains those who do not permit their children any direct involvement with illegal drugs. This leaves several possible ways to treat the topic of the adults' own involvement with drugs and how open they are about it. Do they let the kids know they smoke pot? Moreover, do they do it in the children's presence?

Overt

The great majority of our subjects openly smoked in front of their children, defining marijuana as an accepted and natural pastime. Even parents who withhold it from their young children hope that the kids will someday grow up to be like themselves. Thus, they smoke pot overtly. These marijuana smokers are divided on the issue of other drugs, such as pills and cocaine.

a. Permissive

One group considers it acceptable to use any drug in front of the children. Either they believe in what they are doing and consider it right for the kids to observe their actions, or they don't worry about it and just do it.

b. Pragmatic

A larger, practically oriented group differentiated between "smokable" drugs (pot and hashish) and the others (cocaine and pills), finding it acceptable to let children view consumption of the former group, but not the latter.

Rationales varied for this, ranging from safety to morality:

> Well, we have smoked hashish around them but we absolutely **never ever** do coke in front of them because it's a white powder and if they saw us snorting a white powder there goes the drain cleaner, there goes the baby powder. Anything white, they'll try it; and that goes for pills too. The only thing they have free rein of is popping vitamins.

Fred expressed his concern over problems this might engender in the preservation of his children's moral fiber:

> If he sees me snorting coke, how is he going to differentiate that from heroin? He gets all this anti-drug education from school and they tell him that heroin is bad. How can I explain to him that doing coke is okay and it's fun and doesn't hurt you but heroin is something else, so different and bad? How could I teach him right from wrong?

c. Capricious

A third group is irregular in its handling of multiple drug viewing and their offspring. Jon and Linda, for instance, claim that they don't mind smoking before their child but absolutely won't permit other drugs to be used in his presence. Yet in fact they often use almost any intoxicant in front of him, depending on their mood and how high they have already become.

In our observations we have never seen any parent give a child in the tinydoper range any kind of illegal drug other than marijuana and, extremely rarely, hashish. Moreover, the treatment of pot has been above all direct and open: even those parents who don't permit their children to join have rejected the clandestine secrecy of the behind-closed-doors approach. Ironically, however, they must often adopt this strategy toward the outside world; those parents who let it be known that they permit tinydoping frequently take on an extra social and legal stigma. Their motivation for doing so stems from a desire to avoid having the children view pot and their smoking it as evil or unnatural. Thus, to de-stigmatize marijuana they stigmatize themselves in the face of society.

Conclusions

Tinydoping, with its combined aspects of understandably innovative social development and surprising challenges to convention, is a fruitful subject for sociological analysis. A review of historical and cultural forces leading to the present offers insight into how and why this phenomenon came to arise. Essentially, we are witnessing the moral passage of marijuana, its transformation from an isolated and taboo drug surrounded by connotations of fear and

Table 21.1　Sequential model of social change: the diffusion and legitimization of marijuana

	Stage	Carriers	Marijuana
I	1940s	Stigmatized outgroup	Blacks
II	1950s	Ingroup deviants who identify with stigmatized outgroup	Jazz musicians
III	1960s	Avant garde ingroup members	College students and counter culture
IV	1970s	Normal ingroup members	Middle class
V	1975+	Sacred group	Children

danger, into an increasingly accepted form of social relaxation, similar to alcohol. The continuing destigmatization of pot fosters an atmosphere in which parents are willing to let their children smoke.

Marijuana's social transition is not an isolated occurrence, however. Many formerly deviant activities have gradually become acceptable forms of behavior. Table 21.1 presents a general model of social change which outlines the sequential development and spread of a conduct undergoing legitimization.

Particular behaviors which first occur only among relatively small and stigmatized outgroups are frequently picked up by ingroup deviants who identify with the stigmatized outgroup. In an attempt to be cool and avante garde, larger clusters of ingroup members adopt this deviant practice, often for the sake of non-conformity as well as its own merits. By this time the deviant activity is gaining exposure as well as momentum and may spread to normal ingroup members. The final step is its eventual introduction to sacred groups in the society, such as children.

[...]

References

Douglas, Jack D. 1976. *Investigative Social Research*, Beverly Hills: Sage.

Gusfield, Joseph R. 1967. "Moral Passage: The Symbolic Process in Public Designations of Deviance," *Social Problems*, 15, II, Fall.

Simon, William and John H. Gagnon. 1968. "Children of the Drug Age," *Saturday Review*, September 21.

Questions

1 How does the socialization process of marijuana smoking compare and contrast with those who learn to smoke later in life? How might broader cultural knowledge impact the learning process at a later age?

2 How might teaching children moderate and responsible drug use at a younger age benefit them later in life? How young is too young? Who do you think should be responsible for defining a lawful age threshold: parents, government, doctors? Why?

3 How does this article make you feel about addressing the topic of drugs with your own children in the future? Which set of parents do you most identify with? Why? How is marijuana use in the presence of children viewed today? Have we seen the "moral passage" of marijuana the authors discussed? Why or why not?

Grappling with the Medicated Self
The Case of ADHD College Students

Meika Loe and Leigh Cuttino

Meika Loe and Leigh Cuttino build on some of the ideas we raised in the introduction to our last selection about the relation between young people and prescribed pharmaceuticals. They address the interesting question of how children who have been raised on pharmaceuticals manage as they age and move out of the house. Although Vecitis notes that the use of drugs such as Ritalin and Adderall is widespread in college for studying, people who have a broader relationship to them may, at some point, re-think their dependence on these substances. This broaches the issue of the nature of our medicated society, where more people are taking prescribed drugs than ever before. High school and college health centers are overwhelmed refilling drugs for treating not only ADHD, but asthma, sexually transmitted diseases, and psychoactive disorders such as anxiety, depression, and panic disorder.

How do people feel about their dependence on these drugs over the life course? How does this compare to the way they feel about street drugs? Are there pull and push factors such as Spicer described for American Indians? What social groups form the relevant context within which these students make their decisions: their family, their racial/ethnic community, and/or their peers? How does their relative affluence affect their feelings about their control over their selves and their drug use? Is this kind of licit drug use a gendered behavior? What kinds of pharmaceuticals are more often used by men versus women? Finally, where do the college years stand, over the life course, as an age span in people's general drug-using careers? What kind of expectations does society have about the appropriateness of drug use at this age versus older or younger periods? How does this compare with Vecitis' college drug users?

Drugs and the American Dream: An Anthology, First Edition. Edited by Patricia A. Adler, Peter Adler, and Patrick K. O'Brien.
© 2012 John Wiley & Sons, Inc. Published 2012 by John Wiley & Sons, Inc.

Over the past two decades an astonishing number of children, adolescents, and, more recently, adults in the United States have been diagnosed with attention-deficit/hyperactivity disorder (ADHD) and prescribed treatment in the form of medications such as Ritalin and Adderall.[1] In 1998 over five million children had prescriptions for Ritalin – a fivefold increase over eight years and an extension of a social phenomenon that Lawrence Diller (1999: 2–3), the author of *Running on Ritalin,* calls "a white middle class suburban phenomenon." Nearly eight million children have been diagnosed with ADHD, and the demographics cut across traditional race and class lines. The picture is clearly gendered: almost 10 percent of ten-year-old boys in the United States take stimulants for ADHD, while only about 5 percent of ten-year-old girls do. It is an age-based phenomenon as well, with ADHD generally diagnosed in childhood or early adolescence, although this may be changing as the adult ADHD market expands. And the phenomenon remains uniquely American; the United States consumes between 80 and 90 percent of the Ritalin available in the world.

[...]

The present analysis is focused on the case of ADHD college students as they negotiate medicated selfhood. Specifically, we ask, "How do elite college students come to terms with selfhood in the context of pharmaceutical use?" While a significant amount of sociological scholarship is focused on identity and its renegotiation in the context of illness, our case study focuses on identity in the context of pharmaceutical use, which can be much more salient for students than medical diagnosis or illness. [...] For ADHD college students, questions about identity revolve around psychostimulant use in relationship to self, body, and performance.

Our informants have come of age in the pharmaceutical era, where prescription drugs are available, accessible, and advertised as commodities attached to lifestyles. They are members of the so-called Ritalin generation (or "RX generation"), that is, the largest US cohort of children to receive prescription behavior modification treatment in the early 1990s (they were in kindergarten at that time). These students have grown up in what has been called a "rapid-fire culture," where a fast pace and constant stimulation have created an addiction to the technologies and social institutions that allow them to persist. [...]

Methods

Interviews were conducted to understand how college students construct and manage identity in the context of pharmaceutical use. Qualitative data allowed us to capture identity and meaning making in process. Our sixteen student informants attend a selective private liberal arts college in the Northeast; eight are male and eight are female. To recruit informants, signs were posted in several campus buildings asking for student volunteers who had been diagnosed with ADHD and had taken prescription medications. Accordingly, all informants have been diagnosed with ADHD and prescribed treatment in the form of prescription stimulants at some point in their lives; fourteen have active prescriptions. The interviews were conducted at the informant's place of choice and ranged from thirty to ninety minutes long. During each interview, students were asked to reflect on their experiences with diagnosis and treatment for ADHD, as well as on their educational background and understanding of success. [...]

While this sample is not generalizable to all ADHD students attending colleges, our data reveal patterns in identity construction that may likely resonate with similar sample populations, including middle- and upper-class ADHD students attending elite schools, as well as the larger population of adults taking psychotropic medication. Like the majority of college students currently diagnosed with ADHD, our informants self-identify as white and middle, upper middle, or upper class. These students are in advantageous positions; their economic resources have given them the ability to seek out physicians, obtain medical treatment, and engage in consumption-based body projects. This location in medicalized worlds means that these students have defined their own bodies as deficient or have been diagnosed as such by medical experts. These students have also chosen to take stimulants in college, while we presume that some members of the Ritalin generation with access to these same resources elect not to use medication in this context.

[...]

Understanding Medicated Identity in the Collegiate Setting

[...] ADHD students situate their use of prescription stimulants in the context of an academic ethic. In general, many express some awareness of the interplay between body and society; while they believe that they are biologically different than others, they also realize that their environment plays a crucial role in the construction of self. The following two quotes are from students who are perhaps most skeptical of the biological aspect of ADHD. Both individuals imply that diagnoses and subsequent treatment may emerge from an inability to meet the demands of social environments. The first quote is from Matt, a senior diagnosed in college, an environment that he implies creates disordered bodies:

> The thing with having ADHD ... I don't really believe in it that much, even. I think Adderall helps, but I think it helps everyone. ... I don't know if ADHD is one of those things that you have [biologically] so that you *need* to take medicine. I didn't need it before ... and now that I'm taking it I'm just as with it ... the situation just changed. Maybe people are situationally ADD.

Kristin, a junior diagnosed and prescribed stimulants the summer before she went to college, explains her diagnosis as a result of social learning and environment, an explanation that is similar to DeGrandpre's (1999) argument that ADHD is a result of a "rapid-fire culture" that has changed human consciousness:

> KRISTIN: I knew I didn't have super severe ADD. ... I thought I probably had ... some level of it. But, I don't know. I didn't really believe in it until I was diagnosed with it [laughs].
> INTERVIEWER: What do you mean by "believe in it," exactly?
> KRISTIN: I mean, I just see [ADHD] as a product of our society. ... I mean if you're in Bolivia, working day to day, you don't really have ... you're living for the moment, you know. ... I see it as something about stimulation. You know, television, video games, all this. ... it's what keeps you interested, what keeps you going to the next thing and matches your attention. And so if you don't have those things ... that level of stimulation isn't needed to get to the next point.

Interestingly, both Matt and Kristin state that they didn't "believe" in ADHD prior to being diagnosed, seeing it as a social construct in the context of changing social expectations. After being diagnosed, however, each is forced to make a connection between social environment and individual bodies. If their bodies are deficient or dysfunctional, social environments are to blame. Matt and Kristin also blame themselves for not being able to keep up with social expectations. However, while they may see ADHD as a product of social expectations, they may not go far enough in analyzing how they themselves interact with and contribute to these environments through their pharmaceutical use.

In every interview, informants note the challenges of the college environment. As Kadison and DiGeronimo (2004: 12) note, "When kids go off to college, society expects that their identity will shift from being dependent children to being responsible adults, but as students ... find out, this expectation and the reality of the experience often clash." When individuals enter new environments, they are often faced with new challenges and situations that they may not be equipped to overcome. Identity may feel threatened, in that a once well-defined and capable self is suddenly questioned by the perceived threat of failure or the inability to perform as that self was once able to. The transition to college requires that students reevaluate selfhood in the context of new demands and expectations. Some have found that medication can smooth a difficult transition.

Diagnosed with learning disabilities at a young age, Mary was not officially diagnosed with ADHD until after her second semester of college. She discusses here how a demanding college academic ethic led to a reevaluation of her self-identity:

> It was a combination of me no longer being at home with my parents over me. And I mean, I was pretty much trying to get by the same way I did in high school ... not reading until tests ... and I couldn't, I mean I was staying up for like three nights straight, two nights straight trying to read like, astronomy ... the entire textbook for a test but I couldn't ... and then I was failing the tests. So, basically it was. ... I was pretty much the same but the school demanded that much more of me so I couldn't ... get by.

Like Matt and Kristin, Mary's narrative suggests a stable sense of self in a changing context. She describes herself as "pretty much the same," but in an environment that holds her to a new level of expectation. Her new ADHD identity seems to emerge from a sense of inadequacy, a realization that she was unable to handle the challenges that college presented. In the campus context, she is ADHD, and she self-medicates to meet academic expectations. But outside the classroom and the library, Mary retains her "authentic" self, a self that is not considered disordered.

Similarly, Ali, a junior diagnosed and first treated at age seven, describes her un-medicated self as "normal." When she is medicated, she believes she can function at a higher level, a level that the college educational system seems to demand.

> I mean, I still can function totally fine. I function totally normally in society without being on medication, it's not an issue with that. So like that's another interesting aspect of it. 'Cause it's like … well, I still could function, maybe not as well. … I'm not going to function at a level which, we, as a society … let's say like, higher education's sort of class, that kind of class, wants me to. I wonder, at what level … if so many people have ADD … at what level it is just because of the standards we hold over everyone and the expectations of the school system and the work world.

Ali knows that she is capable of performing, but she also realizes that she has chosen to partake in an academic environment that is often highly competitive. The challenge of handling a rigorous course load, creating a new work ethic, and establishing independence away from parental support is often unsettling to the student entering college. As in the following quote from Sean, medication is something he leans on in the absence of parent- or school-imposed structure.

> Everything is so much more on us. That *we're* in control and *we* have to manage our time and *we* have to get it done, and there are no teachers there. You know, your professors tell you it's due on a specific date and that's about it. But yeah, you don't have [parents around]. Like my parents … were always there … to help me along. But now, it's all on us, or on me. … I've sort of realized how helpful the treatment can be. And at least for me, how necessary it is to get things done.

In this section, Sean, Ali, Matt, Kristin, and Mary suggest that pharmaceuticals make it easier to manage new (sometimes unrealistic) demands and expectations placed on the college student, and thus diagnosis and treatment are rationalized in this context of perceived academic necessity. Therefore, for the ADHD student, prescription medication serves as a tool to discipline behavior and enhance a sense of self-control. Perceived self-control is central to students' belief in the possibility of achievement; the greater the sense of perceived self-control, the greater the belief in the possibility of achievement. However, this is not the end of the story for our informants. While they are actively making sense of their disordered bodies in the context of externalized and internalized college performance expectations, they also see their "need" for prescription medication as frustrating and problematic, revealing the paradox of medical self-control.

Managing Identity and the Paradox of Medical Control

ADHD students seem to be caught in the paradox of medical control as they describe their own pharmaceutical use in the context of need, dependency, or lack of control. Below, Sean, Mary, and Kristin reveal how the process of medication is one of compromise, or "give and take." For them to "fit" with what they see as the academic ethic, they are willing to at least temporarily allow a foreign substance to control their behaviors and discipline their bodies. In other words, in order to *have* control, they must allow themselves to *be* controlled. As a result, their words convey a level of ambivalence about their relationship with prescription medicine:

> SEAN: I guess since I sort of … control it myself … that I only take it when I think I need to … I guess, I don't know. I like it I guess. I think I like it. I don't like the fact that I need it, but I like the fact that I have it."
> MARY: It kind of sucks [needing] medication … to do well in school. But the fact that I know I can do it, on medication. … I just feel like, it's kind of … give or take, almost. It's like, … fine, but now I'm … just as smart. So … take it with a grain of salt.

KRISTIN: There are pros and cons. Because like … certain things in terms of my school work … that are kind of … out of control enough that … without a sort of support system, without doctors helping me, I don't know how I'd … take that. I don't know if I would be able to … be in school.

Fear of drug dependency is only heightened for students caught up in college performance culture who see ADHD bodies as limiting success and future prospects. In an attempt to confront ambivalence, many of our informants have created approaches to constructing selfhood by attempting to maximize self-determination and minimize medical control. In these ways, ADHD students are managing what they perceive as fragmented identity: the division of the medicated and nonmedicated self. These strategies allow students to believe they are protecting their "authentic" selves and minimizing the need for medicated identities. Students report using three strategies to manage ambivalence and drug dependency (and in turn, preserve a sense of one's "true self"): self-dosing, avoidance of academic risk, and going off the drugs.

The vast majority of students we spoke with manage pharmaceutical dependency by asserting control of their medication and related bodily regimes. Many times this requires taking the doctor and parent out of the equation and self-medicating in ways that protect their sense of coherent selfhood. To do this, students practice "reflexive identity maintenance," weighing the costs and benefits of their medicated and nonmedicated identities and approaching each strategically. In this way they can appropriate and reappropriate identity as they see fit. For some, this means segregating their work and social lives, self-medicating and acknowledging ADHD only "when necessary" in the context of academic success, while purposefully not medicating or identifying as "deficient" in the context of social success, as Sean suggests above. Many see this approach as achieving success in both realms, protecting their authentic self and "personality" and leveraging this at times to achieve academic success.

For example, Kate makes a distinction between her academic and her social self, insisting that her Ritalin self (which is achieved only when necessary) feels "fake" in contrast to her authentic and familiar "social" self. In this way she temporarily trades on her sense of

authenticity in order to feel good about herself academically.

I guess like I'm happier with who I am when I'm not on drugs like Ritalin. … I feel better about myself like academically, like when I'm on it, but, not like, you know, socially. To me [the effect of Ritalin] is like – feeling physically drained and like almost fake 'cause it's not like who I am, you know?

[…] [M]ost student informants seem to construct their nonmedicated bodies as primary, normal, and essential (natural), despite having spent years (sometimes the majority of their lives) on medication. Anne, a junior diagnosed with ADHD in her senior year of high school, has a prescription for a time-release and fast-acting Adderall pill daily. An ongoing relationship with medicine has resulted in a nonchalant integration of "medical talk" into her personal narrative. It has also resulted in a decision to self-medicate based on what she perceives as periods and degrees of need.

ANNE: I don't take the short-acting every day. I take the time-release every morning. … I eat breakfast and I take it, so around like … like eight? And then, if I have other work, I'll take the other one. … I actually won't even take a whole one, sometimes. … so when I don't have a lot of work, I'll take a half one.
INTERVIEWER: So do you take those everyday…?
ANNE: Not everyday. I don't take the time-release like, on the weekends when I don't have any work to do. I only take it when I really have work to do, or if I have to sit through class. … Yeah, or like sometimes [laughs] when I have a really long movie, I'll take them, because I can't like concentrate on a movie for like that. … long. But … I don't take it on a daily basis.

Students seem to enjoy the ability to pick and choose when they take their medication, as it means that they can assume their "medicated identity" only as needed. For Kristin, like Anne, self-medicating involves making decisions about dosage and drug variety, again effortlessly integrating "medical talk" into her self-narrative:

Initially [I took] the 20 mg time release, um, but eventually I switched off of that because … I didn't want to be on it for the whole day if I didn't need to be. ... It helps me mainly for classes, more so than doing work ... and so I'd wanna take it in the morning before classes, but by being on the time release, that kind of obliged me to be on it the whole day, even if I didn't want to be. And so I prefer to take the one in the morning and if I want, or if I need it, or if I have a lot of work in the afternoon or lab, then I'll take it. But if not, then I won't have to be on it.

Self-dosing allows students like Anne and Kristin to preserve a sense of authentic selfhood when not playing the role of the student. Below, Nathan explains why he chooses to take his prescription medication only in certain contexts. Being "himself" is preferable and synonymous with being off medication. However, Nathan is willing to shift identity for the purpose of work:

I feel like I'm kind of different. ... like I'm more subdued and ... more concentrating on things, rather than being like, myself and being spontaneous. I feel like it's more like, focused energy. It's good for working but ... I don't really feel like being on it all the time I guess.

While self-dosing minimizes the length of time that individuals are "controlled" by medication, it also means that they are constantly shifting between their medicated and nonmedicated identities. The question follows: Why not stop treatment? If it causes identity conflict or distress, the answer seems simple enough. However, giving up treatment means scaling down aspirations, which can be perceived as a form of failure. Further, many informants have taken medication for so long that they are equally as attached to their medicated self as they are to their "authentic" self. Doug, who was diagnosed at the age of seven, speaks to this point:

I don't like the idea ... that the person I'm most like is the person who I am when I am taking medication ...when there's chemicals that are running through my ... that aren't naturally there. But I find more and more, that when I don't take it, I don't act as someone that I think that I am or who I'd like to be ... that I feel like I can't do anything. So ... I don't know what to do about that.

As his narrative implies, Doug has been on medication so long that he has become more comfortable with his medicated identity than with his nonmedicated one — so much so that he has actually begun to question and even dislike the latter. Rather than feel physiologically "disrupted" because of illness, Doug grapples with medical disruption and its effect on his body. Both he and Ali express these feelings of disruption through a form of medicated body ambivalence, where the medicated body is juxtaposed against the nonmedicated body against the backdrop of personal and academic success. Ali, who was also diagnosed at seven, expresses a similar form of medicated body ambivalence, stating that her sense of self is challenged and changed on medication. She tries to "deal with" the fact that her medicated "personality" is more normal than not.

I think it's messed up and twisted that I've been on study medications since first grade. I think it's ... I can't say really a moral debate but, just a debate internally about how I feel about it because I know ... there's no way I would be at [this school] without it. ...And at the same time ... [just thinking] how much [taking a pill] can change your personality ...who you are is ... challenged. I mean I can deal with it. It's easy for me to rationalize it in the sense that I've taken it for so long I can just not think about it ... which is what a lot of people do.

As a sense of identity conflict heightens, some students have chosen alternative, nonmedical routes to managing their performance and avoiding failure. One route is "cooling out," the process whereby individuals avoid the "hard no" and redefine their future on more "realistic" terms. This process ensures that individuals are able to remain successful, even if their aspirations have been scaled down. In fact, Kathleen Nadeau's (1994) *Survival Guide for College Students with ADD or LD* offers many tips that suggest the avoidance of certain requirements may prove difficult for this type of student. For Mary, who has been diagnosed with both ADHD and learning disabilities, the cooling-out process is especially central:

I pretty much know my strengths and weaknesses. So I know I can't take a history course because I'm not at all oriented in history. I'm pretty good in math ... I'm pretty math-oriented. And I love education courses and I love sociology courses and [I'm] taking classes I know I'll be fine in. ... I'm not going to go and throw myself in a Poly Sci course when I know nothing about it. So, ... I don't really push myself to take courses that I'm not going to do well in. I take courses that I'm interested in that I expect myself to do well in.

Mary's strategy is to orient her choices around that which she perceives she will be able to accomplish. By avoiding certain subjects, she is able to ensure performance, guard against failure, and gain a sense of control in the context of her surrounding environment. With many students approaching college in this way, the cooling-out process is what *allows* "society to continue to encourage maximum effort without major disturbance from unfulfilled promises and expectations" (Clark 1960: 576).

In this context of strategic avoidance, the academic ethic is reinforced and rarely questioned. Although Mary has strategically avoided certain classes, it is clear that she still resorts to her prescription medication as a tool to meet demands and expectations. However, cooling out enables her to minimize the use of prescription medication, as she perceives her nonmedicated self as more capable of excelling in other areas.

Perhaps the easiest way to reconcile ambivalent identities is to stop using prescription medication altogether – a strategy that is particularly courageous and rare while students are still in college. Dylan and Homer both struggled with what they describe as stimulant drug dependency, largely because of self-dosing habits and perhaps unknowingly violating "normal dosage" amounts. Both have since sworn never to go back to these prescription drugs. Instead, each trained himself to reverse ADHD symptoms by using study skills or various relaxation techniques.

DYLAN: All Adderall does is make you think that you can do those eight things at once and really stretch yourself out; especially if you are as hyperactive as I am – Adderall is not the answer. The answer is meditation, the answer is yoga, the answer is smoking weed, the answer is having sports so like you're relaxed when you're not doing sports.

HOMER: I refuse to take the drug now – [so] I've had to come up with like techniques. Like I have to take breaks incessantly, if I don't then I will burn out. Like if I'm reading something, I have to, if I really wanna retain it, like I've gotta write, like, underline

things – and then write next to it reminder words. ... and that's been real helpful.

For Dylan and Homer, training the ADHD body to fulfill the academic ethic doesn't require medication. In their case, medication made things worse. Medicine-free, they report feeling more in control of their bodies and "healthier than ever."

[...]

Looking to the Future

As ADHD students look to the future, many believe they would not have made it in (or even to) college without their medication. Following college graduation, they face a postindustrial world where flexibility, adaptability, and optimization can be central to success. At the same time, as they enter the work world, many want to leave behind the drugs they associate with years of schooling and academic performance. This means embracing and entering the world with (unmedicated) ADHD bodies and finding work that fits with one's sense of self. For example, Lauren, who has embraced her ADHD diagnosis, describes her body not as "deficient" but as overly ambitious, wanting to do a billion things at once. Thus, she feels she is a perfect fit for her career choice, an ER doctor. Nathan is looking for a career and a lifestyle that suits someone with his unique attributes, perhaps in finance. He says, "Having ADD really makes me ... ready to go for like, a city kind of lifestyle. Very fast-paced." Matt says that choosing a routinized, structured job will eliminate his need for a stimulant.

Sean is not sure what people in his generation should do with their pills. For him, ADHD medication may be necessary in the context of school-based behavioral expectations. When schooling is completed, one's drug regimen should end as well. Following this thinking, using prescription stimulants on the job constitutes "cheating" in his mind. (He makes a distinction between a legitimate need for the drug in calming down a hyper child and using a drug in the workplace to enhance performance.)

I guess maybe, people a couple years older than us will be the first to be taking it as kids and into their professional life. I mean, ... let's say if I go into banking, if I can take it everyday, I'd be so much more effective than if not. So I could imagine that it could be really good. ... I feel like I'd be cheating though. It's like a performance enhancing drug, to some degree ... in the workplace.

Mary is also a strong believer in the school environment justifying the need for medication. For her, being an educator is going to take just as much concentration and focus as being a student, so she thinks she will continue to take medication:

> I think I'm potentially going to be a teacher ... and I think I need to be able to you know, go home from work and grade papers all night, and I think I'm going to have to definitely ... stay on it for at least a little while.

Ali, Sean, Doug, and Dylan have been using stimulants since elementary school. Perhaps because of their extended use, they are the most critical about prescription drugs and identity. Of the four, Dylan has already decided to take himself off of his medication, and the rest tentatively plan to do so when they graduate from college. For those students still in school, they continue to reconcile identity, medicine, and success. Kristin, now a proponent of behavior modification coupled with prescription stimulant use, recently hired an "ADD coach" with whom she speaks by phone regularly. She recommends this approach to all ADHD students, suggesting that they can benefit from "just something as simple as [someone] calling to make sure you're doing your work." Ali plans to try to take a test without her pills, has quit sports, and feels good about getting involved in outdoor education. Doug has three more years of college, and his goals are simple: "I want to make myself into a person that I feel happy with." He has yet to decide if prescription drugs are part of that formula or not.

Discussion

This article has attempted to delineate a case of "the medicated self." [...] In the context of pharmaceutical use, ADHD students face a difficult situation in the pursuit of a coherent sense of self. To some, giving up their perceived "authentic" identity means being permanently controlled by medicine that blots out their own unique personalities. Giving up the "medicated" identity means losing the ability to manage performance and achievement. Willing to relinquish neither one nor the other, pharmaceutical ambivalence persists for ADHD college students. To manage this conflict, many students accept and rationalize situational medical control while employing strategies designed to emphasize agency and preserve a sense of authentic selfhood. In this context, what we call strategic pharmaceutical use becomes a way to occupy a middle ground between medical optimization and authenticity. [...] Interestingly, while students justify strategic pharmaceutical use in the context of an academic ethic, they may not see how, by using prescription drugs to normalize, enhance, or fix themselves, they are contributing to the social expectations to which they are responding.

[...]

One question came up in almost every interview: What does it take to ease off medication that has been integrated into an identity and sense of potential for years – in some cases the majority of a lifetime? Or, as Ali says, "At what point do you stop?" By the end of college, many ADHD students express an interest in returning to their "authentic selves" and leaving their medication behind. After years of disciplining their bodies and selves to fit within narrow academic contexts and standards, ADHD students express hope in choosing future work environments that "fit" with their conception of self. However, will these students find work that fits with their unique attributes? In the context of expanding adult ADHD and prescription drug use in the workforce, will students be able to sever ties with a medication they associate with success and potential and feel confident without medical support? Future research should track this generation as they face the demands and expectations of a new work environment. As they graduate from college and join the workforce, ADHD students will be expected to establish independence and begin a life of their own. What role will medications play, and how will they come to understand their new identities? Answers to these questions carry important implications not only for future generations of prescription drug users but for society as a whole.

Concerns about stopping medication reveal a still-prevalent irony in our society; students must confront an antimedication macro social bias combined with widespread prevalence of pharmaceutical use. This is the crux of the dynamic tension within the individuals we interviewed and within the society at large; pharmaceutical performance enhancement on a macro level may be highly stigmatized and perceived as cheating, but individuals, particularly in the context of perceived medical need, can evade blame. [...]

Note

1   The number of youths in this country taking prescribed psychotropic drugs – in other words, drugs that alter behavior, emotion, or perception – increased by as much as 300 percent overall from 1987 to 1996. Youths (defined by the study as being under the age of twenty) use psychotropic drugs almost as often as adults do now. The most pronounced increases – 700 percent among youths on Medicaid and 1,400 percent among youths enrolled in HMOs – came in the use of amphetamines (mainly dextroamphetamine sulfate, which is used to treat attention deficit disorder). Antidepressants were the second most-commonly prescribed medication.

References

Clark, Burton. 1960. The "Cooling-Out" Function in Higher Education. *American Journal of Sociology* 65(6): 569–76.

DeGrandpre, Richard. 1999. *Ritalin Nation: Rapid-Fire Culture and the Transformation of Human Consciousness.* New York: Norton.

Diller, Lawrence. 1999. *Running on Ritalin: A Physician Reflects on Children, Society, and Performance in a Pill.* New York: Bantam Books.

Kadison, Richard and Theresa DiGeronimo. 2004. *College of the Overwhelmed: The Campus Mental Health Crisis and What to Do about It.* San Francisco: Jossey-Bass.

Nadeau, Kathleen. 1994. *Survival Guide for College Students with ADD or LD.* Washington, DC: Magination.

Questions

1   How might the use of Ritalin and/or Adderall ease the pressures associated with academic pursuit? Furthermore, how might these stimulants be used to juggle the academic life and social life for university students?

2   In the article, some students had become more comfortable with their medicated identity. Should this be considered a form of substance dependence? Why or why not?

3   How are university students using stimulants such as Ritalin and Adderall today? Are students using these stimulants for recreational or instrumental purposes?

Marginality among Older Injectors in Today's Illicit Drug Culture
Assessing the Impact of Ageing

Tammy L. Anderson and Judith A. Levy

Where do older drug users go? Tammy Anderson and Judith Levy address the issue of change in drug-using scenes through their study of older heroin and cocaine addicts in Chicago. Just as the world shifted between the period during which we wrote "Tinydopers" and the present, the mostly Black men in this study witnessed the transformation of their drug environment from one dominated by an ethos of trust, common interests, and community to one where violence, competition, and exploitation are the norm. It is common that people engage in criminal behavior, including drug using and drug dealing, with others of similar age, race/ethnicity, social class, and gender, but these drug injectors have aged out of their cohort. Consequently, they face significant difficulties in navigating the new, mean, and rough streets they encounter.

How do the problems these drug users face compare to those of younger people? How do social norms about age and drug use impact on them from the outside (the way they are treated by others)? From the inside (they way they regard themselves)? How do the problems of aging intersect with the problems of drug addiction, minority race, and poverty? How does this compare to the aging process of the Mexican-American gang members? What can we infer from this about the life course of drug-using?

Introduction

Years ago, Robert Park (1928) wrote about the difficulties of the 'marginal man', someone whom [he] described as living in two separate cultures but not fully a member of either. Such dual positioning produced numerous personal consequences and the potential for an unstable and stressful identity. Used traditionally to describe immigration experiences, the concept was broadened to include a variety of situations and settings where individuals live on the periphery of two modes of life that can produce a divided self. Park's concept has rarely been applied to studies of deviance, although deviance scholars have discussed marginality at length.

Drugs and the American Dream: An Anthology, First Edition. Edited by Patricia A. Adler, Peter Adler, and Patrick K. O'Brien.

'Deviants' are rarely fully deviant: typically they keep a foot in the conventional world and assume socially valued identities by engaging in acceptable and productive activities while possibly concealing their deviance. [...] At the other end of the spectrum are those who are marginal both to mainstream society and the subcultures that define their deviance. [...]

These issues of people holding dual citizenship in both the straight and deviant world inform our analysis of older injecting drug users (IDUs). Indeed, the subculture of street life, including drug use, is made up of many small groupings formed at different times and for a variety of purposes. Older street addicts hold allegiance to social networks that are organized around illicit drug use, but they also operate typically in the conventional world of family, neighbourhood and general social life. Long-term chronic drug abuse restricts older IDUs' full integration into mainstream culture. However, over time, and with the social restrictions and infirmities of advancing age, our data show that older injectors also find themselves additionally marginalized by being socially relocated by varying levels of choice and coercion along the periphery of the drug world. Being an older injecting drug user, we argue, is to become marginal among the marginal.

This paper explores the joint influences of ageing and social change on the creation of marginality within a deviant population. Our analysis considers how the more common physiological and social aspects of ageing in concert with the demands of a changing drug culture influence core positioning within the latter. Our findings advance the literature on both deviance and ageing by showing how they intersect within the social context of marginality. In short, the displacement of older injectors from a comparatively central position in what our respondents refer to as the 'Old School' (the drug culture of the 1950s to the 1970s) to a marginal and alienated position in today's 'New School' tells us much about the social and physiological consequences of growing older within a changing cultural context.

Our data add to Park's formulation by illustrating the complexities of marginality that his theory failed to envision. As Weisberger (1992; 429) observes:

The marginal person is not only unable to sever ties with his or her own culture and to merge into the new one, but also is unable to return to the native culture or shrug off the influence of the new one.

Weisberger (1992) maintains that Park addressed the first matter (severing ties with the old and merging into the new), but neglected to consider the second (the inability to return to the native culture or to escape the sway of the new). The second matter is especially relevant for our analysis.

Weisberger (1992) delineated four responses to marginality as a human predicament: (1) a *return* to a host culture or an old way of life; (2) *transcendence* that involves overcoming the opposition of two opposing cultures; (3) assimilation through absorption of a host culture's standards: and (4) *poise* that entails a refusal or inability to resolve the ambivalence of marginality despite possible cost in loneliness, anxiety or increased personal tensions. Our data show that returning to the 'Old School' is impossible for the older injectors whom we studied as the drug world of their youth no longer exists. Transcending the cultural contradictions that separate the Old School from the New School as a means to overcome their marginality also is unlikely. Health complications due to ageing that have resulted in a diminishing social status restrict older users' full participation in today's drug world. These same attributes also limit possibilities for assimilation. Instead, the older injectors we studied adopt a position of 'poise' to their predicament by clinging to the self-identity and cultural values of the past while taking an increasingly marginal position within the new. Although they protest their dislocation, they perceive themselves powerless to adjust to the social norms and physical demands of full membership in the drug world that currently exists. Because the poise adaptation represents the loneliest and most isolated position of all we maintain, and our data reveal, that being an older IDU in today's drug scene is fraught with loneliness, stress, and fear of victimization.

Our respondents' experiences of growing older as IDUs tell us much about the personal conflicts and consequences of a life-time of chronic drug dependency. They also teach us about two important matters of general social interest and scientific inquiry that transcend the substantive issues of drug use: (1) the impact of the ageing process on identity and status;

and (2) the meaning and experience of becoming marginal in a social context where one initially enjoyed the privileges of full integration. Park's concept of marginality assumed that people are thrust into dual allegiance either through circumstances of birth or by relocating from one social world to another. Our analyses show that a third possibility exists: marginality may arise when social worlds change but individuals who are committed to them cannot adapt.

[...] We then discuss the age-related issues that fostered our respondents' marginality and their adaptation of poise in today's drug scene. We conceptualize poise as did Weisberger (1992): the failure or inability to resolve the ambivalence of marginality despite its personal costs. We end with a discussion of theoretical and policy-oriented implications.

Analytical Approach

In the fall of 1998, the National Institute of Aging funded a small exploratory study of ageing, drugs and HIV risk among injecting drug users over the age of 50 years. The study evolved from the second author's grant from the National Institute on Drug Abuse, 'Partners in Community Health.' The Partners project was located in a converted storefront within a high crime, economically depressed neighborhood on the west side of Chicago. It employed a two-person (one male and one female) outreach team, both of whom were former injecting heroin users indigenous to Chicago's west side, to recruit 1066 active IDUs for HIV counseling, testing, and partner notification. As part of their community outreach and recruitment duties, the team walked through neighborhoods, copping areas, and shooting galleries daily, delivering AIDS education and prevention materials. During their strolls, they recruited active IDUs for participation in the research component of the Partners project. The recruits, all of whom were active injectors, tended to be polydrug users (some combination of heroin, crack, cocaine or amphetamines). Most were African-American or Latino, and about 40% were female. Ages ranged from 18 to 68. Approximately 21% (n = 222, 179 male and 43 female) of the 1066 IDUs enrolled in the Partners project were 50 years of age

or older. These older users formed the sampling pool for the present study.

Using convenience sampling, we recruited 40 older IDUs to address the topics of ageing, drug use, and HIV risk. We began recruitment by contacting those enrolled most recently in the Partners project because their addresses were the most current. Although the Partners' sample was 40% female, only 16% of the women were over the age of 50 years. We choose to over-sample women from the Partners project for the present qualitative study to obtain adequate gender representation. Participants received $25.00 as compensation for the time spent being interviewed. We reached saturation for our research objectives with 40 respondents.

[...]

Profile of respondents

Our respondents were between the ages of 50 and 68. Most were black (96%), male (63%), parents (90%) and single (80%). Many lacked the educational skills necessary to compete in today's labor market, an attribute that probably contributes to their marginaiity from conventional society. For example, 37% had not completed high school, while 63% had a high school diploma or slightly more. None were college graduates. Twenty-four percent tested HIV seropositive.

Self-reports of the injection of heroin, cocaine, and the speedball mixture of heroin and cocaine provide indirect evidence of extensive interaction in Chicago's west side drug markets. For example, 88% of the respondents reported having injected heroin in the past month, with 49% having done so more than 20 times. Although ours was a study of injecting drug users, 43% also reported smoking crack in the past month with 10% reporting doing so more than 20 times. Although crack is smoked most often, we found 8% of the respondents had injected it in the past month.

Results

The Old School

The period of the 1960s and 1970s in which our respondents began injecting drugs as teens and young adults corresponds to one of the nation's harshest periods of national drug policy. Due to the severe legal penalties for selling or using narcotics, fear of arrest and incarceration helped to create a covert camaraderie among buyers and sellers. Drug marketing and illicit substance use occurred typically under a cloak of social concealment characterized by stealth and self-serving mutual protection. Ralph explains, 'it was like a secret fraternity … [we] didn't let anybody else know that we was using [drugs] but another dope fiend.'

The norms and practices of the Old School, as our respondents call it, developed as a product of this subcultural environment. This term, when used in this context, refers to an ideological system attributed to the drug culture of the 1950s to the 1970s, replete with a proscribed set of behaviors believed to govern how and with whom illicit drugs should be purchased and consumed. According to our respondents, the mores of the Old School differ sharply from the practices and normative expectations of today's illicit drug world with its emphasis on high volume marketing, violence, and predatory behavior. [...] [O]ur respondents described drug users in 1969 as a community bonded by common interests and cooperative partnerships with other addicts to raise money for drugs and drug paraphernalia. Heroin use formed the core of social interchanges, and drug acquisition absorbed much of the user's time. Wistful for what they remember with nostalgia as the more fraternal drug culture of the past, older users find that they must now conform to the social demands and practices of the new.

The extent to which such moral codes or 'schools' actually exist and operate among drug users of any generation is questionable. Like all value systems, our respondents' perception of what constitutes the Old School is subject to competing interpretations and the biases of nostalgia and imperfect memory. As a result, their accounts of its existence probably represent an idealization of how things 'should' be rather than how they actually were. Nonetheless, the values of the Old School are real to the older injectors whom we studied, and they serve as an organizing framework for how they view their lives both past and present.

Drug use in the Old School

Drug use in any era is largely a social enterprise that requires initiation into its practices and the cultivation of useful contacts to maintain. In the Old School

environment, as is true today, a friend, family member or acquaintance served typically as the neophyte's or occasional user's conduit to drugs and the drug world. Indeed, initiation into drug use both past and present tends to occur through close affinitive ties for most nascent users. However, in the Old School when such interpersonal resources dried up or personal need outstripped available supplies, procurement of drugs might entail a trip to one of the 'dope pads' that operated as small retail drug outlets in buildings throughout the city's high crime neighborhoods. David explains how this purchasing route worked:

> You didn't go to the streets. You went to somebody's house … call them … slide the money through the door, something like that. Or you know, knock on the door and come in and sit down. They show you what they going to give you and you get it and you leave. That's how it was.

In general, the 'dope pad' system to which David refers functioned as a small cottage industry in many urban areas throughout the 1960s to the 1980s. The system typically provided income through drug sales for a boss and two or three underlings. Besides supplying illicit substances and providing some level of security for themselves and their customers, the small-scale entrepreneurs of the dope pad system also offered other services such as renting or selling drug injection equipment and performing injecting services for novices or the queasy. Rarely organizationally stable, the lines between users and sellers often blurred or switched as practitioners changed roles. Henry described his experience in going from dealer to user:

> She [a customer] came in and bought five keys. I made $40,000 dollars in an hour … I kept those people [regular customers] about a year or so: But the drugs began worrying the hell out of me. 'This must be good. This got to be good.' … I had been taught-a guy told me, 'don't you never mess with it. You never mess with it.' But my curiosity got the best of me. I put me two lines down and I snorted it.

In contrast to the advantages of sampling one's merchandise as a dealer, access to the wares of a dope pad in the Old School rested more commonly on having someone initially steer the novice toward a seller and then vouch for the customer's trustworthiness, but even experienced IDUs depended upon identifying a constant source of heroin that was readily accessible, affordable, and chemically acceptable. Thus a practical incentive existed for both buyers and sellers to cultivate a ready and ongoing relationship based on some level of mutual knowledge and trust. The buyer needed a dependable source of drugs: the seller required a steady, reliable and discreet supply of repeat customers. The result was the formation of a subculture of individuals, bonded by common interest, whose actions 'in the life' *were* mutually organized around the marketing and/or use of illicit substances.

While based on need and social convenience, this illicit fraternity might also take on shades of paternalism and affective concern—at least in the memories of our respondents. Marla describes a kind of social kinship she recalls from the past:

> See each school got they own thing. See our school, we was taught never to see another addict sick. We were taught to share and the New School don't believe in that. They don't care if you're dying. You're dying: Just die!

Leroy recounts the paternal association that he remembers between users and dealers:

> When I was coming up, you understand, I was buying drugs from drug houses. ... The old-days, they looked out for the older guys. They looked out for the drug users, and on a Sunday if you didn't have no money to buy none with, they give you a bag.

Of course, other users' descriptions suggest that not all user/user or dealer/buyer relationships were as benevolent as Marla's and Leroy's memories suggest: but the close social interaction of users with dealers, and the cycle of going from one role to the other, created the opportunity and helped to encourage the development of some level of perceived fraternal ties. Like all subcultures, language and the normative protocols of membership in the Old School served as a boundary separating those who were legitimately part of 'the life' from those who were not. 'Squares' (non-users) and others outside the drug culture were viewed with suspicion and purposefully excluded from the secrets that insiders knew. The belief that drug consumption should occur outside the home and away from family and home life was common. Children in particular were to be shielded from the sight, if not always the knowledge, of their elders' use.

Protection of the young and the adolescent also extended to proscriptions against their initiation into drugs. Under the ideology of the Old School, selling or distributing drugs to youth constituted a serious breach of ethics. Of course, such breaches did occur, perhaps on a regular basis. Most of the respondents in this sample began their drug use as teens. This circumstance suggests that the age-graded boundaries guarding appropriate use may have been more permeable than generally recognized or acknowledged by today's older user. Faupel (1991) observed that seasoned habituates of this era tended to view violations of the mores prohibiting aiding youthful drug involvement as the work of improperly socialized, newer users. Perhaps this explanation helped veteran users to maintain their belief in the existence of a community and moral order governing illicit drugs within which they acted with honor and integrity.

Presentation of self

The idealized self-image sought by the older IDUs that we studied parallels that of the 'cool cats' who Finestone (1957) describes so richly in his now-classic work. Finestone argues that the imagery of the cat, with its ability to give form and purpose to its own isolated world, substituted in the 1950s and 1960s for the more traditional models of social mobility that were denied to youth reared in the impoverished black ghettos of that era. The 'cool cat' notion of a self-image built on style, grace, and sensual hedonism was particularly salient for our respondents in Chicago – a city that continues to pride itself on the legacy of the neighborhood club scene with its smoky atmosphere, behind-the-scenes drug use, cool jazz and blues.

Our respondents, many of whom grew up in poor, segregated neighborhoods of that era, were socialized in the Old School to believe in the importance of presenting the right appearance. As was true in other major cities, looking 'good' was central to the identity of the illicit user. Male IDUs sought to gain and maintain street respect by operating with style, dignity, and polish. Mike explains, 'See my lifestyle had been always been smooth, you know a smooth hustle.' Women IDUs sought a personage of glamour, excitement, and liberation. Sally, an attractive woman in her early 50s. describes the allure of the late 1960s drug world and her self-perceived place within it:

> That was '67, I believe it was, and that's when the ladies, and the light, the attire, the bright lights, the honking of the horns [attracted me]. –I'm on Broadway [a street in Chicago once known for its club scene] looking up at the sky filled with lights and I'm like, 'yeah. This is where I want to be.'

Sally was far from alone in making this judgement. An unknown number of poor women with few prospects for advancement have perceived the mores and practices of the 'fast life,' including its emphasis on drug use, as a chance to gain otherwise unobtainable prestige, fast paced excitement, and monetary rewards.

Under the Old School ideology, how users procured money and/or drugs could add or detract from one's presentation of self as slick or dignified. Dealing drugs brought respect and prestige while also guaranteeing a central role in the street scene. Typically, such male respondents were small-time marijuana and/or heroin sellers although they might dabble in other substances. Minor theft, con games, gambling (shooting pool, dice, and playing cards), or legitimate work in the informal economy supplemented or provided alternative sources of income.

The New School

Over the 30–40 years of drug use, the older IDUs we studied have seen the drug scene change from a cottage industry at the local level to a more sophisticated and complex trafficking system. While not entirely dead and with some vestiges still operating, the Old School has been transformed into the 'new.' Drug marketing in the New School has become increasingly a lucrative enterprise with a large and complex staffing characterized by a hierarchical division of labor that includes dealers, street-level sellers, touts, steerers, look-outs, and drug baggers. Dope pads continue to exist, but they operate

alongside a wider range of 'copping spots' than appear typical of the 1960s, 1970s, and 1980s. Abandoned buildings join private homes and apartments as copping grounds and shooting galleries where drugs commonly are purchased and used. Street-level distribution is common with touts and 'steerers' openly hawking their wares.

Street gangs often dominate the network of suppliers and these affiliations, along with those of competing interest groups, bring their own code of ethics to the scene. Jankowski (1991) notes that the ideology and marketing arrangements of today incorporate a strong entrepreneurial ethos comprised of five core values. First, today's trafficking stresses an ideology of Darwinian competition for financial rewards in which unsuccessful combatants are deemed inadequate and inferior. Secondly, it values material accumulation as a means to improve leisure time, personal comfort, and life-style. Thirdly, it emphasizes the rewards of status-seeking, prestige, and reputation. Fourthly, it encourages preoccupation with planning activities that will bring fortune and fame. Finally, it honors risk-taking even when it involves violence. Dembo et al. (1993), for example, found that a significant majority of today's drug dealers have killed or seriously hurt someone.

Drug sales are orchestrated in the New School to maximize volume and distribution. 'Crew bosses' operate 'runner systems' involving large teams of workers who service drive-up customers or a pedestrian crowd. Transactions are conducted in public spaces and are readily observable to those who know where to look. This openness and easy availability contrast sharply with Old School marketing methods in the memories of old timers. George explains:

> When I was coming up, you understand. I was buying drugs from drug houses. ... Nowadays, you buy drugs along the comer. At that time, you know, it wasn't like it is now where the kids be on the corner hollering 'rocks and blows.'

Mieczkowski (1992) notes that the 'crew system' of distribution in what we call the New School offers sellers at least three advantages. First, it permits sellers to escape the confinement of a fixed selling location. As a result, police interference and the chances of arrest for drug dealing are reduced. Secondly, the common practice of using minors as street-level operators offers an easy-to recruit, cheap and relatively controllable source of labor while also protecting adults who run the operations behind the scenes from legal difficulties and prosecution. Finally, the easy access of buyers to sellers permits achieving greater sales volumes than possible in a closed, covert system.

Drug use and relationships with dealers

Despite its clear advantages to the seller, benefits to the buyer are less easily discerned. Assuming that our respondent's accounts of the past are accurate, the paternalism reported in the era of the 1960s and 1970s appears to have dwindled along with the granting of 'perks' to faithful buyers that this relationship entailed. Consumers complain of violence and a perceived power inequity between buyer and seller that is exacerbated by differences in age, gender, and prestige, as Edward complains of the frustrations and interpersonal indignities of queuing up to buy drugs:

> They keep telling you 15 minutes, 15 minutes and you stand there for a hour. I say, 'fuck it. I'm gone. I see you.' Cause [if you complain], they will tell you to 'shut the fuck up,' or you know, 'get the fuck out my way.'

Such interpersonal conflict is reinforced by the tendency for sellers and users to inhabit separate social spaces due to gender, age grading, and the impersonal characteristics of contemporary drug transactions. While faces might be familiar, few interpersonal relationships exist between users and dealers in the New School, as well as little bonding, solidarity, and shared identity.

Presentations of self

Presentations of self in today's New School also noticeably differ from the 'suave,' 'slick,' images sought several decades ago. Street reputations are organized around being 'bad,' a judgement that can be enhanced or bought through the threat or actual act of violence. Older IDUs describe today's dealers and their underlings as wanting to be perceived as powerful, macho, and willing to use violence to get what they want. Sam notes that they all 'sound like young gladiators, all they want to do is fight and stuff like

that.' Sam went on to offer an example of a violent exchange that occurred when a young buyer, who was a newcomer in the neighborhood, partly overheard the whispering of a husband and wife as they queued up for a drug purchase:

> Just the other day I was in line copping. This guy [the husband] say something to his wife about him [the newcomer]. I don't know what he said. But uh this kid say [to the wife], 'what did he say to you:' and she said 'nothing,' and he said, 'no, no, fuck that. What did he say to you.' Then this girl said, 'I tell you what he said.' He said, 'I'm tired of these motherfuckers coming over here copping.' He [the newcomer] turned to the husband and said, 'I thought that's what you said. Didn't I tell you about that bullshit man.' Shot him [the husband] in the leg.

Exposure to such acts of violence often becomes a focal point in the process of self-questioning that begins when older users realize that the culture of drug use into which they were socialized as youth has changed. Taken-for-granted assumptions about the streets and their place within it form an impetus for self-re-examination. Ralph summed up what he concludes about his own ability to compete as a central figure in this aggressive environment:

> When I was younger I used to say, 'separate the eagles from the sparrows,' you know. But now it's just crazy. I'm a sparrow now. I was a eagle back then when I had my health. But now I'm a sparrow. I know I'm going to fall dead.

From Center to Margin

Having described the changes over time in the social context of injecting drug use, we now elaborate on the age related processes that have helped relocate our respondents from their former central location in the Old School to their marginalized position in today's drug culture. Our discussion focuses on identity because it was a central concern of Park's and remains so in more recent studies of deviance and marginality. [...] Our premise is that various aspects of the ageing process render our respondents unable to retain their central location in the drug subcultures of today, what our respondents refer to as the 'New School.' The marginalization outcome is ultimately therefore an identity problem. Older injectors cannot effectively negotiate the identity scripts located in this more modern social context. Examination of the biological and social aspects of ageing and chronic drug use helps to explain this disconnect, and these two influences are explored below.

Biological ageing

Physiological changes mark the process of growing older and typically include the possibility of increased illness and disability. The socio-biological consequences of chronic drug use and living the hard life of drug dependency exacerbate further this normal ageing process. Our respondents told of the following health problems: abscesses, arthritis, injured legs and shoulders, gastrointestinal problems, collapsed veins, chronic body pain, bronchitis, cancer, cirrhosis of the liver, colon problems, diabetes, emphysema, gunshot wound side-effects, hypertension and related cardiovascular issues, hepatitis C, liver dysfunction, HIV complications, mental health problems (e.g. depression), sinusitis, swollen limbs, and scarred hands.

In addition to such health declines, most injecting drug users eventually confront problems with 'burned up' veins—a condition exacerbated by age. To compensate, those for whom injection has become extremely difficult often switch to snorting drugs, relying on others ('hit doctors') to help with injection or 'skin-popping' (intramuscular injection). Associated with low status among users, Kenny describes the latter practice:

> Your veins get hard. They died out. You killed them and they gone, and then you can no longer have no more veins. Then you have to skin pop it. Then you keep skin-popping it and your body start rotting with them abscesses. My girlfriend I want to go on a program [methadone].

Such problems in delivering drugs to the body tend to set the older injector apart from the mainstream drug scene with its emphasis on youth and invincibility. Furthermore, research on ageing and identity has linked problems and physiological declines associated with age

to a sense of diminished self-worth and self-control. Our respondents' descriptions of themselves and their lives are consistent with this literature. Older users can do little about the health declines of age except to rely on poise to minimize their effects.

Social ageing

George (1998) has documented how the ageing process exacerbates the desire for self-protection and reduces risk-taking. Our respondents told us of how, as they aged, fear of victimization by younger users caused them to shift increasingly from active participation in the general drug scene to covert drug use along its periphery as a protective adaptation against harm. In addition to such self-imposed isolation (marginalization), the health consequences of ageing rendered them less physically fit and demanded that they find less challenging ways to obtain money and drugs. As Courtwright et al. (1989) also found when studying the generation of older users who predate our study respondents, hustling strategies shifted from potentially profitable high-risk illegal pursuits such as drug dealing and robbery to comparatively lower-risk legal and illegal hustles such as boosting (petty stealing) and reliance on public assistance and money from family members Such latter activities buy little status in the contemporary drug culture, where the currency for respect lies typically in ruthlessness, control, physical superiority, or dollars (Dembo et al. 1993).

Conclusions

For many years, researchers in the study of drug abuse subscribed to the 'maturation hypothesis' which posits that illicit substance users [mature out of drug using behavior as they age under the pressures and trials of living the life. Despite numerous attempts through the years to test this hypothesis results proved ambiguous and conclusions open to argument. More recently, the AIDS epidemic has added important insight to the controversy. As projects around the country began to recruit active addicts for HIV counseling, testing and AIDS interventions, an unanticipated number of participants turned out to be over age 50. Rather than having 'matured out' of the life, these older survivors of an earlier era remained active but hidden.

Such a change in how older injectors maintain their drug use in late adulthood calls attention to how age, period, and cohort effects can intersect. As data from the drug abuse treatment studies show, each birth cohort of illicit drug users' initiation into illicit drug use is associated with a particular drug and pattern of use. Our respondents began their hard-core drug use primarily as heroin users during a historical period where heroin was the serious drug of choice. As they aged they switched drugs and modes of operating on the street to accommodate the biological and psychosocial changes that negated their ability to maintain their former drug using careers.

How much of the changes we found are due to age versus the effects of social change, separating out the influences of age, cohort, and periodicity, is extremely difficult when analyzing any birth cohort or generation or people given the close relationship of these factors. We did not attempt this task in our analysis. Instead, we observe that it is the very conflux of the three factors—age, cohort and period effects—that over a life-time of drug use force our respondents from center position in the drug culture of their youth to the margins of the drug culture within which they participate in old age. Thus, we leave it to others to determine how much one of any of the three factors contributes to the total process.

[...] [H]eroin and other drug epidemics occur under conditions of open marginality when a societal group that shares a common identity undergoes rapid social change. Drug epidemics emerge and are identified as such through public discourse, at a specific historical time when the ensuing gap between expectation and reality produces sufficient stress to propel group members into serious and chronic drug use that comes to public attention.

Our findings suggest that age may factor into this process. Rather than older injectors' movement toward increased marginality spurring a new drug epidemic of their making, or their plight resulting in public notice that becomes fodder for declaring an epidemic, their situation in old age represents an adaptation to a drug epidemic of an earlier time. Under pressures of age and social change, and unable to transcend their marginality or to assimilate fully, they can do little more to put a positive spin on their situation than to cling to treasured memories of the past and to occupy the present with poise. As Goffman (1961) suggests of the marginalized person in general, they have become 'locked into a position and coerced into living up to the promises and sacrifices built into it.' This lonely adaptation of poise—the failure to resolve the ambivalence of marginality, but rather to abide within it through nostalgia and longing—ushers in numerous personal tensions for the ageing drug injector and produces a daily existence that is both turbulent and stressful.

We think of the fates of the older injectors we have studied as caught up in generic processes of social change, and accordingly the question becomes one of what happens when society changes but some of its members do not. Sometimes such people become displaced workers, as when automation replaces craft skills; sometimes they become homeless, as when low-rent apartment buildings are gentrified. In the case of older drug injectors, they become marginal among the marginal of society, or perhaps stated another way they become deviant among the deviant. What we see in our own data therefore is an instance of generic and classical problems of persistence and change. Instead of reconstructing identity scripts formed during the Old School to conform to contemporary norms and practices our respondents opt, and to some degree are forced, to remain committed to their pasts. While it may be typical for older adults to live in a world they do not recognize as the one of their youth, the older injector has few options but to persist in the present. This is the essence of poise.

[...]

References

Courtwright, D., Joseph, H. and Des Jarlais, D. (1989) *Addicts Who Survived: An Oral History of Narcotic Use in America.* Knoxville, TN: University of Tennessee Press.

Dembo. R., Hughes. P., Jackson, L. and Mieczkowski. T. (1993) Crack cocaine dealing by adolescents in two public housing projects; a pilot study. *Human Organization,* 52, 89–96.

Faupel, C. E. (1991) *Shooting Dope: Career Patterns of Hard-Core Heroin Users.* Gainesville, FL: University of Florida Press.

Finestone, H. (1957) Cats, kicks, and color. *Social Problems,* 5, 313.

George, L. K. (1998) Self and identity in later life: protecting and enhancing the self. *Journal of Ageing and Identity,* 3(3), 133–52.

Goffman. E. (1961) *Encounters.* Indianapolis: Bobbs-Merrill.

Jankowski, M. S. (1991) *Islands in the Street.* Berkeley, CA: University of California Press.

Mieczkowski. T. (1986) Geeking up and throwing down: heroin street life in Detroit. *Criminology,* 24, 645–66.

Park, R. E. (1928) Human migration and the Marginal Man. *American Journal of Sociology,* 33, 881–93.

Weisberger. A. (1992) Marginality and its directions. *Sociological Forum,* 7, 425–46.

Questions

1   Why do older injecting users become the "marginal among the marginal" in this deviant population? What may be examples of this occurrence in other drug subcultures? How might gender impact this marginality?

2   According to the respondents, how did the "old school" differ from the practices and expectations of today's drug world? Do we see such sociocultural shifts in other arenas of the drug world? Are people using and selling drugs differently today?

3   How did biological aging and social aging operate for the injectors? How might various forms of aging operate in other drug using subcultures? What are some other reasons users may age out of drug use not mentioned in the article?

24

Baby Boomer Drug Users
Career Phases, Identity, Self-Concept, and Social Control

Miriam Williams Boeri, Claire E. Sterk, and Kirk W. Elifson

Miriam Boeri, Claire Sterk, and Kirk Elifson offer us another view of aging drug users with their study of older baby boomer heroin and methamphetamine injectors in Atlanta. Like Vecitis, they offer a four-fold table differentiating adaptive styles by people's ability to maintain control over their drug use and their adoption of conventional legitimate versus illegitimate nonconventional social roles. Their study aims to reveal the relationship between people's control over their drug use and their ability to attain and hold respectable social and occupational roles. Featuring a sample population more integrated by age and race, this study reveals an enormous variety in how users aged over their careers in drug use, with some faring moderately well and others suffering.

In contrast to some of the other studies, you may want to think about the role of pharmacology in influencing drug users' life outcomes, since differences prevailed between the methamphetamine and heroin addicts. This study's diverse population also makes it difficult to characterize the effects of ethnic subculture, gender power, and social class. Instead, what factors does it emphasize in discussing the career trajectories of users? In reading this article you may want to think about the role of conventional society in holding drug addicts from falling to the lowest rungs of despair and complete loss of self-control. How might this influence your thoughts about public policy toward injecting drug users?

Research on illicit drug use has been guided by a wide range of sociological and criminological theoretical approaches. In this article we build on existing studies of illicit drug use that have applied theories of self-control. [...] We view self-control as a measure of the level of control over drug use (including controlled use and loss of control). In addition, we draw on aspects of internal control processes, primarily social bonding and social learning through commitment to social roles.

In this study we examined drug use patterns and social roles of opiate and stimulant use over the life course. Our sample of 65 baby boomers[1] includes both heroin and methamphetamine users.[2] Based on in-depth interview narratives, we developed a typology focused on dimensions of self-control and social control. Four phases of drug use emerged from the data: controlled users, marginal users, hustlers, and junkies. Drug users in the controlled user phase have control over their drug use and maintain legitimate and conventional social roles. Those in the marginal phase maintain legitimate, conventional social roles, but are losing control over their drug use. Users in the hustler phase are involved in illegitimate roles, such as dealer, hustler, and sex worker, but they must maintain some control over their drug use. Finally, the users in the junkie phase have lost control over drug use and have lost all legitimate and illegitimate social roles except the role of drug user. The study participants' identity and self-concept are employed as descriptive illustrative themes. While we are not focusing on specific cause-and-effect relationships, in this exploratory study we ask how the salience of social roles and changes in levels of control, loss of control, and regained control are depicted in individual biographies among a diverse older population of drug users.

[...]

Methods

Data for this study were derived from a larger research project on drug trends in Atlanta, Georgia, including sociodemographic characteristics, use patterns, and drug use careers among active users of heroin or methamphetamine. Heroin and methamphetamine were selected because the epidemiological trends regarding these drugs were showing the most increase, particularly for the baby boomer age group. [...] In this article, we used data on baby boomer drug users. We defined baby boomers as those participants who were at least aged 35 in the year 2000.[3] To be eligible for inclusion in the sample for this article, study participants met the following criteria: (1) were 35 to 54 years old in the year 2000; (2) used methamphetamine or heroin at least once in the last 30 days prior to the interview and at least six times in the last six months; (3) were not in substance abuse treatment, prison or jail, or any other institutional setting; and (4) were able to conduct the interview in

English. Failure to meet all of the above criteria was the only reason for not including potential participants and no participants were dropped from the baby boomer sample.

[...]

Typically, recruitment involved spending many hours walking city streets and neighborhoods, frequenting establishments, and talking to potential participants while collecting ethnographic data. Recruitment flyers were posted in a wide variety of public settings to advertise the study and to engage potential study participants. Snowball or chain-referral sampling was employed, including asking ineligible individuals for referrals. Study staff acted simultaneously as recruiters, ethnographers, and interviewers. For this article, we selected baby boomers only. Three men and two women of different racial and ethnic backgrounds conducted the interviews. The authors of this article trained all interviewers, and one author conducted the majority of the baby boomer interviews. Regular project meetings were held to discuss new findings and theoretical sampling methods. [...] The data collection consisted of a closed-ended questionnaire and an audiotaped, in-depth life history interview. Each participant was paid $15 for each part of the interview, or $30 in total. [...]

The sample included 65 baby boomer drug users. Approximately two-thirds were men. The ages of study participants ranged between 34 and 54 years (median 41) at the time of the interview. Three-fifths identified as white, followed by two-fifths African American. In terms of their educational attainment, one-fifth had less than a high school diploma or the equivalent thereof, and three-fifths of the study participants had some college education, a college degree, or a graduate degree. Over one-third were employed either full time (21.5%) or part time (16.9%). Typical living conditions were in own house or apartment (30.8%) or in someone else's house or apartment (27.7%). Among the study participants, 12.3% were homeless.

Typology of Older Drug Users

We developed a typology to categorize respondents according to reported level of self-control over their

Table 24.1 Typology of drug user phases

	Maintains control	*Low/lost control*
Mainstream legitimate conventional roles	*Controlled users* N = 23 (35.4%) Maintains social roles and control over drug use	*Marginal users* N = 12 (18.5%) Maintains social roles but losing control over drug use
Nonmainstream illegitimate nonconventional roles	*Hustlers/dealers/sex workers* N = 23 (35.4%) Lost conventional social roles but maintains some control over drug use	*Junkies* N = 7 (10.8%) Lost all social roles and control over drug use

drug use (maintaining self-control and losing or loss of self-control) and their level of continued involvement in mainstream or nonmainstream social roles. The level of self-control over drug use was derived from quantitative data on the number of days and the number of times drugs were used in the last 90 and 30 days prior to the interview. In addition, changes in the amount of drug use during these time periods as well as responses to survey questions regarding control over drug use were considered in assigning the level of self-control for each participant. An understanding of the study participants' involvement in various social roles was derived from the quantitative data on current family relationships, partners, marital status, occupation, living arrangements, and income sources. This information was supplemented with qualitative data on topics such as the salience of mainstream and illegitimate social roles, involvement in drug use role, the extent to which drug use interfered with functioning in mainstream social role, role attachment, time spent in the role, and the gain or loss of roles in the previous three months.

The typology consisted of four categories: controlled users, marginal users, hustlers, and junkies (see Table 24.1). Controlled users were studied in the 1960s. However, they have been understudied in more recent decades, with some notable exceptions. Marginal users often are defined using addiction criteria, while social roles seldom are addressed. Only a few studies have explored how having something at stake helps marginal users control their drug use. The hustler and junkie have been depicted in literature as the same social role, but in this article we distinguish between the two. We want to reemphasize that these drug use types do not represent developmental or static categories. Similar to the typology developed by Faupel (1991) the categories in this typology refer to "phases" of use that describe the user's current drug use behavior and social roles. In addition, this model is not depicting a developmental path in the drug career. Although users may move from one phase to another, this does not necessarily occur as a developmental process or in a particular order that requires transitioning through all phases. For example, some users were "controlled users" who became "junkies" without ever having been "marginal users" or "hustlers."

First, we highlight differences found between the methamphetamine and the heroin users within each phase. Next, we portray the lives of the drug users in each phase as illustrated through participants' quotes on identity and self-concept. We want to acknowledge that social stigma of methamphetamine users has increased since the data were collected, which may affect the identity and self-concept of current methamphetamine users that is not reflected here.

Controlled user phase

The two most common mainstream social roles among the baby boomers in the controlled user phase were family roles (such as being a parent or being someone's partner) and legitimate work roles. A central theme in their narratives was their ability to maintain or regain control. In addition, the users in this phase often referred to intervention strategies that allowed them to respond to the potential loss of control. These included temporarily ceasing use, cutting down on use, shifting the route of administration, or seeking drug treatment.

Methamphetamine users were more likely than heroin users to indicate controlled use, with 50 percent (16) of the methamphetamine users being controlled users as compared to 21 percent (7) of the heroin users. Most of the controlled methamphetamine users took the drug primarily for functional reasons, often related to their work performance. A tailor, whose methamphetamine use was controlled, indicated that it helped her to focus on her work, stating, "I sewed and … I got the details down so well on this and everything. This is really an opportunity drug here."

Among the controlled heroin users, being able to handle withdrawal symptoms was a common theme. One controlled heroin-using female said, "I have never felt any withdrawal. … I've never felt like … a person told me that I should feel like I was aching and hurting. I never felt sick that way." Those controlled heroin users who did experience withdrawal symptoms reported either seeking drug treatment or adjusting their use in order to regain control over their use.

Others described how the salience of certain mainstream social roles helped them maintain their drug use or motivated them to gain control when their drug use escalated. One long-time heroin user indicated that the importance he gave to his role as a grandfather facilitated his control. He described feeling guilty if he had to leave his grandchildren because of withdrawal symptoms. Recently, he enrolled in a methadone maintenance program hoping to regain control over his heroin use.

Identity and self-concept

All users in the controlled phase expressed the importance of keeping the prominence of their drug use role under control. Consequently, their narratives were full of references to social roles other than being a drug user. Some study participants referred to their conventional social roles as "priorities." When asked about the characteristics of controlled methamphetamine users, one older woman answered: "Probably depends on their priorities in life, whether they're more focused on work and/or family or relationship." A 37-year-old heroin user who lived with his mother illustrated how his priority of being a good son limited his use: "I'm not going to use at home. I never got high at my house in my life. I don't get high

at home – give it away or sell it before I go home. … Never had dope bags in my mama's house in my life."

The desire to maintain an effective work role also contributed to curtailing the drug use role. For example, one controlled user indicated that as his work was important to him, he controlled his methamphetamine use by using only on Saturdays. He also pointed out that his use pattern was designed to pass a potential drug test at work: "… that's another reason why I don't do it during the week. Just [be] cause, you know, I know if I, even if I do it on Sunday, if I'm pulled that week, I can go pee on Friday and it will pass [the drug test]."

Interview data revealed that the user's self-concept played a role in control of use. For the 37-year-old heroin user quoted above, being a good son in the eyes of his mother overrode his drug use role. He expressed concerns about the consequences if he ever would lose his self-concept as a respected son, emphasizing, "[F]or her to find out – that would really hurt me." Another controlled heroin user portrayed a concept of self that included the drug-using role only when around friends who used. He said he used "to impress them, to fit in," but he specified that he was still in control: "[Be]cause I can be in their presence and still don't do it if I'm not in the mood to use it – and they still do it."

As mentioned previously, among controlled users who are moving in the direction of losing control, being able to regain it was essential. Their narratives showed that their self-concept acted as a strong motivating force. One older male claimed to have recently regained control of heroin use by switching from injecting to snorting heroin. Snorting heroin allowed him to function more effectively as a husband.

Another controlled heroin user showed evidence of conforming to the standards set by society for being a "good" father: "I don't neglect my son. I think I'm doing a pretty good job with him in spite of being on heroin. We always have had a place to stay. We've always had food on the table. He goes to school."

A recurring feature of the controlled methamphetamine users was a self-concept as a hard and able worker. One methamphetamine-using decorator appeared proud that his coworkers tell him, "I'm faster than anybody they've ever met in their lives. I can disassemble a room in no time flat and put it back together in no time flat." A female who started using methamphetamine late in life indicated that she takes the drug only for her work role:

> I work drugged, which I know sounds stupid, but it's not a social situation for me ... the only reason that I ever did the drug in the first place was for a physiological need to be able to get up and go. And maybe it's because I was older, you know, when I tried it the first time.

Marginal user phase

Drug users in the marginal user phase are those who maintain conventional and legitimate social roles but who indicate a periodic and/or increasing loss of control over drug use to the point that it is beginning to interfere with their ability to maintain mainstream social roles. Frequently, marginal users were "oblivious" to their emerging drug use-related problems. Approximately 18.5 percent of both groups of users (six heroin users and six methamphetamine users) were marginal users. We found little difference between heroin and methamphetamine users in this phase other than the amount of time spent in work-related roles was greater for methamphetamine users. Being a marginal user tended to be a transitional phase; either the user would regain control and become a controlled user, or the use would escalate, pushing the user to become a hustler or junkie with greatly decreased involvement in mainstream social roles. For example, one marginal user previously controlled her methamphetamine use because of financial constraints. So far, she had been able to prevent herself from becoming overly involved in illegal activities to support her habit. However, her story indicated she was slipping:

> Money is the issue. [My partner] gets disability, and I have money from my parents ... and I work a little bit here and there. Doing odd jobs ... I do everything from grocery shop for people to pick up their dog. I'll do anything for money just as long as it's above board. I'll even go so far as to um ... I quit dealing in 1997, for all intents and purposes, I have. The most I'll do is, um, a prescription for Vicadone will come along and, uh, I know a couple [of] people, one in particular, who likes it. He'll pay lop dollar for it, straight and confidential, very cool. ... That's eighty, ninety bucks in my pocket. Sometimes two hundred bucks in my

pocket. That's about as close as I get to the line when it comes to [participating in] illegal [activities].

This older woman is an example of a marginal user who is drifting into becoming a hustler. Yet to her it was important that she did not become a drug dealer, despite her involvement in drug sales.

Identity and self-concept

Those in the marginal user phase frequently become publicly known as drug users. For some, being identified as a drug user took place at work or at home, and for others it occurred upon arrest. Once labeled as a drug user, many recounted experiences of lost employment, broken relationships, and decreased social support. In other words, the identification as a drug user created broken social bonds. Frequently, this loss triggered greater lack of control over their drug use.

Some marginal users described intensive attempts to hold onto their legitimate social roles or to fight the stigmatization of a drug user identity and subsequent loss of mainstream social roles. The story of one marginal user who self-defined as a heroin "addict" exemplified the influence of social roles and their loss, as well as the fluidity of the marginal category. This 50-year-old male said he had been addicted to prescription opiates, which allowed him to remain in a controlled user phase, but he turned to heroin after losing one of his cherished work roles:

> I was what they call a half-assed functioning addict ... I had to get high before I can go to work, but I would go to work (laughs) and make money ... Oh, it wasn't controlled. I mean, because I had a habit. You had to do it every day. but I did what I had to do. I cooked, I cleaned, and I went to work.... Sometimes I may have just got tired of going so far away to work or just the monotony of the job, period. You know a lot of times you get tired, um, when you're an addict, you get tired of shit quick (laughs).

In this quote, the user discussed social roles and control in apparently contradictory terms. Using an addict/nonaddict dichotomized view of self-control, the user believed he had no control. However, if we accept any control over drug use as indicating a level of control, then we can see this user did have some self-control. First, he stated that he maintained a functional work role simultaneously with his user role. Eventually he "tires" of the work role, which was a low-paying warehouse position. Second, although he said he did not control his habit, he also explained that he maintained sufficient control to work and to take care of his home life. For instance, he described being engaged with cleaning and cooking. Further into the interview, he revealed that prior to his most recent job he had lost his position as a welder when his drug test was positive. He seemed to have been able to control his drug habit while he was a worker. However, once identified as a drug user at work, he lost his job, independent of his past performance. Even though he found other employment, he was bitter about the urine test, and he perceived his new job in a warehouse as below his status. Gradually, he identified primarily as a drug user and could not find ways to regain control.

Some marginal users sought assistance from family members and friends in their effort to maintain conventional social control. For example, a male methamphetamine user who was very close to his mother indicated that she was supportive despite her feelings about his drug use.

> I think, she has to be careful, you know, but I think she is careful in front of me, you know, and tries real [hard] just to be supportive, and, you know, not to let me know how bad it is for her. It's very disappointing for her, yeah.

Other baby boomer marginal users recognized a growing prominence of their drug use role. Instead of seeking support, they focused on hiding their habit from friends and family. Efforts to maintain salient mainstream social roles became part of their survival strategy. For example, one financially successful methamphetamine user indicated that the work role helped to keep a marginal user status:

> I noticed that methamphetamine is big in the working class. People get up, eat, do some more [methamphetamine] and go to work ... I mean you need to go to work, so regardless of the negative impact [of methamphetamine] on your body, you're going to do some more and go.

Another methamphetamine user who continued in a mainstream work role explained that he had become paranoid and began hallucinating recently, although he still thought that he appeared "normal":

> Like, people, like hiding behind trees, hiding behind bushes, watching me, you know, just stuff like that. Police, sometimes I can't get out of the house to go to work 'cuz I'm surrounded by the police and I'm afraid to leave 'cuz they'll arrest me. Well, it's gotten to the point that I can't tell the difference, but I have to kinda pretend like I do so I don't really ... so I look normal.

A heroin-using female in the marginal phase was worried about her drug-using role affecting her family role. Currently in a committed relationship with another female, she indicated that her self-concept as a loving partner was more important to her than using heroin:

> If it came to the point where I saw that the drugs was gonna break up my family, my wife was gonna leave me or somethin' like that, I'd leave it alone. But it's never gotten to that point. I don't even think she realizes that.

The marginal users in these examples cling to their traditional mainstream social roles. Because of increasing difficulty in controlling drug use, they are likely to lose all conventional social roles. Frequently, marginal users face the choice of entering drug treatment, as a sign of wanting to regain control over their habits, or losing conventional social roles.

Hustler, dealer, and sex worker phase

Drug users in this phase are those who have lost or abandoned their legitimate conventional social roles and have acquired salient illegal or nonconventional social roles, such as street hustlers,[4] drug dealers, or sex workers. Some hustlers began experimenting with a particular hustle while in the marginal phase. Others did not have any previous familiarity with hustling activities. The study participants who had been publicly identified by others as drug users while they were in the controlled or marginal phases subsequently faced the loss of a regular income, loss of social support from relatives and friends, and, in some cases, arrest and jail or prison time. These experiences influenced their current hustling role. Almost twice as many of the hustlers in the sample were heroin users compared to methamphetamine users, with 21.9 percent (7) of the methamphetamine users and 48.5 percent (16) of the heroin users categorized as hustlers.

Typically, when users are in this phase they live on the edge of society. Their drug use dominates many aspects of their lives as they lose or give up legitimate social roles. However, their most salient social role is not that of being a drug user but a nonconventional role such as street hustler, dealer or runner[5] of drugs, or sex worker. Their narratives called attention to how they controlled their drug use sufficiently in order to function successfully in their hustler role. For example, a heroin-using respondent who was a former dealer said that he could no longer sell drugs because he used too much and became dangerously indebted to his suppliers. A female drug runner explained that she decreased her heroin use to two bags a day in order to keep running heroin. She described what self-control means in order to function in this phase of hustling, dealing, or sex work:

> There's the big difference right there. Some of us are using and some of us are abusing. I'm a user. I get it for the sickness to get off me, so I'll be well and can function. Other people do it like I said – they sit around all day, have nothing to do but to do dope 'cuz they like the dope. 'Cuz they love the dope.

A substantial proportion of the methamphetamine users experienced difficulty in maintaining social roles other than their drug use role once their habit became uncontrolled. Among the heroin users, on the other hand, the loss of social roles (legitimate or illegitimate) often was attributed to their stigmatization of being a heroin user. In other words, among the heroin users in our sample the loss of social roles was less directly related to their use but rather a result of the way in which they were labeled. We draw attention to the fact that in the past year methamphetamine has become more widespread and methamphetamine use has become more highly stigmatized as panic over methamphetamine abuse is rising in the area where this study was conducted. The labeling effects on methamphetamine users may be more relevant currently.

Identity and self-concept

When describing their identity through social roles other than the drug user role, many hustlers explained that there was some process of specialization that took place. They performed better or were more comfortable with some unconventional roles than

other unconventional roles. Others described the unpredictability of succeeding. One of the older heroin-using pimps recalled:

> But there are times … especially being a hustler, quote, "a pimp." Sometimes the girl will run off and won't bring you no money. Sometimes the hustle game doesn't work and you can't get it and you're sick. I've been sick today and I'm really struggling to do this interview.

However, the main key to being a successful hustler was maintaining sufficient control over his heroin habit. This is captured in the following quote:

> I'm kind of just staying where I'm at right now … the best I can. I don't really want to get more, because it's getting harder to hustle money and stuff. So I'm trying to stay just where I'm at. Just keeping from being sick really … that is what I'm doing.

The meanings the hustlers attached to their illegitimate social roles are barometers of their self-concept. It was not uncommon for drug dealers to view themselves as higher up the hustler hierarchy than, for instance, drug runners or sex workers. Among the sex workers, we learned that status reflected the type of clientele they served. One of the baby boomer methamphetamine users who hustled wealthy gay males said:

> Hustling is easy money and … also it makes me feel worthwhile. Even though they [the customers] were all talking shit, I heard them saying nice things about me. … Basically, I met a lot of nice people. I still have a couple of people that I've known for 18, 20 years. … I got a GED [General Education Diploma] … I think I'm a pretty smart guy and most of that comes from all the tricks and people I've met over the years.

Yet the baby boomer dealers gave little evidence of taking pride in their role as a dealer, and some referred to dealing or running drugs as a necessary activity because of their habits. As one older heroin user expressed his disdain: "No, I don't like it at all. It's just something that I'm caught up in because of my heroin habit. I mean, I don't like it because I'm dependent. You're dependent upon other people, you know what I'm saying?"

Having lived the life of a drug user for many years, most of the dealers were no longer infatuated with the high-risk role of dealing and running drugs. One heroin dealer lamented, "I haven't had a job in like eight years, seven years. I am trying, though, at this point in my life, to get that schedule back." In addition, being a "cool hustler" seemed to be the label for the younger hustlers, as evidenced by the way aging hustlers talked about their role as "just an old hustler." The baby boomer hustlers and sex workers realized they are despised by many people. Some desired to have a legitimate work role. When asked about future plans, an older hustler echoed the same response heard from other aging dealers and sex workers: "I'm gonna get a job."

Although dealing and running drugs appear to be preferable to hustling and sex work as a way of maintaining heroin dependence, the hustler and sex worker manage to maintain a self-concept that is a figurative step above the junkie. Following the guidance provided by the study participants, we did not include panhandling as a hustle. Although panhandling often is viewed as a form of hustling, in our sample the drug users in the hustling phase did not include panhandling as one of their support sources. They also indicated that the hustles they conducted were not as low as panhandling. As one hustler commented when referring to street-dwelling junkies, "I can't be one of these street people who is dirty all the time and panhandles. I can't panhandle – it's just not me."

Junkie phase

The daily life of drug users in the junkie phase was organized around the drug use role. Few mentioned any current family roles, work roles, or any other mainstream social role. Most, however, recounted memories of having held such roles. In addition, they described having failed at maintaining illegitimate roles other than being a drug user. Their days are centered on moving from one fix to the next. The lack of social routines other than drug using is the most evident characteristic of the users in the junkie phase. A main theme in the junkies' narratives was their desire to regain sufficient control over their drug intake so that they could incorporate roles, legitimate or illegitimate, other than being a drug user.

Four of the baby boomer junkies were heroin users and three used methamphetamine. This constituted 12.1 percent and 9.4 percent, respectively, of the heroin and methamphetamine users studied. There was little difference between the heroin- and methamphetamine-using junkies, indicating that both drugs may be equally devastating in terms of loss of social roles and loss of control.

These are the users that have exhausted all resources and sources of help except for public shelter and treatment facilities. All of the junkies were street dwellers who lived near their source of heroin and bought drugs with money made through panhandling and/or petty theft. In addition, all reported living in a violent social environment. One heroin junkie, who formerly lived in a middle-class neighborhood, described his current situation living under a bridge:

> I've been robbed at gunpoint; had three skull fractures; was pistol-whipped in the back of my head. I've had every rib in my body broken, [and] my bladder ruptured where I was urinating blood for two weeks.

We also learned that some of the many attempts by the junkies to acquire other social roles are temporarily successful. Several junkies described having had a hustle that worked for a while or having been engaged in a mainstream social role. Eventually, however, they lost those roles as they became users who, as expressed by one junkie, "would do anything for a hit."

The lack of self-control the junkies had over their drug use was evident in all their narratives. One methamphetamine user in the junkie phase indicated that the only way he controlled use was when he ran out of money. Many of them indicated that they might be near the point of death by overdose, and some of the heroin users suggested this was desirable. One older heroin user said that overdosing on heroin "is the only way I want to go." Paradoxically, all had hopes of being drug-free within a year if they were still alive, and some expressed a desire to go into treatment "soon."

Identity and self-concept

Users in the junkie phase identified as societal outsiders who have been marginalized all their lives. One baby boomer methamphetamine-injecting junkie who self-identified as "a full-fledged street junkie" explained:

> I'll say I'm addicted to this but the hell with it, I'm not gonna quit taking it because most of my life, I wasn't able to hold a job. I wasn't able to sit and focus on

anything. And the reason being [and because of this], my parents sent me to a psychiatrist all of my life, and in and out of institutions. I was hospitalized at least 60 times.

The role-related behavior that describes the junkie's identity revolves around living on the street, panhandling, copping, and shooting their drug. One junkie explained his current life as a panhandler: "I tell them a story. Con them. ... You would be surprised how quickly somebody will give me their $10 bill. Like that. I talk to maybe 10 people. ... I take a break and get high and I'm back."

Most users in the junkie phase identified as being a person with an incurable addiction. One older heroin junkie said:

I believe I have a disease. It's called an addiction. ... Well, I'm genetically predisposed. I don't know, where, somewhere down the road somebody had it and just passed it on somewhere, and it came upon me.

A few users in this phase attributed their current state to their own shortcomings. A methamphetamine junkie who self-identified as gay explained:

My dad started callin' me worthless and called me a sexually transmitted disease, ya know. ... I was pissed off. I didn't think anyone wanted to be around me because of that. 'Cuz he wasn't ever there. What's wrong with me? Do I stink or somethin? I don't know. It's all kinds of different shit. But basically, I was pretty much a loner. I can't recall having friends growing up.

The junkies portrayed a despondent self-concept of users who can never regain control. One heroin-using junkie explained:

I'll use the analogy of the burner on the stove, okay? You touch the burner on the stove when it's hot, and you never touch it again. Okay, and I lose my job because of dope, and what do I do? I go do some more dope as opposed to going, "Damn, I can't believe I did that." I mean, common sense would kick in, in a normal person, and they would quit the dope, and they would definitely try to get their shit back together.

Most often, the junkies revealed self-concepts that they were somehow inferior, or they had problems others did not have and therefore they could not cope

with life. Lack of coping skills was a common theme in the narratives. One female heroin junkie explained how she relapsed and gave up an important work role: "I want the escape. I want the total escape from being an adult, from all the responsibilities, from all the worries, from all the stress, I just, I don't want – I don't want it, I just want to escape."

Yet when talking with them, we often heard the shame they felt. The current stigmatized position of a formerly upper-middle-class man who became an aging heroin junkie was revealed as he described his present homeless situation:

And as you begin to get closer to being broke, and as you begin to burn all your bridges, you know, people stop supporting you, or enabling you, whichever one it is. And finally you get to the point, you know, growing up like I did, you're not used to the – the thought of being in the street is, is foreign. ... 'Cause, it's, it's, it's not how, it's not how, you know, I was raised up originally.

Discussion

In this article, we examined the life stories and current social roles and use patterns of baby boomer drug users. [...] We explored how users are able to maintain salient social roles and/or control of their drug use. When the users recounted loss of conventional social roles, we examined how self-control was affected. Conversely, when users began to lose control of their drug use, we noted how social roles in mainstream society were affected, paying close attention to how social roles and self-control were related to turning points and transitions in the drug career. Because of the wide range of baby boomer-aged users (from controlled users to those who reported being out-of-control, and from users with conventional social roles to users living and begging on city streets), this study contributes much-needed insight on stability and change in control of drug use over the life course.

[...]

Although users with legitimate roles (controlled users), as well as users with illegitimate roles (hustlers), indicated control over their drug use, there are some differences between these two phases of use. For example, in contrast to the controlled use of those in the hustler phase, the drug users in the controlled user phase reported stable drug use, strong social roles in mainstream society, and no criminal behavior other than drug use. Another surprising finding is the difference between methamphetamine and heroin users in terms of control over drug use. We found that methamphetamine users who maintain control over drug use are more likely than heroin users to maintain involvement in mainstream social roles, whereas heroin users who maintain control over drug use are more likely to be involved with nonconventional roles. This difference in involvement in social roles "disappears" once control is lost. In other words, the substance used is no longer relevant when control is not maintained. Our narrative data suggested that methamphetamine is considered a "functional" drug when used in a controlled manner.

[...]

Notes

1   As the average age of the U.S. population increases, an interest in aging drug users is emerging. Charles Winick (1962) stated that most drug users mature out of drug use by the time they reach the age of 35, and epidemiological data consistently show that younger age groups constitute the largest proportion of illicit drug users. Recent epidemiological data reveal that the 35 years and older age group is the fastest growing subgroup of drug users and the largest age group using heroin and methamphetamine (SAMHSA 2004). While ample research on former drug users aged 35 years or older exists, research on active users in this age group is limited (Anderson and Levy 2003). An older population of drug users, rather than younger populations, includes a broader range of users and user experiences.

2   Heroin is a depressant and methamphetamine is a stimulant. Whereas depressants lower the energy level of the nervous system, stimulants make the user feel more energetic and alert. We recognized the differences in the drug use patterns and social roles of opiate versus stimulant use over the life course.

3   According to the U.S. Bureau of Census, the years of birth for baby boomers are 1946–1964. However, different scholars use various years to designate the beginning and ending of the baby boom generation, generally starting in 1945 or 1946 and lasting until 1964 or 1965.

4   A hustle is usually an illegal activity. Agar (1973) lists stealing, dealing, pimping, confidence games, and prostitution as common hustling activity among heroin users.

5   The respondents' narratives implied a distinction between dealer and runner. A runner acts as intermediary between buyer and dealer.

References

Agar, Michael. 1973. *Ripping and Running*. New York: Seminar Press.

Faupel, Charles E. 1991. *Shooting Dope: Career Patterns of Hard-Core Heroin Users*. Gainesville, FL: University of Florida Press.

Questions

1   How do you think the career processes of the people in this study were affected by their demographic characteristics such as race/ethnicity, class, and gender?

2   How might these drug users have been differently affected had they used less addictive drugs? Pharmaceuticals? More or less available drugs?

3   What factors seemed to affect the way people "learned" to control their drug use? How might this insight affect your views on social policy and how we should treat drug users? How does this impact on your view of the difference between drug users and drug abusers?

Part III

Drug Lifestyles

We turn now to the lifestyles, economics, and violence associated with drug using and trafficking. This part depicts the everyday lives of drug users, some of the common issues that are important to them, the problems they face and how they deal with them, and the hierarchies and opportunities in the world of drugs and crime. Although not the dominant emphasis in this part, you may still note the influence of some of the demographic, sociological factors discussed in the previous part on different types of drug users.

Here, we provide information about how drug users manage their lifestyles while still doing drugs. It should be noted that not all drug users are abusers – far from it – so that some people can consume copious amounts of drugs and alcohol with few destructive effects on other aspects of their lives, such as family, work, education, and recreation. Yet, we have all witnessed people who have allowed drugs to take over their lives, as they become enslaved by the substances, the lifestyle, and the enticements to continue to do more. Yet, as drug researchers have pointed out for decades, being a drug user is not an easy "job." One has to still manage much of everyday life, including earning money, parenting, staying healthy, going to school, and performing the practical duties of living, such as shopping, banking, being groomed, having friendship and romantic relations, and raising families. Thus, managing a drug lifestyle becomes a part of people's daily rituals.

In addition to maintaining their lifestyles, people also have to come to terms with the economics of drugs. Whether it be the single user on the street, a gang that operates in a drug-selling environment, or the giant cartels responsible for importing many of the drugs consumed in America, there are economic features of the business that people must adhere to in order to continue their drug use or dealing. Since many drugs are sold in an illegal marketplace, unique circumstances prevail that must be followed in order to continue drug selling and use. These economic dimensions are also highlighted in Part III.

Finally, not all, but some, drugs are richly associated with violent subcultures. One of the major problems associated with drugs is that the context of smuggling, distributing, selling, and using them might involve or precipitate violence. This section, then, explores the oft-cited drugs–crime connection, and examines to what extent the correlation between these two variables is representative of a drug-using subculture or other aspects of people's worlds that lead to brutality.

Drugs and the American Dream: An Anthology, First Edition. Edited by Patricia A. Adler, Peter Adler, and Patrick K. O'Brien.
© 2012 John Wiley & Sons, Inc. Published 2012 by John Wiley & Sons, Inc.

Managing Drug Use

25

Club Drug Use and Risk Management among "Bridge and Tunnel" Youth

Brian C. Kelly

Drug users are aware of the potential health risks posed by the substances they imbibe, and are often motivated by both their own concerns and their evaluation by others in the way they deal with these issues. Brian Kelly shows the extreme sophistication young, White club users from the outer boroughs and suburbs of New York City have in planning their drug use. The government often embarks on public service "fear" campaigns, such as the one launched against ecstasy, to tamp down the demand for illicit substances. To what extent do you think young people give credibility to various sources of information about such drugs? What are other avenues for obtaining information that are considered more reliable? How planned or controlled are young, affluent drug users about their drug use? What kinds of outside groups affect their patterns of use the most, from their families, to their ethnic/racial subcultures, their peers, the media, the government, or the larger society more generally? How do these people's involvement in the kinds of social roles discussed by Boeri, Sterk, and Elifson affect their identities and self-control with regard to drugs? What kinds of societal resources do they possess and use?

How do these clubbers represent typical or atypical patterns of drug use for their age? For their race/ethnicity? For their social class? Are these people "righteous dopefiends?" Do you accept their descriptions of the precautions they take as legitimate or do they appear to be rationalizations? Finally, how controlled are they in their drug use, and how likely are they to progress to harder drugs or into more dangerous drug-using careers?

Drugs and the American Dream: An Anthology, First Edition. Edited by Patricia A. Adler, Peter Adler, and Patrick K. O'Brien.
© 2012 John Wiley & Sons, Inc. Published 2012 by John Wiley & Sons, Inc.

Introduction

Club drugs emerged as a significant recreational drug phenomenon during the 1990s. Ecstasy is perhaps the substance most commonly associated with the term "club drugs"; its use surged in the late 1990's through an association with club and rave subcultures. Dramatic increases in ecstasy use among high school aged youth from 1996 to 2001 were found, with lifetime prevalence rates doubling during that time period. In addition, the Drug Abuse Warning Network data demonstrated that ER mentions of MDMA in New York increased fivefold from the second half of 1998 to the first half of 2000 suggesting that problematic use became more frequent during that span. However, since 2001, rates of ecstasy use have plateaued, indicating that the diffusion period of the drug cycle has ceased and we have now entered a period of stabilization. Nonetheless, ecstasy remains a widely used substance. Kelly, Parsons, and Wells (2006) found that almost half of young adults who attend nightclubs in New York City had used ecstasy during their lives. More than one out of five of these young adults reported recent (past three months) use of club drugs (Kelly, Parsons, and Wells, 2006). Other club drugs, including ketamine and GHB, followed a drug cycle similar to ecstasy, having plateaued since 2001. These stable patterns of use indicate the entrenchment of ecstasy and other club drugs and their continued potential for posing risk to youth and young adults. The associated wave of methamphetamine use, which remains a "club drug" rather than street drug in New York, appears to follow a different pattern as it continues to diffuse on the East Coast well into the first decade of the 21st century.

The use of any of these substances contains inherent risks. Public health professionals have identified a range of risks associated with club drug use, including cognitive impairment, hyperthermia, depression, addiction, sexual risk taking, HIV infection, coma, or death. Yet, the understanding of risk among youth remains complex. As noted by social anthropologist Mary Douglas, "The public definitely does not see risk in the same way as the experts" (1992, p. 11). This certainly could be said about the risks associated with club drugs. Youth understand risks related to club drug use in complicated yet calculating ways. The importance of understanding such "folk models" of risk has been underestimated. Though these models of risk no doubt underscore the extent to which information about the dangers associated with drugs use has been disseminated amongst the populace, these models serve a more important function in examining the practice of club drug use. The primary significance of understanding folk models of risk relates to the way in which they inform drug use practices, which can be either risky, protective, or perhaps more likely a combination of both. Thus, folk models of risk constitute the basis of an informal logic which underlies the drug practices of youth.

It is sometimes assumed that youth use club drugs because they lack either the awareness or knowledge of dangers associated with these drugs. Yet, research on club drug-using youth does not support this. Given sufficient resources, youth often fully recognize that they take risks when using club drugs such as ecstasy. In fact, they often have a clear cut sense of what specific dangers are being risked when they take club drugs. This is perhaps because youth enjoy a truer sense of risk than professionals allow them. Professionals often privilege danger when assessing risk. But, risk is actually a two-sided proposition; with danger on one side and some sort of potential payoff on the other. Individuals take risks when the potential payoff feels valuable in the face of potential danger. Such dangers are possible – not certain or perhaps even probable – and club drug-using youth recognize them as such when they make risk assessments. The conceptions of risk among these youth readily account for dangers associated with club drugs.

[...]

Methods

The data for this paper are drawn from an ethnographic study of club drug use among "Bridge and Tunnel" youth in the New York City metropolitan area. Bridge and Tunnel is local vernacular for youth who live in suburban neighborhoods surrounding New York City but "party" in Manhattan. These youth are engaged in both urban social scenes as well as their everyday suburban existences and as such provide a window from which to examine the phenomenon of club drug use in both urban and suburban locations.

[...] I conducted informal interviews about club subcultures and club drugs during participant-observation at clubs and raves where Bridge and Tunnel youth socialize. [...]

[...] The in-depth interview cohort consisted of youth recruited at the designated venues directly and independently of one another, avoiding network sampling methods such as snowball sampling, in order to capture as full a range of variability as possible. Inclusion criteria for the in-depth interview cohort were individuals (a) who were between the ages of 18 and 25, (b) who reported the use of one of four club drugs – MDMA, ketamine, methamphetamine, or GHB – within the previous year, (c) who resided in a suburban county outside New York accessible by public transport, and (d) who were willing and able to consent to participation. [...]

The data for this paper was drawn primarily from the interviews with 40 Bridge and Tunnel youth hailing from New Jersey, Long Island, and the Mid-Hudson suburbs of New York City. They ranged in age from 18 to 25 with an average age of 21 years. They had an average monthly income of $1,800, with a range of $600 to $4,000 from a variety of jobs, such as part-time florist, selling drugs, and marketing analyst for a multi-national corporation. As a group, they were well educated, with most either currently enrolled in college or having already completed college. The cohort consisted of 28 White, seven Latino, three Asian, and two youth of "mixed" race. Ecstasy was the primary club drug utilized by these youth, which supports existing prevalence data. Each member of the cohort had used ecstasy during the course of his/her life. Ketamine had been used to a lesser degree amongst this group though was still prevalent. Methamphetamine and GHB had been used by very few participants. Thus, ecstasy resonated most predominantly in the lives of these Bridge and Tunnel youth. For this reason, the focus of the following discussion of risk management strategies revolves primarily around MDMA, but other club drugs are discussed where relevant.

Results

Knowledge acquisition plays a key role in the development of particular conceptions of risk. Youth weigh risks based upon knowledge cultivated about these substances alongside that of the potential payoffs, and they practice club drug use accordingly. In a certain sense, it is the foundational practice of risk management. As Tony, a 22-year-old White male, noted, "You're not supposed to be on drugs. The smartest thing you can do while you're on drugs is research about it. Know what you should be doing. Know what you shouldn't be doing."

As I will explain here, youth engage in a wide range of risk management practices. The following descriptive epidemiological profile highlights some of the risk management practices strategically employed by youth, practices which grow out of how they conceive of risk. Some of these practices have grown out of and have been transmitted by means of organized harm reduction movements within club and rave scenes; other practices are indigenously cultivated ways of strategizing about risk. Here, I will highlight certain "key" risk management practices regularly encountered and routinized within club subcultures: regulated water consumption, "chilling out," moderation, avoidance of alcohol, pre-loading and post-loading, social network utilization, and pill testing.

Regulated water consumption

Given their recognition of the potential harm of hyperthermia, youth practice a variety of risk management strategies to reduce its likelihood. Access to water is of primary concern to these youth. Rave-related harm reduction organizations have made water consumption a central message directed at youth who use ecstasy. This message has seemingly permeated rave and club scenes in New York, even to youth without direct contact with such organizations. When I talked with George about what he thought was an important health issue related to ecstasy consumption, he remarked, "I'd say the most important is for people to have water. And the fact that they charge $4 or $5 for water is pretty bad too. People get dehydrated, they could die, you know." Youth consciously consume water in an effort to lower the risk of dehydration and overheating. Regular water consumption has become a practice so common in the club and rave scenes that it has been simply incorporated into other activities during a night out. Even youth who no longer consume ecstasy, or are not consuming on that particular evening, drink water somewhat instinctively throughout the night. In that sense, water consumption has become somewhat of a naturalized practice within these scenes.

So as to avoid the high cost of what is in fact a necessary natural resource, many youth purchase a bottle of water at the beginning of the evening and refill the bottle with tap water from a bathroom sink throughout the course of the night. At some events or particularly busy evenings, lines form in the men's room, not for the urinals, but for access to the sinks. For example, while conducting fieldwork at a rave during the summer of 2003, I saw the fundamental importance of water access to these youth, Midway through the evening, the venue shut off the cold water in the men's bathroom so as to prevent patrons from refilling their bottles with cool water. There was extreme vocal protest in the men's room as guys cursed and yelled when they filled their bottles with hot water. Later on in the evening I spoke with some young women and the subject happened to come up during the course of our conversation. I mentioned that I wished I could fill my bottle at the tap in the bathroom. Immediately, one of the girls said to me, "Oh my God, did you know that they shut the cold water off on us. That's so fucked up isn't it? People could die because of that shit." She then went on a profanity laden tirade against the venue management.[...]

Chilling out

"Chilling out" is another strategy used by ecstasy-using youth to minimize the likelihood of hyperthermia. The objective of "chilling out" is just that; youth take regular breaks from the hot dance floor and relax in a location in the club with lower ambient temperature in the hopes of cooling down and maintaining normal body temperature. It serves the purpose of reducing the risk not only of overheating and dehydration but also of muscle cramps. It is important to note, however, that these breaks are not simply due to fatigue; rather, they are structured into

the evening to reduce the risk of a variety of health problems. George noted, "If I take E, I can dance probably for like six hours straight. I'm like that all night. As long as I have water and I take a couple of breaks, I'm good." For George, who could see himself dancing for six hours straight based upon energy alone, his breaks are simply woven into his routine of dancing all night long. He strategically takes these breaks to reduce his risk of overheating and cramping.

Yet, others mentioned that they chill out after using stimulant drugs to come down from a high that was "too high" for them. Andy said, "That time, I did speed for energy. It was a pill but totally different from an e-pill. I don't know though I felt like so hyper and my heart was pounding and I had to go chill for a while. I went and got something to drink and just chilled with my girl. You know, we just like stood and watched everyone else for like a half hour and then I was good. We went and danced after that. That was the last time I did speed though."

Some clubs and raves have "chill out" rooms specifically designed to accommodate this practice of breaks for relaxation and cooling off. Chilling out and the designation of specific "chill out rooms" has become such a common practice that ecstasy users and non-users alike partake in their use. I came to fully appreciate these rooms myself during my first summer of fieldwork. The following excerpt from my fieldnotes describes the sensation of leaving a main dance floor for a chill out room.

It was hot as hell. Despite that the AC was on, the club was filled with people dancing into a frenzy in the early hours of a hot Sunday morning. I guess there was only so much an AC system can do when it's exceptionally humid outside and there's a thousand people packed into a room on the inside. I felt swamped on the dance floor. My shirt had soaked through with sweat even though I was really hanging out on the dance floor watching other people more than I was dancing. I squeezed my way through the crowd towards the bathroom and then headed towards the chill out room. As soon as I walked through the entry way, a cool breeze rushed over my body, almost instantly chilling the sweat on my arms. I wouldn't have minded a few goosebumps right then. At the time, I was surprised to see as many people in there as I did, but looking back on it, it makes complete sense given how hot the dancefloor was. I squeezed in on a bench between two groups of people and sat down for a few minutes before going over to the bar to grab a Red Bull for a bit more energy. I put the cold can on the back of my neck before I opened it and felt even more relief. The DJ in the chill out room had really relaxing music on, some kind of ambient music I guess, and it almost made me want to lie down on the floor and take a nap if the floor wasn't so skanky. After fifteen minutes or so of hanging out in the chill out room, I felt refreshed and my wet shirt was starting to almost feel damp and cold, so I headed back out into the main room.

As the excerpt shows, chilling out has developed important uses for non-drug users in addition to those using ecstasy and other club drugs. It doubles as a risk management strategy for those who use club drugs and an oasis of relief for those who do not.

Moderation

Though managing imminent harms such as over-heating perhaps seems natural, youth also engage in a variety of practices aimed at minimizing potential long-term harms as well. Moderation is a key strategy employed to minimize both the acute risks and the long-term risks, such as memory loss, of ecstasy use. Some youth attempt to moderate their intake via frequency of use; others do so by minimizing quantity during use; while still others will only use in specific locations. Often, youth employ a combination of these strategies.

Many club drug-using youth conceive of the risk of neurotoxicity to be dependent upon how much and how often ecstasy is consumed. When asked about what people risk when consuming ecstasy, Andy remarked, "I think that it depends on how much they try to take per week. You really should not even use it once a week; maybe once a month is pretty good. People who take it once a week or even more than that, I think that's pretty risky." Andy specifies later on in the interview that by "risky" he is concerned about the risk of memory loss and depression. One practice is strategically using ecstasy, perhaps saving it for special occasions, such as a birthday or holiday. Jane discussed how she doesn't use ecstasy every time she goes out to a rave or club. [...] Many of these youth

try to use ecstasy less than once per month, which was generally supported by the average consumption in the past year among this small sample, roughly 13 times.

Though the practice of "stacking" and "boosting" – respectively consuming multiple pills at one time and re-dosing at regular intervals – has been reported in the literature, many youth are like George, who "try not to take too much of it." Some youth also reported the practice of consuming ecstasy in increments rather than in larger doses. For instance, some youth reported consuming ecstasy pills in ½-pill increments until they achieve the "appropriate" high and maintain it in that same fashion. The following fieldnote excerpt, in which I ran into Tony on the dance floor at a club, highlights this practice.

> After greeting each other and exchanging the normal pleasantries, I asked him how the night was going for him. He told me that his "roll" was wearing off and he needed to take another ½ pill of ecstasy. "Why a half-pill?" I asked, somewhat confused. He replied, "Moderation brother, moderation. I got to take care of my brain." I asked him what he meant, still somewhat confused since generally my own idea of taking care of my brain would preclude ecstasy consumption. After he paused with a stylish dance move, he explained that he wanted to achieve his "roll" – the high derived from ecstasy use – with as little ecstasy as possible because he asserted that the degree of brain damage is dependent upon quantity consumed.

The purpose of taking pills in increments is to induce a certain high while minimizing the amount of ecstasy consumed. Given that risk is perceived to be dose-related, they attempt to reduce risk by consuming a minimal amount.

Other youth practice moderation by trying to consume ecstasy only in certain locations. Thus, some youth have a rule that they only use in "safe spaces." Such safe spaces are locations that the youth have identified as both familiar and with accessible assistance should a negative health event occur. The young women I interviewed often attempted to be discriminating about the locale of their ecstasy use. As Vicky said, "If I take E when I go out into the city, it's gotta be a place that I know. Like, I probably have to have been there at least once and know it's not like a shady place or anything like that. And I really don't like to roll until I've already gone inside and didn't get like a bad vibe from the place." Such a practice has the effect of limiting when and where youth consume ecstasy, again moderating consumption.

Alcohol avoidance

Alcohol use is entrenched in club subcultures, though perhaps less so in the rave scene. Many participants in the club scene who do not use illicit substances are consumers of alcohol. However, a number of ecstasy taking youth proscribe alcohol consumption when under the influence of ecstasy. Their main concern relates back to the related practice of water consumption. They are concerned about dehydration and overheating. Ed's comment best illustrates this: "Well, when I'm rolling and they're decent pills I really don't need alcohol really. But, it's also like, E-pills dehydrate you as it is and when you drink you get dehydrated too, so I'm not gonna get like double dehydrated you know. That's why I just drink water." Thus, Ed's decision to not mix alcohol and ecstasy is aimed at managing the inherent risk of dehydration with ecstasy use.

Others assert that ecstasy and alcohol should not be mixed because of increased after-effects. For instance, Vicky described why she avoids alcohol when she uses ecstasy. She said, "Like I said, you feel terrible after using ecstasy. I feel like all cracked out afterwards. And I don't like hangovers. Drinking gives you a hangover, right. So, I don't want to feel cracked out from ecstasy and have a hangover at the same time. I'd be like a retard for a week." Thus, avoiding alcohol is aimed at reducing the adverse after-effects of partying with both substances. Yet, while avoiding alcohol when using ecstasy minimizes the risk of adverse outcomes for many youth, it is by no means a universal practice. Other youth I encountered in the club and rave scenes regularly drank alcohol and used ecstasy concurrently. [...]

Pre-loading and post-loading

"Pre-loading" and "post-loading" are strategies aimed at minimizing the likelihood of certain acute and long-term risks of ecstasy use. When pre-loading and post-loading, youth consume other substances perceived to mitigate the negative effects of ecstasy use, primarily the potential for depression and neurotoxicity. Pre-loading is the practice of routine ingestion of these substances prior to the use of ecstasy, perhaps planned as far in advance as a few days before the use of ecstasy. Post-loading, conversely, is the practice of ingesting certain substances during the "come down" or after the ecstasy experience. Youth use a variety of substances for pre-loading and post-loading, such as 5-HTP, SSRI's, Ginko Biloba, St John's Wort, Vitamin C, and multivitamins.

5-HTP and SSRI's are used in pre-loading and post-loading to mitigate both depression and neurotoxicity. Andy discussed his experiences with pre-loading and post-loading in a positive light. He said, "Without it (pre-loading and post-loading with 5-HTP) my mind would feel as if … it's kind of like right after the day I took E, my mind would feel totally blank and I would feel like a hangover I guess. I can't think. I can't concentrate on anything. It's as if my mind was shut down for the next couple of days. But if I do take it, the 5-HTP, I can go on with my normal day." He also described using Prozac in a similar way, "There are some people who take Prozac. I could get Prozac and I've tried using Prozac but it pretty much works the same way." He also noted that taking 5-HTP has dramatically reduced his post-E depression.

Other youth use supplements for specific purposes. St. John's Wort, for example, is used by some youth specifically to ward off post-E depression. Ginko Biloba is said to reduce the hangover and "cracked out" feeling for some. Youth also report taking Vitamin C, which is also rumored to enhance the ecstasy high, and multivitamins in an effort to "replenish the body."

Social network utilization

Many youth argued for the importance of social networks for reducing the potential for harm associated with ecstasy use. Friends and other people "you can trust" played an important role in establishing risk management practices. The importance of knowledge cultivation was mentioned earlier. Social networks comprise a key source not only for the acquisition of drugs, but also for the discussion of knowledge related to club drugs as well as strategies for mitigating their harms. [...]

Social networks play a key role in monitoring the acquisition of ecstasy pills. Many youth have concerns about adulterated pills. Youth argue that not all ecstasy pills are equal risks and thus steps should be taken to minimize potential harms. By this logic, ecstasy pills should not be purchased at clubs or from unknown people. This is not only aimed at minimizing the potential for arrest but is also aimed at reducing the potential for buying "a pill that is filth," as Tony put it. The perception is that by acquiring the pill from "someone you know," you are less likely to be given pills with adulterants. Whether this assessment is in fact correct remains to be seen. It likely reduces the chance that one would deliberately be given bad pills, but does not solve the larger problem of the significant adulteration of the United States' ecstasy market. Nonetheless, conceptions of risk about adulterated pills shape the way youth pursue their drug acquisition.

Many youth also stress that the consumption of ecstasy should only occur in the presence of friends whom "you can trust." Trustworthy friends provide a source of assistance if any negative health events were to occur. Mandy, an 18-year-old Latina, said, "I personally would not [use club drugs] without having at least three really good friends with me that I could trust. I know that if I disappeared for a hot second they would be searching everywhere for me. Make sure you go with people that you trust." Mary echoed those sentiments when she said, "Make sure you're with reliable people. Don't do it with somebody that… like my friend who likes to wander away, I just wouldn't do it with her you know." Thus, it is not simply a matter of having people around but trustworthy people who can supply instrumental support if the need arises.

The use of social networks for specific instrumental support remains key for youth who have failed to adhere to the principle of moderation. Mandy described a story of caring for a friend who had used too much ketamine at a rave: "Well, halfway through the night, one of them (a male friend) went into a K-hole. Like, we saw he was just kind of standing there like he was totally out of it and we

knew he was doing K. So, me and my other friend brought him over by the side. We just kind of sat around there for a while which kind of sucked but I'm not gonna be a bitch and just leave him there. You know, he was in a K-hole so I couldn't leave him there. After a while, he just kind of got up and we went back (to the dance floor)." Thus, as she explained, Mandy teamed with her other friend to watch over a friend heavily intoxicated by ketamine until he recovered sufficiently from his ketamine induced stupor.

[...]

Ecstasy pill testing

As noted earlier, adulteration of MDMA is a key concern among ecstasy using youth. Besides acquiring ecstasy pills through social networks to reduce the likelihood of being given bad pills, youth also make use of ecstasy-testing procedures. These testing procedures function in a variety of different ways. Youth may directly test pills, seek out pill-testing operations at events, or work with laboratories set up for pill testing. Youth who tend to engage in these practices demonstrate a fair amount of sophistication with regard to their knowledge acquisition about the drugs. They tend to be amongst the members most knowledgeable about drugs within their networks.

Those who test pills typically do so using ecstasy self-testing kits. Ecstasy pill testing kits are available from small companies and harm reduction organizations. With the kit, users apply chemical solutions to shavings of an ecstasy pill. When added to the pill shavings, the chemical solutions will turn one of several colors, indicating the presence of certain substances, or no color at all, indicating none of the specific substances the pill tests for are present. For example, when added to a pill containing MDMA, the solution will turn a purplish-black. However, a limitation of these pill testing kits is that they test merely for the presence of substances and cannot provide indications of the level of purity. A pill may test positive for MDMA but still contain other substances or contaminants. Nonetheless, these pill testing kits are highly regarded by many ecstasy-using youth.

[...]

Other individuals use on-site pill testing provided by harm reduction organizations. At club and rave events, pill testing can have an effect of deterring the use of adulterated pills. The following fieldnote illustrates the reaction of one ecstasy user after having his pill tested by a local chapter of DanceSafe. Members of the local chapter set up a table to provide free pill testing at this event.

> A kid came by the table while I was there. He was a young guy, tall and lanky, perhaps Dominican if I had to guess, and was with a shorter White male friend. He had a red pill that he wanted tested. The two members of the DanceSafe team obliged and scraped a shaving off and tested his pill. After applying the necessary chemical solutions the pill shaving did not change any color, which meant that it came back negative for the presence of MDMA and a few select other substances. The team explained the details of the test and told him that the test suggested the pill contained no MDMA. He asked them what he should do. One member responded that they had no idea what the pill was and that they couldn't offer any advice on what he should do, they could just perform the test. The young guy had a look on his face that suggested he was pissed. He looked at the pill for a second and then tossed it into an area along the wall with plants and bushes, I overheard him say to another onlooker that he had brought the pill with him from the outside and did not purchase it there. He then set about with his friend to find a different supply.

Thus, provided with information that his pill did not contain MDMA, the young man chose not to use the drug despite having spent money on it. He subsequently disposed of the pill. [...]

A third type of pill testing occurs among club drug-using youth. Though infrequent, some youth discuss making use of laboratories that publish the results of their pill testing on the internet. Besides using home testing kits, Paul also discussed making use of such a laboratory. He said, "Well, there's also this website, Ecstasy Data, that people send pills to and they use their lab to break down the whole pill and tell you exactly what's in there and then they post all their results online. I sent a pill in once, but I'm not an asshole who's going to send in like a $10, $20 pill every few months. What I usually just do is check the results [on the website] from like the Northeast, like New York, Jersey, Connecticut. I look at the results and see if there's any pills I know about or, you know, pills I took, so I can figure out exactly what's in them. Then I know if there's a brand I gotta avoid, you know." Ecstasy-using youth can either anonymously send in their own pills or simply review the results of pills others have sent in. Through gas chromatography and mass spectrometry scientists at these laboratories can analyze the ecstasy pills with far more precision than a home testing kit. They give specific results of all of their tests on their website, which is free of charge. [...]

Discussion

Club drug-using youth provide a grounded example of the translation of thought into practice. They have particular conceptions of risk in their lives and implement these conceptions into efforts designed to manage the risk in their lives. These practices demonstrate how risk is fundamentally dependent upon social context. Their understandings have a rich complexity that cannot be translated into some sort of dogmatic "if ... then" statement. Club drug-using youth account for the gray areas of risk and engage in risk management practices to effect some sort of positive outcome in the face of harm. Though normative within club and rave subcultures, it remains unclear to what extent these risk management practices extend beyond the subcultural realm.

[...]

These youth of the DARE generation grew up in a time where they were encouraged to "Just Say No." They witnessed dogmatic educational efforts and were subjected to a banking educational model, as if filling their minds with messages of harm would eliminate drug use. It struck a chord with some, but not all, youth of this generation. In recognizing the nuances of risk, these youth resist the dogmatic drug education efforts aimed at them. Nonetheless, I have found them to be quite willing to listen to professionals, but they want to engage in dialogue about the significance of potential dangers in their lives, rather than simply be instructed that drugs can be harmful.

Greater efforts must be made by health professionals to direct harm reduction methods to these youth rather than solely bombard them with messages of danger as it is harm reduction measures that they respond within their own subculture.

[...]

References

Douglas, M. 1992. *Risk and blame: Essays in cultural theory.* New York: Routledge.

Kelly B. C., Parsons, J. T., and Wells, B. E. 2006. Patterns and prevalence of club drug use among club-going young adults. *Journal of Urban Health,* 83, 884–95.

Questions

1   Why do you think experts may overestimate the dangers of drug use? Who are these "experts" and why are they considered experts? How might social power enhance their credibility? How did the respondents in the article construct their own danger knowledge? How do you feel about what you hear from doctors, clinicians, and the government sources concerning drug dangers?

2   What are some of the risk management strategies discussed in the article? What are some other examples of risk management strategies for other drugs? Do you think risk management strategies should be included in formal drug education? Why or why not?

3   How important are social networks for the dissemination of drug knowledge and risk management strategies? Do you think purchasing drugs from people you know is safer? What about doing drugs in the presence of people you know? Why or why not? What do you think the main reasons are behind adulterated ecstasy pills? How might prohibition policies exacerbate the dangers of attending raves and using associated drugs?

"I'm a Health Nut!" Street Drug Users' Accounts of Self-Care Strategies

René D. Drumm, Duane C. McBride, Lisa Metsch, Melodie Neufeld, and Alex Sawatsky

René Drumm, Duane McBride, Lisa Metsch, Melodie Neufeld, and Alex Sawatsky offer an interesting contrast to the lifestyle of drug users from Kelly's population because their subjects fall at the lower end of the socioeconomic scale and use different drugs. To what extent do these Black street addicts take the kinds of precautions to protect their health as we saw in the previous selection? How important does it seem to be to them? How legitimate or "righteous" do you think their claims of health protection appear, especially compared to those in the last selection? How do they compare in their health concerns and precautions to the homeless injecting drug addicts described by Bourgois and Schonberg? To what can you attribute these similarities and differences?

How do their resources compare to those of the club drug users? What similarities do you see between these populations and their drug use and lifestyles? What characteristics differentiate them? Where do they stand in the arenas of conventionality, identity, and self-control introduced by Boeri, Sterk, and Elifson? Given the differences in these two groups' resources, what does a comparison of these two populations tell us about some of the norms and values of drug users more generally? Finally, how are these people influenced by the social contexts of family, subculture, peers, and community in which they are embedded?

Drugs and the American Dream: An Anthology, First Edition. Edited by Patricia A. Adler, Peter Adler, and Patrick K. O'Brien.
© 2012 John Wiley & Sons, Inc. Published 2012 by John Wiley & Sons, Inc.

Introduction

The daily lives of street drug users have been of considerable concern to researchers, policy makers, and the general public. Researchers have spent decades documenting the personal and social consequences of the use of heroin, cocaine, crack, and methamphetamine. Research indicates that drug users engage in significant levels of criminal activity related to their drug use, have much poorer health than nondrug using populations, have higher rates of mental illness such as depression, and live lives dominated by the search for the next drug "hit." Generally, the literature also suggests that street drug users represent a high economic cost to society.

Intended or not, describing only the problems of drug users often implies that they passively respond to the experiences and consequence of their use. The implication is that drug users are acted upon by external circumstances to such an extent that they are no longer actors with any control over their daily lives. Focusing only on problems and deficits among drug users reinforces these stereotypes. There is another tradition of research that focuses on street drug users as often successful actors in a complex social and interpersonal world. Examples of this research cover three decades and include work by such scholars as Preble and Casey (1969), with their emphasis on street addicts actively engaged in "taking care of business," and Stephens (1991), with his integration of role theory with street heroin use. Stephens saw street heroin addicts as playing an active role in the construction of their daily lives – how those lives were lived and often successfully managed. The implications of this tradition of research suggest that a significant part of being a street drug user involves the successful negotiation of a wide variety of complex situations as well as meeting very basic health and safety needs.

It is the purpose of this qualitative analysis, using a population of street injecting and chronic drug users in Miami, to focus on users' attempts to prevent major health consequences associated with drug use, manage health consequences that occur, and develop strategies to improve their health. The data suggest that street drug users do not passively accept the health consequences of use, but rather actively engage in behaviors that attempt to ameliorate damage to their health as well as behaviors specifically designed to improve their health. [...]

Methods

Sample characteristics

This study draws upon face-to-face in-depth interviews conducted with a subsample (n = 28) of the study population of a larger community-based research project. The overall project focused on health services needs, barriers in meeting those needs, and utilization of health services among 1,479 chronic drug users and nondrug users in Miami/Dade County Florida. The face-to-face interviews occurred as a follow-up to the larger quantitative study. The purpose of the in-depth interviews was to clarify the quantitative data and to uncover any missing aspects of health care in this population.

Sample eligibility and recruitment

Indigenous outreach workers recruited participants over the age of 18 from neighborhoods that have high rates of drug use and sexually transmitted diseases (STDs). [...] Workers screened prospective study participants for eligibility on the basis of the active use of either injection drugs or crack cocaine. Screeners confirmed the self-reported use of heroin or cocaine within the previous 48 hours using toxicology screens (using ONTRAK from Roche Diagnostic System) and visual screening for recent track marks. To be eligible, study participants could not have participated in drug treatment within 30 days prior to study enrollment.

Two anthropologist-trained interviewers conducted face-to-face, qualitative, in-depth interviews with the participants. Participants responded to general questions in an open-ended, conversational format, using an interview guide containing an outline of topics to be covered in the interview. The interviews focused on documenting health care needs and problems as well as barriers and facilitators to receiving care when needed. [...]

The study outreach center, which is located in one of the neighborhoods where many drug users either live or hang out, provided a venue for all of the interviews. Participants received a small monetary incentive as well as information on local health services resources to encourage participation. Interviewers conducted the sessions in private, providing assurances of confidentiality, including notification of a NIDA Certificate of Confidentiality. Study procedures for the protection of human subjects received approval from the University of Miami's Institutional Review Board before collection of data.

[...]

Findings

In this sample, in spite of their continued drug use, participants drew on a variety of strategies to stay healthy and address their health care needs. [...] While the types of strategies varied from participant to participant, the theme of proactive self-care remained strong throughout the data. All participants mentioned at least one strategy of self-care in response to interview questions.

The research team identified five self-care domains discussed by the study participants. These include strategies to improve nutrition, increase physical activity, address medical concerns, regulate substance use, and reduce sexual risk. [...]

Nutritional self-care strategies

The most predominant theme in the data pertained to nutritional strategies participants used to maintain or improve their health status. Participants reported paying attention to both the quantity and quality of their nutritional intake. In terms of quantity, participants focused on getting enough food and eating regularly. Themes around food quality included increasing foods that they saw as health inducing as well as eliminating or reducing foods they believed to be unhealthy. These data indicate a concerted effort by participants to consume foods that they believe have greater nutritional value, which may in turn favorably impact their health. The following quotations illustrate participants' efforts to choose fruits and/or vegetables over other types of foods.

MICHAEL (A SINGLE 39-YEAR-OLD AFRICAN AMERICAN): I'm a health nut. It shows in the food I eat. I'll eat meat, but I'm a vegetables and fruit man, and a little sweets. [...]
INTERVIEWER: What type of things do you eat?
FRED (A 43-YEAR-OLD UNEMPLOYED HIGH SCHOOL GRADUATE): Things God put on the earth for us.
INTERVIEWER: What do you mean?
FRED: Fruit, vegetables, nuts. Those type of things.

Besides making efforts to include more fruits and vegetables in their diets, some participants supplemented their diet with vitamins.

INTERVIEWER: So what do you do on your own to stay healthy?
DONNA: Oh, I take my vitamins every day, and you know I take, oh God, I let me see, so many vitamins. I got like six or seven different kind of vitamins I take. And iron and you know I drink as much water as I possibly can drink. [...]

While many participants made efforts to incorporate fruits, vegetables, or vitamins, other participants focused on eliminating or reducing unhealthy foods in their diets. The types of foods participants wished to decrease included salt, coffee, soda, junk food, fried or greasy foods, and red meat. The following quotations exemplify participants' decisions to cut back on or stop using food choices they saw as unhealthy.

INTERVIEWER: What are some of the other things you do, to try to stay healthy?
LAVERNE (A 41-YEAR-OLD HISPANIC MALE): Eat right. No salt. Not too much of this, not too much of that. Really, it's a diet. No salt. Almost no flavor, everything have to be without salt. [...]
MARIE: I cut down on the grease [for my liver condition], 'cause I eat a lot of greasy food. That's really bad. Especially with high blood pressure and all of that.

While participants reported efforts to improve the quality of their food intake as illustrated above, participants also sought to increase the quantity of food they consumed. For many street drug users, getting enough food can be a challenge. These data indicate that the participants were cognizant of the amount of food they ate and were weight conscious or concerned about gaining or maintaining a certain weight. The following quotations describe participants' concerns about eating to maintain or gain weight.

> INTERVIEWER: So what do you do to stay healthy to keep your T-Cell count up?
> KEISHA: A lot of eating. The last time I was in here I weighed like 105 pounds. So far, I'm up to 178. [...]
> GEORGE (A 28-YEAR-OLD HIGH SCHOOL GRADUATE): So I'm eatin' a lot better, than what I was. I've gone from one meal a day to two good size ones and a whole lot of snacks in between. So that part is gettin' better. I think my weight will start coming back up to where it was.

Physical self-care strategies

The study participants reported using a variety of ways to get physical exercise. Participants discussed walking, swimming, playing basketball, roller skating, and sleeping. The following quotes illustrate the ways participants engaged in physical activities.

> [...]
> MARIE: I walk a lot. God almighty, I walk a lot.
> DON (A 46-YEAR-OLD AFRICAN AMERICAN HIGH SCHOOL GRADUATE): I go swimming.
> JOSHUA (46-YEAR-OLD): I'm out there playing basketball with the young guys. [...]
> ALAN: Eat and rest. Like in other times where I was getting high, I'd stay up two and three days, where [now] I go to sleep every night. [...]

Medical self-care strategies

Medical self-care strategies encompass a variety of methods participants used to care for or prevent physical disease. The predominant types of medical self-care strategies include taking care of routine ailments, engaging in nonconventional doctoring, flushing the system, and using the formal health care system. Routine ailments consisted of afflictions such as migraine headaches, skin infections, calluses, and sore throats that generally do not require professional medical intervention.

Routine ailments: Over-the-counter treatments

The two primary ways that participants addressed routine ailments included using over-the-counter medications and home remedies. The types of over-the-counter medicines participants reported using included Nyquil, Motrin, Tylenol, and Listerine. The following quotations illustrate participants' use of over-the-counter medications.

> LAVERNE: Listerine is pretty good (to help sore throats).
> INTERVIEWER: And how did you come to the conclusion that Listerine was good?
> LAVERNE: Everybody will tell you. The doctor will tell you. And it's really good. Because when you do gargle with that, you see all that stuff coming out. It's good. You gotta' know that it's just...it's good. But Listerine taste nasty, get the job done. [...]
> INTERVIEWER: What do you do for your headaches?
> GEORGE: I go buy a couple of Tylenol from Jack...that's it.

Routine ailments: Home remedies

Aside from using over-the-counter medicines to manage routine ailments, participants shared ways in which they took care of common conditions by using home remedies. Deborah refers to herself as an expert in herbal remedies and identified marijuana as a herb with medicinal qualities. Deborah views marijuana tea as a home remedy for a variety of ailments.

> DEBORAH: Shit, I been drinking marijuana all my lifetime coming in to Miami before I even put a piece of paper and smoke it.
> INTERVIEWER: You drink marijuana?
> DEBORAH: Yeah it's a herbal tea.
> INTERVIEWER: Uh-huh?
> DEBORAH: Shit that's the best remedy you can ever have.

Fred shared how he uses heroin to cope with intense migraines: "I try and get some heroin and some hot towels, or take a hot bath. To open up my blood vessels and it just alleviate some of the pain."

Nonconventional doctoring

Behaviors designated as nonconventional doctoring included activities that normally are addressed by professional health-care providers such as setting a fracture or draining an abscess. Participants reported these methods as preferred alternatives to seeking out professional medical treatment. Participants shared ways that they would avoid doctor visits by performing feats of home doctoring, as illustrated in how Don took care of a broken bone:

INTERVIEWER: How long ago was your broken bone?
DON: Oh about 6 months ago. I went to the hospital, but I didn't stay to have them treat it. They was talking about a cast and I...I just wrapped it up myself with a bandage and a piece 'o wood and went home. I really don't like hospitals. Ahh...got an ole' saying that you know, hospitals for the living and the dead and I try to stay away from 'em you know. I looked at the x-rays and I felt that I could've dealt with the compound fracture so I dealt with it.

Another example is Henry's way of treating abscesses received from intravenous drug use:

Well I went ahead and took a new syringe that I had and I stuck it in the, ahh, abscess and drew out the poison and, ahh, pressed and put pressure on it and everything and I drained it and everything and after it showed red blood started coming out, then I went ahead and swabbed everything with alcohol and peroxide and then bandaged it with some ointment over the little wound there and kept it constantly ahh, clean and bathed with alcohol and peroxide. It eventually healed.

Flushing the system

A minority of participants mentioned their practice of "flushing the system" to maintain good health. Participants reported that the purpose of flushing is to decrease the impact of drug use or rid their bodies of some infection. Methods of flushing the system included using antibiotics, drinking fruit juice and physically sweating out poisons. The following quotes from participants illustrate flushing out the system.

DONNA: And every now and then as bad as I hate it, I drink those nasty juices you know like prune juice and different things to flush the system you know. I do that as well, every other week. You know I try to do what I can.
MANDY (SINGLE 42-YEAR-OLD AFRICAN AMERICAN): I take antibiotics for my legs and I clean out my system.

CURTIS (MARRIED 50-YEAR-OLD HISPANIC): I need to clean my system out and get rid of all the poisons. You know, sweat it out, urinate it out, and relieve myself, you know. I sweat it out. I gotta' get all this poison and chemicals out of me.

Formal health care

While most participants reported attending to medical needs primarily without professional medical help (avoiding the formal health care system), others actively pursued formal health care and reported complying with their health care provider's directives. Participants reported engaging in regular office visits, going to the dentist, and taking prescription medicines.

INTERVIEWER: So does that mean that you go regularly to see a doctor?
KEISHA: Every six months.
DEBORAH: I go to the dentist every month.
INTERVIEWER: So are you taking the medication for your hepatitis?
CLARENCE (A 51-YEAR-OLD AFRICAN AMERICAN): Yes.
INTERVIEWER: And how often do you take them (antibiotics) now?
CLARENCE: Ahh... once a day.

Substance use regulation

Another self-care domain that emerged in this analysis was regulating substance use. Participants expressed general dissatisfaction of the substance dependence programs because of many program's emphases on traditional abstinence-only approaches. These approaches clearly did not succeed with these participants.

Instead of using established treatment approaches, participants developed creative strategies to manage substance use in an attempt to slow or decrease its harmful effects. These strategies include substituting another substance for their primary addictive drug, consciously using less of their primary drug (cutting back), and taking precautions for safer drug use.

Drug substitution

While most participants identified themselves as polydrug users, most had a drug of choice – one particular drug that they saw as problematic. Drug substitution occurred when users would make a conscious choice to not use their preferred drug in an effort to curb drug use. The following quotes from participants illustrate substituting one substance for another in an effort to reduce the use of heroin.

> SALLY (A WIDOWED 35-YEAR-OLD): I couldn't get off the booze so, ahh, I was told by someone I really trusted it [using heroin] would help me get off alcohol, cause it would keep me down so I could get off booze. And see, that's how I kick heroin too. I'll kick heroin, I'll drink. And so then that helps. I use 'em to kick each other. [...]

Cutting back

About half of the participants mentioned some attempt to use drugs or alcohol less frequently or in smaller amounts. Cutting back included any efforts participants made to use substances less. The following quotes illustrate participants' efforts to reduce their drug use.

> GEORGE: Actually I'm feeling a lot better. I ain't drinking as much.
> INTERVIEWER: How much do you think you've cut down?
> GEORGE: Going from 10 to 12 quarts a day to maybe three 16 ounces a day.
> INTERVIEWER: You said you've been using less?
> JACKIE (A 33-YEAR-OLD AFRICAN AMERICAN IN A COMMON LAW MARRIAGE): A lot less yeah. And I'm still doing the average, I think I got a month about maybe three- or four-hundred dollars for dope. [...]

Several participants reported specifically cutting back on alcohol because of their fears about potential or realized liver damage. The following quotes from participants exemplify these concerns.

> [...]
> DONNA: I'll be real careful with my liver. You know that's another reason why I can't [drink], just let myself go like everybody else out there does. You know if I do that it's gonna' kill me. My liver is not in good shape.
> CURTIS: I don't wanna' be one day with my liver blowing up on me, you know. So, I've been trying to, well, I stopped, like I said.

Safer drug use

While some participants tried to cut back on drug use, others engaged in self-care by exposing themselves to less risk while using. For example, Sara contained her use of drugs to one partner only: "Well I just do it [shoot heroin] with my husband, that's all. I don't go out and share needles with anybody else or get high with anybody else. It's just me and my husband." Another strategy of safer drug use was to use only their own equipment. Martha shared, "I try not to use drugs or use anybody else's equipment, you know, like their pipes or whatever."

Sexual self-care

Most often, drug users mentioned sexual self-care strategies in conjunction with taking precautions against either contracting or passing on the HIV virus. Participants took care of themselves sexually by using condoms and by abstaining from sexual activity. The following quotes illustrate participants' efforts to use condoms and abstain from sexual relationships in an effort to care for themselves and their sexual partners.

> [...]
> KEISHA: But I use my protection. They know I got it [AIDS]. As a matter of fact I don't use one (condom). I use like two, to be on the safe side.
> DEBORAH: I haven't had no one in the last two and a half years since I been told [I'm HIV positive]. I haven't had no sex with nobody.

Discussion

This study documents the strategies chronic drug users employ to manage their health issues. Strategies emerged around nutritional, physical, substance use, medical, and sexual domains of care. These strategies indicate addicts' substantial knowledge about health issues and considerable commitment to manage health risks while at the same time continuing to be chronic drug users.

[...]

Overall, these data show that chronic drug users were actively involved in managing and improving their health and that they attempted to take self-protective actions, even while continuing to engage in active drug use. Documenting these positive and constructive strategies is important because many prior published studies have focused on how chronic drug users often do not view health care or self-care as highly salient, especially in comparison to the competing roles associated with obtaining drugs and maintaining their drug using lifestyles. It is also possible that, by engaging in these health strategies, chronic drug users may be able to use illicit drugs with less internal conflict or cognitive dissonance because they are taking other actions to protect their health. [...]

[...] [T]he present study documents various self-care strategies carried out by chronic drug users to actively take control of their health and (sometimes) to reduce their drug use. Given the public health importance of reducing drug use, stemming the spread of HIV through reduction in risk behaviors, and the overall value placed on physical exercise and nutrition, it seems appropriate that interventions conducted with chronic drug users should take into account these self-protective behaviors. This approach would certainly be welcomed by drug users, who are traditionally stigmatized and viewed as deviant populations in the communities in which they live.

References

Preble, E. A. and Casey, J. J. Jr 1969. Taking care of business: The heroin user's life on the street. *International Journal of the Addictions, 4*, 2–9.

Stephens, R. 1991. *The street addict role: A theory of heroin addiction.* Albany: State University of New York Press.

Questions

1 According to the article, focusing only on the problems of drug users implies they are acted upon by external circumstances to such an extent that they are no longer actors with any control over their daily lives. How did the drug users in the article exhibit personal agency? What may be some external structural factors that have taken control away from these street level drug users?

2 Do you think the health strategies discussed by the drug users in this article might simply be discursive tools they used to excuse or justify their drug use? How might their claims to pursue a healthy lifestyle be an attempt to claim a more normative existence?

3 How do the health strategies discussed in this article challenge some of the preconceived notions and/or stereotypes our society has about street level drug users? How do their healthcare strategies compare and contrast with drug users of a higher socioeconomic status?

Latino Gay Men's Drug Functionality

José A. Bauermeister

José Bauermeister introduces us to the world of Latino gay men who do club drugs in this Bay Area study. Like Boeri, Sterk, and Elifson, he examines the relationship between two variables: membership in drug-using social networks and the ability to maintain a relationship of functionality and control over one's life and drug use. Bauermeister introduces a four-fold typology of drug users that presents a continuum of social networks and social support. Unlike the White, suburban clubbers in Kelly's study, these men primarily smoke crystal methamphetamine, and sometimes find themselves unable to moderate their usage patterns. You may want to ask yourself as you read this how these drug users are relatively influenced by the pharmacology of their drug as opposed to the lifestyle associated with their sexual orientation. Is this an issue of biochemistry, set, or setting? What role models might they be following in making decisions about becoming involved with drugs? What factors seem to influence their becoming more engaged to the point where they may lose control? To what extent do you think the bulk of the users in this scene manage their drug lifestyles successfully? What does Bauermeister seem to think may be helpful in leading them to regain functionality in their lives? Finally, how do the roles and responsibilities of these young Latino men differ from some of the Latino women we have read about, or from women embedded in similar ethnic subcultures?

Introduction

Several studies have evidenced a high prevalence of drug use among gay men and particularly high rates of drug use have been found in gay community epicenters like San Francisco's Castro District. This drug use among gay men has been associated with the desire to "escape" the reality in which they live and, furthermore, become a conduit for expressing their desires, whether sexual, emotional, or social. Taken together, these findings are worrisome given the association between substance use and risky sexual behaviors. [...] While research with White drug-using

Drugs and the American Dream: An Anthology, First Edition. Edited by Patricia A. Adler, Peter Adler, and Patrick K. O'Brien.
© 2012 John Wiley & Sons, Inc. Published 2012 by John Wiley & Sons, Inc.

populations suggests that not all drug use leads to addictive behaviors, we know very little about how drug use impacts other aspects of Latino gay men's lives.

Physiological and behavioral processes may moderate abusive drug use across individuals. The human body can create tolerance to drugs, increasing the threshold required to feel the expected physiologic rewards bestowed by drugs. Thus, the intake frequency and quantity of a drug may not always predict its harm to an individual. Behaviorally, drug users may learn to regulate their drug use without spiraling out of control and harming other life domains. Because drug use is a time-consuming behavior, drug users must accommodate their drug use with other social activities. Several researchers have suggested that the degree of addiction be categorized as a continuum ranging from functional to abusive. An individual's ability to maintain the drug-using habits from disrupting and damaging their lifestyle determines the extent of the addiction. From this perspective, functional users are able to partake in drug-using behaviors without compromising or damaging social responsibilities (e.g., work, family, friends, romantic relationships). Conversely, abusive drug users are characterized by having an unregulated drug intake leading to an inability to maintain their social and economic responsibilities. Unfortunately, the authors could not find any studies that explored how and why drug-use and abuse patterns emerge, establish, and maintain among Latino gay men. Consequently, they know very little about how drug use functionality and drug abuse may resonate in Latino gay men's lives. Through this study, the author hopes to gain some insight into this matter.

[...] [R]esearch suggests that drug users' social networks may explain drug use regulation. Interestingly, the effects of social networks on drug use behavior are not always positive (reducing or regulating drug use). Numerous studies have found that linkages to certain social networks may actually increase drug intake and disrupt drug regulation. [...] Social support can be categorized into four types of supportive behaviors: emotional support (i.e., love and caring), appraisal support (i.e., constructive feedback, social comparison, and affirmation), informational support (i.e., information, suggestions, and advice), and instrumental support (i.e., access to tangible aid, resources, and services).

For Latino gay men in the United States, social support may be scarce due to disconnections within their social networks. Social discrimination embodied by sexual prejudice, homophobia, and racism may compromise the availability and/or accessibility of these safety nets. The membership of Latino gay men within both the Latino and homosexual communities may lead to increased isolation. In the Latino community, homosexuality may curse an individual to experience stigma, ridicule, and segregation from his family, friends, and community. Within the gay community, Latino gay men feel alienated from the mainstream gay community due to cultural differences and their tendency to be sexually objectified. In an attempt to cope with their social isolation, Latino gay men may recur to drugs as one of the mechanisms to enhance their social connections. However, scant attention has been given to the social networks encircling Latino gay men drug users. Furthermore, we do not know whether and how social networks help Latino drug-using gay men regulate their drug use through the provision of social support. [...]

In light of the current scarcity of knowledge about drug use among Latino gay men, it is important and appropriate to begin with an open-ended, qualitative approach. Using qualitative data collected from 70 semi-structured interviews with Latino gay men living in the San Francisco Bay Area, the study has three objectives. First, the author describe how Latino gay men gain access to drugs through their participation in venue-specific social networks. Second, I illustrate different drug-using patterns among socially connected and disconnected Latino gay men. Finally, I comment on how social support within LGM's social networks influenced drug use regulation and recovery from drug abuse. Based on my findings, the author suggests the development of culturally appropriate social network and social support prevention and harm reduction interventions.

[...]

Results

Exploring new world: Exposure to drugs

While a few Latino gay men confided that they had used drugs prior to moving to the Bay Area, most participants began using drugs when they moved to the Bay Area as a mechanism to alleviate the loneliness caused by the absence of the social networks left behind. As shown in Figure 27.1a, LGM participants sought to create new friendships by socializing and exploring the Bay Area's social venues, including settings where drugs were unavailable (e.g., workplace, church, chat rooms) as well as obtainable (e.g., dance clubs, bars, sex clubs). Attending the drug-present venues with greater frequency, Latino gay men mentioned befriending other gay men in these venues. As part of their socializing process, LGM consistently mentioned being offered drugs gratuitously by these acquaintances.

[...]

"Clash of worlds": Regulating drug use

Latino gay men reported differing drug use habits, ranging from functional to abusive substance use. Several Latino gay men self-identified as being "functional drug users" during their interview. In his interview, Julio gave an interesting description of how functional versus non-functional drug users differ based on how their drug use impacts the rest of their lives.

> JULIO: ... Well, there are functional drug addicts and drug addicts who are not functional, that is the way I understand it [...] To me, the drug addicts who are not functional are those who are in the crack houses, who are lying around on the streets, who are with their pipe on the streets and that is all they do all the time. And the functional ones are the ones who do drugs but can work, can think, who can ... you understand what I'm telling you? They can lead a normal life. Normal. That are, as I understand it ...
>
> INT: And how would you say your drug use compares with that of your friends? How would it compare?
>
> JULIO: Well, like I mentioned, I don't think I'm addicted, because I'm not spending my money on it, I'm not wasting my last cents on it. And I can still function like throughout the week, like work and take care of my business and stuff. And there's people that they just depend on that every day.

Across the narratives, LGM functional users highlighted the importance of regulating their drug use to avoid monopolizing other aspects of their lives, including their health, their jobs and finances, as well as their relationships with family and friends. Functional users narrated how they prepared for drug sprees by nourishing their body beforehand, as well as separating time to recover from the drug's effects in order to avoid negative social outcomes. Mauricio, a 34-year-old Colombian man working as a waiter, stressed during his interview how he avoids "flaking out" by planning ahead when he's going to use drugs and ensuring that it won't conflict with other responsibilities.

> MAURICIO: I try not to flake out. I kind of try to plan when I'm going to do ecstasy and/or speed or something like that because I don't want it to interfere with the rest of my life. You know, so I kind of block out a couple of days, you know, and it's happened on occasion that somebody will come up and go, hey, do you want to get high and it's like okay, I have this and this to do, but I'll call and cancel, or you know ...

Functional drug users also described their drug-using behaviors as temporary. During most of the interviews, for example, functional drug users explained that they planned to stop using drugs once they had their share of fun. Pedro, for example, is a 26-year-old Mexican immigrant working part-time in a café. Like many other functional users in their interviews, Pedro underlined how his drug use would become "boring" if it became a necessity in his life.

> PEDRO: I guess what goes on in my mind is like yeah, I could enjoy it for now, but I don't see myself doing this for a long time. You know what I mean? ... I could not see myself making that part of my life. Like I couldn't see myself going out to a club and smoking out as a way of life or anything. It would be completely boring for me.

In addition, other functional drug users described their participation in the drug world as transient. As illustrated in Figure 27.1b, many functional users recounted entering and exiting drug-using social networks, without feeling like they fully belonged in them.

Antonio, a 37-year-old gay Mexican American, had much to say about this issue. In Antonio's interview, he describes his drug-using social network as part of his "outside world," suggesting a partial convergence between drug and non-drug-using networks in

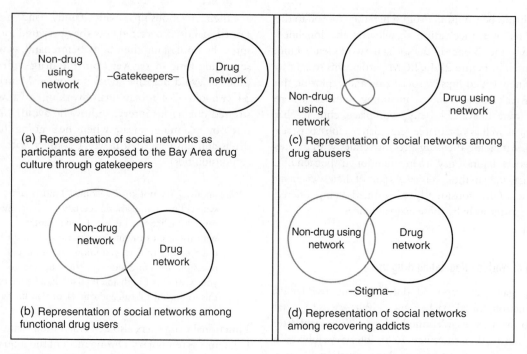

Figure 27.1   Drug use continuum

his life. Interestingly, Antonio also states how disempowering it is to be "connected" to this drug world at times because he sees the toll drugs like ecstasy are having on some members of his community.

> INT: I want you to describe to me that drug world as seen through your eyes and what your place in that world is ...
>
> ANTONIO: Um, it's very indirect because I don't really associate with ... even though the people that I know are actively users, we've sort of become part of my outside world. I've always felt while I was growing up ... like drugs [are] retarded. ... I mentioned, I'd never seen ecstasy. Like all these people keep talking about ecstasy [...] I see it as this big monster that's really affecting some of the people that I know and some of the people that I don't know but as a gay man or as a Chicano man, I sort of feel connected to and there's nothing I can do about it. So it's very dis-empowering and very ... almost a helpless situation that I can't do anything about.

Other functional users recognize that they belonged to both worlds during the interview process. In Julio's case, for example, he suddenly realizes his social

networks have converged as he describes the Bay Area's drug world in the interview.

> INT: Can you tell me about the drug world, where guys like you use drugs. How ... what's your relationship to this world and ... what is it like?
>
> JULIO: Um, I don't know. I mean, I'm friends with a lot of people that do drugs. But I don't feel like I'm in their circle ... Like ... I mean... maybe I am! It does feel like you're in the circle because you have always got to go through somebody.

While acknowledging that they belonged to both social networks, functional users mentioned having the ability to regulate their drug use by having access and support from members of non-drug and drug-using networks. Interestingly, the type of support provided by these social network members had different functions in participants' drug regulation. Functional users narrated how they obtained informational support from other drug users prior to consuming the drug. In some instances, drug-using peers provided tangible support by increasing access to drugs that are reliable in their potency and chemical content. Most often, however, drug users in their social networks provided LGM with informational support by detailing how much and what type of substance to consume, how to determine the quality of the drug, when to use it, and the consequences/side-effects tied to each drug. Felipe, a 26-year-old Mexican gay man, narrated how various friends and acquaintances tried to dissuade him from using crystal-meth by providing him with informational support. Curiously, Felipe interrupts himself by acknowledging that his friends' warning was accurate once he tried crystal-meth.

INT: Was that the first time you had heard of that drug [crystal], or …?
FELIPE: I'd heard about it before from someone who used it and also had incredible sex, he told me it was incredible, that … But he said, "But I don't recommend you use it" (laughing). Yes, really. Yes, yes, it's true. That person told me about, about this drug. And I have never heard of it before. It's not common in Mexico … and he said he'd used it and felt that and I said, "Wow, I'd like to try that some day." He said, "I don't recommend using it, or this or that could happen." Everything he told me could happen, did wind up happening to me.
INT: So you were talking with them about it. …
FELIPE: Yes, um, they were telling me about their experiences [with crystal]. They told me that it wasn't good to, to take it, to take that drug very often, that maybe if I used it recreationally … then maybe I could, um, maybe have a good time with it. But that I shouldn't get hooked on it, that I shouldn't get hooked on that drug. That it wasn't, wasn't very good, it could lead to a lot of things. By the way, I will never forget the saying they told me that day. They said, "Crystal[meth] robs you of everything, even your soul."

Simultaneously, functional users attributed their drug regulation to having non-drug-using friends monitor them. Participants feared letting down the people who cared about them (e.g., parents, siblings, boyfriends, friends, and workmates). Functional users narrated how their non-drug-using friends helped them avoid spiraling out of control, highlighting the importance of receiving emotional and appraisal support in their drug regulation. Jose, a 44-year-old Cuban immigrant working as a waiter, feared he was losing grip of his regulated drug use. During his interview, Jose talked about how he sought out the help of his three best friends when he felt his life spiraling out of control. Interestingly, Jose highlighted how the help provided by one of his friends was not perceived as supportive.

INT: And you felt you were getting into a problem and you called–
JOSE: No, I got – I was in a problem […]
INT: And you called a friend? […]
JOSE: Well, you know, my transgender friend, I can't say the name– She uh–give me a big speech about drugs and smoking … You, you, you talk to her about something like that, she assumes the professional [role], uh–you know, words – [a] social worker attitude, which I hate, you know – "You know what it does to you?" "You know" this, "you know" that! I say, "That's not what I'm calling for!" You know what I mean–I called my other friend and I call my friend in Boston and, you know, they walked me through it. You know.
INT: What did they do?
JOSE: Oh, you know, they remind me who I was and how you know, who I been all my life and how, you know, I'm a frontal freak, you know, and I have to control my life.

"The world of lost souls": Spiraling into drug abuse

While all LGM feared the repercussions of drug abuse in their lives, some participants acknowledged having difficulty with regulating their drug intake and self-identified as addicts. Gabriel, a 22-year-old Mexican American, illustrated how his drug intake transitioned from functional to abusive as he described his personal drug use to the interviewer.

INT: How would you describe your own personal drug use? What name would you give it?
GABRIEL: Abusive … umm, extreme … uncontrollable. … addictive. I mean I, I'm, I know, there is no doubt in my mind that I'm addicted to it. There's no doubt in my mind that uhm, I use them too much. I mean uh, I, I had a point like, I mean it has never been so intense as it is at this point in my life. Right now at this, this whole like past, like this year and last year.
    It's never been this way, you know, it's like, I was always working first and maybe like twice a month I would buy like a quarter of crystal, maybe one hit of E [ecstasy] and enjoy my weekend and I was good for

a month. And then I would go home and relax and so really I think, the drugs like took me to this part, this like spot in my life where I feel like shit and now that I feel like shit, I want to get high to forget about it, you know, and it doesn't work that way.

Most often, intermittent cravings for drugs led some Latino gay men to be unable to plan their drug intake. Drug abusers narrated how they began doing drugs without planning ahead. Later in the interview, for example, Gabriel recounted what happened with his last paycheck before he lost his ability to regulate his drug intake:

GABRIEL: It was a Friday evening, I was at work where it all begins, you know. I'm sitting there and I have my check in my hand. I just got paid and I'm telling myself in my head, we're not going to do the same thing we did last time. No. We're going to put it aside and we're going to save money, you know, we're not going to buy any drugs. We're going to go home and relax. And so I go okay, I can do that. So, I go cash my check on my lunch break that day, that Friday afternoon and I come back after eating lunch and I got to work and I'm already starting to like little thoughts in my head, you know, Friday night party. I think. … well … you get in for free so I'm not wasting any money there. And I don't need drugs to party […] My roommate gets home and we start getting high smoking crystal meth […] around 11 o'clock, I walk up to [club]. I get in line, I go in, you know, I, oh I forgot, I bought a bag of Special K, I bought that from my uhm, for my roommate […] I'd set aside like 200 bucks and brought 100 with me. Okay, I set some money aside, so I had accomplished part of my goal.
    […] On Sunday, I go back to my house and I'm so furious that, you know, I didn't get to hang out with anybody like at an intimate level. So furious that I have now 2 dollars in my pocket from the like 375 that I had gotten paid, uhm, scared that I'm going to get thrown out because my roommate knows that I got paid and I have nothing to show for it. Uhm, scared that I'm going to be hungry for the next two weeks and I don't know how I'm going to get my food. […] the drugs still having an effect in my mind and … I end up having such a massive headache, my body is so drained, I can barely stand, uhm, and I have nothing to like, to like survive on. You know, I have no food that I bought, there's no groceries, there's no

cigarettes to like relax me, there's no pot. … There's nothing. Everybody's at work and I'm sitting in the house, skinny, tired, sweaty … I take a shower and I just sit there. And I, I'm miserable for the evening and I don't sleep until like Monday evening because I can't sleep all of Sunday.

Sporadic drug use has serious repercussions in drug abusers' lives. Across the narratives, drug abusers narrated how their inability to regulate drugs led to being evicted, losing a job, or discontinuing their education. Javier, a 19-year-old Mexican American who moved to the Bay Area when he was 17, narrated how his drug abuse has disrupted his life, including losing his housing and recurring to sex work for money.

INT: … How would you say your life is going right now?
JAVIER: Right now, because, you know, I've gotten more deeper into my drug use, that I think that it's falling apart, really. Or until my brother came today (laughs). So, but yeah, it's been falling apart because I've been on the street for the last couple of weeks. And it hasn't been too pretty (laughs). So …
INT: And, falling apart in the sense that you've been in the streets or in other ways as well?
JAVIER: Um, other ways as well. I mean, I've given up trying to look for a job and just getting back on the road that I was before because I'd rather party instead of, you know, work or whatever.
INT: And what was the road you were on before?
JAVIER: The road that I was on before, I, I was working … I had a hotel [room], you know, I was going for my GED. And I got two of the tests done, my math test and my writing test. So, I just got three more to go. But, yeah, I was doing very good.

When some participants began overusing drugs, drug-using and non-drug-using friends confronted them about their non-monitored drug use. Participants discussed how judged they felt when their friends confronted them about their drug use. Even when they agreed with their peers, participants narrated how unworthy they felt of receiving affection or support to overcome their drug-abusing habits. Most often, drug-abusing participants narrated how they stopped interacting with non-accepting members of their social networks. Feeling estranged from their peers and requiring greater access to drugs to cope with their social isolation, drug abusers narrated how they incrementally embedded themselves into drug-using networks by establishing intimate relationships with other drug users.

The social disconnection and the drug abuse slowly led the abusers to interact with only two types of individuals: functional drug users or drug abusers. In this context, drug abusers felt trapped because they had drug-using friends constantly reinforcing their habits by providing substances and company to consume drugs. Other times, drug-abusing participants narrated how strangers would approach them unexpectedly to ask if they wanted to use drugs together. As shown in Figure 27.1c, the tapered network increases the availability and accessibility of substances and makes it impossible for drug abusers to avoid leaving – even if temporarily – the drug world. Fernando, a 46-year-old Cuban immigrant currently on AIDS disability, had this to say about the presence of drugs in his environment:

FERNANDO: Sometimes I don't want to do absolutely any … sometimes I would like to not do any more drugs again in my life. But I don't know how … there is something that tells me to do it. I live in a … in a building where everyone is addicted, the one who doesn't use crack uses speed, the one doesn't use speed, use chiva, the one who don't use chiva use … (laughs) … like … everything … It is a everyone has done it. So it is very easy to get drugs there. And people exchange it for marijuana … so … everything, everything it's a … drugs, drugs, drugs transactions.

INT: Wow. So when you need crack, all you need to do is simply go upstairs?

FERNANDO: Exactly (laughs). Oh, it makes me so sad … that is what one has to do … go up a floor, or they … or they knock on my door, someone is always going to want some sort of party. "Oh, let's go to the bar!" I mean, the person who is … the person who is using the drug is always going to want to share with another one.

Drug-abusing participants constantly narrated how they wished the interviewer could understand the feelings that led to abuse and the effort it takes to keep their drug intake regulated, especially during moments where support is lacking. Drug-abusing participants frequently voiced imageries of denigration, entrapment,

and despair when referring to this drug world. Later on in his interview, Gabriel narrates:

GABRIEL: … I just want to go somewhere because I'm tired of being stuck. I'm tired, I've wasted 4 years on partying. It's like I'm still here and I mean it's no different than 4 years ago today. Same shit, same story, same people, same drugs, same sex and everything.

"Never hitting bottom again": Recovering from drug abuse

Several functional drug-using participants disclosed abusing drugs some time in their lives. Latino gay men describing themselves as "ex-abusers" commented on their desire to reclaim their previous way of life. Feeling overwhelmed with their drug abuse, ex-abusers sought support outside of the drug world, whether from other ex-abusers or non-drug users.

Participants highlighted how reconnecting with non-drug-using social networks facilitated their ability to recover from abuse. The availability of loved ones to provide support while the drug user rehabilitated seemed central in their narratives. Ex-abusers narrated how their recovery was enabled by having access to friendships where the ex-abusers could talk about their drug problem. In most instances, ex-abusers narrated how the emotional support provided by non-drug-using friends and family made them feel loved and important while they attempted to leave their drug abuse behind. Ex-abusers repeatedly voiced that they would never spiral out of control again because they felt they had people counting on them. Felipe told the interviewer how his family reached out to him when he attempted to recover from his drug abuse:

INT: You mentioned your aunt and uncle. Does your family know you've used drugs besides alcohol?

FELIPE: Yes. They know–

INT: What do they know and who knows what?

FELIPE: Ha (chuckling). Everyone knows. They know about the problem I had with Crystal[meth], they know about the emotional problems I had, um, I lost a job. Um, they know about the problems I was having with my partner. I was having trouble financially too. They know all that. My family gave me a lot of support.

INT: Okay. And when you say "family," not just your aunt and uncle, but also your parents and …?

FELIPE: My parents called me every day, my sister cried with me on the phone and …

INT: Your three brothers?

FELIPE: Them too. Everyone knows about my problem with drug addiction.

INT: And you felt supported?

FELIPE: Very much. Thanks to them, I think, because they made me feel like I was home again. Yes, they really supported me.

In some narratives, loved ones also provided tangible support. One participant, for example, narrated how he agreed to go to a treatment clinic after his partner spoke to him about seeking help.

While the access of social support was essential to ex-abusers' recovery, access to social support wasn't always readily available. In several interviews, drug-abusing participants narrated how they sought support from other drug users as they tried to regain control of their drug use. Whereas ex-abusers spoke about finding non-drug users willing to assist them, some of these men also narrated how previous recovery efforts were sometimes unsuccessful due to the presence of drug users who rejected and stigmatized them further.

Ex-abusers who sought support from functional drug users had limited success. As shown in Figure 27.1d, once ex-abusers reestablish ties with non-drug-using social networks, they distanced themselves from their drug-using peers by stigmatizing them. Most often, functional users seeking to escape and cope with their own problems through drugs were uninterested in listening to the abuser's problems. Consequently, functional users, with and without a history of drug abuse, distanced themselves cognitively from support-seeking drug abusers. Stigma toward the drug world promotes a social comparison between functional drug users and drug abusers that helps to maintain both social networks from converging too much. After expressing how difficult it was to transition back from abuse into functional drug use, Antonio narrated how he learned to access the drug world temporarily without feeling like a part of it. In so doing, he highlights how he discontinued his friendships with "those people," referring to drug abusers.

INT: What's your relationship with that world? Briefly …

ANTONIO: Uhm–No–It's, it's not a relation. I don't k … I, I don't keep friendships with those people. I keep that, that relationship anonymous in a way that, you know, I go when I want it, you know, I when I felt like [a] really bad boy.

As a result of this "othering," drug abusers wishing to recover may find the access to social support difficult. Consequently, ex-abusers were unaware that they were perpetuating the barriers that they encountered when they attempted to recover from their drug abuse.

Discussion

Our analyses suggest that the availability and accessibility of drug and non-drug social networks influences the likelihood of receiving social support. The presence of social networks in which Latino gay men receive social support seemed to protect them from spiraling out of control. The availability of informational, emotional, appraisal, and tangible support may facilitate LGM's drug regulation. Among the men interviewed, the availability of non-drug social network members who provided social support was strongly linked to LGM's drug functionality. Taken together, these findings suggest that Latino gay men need secure social spaces where they may explore, express, and share their feelings, experiences, and connect with other community members.

As Antonucci (2001, p. 438) writes: "It is not so much skin color or country of origin that is of interest, but the fact that group membership is associated with specific advantages, disadvantages, expectations, and dependencies that may fundamentally influence the individual's experience and interpretation of social relations." Kaniasty and Norris (2000) and Barrio (2000), for example, found cultural differences when support-needing individuals decided to solicit social support from network members. Latino cultural beliefs, for example, may add increased value to a person's capacity to carry his/her own weight and not inconvenience network members. In their findings, these authors find social support was only activated within this population when Latinos were overburdened by their problems. We find similar results in our analyses.

Although it is clear that individuals who have social support available in their networks tend to have better outcomes than those who do not, it is important to understand the population's needs to best serve them with our efforts. Functional drug-using participants, for example, voiced that they did not always receive social support from their social network members. Some social network members provided aid intended to be positive, yet were perceived as unhelpful and disapproving by drug users. Among drug abusers, the availability of safety nets facilitated reconnections with non-drug-using social networks and allowed the abuser to curtail his drug intake to a functional level or stop using drugs altogether. Furthermore, we found functional drug users consistently recurred to downward social comparisons and "othering" when

talking about their drug-abusing counterparts. Downward social comparisons and "othering" have been found to negate the beneficial effects of social support within social networks. These findings highlight the importance of considering the presence of stigma toward drug abusers.

[...]

References

Antonucci, T. (2001). Social relations: An examination of social networks, social support, and sense of control. In J. E. Birren and K. W. Schaie (eds.), *Handbook of the Psychology of Aging*, pp. 427–53. San Diego: Academic Press.

Kaniasty, K., and Norris, F. (2000). Help-seeking comfort and receiving social support: The role of ethnicity and context of need. *American Journal of Community Psychology*, 28(4), 545–81.

Questions

1 According to the article, several researchers have suggested that the degree of addiction be categorized as a continuum ranging from functional to abusive. How do you think such a scale should be conceptualized? What indicators do you think we should use to distinguish between functional and abusive?

2 How might gender and sexuality reduce the availability and/or accessibility of social support networks for drug users? What about race and ethnicity? What are some examples? How might this impact the drug user and their drug using functionality?

3 How did planning seem to operate as a method of maintaining drug using functionality for the informants in the article? What are examples of drug use planning you see operating in the world around you? How does this form of moderation encourage functional use? How might socioeconomic status contribute to the ability to plan and moderate drug use?

28

Cannabis, Consciousness, and Healing

Wendy Chapkis

Following a slightly different vein, Wendy Chapkis' approach to studying the drug-using lifestyle focuses on the effects of medical marijuana. At the same time as most proponents are de-emphasizing the role of the "high" in discussing the healing properties of the drug, Chapkis and her subjects, drawn from a drug alliance for people with life-threatening illnesses, openly tout the benefits of marijuana's effects on their health and feelings of well-being. You may want to compare and contrast the sensations they describe and compare them to those of people around you who use this drug. Are they the same? Does these subjects' status as dying and the pain or anguish they have undergone prior to being accepted into this cooperative cause a difference in the ways college students experience getting high? How do these both compare and contrast with the depictions found in the media? What fears do these people have about losing control over their drug use and is this a common problem? Why or why not? To what extent are their usage patterns influenced by their race/ethnicity, their socioeconomic status, or their health? Finally, why is discussing the actual nature of the drug high such a taboo topic among most proponents of medical marijuana?

Introduction

The consciousness-altering properties of cannabis are generally understood by prohibitionist policy-makers as a critical impediment to the drug's designation as a medicine. Indeed, for many, the claim that cannabis is of any therapeutic value is a ruse employed not for the benefit of the dying but for those dying to get high. In response, many medical marijuana advocates downplay the drug's popular psychoactive effects, instead choosing to emphasize the role marijuana can play in managing pain, calming chemotherapy-related nausea, enhancing appetite in patients suffering from AIDS-wasting, relieving muscle spasticity associated with multiple sclerosis (MS), reducing intra-ocular pressure for glaucoma sufferers, and controlling seizure activity among epileptics. It is as if the high which makes the drug an attractive recreational substance either disappears

Drugs and the American Dream: An Anthology, First Edition. Edited by Patricia A. Adler, Peter Adler, and Patrick K. O'Brien.
© 2012 John Wiley & Sons, Inc. Published 2012 by John Wiley & Sons, Inc.

with medical use or is nothing more than a trivial side-effect unrelated to the plant's therapeutic value. But in-depth, semi-structured interviews with 42 patients affiliated with one California-based patient–caregiver cooperative, the Wo/Men's Alliance for Medical Marijuana (WAMM), suggest that for many patients the consciousness-altering properties are an important part of the plant's therapeutic value.

Method

This article is part of a book-length project, *Dying to Get High*, focusing on the politics of medical marijuana use and provision. It is based on a decade of ethnographic research with WAMM, a medical marijuana cooperative in northern California. The primary research method was participant observation involving attendance at weekly membership and distribution meetings, and participation in volunteer work, including in the collective's medical marijuana garden.

[…]

Members of the Wo/Men's Alliance for Medical Marijuana are primarily low-income patients living with life-threatening illnesses such as cancer and AIDS or with such serious chronic conditions as post-polio syndrome, spinal cord injury, epilepsy, or MS. The organization was founded in 1996 and currently has roughly 130 members using medical marijuana and another 30 supporting members serving as primary caregivers. In order to become members of WAMM, each patient participant is required to obtain a physician's written recommendation stating that cannabis might prove useful in managing specific symptoms associated with their illness, disability, and course of treatment.

The number of members the program can accommodate is limited by the amount of marijuana the organization is able to grow. There is an extensive waiting list to join the group; with more than 80% of members living with a life-threatening illness, the standing joke is that people 'are literally dying to get into WAMM.' The organization is not a 'Buyers' Club,' I need to point out. Medicinal products are made available to the membership without charge and according to need. Instead of paying for marijuana, members are encouraged, as their health permits, to

contribute volunteer hours to the organization through such activities as working in the garden; assisting with fund raising; making cannabis tinctures, beverages, capsules, and baked goods; volunteering in the office; and helping dying members with informal hospice support.

The organization's survival is never secure and made all the more difficult because of the dual challenges of dependence on an ill and impoverished membership and ongoing threats from the federal government. Out of political necessity, members not only raise funds and an annual crop of cannabis, but they also have had to expend significant resources fighting the federal government in court. In 2004, the organization made history when it secured a federal injunction protecting the group and its members from interference by the DEA. For a little over a year, WAMM operated the only fully legal medical marijuana garden in the United States. The injunction protecting WAMM was lost in the aftermath of the 2005 Supreme Court Gonzales v. Raich ruling against medical marijuana patients. Despite the renewed risk, WAMM members continue to meet weekly, sharing their reduced supply of marijuana.

Marijuana: A Dangerous Drug With No Medicinal Value?

Marijuana is a prohibited substance, the use of which is illegal under federal law in all circumstances, including physician-recommended medicinal use in states with medical marijuana laws.[1] The drug's placement within the most restrictive federal drug category, Schedule 1, relies on the assertion that cannabis is both dangerous and has no accepted medical use.

However, evidence for this assertion is lacking, despite the fact that the US federal government has invested millions of dollars seeking to establish the dangers of the drug. In the 1980s alone, federal funding for research into risks associated with marijuana use increased nearly tenfold. But no clear evidence has emerged of physical harms associated with cannabis use beyond those related to the popular delivery system of smoking. […]

Not only is the drug strikingly safe, but evidence is accumulating of the medicinal value of the plant and its constituent compounds. [...] In the face of this growing evidence of the drug's therapeutic potential and in the absence of evidence of significant harm, continued federal prohibition of marijuana increasingly depends on the claim that, because of the plant's psychoactive properties, the drug carries a 'high potential for abuse'. This claim, too, however, rests on unstable ground, undermined by the government's own contradictory policies on synthetic versus natural THC. THC — delta-9-tetrahydrocannabinol — is the most psychoactive component of cannabis. A synthetic version of the substance, dronabinol (Marinol), has been available on prescription in the U.S. for more than 20 years. In 1999, synthetic THC was deemed so safe, with such a low risk of abuse, that dronabinol became the only drug ever moved from Schedule II to Schedule III. [...]

These contradictory claims, about the established safety of synthetic THC and the risks of natural THC, depend largely on the definition of the former as medicine and the latter as having 'no accepted medical use.' If there is no legitimate use for marijuana, then a 'high potential for abuse' can easily be established: all use can be defined as abuse. For federal drug regulators committed to the continued prohibition of marijuana, the real problem with botanical cannabis is not that it is unsafe, therapeutically ineffective, and highly addictive, but rather that it may be none of these.

In the face of growing evidence for the safety and therapeutic promise of cannabis, attempts to maintain federal control are beginning to shift away from absolute prohibition to efforts at pharmaceuticalization. The first prescription drug composed entirely of botanical cannabis, Sativex, has already been approved in Canada and is working its way through the FDA approval process in the United States. The manufacturer of Sativex, GW Pharmaceuticals, insists that this product is different from marijuana because patients who use it don't get high. According to the company's website:

> By careful self-titration (dose adjustment), most patients are able to separate the thresholds for symptom relief and intoxication, the 'therapeutic window,' so enabling them to obtain symptom relief without experiencing a 'high.' Patients emphasize that they seek to obtain the medical benefits without intoxication. (GW Pharmaceuticals, 2007)

Here GW Pharmaceuticals makes the politically useful claim that, unlike recreational users of cannabis, legitimate patients reject the high as both unnecessary and unwelcome as well as entirely unrelated to the 'medical benefits' of the drug.

But many medical marijuana users, physicians, and researchers — including at least one scientist affiliated with GW Pharmaceuticals itself — dispute such claims. Dr William Notcutt (2004), a medical researcher involved with the development of Sativex, acknowledges the psychoactive effects of the drug but answers critics by arguing that such effects are, in themselves, therapeutic:

> There are many health professionals who perceive that a mild psychoactive effect from the drug is somehow wrong. This only seems to be of concern to those who do not treat patients in pain or distress.... Elevating the mood of a patient whose life is miserable because of chronic, untreatable pain would seem to be a worthwhile goal. (p. 293)

The real problem, according to Notcutt, is that the effect has been stigmatized by the drug's counter-cultural origins: 'The terms "high" or "stoned" belong to the hippy era and should be avoided in the context of medicinal cannabis. Euphoria, dysphoria, etc. are more appropriate descriptors of these effects' (p. 293).

Findings

Cannabis and a sense of wellness

Whether the effect is called a high, euphoria, or simply an enhanced sense of wellness, the psychoactive effects of marijuana are a frequently-commented-on aspect of the drug's medicinal value in interviews with WAMM patients. 'Jon,' a 37-year-old WAMM member living with HIV, for example, observes:

> Marijuana lifts me up past whatever symptoms I have at the moment and creates this sense of wellness and well-being that allows me to just function very much the way I could before I was HIV positive. I really feel like the worst symptom of HIV is how drained it makes you feel. The feeling of well-being that we all take for granted when we are healthy, that mental state disappears when

we feel sick. So when I'm stoned, I'm able to just rise above it and press on. I love that. It's a good thing. People who are well might not understand this. When you are really sick it affects your desire to live. If you are constantly ill for a long period of time, you can feel like it's not worth climbing back up the ladder. Because every step back is a struggle. So if you can take some substance to make you feel well, even for a brief moment in time to remind you what that's like, it's invaluable.

The need to battle situational depression and to regain some sense of wellness is commonplace among those living with chronic pain or life-threatening illness. This struggle can be intensified by the effects of some prescription pain medications. WAMM member Suzanne Pfeil uses a range of pharmaceutical drugs to control severe neuropathic pain associated with post-polio syndrome. She observes:

Some of the pharmaceuticals will take the pain down a notch but most of them are depressants – especially the muscle relaxers and pain pills – so they take your mood down. What I find is that I'm getting the edge taken off the pain but I'm also getting depressed. So, when I get a pain flare, I smoke [marijuana] and it helps to relieve the pain and relieve the spasms but it also means I don't get as depressed. Marijuana never fails to lift my mood. I smoke and think, 'Okay, I'm just going to have to go with the pain today. It's beautiful outside and I'm going to go tool around the garden in my chair.' It takes you to another level mentally of acceptance about being in this kind of pain. So when I'm in that 'I can't handle this another minute' stage, it produces a positive shift and I can go on to something else. The other drugs I'm prescribed have such major side-effects, but if I smoke a joint, the biggest side-effect is a mental lift. And that's a side-effect I can live with.

It is significant that Suzanne doesn't claim that cannabis fully masks her pain, but rather that it produces a shift in attitude toward pain. This was a frequent formulation by WAMM members discussing the effects of cannabis on pain management and depression. […]

Productivity and amotivational syndrome

[…] Suzanne Pfeil […] and Jon suggest that marijuana enhances one's ability to function in the world. This runs counter to a popular narrative about the dangers of marijuana in undermining productivity.

Some WAMM members spoke directly to the question of whether the consciousness-altering properties of the drug were an impediment to certain kinds of activity. […] 'Rev. Sonny,' a former Baptist minister who began to use marijuana medicinally to manage side-effects from cancer chemotherapy, observed a similar shift in what he perceived to be the effect of marijuana on his concentration and productivity:

I never would have guessed that I would ever be using marijuana medicinally when I was well. I always said that it was written in heaven that I couldn't smoke marijuana because it had such an effect on me. I just got really stoned, you know? But something changed when I got sick. I never would have believed it, but now I can function perfectly well with marijuana. In fact, I notice that it not only takes away my pain but I can get really focused on things. I can get really into a project if the distractions leave me alone. The only side-effect I really notice is forgetting things. But I don't have a lot that I really have to remember right now.

One complicating factor in attempting to identify the specific effects of the medical use of cannabis is that most patients suffering from serious illness – including most WAMM members – take a range of pharmaceutical drugs in addition to their marijuana. It can be difficult to identify which drug (or interaction between drugs) is causing a particular effect. […]

But not all medical marijuana patients agree that reduced productivity necessarily accompanies disease or disability. Many WAMM members are adamant about their desire to remain as productive as possible in the face of their physical challenges. These patients tend to emphasize the ways in which marijuana enhances function. 'Cher,' a woman in her early 50s disabled by a serious seizure disorder and chronic pain, for example, argues that marijuana has contributed to her ability to return to work:

Marijuana makes the pain easier to deal with. I won't say that it eliminates it – that would be overstating it. But it certainly makes it less of a nightmare so I can function. That's really important to me, to be able to function. From age 25 to 35 I couldn't work because my seizures were so frequent and I was in so much pain. Now, when I hear people talking longingly about retirement,

I realize how little they know about being useless. They are in for a big surprise. It is devastating to be useless.

[…]

This characterization runs contrary to decades of federal anti-drug education, which has emphasized the risks of so-called 'amotivational syndrome.' Marijuana users were described in a 1974 Senate hearing, for example, as existing in a state of 'apathy approaching indolence' (Sullum, 2003, p. 108). Similarly, a 1998 pamphlet produced by the National Institute on Drug Abuse depicts those who use marijuana as 'not caring about what happens in their lives, [demonstrating] no desire to work regularly, [experiencing] fatigue, and [exhibiting] a lack of concern about how they look' (p. 110). WAMM members are well aware of that stereotype. 'Charles,' a 42-year-old living with AIDS, points out:

> My [AIDS-related anti-viral] meds give me 24/7 flu-like symptoms. Under those conditions, it can be difficult to force myself to do more than to sit around and mope. Marijuana helps with that. I crack up when I see anti-drug television commercials about marijuana causing a lack of motivation or something. That's you; that's not the marijuana. If you are procrastinating, that's just you. Blaming it on the marijuana is an excuse. It never gets in the way of me doing what I need to do. In fact, when I'm at home and I medicate, I'm very productive. I take care of things I need to do around here. That's when I get things accomplished. It breaks through my procrastination.

Tolerance

[…] This claim may also reflect the fact that the intensive medicinal use of any substance may create some measure of tolerance and diminished effect. In fact, many WAMM members report that the euphoric effects of cannabis remembered from prior recreational use (or from the early days of their medicinal use) diminished or disappeared over time. Hal, for example, explains that as he became more accustomed to the drug as a medicine, its effects seemed to change:

> After a couple of months, I found that I wasn't getting high as much as I was getting calm. It took a couple of months though. At first, I'd smoke and get really high

and have a wonderful afternoon or evening or whatever. But then it started to change and I just got calm.

Establishing a clear difference between consuming cannabis in a recreational setting and consuming it in a medicinal setting is a priority for those WAMM members with a history of drug abuse and recovery. By drawing a line between 'getting loaded' and 'taking medicine,' these individuals are able to maintain their sense of sobriety while using cannabis therapeutically. Inocencio Manjon-McFaline, a 54-year-old cancer patient and former cocaine addict, describes the difference as profound:

> For me, the decision to start using marijuana was really hard. I had a long history of using drugs. You name it, I used it. I spent time in Vietnam where I got into injectable drugs and then I was in central America for 28 years working with the canine section at an international airport. What it amounted to was taking all the cocaine and putting it in my back pocket. I had at my disposal whatever I wanted. In 1988, I quit, cold turkey. I stopped everything – cigarettes, alcohol, coffee, drugs – everything that I was addicted to. Completely clean. Given the amount of cocaine I'd been using, cleaning up was so painful I keep a good memory of it. So when my doctor suggested marijuana to me about four years ago, I said, 'No, I don't want to start that.' I was really against it. For me to start smoking was like, did I fail? After all those years of being clean? For what? But it got to the point where it was only a choice between which pain relievers I would use – oxycontin or marijuana. I decided to stop the oxycontin and try the marijuana.

In his description of his current use of marijuana for pain relief, Inocencio Manjon-McFaline emphasizes the profound difference in the effect of the drug when used medicinally rather than recreationally:

> What's strange now is that I don't feel the effects [from marijuana] that I remember from when I would smoke it before, smoking to get loaded. It's a different time for me. I'm not smoking it looking for a high. Maybe it's just psychologically different knowing I'm smoking it for medicinal use. But I haven't felt loaded. I smoke only for the pain. It gets me out of there, out of that frame of mind. I'll smoke and I'll tend to focus on what I want to focus on. Generally, that's my breathing and my heartbeat. And I'll get really into plants. I just really get into that and forget about pain. Every breath I take is a blessing.

Mind set and setting

In attempting to establish a clear difference between recreational use and medical use, Manjon-McFaline's comments also raise the important question of what it means to get high. Clearly, he is no longer looking to 'get loaded' and argues that he no longer gets high. However, his description of his medicinal use suggests that marijuana assists him in not only dealing with pain and nausea but also in focusing on his breath, on his heartbeat, on the blessings of being alive. This echoes reports by many recreational users of the psychoactive effects of the drug. The difference may be that this state seems more altered when there are more conventional demands making claims on a user's time.

A present-tense focus, attention to the breath, and a renewed delight in living may not feel altering so much as confirming or enhancing in the context of terminal illness. In other words, at least some of the differences patients report in the effects of the drug when taken medicinally may be attributable to what Norman Zinberg (1984) refers to as the effects of 'set' (the user's mindset) and 'setting' (the context in which the drug is taken). A substance taken in expectation of pleasurable intoxication by a healthy individual may produce a substantially different effect than that experienced by an individual living with a life-threatening illness or in chronic pain. In short, partying and medicating are different. [...] This nuanced description of the range of effects that can be experienced from the same substance by the same user, when consumed in contrasting settings, challenges the notion that a clear-cut distinction can be made between patients who don't get high and [...] 'dope heads' who do.

In contrast, WAMM members describe a complex relationship to the drug depending on circumstance and intention. In one setting, a patient may be using marijuana specifically for physical symptom relief, while in another situation marijuana may be consumed with an expectation of deepened relaxation, introspection, or enhanced creativity. [...]

Stoned realizations

[...] WAMM members [... describe] the therapeutic use of marijuana as targeted at more than physical symptom relief. Many emphasize the role the drug plays in allowing them to face difficult emotional issues with diminished anxiety. [...]

[...] [P]atients report that the introspective effects of cannabis allow them to reflect on, and in some cases resolve, issues unrelated to their illness. 'Sarah,' a 54-year-old living with MS, uses cannabis to control pain but acknowledges that increased introspection is a welcome side-effect:

> I certainly wouldn't put the altered consciousness thing as a primary effect for me. Though I have to say that the last two or three years have certainly been very surreal largely because my father was in the process of dying. It was interesting to see how marijuana maybe turned my head with regard to that, to his problems and insights into my own behavior. It was probably helpful in letting me just dwell longer in my mind on that particular topic and try to get to the bottom of things that had been brought up in one conversation or another. I think I was able to look at my life a little differently as a result.

Such 'stoned realizations' are often discussed by WAMM members with a knowing nod to the drug's counter-cultural past. 'Alicia,' a 34-year-old breast cancer survivor, for example, observes:

> If I'm in a really high realm of pain, then I don't get any pleasure from pot at all. It just helps stop the torture. But there are also times when the pain is not nearly so bad; bad enough to treat but not in the upper stratosphere. Then marijuana is also a relaxing experience. It's not, you know, like something from the old psychedelic movies of the 70s, but there is a certain pleasure factor in there as well as the absence of pain. And it does lead to a certain degree of introspective enlightenment, a sort of free-form thinking. This is such a cliché that I feel like I need to have 'Stairway to Heaven' playing. But it does inspire introspective thought. Like I say, it's so cliché but it's definitely true. I remain very aware when it's occurring. I had something like that happen just last night. I was thinking about some family stuff – I have a very screwed up family. And I had a revelation that actually made sense to me about forgiveness. Now could I have had those kinds of thoughts if I weren't stoned? Definitely. Definitely I could have. Would I have, though? That's a different matter. Generally in a non-stoned state, I wouldn't even bother to think about those kinds of things. It's being in that altered state that you think, 'Hhmmm ... this is interesting,' as opposed to, 'what else is on TV?'

[...]

Escape from reality

A common objection in the anti-drug literature to the high associated with psychoactive drugs is that altered consciousness offers only a distortion of, or escape from, reality. The implication is that escape is somehow unworthy or undesirable. However, in the context of chronic pain or terminal illness, one might question whether reality isn't greatly over-rated. As Jane Wagner and Lily Tomlin observe, '[R]eality is the leading cause of stress amongst those in touch with it' (Wagner, 1986, para. 4).

Susan Durst, a 62-year-old WAMM member with cancer, for example, struggles not only with physical pain but with poverty and social isolation related to her illness:

> I eat about an eighth or a sixteenth of a [marijuana] muffin in the morning, mostly to help with stopping all this anxiety and fear and this 'poor me.' It stops the fear, it stops the worrying. It isn't just the fear of the cancer, it's the poverty, it's the fear of being evicted, it's all of it. My world feels like it is closing in, closing down. My secret pleasure is watching baseball on television. To eat a little bit of muffin or drink a little bit of [cannabis infused] milk and just lay back and watch the game is right now kind of bliss for me. Marijuana alters your thought processes, gives you a little sense of well-being, and takes away some of the minor bone pain. During the chemo, it helped to take the edge off and it made me believe I was getting better, and it made me able to sleep, to live in that awful mess and not fret about it too much.

For some patients, like Pamela Cutler who is facing terminal illness at an early age, marijuana use reportedly softens the focus on death:

> Marijuana kind of helps dull the reality of this situation. And anyone who says it's not a tough reality … I mean your mind will barely even take it in. It does dull it and I don't think there is anything wrong with that if I want to dull it. That's fine. I was diagnosed with breast cancer and had a radical mastectomy. The whole thing was a big shock. I mean, I was 36. I was like, 'What?' And ever since then it's been like a roller coaster: okay, it's spread to my bones, and then it's spread to my lungs, and then my

liver. Marijuana makes it easier to take for me. It doesn't really take it away. It just dulls the sharpness of it – like, 'Oh my god, I'm going to be dead.' I just think that's just incredible.

Similarly, Charles argues that the need to escape occasionally is both valid and understandable in the context of living with AIDS:

> Since I tested positive in 1990, my life has been a real roller coaster ride. On my worst days, it's hell, a living hell. I lie in bed, or on the couch, or on the floor. The meds make you so sick, you can't even cope with yourself, let alone the outside world. By 'cope' I mean how many times do you have to run to the bathroom, for instance. The diarrhea is awful. And the first thing they want to do is give you another pill to stop it. I'm not taking another pill. I'd rather smoke marijuana. It can help put you in a different state of mind. I mean, I've never had a life-threatening disease and now I was watching everyone die in front of me. I wasn't just getting high anymore; it let me think about why I am still here after they are all gone. With marijuana, I can get high and let it all go. But at the same time, it also makes it possible for me to eat, to deal with the nausea, the insomnia, and all that. So it's not just an escape. Absolutely not. And even if it was, why would that be such a bad thing?

As Pamela Cutler and Charles suggest, the psychological dimensions of serious and life-threatening illness can be as important to treat as the physical symptoms. Under such circumstances, healing modalities associated with palliative care – for example, pain relief and anxiety reduction – may be more relevant than heroic measures intended to cure. As Dr Bal Mount, founder and director of the Palliative Care Unit at the Royal Victorian Hospital in Montreal, observes, '[H]ealing doesn't necessarily have to do with just the physical body. If one has a broader idea of what healing and wellness are, all kinds of people die as well people' (quoted in Webb, 1999, p. 317).

Dependence

Discussions about appropriate treatment often include debates about the benefits of adequate pain relief measured against the risks of dependence on often highly addictive prescription pain medications. WAMM members are aware of this problem, arguing that their marijuana use allows them to reduce their dependence on more dangerous pharmaceutical drugs. 'Silverknight,' who suffers from chronic pain due to a broken back, observes:

I'm careful not to ever abuse my prescription drugs – in fact, that is part of the reason to use marijuana, to cut the need for those pain relievers that are very addictive. With the heavier strains of marijuana, I can take half [a prescription pill]. That's all I'll need.

But she also raises the issue of the responsible use of medical marijuana:

Even with the marijuana itself, you have to know what you're doing. Some of the strains are pretty strong and I know not to smoke too much and not to mix it with some of the prescription drugs that I have for pain. I look at marijuana as a friend, a medicinal helper, a spiritual helper, a wonderful thing. But I also know the parameters. Do you want to be knocked out stoned? Not me. I want to be able to alleviate the pain I'm having. It's like taking any other drug to help you: be responsible. I think you can abuse anything and, sure, some people do develop some type of dependence on marijuana that's not good. I mean, like Valerie says [Valerie Corral, the co-founder of WAMM], 'Once you are "there," why continue to smoke, smoke, smoke?' You are already there. So what is that? Why is that person picking up another joint? That's a concern. I've been in that place myself but I recognized it. I had to say to myself, 'Okay, now, you're there. You can always get there again. Just enjoy this; it's not going to be taken away from you.' That's the old fear. But with WAMM, you don't have to go out on the street and try to find it. You are in a safe situation where there will be more.

[...]

Conclusion

As these accounts suggest, medical marijuana patients have varying relationships to the drug and experience a range of effects from its use. Each of the 42 patients interviewed described marijuana as an effective alternative, or adjunct therapy, to more dangerous

pharmaceutical drugs. Most, though not all of them, also argued that the plant's medicinal value was closely related to the consciousness-altering effects of the drug. For those patients, it was difficult or impossible to separate the medical benefits of the drug from its effects on mood and cognition.

A growing body of research seems to confirm the anecdotal evidence provided by WAMM members, regarding both the drug's therapeutic value and the relationship between the consciousness-altering properties of the plant and symptom relief. Researcher Norman Zinberg (1979), for example, observes that the anti-nausea effects associated with cannabis 'accompany the existence of the "high" state. It is when the high wears off that we have learned to expect the onset of nausea and vomiting' (p. 137). Similarly, in 2006, researchers studying the therapeutic effectiveness of marijuana as an adjunct therapy in the treatment of hepatitis-C reported that patients who used marijuana were significantly more likely to complete a difficult treatment protocol and to have a positive outcome from it; six months after treatment ended, 54% of the marijuana users were virus-free compared to only 18% of those who had not used cannabis (Weiss, 2006). The researchers concluded that cannabis might have some specific virological effect in fighting the virus, but that it was much more likely that marijuana helped patients tolerate the treatment better by 'reducing depression, improving appetite and offering psychological benefits' (p. 2).

[...]

[...] [P]atients who find that cannabis does work well may have some concerns about the high. Any possibility of impaired performance or psychological dependence suggests that patients would be well served by warnings in place for other legal – although far more dangerous – medicinal and recreational substances. However, the continued outright prohibition on marijuana use, even for medical purposes under the supervision of a licensed physician, is insane. That such policies continue to be enforced by the US federal government despite growing scientific evidence of efficacy and safety suggests that the needs of drug warriors and pharmaceutical manufacturers are still being prioritized over those of seriously ill patients seeking relief.

Note

1   Eleven states have currently legalized marijuana for medical use, although the drug is still illegal under federal law.

References

GW Pharmaceuticals. (2007). *What Is Sativex?* Retrieved January 16, 2007, from http://www.gwpharm.com/faqs. asp#faqs2.

Notcutt, W. (2004). Cannabis in the treatment of chronic pain. In G. Guy, B. Whittle, & P. Robson (eds), *The medicinal uses of cannabis and cannabinoids* (p. 293). London: Pharmaceutical Press.

Sullum, J. (2003). *Saying yes.* New York: Penguin.

Wagner, J. (1986). *The search for signs of intelligent life in the universe.* New York: Harper and Row.

Webb, M. (1999). *The good death.* New York: Bantam.

Weiss, R. (2006, September 13). Marijuana aids therapy. *Washington Post*, p. A02.

Zinberg, N. (1979). Cannabis and health. *Journal of Psychedelic Drugs*, 11: 135–44.

Zinberg, N. (1984). *Drugs, set, and setting.* New Haven, CT: Yale University Press.

Questions

1   According to the article, for federal drug regulators committed to the continued prohibition of marijuana, the real problem with botanical cannabis is not that it is unsafe, therapeutically ineffective, and highly addictive, but rather that it may be none of these. Do you think the billions of dollars spent on the War on Drugs would be justified if marijuana were a legal and regulated substance? How do the patient stories in the article compare to the anti-marijuana discourse in the United States?

2   According to the article, how are the psychoactive effects of marijuana therapeutic? What are some other ways, not mentioned in the article, that the psychoactive effects of marijuana might be therapeutic? How might users who do not identify as medical marijuana patients benefit from marijuana use?

3   Why do you think some WAMM members in the article felt a diminished effect to marijuana's psychoactive properties after intensive medicinal use? Do you think this is a physiological tolerance or a socially learned tolerance? Why? How might "mind set and setting" impact a patient's experience using marijuana differently than that of a recreational user?

29

The Dealing Lifestyle

Patricia A. Adler

This excerpt from Patti Adler's classic study of upper-level marijuana and cocaine smuggling in the 1970s focuses on the lifestyle of Southwest County drug traffickers. White, moderately affluent, often professional, and with little prior criminal experience, these mostly men and their flashy girlfriends were heavily motivated in their illegal behavior by the sex, spontaneity, and freedom of their hedonistic lifestyle. Despite the need for secrecy, they also enjoyed the ego gratification they derived within their subculture from the danger and status of their law violations.

Reading through this selection, consider the role of the dealers and smugglers in this community and their women. To what extent do they follow similar gender roles to other portrayals we have seen such as Mohamed and Fritsvold's college dealers and Peralta's college drinkers, both from predominantly White middle- to upper-class settings? How might they compare to the gender roles depicted in Latino, Black, American Indian, and Asian-Pacific Islander communities?

Do these people have the kinds of issues with functionality and control that we have seen in other settings? Why and why not? To what extent are they integrated into or insulated from the larger community around them? How might their involvement in this highly illegal activity be affected by their age? Their race/ethnicity? Their socioeconomic status? What role do these traffickers' families of origin or creation play in their drug using and/or dealing? What role does this historical point in time play in their activities? Do they feel the need to justify their behavior or their health like some of the street drug addicts about which we have read? Why or why not? How credible would they be?

Drugs and the American Dream: An Anthology, First Edition. Edited by Patricia A. Adler, Peter Adler, and Patrick K. O'Brien.
© 2012 John Wiley & Sons, Inc. Published 2012 by John Wiley & Sons, Inc.

This is a study of a community of drug dealers and smugglers and the social scene they inhabit. These operators constitute the drug world's upper echelons, as they import and distribute tons of marijuana and dozens of kilos of cocaine at a time. In part, the extremely illegal nature of their trafficking activities makes these individuals cluster together for both business and social relations, forming a deviant subculture which reflects common norms and values. This subculture provides guidelines for their dealing and smuggling, outlining members' rules, roles, and reputations. Their social life is deviant as well, as evidenced by their abundant drug consumption, extravagant spending, uninhibited sexual mores, and focus on immediate gratification. They are the jet-setters of the drug world, living the fast life, pursuing the whim of the moment.

[...]

The methods I used to study this group were direct and personal. With my husband as a research partner, I spent six years in the field (from 1974 to 1980) engaged in daily participant observation with members of this dealing and smuggling community. Although I did not deal myself, I participated in many of their activities, partying with them, attending social gatherings, traveling with them, and watching them plan and execute their business activities. I thus came to know members of this subculture, and formed close friendships with several of them. In addition to observing and conversing casually with these dealers and smugglers, I conducted in-depth, taped interviews, and cross-checked my observations and their accounts against further sources of data whenever possible. After leaving the field, I continued to conduct follow-up interviews during periodic visits to the community until 1993.

[...]

The Setting: Southwest County

Located within the sunbelt of the southwestern United States, Southwest County was composed, in part, of a handful of informal beach towns that dotted the Pacific Ocean. [...]

The local surf subculture pervaded the area, creating an ambience that was centered around outdoor living, natural food, good health, physical narcissism, relaxed good vibes, and a general lack of future-orientation. Here, the quest for youth prevailed, and individuals of all ages thought and acted with an intentional freedom and exuberance.

This area was further divided into homogeneous pockets of people who clustered together along racial, age, and economic lines, living in relative separation from each other. Southwest County dealers and smugglers carved out their niche in "Grass City" (a small village of approximately 7,000 people) and the two smaller towns on either side of it. Grass City was peaceful during the daylight hours, as shoppers, beachgoers, and surfers pursued their activities. At night, though, the nightclubs, bars, and restaurants were enlivened by drug traffickers and their entourages. Spending ran high, helping to keep the local community afloat financially.

Several features of Southwest County, and particularly Grass City, combined to make this area attractive to the upper-level dealing and smuggling set. First, its proximity to the Pacific Ocean and the Mexican border placed it at a strategic advantage for the wholesale drug business. It functioned as a point of entry along both land and water frontiers. Second, the local surf subculture provided a compatible social climate for drug traffickers, as dealers and smugglers shared many norms with this drug-using, present-centered group. The drug world and surf subcultures thus had a degree of sympathy toward and reciprocal influence over each other. [...]

The People

The exact size of Southwest County's upper-level dealing and smuggling community was impossible to estimate. People tended to be very secretive, hiding their identity and actions from outsiders. They also varied their involvement with dealing, frequently dropping out and reentering the scene. During the course of my six years of participant observation research with members of this group, I was able to observe closely 65 dealers and smugglers, conducting intensive, taped interviews with 24 of them. In addition, I observed and interacted with numerous other drug world members, including dealers' "old ladies" (girl friends and wives), friends, and family members, who constituted the dealers' and smugglers' social group.

At these upper levels, Southwest County's drug crowd was quite homogeneous. Participants were predominantly white, came from middle-class family backgrounds, and had a low degree of prior criminality. The dealers' and smugglers' social world contained both men and women, but most of the serious business was conducted by the men, who surrounded themselves with beautiful but flighty "dope chicks." While all of the smugglers I studied were men, about one-tenth of the drug dealers in my sample were women. This primarily included dealers' ex-old ladies who had learned the business from their former mates, and women who had dealt or begun dealing jointly with their spouses. Members of this dealing and smuggling community ranged from 25 to 40 years old. This was an older group than that described by most other studies of drug dealing, which, as with much academic research, focus on student and university-related populations. My sample included people who had progressed beyond the low levels of trafficking commonly found among these younger populations, and had moved up to the larger quantities where the opportunities for profit were greater. In addition, many of those I observed were recruited into the drug world, by their peers, at a later age, thus bypassing the lower levels entirely. My subjects' experiences in traveling around the country to buy and sell drugs at the upper levels suggested that this age range was predominant among the people who dealt at this level.

[...]

The Fast Life

[...] Southwest County dealers and smugglers led lives that were seldom dull. Abandoning the dictates of propriety and the workaday world, they lived spontaneously and intensely. Drug traffickers rejected society's normative constraints which mandated a lifestyle of deferred gratification, careful planning, and sensible spending. Instead, they embraced the pursuit of self-indulgence. Whether it was the unlimited availability of their favorite drugs, the illusion of the seemingly bottomless supply of money, the sense of power and the freedom they attained, their easy access to sexual satisfaction, or merely the excitement associated with the continual dangers they faced, the dealing crowd was strongly driven by the pleasures they derived from their way of life. This lifestyle was one of the strongest forces that attracted and held people to the drug trafficking business. It was therefore largely responsible for the set of traits which comprised the dealers' personality; only those people who found the reward system enticing enough to merit assuming the risks were persuaded to strive for greater involvement in this world. [...]

The lifestyle associated with big-time dealers and smugglers was intemperate and uninhibited. Dubbed the fast life, or "flash," it was characterized by a feeling of euphoria. So pleasurable was life that nobody worried about paying the bills, running out of drugs, or planning for the future. Dealers and smugglers plunged themselves fully into satisfying their immediate desires, whether these involved consuming lavish, expensive dinners, drugging themselves to saturation, traveling hundreds of miles to buy a particular item that caught their eye, or "crashing" (sleeping) for 15–20 hours at a time to make up for nights spent in unending drug use. Those who lived in the fast lane sought an intensity that disdained the boredom of security and the peace of calm quietude. They were always on the run, rushing back and forth between partying and doing business, often intermingling the two. Schedules and commitments were hard to maintain, since people were apt to pursue the unexpected at any time or get caught in a run of drug consumption that could last for hours or even days. One coke dealer commented on the frequency of his partying:

> When we're sitting around the house with friends that are into dealing it always turns into a party. We do a lot of drugs, drink a lot, and just speed rap all night.... It's a full time thing; we're basically decadent 24 hours a day.

Those who lived the fast life were the *beautiful people*, bedecked with expensive adornments such as flashy clothes, jewelry, and sports cars. When they entered a restaurant or bar they ordered extravagantly and tipped lavishly. They grew up to reattain a childlike innocence by escaping the unpleasant responsibilities of adult life, while seizing the opportunity to surround themselves with anything money could buy. In their own eyes, they were the ultimate "in crowd."

The dealers' and smugglers' fast life emulated the jet set with all of its travel, spending, and heavy partying. Private planes were diverted to carry a smuggler's entourage off for a week in Las Vegas where they all drank, gambled, and saw the shows. At other times it was off to the Pacific Islands for sunbathing and tropical drinks, to the mountains for skiing, or to famous spas, where they luxuriously exercised and rejuvenated themselves. In contrast to those children of inherited wealth, though, dealers and smugglers had to work for their money. Their lifestyle was characterized by a mixture of work and play, as they combined concentrated wheeling and dealing with unadulterated partying. Yet, like jet-setters, they ultimately became bored and sought ever-greater excitement, usually turning to drugs for their most intense highs.

Members of the "glitter crowd" were known for their *irresponsibility* and *daring*, their desire to live recklessly and wildly. They despised the conservatism of the straight world as lowly and mundane. For them, the excitement of life came from a series of challenges where they pitted themselves against the forces that stood in their way. Although they did not create arbitrary risks, dealers and smugglers were gamblers who enjoyed the element of risk in their work, being intoxicated with living on the edge of danger. They relished more than just the money; they reveled in the thrill-seeking associated with their close scrapes, their ever-present danger, and their drug-induced highs. Gone was the quiet, steady home life of soberly raising children and accumulating savings, as they set themselves on a continuous search for new highs. They exalted freedom, the ability to pick up and "blow" without having to answer to anybody. One dope chick who had spent the past several years moving from relationship to relationship with various big dealers discussed her sense of freedom:

> Now I can do anything I want and not have to worry about someone telling me not to do it. One day I just woke up and said to my little girl, "Honey, pack your clothes. We're going to Hawaii."

Drug dealers lived for the present, surrounding themselves with the maximum pleasures they could grab. They did not, as the middle class ethos suggested, live in reduced comfort so that they could enjoy the fruits of their labor at a later date. In fact, the reverse was true. The beautiful people seized their happiness now and deferred their hardships for the future; they lived for the moment and let tomorrow worry about paying the tab. One dealer's old lady elaborated on this *mañana* effect:

> It was always like, tomorrow, tomorrow. You write a check, you think you'll cover it tomorrow. It was like that. We went through a lot of stuff like that.

Money lay at the base of their exhilarating madness, more money than most could ever have imagined. The gigantic profits that could be accumulated after even a short period of smuggling or heavy dealing could run into hundreds of thousands of dollars a year, which seemed like an endless supply to most participants. Sometimes they became so overcome by their material wealth that they just gloried in it. One novice dealer exclaimed:

> We were like little children in a big fancy palace playhouse. We'd dump all our money on the living room floor and we'd roll in it.

Most initiates could not imagine how to spend this much at first, but they soon learned. After even a short period they found themselves laughing when hundred dollar bills came out of laundered shirt pockets, crumpled and torn from the wash. By then money had become something to be spent without care on the fulfillment of any whim. One member of a smuggler's crew recalled:

> Money meant nothing to me. Like, if some guy gave me a $100 bill I'd go out and burn it or cut it in half for all I cared.

This overabundance drove them to generate new needs, to search out new avenues of spending. As one dealer illustrated:

> At the height of my dealing I was making at least 10 grand a month profit, even after all my partying. When you have too much money you always have to look for something to spend it on. I used to run into the stores every day to find $50, $60 shirts to buy because I didn't know what else to do with the money, there was so much.

Drugs were also a big part of the fast life. Smugglers and dealers took personal consumption for themselves and their entourage as a basic cost of doing business, to be siphoned out before profits could accumulate, so drugs flowed freely, without care for expense. High-potency marijuana and hashish were smoked in moderation by many, most noticeably among the marijuana traffickers. Alcohol, particularly wine and champagne, was consumed regularly, often along with other drugs. Cocaine, however, was used heavily, its presence pervading the entire dealing community. They typically "coked" themselves to saturation, and it was not uncommon for a dealer to snort more than an ounce a week (market value: $2,000–$2,200) during periods of heavy partying. One cocaine dealer estimated how much he and his old lady took out for their "own heads":

> As much as we wanted, which was a lot. We used a couple of grams a day at least, that was nothing. We could go through a quarter [of an ounce], you wouldn't believe it. We used big ziplocs, the large size, for our personal stash. We'd stick a big spoon in it and just dump it out on the mirror. One time I dropped an ounce down the front of my shirt when I went to take a toot [snort] and the bag ripped. I just brushed it off, it was nothing.

[...]

Another component of life for Southwest County's beautiful people was the *casual sex scene*. Although many members of the community were married and had children, they openly broke the bonds of marital fidelity to explore their sexual urges. Casual attractions, although not the only mode of sexual fulfillment, were a commonly accepted part of life. This open sexual promiscuity was legitimated by the predominance of the hedonistic ethos which infused the dealing and smuggling community. The ease with which they engaged in casual sexual relations indicated their openness toward sexual self-indulgence as a subculturally accepted norm, overriding the contrary sexual mores of the greater society.

Many male dealers and smugglers went out with their male friends to pick-up bars, looking for one-night stands. Some kept old ladies on the side and set them up in apartments. They also played musical old ladies, shifting from one to another as they got tired of each one. Extramarital flings were not limited to the men, though, as married women frequently went out for a night with the "girls" and did not come home until sunrise. Marital relationships often became taken for granted in the light of this emphasis on immediate attractions, and divorce was common.

Dealers' old ladies formed an interesting part of the drug scene, because although their role was occasionally active, it was more often passive. Some women ran their own drug businesses. Of these, most entered dealing through the connections they made while living with a male dealer. Typically, after a breakup, these women needed money and realized that they had the knowledge to attempt doing business on their own. Not all women who tried to establish themselves as drug traffickers were successful, however. This lack of success rested, in part, on certain qualities essential to the profession and in part on the reactions men had to working with them. [...] [A]s one marijuana trafficker complained:

> Among the guys I know, a lot of them are reluctant to deal with girls. Girls don't seem to bend as well as guys do. Like girls seem to be a lot more high-strung, or they get more emotional if something doesn't go down right. Like guys seem to have more patience involved in it.... And girls are a lot more greedier than guys, they want a bigger cut normally for some strange reason.

This was not a universal complaint. Others found nothing wrong with working with women and did not reject them as associates. One cocaine dealer gave his view on women dealers:

> Out here there's lots of them, as equal with guys. The first person who gave me my first front was a lady and I'm still good friends with her. I really have no preference for dealing with either sex.

Most people agreed, though, that men chauvinistically bent the rules for the "ladies." For instance, women were given more time to pay back money they owed, and were less likely to have to adhere to standard operating procedures for dealing, such as weighing or performing tests for quality on drugs that they sold. This chauvinism could be favorably manipulated, as one female dealer admitted:

> Chicks have a great advantage, especially when you use it in an unfair way, which you can when you're a chick.

Women, as I have discussed, were also used by male dealers and smugglers as employees. Smugglers felt that women were less vulnerable to the suspicions of police or border agents. Positions in which women were often employed included transporting money or drugs, locally, around the country, or across international lines, and operating stash houses.

The majority of women in Southwest County's drug world took a more passive role, however. A crowd of dope chicks formed part of the entourage which surrounded big dealers and smugglers. Universally beautiful and sexily clad, they served as prestigious escorts, so that dealers could show them off to other members of the community. The motivation for these women was to share in the fast life's drugs, money, glamor, and excitement, as one dealer's wife explained:

> Some chicks use their looks as a way of getting a man or some coke or their money or whatever. Those girls are like prostitutes – they put themselves where they know they can accomplish what they're really looking for.

In return, they were expected not to intrude on any of their companions' social or business relations. One dope chick offered this explanation of the reciprocal relationship:

> I guess he just wanted someone to look pretty and drive his Pantera, so that people would say, hey so-and-so's got a real foxy-looking chick.

Beyond appearance, dealers looked on these women as sex objects. A married smuggler explained the rules of the game:

> Sex is important in that they can make love to that lady because they're stimulated by her. They're gonna live with her and ball her, but yet they can make love to another lady too.

When it came to personality, however, less dynamic stimulus was required. A major coke dealer was frank about his colleagues' attitudes on this point:

> The guys want a chick who will hang on their arm and go places with them and they don't really have to relate to her, because they would actually prefer if the chick was dumb enough to where they could leave her with a couple of bottles of wine and say I'm going out to do some business, I'll see you in the morning. They want a chick who will accept where she's at and have enough brains to know when to shut up.

[...]

Motivations for Dealing

Two dominant motivations fueled the drive to traffic in drugs: *hedonism* and *materialism*. The latter was the more readily apparent of the two, and has been cited by most sociological accounts of other illegal occupations as the primary enticement. Certainly, none of the dealers or smugglers I observed could have earned as much money in as short a time by legitimate means. Their drug profits enabled them to surround themselves with the kind of material possessions they coveted: fine food, clothes, cars, electronic equipment, and, above all, money itself, as a symbol of success and power. The lure of extravagant wealth thus served to both recruit and hold people to this enterprise.

A second source of motivation, more compelling than the first, however, was the hedonism inherent in the lifestyle. Southwest County drug traffickers pursued a style of life filled with the pleasures of unlimited drugs, sexual promiscuity, personal power, high status, freedom, risk, and excitement. Yet the acceptance of hedonism as a forceful motivation underlying criminal behavior remains controversial in the literature. Some studies, particularly those focusing on materialism, have decried this as a secondary, irrelevant, or nonexistent dimension of deviant occupations, considering illegal work as mundane as its legal counterpart. Others, however, have pointed to the thrills, sexual opportunities, and deviant lifestyle as equal in their attraction and reward to materialistic compensations. For Southwest County dealers and smugglers, the fast life became the central part of their existence. While they might have been initially drawn to trafficking out of materialism, they soon became addicted to it out of hedonism. Once people had become sufficiently exposed to the enchantment of the fast life, enamored with their feelings of importance, and used to wantonly consuming money and drugs, they were willing to continue drug trafficking to support themselves in this style. The myriad pleasures reinforced one another, overwhelming even the once soberly directed individuals. Thus, the dealing lifestyle, through its unmitigated hedonism, both attracted pleasure-seeking individuals into the drug business and transformed others, through its concentrated decadence, into pleasure seekers, combining its thrust with materialism in ensuring their continuance in this line of work.

Questions

1 How might the demographic homogeneity of Southwest County's drug crowd have protected them from the suspicion of the law? How might their lifestyle have attracted attention of law enforcement?

2 How did gender operate in the higher echelons of this drug dealing world? How do these gender dynamics compare and contrast with those in the legitimate world? Why do you think most of these high level traffickers were men? Have things changed in the illegitimate marketplace? Why or why not?

3 How are the motivations for dealing discussed in the article related to the pursuit of the "American Dream?" Why do you think the dealers in the article chose illegitimate means over legitimate means to achieve their goals and desires?

The Economics of Drugs

30

Women in the Street-Level Drug Economy
Continuity or Change?

Lisa Maher and Kathleen Daly

Returning to the tough, poverty-stricken streets of New York, Lisa Maher and Kathleen Daly focus on the economic activities women take within this crack cocaine scene. How do the primarily Hispanic and Black women's roles in this setting compare to those of Adler's affluent, often professional, traffickers? Does it make a difference that many of the women Adler encountered had been college educated while most of Maher and Daly's subjects never graduated from high school?

How do the activities of these urban ghetto dwellers compare to the women Dunlap, Golub, and Johnson described in a similar environment who were nearly all Black? Is this a question of opportunity structure, subcultural gender roles, physical attributes, or some of each? Why do these largely Latino women seem so liberated from household, childrearing, and family obligations, especially compared to Hardesty and Black's Latinos and Joe Laidler's Asian-Pacific Islanders?

How does the structure of the dealing operations described here seem to compare to the upper-level traffickers from Adler's study? Do they have similar levels of violence? What might account for some of the differences? How does the domestic violence in relationships compare to Joe Laidler's Asian-Pacific Islanders, Spicer's American Indians, and Dunlap, Golub, and Johnson's Black ghetto dwellers? Are these similarities or differences primarily racial/ethnic, class, or occupationally affected? Why do you think Maher and Daley do not report on any of the women in this scene being involved in prostitution? Finally, do you think these women are liberated or not, and if so, liberated from what?

Drugs and the American Dream: An Anthology, First Edition. Edited by Patricia A. Adler, Peter Adler, and Patrick K. O'Brien.
© 2012 John Wiley & Sons, Inc. Published 2012 by John Wiley & Sons, Inc.

Images of women in the contemporary drug economy are highly mixed. Most scholars emphasize *change* in women's roles in US drug markets of 1960–1985, organized primarily around heroin, compared to women's roles in more recent drug markets with the advent of crack cocaine. Some emphasize *continuity* from previous decades. Others suggest that both change and continuity are evident, with women inhabiting "two social worlds": one of increased participation in, and the other of continued restriction by, male-dominated street and drug networks.

One should expect, on the one hand, to see variation in women's positions in the drug economy. Research on drug markets in New York City, Miami, Washington, DC, Detroit, Chicago, Milwaukee, Los Angeles, and the West Coast reveals differences in the racial and ethnic composition of participants and who controls markets, the kinds of drugs sold, how markets are organized, and participants' responses to law enforcement. Such differences are likely to affect women's positions and specific roles.

At the same time, the varied characterizations of women's roles reflect differences in the theoretical assumptions and methodological approaches taken by scholars. For example, women's increasing presence in the drug economies of the late 1980s and early 1990s is said to reflect (1) emancipation from their traditional household responsibilities, (2) an extension of their traditional household responsibilities, and (3) the existence of "new opportunities" in street-level drug markets, especially with increased rates of incarceration of minority group men. These explanations reveal different assumptions about changes (or not) in the gendered structure of drug markets and about the links (or not) between women's participation in crime and their domestic responsibilities.

[...]

This article presents the results of an ethnographic study of women drug users conducted during 1989–92 in a New York City neighborhood. We assess whether women's involvement in US drug markets of the mid-1980s onward reflects change, continuity, or a combination of change and continuity from patterns in previous decades. We find that [...] crack cocaine markets have not necessarily provided "new opportunities" for women, nor should such markets be viewed as "equal opportunity employers". Our

study suggests that recent drug markets continue to be monopolized by men and to offer few opportunities for stable income generation for women. While women's *presence* on the street and in low-level auxiliary roles may have increased, we find that their *participation* as substantive labor in the drug-selling marketplace has not.

[...]

Research Site and Methods

Research site

Bushwick, the principal study site, has been described as hosting "the most notorious drug bazaar in Brooklyn and one of the toughest in New York City" (*New York Times*, October 1, 1992: A1). [...] In 1960 the population was 89% white, 6% black, and 5% Hispanic. By 1990 it was 5% white, 25% black, and 65% Hispanic (Bureau of the Census, 1990). In 1990 Bushwick was Brooklyn's poorest neighborhood with a median household income of $16,287; unemployment was twice the citywide rate; and more than half of all families and two-thirds of all children lived under the official poverty line.

Fieldwork methods

Preliminary fieldwork began in the fall of 1989 when the senior author established a field presence in several Brooklyn neighborhoods (Williamsburg, East Flatbush, and Bushwick). By fall 1990 observations and interviews were intensified in Bushwick because it hosted the busiest street-level drug market in Brooklyn and had an active prostitution stroll. As fieldwork progressed, it became apparent that the initial plan of conducting interviews with a large number of women crack users was not, by itself, going to yield a complete picture. For example, few women initially admitted that they performed oral sex for less than $20, and none admitted to participating in sex-for-crack trades.

By the end of December 1991, interviews had been conducted with 211 active women crack users in Williamsburg, East Flatbush, and Bushwick. These were tape recorded and ranged from 20 minutes to

3 hours; they took place in a variety of settings, including private or semiprivate locations (e.g., apartments, shooting galleries, abandoned buildings, cars) and public locales (e.g., restaurants, parks, subways, and public toilets). From January to March 1992, a preliminary data sort was made of the interview and observational material. From that process, 45 women were identified for whom there were repeated observations and interview material. Contact with these women was intimate and extensive; the number of tape-recorded interviews for each woman ranged from 3 to 15. Unless otherwise noted, the research findings reported here are based on this smaller group of 45 Bushwick women.

Profile of the Bushwick women

The Bushwick women consisted of 20 Latinas (18 Puerto Ricans and 2 Dominicans), 16 African-Americans, and 9 European-Americans; their ages ranged from 19 to 41 years, with a mean of 28 years. At the time of the first interview, all the women used smokable cocaine (or crack), although only 31% used it exclusively; most (69%) had used heroin or powder cocaine prior to using crack. The women's average drug use history was 10.5 years (using the mean as the measure); heroin and powder cocaine initiates had a mean of about 12 years and the smokable cocaine initiates, about 6 years.

[...]

Structure of New York City crack markets

Street-level crack markets have frequently been characterized as unregulated markets of freelancers engaged in individual entrepreneurial activity. Some evidence suggests, however, that once demand has been established, the freelance model may be superseded by a more structured system of distribution. When the crack epidemic was at its peak in New York City during the late 1980s, Bushwick (like other neighborhoods) hosted highly structured street-level drug markets with pooled interdependence, vertical differentiation, and a formal, multi-tiered system of organization and control with defined employer–employee relationships. This model is similar to the "runner system" used in heroin distribution.

In selling crack cocaine, drug business "owners" employ several "crew bosses," "lieutenants," or "managers," who work shifts to ensure an efficient organization of street-level distribution. Managers (as they were known in Brooklyn) act as conduits between owners and lower-level employees. They are responsible for organizing and delivering supplies and collecting revenues. Managers exercise considerable autonomy in the hiring, firing, and payment of workers; they are responsible for labor force discipline and the resolution of workplace grievances and disputes. Next down the hierarchy are the street-level sellers, who perform retailing tasks having little discretion. Sellers are located in a fixed space or "spot" and are assisted by those below them in the hierarchy: lower-level operatives acting as "runners," "look-outs," "steerers," "touts," "holders," and "enforcers." Runners "continuously supply the sellers," look-outs "warn of impending dangers," steerers and touts "advertise and solicit customers," holders "handle drugs or money but not both," and enforcers "maintain order and intervene in case of trouble."

In New York City in the early 1990s, it was estimated that 150,000 people were involved in selling or helping to sell crack cocaine on any given day. Crack sales and distribution became a major source of income for the city's drug users. How, then, did the Bushwick women fit into this drug market structure? We examine women's involvement in a range of drug business activities.

Selling and distributing drugs

During the entire three years of fieldwork, including the interviews with the larger group of over 200 women, we did not discover any woman who was a business owner, and just one worked as a manager. The highly structured nature of the market in Bushwick, coupled with its kin-based organization, militated against personal or intimate sexual relationships between female drug users and higher-level male operatives. To the limited extent that they participated in drug selling, women were overwhelmingly concentrated at the lowest levels. They were almost always used as temporary workers when men were arrested or refused to work, or when

Table 30.1 Bushwick women's roles in the drug economy, 1989–92

	N	%
No role	26	58
Had some role	19	42
	45	100

Of the 19 women with roles in the drug economy during the three-year study period, the following shows what they did. Because most women (N = 13) had more than one role, the total sums to greater than 19.

Selling and distributing roles	
Owner	0
Manager	0
Regular seller	0
Irregular seller	7
Runner	0
Look-out	0
Steerer or tout	9
Holder	0
Enforcer	0
Selling/renting paraphernalia	
Works sellers	4
Stem renters	6
Running a gallery	3
Copping drugs for others	14
Other drug business hustles	
Street doc	1

Note: While we have tried to be precise, we should note that it can be difficult to characterize women's roles – not only because drug markets are fluid and shifting but also because some women had varied mixes of roles over time.

it was "hot" because of police presence. Table 30.1 shows how the 45 women were involved in Bushwick's drug economy.

Of the 19 women (42%) who had some involvement, the most common role was that of informal steerer or tout. This meant that they recommended a particular brand of heroin to newcomers to the neighborhood in return for "change," usually a dollar or so. These newcomers were usually white men, who may have felt more comfortable approaching women with requests for such information. In turn, the women's perceptions of "white boyz" enabled them to use the situation to their advantage. Although they only used

crack, Yolanda, a 38-year-old Latina, and Boy, a 26-year-old African-American woman, engaged in this practice of "tipping" heroin consumers.

> They come up to me. Before they come and buy dope and anything, they ask me what dope is good. I ain't done no dope, but I'm a professional player.... They would come to me, they would pay me, they would come "What's good out here?" I would tell them, "Where's a dollar," and that's how I use to make my money. Everyday somebody would come, "Here's a dollar, here's two dollars." (Yolanda) [What other kinds of things?] Bumming up change. [There ain't many people down here with change.] Just the white guys. They give you more faster than your own kind. [You go cop for them?] No, just for change. You tell them what's good on [the] dope side. Tell them anything, I don't do dope, but I'll tell them anything. Yeah, it's kicking live man. They buy it. Boom! I got my dollar, bye. (Boy)

[...]

Early in the fieldwork period (during 1989 and early 1990), both men and women perceived that more women were being offered opportunities to work as street-level sellers than in the past. Such opportunities, it turned out, were often part of a calculated risk-minimization strategy on the part of owners and managers. As Princess, a 32-year-old African-American woman, observed, some owners thought that women were less likely to be noticed, searched, or arrested by police:

> Nine times out of ten when the po-leece roll up it's gonna [be] men. And they're not allowed to search a woman, but they have some that will. But if they don' do it, they'll call for a female officer. By the time she gets there, (laughs) if you know how to move around, you better get it off you, unless you jus' want to go to jail. [So you think it works out better for the owners to have women working for them?] Yeah, to use women all the time.

As the fieldwork progressed and the neighborhood became more intensively policed, this view became less tenable. Latisha, a 32-year-old African-American woman, reported that the police became more aggressive in searching women:

> [You see some women dealing a little bit you know.] Yeah, but they starting to go. Now these cop around

here starting to unzip girls' pants and go in their panties. It was, it's not like it was before. You could stick the drugs in your panties' cause you're a female. Now that's garbage.

[…]

In previous years (the late 1970s and early 1980s), several Bushwick women had sold drugs in their roles as wives or girlfriends of distributors, but this was no longer the case. During the three-year study period only 12 women (27%) were involved in selling and distributing roles. Of this group of 12, only 7 were able to secure low-level selling positions on an irregular basis. Connie, a 25-year-old Latina, was typical of this small group, and in the following quotation she describes her unstable position within the organization she worked for:

> I'm currently working for White Top [crack]. They have a five bundle limit. It might take me an hour or two to sell that, or sometimes as quick as half an hour. I got to ask if I can work. They say yes or no.

Typically the managers said no to women's requests to work. Unlike many male street-level sellers who worked on a regular basis for this organization and were given "shifts" (generally lasting eight hours), Connie had to work off-hours (during daylight hours), which were often riskier and less financially rewarding. Temporary workers were usually given a "bundle limit" (one bundle contains 24 vials), which ensured that they could work only for short periods of time. As Cherrie, a 22-year-old Latina, said,

> The last time I sold it was Blue Tops [crack]. That was a week ago. [What, they asked you or you asked them to work?] Oh, they ask me, I say I want to work. [How come they asked you?] I don't know. They didn't have nobody to work because it was too hot out there. They was too full of cops.

Similarly, although Princess was well-known to the owners and managers of White Top crack, had worked for them many times in the past year, and had "proved" herself by having never once "stepped off" with either drugs or money, she was only given sporadic employment. She reported,

Sometime you can't [sell]. Sometime you can. That's why it's good to save money also. So when you don't get work. [How come they wouldn't give you work on some days?] Because of some favor that someone might've done or y'know, jus' … [It's not like they're trying to punish you?] No, but they will do that y'know. Somebody go and tell them something, "Oh, this one's doin' this to the bags or this one's doin' this to the bottles." OK, well they check the bags and they don' see nothin' wrong, but they came to look at it so they're pissed off so they'll take it away from you, y'know.

Violence and relationships

In addition to being vulnerable to arrest and street robbery, street-level sellers who use drugs constantly grapple with the urge to consume the product and to abscond with the drugs and/or the money. Retaliation by employers toward users who "mess up the money" was widely perceived to be swift and certain. Rachel, a 35-year-old European-American woman, said,

> Those Dominicans, if you step off with one piece of it, you're gonna get hurt. They don't play. They are sick people.

The prospect of violent retaliation may deter women from selling drugs. Boy, a 26-year-old African-American woman, put it this way:

> I don' like their [the managers'] attitude, like if you come up short, dey take it out on you … I don' sell no crack or dope for dese niggers. Because dey is crazy. Say for instance you short ten dollars, niggers come across you wit bats and shit. It's not worth it, you could lose your life. If dey say you are short, you could lose you life. Even if you were not short and dey say you is short, whatever dey say is gonna go, so you are fucked all the way around.

[…]

Relationships in the drug economy are fueled by contradictory expectations. On the one hand, attributes such as trust and reliability are frequently espoused as important to drug-selling organizations. On the other hand, ethnographic informants often refer to the lack of trust and solidarity among organization members. This lack of trust is evident in the constant "scams" sellers and managers pull on each other and the ever-present threat of violence in owner–manager–seller relations.

Strategies of protection and "being bad"

Women who work the streets to sell or buy drugs are subject to constant harassment and are regularly victimized. The Bushwick women employed several strategies to protect themselves. One of the most important was the adoption of a "badass," "crazy," or "gangsta bitch" stance or attitude, of which having a "bad mouth" was an integral part. As Latisha was fond of saying, "My heart pumps no Kool Aid. I don't even drink the shit." Or as Boy put it,

> Ac' petite, dey treat you petite. I mean you ac' soft, like when you dress dainty and shit ta come over here an' sit onna fuckin' corner. Onna corner an' smoke an you dressed to da teeth, you know, you soft. Right then and there you the center of the crowd, y'know what I'm sayin'? Now put a dainty one and put me, she looks soft. Dey look at me like "don't fuck wid dat bitch, she looks hard." Don' mess wit me caus I look hard y'know ... Dey don't fuck wit me out here. Dey think I'm crazy.

Acting bad and "being bad" are not the same. Although many Bushwick women presented themselves as "bad" or "crazy," this projection was a street persona and a necessary survival strategy. Despite the external manifestation of aggression, a posture and rhetoric of toughness, and the preemptive use of aggression, women were widely perceived (by men and women alike) as less likely to have the attributes associated with successful managers and street-level sellers. These included the requisite "street cred" and a "rep" for having "heart" or "juice" – masculine qualities associated with toughness and the capacity for violence. Women's abilities to "talk tough" or "act bad" were apparently not enough to inspire employer confidence. Prospective drug business employers wanted those capable of actually "being bad." Because female drug users were perceived as unreliable, untrustworthy, and unable to deploy violence and terror effectively, would-be female sellers were at a disadvantage.

Selling drug paraphernalia

In Bushwick the sale of drug paraphernalia such as crack stems and pipes was controlled by the bodegas, or corner stores, whereas syringes or "works" were the province of the street. Men dominated both markets although women were sometimes employed as part-time "works" sellers. Men who regularly sold "sealed" (i.e., new) works had suppliers (typically men who worked in local hospitals) from whom they purchased units called "ten packs" (10 syringes). The benefits of selling syringes were twofold: the penalties were less severe than those for selling drugs, and the rate of return was higher compared to the street-level sale of heroin or crack.[1]

The women who sold works were less likely than their male counterparts to have procured them "commercially." More often they "happened across" a supply of works through a family member or social contact who was a diabetic. Women were also more likely to sell works for others or to sell "used works." Rosa, a 31-year-old Latina, described in detail the dangerous practice of collecting used works strewn around the neighborhood. While she often stored them and later exchanged them for new works from the volunteer needle exchange (which was illegal at the time), Rosa would sometimes select the works she deemed in good condition, "clean" them with bleach and water, and resell them.

Although crack stems and pipes were available from neighborhood bodegas at minimal cost, some smokers chose not to carry stems. These users, almost exclusively men, were from outside the neighborhood. Their reluctance to carry drug paraphernalia provided the women with an additional source of income, usually in the form of a "hit," in exchange for the use of their stem. Sometimes these men were "dates," but more often they were "men on a mission" in the neighborhood or the "working men" who came to the area on Friday and Saturday nights to get high. As Boy put it,

> I be there on the block an' I got my stem and my lighter. I see them cop and I be askin' "yo, you need a stem, you need a light?" People say "yeah man," so they give me a piece.

An additional benefit for those women who rented their stems was the build up of crack residues in the stems. Many users savored this resin, which they allowed to accumulate before periodically digging it out with "scrapers" fashioned from the metal ribs of discarded umbrellas.

Some women also sold condoms, another form of drug-related paraphernalia in Bushwick. Although condoms were sold at bodegas, usually for $1 each, many of the women obtained free condoms from outreach health workers. Sometimes they sold them at a reduced price (usually 25 cents) to other sex workers, "white boyz," and young men from the neighborhood. Ironically, these same women would then have to purchase condoms at the bodegas when they had "smoked up" all their condoms.

Running shooting galleries

A wide range of physical locations were used for drug consumption in Bushwick. Although these sites were referred to generically as "galleries" by drug users and others in the neighborhood, they differed from the traditional heroin shooting gallery in several respects. Bushwick's "galleries" were dominated by men because they had the economic resources or physical prowess to maintain control. Control was also achieved by exploiting women drug users with housing leases. Such women were particularly vulnerable, as the following quotation from Carol, a 40-year-old African-American woman, shows:

> I had my own apartment, myself and my daughter. I started selling crack. From my house. [For who?] Some Jamaican. [How did you get hooked up with that?] Through my boyfriend. They wanted to sell from my apartment. They were supposed to pay me something like $150 a week rent, and then something off the profits. They used to, you know, fuck up the money, like not give me the money. Eventually I went through a whole lot of different dealers. Eventually I stopped payin' my rent because I wanted to get a transfer out of there to get away from everything, 'cause soon as one group of crack dealers would get out, another group would come along. [So how long did that go on for?] About four years. Then I lost my apartment, and I sat out in the street.

The few women who were able to maintain successful galleries operated with or under the control of a man or group of men. Cherrie's short-lived effort to set up a gallery in an abandoned burned-out building on "Crack Row" is illustrative. Within two weeks of establishing the gallery (the principal patrons of which were women), Cherrie was forced out of business by the police. The two weeks were marked by constant harassment, confiscation of drugs and property, damage to an already fragile physical plant, physical assaults, and the repeated forced dispersal of gallery occupants. Within a month, two men had established a new gallery on the same site, which, more than a year later, was thriving.

Such differential policing toward male- and female-operated galleries is explicable in light of the larger picture of law enforcement in low-income urban communities, where the primary function is not so much to enforce the law but rather to regulate illegal activities. Field observations suggest that the reason the police did not interfere as much with activities in the men's gallery was that they assumed that men were better able than women to control the gallery and to minimize problems of violence and disorder.

Other factors contributed to women's disadvantage in operating galleries, crack houses, and other consumption sites. Male drug users were better placed economically than the women in the sample, most of whom were homeless and without a means of legitimate economic support. When women did have an apartment or physical site, this made them a vulnerable target either for exploitation by male users or dealers (as in Carol's case) or for harassment by the police (as in Cherrie's). Even when a woman claimed to be in control of a physical location, field observations confirmed that she was not. Thus, in Bushwick, the presence of a man was a prerequisite to the successful operation of drug-consumption sites. The only choice for those women in a position to operate galleries or crack houses was between the "devils they knew" and those they did not.

Copping drugs

Many Bushwick women supplemented their income by "copping" drugs for others. They almost always copped for men, typically white men. At times these men were dates, but often they were users who feared being caught and wanted someone else to take that risk. As Rachel explained,

> I charge them, just what they want to buy they have to pay me. If they want twenty dollars they have to give me twenty dollars worth on the top because I'm risking my

free time. I could get busted copping. They have to pay me the same way, if not, they can go cop. Most of them can't because they don't know the people.

Those who cop drugs for others perform an important service for the drug market because as Biernacki (1979: 539) suggests in connection with heroin, "they help to minimize the possibility of infiltration by undercover agents and decrease the chance of a dealer's arrest." In Bushwick the copping role attracted few men; it was regarded by both men and women as a low-status peripheral hustle. Most women saw the female-dominated nature of the job to be part of the parallel sex market in the neighborhood. Outsiders could readily approach women to buy drugs under the guise of buying sex. As Rosa recounted,

> You would [be] surprise. They'd be ahm, be people very important, white people like lawyer, doctors that comes and get off, you'd be surprised. Iss like I got two lawyer, they give me money to go, to go and cop. And they stay down over there parking.... [How do you meet them?] Well down the stroll one time they stop and say you know, "You look like a nice girl though, you know, you wanna make some money fast?" I say, how? So they say you know, "Look out for me." First time they give me like you know, twenty dollars, you know. They see I came back, next time they give me thirty. Like that you know. I have been copping for them like over six months already.

Sometimes this function was performed in conjunction with sex work, as Latisha's comment illustrates,

> He's a cop. He's takin' a chance. He is petrified. Will not get out his car ... But he never gets less than nine bags [of powder cocaine]. [And he sends you to get it?] And he wants a blow job, right, okay. You know what he's givin' you, a half a bag of blue (blue bag cocaine). That's for you goin' to cop, and for the blow job. That's [worth] two dollars and fifty ... I can go to jail [for him]. I'm a piece of shit.

Women also felt that, given the reputation of the neighborhood as very "thirsty" (that is, as having a "thirst" or craving for crack), male outsiders were more likely to trust women, especially white women, to purchase drugs on their behalf. Often this trust was

misplaced. The combination of naive, inexperienced "white boyz" and experienced "street smart" women produced opportunities for additional income by, for example, simply taking the "cop" money. This was a calculated risk and sometimes things went wrong. A safer practice was to inflate the purchase price of the drugs and to pocket the difference. Rosa explained this particular scam,

> He think it a ten dollar bag, but issa five dollar. But at least I don't be rippin' him off there completely. [But you're taking the risk for him.] Exactly. Sometime he give me a hunert dollars, so I making fifty, right? But sometime he don't get paid, he got no second money, eh. I cop then when I come back the car, he say, "Dear I cannot give you nothin' today," you know. But I still like I say, I gettin' something from him because he think it a ten dollar bag.

Similar scams involved the woman's returning to the client with neither drugs nor money, claiming that she had been ripped off or, less often, shortchanging the client by tapping the vials (removing some crack) or adulterating the drugs (cutting powder cocaine or heroin with other substances). These scams reveal the diversity of women's roles as copping agents and their ingenuity in making the most of limited opportunities.

[...]

Discussion

A major dimension of drug economies, both past and present, is the "human qualities" believed necessary for the performance of various roles. Opportunities for income generation are defined, in part, by who has the necessary qualities or traits and who does not. These traits, whether grounded in cultural perceptions of biology and physiology (e.g., strength and capacity for violence), mental states (e.g., courage and aggressiveness), or kinship (e.g., loyalty and trustworthiness), are primarily differentiated along the lines of gender and race-ethnicity. In this study, we found that women were thought to be not as "strong" as men and that men, particularly black men and Latinos, were thought to be more "bad" and capable of "being bad." The gendered displays of violence that men incorporate into their work routines not only cement their solidarity as men, but also reinscribe these traits as masculine. As a consequence, men are able to justify the exclusion of women from more lucrative "men's work" in the informal economy. All the elements of underworld sexism identified by Steffensmeier (1983) – homosocial reproduction, sex-typing, and the qualities required in a violent task environment – featured prominently in Bushwick's street-level drug economy.

The significance of gender-based capacities and the symbolism used to convey them was evident in the women's use of instrumental aggression. Boy's discussion of how to "dress for success" on the streets reveals that power dressing is "dressing like a man" or "dressing down." It is anything but "dressing dainty." Both on the street and in the boardroom, it appears that a combination of clothing and attitude makes the woman. In the drug business, conveying the message "don't mess with me" is integral to maintaining a reputation for "craziness," which the women perceived as affording them some measure of protection.

The Bushwick women's experiences within a highly gender-stratified labor market provide a counter to the romantic notion of the informal drug economy as an "equal opportunity employer." Their experiences contradict the conventional wisdom, shaped by studies of the labor market experiences of minority group men, that the drug economy acts as a compensatory mechanism, offering paid employment that is not available in the formal labor force. While in theory the built-in supervision and task differentiation of the business model, which characterized drug distribution in Bushwick, should have provided opportunities to both men and women, our findings suggest that sellers were overwhelmingly men. Thus, the "new opportunities" said to have emerged with the crack-propelled expansion of drug markets from the mid-1980s onward were not "empty slots" waiting to be filled by those with the requisite skill. Rather, they were slots requiring certain masculine qualities and capacities.

[...]

Note

1   Street-level drug sellers typically made $1 on a $10 bag of heroin and 50 cents on a $5 vial of crack. Syringe sellers made at least $1.50 per unit, depending on the purchase price and the sale price.

References

Biernacki, Patrick. 1979. Junkie work, "hustles," and social status among heroin addicts. *Journal of Drug Issues* 9: 535–49.

Steffensmeier, Darrell. 1983. Organization properties and sex-segregation in the underworld: Building a sociological theory of sex differences in crime. *Social Forces* 61: 1010–32.

Questions

1   How do women's roles in the street-level drug economy compare and contrast with women's roles in upper echelon drug trafficking? What might account for these similarities and/or differences?

2   As women's opportunities have evolved and increased in the formal labor force over the last few decades, why do you think the same has not occurred in the illegitimate marketplace? Do you think the legalization and regulation of drugs would present equal opportunities for men and women in a new marketplace? Why or why not?

3   How might women working as street-level drug dealers be more vulnerable to the risks of violence than their male counterparts? How might the protection strategies used by women in the article, "acting bad" or "talking tough," actually perpetuate violence against them? How did the police contribute to the gender dynamics of the illegal marketplace?

An Economic Analysis of a Drug-Selling Gang's Finances

Steven D. Levitt and Sudhir Alladi Venkatesh

Building on Maher and Daley's description of the stratification hierarchy of drug dealing, Steven Levitt and Sudhir Venkatesh report on their investigation of inner-City Chicago crack dealing gangs. Living in the projects, these poor, Black men come from the lowest rung of the socioeconomic strata. This selection discusses the occupational structure of this gang, the earning potential of people at the various rungs, the risk of violence, and then compares what a person from this background could earn working at a minimum wage job, such as at McDonalds, to holding the most common gang dealing job: the foot soldier.

As you read this, you may want to think about the contrast between these drug dealers and Maher and Daley's women, Valdez, Nowotny, and Cepeda's Mexican Americans, Mohamed and Fritsvold's college dealers, and Adler's upper-level dealers and smugglers. Ask yourself what these groups have in common and what differentiates them. How are the drug markets portrayed differently in structure, fluidity, composition, profitability, and violence? What kinds of factors cause these differences: the drugs, the social class, the racial/ethnic composition, the gender, the time period, the location, or others? How does this compare to the image of drug dealing conveyed for organized criminals, such as the Mafia, in popular films and television?

Do you buy the argument the authors put forth about how gang earnings compare to minimum wage jobs? Do you think the gang members would? Aside from money, what sorts of other benefits do people gain from this kind of gang membership and dealing? What other options seem to be available to them? Finally, is there anything we could do to change that?

Drugs and the American Dream: An Anthology, First Edition. Edited by Patricia A. Adler, Peter Adler, and Patrick K. O'Brien.
© 2012 John Wiley & Sons, Inc. Published 2012 by John Wiley & Sons, Inc.

Street gangs have a long history in American cities. Until recently, gangs were organized primarily as social peer groups. Any economic activities were of secondary importance. The last two decades, however, have given rise to a dramatic transformation in street gangs, or what Taylor [1990] terms their "corporatization." When crack became widely available in the mid-1980s, sold in small quantities in fragmented street-corner markets, street gangs became the logical distributors. The potential profit in drug dealing dwarfed that previously available to gangs through other criminal channels. As a consequence, gangs became systematically involved in the distribution of various narcotic substances including heroin and crack-cocaine.

[...]

A number of researchers have estimated the returns to crime and drug selling through the use of self-reports. The returns to drug selling tend to be much greater than that of other criminal activities, with frequent drug sellers reporting mean annual incomes in the range of $20,000–$30,000. Studies relying on ethnographic observation, however, find much lower values for drug-related earnings. One explanation for this discrepancy is that the self-report and ethnographic studies have focused on very different populations. The self-report studies have tended to survey independent drug dealers, i.e., those with no gang affiliation, whereas ethnographic research has focused on low-level members of a hierarchy. Independents are likely to have greater ability, experience, and access to capital than "foot soldiers" who sit at the low end of the street gang's organizational hierarchy. Our data, which span the levels of a gang hierarchy, from rank-and-file members to imprisoned leaders, offer a partial solution to this problem. Higher-level gang members may tend to have similar characteristics to independents.

In contrast to the returns to crime, there has been little attention paid to the "career path" of gang members, market structure, organizational forms, competitive strategies, and how economic activity is structured in the absence of legally enforceable contracts. In this paper we are able to directly analyze for the first time a wide range of economic issues related to gangs and drug distribution. We do so through the use of a unique data set containing detailed financial information over a recent four-year period for a now-defunct gang. These data were maintained by the leader of the group as a management tool for tracking the gang's financial activities and for monitoring the behavior of gang members. Updated monthly, the data include breakdowns of costs and revenues into major components, as well as information on the distribution of profits as wages to gang members at different levels of the hierarchy. Information on both price and quantity is included. These financial data are supplemented with information on the numbers of violent deaths, injuries, and arrests of gang members over this period, as well as interviews and observational analysis of the gang. While the data suffer from important limitations and a number of potential biases (which appear below), they nonetheless represent a substantial improvement on previously available information.

Using these data, we analyze the extent to which the individual and collective actions of gang participants can reasonably be characterized as emanating out of economic maximization. We address three different issues in this regard. First, we examine the economic returns to drug dealing relative to legitimate labor market activities. The higher the returns to drug selling, the more likely it is that the economic aspects of the gang are paramount. We then consider the causes and consequences of gang wars. Finally, we analyze the risk trade-offs made by gang members and whether these can be reconciled with optimizing decision making.

A number of insights emerge from the paper. Street-level sellers appear to earn roughly the minimum wage. Earnings within the gang are enormously skewed, however, with high-level gang members earning far more than their legitimate market alternative. Thus, the primary economic motivation for low-level gang members appears to be the possibility of rising up through the hierarchy, as in the tournament model of Lazear and Rosen [1981]. The average wage in the gang (taking into account all levels of the hierarchy) is perhaps somewhat above the available legitimate market alternatives, but not appreciably higher.

Gang wars are costly, both in terms of lost lives and lost profits. Almost all of the deaths of drug sellers are concentrated in war periods. Moreover, the violence keeps customers away. This negative shock to demand is associated with a fall of 20–30 percent in both the price and quantity of drugs sold during fighting, and the drug operation becomes far less profitable. In spite of this, the gang discussed in this paper fights with rivals roughly one-fourth of the time. Gang wars are also an extremely costly means of dispute resolution, but given the absence of legally enforceable property rights and contracts, other means of resolving conflicts may be circumscribed. There is also evidence that frequent gang wars are the result of an agency problem, namely the desire of low-level gang members to build a reputation for toughness may be in their personal interest, but will almost assuredly be costly to the gang as a whole. [...]

Finally, drug selling is an extremely dangerous activity. Death rates in the sample are 7 percent annually. Given the relatively low economic returns to drug selling noted above, the implied willingness to accept risk on the part of the participants is orders of magnitude higher than is typically observed in value of life calculations. This suggests either that gang members have very unusual preferences, that the ex post realization of death rates was very different than the ex ante expectation, systematic miscalculation of risk, or the presence of important noneconomic considerations.

Based on these findings, we conclude that even in this gang – one of the most economically sophisticated and successful gangs – the decision making of members is difficult (but not impossible) to reconcile with that of optimizing economic agents. Certainly, economic considerations play an important role in the decisions of members and the activities of the gang. However, we find that social/nonpecuniary factors are likely to play an important role as well. Of course, all of these conclusions are based on the analysis of a single gang's experience. The degree to which these results are broadly generalizable remains an open question.

The Gang and the Social, Economic, and Competitive Environment in Which it Operates

The gang for which we have data is located in an inner-city neighborhood in a large, industrial American city. [...] Residents of the area are almost exclusively African-American (over 99 percent), as are all of the gang members. The labor market experiences of the residents, particularly males, are far worse than those in the United States as a whole. Unemployment rates for males in 1990 were over 35 percent – six times higher than the national average. In addition, over 40 percent of males were not in the labor force. The female unemployment rates are roughly half of the male unemployment rate.

Children in the neighborhood experience high probabilities of adverse economic circumstances. Over half of the children were below the poverty line at the time of the 1990 census. More than three-quarters of all children live in single-parent families, and 60 percent are in families that receive public assistance.

Median family income is $15,077 annually, less than half of the national average. A small fraction of the census tract is public housing, although the immediate neighborhood in which the gang operates does not include any large-scale public-housing complexes. Roughly half of adults in the community do not have a high-school diploma. Only one in twenty residents has a degree from a four-year college, compared with one in five Americans generally.

[...]

The organizational structure of the gang as a whole is shown in Figure 31.1. We use the titles used by the gang, except where those titles would reveal the gang's identity. The structure of the organization is simple compared with most firms of comparable size. The toplevel of the organization is made up of what we broadly denote the "central leadership." This body is chaired by four to six individuals with responsibility for devising the long-term strategies of the multistate organization, and maintaining relationships with suppliers and affiliates in other regions of the country. The central leadership also includes approximately twelve persons who are responsible for collecting dues, overseeing recruitment of new members, allocating punishments, and serving as liaisons to the community. Roughly one-third of these leaders are imprisoned at any given time. The next tier in the organization is a group of "local gang leaders" with specific territorial responsibility for one or more localized gangs. In the organization we study, there are

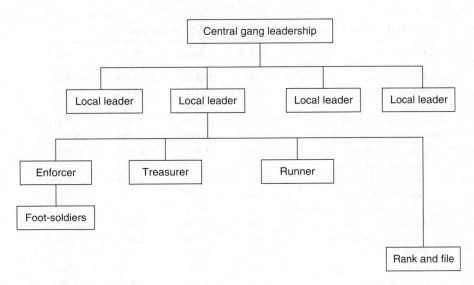

Figure 31.1 Organizational structure

roughly 100 of such gang leaders. Reporting in to each gang leader are three "officers." The "enforcer" is responsible for ensuring the safety of group members, the "treasurer" manages the liquid assets of the group, and the "runner" performs the risky task of transporting large quantities of drugs and money to and from the supplier. Reporting to the enforcer are the "foot soldiers" who serve as street-level drug sellers and from whose ranks future officers and leaders arise. Foot soldiers are typically 16–22 years of age, although potentially much older. At the periphery of the gang is a "rank-and-file" member pool who span all ages (the age range in the group we study is 14 to 40) and who have little formal responsibility for drug selling. Rank and file, unlike foot soldiers and higher gang members, pay dues to the gang, in return receiving protection, status, and a reliable supply of drugs for those who deal independently.

The structure of the overall organization is similar to that of a franchised company. Gang leaders pay a fee to the franchisers (central leadership), but are the residual claimants on the profits accruing to their franchise. In return for those tribute payments, higher-ranking leaders ensure that a local gang has sufficient protection (both on their turf and in prison), stable alliances with other gang sets such that gang members can travel to other areas of the city with relative safety,

access to reliable sources of wholesale drugs, and the possibility for members to rise up the hierarchy into the upper echelon, where personal revenue and power are considerably enhanced. The individual, local gang units, like separate franchise owners, have relatively little interaction with one another.

The data that we have are for just one gang within the larger organizational structure. That gang is overseen by a local gang leader, and has one enforcer, one treasurer, and one runner at any given point in time. The number of foot soldiers ranges between 25 and 75 over the period examined, and there are 60 to 200 rank and file. At any given point in time, roughly one-fourth of the males aged 16–22 in the neighborhood are foot soldiers.

[...]

Data and Descriptive Statistics

The data set contains detailed financial information on the activities of the gang described above on a monthly basis for a recent four-year period. The data were originally maintained by the leader in control of the gang, and they were updated each month by the enforcer, who compiled the information by hand. The data end abruptly with the arrest of the gang leader

Table 31.1   Gang finances by year, monthly averages in 1995 dollars

Category	Year 1	Year 2	Year 3	Year 4
Total revenues	18,500	25,600	32,000	68,400
Drug sales	11,900	19,100	24,800	53,000
Dues	5,400	5,200	5,100	9,600
Extortionary taxes	1,200	1,300	2,100	5,800
Total nonwage costs	8,100	11,600	14,000	25,200
Cost of drugs sold	2,800	4,000	5,000	11,900
Tribute to gang hierarchy	3,200	4,400	5,000	6,000
Mercenary fighters	1,000	1,000	1,300	1,200
Funerals/payments to families of the deceased	300	1,200	0	1,100
Weapons	300	400	300	1,800
Miscellaneous expenses	500	800	2,400	3,200
Total gang wages	6,200	8,000	9,500	32,300
Officers	2,600	2,600	2,100	3,300
Foot soldiers	3,600	5,400	7,400	29,000
Net profit accruing to leader	4,200	6,000	8,500	10,900
Monthly wage per foot soldier	140	200	180	470
Price and quantity of drugs sold:				
Quantity	1,310	2,054	3,109	7,931
Price	8.64	9.18	8.00	6.69

and other officers. Shortly thereafter, the gang, weakened by these arrests and beset by infighting, was overpowered by rivals, its turf divided between enemy gangs. The gang we study is no longer in operation. Most of the former gang members have since abandoned drug dealing. The person who supplied us the data is a former gang member with ties to the gang that tracked the data (although he was not necessarily directly affiliated with this particular group). Our informant, after serving a prison sentence, now holds a full-time job in the legitimate sector. For obvious reasons, we have accommodated his request to remain anonymous.

Given the unusual nature of the data, it is important to consider both its reliability and the degree to which it is representative of gangs more generally. On the most basic question of authenticity, we have no reason to doubt that the data actually represent the financial records of the gang. In terms of understanding the possible biases in the data, it is worth noting that it served two purposes: (1) a tool for managing the day-to-day operations of the gang, much as a CEO

relies on management information systems (MIS) data in a firm, and (2) a means of tracking operations for reporting to higher levels in the gang hierarchy. [...]

The data contain monthly breakdowns of the major sources of revenues and expenditures for the gang. Table 31.1 presents monthly averages for each of the four years covered. [...] Revenues are broken down into three sources: proceeds from drug sales (almost exclusively crack-cocaine), dues from gang members, and "street taxes," i.e., money extorted from individuals (and occasionally companies) conducting business on the gang's turf. Examples of those required to pay street taxes would include grocery store owners, gypsy cabs, people selling stolen goods, and those providing services such as auto or plumbing repair. Average monthly revenue from all sources for the gang rose from $18,500 to $68,400 over the period examined. [...] Proceeds from the sale of crack are the gang's major source of income, and growth in drug sales accounts for virtually all of the increase in revenue over time. Dues collected from gang members are nearly constant until the final year, when the gang membership expands dramatically with the expanded turf. It is important to note that in this gang, core gang members (i.e., officers and foot soldiers) were not required to pay dues. Only the peripheral members of the gang (i.e., rank and file) paid these fees.

Although the revenue numbers may appear low, "back-of-the-envelope" calculations suggest that they are reasonable. Using these revenue figures and average dollars per sale of $10, we estimate that the number of sales per hour by a drug-selling team ranges from five to twelve over the sample. That frequency of sale is consistent with self-reports of the participants as well as recent observational data we have collected in similar neighborhoods.

In the original data, the nonwage costs are broken down into six categories: costs of drugs sold, payments to higher levels of the gang, weapons, payments to mercenary fighters (nongang members who are hired for short periods of time to help fight in gang wars), funeral costs and payments to families of the deceased, and miscellaneous expenses.

The greatest nonwage expenditure of the gang was the regular tribute payment to higher levels of the gang. Such payments amount to almost 20 percent of total revenues. Expenditures related to drugs comprise the next largest nonwage cost component, accounting for 15 percent of total revenue, and almost 25 percent of drug sales. The price paid by the gang to obtain powder cocaine, which is subsequently transformed into crack by the gang for resale on the street, declines roughly 35 percent over the sample period, reflecting a citywide decline in the price of bulk cocaine. Surprisingly, there appears to be substantial imprecision in the measurements used in these bulk drug transactions. Standard units such as kilograms and pounds are not used by the gang (although the supplier does use such units). Quantities instead are described in various "street" units that we are able to only roughly translate into kilograms. Thus, we report our results in an artificial unit ("bags") that approximates the standard quantity in which street sales occur, rather than in kilograms. While this choice of units is essentially arbitrary, it has the attractive feature of roughly capturing the number of sales made by the gang in a month. A bag contains an extremely small quantity of crack-cocaine (e.g., a few pebbles) and typically sells for about $10 on the street. By our calculations, between 10,000 and 15,000 bags can be produced from one kilogram of powder cocaine, making the street value of a kilogram of pure cocaine converted into crack between $100,000 and $150,000.

[...]

Another important expenditure item is for mercenary fighters known as "warriors" whom the gang hires on a retainer basis to fight in wars. Fees for warriors are roughly $2,000 per person per month of service. The warriors have various duties including guarding areas where drugs are sold, occupying front-line positions on the gang's turf, and performing drive-by shootings. The use of hired warriors declines at the end of the sample as the gang increasingly chose to use internal resources (foot soldiers) for fighting rather than contracting-out this task. This decision on the part of the gang appears to be linked in part to its difficulty in controlling the expanded turf, over which the gang had no inherent legitimacy. The original territory was much easier to defend because the gang's roots were in their original neighborhood and the "original" gang members continued to reside there. Furthermore, prior to expansion, all of the gang violence involved the gang to the north. After the takeover, the gang's enemies increase in number, leading to a rise in the baseline frequency of violence when discrete wars are not taking place. Consequently, developing this fighting expertise within the organization became more valuable.

Funerals and related expenses such as compensating victims' families are costly to the gang. Typically, for a foot soldier who is killed, the gang pays $5,000, or approximately three years of foot-soldier wages, to his family for compensation and funeral services. Such payments are viewed as extremely important by the gang leaders, both to maintain community support for the gang and because, in the words of one gang leader, "*You got to respect family.*" Interestingly, when the gang expanded, members conscripted from the former rival outfit were treated much less generously than were those who belonged to the original gang.

The purchase of weapons, at a cost of $300–$400 per month, is initially a relatively small component of gang costs. Expenditure on weapons increases dramatically in the final year, both due to increased fighting, and because the gang reduced its reliance on outside warriors, choosing instead to defend itself. Combined with miscellaneous expenses, all of these nonwage costs total to just less than 50 percent of revenues.

The remainder of the revenues are distributed as wages to gang members, or are retained by the gang leader as profits. The earnings of the gang members involved with drug distribution are the focus of the next section.

The Economic Returns to Drug Selling in the Gang

In this section we attempt to measure the economic return to selling drugs in the gang. We begin with the "official" data reported in the gang's books. Later, we incorporate "off-the-books" sources of income as well.

An individual's rank within the gang is of critical importance for his personal remuneration. The local gang leader is the residual claimant on drug profits. As shown in Table 31.1 the gang leader retains between $4,200 and $10,900 a month as profit, for an annual wage of $50,000–130,000. This value is well above what leaders could hope to earn in the legitimate sector given their education and work experience. For instance, a former leader of a rival gang is now employed in the legitimate sector at an annual salary of $16,000. His legitimate sector wage may be lower than it otherwise would have been, however, due to his intervening years spent in prison.

The officers each earn roughly $1,000 per month. This wage is relatively constant, although in war periods reductions sometimes occur. These tasks are generally full-time jobs (in the sense that the people who perform them would be unlikely to be concurrently employed in the legitimate sector, although they may not strictly involve 40 hours of work per week). The standard of living associated with holding these jobs is only slightly higher than a full-time minimum wage job.

This gang is unusual in that foot soldiers for the most part received a flat wage. Compensation was not directly linked to the volume of sales. Their wage depended both on the number of shifts in which they distributed crack and on their position within their drug-selling team. Crack was sold in teams of six foot soldiers, with a team leader, a carrier who delivers the goods, two laborers who package the goods, make change, etc., and a lookout. Wages were highest for the team leader and lowest for the lookout who is typically an entry level foot soldier.

[...]

Official monthly payments to each foot soldier are low: only $200 per month or less until the final year. Based on observation and discussion with the gang leader, we estimate that the typical foot soldier worked four four-hour shifts per week selling drugs, and performed approximately four hours of other tasks for the gang, for a total of twenty hours of work per week. Hours worked per person appear to have stayed relatively constant over time. The increased demand for labor by the gang was accomplished through an expansion of the number of foot soldiers from approximately 25 at the beginning of the time period to over 60 in the final year. Based on these estimates of hours worked, the hourly wage earned by the typical foot soldier was below the federal minimum wage.

While these foot-soldier wages are strikingly low, [...] it is hardly surprising that foot-soldier wages would be low given the minimal skill requirements for the job and the presence of a "reserve army" of potential replacements among the rank and file. [...] Empirically, the behavior of the foot soldiers suggests that they are not well off financially. First, gang members below the level of gang leaders live with family because they cannot afford to maintain a separate residence. Second, many foot soldiers also hold low-paying jobs in the legitimate sector, typically working as service-sector employees in shopping malls and fast-food restaurants, performing physical labor such as demolition, or working in small local businesses like dry cleaners or grocery stores. We estimate that 75–80 percent of the foot soldiers are employed in the legitimate sector at some point over the course of a year. Job tenure, however, is generally quite low, so that perhaps only 40–50 percent of the foot soldiers are employed in the legitimate sector at any given point in time. Previous research suggests that even among well-paid drug sellers, more than 25 percent participate in the legitimate economy. The higher numbers we obtain for legitimate labor market participation are consistent with the lower drug-related earnings of the foot soldiers in our sample.

[...]

Given the enormous gap between the wages of the foot soldiers and those higher up in the gang, the most reasonable way to view the economic aspects of the

Table 31.2   Gang participation as a tournament

	Estimated hourly wage including only official income sources			Estimated hourly wage including both official and unofficial income sources		
	Average wage for all gang members	Gang leader wage	Foot soldier wage	Average wage for all gang members	Gang leader wage	Foot soldier wage
Year 1	$4.80	$25.20	$1.70	$ 5.90	$32.30	$2.50
Year 2	$5.90	$36.00	$2.40	$ 7.40	$47.50	$3.70
Year 3	$5.60	$51.00	$2.20	$ 7.10	$65.90	$3.30
Year 4	$8.70	$65.40	$5.60	$11.10	$97.20	$7.10

decision to join the gang is as a tournament, i.e., a situation in which participants vie for large awards that only a small fraction will eventually obtain [Lazear and Rosen 1981]. Gang members themselves appear to be keenly aware of this, as evidenced by the following quote from a foot soldier: "You think I wanta be selling drugs on the street my whole life? No way. But I know these n------ [above me] are making more money, and it's like, people don't last long doing this s---. So you know, I figure I got a chance to move up. But if not, s---, I get me a job doin' something else."

Table 31.2 presents empirical documentation of the tournament aspects of gang participation. [...] Columns 1–3 present average wages under the assumption that the official data fully capture the wages and profits to the organization. Columns 4–6 adjust the official data under the assumption that the gang leader fails to report 10 percent of drug revenues and the foot soldiers skim an additional 15 percent. Focusing on that second set of estimates, which we believe to be more representative, the average wage in the organization ranges from $5.90–$11.10 during the sample period. This value is above legitimate market wages available to the foot soldiers, who, as poorly educated inner-city youths, are unlikely to earn much more than the minimum wage. As discussed later, however, the wage premium earned by gang members is quite small given the enormous risks associated with selling drugs.

Table 31.2 demonstrates the enormous skew in the distribution of wages within the gang. The gang leader earns 10–20 times more than the average foot soldier. While this earnings gap is small compared with frequently cited numbers about CEO pay, it should be noted that the gang leader to whom we refer has only

a few hundred employees, and is two levels in the hierarchy below those who run the gang organization. [...] To the extent that employees of franchises appear to be paid more than the foot soldiers, the distribution of wages is more skewed in the gang than in the typical franchise.

[...]

The Dangers of Drug Selling and the Willingness of Gang Members to Accept Risk

Table 31.3 presents information on the frequency of adverse events in our sample, expressed in terms of likelihood per gang member per month. Results are separately compiled for war and nonwar months before and after the takeover, and for the transition period. These data are based on field notes compiled concurrent with the events. The number of deaths is complete and accurate. The counts on injuries and arrests represent lower bounds as some of these might have been left out of the field notes. Unfortunately, we do not have good information on time served in jail or prison by the gang members as a consequence of these arrests.

Table 31.3 highlights the tremendous risks associated with participation in the drug trade, at least in this particular gang during times of fighting. The per-person likelihood of death ranges from 1 to 2 percent a month during gang wars and the transition period. Using the actual number of months in the sample falling into each category (listed in the bottom row of the table), it is possible to construct the cumulative frequency of adverse events per gang

Table 31.3   Frequency of adverse events

| | Likelihood of occurrence per person-month | | | | | |
| | Preexpansion | | | Postexpansion | | |
Adverse event	Gang war	No gang war	Transition period	Gang war	No gang war	Cumulative frequency over four-year period
Violent death	0.012	0	0.018	0.021	0.002	0.277
Nonfatal wound or injury	0.078	0.033	0.100	0.075	0.051	2.40
Arrest	0.155	0.103	0.214	0.219	0.133	5.94
Number of months in sample	9	17	5	3	8	42

member over the four-year period observed. That number is displayed in the last column of Table 31.3. Gang members who were active for the entire four-year period had roughly a one in four chance of dying. Furthermore, there was an average of over two nonfatal injuries (mostly gunshot, but some due to knives or fists) per member, and almost six arrests. The risks associated with selling drugs in this sample are astonishing. By comparison, homicide victimization rates for black males aged 14–17 in the United States are roughly 1 in 1000 per year, about 1/80 the rate we observe in this sample. Even among rank and file of this gang (those affiliated with the gang, but not actively engaged in the drug trade), homicide rates are only about 1 in 200 annually in our sample.

Using the frequency of adverse events, it is possible to calculate a rough estimate of the willingness of the foot soldiers to accept risk of death or, extrapolating, the implicit valuation they place on their own lives in the current context. In order for such calculations to be reasonable, the participants must be relatively well-informed about the rewards and risks, and the ex post outcomes must be consistent with ex ante projections. We generate estimates using four different possible comparisons. In each instance, we focus only on the likelihood of death, ignoring differences in the number of injuries or arrests. [...]

The first comparison is between foot-soldier wages in war and nonwar months in the preexpansion portion of our sample. The average monthly wage in war and nonwar months is calculated to be $250 and $150, respectively, or a $100 differential. Given an observed differential in the chance of violent death of .012 per month from Table 31.3, the implied value

of a life is a little over $8,000. This number may be unrealistically low because foot soldiers may be compelled to sell drugs during war months through threats of punishment – in some gangs compulsion may be quite pronounced with high exit costs. Furthermore, to the extent that heroic actions in wars are rewarded with promotions, this static analysis may not adequately capture the trade-offs involved in war months. Certainly, acts of heroism by soldiers in wartime periods are not uncommon, further calling into question the relevance of this particular calculation as a measure of willingness to accept risk.

A second possible approach relies on a comparison of foot soldier wages pre- and postexpansion. In contrast to the previous measure, this calculation may systematically overstate the value of a life since the overall profitability of the drug operation is increasing over time. Thus, part of the wage increase may not be due to the increased risk in the latter part of the sample, but to other factors. Taking a weighted average over all relevant months, average foot-soldier wages rise from $185 per month before expansion to $570 after expansion. [...] This approach yields an implicit valuation of $127,000 on a foot-soldier life.

The final two comparisons are between gang wages and market wages (both before and after expansion). We use an (after-tax) market wage of $4.00 as the baseline. We also assume that the likelihood of violent death is zero for nongang members. The *average* gang wage before expansion is $6.60. Assuming twenty hours of work a week, the gang premium translates into an extra $220 per month. Given a .00415 chance of death per month, the implicit valuation on life is $53,000. A similar calculation for the postexpansion period yields a valuation of $90,000. Note that these last two comparisons may overstate the willingness to accept risk if gang work is more pleasant than a formal-sector job or there are nonpecuniary benefits associated with gang membership.

In all four scenarios examined, foot soldiers demonstrate an apparent willingness to accept risks of death in return for small amounts of financial compensation. The values obtained in this paper are far below those typically found in the literature. Our results are consistent with the matter-of-fact manner in which foot soldiers speak about death. For instance, one nineteen-year-old foot soldier described his situation as follows, "It's a war out here, man. I mean everyday people struggling to survive, so you know, we just do what we can. We ain't got no choice, and if that means getting killed, wells---, it's what n------ do around here to feed their family."

[...]

Conclusion

This paper provides the first detailed analysis of the financial activities of an entrepreneurial street gang. The data imply that for this gang drug dealing is not particularly lucrative, yielding average wages only slightly above those of the legitimate sector. Hourly wages for those on the lowest rung of the gang hierarchy are no better than the minimum wage. The wage structure within the gang is highly skewed, however, so that the more reasonable way to measure the economic rationale for gang participation is in the context of a tournament. Gang wars are extremely costly in terms of injuries, death, and profits. Nonetheless, fighting takes place over roughly one-fourth of the sample. The willingness to accept a risk of death among gang members appears to be extremely high.

Taken as a whole, our results suggest that even in this financially sophisticated "corporate" gang, it is difficult (but not impossible) to reconcile the behavior of the gang members with an optimizing economic model without assuming nonstandard preferences or bringing in social/nonpecuniary benefits of gang participation. Similarly, while certain business practices such as frequent gang wars and pricing below marginal cost can be fit into a framework of economic maximization, the possibility of suboptimal decision making cannot be eliminated from consideration.

[...]

References

Lazear, Edward, and Sherwin Rosen, "Rank Order Tournaments as Optimum Labor Contracts, *Journal of Political Economy*, 89 (1981), 841–64.

Taylor, Carl, *Dangerous Society* (East Lansing: Michigan State University Press, 1990).

Questions

1   How do you think the lives of the middle- to upper-class drug dealers in Adler's article compare and contrast with those of the higher-level gang members in this article? How do both differ from the low-level street dealers? What role do you think race and/or socioeconomic status might play in these differences? What about geographic location?

2   How does the bureaucratic structure of the gang in the article resemble that of a legitimate business or corporation? How does this article dispel or confirm commonly held myths about the lives of inner-city drug dealers? Why do you think so many of the foot soldiers also participated in the legitimate labor force?

3   According to the article, given the enormous gap between the wages of the foot soldiers and the higher-ups in the gang, the most reasonable way to view the economic aspects of the decision to join the gang is as a tournament. How does the idea of a "tournament," as presented in the article resemble the quest for the American Dream in our society?

Crime and Violence

The Drugs/Violence Nexus
A Tripartite Conceptual Framework

Paul J. Goldstein

Paul Goldstein examines the relationship between drugs and violence in this classic selection drawn from New York City Black ghettos. He suggests that there are certain kinds of violence typically associated with drugs, and that drug violence occurs in predictable times, places, and ways. As you read this, you may want to think about which drugs are the most likely to be associated with violent activity and which the least. Does this run contrary to media-generated impressions? Which of these might need to be corrected? How might Goldstein's conceptions be different if he was conducting his research on a different racial/ethnic group? Gender group? Age group? Class group?

Does his depiction fit with some of the other portrayals we have read about? What do you think about the psychopharmacological model? What other readings might challenge this, if any? What about the economic-compulsive model? Would this apply to different drugs or different populations? What about the systemic model? Would this apply to different rungs of dealing, different geographic locales, different periods in time, different racial/ethnic groups, different gender groups, or different age groups? How do you think this compares to the gang dealing portrayed by Levitt and Venkatesh and Valdez, Nowotny, and Cepeda? Is individual drug dealing more or less violent than that conducted by organized groups? Why?

Drug use, as well as the social context in which that use occurs, are etiological factors in a wide range of other social phenomena. Drug use is known to be causally related to a variety of physical and mental health problems, crime, poor school performance, family disruption, and the like. Previous research has also consistently found strong connections between drugs and violence.

[...]

The drugs/violence nexus also appears consistently in newspaper headlines. For example, a seventeen year old boy who committed suicide by hanging himself in his jail cell had earlier confessed to committing a ritual stabbing and mutilation killing of another youth because he believed the boy had stolen ten bags of PCP from him. A New York City Transit policeman was beaten with his own nightstick and his chin was nearly bitten off by a farebeater who was high on angel dust. A thirty-nine year old mother of three was killed by a stray bullet fired during a fight between drug dealers on the lower east side of Manhattan. A front page headline in the *New York Times* (October 29, 1984) claimed that "Increase in Gang Killings on Coast is Traced to Narcotics Trafficking." Less than a month later, another *New York Times* front page headline announced that "Cocaine Traffickers Kill 17 in Peru Raid on Antidrug Team." A Miami police official was quoted on television as saying that one-third of the homicides in Miami in 1984 were cocaine related.

[…]

While the association between drugs and violence appears strong, and drug use and trafficking appear to be important etiological factors in the incidence of violence, there has been little effort to place this relationship into a conceptual framework to guide further empirical research. The purpose of this paper is to introduce such a framework.

Information for this report was gathered during the course of three separate empirical investigations. Sixty women were interviewed in 1976 and 1977 for a study of the relationship between prostitution and drugs (Goldstein, 1979). Between 1978 and 1982, an ethnographic study was undertaken of the economic behavior of 201 street opiate users in Harlem. Finally, in 1984, I began a study of the relationship between drugs and violence on the lower east side of Manhattan. That study is guided by the conceptual framework presented below.

Drugs and violence are seen as being related in three possible ways: the psychopharmacological, the economically compulsive, and the systemic. Each of these models must be viewed, in a theoretical sense, as "ideal types," i.e., as hypothetically concrete "... devices intended to institute comparisons as precise as the stage of one's theory and the precision of one's instruments allow" (Martindale, 1959: 58–9). In fact, it will be shown below that there can be overlap between the three models. However, this overlap does not detract from the heuristic value of the tripartite conceptual framework.

Psychopharmacological Violence

The psychopharmacological model suggests that some individuals, as a result of short or long term ingestion of specific substances, may become excitable, irrational, and may exhibit violent behavior. The most relevant substances in this regard are probably alcohol, stimulants, barbiturates, and PCP. […]

Early reports which sought to employ a psychopharmacological model to attribute violent behavior to the use of opiates and marijuana have now been largely discredited. In a classic statement of this point, Kolb argued the following.

> There is probably no more absurd fallacy prevalent, than the notion that murders are committed and daylight robberies and holdups are carried out by men stimulated by large doses of cocaine or heroin which have temporarily distorted them into self-imagined heroes incapable of fear ... violent crime would be much less prevalent if all habitual criminals were addicts who could obtain sufficient morphine or heroin to keep themselves fully charged with one of these drugs at all times. (Kolb, 1925: 78)

Kolb's point must be modified in one very important way. He is correct in claiming that ingestion of opiates is unlikely to lead to violence. However, the irritability associated with the withdrawal syndrome from opiates may indeed lead to violence. For example, in previous research on the relationship between drugs and prostitution I found that heroin using prostitutes often linked robbing and/or assaulting clients with the withdrawal experience (Goldstein, 1979). These women reported that they preferred to talk a "trick" out of his money, but if they were feeling "sick," i.e., experiencing withdrawal symptoms, that they would be too irritable to engage in gentle conning. In such cases they might attack the client, take his money, purchase sufficient heroin to "get straight," and then go back on the street. In a more relaxed physical and mental state, these women claimed that they could then behave like prostitutes rather than robbers.

Drug use may also have a reverse psychopharmacological effect and ameliorate violent tendencies. In such cases, persons who are prone to acting violently may engage in self-medication in order to control their violent impulses. Several subjects have reported doing this. The drugs chosen for this function are typically heroin or tranquilizers.

Psychopharmacological violence may involve drug use by either offender or victim. In other words, drug use may contribute to a person behaving violently, or it may alter a person's behavior in such a manner as to bring about that person's violent victimization. Previous research indicates relatively high frequencies of alcohol consumption in rape and homicide victims. Public intoxication may invite a robbery or mugging. One study found that in rapes where only the victim was intoxicated, she was significantly more likely to be physically injured.

It is difficult to estimate the true rate of victim precipitated psychopharmacological violence because many such instances go unreported and, hence, unrecorded in official records. My own research in New York over the last decade indicated that many intoxicated victims do not report their victimization. Such victims say that they do not wish to talk to the police while drunk or "stoned." Further, since they are frequently confused about details of the event and, perhaps, unable to remember what their assailant looked like, they argue that reporting the event would be futile.

Assuming that the psychopharmacological violence is not precipitated by the victim, the victim can then be just about anybody. Psychopharmacological violence can erupt in the home and lead to spouse or child abuse. Psychopharmacological violence can occur in the workplace, on the streets, in bars, and so on. The incidence of psychopharmacological violence is impossible to assess at the present time, both because many instances go unreported and because when cases are reported the psychopharmacological state of the offender is seldom recorded in official records.

Economic Compulsive Violence

The economically compulsive model suggests that some drug users engage in economically oriented violent crime, e.g., robbery, in order to support costly drug use. Heroin and cocaine, because they are expensive drugs typified by compulsive patterns of use, are the most relevant substances in this category. Economically compulsive actors are not primarily motivated by impulses to act out violently. Rather, their primary motivation is to obtain money to purchase drugs. Violence generally results from some factor in the social context in which the economic

crime is perpetrated. Such factors include the perpetrator's own nervousness, the victim's reaction, weaponry (or the lack of it) carried by either offender or victim, the intercession of bystanders, and so on.

Research indicates that most heroin users avoid violent acquisitive crime if viable non-violent alternatives exist. This is because violent crime is more dangerous, embodies a greater threat of prison if one is apprehended, and because perpetrators may lack a basic orientation toward violent behavior. Bingham Dai reported similar findings nearly fifty years ago. His study of the criminal records of over one thousand opiate addicts in Chicago revealed that the most common offenses for which they were arrested were violations of the narcotics laws, followed by offenses against property.

> … it is interesting to note that comparatively few of them resorted to violence in their criminal activities. The small percentage of addicts committing such crimes as robbery, assault and battery, homicide and others that involve the use of force seems to discredit the view shared by many that the use of drugs has the effect of causing an individual to be a heartless criminal. On the contrary, our figures suggest that most of the crimes committed by addicts were of a peaceful nature that involve more the use of wit than that of force. (Dai, 1937: 69)

Victims of economic compulsive violence, like those of psychopharmacological violence, can be anybody. Previous research indicates that the most common victims of this form of drug related violence are people residing in the same neighborhoods as the offender. Frequently the victims are engaged in illicit activities themselves. Other drug users, strangers coming into the neighborhood to buy drugs, numbers runners, and prostitutes are all common targets of economic compulsive violence.

While research does indicate that most of the crimes committed by most of the drug users are of the nonviolent variety, e.g., shoplifting, prostitution, drug selling, there are little data that indicate what proportion of violent economic crimes are committed for drug related reasons. No national criminal justice data bases contain information on the motivations or drug use pattern of offenders as they relate to specific crimes.

Systemic Violence

In the systemic model, violence is intrinsic to involvement with any illicit substance. Systemic violence refers to the traditionally aggressive patterns of interaction within the system of drug distribution and use. Some examples of systemic violence follow below.

1 disputes over territory between rival drug dealers.
2 assaults and homicides committed within dealing hierarchies as a means of enforcing normative codes.
3 robberies of drug dealers and the usually violent retaliation by the dealer or his/her bosses.
4 elimination of informers.
5 punishment for selling adulterated or phony drugs.
6 punishment for failing to pay one's debts.
7 disputes over drugs or drug paraphernalia.
8 robbery violence related to the social ecology of copping areas.

Substantial numbers of users of any drug become involved in drug distribution as their drug-using careers progress and, hence, increase their risk of becoming a victim or perpetrator of systemic violence. Examples of each type of systemic violence mentioned above are readily available.

We recently reported that much of the heroin in New York City is being distinctively packaged and sold under "brand names" (Goldstein et al., 1984). These labeling practices are frequently abused and this abuse has led to violence. Among the more common abuses are the following: Dealers mark an inferior quality heroin with a currently popular brand name. Users purchase the good heroin, use it, then repackage the bag with milk sugar for resale. The popular brand is purchased, the bag is "tapped," and is further diluted for resale.

These practices get the real dealers of the popular brand very upset. Their heroin starts to get a bad reputation on the streets and they lose sales. Purchasers of the phony bags may accost the real dealers, complaining about the poor quality and demanding their money back. The real dealers then seek out the purveyors of the phony bags. Threats, assaults, and/or homicides may ensue.

A common form of norm violation in the drug trade is known as "messing up the money." Basically, this involves a subordinate returning less money to his superior than is expected. For example, a street dealer is given a consignment of drugs to sell and is expected to return to his supplier or lieutenant with a specific amount of money. However, for any of a variety of reasons, he returns with too little money or fails to return at all. Some of the reasons why he might be short on his money are that he used some or all of the drugs himself; he sold all of the drugs, but then spent some or all of the money; he gave out too many "shorts," i.e., he sold the drugs for less than he should have; he was robbed, either of his drugs or of the money that he obtained from selling them.

When a street dealer fails to return sufficient money, his superior has several options. If only a small amount of money is involved, and the street dealer has few prior transgressions and a convincing justification for the current shortage, his superior is likely to give him another consignment and allow him to make up the shortage from his share of the new consignment. Other options include firing the street dealer, having him beaten up, or having him killed.

In a recent study, a lieutenant in a heroin dealing operation had been rather lax in supervising the six street dealers working under him. Just about everybody was "messing up the money," including himself. One day the supplier and two "soldiers" picked up the lieutenant and took him for a ride in their car. The lieutenant was afraid that he was going to be killed. However, after cruising for a while, they spotted one of the street dealers who had been "messing up the money." The two soldiers jumped from the car and beat him with iron pipes. They positioned him in the street and drove the car over his legs, crippling him for life. The supplier then suggested to the lieutenant that he would be well advised to run the operation more tightly in the future.

An interesting addendum to this discussion is that the "code of the streets" dictates that "blood cancels all debts." In other words, if a street dealer has "messed up the money" and is subsequently beaten up or wounded, then he no longer owes the money. The shedding of blood has cancelled the debt.

The above account illustrates a direct punishment for a norm violation. Violence may also arise in the course of a dispute that stems from a norm violation. I was recently told of such an incident. A drug dealer operated out of an apartment in New York City. Prospective purchasers would line up in the hallway of the apartment house and give their money to a young Hispanic woman who worked for the dealer. The woman would then get the drugs from the dealer and give them to the buyers. Dealers seldom allow customers into the space where the drugs are actually kept.

One day the line was long and three Black men waited patiently to make their purchase. Finally it was their turn. However, the woman bypassed them in favor of two Hispanic men who were at the back of the line. The Hispanic men made a large purchase and the woman announced that the dealer had sold out for the day. The Blacks were furious. An argument ensued, shots were fired, and one of the Hispanic men was killed. The norm violator in this case, the woman, was fired by the dealer.

A common precipitator of violence in the drug scene is the robbery of a dealer. No dealer who wishes to stay in business can allow himself or his associates to be robbed. Most dealers maintain an arsenal of weapons and a staff that knows how to use them. A subject in a recent study reported going with two friends to "take off" a neighborhood social club that was a narcotics distribution center. In the course of the hold-up they shot one of the employees and beat up several other men and women. In retrospect, the subject admitted that they had probably used excessive force, but that at the time it had seemed justified because they were outnumbered about fifteen to three. One of the victims recognized one of the robbers. This robber was later shot to death in the street.

The Pulitzer Prize winning study of narcotics trafficking, *The Heroin Trail*, documents many instances of systemic violence. One concerns Joseph Fucillo, a Brooklyn drug dealer who became a police informant in 1972.

> One day, as his wife watched from the window of their home in the Bensonhurst section of Brooklyn, Fucillo backed his car out of the driveway, and two men in ski masks walked up to it. Two guns fired rapidly and seven bullets went into Fucillo's head. He died. (*Newsday* Staff and Editors, 1974: 226)

A pimp stated that he would never allow a "junkie broad" to work for him. One of his reasons was that an addicted woman might be easily turned into an informant by the police. When asked what he would do if one of his women did start to use narcotics, he replied that if she didn't know too much about his activities he would just fire her. However, if she did know too much, he would kill her (Goldstein, 1979: 107).

New York Magazine reported an event that was tragic both in its consequences and in the fact that it is so typical of the current drug scene.

> Sylvester, a 16 year old boy, is stabbed in the chest … in the Crown Heights section of Brooklyn. He is taken to St. Mary's Hospital and dies a short time later. According to a witness, Sylvester sold marijuana to a group of adolescents a few days before the incident. His customers were apparently dissatisfied with its quality. Tonight the teenagers, a group of about eight or ten, find Sylvester on the street and complain about the bad grass. The leader of the group, John Green, demands their money back. Sylvester then picks up a couple of bottles and throws them at the group, running away down the block. The teenagers chase Sylvester down Lincoln Place where he picks up a stick and starts swinging. Knocking the stick out of his hand, John Green plunges a four inch knife into Sylvester's chest. Green and the others escape from the scene. At one P.M. Sunday afternoon, in apparent retaliation for the Sylvester murder, John Green is shot once in the left rear side of the body. He too is taken to St. Mary's, where he too dies. (Goro, 1977: 31)

Violence associated with disputes over drugs have long been endemic in the drug world. Friends come to blows because one refuses to give the other a "taste." A husband beats his wife because she raided his "stash."

The current AIDS scare has led to an increasing amount of violence because of intravenous drug users' fear of contracting this fatal disease from contaminated "works." Some sellers of needles and syringes claim that the used works that they are trying to sell are actually new and unused. If discovered by would-be purchasers, violence may ensue. I was recently told of one incident that allegedly led to the death of two men. A heroin user kept a set of works in a "shooting gallery" that were for his exclusive use. One day another man used these works. The owner of the works discovered what had happened and stabbed this man to death. He later stabbed a friend to death who was present when the stranger had used the works, had done nothing to stop him, and had failed to inform the owner of what had happened.

The social ecology of copping areas is generally well suited for the perpetration of robbery violence. Most major copping areas in New York City are located in poor ghetto neighborhoods, such as Harlem. In these neighborhoods, drug users and dealers are frequent targets for robberies because they are known to be carrying something of value and because they are unlikely to report their victimization. Dealers are sometimes forced to police their own blocks so that customers may come and go in safety.

A subject in a current study earns money by copping drugs for other people. He stated that he was recently forced to protect one of his clients by fighting off two would-be robbers with a garbage can lid. Interestingly, he knew the two attackers from the street, but he claimed to harbor no ill will towards them. He stated that they did what they had to do and he did what he had to do.

Victims of systemic violence are usually those involved in drug use or trafficking. Occasionally, noninvolved individuals become innocent victims. The case of a woman being killed by a stray bullet fired in a dispute between rival drug dealers was cited earlier. Several cases have been reported where whole families of drug dealers, including wives and young children, have perished in narcotics gang wars. However, the vast majority of victims of systemic violence are those who use drugs, who sell drugs, or are otherwise engaged in some aspect of the drug business.

Various sources have stressed the importance of what I have termed the systemic model in explaining drugs/violence relationships. Blum (1970) points out that, with the exception of alcohol, most drug users are not violent but that this point does not apply to the typical dealer for whom there is strong evidence linking drugs and violence. Smith (1972) in his discussion of amphetamines and violence in San Francisco's Haight-Ashbury district, stated that the primary cause of violence on the streets was "burning," i.e., selling phony or adulterated drugs. Several sources suggest that studying the area of systemic violence

may be more important than the study of the relationship of drug use to crime on the level of the individual user.

> Racket associated violence, a result of the intense competition for enormous profits involved in drugs, is flourishing. This is not the "crime in the streets" which is often associated with drugs, but an underworld in which ordinarily those people suffer from violence who in one way or another have become related to the traffic. (Fitzpatrick, 1974: 360)

> Because these criminal entrepreneurs operate outside the law in their drug transactions, they are not bound by business etiquette in their competition with each other, in their collection of debts, or in their nondrug investments. Terror, violence, extortion, bribery, or any other expedient strategy is relied upon by these criminals. (Glaser, 1974: 53)

> Where a commodity is scarce and highly in demand (as may be the case with drugs), extreme measures of control, i.e., homicide, may be involved. Further, in areas of high scarcity and inelastic demand, bitter arguments centering on the commodity are likely to ensue. When such arguments take place in a subculture where violence is the modus operandi, and where implements of violence, e.g., guns, are readily available, homicide is likely to be the result. (Zahn, 1975: 409)

Zahn pointed out the importance of systemic violence in her recent study of homicide in twentieth century United States. She showed that homicide rates peaked in the 1920s and early 1930s, declined and levelled off thereafter, began to rise in 1965, and peaked again in 1974. This analysis led to the following conclusion.

> In terms of research directions this historical review would suggest that closer attention be paid to the connection between markets for illegal goods and the overall rate of homicide violence. It seems possible, if not likely, that establishing and maintaining a market for illegal goods (booze in the 1920s and early 1930s; heroin and cocaine in the late 1960s and early 1970s) may involve controlling and/or reducing the competition, solving disputes between alternate suppliers or eliminating dissatisfied customers…. The use of guns in illegal markets may also be triggered by the constant fear of being caught either by a rival or by the police. Such fear may increase the perceived need for protection, i.e., a gun, thus may increase the arming of these populations and a resulting increased likelihood of use.

For the overall society this may mean a higher homicide rate. (Zahn, 1980: 128)

It was stated above that the three models of the drugs/violence nexus contained in the tripartite conceptual framework should be viewed as ideal types, and that overlap could occur between them. For example, a heroin user preparing to commit an act of economic compulsive violence, e.g., a robbery, might ingest some alcohol or stimulants to give himself the courage to do the crime. This event now contains elements of both economic compulsive and psychopharmacological violence. If the target of his robbery attempt was a drug dealer, the event would contain elements of all three types of drug related violence.

The conceptual framework allows the event to be effectively analyzed and broken down into constituent parts and processes. The roles played in the event by different sorts of drugs can be explicated. In the above example, the need for money to purchase heroin was the primary motivation for the act. Alcohol and stimulants were ingested after the act was decided upon because of the robber's need for courage and, presumably, because prior experience with these substances led the perpetrator to believe that they would serve that psychopharmacological function.

The choice of target, a drug dealer, is open for empirical investigation. It may turn out that the reason the heroin user needed to commit the robbery was because that dealer had cheated him earlier in the day on a drug purchase, perhaps selling him "dummy" bags. Our robber, needing to "get straight" and not having any more money, decides that robbing this unscrupulous dealer would be an appropriate revenge.

Several subjects in our studies reported committing economic compulsive acts out of fear of becoming a victim of systemic violence. These were street dealers who had "messed up the money" and who were terrified of what their superiors might do to them. Some had already been threatened. This motivated them to do robberies as a quick way to obtain the money that they owed.

Thus, as the concepts are employed, a fuller understanding of the event emerges. The roles played by specific drugs become clearer. The actor's motivations and the process by which he undertakes to commit a robbery are elaborated upon.

If the above events were to be examined in official crime records, assuming they were reported, they would be listed as robberies. Victim–perpetrator relationships would probably be unknown, though they might be listed as "acquaintance" or "stranger." No mention of drugs would be made.

Victims of systemic violence frequently lie to the police about the circumstances of their victimization. Not a single research subject whom I have interviewed who was the victim of systemic violence, and who was forced to give an account of his or her victimization to the police, admitted that he or she had been assaulted because of owing a drug supplier money or selling somebody phony or adulterated drugs. All such victims simply claimed to have been robbed.

It would make little difference if the robbery were to develop into a homicide. The classification of the event would change from robbery to homicide, but victim–perpetrator relationship and nature of the homicide would remain unknown or be coded in such a broad fashion that the information would not be very useful. No mention of drugs would be made. Attention will now be focused on the quality of data available on the national level to elaborate on the drugs/violence nexus.

[…]

Summary and Conclusions

Drugs and violence were shown to be related in three possible ways: psychopharmacologically, economic compulsively, and systemically. These different forms of drug related violence were shown to be related to different types of substance use, different motivations of violent perpetrators, different types of victims, and differential influence by social context. Current methods of collecting national crime data were shown to be insensitive to the etiological role played by drug use and trafficking in creating violent crime.

No evidence currently exists as to the proportions of violence engaged in by drug users and traffickers that may be attributed to each of the three posited models. We need such data. My own impression, arising from research in New York, is that the area of systemic violence accounts for most of the violence perpetrated by, and directed at, drug users.

Systemic violence is normatively embedded in the social and economic networks of drug users and sellers. Drug use, the drug business, and the violence connected to both of these phenomena are all aspects of the same general lifestyle. Individuals caught in this lifestyle value the experience of substance use, recognize the risks involved, and struggle for survival on a daily basis. That struggle is clearly a major contributor to the total volume of crime and violence in American society.

References

Blumm, Richard and Associates. 1970. *Students and Drugs*. San Francisco: Jossey-Bass.

Dai, B. 1937. *Opium Addiction in Chicago*. Montclair: Patterson Smith.

Fitzpatrick, J. P. 1974. Drugs, Alcohol and Violent Crime, *Addictive Diseases*, 1: 353–67.

Glaser, D. 1974. Interlocking Dualities in Drug Use, Drug Control and Crime, in Inciardi, J. A. and C. Chambers (eds.), *Drugs and the Criminal Justice System*. Beverly Hills: Sage Publications.

Goldstein, P. J. 1979. *Prostitution and Drugs*. Lexington: Lexington Books.

Goldstein, P. J., D. S. Lipton, E. Preble, I. Sobel, T. Miller, W. Abbott, W. Paige, and F. Soto 1984. The Marketing of Street Heroin in New York City, *Journal of Drug Issues*, 14: 553–66.

Goro, H. 1977. Saturday Night Dead, *New York Magazine*, 10: 31.

Kolb, L. 1925. Drug Addiction and its Relation to Crime, *Mental Hygiene*, 9: 74–89.

Martindale, D. 1959. Sociological Theory and the Ideal Type, in Gross, L. (ed.), *Symposium on Sociological Theory*. New York: Harper and Row.

Newsday Staff and Editors 1974. *The Heroin Trail*. New York: Holt, Rinehart and Winston.

Smith, R. 1972. Speed and Violence: Compulsive Methamphetamine Abuse and Criminality in the Haight-Ashbury District, in C. Zarsfonetis (ed.), *Drug Abuse: Proceedings of the International Conference*. Philadelphia: Lea and Febiger.

Zahn, M. A. 1975. The Female Homicide Victim, *Criminology*, 13: 409.

Zahn, M. A. 1980. Homicide in the Twentieth Century United States, in Inciardi, J. A. and C. E. Faupel (eds.), *History and Crime*. Beverly Hills: Sage Publications.

Questions

1 With regard to crime and violence, what does the psychopharmacological model fail to explain? What does the economic-compulsive model fail to explain?

2 How might the regulation and control of drugs reduce the crime/violence discussed in this article? With regard to the three models of crime/violence, where would a policy change have the most impact?

3 Why are illegitimate forms of social control so popular in the illegal drug world? How are the options for dispute resolution hindered in the illegal marketplace?

33

Managing Retaliation
Drug Robbery and Informal Sanction Threats

Bruce A. Jacobs, Volkan Topalli, and Richard Wright

Bruce Jacobs, Volkan Topalli, and Richard Wright report on a highly dangerous occupation: robbing drug dealers. Fans of *The Wire* may think, in reading this selection, about the exploits of a favorite Baltimore character, Omar Little, whose exploits and lifestyle in this occupation were daring and dangerous. This selection draws on research conducted among an extremely hidden population: Black, inner-city, men who were buried deep into a St Louis criminal underworld. These drug robbers took advantage of dealers' lack of recourse to legitimate protection to steal from criminals earning a lucrative living. Jacobs, Topalli, and Wright discuss topics of high fascination such as their target selection, their ways of protecting themselves, and their rationalizations.

Into which of Goldstein's categories of violence would these people fall? How do they compare to other readings such as Valdez, Nowotny, and Cepeda and Levitt and Venkatesh? Do you think that other types of dealers, such as Mohamed and Fritsvold's college dealers, and Adler's upper-level dealers and smugglers, faced these kinds of problems? Why or why not? Finally, even though they indicate that their sample is all male, they provide data on a woman drug robber. What does Maher and Daley's article about women in the drug economy suggest about how women would fare here? What might be their advantages and disadvantages?

Since its earliest days, criminology has sought to understand how the threat of official sanctions influences the behavior of would-be criminals. Conventional wisdom holds that the more certain and severe the sanction, the less likely individuals will offend. "Informal" sanction threats also have attracted considerable scholarly attention, with particular emphasis placed on the role of shame and embarrassment. Initially attractive deviant actions, it is said, become decidedly less appealing when such conscience-linked variables are factored into the decision-making process. Some analysts have gone so far as to suggest that the extralegal consequences of offending may be the "real deterrent and that formal punishment is important only insofar as it triggers informal sanctions."

The notion that informal sanction threats influence criminal decision-making is perhaps the most important

Drugs and the American Dream: An Anthology, First Edition. Edited by Patricia A. Adler, Peter Adler, and Patrick K. O'Brien.

contribution to deterrence theory in the past 15 years. Notably absent from this contribution, however, is an examination of the ways in which the risk of victim retaliation – arguably, the ultimate informal sanction – mediates offender decisions. Indeed, we find it striking that the issue of deterrence has been discussed since the time of Beccaria and Bentham, yet retaliation has received so little attention from researchers.

On its face, retaliation would appear to be a serious consequence of many offenses, especially those perpetrated against victims who themselves are involved in crime. Certainly the threat of retaliation is widely assumed in criminological discussions of organized crime, gang violence, and drug dealing. To hear criminologists talk, offenders who engage in these activities risk swift and potentially fatal consequences at the hands of their victims. Paradoxically, such discussions often are coupled with the observation that a major benefit of preying on fellow criminals is that they cannot go to the police. But why should offenders elect to reduce their chances of getting arrested at the cost of increasing their odds of being killed? What is it that allows them to accept this putatively greater risk?

Despite ample speculation on their part, criminologists lack any systematic empirical data on whether and, if so, how the threat of victim retaliation influences criminal behavior before, during, and after offenses. This lack of data represents a crucial gap in our understanding of both deterrence and the contagion-like processes through which violence is contracted and contained. If, as some have suggested, the spread of violence is a public health problem, then we must develop a better understanding of the precise mechanisms that facilitate or impede its transmission from one offense to another. To this end, the present paper examines how active drug robbers – individuals who take money and drugs from dealers by force or threat of force – perceive and respond to the risk of victim retaliation in real-life settings and circumstances.

[...]

Method

The data for our study were obtained during in-depth interviews with 25 currently active drug robbers recruited from the streets of St Louis, Missouri. Historically, St Louis has had one of the largest illicit drug markets in the Midwestern United States. In many neighborhoods, marijuana, PCP, crack, and heroin are sold openly and available throughout the day. St Louis arrestees persistently have high rates of cocaine-, opiate-, and marijuana-positive urine specimens; they are among the highest of the 24 cities measured in the Drug Use Forecasting program (now called Arrestee Drug Abuse Monitoring, or ADAM). Emergency room cases involving hard drugs mirror other large metropolitan areas and indicate a high degree of street drug institutionalization.

Among the most socially distressed areas in the St Louis metropolitan area, the neighborhoods from which our offenders were recruited generally outrank other local sectors in the percentage of people living at or below poverty, citizens unemployed or on welfare, school drop-outs, drug arrests, and various other indicators of poor health. The neighborhoods and contiguous blocks have all of the earmarks of "urban dead zones": abandoned buildings, burned-out tenements, garbage-strewn vacant lots, and graffiti-splashed walls.

The drug robbers were located through the efforts of two street-based African-American field recruiters, both of whom were themselves active members of the criminal underworld. One of these individuals had taken part in a previous research project, and impressed us as being more reliable than most of his colleagues. The second was his associate, a person who quickly proved himself to be competent and dependable. Each had extensive connections to networks of street offenders and, within those networks, enjoyed a solid reputation for integrity and trustworthiness.

Trading on their trust, the field recruiters began by approaching relatives, friends, and acquaintances whom they knew to be active drug robbers. They explained our research objectives and told prospective respondents that they would be paid $50 for participation. It is a cardinal rule of street life that one should never do anything for nothing. Although $50 may seem to be a substantial sum, it is important to remember that most of these offenders could have earned much more through crime, and, from their perspective, crime may have appeared to be less risky than talking to strangers about their law-breaking. Once the field recruiters' initial source of active drug robbers was exhausted, they turned to referrals provided by earlier interviewees to further expand the sample.

[...]

The drug robbers in our sample ranged in age from 15 to 46; the mean age was 29.6. All of them were African American; all but four were male. There is no way of knowing how well this sample represents the total population of active drug robbers, but it confidently can be said to over-represent African-American offenders. No doubt the racial composition of our sample reflects the social chasm that exists between African Americans and whites in the St Louis criminal underworld. These offender groups display a marked tendency to "stick to their own kind," seldom participating in overlapping criminal networks. The fact that both of our field recruiters were African American meant that they had few realistic opportunities to establish bonds of trust with white offenders; they simply had little day-to-day contact with them.

[...]

Retaliatory Threat Management

Although drug robberies are seldom reported to the police, those who commit them risk grave *extralegal* consequences. Victim dealers, unable to report the robbery to authorities, have a strong incentive to retaliate. To do otherwise risks being labeled a "mark," opening oneself up to even more exploitation. Street sellers, moreover, very often sell on consignment. To the extent that they must answer to someone else for lost cash and drugs, their need for retribution will be enhanced: The wrath of higher level suppliers can be swift and severe, and to chance it is unwise. Insofar as drug market participants are impulsive, short-run thinkers, vengeance may become the only "proper" course of action. The drug robbers we interviewed well understood these issues and, in response, developed particular tactics to manage the threat. We present these tactics through a three-part typology consisting of intimidation, anonymity maintenance, and hypervigilance.

Intimidation

First and foremost, the drug robbers wanted to choose dealers whose retributive potential was weak. Fundamentally, good targets were soft, bad ones were hard. By definition, soft targets are easily intimidated and unlikely to retaliate. Even a cursory review of the drug literature indicates that sellers make for pugnacious and formidable prey. Common sense suggests that they must be so to have any chance of survival in the cut-throat world of the streets. Yet, our offenders claimed that soft dealers were "everywhere." A reflection of drug market circumstances unique to St Louis or of the particular experiences of our respondents, such comments highlight an important perception that guided their actions. As Ray Dog put it, "[D]ope dealers out here right now today man, are straight up chumps. They are chumps. They are punks ...They are the weakest...." Do-dirty declared that dope dealers were "the most punk ass niggers in the world." Darnell used this stereotype to hone in on one particularly easy mark:

> He was a motherfucker that had all this dope and money but he was a bitch, real soft, you know what I'm saying? He was more like a little girl. He was the kind that did his feet and his hands, got his nails done, you know what I'm saying, had a couple of tough [friends] but he stayed by his self. Personally, I thought the motherfucker was gay but he wasn't, you know what I'm saying?

As a general rule, streetcorner dealers were perceived to be softer than those who sold from houses (typically in larger quantities). Our respondents suggested that street dealers tended to be young and, surprisingly, unarmed – presumably to avoid the double sanction of drug and weapons possession. We also know, from the literature, that curbside drug dealers often lack the organizational wherewithal required for even mundane retaliatory action. Their freelance, individualistic orientation simply is not conducive to focused payback. This is especially true for those who deal in high-volume, competitive sets (on which many of our offenders committed their drug robberies). Time spent seeking retaliation can better be spent making money, and for many, the opportunity cost of lost sales may be too high to justify the effort. As Blackwell put it, "I don't think I'm ... gonna get retaliated back on by them cause they want to go back on they corner and sell drugs. That's what they do, sell drugs."

Targeting soft dealers, however, meant little in the absence of intimidation. Even the weakest sellers might be tempted to retaliate later if drug robbers failed to project a fierce enough persona during the offense. The goal, then, was to present a self so indomitable and trigger-happy that victims would not only hand over their possessions without hesitation, but would think twice about seeking out perpetrators later. Menacing presentations were as much dramaturgical as indicative of the performer's "essential" character. To the extent that such performances persuaded victims that the drug robbers' presented hardness was real, the drive for retaliation would weaken.

Both verbal and physical tactics were used toward this end. Expletive-loaded commands, such as (paraphrased here) "Get on the ground, don't move or you're dead motherfucker!," "Bitch, whore, asshole, motherfucker, up it or else!," and a host of others were reportedly voiced with a tone so fearsome as to leave no doubt that the perpetrator was not to be messed with, ever. Pistol-whippings and warning shots drove this message home, underscoring the futility – and peril – of pursuit. "Sho[o]t ... at the ground a few times," Darnell remarked, "let him know I [am] not bullshitting." Or as Kilo commented, "Hit him, hit him with the pistol, strike 'em ... Just smack him with the butt of the gun, you know, in the back of the head somewhere ...." Buck took an even more menacing approach, grabbing his victims around the throat and then letting "them feel that cold steel [of the gun] on the back of they neck. [Cock the gun for] intimidation." Smoke Dog, similarly, pistol-whipped his victim, but only after seizing the booty – seemingly to make a point more than anything else. "I smacked him ... so he grabbed his face and just laid on the ground. I guess he thought I was gonna go on and kill him or whatever but I walked on out ... punk ass nigger." Lamont robbed a dealer of an eight-ball of crack (about three grams) and $100 outside an East St Louis night club – shooting "less than lethal" shots before sprinting away. He made it clear, however, that preventing retaliation was very much on his mind:

He could be having a gun on him too. I couldn't just walk away from him like that, just take that and walk away. He might have shot me in the back, shot me in the back of my head or something ... I shot him to let him know I ain't playing with the .25, bing, bing, bing, bing.... I know he had a gun in his car and he messing around as soon as I walked away. He snuck in his car and might have run up behind me and shot me or something. So I shot him, bing, bing, I'm gonna leave him laying right here and I'm gonna make it to my car. Cause he gots to go to the hospital. Any person that you shot they got to go to the hospital unless you Superman or something, you can take these bullets, they bounce off you, you spit 'em out your mouth or something like Superman did. You a bad man if you can do that.

[...] In nearly all cases, however, offenders endeavored to avoid seriously injuring or killing their victims. Lethal violence may be the best way to pre-empt retaliation, but it is the least desired. Bodies bring heat and negate the primary reason these offenders rob drug dealers in the first place: because they cannot go to the police. As V-O put it, "you kill somebody that's ... 14 years of your life [in prison]. You don't want ... that." Establishing fear in the psyche of the victim, rather, is the name of the game. To instill it in would-be pursuers is to unnerve them and weaken their retributive resolve. [...]

Anonymity maintenance

Though choosing soft dealers and intimidating them into submission may be useful for shaping the "supply-side" of retribution, nothing eliminates the threat of reprisal in the way anonymity can: If victims never know who it is that robbed them, retaliation becomes moot. Nameless and faceless, drug robbers can move through the streets without worry or concern. This is not easy, however; significant effort is required to construct barriers around one's identity. Three particular strategies were used toward this end: stranger targeting, discretion, and disguises.

Stranger targeting

Most of the offenders refused to target dealers with whom they were overly familiar. Acquaintanceships, no matter how weak or shallow, increase the odds of recognition and thus retribution. Preemptive lethal measures, which already have been identified as unattractive to the vast majority of our respondents, might be required as a result. The importance of attending to microstructure in "prequalifying" one's targets was thus undeniable. As Low Down emphasized:

> I ain't gonna rob nobody [I know]. If I rob [him], I'm pretty sure [he] would know my voice ... if I be growing up with you all your life and I robbed you, I would be on the run ... [you gonna be knowing me] since we was like this [younger]....If I rob [an associate] I'll have to kill him cause he will know me and he'll be looking for me....Then I being having to watch my back....I'm not gonna come back and make like it never happened.

[...] Ray Dog insisted that the whole idea of robbing a friend was ridiculous, not because it violated basic loyalties (which are weak to begin with), but because of its sheer impracticality. "I rob strangers better," he said, "because they don't know me. See friends know me, they know your voice, they know how you walk, how you talk, they know everything....You can't [cover up] your face and go up there tell him, 'look nigger, up it.' 'Oh man, Ray, that you man,' you know."

This is not to suggest that known dealers were never targeted; some simply were too good to pass up. A number of drug robbers resolved the dilemma by enlisting a fellow offender, unknown to the mark, to commit the crime. Having accurate information on the dealer's movements, defensibility, support, and goods, the contracting offender would relay this intelligence to their proxy, who then did the job. Such ventures proved lucrative for both parties: Inside information produced a guaranteed and often considerable take that the two offenders would split; use of a surrogate, meanwhile, ensured continued anonymity for the offender who set up the scheme.

Innovations aside, there were important lessons to learn from those who failed to take interpersonal familiarity into account. Low Down, for example, witnessed the slaying of a partner who had robbed one acquaintance-dealer too many. This individual was killed after two prior retaliation attempts. "I stayed away from him," Low Down recalled. "I could have been riding with him and they seen me and thought I had something to do with it." Robbing a stranger-dealer more than once was misguided in a similar

sense; anonymity could no longer be maintained or taken for granted. "You never go back and strike the same [victim]," Do-dirty warned, "never do that.... You rob a person one time then you go back a second time and try to rob them, they gonna be recognizing you." This, according to Lewis, would most assuredly result in a "gun down."

Familiarity, or the lack thereof, was also important in a geographic sense. Many offenders refused to commit drug robberies in or around the neighborhood where they spent most of their time. To do so risked almost certain exposure. As Slim asked, "Why would I rob somebody where I rest my head at? Why would I bring heat where I rest my head at, where I stay at? That don't make sense." YoYo concurred: "If I gonna do some dirt, I don't want [nobody] to know where I stay." Baby Doll put these sentiments into perspective:

> They [victims] know where you stay at, know where you hang out ... [Doing a drug robbery in your "home neighborhood"] that's like putting your life on the line, you know what I'm saying. They can go on up and kill you ....I try to have a safe place to live, lay my head. When I go home I know I'm safe there, I ain't got to worry about nobody kicking my door in or chasing me, chasing me down, something like that you know.

[...] The bottom line is that our offenders realized the importance of not "working" where they slept. Using one or more safe zones as a base of operation, they sought to establish separation between grounds intended for "hunting" and those geared toward habitation. In doing so, the offenders could enjoy an added layer of protection: Even if their anonymity somehow was blown, the likelihood of victims finding them remained small.

Discretion

Stranger targeting aside, anonymity maintenance also meant exercising discretion about what, or how much, one stole from victims. Flashing the spoils of a recent robbery – cash, expensive clothing, jewelry – was a sure-fire way to identify oneself as a "player" who needed to be taught a lesson. Showing off items that could be traced directly back to a specific victim was worse still. Both actions constitute affronts and serve as dangerous proclamations of one's "dirty work." This is especially problematic on the streets, where everybody knows everybody else's business and snitches are a ubiquitous feature of the social landscape. Spanky therefore refused to rip an expensive necklace off of his drug dealer-victim, fearing it would ultimately identify him as the perpetrator:

> I didn't want no chain cause the kind of chain he [victim] got, he had like a fat herringbone with a dagger on it and everybody know that's Bobo chain. [Bobo] seen with a size herringbone that big and if anybody else have it [others] would know it was his and they probably would have got hurt.

Subscribing to a policy of discretion might also call for taking "less." Darnell robbed a big-time house dealer of $10,000 in cash and several thousand dollars' worth of drugs, but left without taking all of the booty. This led him to claim that he really "didn't hurt [the victim] cause if I did, I could have gotten more out of the deal which I knew there was more there ....I see the guy to this day. He might smile ....And to this day, I don't think I really hurt him." Other offenders reported doing the same, settling for as much as they could get quickly, while leaving other valuable contraband behind. Though seemingly counterintuitive behavior for impulsive street offenders, it must be remembered that in these neighborhoods – and in the drug game in general – predation is so common as to be measured in degrees. To the extent that drug robbers moderate the amount they steal, victims might be more prone to chalk the experience up to the game, and move on. Given the rapidity with which drugs and drug income can be replenished (at least by resourceful sellers), such a strategy may be well-grounded.

Perhaps the most vital component of discretion is postoffense silence. On the streets, word travels fast; there is no such thing as discussing a drug robbery in confidence. One never knows when, where, or to whom a story might be repeated. Postoffense boasting was perceived to be both dangerous and stupid. As June Bug explained:

> It don't make no sense to brag about it because see you could be bragging and ain't no telling this [person] might be somebody's cousin or relative, anybody, you see

what I'm saying. So therefore you say to yourself why start bragging about shit? I'm not gonna get a bunch of motherfuckers here, 'I robbed this bitch you dig, and this you dig,' and just see what happened. Her cousin might be there, anybody's sister, brother, any motherfucker.

Ray Dog agreed, declaring that "You don't go around telling every motherfucker that you [did] that. That's how you get yourself killed." Or, as Buck put it, "Why would I tell on myself?....I go to two or three [offender] funerals every year....I don't want to get shot." [...] Loose talk risked having a price put on one's head. On the streets, snitches are a dime a dozen. To down-and-out drug users, even small offers of money or drugs can serve as powerful enticements to tattle. "Crack dealers ... will pay a crackhead to tell [them], you know, where this person [drug robber] at," Baby Doll explained. "You don't let anybody know what you're doing." Three Eyes agreed: "[You tell and] the next person get jealous or get mad at you, turn you into the dope dealer for some money just for the information."

Disguises

As an anonymity maintenance device, few techniques trump the use of a good disguise. Recall that these offenders inhabit the same social world as their victims. Absent a disguise, they could easily be recognized later (even by stranger targets) or described to someone who knew their identity and whereabouts. "I don't never rob nobody without no mask," Low Down proclaimed, "because they'll [dealers] come back and kill me." "I don't want nobody to know me," Lewis added. "I might ride back down through the same street [sometime] ... and he [past victim] might say, ... 'damn, there goes the dude that robbed me right there.' ... I would rather be safe than sorry." Ski masks were the cover of choice for most. As Smoke Dog observed:

> I'll wear a [ski] mask so they can't see my face ....[Some] of them, I be right in they faces laughing and they don't even know I'm the one that robbed them last night.... That's cold ain't it?....I'm sitting here talking to you, riding in your car with you, you don't even know I'm the one that kicked in your house, put your baby's momma on the ground, you don't even know.

Other drug robbers donned ball caps and dark clothing, wrapped bandannas around their faces, shaved their beards or heads in particular ways, or used nighttime as natural camouflage. "I don't rob nobody in broad daylight," Low Down explained. "Too many people be out [and they can recognize you]." "You ride around, dark, you know," Do-dirty added. "Got some dark glasses on, you know, I might have a camouflage outfit on. I got a couple of camouflage outfits, army outfits, camouflage you know. What they call Ninja suits you know ... put my glasses on with a cap." Ladybug claimed to dress like a street drug user, all in black, adding her "little hat" and "little glasses" to accessorize the look and make her less detectable. "I don't give a fuck if they [victims] see my face today or tomorrow," she boasted, "they don't know who the fuck I am [because I've changed my appearance since I robbed them]." She also claimed to wear a number of different wigs throughout a given week to ensure her continued anonymity. This strategy came in handy when she ran into a previous victim at a local White Castle (fast-food restaurant):

> This ... dude ran up on me, pulled a gun, he was like, 'I remember you!' [You robbed me!]. I said, 'you don't even know me. What's up?' 'Oh, I'm sorry,' [he said], 'I thought you was this other gal.' No I don't trip off these little punk ass niggers.

Failing to disguise one's identity could have fatal consequences. Smoke Dog neglected to do so on one occasion, with near disastrous results. "Dude ... rolled down the city [later], started shooting at me and I started shooting back, me and my little partner. Started shooting back. He [drug robbery victim] jumped in his car and rolled off." Apparently, these gun battles continued well after the offense. "We was going to war," Smoke Dog declared. "Every time I see him he shoot at me, it's like that, we shoot at each other." The "war" stopped only when Smoke Dog's antagonist left town, which, of course, he claimed credit for: "I guess he got scared or whatever .... I broke him."

Disguises do possess a significant drawback, however; they make it difficult for drug robbers to capitalize on the element of surprise. A popular modus operandi among our respondents, for example, involved acting like customers who wished to purchase drugs. This allowed them to cover their true intentions until the last possible moment. Wearing a mask makes this impossible. "You don't come up out of the [neighbor]hood with no disguise on talking about can you cop [drugs]," Spanky explained. "'Cop what? Who are you?' ... [That'll get you shot]."

Hypervigilance

No matter how effective their retaliatory management strategies, no single tactic or combination of tactics was foolproof. The effects of intimidation can wear off. Soft targets might enlist the services of a hit-man. Word of a drug robber's identity or whereabouts can leak. Anonymity might be breached by the most innocuous of chance encounters. The more recent a robbery, the more troublesome run-ins can become: victims' memories are fresh, their sensitivity to interpersonal cues acute, and their thirst for revenge parching. Even with a mask, cues such as voice, demeanor, gait, size, and height remain tell-tale signs for especially attentive victims. Indeed, masks could draw only more attention to such factors during the robbery; essentially, they were the only things to attend to.

Our offenders thus devoted a significant portion of their day-to-day cognitive resources to minimizing the prospect of postoffense victim contact. Hypervigilance, the near obsessive attention to one's surroundings and the behavior of others, became the order of the day. As a general rule, offenders expected to be sought out by victims for hours, days, weeks, or even months after any given drug robbery. Measures had to be taken accordingly, given that dire consequences await those who let their guard down:

> You got to watch. I mean you could be inside some store, anybody walking behind you, you got to be like this here, man. You got to look around corners, you got to look around everywhere, you see what I'm saying? I mean even when I go to my mom's house sometimes, I got to walk around through the back, go around to the backyard, look around in the yard, see if anybody back there .... You stop coming outside during the day, you come out at nighttime .... Because during the day they notice you during the day. See at night it's dark. They might see you in a car or something. Then you change a lot .... You got to change your whole personality toward a lot of things. You got to change your attitude. (Ray Dog) [...]

To the middle-class observer, such behavior may seem paranoid. For drug robbers, it is both functional and necessary. The threat of retaliation has a long half-life, making it necessary for these offenders to keep their heads up and their eyes open. Indeed, most of our respondents insisted that attending to one's environment could never really be suspended, and as the frequency and magnitude of their offenses increased, the need for sustained vigilance rose. "The more you rob," Do-dirty explained, "you always gonna run into [victims] because St. Louis is too small. You bound to run into him. Ain't no place you hide in the city of St. Louis at all." "I see a lot of people that I done shit to," Darnell added. "I mean I laugh on the inside [but] I always keep my eyes open. My uncle told me, 'you know you've done a lot of wrong to these guys. Now that you're getting your life together [getting off heroin], you really got to keep your head up. Cause there is a time when all this shit might come back on you and when you are ready to face it, then face it.'" [...]

Decisions about whether, when, or how to return to the actual offense site (or to contiguous areas) underscored the extent to which hypervigilance constrained the drug robbers' postoffense movement patterns. Most interviewees steered clear of these locations for several weeks to several months. "You give it three or four months before you roll back through there," Do-dirty explained. "And even then, you don't be riding in your car ... [dude might see you and] he might tell his partner, 'man, that's the dude that robbed me' ... 'that's the dude that got you?' And his partners come around the corner with a pistol and when you look up they gonna hit you." Blackwell claimed to wait a "good four months" before returning. By then, he argued, "they probably ain't worried about it." Baby Doll insisted that she might never be able to go back to an area in which she had done a drug robbery. Paradoxically, she recognized that her crack habit was so powerful that she might have to go back:

> If I can't find no drugs in the area where I'm hanging out, shit, I say 'oh well,' I got to creep over this way [to a set where she had robbed]. I got to do a little creeping you know ....I'll take a chance ....

Indeed, sometimes simply knowing that one had to "watch out" was not enough to energize evasive conduct. Given the drug robbers' street-focused lifestyle and frequent consumption of hard psychoactive drugs, their decision-making abilities often were less than sharp. Drinking and drug use are not conducive to clear thinking, and blunted judgment could result in potentially fatal consequences. Baby Doll, for example, recounted a revenge drug robbery in which she targeted a dealer who had raped her a few months previously. The victim sought immediate retaliation, but was not successful: As Baby Doll put it, "He rolled around looking for us [that night] and he went and got I guess a couple of his partners and stuff and they was on the streets. Shit, I had to stay off the street at least about a good month, at least around in that area you know." Apparently, however, she went back too early – a decision no doubt influenced by her drug-induced state of intoxication:

> There was one particular time, I was high, tripping, I was coming down Sarah [Street]. I didn't even think about it [the prospect of retaliation], you know, when you're high you forget about these things. [Her previous victim] pulled over and he had his little partner with him ....He jumped out of the car, his friend jumped out. I just took off running. I was running, I was running, running for dear life ....So one of them was riding around and the other one was on foot. So then his friend, they couldn't find me you know ....I hid down in this vacant building in the basement you know, underneath the steps .... I don't know, something just saved me but he didn't catch me ....I waited there and it came to me, I said, I knew it [the drug robbery] would come back on me.

The task of hypervigilance was complicated by the drug robbers' nomadic ways. Most of them claimed to never "lay their heads" in one place or area for long, staying with kin, friends, girlfriends, and associates for small intervals of time. "I'm a floater," Slim illustrated. "I can't believe in just sitting there and letting roots grow up under my feet. I like to move, I like to stay on the go." In one sense, the offenders' free-ranging lifestyles gave them a much better chance at avoiding payback. Mobility allows them to avoid "hot" areas (e.g., places where they have committed drug robberies) and provides greater access to hiding places. In another, it carried significant risks of its own by increasing the odds of chance encounters. This is especially true given the dense microstructure of the streets. [...] Bus stops, mini-malls, grocery stores, bars, theaters, and fast-food restaurants emerge as contexts fraught with potential risk.

One important and widespread response to this risk was to carry a firearm at all times. As Curly put it, "Never get caught without [your gun], never. When I get out of the car I got it, man, I don't get out of the car without it. Even if I'm getting out of the car to socialize, man, I got it man." Lamont agreed, proclaiming that "I always have big magnum [.44] with me. Big magnum is always with me ....I ride dirty every day, every day, got to ....I'm strapped up, believe me, I'm strapped up ....That big magnum gonna get busy. That's a quick loader too, he gonna get busy ...." Ray Dog was even more emphatic, insisting that "You got to sleep with your pistol, you got to eat with your pistol, you got to go to the bathroom with your pistol, you got to take a shower with your pistol ...everywhere you go you got to take your guns with you."

Bolstered by the confidence that only an ever-present firearm can provide, most offenders believed they could handle anything that came their way:

> [...] Come with a gun. Come with your army, ... cause it gonna take an army to take me down ... you gonna kill me or I'm gonna kill you ....I come to a fight with a big old .45 because ... when they see that big old .45 with a nine inch barrel on here, they bags up, they bags up. (Do-dirty)

Offenders with violent kin and friends were emboldened further by the knowledge that, even if they could not handle a particular situation personally, the slack could be taken up by others:

> I got seven brothers, seven brothers and 13 youngsters, all of them straight up trigger-finger crazy ... anything that happen to me, anything that goes down, I tell them where everything is, tell them where this is, this person did it ....That's a war, you know, that's a straight up war. (Ray Dog) [...]

To some extent, comments such as these strain credulity. Street offenders hold each other in low esteem and relationships among them – even those who call each other "partner" – hinge on mutual distrust. Solidarity in the traditional sense of the term barely exists. Though some offenders seemed to recognize this contradiction, many held onto the belief that they somehow would be covered in the event of reprisal. Talk of being covered may provide all of the reassurance necessary; security comes in saying the words.

Discussion

Drug robbery is an offense with potentially grave extralegal consequences. Unable to report the crime to police, drug dealers have a strong incentive to retaliate. This article has examined how drug robbers perceive and respond to this threat. Three strategies were explored to this end: intimidation, anonymity maintenance, and hypervigilance. Intimidation deters dealer-victims from seeking retribution, anonymity maintenance prevents them from knowing whom to pursue, and hypervigilance reduces the likelihood that any given retaliatory strike will be successful. [...]

Even if strictly adhered to, such tactics clearly are not foolproof. Some have a real potential for creating the opposite of their intended effect. Intimidation, for instance, may squelch within-offense resistance, but might also incite emasculated victims to seek reprisal with even greater resolve. Weapons provide protection, but can entice their carriers to (1) lay low for shorter periods of time, (2) travel to areas that otherwise would be considered off-limits, or (3) be less vigilant. Targeting "strange" drug sets ensures greater anonymity, but may confound a quick getaway (assuming escape routes are less known). Enlisting others to watch one's back engenders security, but exposes offenders to the hazards of gossip (particularly given the precarious loyalty and shifting alliances of the streets). Hypervigilance is functional, but also is emotionally draining. Ultimately, it may be suspended altogether in favor of a fatalistic, "fuck it" mentality that emboldens offenders to commit even more crimes, or leads them to dismiss the importance of retaliatory threat management in favor of preemptive incapacitation [...]. Both function to increase the offenders' aggregate risk.

Pitfalls aside, one could argue that the tactics described in this paper have generic importance outside the realm of drug robbery. They may be part and parcel of a more general decision-making calculus reflected in all forms of victimizing behavior. The drug robbers' practice of intimidating dealers is not wholly unlike threats made against "ordinary" (noncriminal) victims to prevent pursuit. Disguises, discretion, and hypervigilance are analogous to the behavior of any prudent bank robber or street mugger seeking to elude those who might seek them out. The difference is that law-abiding victims, almost by definition, are unlikely to retaliate. Typically, they lack the knowledge, skill, and disposition to do so, as well as the moral conviction to take the law into their own hands (and thus break it). Formal justice exists to shoulder their burden. Fortunately, for would-be offenders, the same tactics that discourage retaliation also may reduce the victim's willingness to seek official redress.

[...]

Questions

1 What model from the previous Drugs/Violence Nexus article most resembles the criminal and/or violent activity discussed in this article? What were the main motivations of the offender?

2 What were the tactics developed by the drug robbers to manage retaliation? Why are informal sanctions, rather than formal sanctions, most feared by drug robbers? Do you think the prevalence of drug robberies differs on the social class of the dealer? Why or why not?

3 How do you think the current prohibition of drugs contributes to the act of drug robberies? Do you think these drug robbers are any better off financially than the foot soldiers that sell on the streets? Why or why not?

Mexico: Cartels, Corruption, and Cocaine
A Profile of the Gulf Cartel

Stephanie Brophy

Our nation has been transfixed recently with horror stories coming from the Mexican border about waves of violence there associated with the power struggle between competing drug cartels. No book on drugs would be complete without some insight into what's going on there. Stephanie Brophy offers us some history of the different cartels in this drug war, and discusses their relation to governments, to national and international enforcement efforts, and to the global economy. The picture she paints is vicious and bleak. She assesses the political and law enforcement options available, and offers some policy suggestions.

How would you compare this picture to Goldstein's typology of violence? To what kinds of criminal organizations can these be compared? How might the drug decriminalization movement in the United States affect these cartels and their drug trade? What kinds of influence can or should the United States have on criminal cartels in another country? Finally, what kinds of predictable patterns of violence do we see in this situation?

Introduction

It is an open secret that if you are going to visit Mexico it would be wise to avoid the northern border towns. Mexico's border with the United States is one of the hottest zones of fighting between federal security forces and organised crime groups. Here, in towns such as Nuevo Laredo (which is within walking distance to the US border), it is not uncommon to see Mexican troops in full battle gear driving through the streets in trucks mounted with machine guns.

In 2007, there were 2,713 organised-crime related homicides in Mexico. So far this year [2008] there have been 1,021 murders ascribed to drugs and organised crime. The four largest organised crime groups (better known as drug cartels) in Mexico are the Gulf cartel, the Juérez cartel, the Tijuana cartel, and the Sinaloan Federation cartel [see Figure 34.1]. This text specifically examines the Gulf cartel's activities and the accompanying implications for both Mexico and the United States.

The Gulf cartel is a major organised crime group in Mexico whose primary interests lie in drug-trafficking.

Drugs and the American Dream: An Anthology, First Edition. Edited by Patricia A. Adler, Peter Adler, and Patrick K. O'Brien.
© 2012 John Wiley & Sons, Inc. Published 2012 by John Wiley & Sons, Inc.

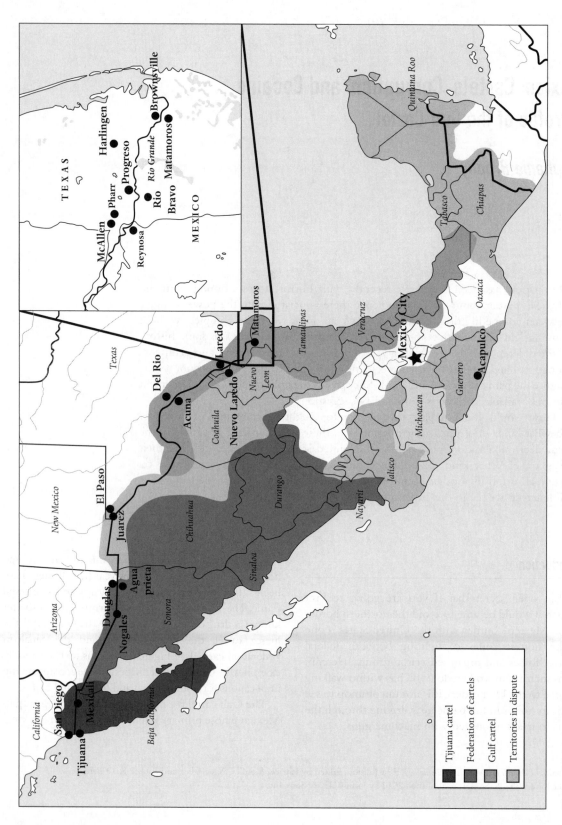

Figure 34.1 Areas of cartel influences

Its principal operations are based out of the cities of Nuevo Laredo, Miguel Alemán, Reynosa, and Matamoros. Other important operations are in Monterrey and Morelia. It also retains a presence throughout the entire country of Mexico and across the United States, and has cemented ties with street and prison gangs in the US.

The Office of the Attorney General of the Republic (PGR) stated that the presence and violent activity of the Gulf cartel exceeds that of the other organised crime groups in Mexico. Armament seized from the Gulf cartel includes M72 and AT-4-type anti-tank rockets, 37 mm MGL rocket launchers, RPG-7 rocket launchers, fragmentation grenades, and 37 and 40 mm grenades.

Origins and Early Growth

The Gulf cartel, and Mexican drugs cartels in general, originated in the 1920s and 1930s in response to demand for smuggling both people and contraband into the United States.

Throughout the 1970s and 1980s Colombian cartels, such as the Cali and Medellín cartels, dominated drug-trafficking and were more powerful than the Mexican cartels. During these years, the Gulf cartel acted as a middleman between Colombian cocaine and the US market. However, because most Colombian cocaine was shipped via the Caribbean at this time, the role of the Gulf cartel in trafficking the Colombian cocaine was minimal.

US anti-drug operations began to focus on the Colombian–Caribbean drug-trafficking connections in the early 1990s. This forced the Colombians to use Mexico as their primary smuggling route. As pressure on the Colombian cartels mounted, a number of meetings took place between the Mexican and Colombian cartels. It was during the early 1990s that the then-leader of the Gulf cartel, Juan Garcia Abrego, cut a major deal with the Colombian cartels. The deal Garcia Abrego made was that the Colombians would forfeit half their cocaine shipment to the Gulf cartel instead of paying cash; the Gulf cartel would then assume the risk of selling it, but take the profits themselves. This deal is responsible for the explosion of the Gulf cartel's power and wealth.

[...]

The Enforcers: Loz Zetas

'Zetas are an armed group. They pick up people. They kill them. They kidnap them. They rob their houses. They find a way to make people disappear'. Like other criminal enterprises, the Gulf cartel employs *sicarios* (translated as hit men). What makes the Zetas unique, however, is that they operate as a private army for the Gulf cartel. For both Mexican and US authorities, the Zetas are the most dangerous paramilitary group in Mexico because of their willingness to shoot and kill law enforcement officers.

Whereas the Gulf cartel deals primarily in drug-trafficking, the Zetas can be classified as a mafia group. In his study of the Russian Mafia, Federico Varese defines a mafia group as 'a particular type of organized crime group that specializes in one particular commodity'.[1] That commodity is protection. Sicilian mafia specialist Diego Gambetta states that 'the mafia is a specific economic enterprise, an industry which produces, promotes, and sells private protection'.[2]

As such, the Zetas act not only as assassins for the Gulf cartel, but also engage in kidnapping, trafficking arms, money-laundering, drug dealing, and collecting payments for the cartel on its drug routes. Networks are key to Zeta enforcement. Local taxi drivers, food vendors, and other people who observe who is entering and leaving the town serve as look-outs and informants for the Zetas. [...]

The Zetas defend the Gulf cartel's territory in northern Mexico and it is reported that they also control trafficking routes along the eastern half of the US–Mexico border. According to Mexico's Federal Preventative Police, the Zetas have evolved into a sophisticated, three-tiered organisation with leaders and middlemen who coordinate contracts with petty criminals. A US intelligence official confirms this depiction when he stated that the Zetas have evolved into a mafia-style organisation found in Chicago in the 1930s.

The Zetas are believed to have been created in the late 1990s when a group of thirty lieutenants and sub lieutenants deserted the Mexican military's Special Air Mobile Forces Group (*Grupo Aeromovil de Fuerzas Especiales*, GAFE). These elite Mexican troops are reported to have been trained by US forces to combat the drug cartels. It is also believed that the Zetas have forged a working relationship with the street gang Mara Salvatrucha (MS-13) which is active in Central America and the United States.

There is evidence that the Gulf cartel is trying to obtain control of Central American smuggling routes. Daniel Perez, a founding member of Los Zetas, was captured in Guatemala in April of 2008 on charges of involvement in a shootout in southern Guatemala in which eleven people were killed. The Gulf cartel's ties with Guatemala run deep. Kaibiles, deserters of Guatemalan Special Forces, are hired as *sicarios* for the Gulf cartel. For example, they are believed to be responsible for the beheading of two Mexican police officers in Acapulco. The Kaibiles' reputation for brutality precedes them; they are accused of committing gross human rights abuses during Guatemala's civil war.

While the Zetas began as hired hit men for the Gulf cartel, it has been recently argued that the group has itself evolved into a drug-trafficking organisation. It is speculated that since 2007 and Osiel's extradition to the US the Zetas have been slowly taking over the Gulf cartel. It is not unheard of for successful organised crime groups to evolve from mafias that primarily provide protection to monopolies that control a specific commodity to transnational criminal operations with franchises in different regions of the world.

Violence

High levels of violence plague the US–Mexico border, with an especially bloody toll in Nuevo Laredo and surrounding Mexican towns. Chris Swecker, the Assistant Director of the FBI's Criminal Investigative Division, stated:

> ...this bloody drama revolves around the Gulf Cartel drug-trafficking organisation, which dominates the region and commands smuggling operations along this stretch of the American Southwest. One of their enforcement groups, known as Los Zetas, bears primary responsibility for the violence.[3]

The Gulf cartel and its enforcers, the Zetas, are serious players when it comes to using violence. Using high-tech weaponry, such as machine guns and RPGs (rocket-propelled grenades), they carry out attacks and engage in standoffs – in broad daylight – against rival cartels, police, and military forces. Some corpses are found with the letter 'Z' carved in their back, others are burned in diesel-filled barrels.

Mexican Attorney General Eduardo Medina Mora acknowledges the superiority of the cartel's firepower when compared to that of law enforcement. 'The sort of weapons they have are way more sophisticated and powerful than the ones a regular police force has: assault rifles, even grenade launchers, even missile launchers'.

The violence surrounding the Gulf cartel's operations is largely due to the illegality of the drug trade. 'Violence, as the arbiter of the black market, is its [prohibition] natural by-product'.[4] Because the drug trade is illegal, transactions and contracts are made outside the rule of law regulated by the state. Disputes between traffickers are therefore more likely to be settled by either the threat or actual use of force because their business lacks a legal framework. Cartel leaders, knowing that they have no legal recourse if they do not receive their payments, must exert control along the long chain of the distribution network to make sure that the money reliably comes back to them. Violence is a deterrent to would-be double-crossers, rivals, and informants.

However, the ease with which illegal weapons can be obtained is also a contributing factor to high levels of violence. A saying in Mexican customs goes: 'si cabe por la puerta, entonces pasa'. If it fits through the gate, then it enters. Approximately eighty percent of illegal weapons in Mexico are trafficked from the United States. This should not be overlooked.

Co-Opting Law Enforcement

One of the ways in which the Gulf cartel advances its operations is by corrupting or intimidating law enforcement officials. The municipal police in Nuevo Laredo, for example, are reportedly involved in kidnapping competitors of the Gulf cartel and then handing them over to the Zetas. The Zetas either hold them for ransom or torture them to find out information about their drug operations. 'The municipal police, the state police, the ministerial police, the police of the state, the soldiers, the federal preventative police, and the military on the border are bought by the Zetas'. The US State Department's 2007 report on human rights abuses in Mexico states:

> Corruption continued to be a problem, as many police were involved in kidnapping, extortion, or providing protection for, or acting directly on behalf of organised crime and drug traffickers. Impunity was pervasive to an extent that victims often refused to file complaints.[5]

The Gulf cartel demonstrated its influence over local law enforcement when the Mexican Army patrols that were sent to Nuevo Laredo to stem drug-related violence in June 2005 were openly attacked by local police units. This was not insignificant – local police controlled by organised crime groups were taking up arms against federal security forces. In January 2008, local police in Nuevo Laredo, Matamoras, and Reynosa were relieved of duty and disarmed by federal army troops because of their links to drug-traffickers. In Reynosa, the chief of police himself, Juan José Muñiz Salinas, was arrested in April 2008 after only four months on the job on charges of protecting members of the Gulf cartel.

Even the prisons in Mexican are not safe from corruption. Often cartel leaders who are imprisoned continue to run their operations from the cell. They buy-off and/or threaten prison officials. It is largely due to lax prison security and the loyalty of the Zetas that allowed Osiel to continue guiding the Gulf cartel's operations from his cell in La Palma prison after his arrest in 2003.

Traffickers must also corrupt law enforcement officers on the US side of the border. Operation Tarnish Star, an undercover FBI sting operation, resulted in the arrest of 13 US soldiers who pled guilty to taking bribes in exchange for transporting cocaine from Texas to Oklahoma. Military uniforms and vehicles provide protection from police searches and seizures; soldiers, therefore, are prime targets to be bribed by the cartels.

Collecting Taxes

Like the state, the Gulf cartel controls territory. And like the state, the Gulf cartel collects taxes. It does this by demanding *pisos* (tolls) from anyone wanting to run drugs, weapons, illegal immigrants, or any illicit contraband into the US from points in Mexico under its control. One of the Gulf cartel's tax collectors, who also happened to be an ex-cop, was arrested in July 2007 while at a supermarket in McAllen, Texas (across the border from Reynosa) buying a watermelon. An off-duty US drug agent thought that the man with two body guards looked not only suspicious, but also familiar as well. He called the McAllen police as both he and the suspect walked to their cars. A few minutes later Carlos Landin Martinez, 'El Puma', was arrested by the McAllen police. The DEA considered the whole thing a lucky break because Landin was not typically in the US; thus, the DEA rarely had an opportunity to pick him up. Landin was convicted in a US court on January 23, 2008 of nine counts of drug trafficking, conspiracy, and money laundering. [...]

Collecting taxes has long been a source of capital for organised crime groups. However, whether it's the Gulf cartel charging people for crossing 'their' territory, or the Sicilian and Russian mafias charging business owners 'protection' fees, the result is the same: the legitimacy of the state and its role as the protector is eroded.

[...]

Effects of Globalisation on the Transnational Nature of the Gulf Cartel

Technological advances – a key component of globalisation – allow Gulf cartel drug-traffickers to be in constant communication and to change trafficking routes if they suspect their plans have been compromised. 'Mexican cartels are more violent and sophisticated than ever, taking advantage of advances in cellular and satellite technology to evade law enforcement'. Advancing technology also facilitates money-laundering operations, as does the deregulation of financial markets.

Free trade, like advancing technology, is a defining aspect of globalisation. The benefits of free trade in North America are often disputed, but what cannot be denied is that since the signing of NAFTA in 1994, the US and Mexico governments have implemented a number of initiatives focused on ensuring the efficient and uninterrupted flow of legitimate trade between the two countries. Opening borders to licit trade also opens them to exploitation by traffickers.

For example, sister cities Nuevo Laredo, Tamaulipas, and Laredo, Texas are important hubs of US–Mexico trade. Approximately forty percent of Mexican exports to the US, carried by an estimated 6,000 trucks, cross from Nuevo Laredo into Laredo, Texas every day. Nuevo Laredo is an attractive departure point for both legal and illegal commerce headed for the United States. As such, the violent turf wars between the Gulf and Sinaloan Federation cartels over the control of the Nuevo Laredo territory should come as no surprise.

The nexus between globalisation and migration contributes to the Gulf cartel's success. The Gulf cartel exploits its well established land transportation networks to traffic drugs from Mexico into and throughout the United States. Drugs move from Nuevo Laredo to Laredo, then up Route 35, where they fan out across the United States to be distributed across the entire country at the retail level.

The Gulf cartel's international success can also be attributed to its 'remarkable ability to adapt, just as the American syndicates demonstrated in the post-Prohibition era.'[6] They have proven fully capable of expanding and consolidating their operations and markets by networking, by force, and by cutting deals with other drug-traffickers and law enforcement personnel in both Mexico and the United States.

Ability to Harm the State

In the 2007 testimony to the US Senate Committee on Foreign Relations, Thomas Shannon summed up best the United States' opinion on the threat posed by transnational organised crime groups such as the Gulf cartel. Shannon stated:

> Over the past decade, drug trafficking and other criminal organisations have grown in size and strength, aggressively seeking to undermine and intimidate government institutions in Mexico and Central America, compromising the municipal and state law enforcement entities, and substantially weakening these governments' ability to maintain public security and expand the rule of law.[7]

In a 2006 interview two members of the Zetas, the Gulf cartel's paramilitary group, claimed that there are Gulf cartel and Zeta cells operating inside the United States – in Roma, Rio Grande City, and Mission, for example – and warned that more are coming. 'It is not a lie', one said, 'They need to check good because it is true'. A 2007 US Government Accountability Office (GAO) report confirms their claims. The report states that:

> … corruption persists within the Mexican government and challenges Mexican efforts to curb drug production and trafficking. Moreover, Mexican drug trafficking organisations operate with relative impunity along the US border and in other parts of Mexico, and have expanded their illicit businesses to almost every region of the US.[8]

In addition, the 2007 US National Drug Threat Assessment documents that although the drug-trafficking organisations in the United States tend to be less structured than in Mexico, they do have regional managers throughout the country and use Mexican street gangs to distribute drugs at the retail level.

It would be difficult to argue that the Gulf cartel's activities are not actually a threat to the state, that they do not seek political change, but only want to be left alone to conduct their business without interference from the state. It would be difficult to make this argument because in Mexico the Gulf cartel actually *controls* territory and imposes its own rule – often violent – over the population and people who pass through, and in doing so is inherently a competitor of the state which also claims sovereignty over the territory in question.

The Mexican government understands the threat to the state posed by organised crime groups. Soon after assuming the presidency in December 2006, President Calderón declared that the cartels would be denied control over any part of Mexico. He deployed in the neighbourhood of 27,000 military and law enforcement officials in early 2007 to conduct counternarcotics operations in eight states. While the effectiveness of these operations is disputed, the deployment signifies the importance that the state places on the threat posed by the cartels.

The Gulf cartel also subverts government institutions, particularly at the state and local level, by using portions of the large profits made by drug-trafficking to bribe officials. And finally, the Gulf cartel threatens the state because, as their killers continue to operate with impunity, a parallel power structure operating outside the rule of law – and therefore a challenge to state authority – has emerged. The fact that the state does not maintain a monopoly on the violent tools of coercion is quite significant.

[...]

Institutional Capacities of Mexico

Mexico has long been plagued by institutional problems – corruption, weak judiciary, and abusive and ineffective police forces. For example, the 70 year long one-party rule by the *Partido Revolucionario Institucional* (PRI) served as the foundation for institutionalised corruption in Mexico. But the drug trade did not create Mexico's institutional problems; however, it is much nourished by them. Strong democratic institutions, good governance, and the rule of law have yet to fully establish themselves in Mexico because of the historical circumstances and the fact that the Mexican people are not yet fully convinced that democracy and capitalism can deliver the goods. And as Balkan specialist Misha Glenny succinctly concludes, 'Organised crime and corruption flourishes in regions and countries where public trust in institutions is weak'.[9] Consequently, the environment in which the Gulf cartel operates is a relatively healthy one for a drug-trafficking organisation.

Capacity is also lacking because of insufficient material resources. For example, Mexican law enforcement lacks the manpower to track the cartels' use of the Internet to openly threaten specific members of other cartels, to post videotaped murders on YouTube, and to openly recruit new members. Andree Teekel, an analyst for a private intelligence firm based in Texas, stated, 'In the US, posting videos like that would be plain crazy – US law enforcement has guys who do nothing but surf the Internet. But in Mexico, they can get away with it. It shows these cartels are untouchable'.

The Mexican government has focused much of its recent anti-cartel efforts on the Gulf cartel in particular. This pressure has forced the Gulf cartel to reorganise and adapt to increased pressure, especially when leaders and lieutenants are captured or killed. In addition, it has forced the Gulf cartel to fight from two sides – against the government and against other cartels attempting to encroach on its territory. Gulf cartel leaders claim that the government is focusing their anti-cartel campaign against them because the government is under the influence of the Sinaloan Federation cartel.

Mexican government efforts to weaken the Gulf cartel by attacking it from various angles may prove successful in diminishing the power and wealth of the Gulf cartel in particular, but will likely encourage the emergence of another leading cartel (e.g. the Sinaloan Federation) by creating a power vacuum. The demand for illicit drugs remains relatively inelastic; consumers will look to buy from another vendor.

[...]

Measures the State Could Take

The Merida Initiative (*Iniciativa Mérida*) is a security cooperation initiative proposed by the Bush Administration to combat the threats of drug-trafficking, transnational crime, and terrorism in the Western Hemisphere. The President has requested US $550 million, of which US $500 million would go to Mexico, in what the administration hopes will be a US $1.4 billion multi-year security cooperation plan. The logic behind the initiative is that leadership and political will are not enough to succeed in the fight against transnational crime; greater institutional and material resources are necessary. For example, the money funded through the Merida Initiative would go towards providing non-intrusive inspection equipment, ion scanners, and canine units for Mexican customs, for the new federal police, and for the military to interdict trafficked drugs, arms, cash, and persons; technologies to improve and secure communications systems to support collecting information as well as ensuring that vital information is accessible for criminal law enforcement; and technical advice and training to strengthen the institutions of justice – vetting for the new police force, case management software to track investigations through the system to trial, new offices of citizen complaints and professional responsibility, establishing witness protection programmes, helicopters and surveillance aircraft to support interdiction activities, and rapid operational response of law enforcement agencies in Mexico.

The White House Office of National Drug Control Policy (ONDCP) agrees that there is room for improved cooperation between Mexico and the United States. They argue, for example, for an agreement between the two countries allowing US law enforcement personnel to board Mexican-flagged vessels suspected of transporting illicit drugs on the high seas.

Latin American expert Laurie Freeman argues that to see real change the US ought to support broad-based police and judicial reform in Mexico by shifting the focus of US programs from providing police and training equipment to transforming structures, incentives, and controls within police and judicial institutions.

Kent Lundgren, chairman of the National Association of Former Border Patrol Officers (NAFBPO), argues that controlling the border zone in particular is beyond the capabilities of law enforcement alone. He advocates deploying the United States military to the border and then using 'whatever force is necessary to control the border zone'.

Sidney Weintraub contends that decriminalizing drug use in the United States would do more to help Mexico in their battle against the cartels than the current United States drug policy, because removing the prohibition from drugs would lower the profits made by dealers. Weintraub simultaneously acknowledged that 'no US presidential candidate is prepared to take this position'.

Another option is to cut a deal. Howard Campbell, an anthropologist at the University of Texas at El Paso who is working on a book on Mexico's drug traffickers concludes that, 'At some point, Calderón will have to negotiate agreements with the cartels. Calderón knows they can't beat them and so they simply want to control them and that's not such a bad strategy. It's a pragmatic approach'.

Conclusion

Simply put, Mexico is mobbed-up. And a mobbed-up country never bodes well for people looking to live in a free, secure, and stable society based on the rule of law. The perennial problem is the gap between the written law and enforced law. And, where corruption is endemic and organised criminal groups wield military, financial, and territorial power, the gap widens exponentially.

One of the biggest obstacles to stemming the lucrative drug trade that supports the Gulf cartel is the 2000 mile-long land border between Mexico and the United States. Between the 43 legitimate border crossings are miles and miles of open desert, rugged mountains, the Rio Grande River, and other geographic impediments that retard surveillance efforts. Relatively weak government institutions, rampant corruption, easy access to weapons, technological advances, broad transnational networks, and prohibition policies also strengthen the Gulf cartel's position. And, as Baja California's attorney general, Rommel Moreno Manjarrez, pointed out, 'It's impossible for the narco to succeed without the help of the police. The success that the narco has been having is because of the police'.[10]

Ultimately, however, the biggest obstacle to putting the Gulf cartel out of business is overcoming the demand for drugs that serves as the necessary incentive for the continuance of their operations. Where there is demand, prohibition policies, and large profits, organised crime will manifest. What then is the answer?

Focusing US aid programs, as Freeman advocates, on transforming structures, incentives, and controls within police and judicial institutions may be the best way the US could assist the Mexican government in weakening the power of the cartels and weeding out corrupt officials. Simultaneously, Mexican Attorney General Medina's office must be fully supported as they pursue their two main goals which are (1) to remove the enormous economic and firepower of the cartels, and (2) to recover territory currently controlled by the cartels for the people and the state.

Prima facie, liberalising US drug policy to decrease profits made by cartels and the violence that accompanies prohibition regimes seems to be a promising alternative to the status quo. But 'liberalising' drug policy is no easy feat. Should we pursue a policy of harm-reduction? Should possession of small amounts of certain drugs (e.g. marijuana, heroin, and cocaine) be decriminalised? In other words, should the penalty be reduced or abolished for people who use drugs 'recreationally?' If so, what about the sale and production of drugs (from which the cartels gain their profit)? What would be the consequences of full scale legalisation of drugs and their regulation by the state? Would society be better off? Or would legalisation encourage drug use, and thereby create a society swollen with addicts? And would legalisation in one country or region simply displace organised criminal activity to another area, where prohibition policies are still in place? These are some of the difficult questions that policymakers must ask if they are to successfully develop initiatives that enable the state to fulfil its protection duty.

The idea of 'cutting a deal' with the cartels is neither pragmatic nor wise. These are violent organisations whose existence and strength is dependent upon prohibition regimes and a weak and corrupted state. Is it feasible to think that a deal would alter the criminal, violent, and opportunistic mentality of these men and women who benefit from the status quo?

In formulating policies four important factors must be taken into account. The first is that while corruption in Mexico is endemic, it is essential to distinguish between corruption from need and corruption from greed. Secondly, it is important to recognise that once a group or an individual has resorted to violence to resolve disputes, it is very difficult to turn them back to non-violent conflict resolution. In other words, any policy must forcefully oppose the violence, and the people who commit it, that is a mainstay of organised crime. Thirdly, policies that reduce drug-related harm may require tolerating increases in drug use. And finally, policymakers must give proper attention to the fact that 'the narco-trafficker lifestyle of big money, big guns, and big thrills' serves as a sexy incentive to recruit new members. Drug cartels and the lifestyle they advertise and glorify must be delegitimised and alternative opportunities must be made available to those most susceptible to recruitment. This means creating real economic opportunities and pursuing a robust public relations campaign that convinces citizens that the horse to back in this race is the state, not the cartel. Nuanced policies that take these four factors into account will have an increased chance of diminishing the military, financial, and territorial power of the Gulf cartel in particular, and organised crime in general. It is this author's opinion that policy changes within the prohibitionist framework can achieve a reduction in our drug-related problems.

Notes

1   Federico Varese, *The Russian Mafia: Private Protection in a New Market Economy* (Oxford: Oxford University Press, 2001), 4.

2   Diego Gambetta, *The Sicilian Mafia: The Business of Private Protection* (Cambridge: Harvard University Press, 1993), 1.

3   Swecker, Congressional Testimony before the US.

4   Laurie Freeman, *State of Seige: Drug-Related Violence and Corruption in Mexico*, Washington Office on Latin America, June 2006, 16.

5   US State Department, Bureau of Democracy, Human Rights, and Labor, *Country Reports on Human Rights Practices 2007; Mexico*, March 11, 2008.

6   Chris Eskridge, 'Mexican Cartels and Their Integration into Mexican Socio-Political Culture' (paper presented at the International Conference on Organized Crime: Myth, Power, Profit, Lausanne, Switzerland, October 1999), 10.

7   Thomas Shannon, Assistant Secretary for Western Hemisphere Affairs, *Merida Initiative*, Testimony before the Senate Committee on Foreign Relations, November 15, 2007.

8   United States Government Accountability Office, *Drug Control: US Assistance Has Helped Mexican Counternarcotic Efforts, but Tons of Illicit Drugs Continue to Flow into the United States* (Washington DC: Government Printing Office, August 2007).

9   Misha Glenny, *McMafia* (New York: Alfred A. Knopf, 2008), 74.

10 Manuel Roig-Franzia, 'Drug Trade Tyranny on the Border', *Washington Post*, March 16, 2008.

Questions

1   What similar patterns of organized crime and corruption do you see from the Mexico drug trade and the days of alcohol prohibition? What have we learned from history?

2   What do you think have been the main factors contributing to the growth of the Mexican cartels? Why might the dissolution of the Gulf cartel through law enforcement efforts be a futile endeavor?

3   The article discusses measures that the state could take to potentially reduce Mexico's cartel problem. Which of these measures do you think would be the most effective? Least effective? Why? How much is the United States responsible for the drug violence and criminal cartels in Mexico? Why?

35

Systemic Violence in Drug Markets

Peter Reuter

Serving in stark contrast to Brophy, Peter Reuter's analysis portrays the violence in drug markets as more predictable and less pervasive than our media suggest. Although he acknowledges the areas she depicts as one of the more violent hot spots, he differentiates strongly between activities, populations, and scenes that are violent and those that are not. Based on some of the variables we have been considering throughout this book, what factors do you think promote greater or lesser degrees of drug violence: age, race/ethnicity, gender, social class, level of organization, activity, or pharmacology? Are there other factors that he introduces as relevant?

Comparing Brophy's and Reuter's accounts, which inspires a greater level of credibility for you? Are they opposing, or might they both be accurate? If you were a policy maker in the government and you accepted Reuter's analysis, what kinds of actions might you take to make things better?

The markets for illegal goods and services operate without the usual protections against fraud and violence offered by the court system. The state, instead of attempting to facilitate transactions, aims to disrupt them. Contracts cannot be enforced through written documents and the legal system; agreements are made hurriedly, sometimes in ambiguous code, and orally. Territories cannot be allocated through bidding for desirable locations, since there is no enforceable ownership of property for these purposes. All these factors can lead to violence for a variety of purposes.

Yet illegality itself is insufficient to generate high levels of violence in a market. Bookmaking, notwithstanding the drama of the film *The Sting*, was a generally peaceful affair; bookies were more likely to die in bed than on the battlefield of competition. Prostitution, though frequently unsightly and sometimes a nuisance, generates generally modest levels of violence. Even for some drugs the markets generate little violence; marijuana in general does not spark much injury as the result of competitive or transactional disputes.

However, some drug markets are clearly very violent; many participants are at risk of being killed or seriously wounded by others in the same business, either as buyers or sellers, and there are shootings of

Drugs and the American Dream: An Anthology, First Edition. Edited by Patricia A. Adler, Peter Adler, and Patrick K. O'Brien.
© 2012 John Wiley & Sons, Inc. Published 2012 by John Wiley & Sons, Inc.

innocent bystanders. The Mexican drug markets, primarily involving shipments to the US, have had high levels of violence for two decades and, since the election of President Felipe Calderon, have seen simply extraordinary levels. In the first ten months of 2008 there were estimated to be almost 4,000 homicides related to drug trafficking in Mexico. The US crack market was particularly prone to market-related violence when it emerged in the 1980s.

Violence related to drugs is an important source of the public fear about drugs such as cocaine, heroin, and methamphetamine in the United States. The upsurge of violent crime in the 1980s was regularly attributed to the growth of the crack markets in that decade and played a role in the development of the draconian penalties for possession or sale of that drug. The popular memory is selective; the fact that violence declined much more sharply than crack use in the following decade did not change the impression that the sale of crack was ineluctably associated with high levels of market violence. The drug-related wars in Colombia and Mexico have been prominently reported in the US press and have helped reinforce the view that drugs cause violence.

This brief essay explores the sources of violence in drug markets, in particular those that result from the workings of the market itself rather than from the drugs, the "psychopharmacological effects" in Goldstein's [2] tripartite division. The first section presents a theoretical discussion of the sources of violence. I then use that framework to examine first what is known about the source of violence in Mexico's high-level markets and then the high level of violence that characterized the domestic US crack market during the 1980s. The emphasis is on identifying the specific drivers of violence but there is no claim to formal hypothesis testing.

Competitive and Internal Violence

Violence in illicit drug markets can be classified in many ways. Most attention has been given to violence generated by competition among sellers. Less attention has been given to violence within selling organizations, [...].

Criminal organizations are hindered in their internal as well as external transactions by lack of access to the civil courts. Employment contracts cannot be enforced except privately; thus a dispute about responsibilities of a subordinate can quickly escalate to a violent conflict. Managerial succession is complicated by the specificity of reputation within the organization. A promising mid-level manager cannot readily provide evidence of performance to another potential employer; as a consequence higher-level managers get weaker market signals and may withhold deserved merit increases. This gives incentives to lower-level agents to use violence for upward mobility.

Symmetric to successional violence is disciplinary violence. Managers have reason to fear subordinates who can provide evidence against them; the longer the relationship, the greater the potential for harm from informing, because the subordinate acquires more useful information for that purpose. Thus managers may use violence as a tool for reducing the likelihood of being informed on. They have more incentive for doing so than do high-level dealers in transactions with low-level dealers because the information about violence will spread more rapidly and completely to lower level employees in a given organization than to a counterpart set of independent low-level dealers. There are numerous stories of this kind of "prophylactic" violence in Colombian drug dealing organizations.

Thus the violence in atomistic markets has a narrower set of sources (competition and transactions) than that in markets serviced by larger selling organizations (which also include disciplinary and successional acts). Transactions within an organization rather than between independent agents may have lower probability of generating violence because they are part of longer-term relationships, which, through development of trust, allow for other modes of resolution. Which market form generates greater violence from a given set of participants cannot be determined theoretically, but some of the decline in market related violence in the last two decades in the United States may reflect changes in organizational structure.

High-Level Trafficking: Mexico 2006–2008

One reason for expecting violence in retail drug markets is that these markets have geographic specificity. Competition can be a struggle for literal "territory," even if it is only a particularly lucrative street corner. Violators of territorial agreement can be observed because, for efficiency reasons, sales are made at a predictable place and time. However high-level trafficking lacks that specificity; transactions may occur at any place and time; the amounts are large enough and the transactions infrequent enough that the two parties find it more efficient to make prior arrangements rather than rely on intersecting routines for contact. Why then would high-level trafficking organizations enter into extended violent conflicts?

One possible explanation is that the groups are competing not for territories directly but for the rights to pay those corrupt officials who control specific channels, such as landing strips in a province of Guatemala. This is consistent with Schelling's [4] classic conjecture about the US Mafia, namely that organized crime was best thought of as the licensed collector of the rents associated with the franchise held by the corrupt police departments in individual American cities.

I will draw examples of violence in high-level markets exclusively from the drug trade in Mexico, where there are repeated claims that various "cartels" (Sinaloa, Gulf, etc.) fight for control of specific routes. In particular, there have been high levels of violence since approximately the inauguration of President Vicente Fox in December 2000 and even greater levels since 2006, with the election of Felipe Calderon and his decision to launch a military campaign against the traffickers. The domestic drug market in Mexico remains small, so it seems fair to attribute the vast majority of this violence to the export and trans-shipment trade. Given the recency of the events discussed here, there is no scholarly literature to draw on. Instead I rely on newspaper reports and official documents as sources for description of the character of the violence.

It is hard to analyze the violence without reference to the chronic corruption that has long plagued Mexico's drug control (and policing generally). There is a history of corruption cases involving high-level officials; the most prominent involved President Zedillo's senior drug official in 1997, General Jesus Gutierrez Rebollo, who was in the pay of a major trafficking organization. Presidents Fox and Calderon have both attempted to shake up existing arrangements

between police and traffickers by firing large numbers of police at the federal level. Notwithstanding the mass firings, major corruption scandals continue to occur. For example, in October 2008, almost two years into President Calderon's administration and campaign against traffickers, 35 members of the Attorney General's department were arrested for providing information to traffickers. The scandals continue to involve the most senior federal enforcement officials, such as the head of the federal police. There also have been mass firings of narcotics police at the municipal level, in which literally hundreds of officers have been dismissed at one time for corruption.

Why the sudden upsurge in violence?

Though there are no authoritative and consistent measures of drug related killings by year, no one doubts that the figures for 2007 and 2008 are very much higher than in previous years. What might have triggered this increase?

Intensified enforcement may be an important factor, working through at least two channels. First, as a result of tougher enforcement there has been considerable turnover in the leadership of the principal drug trafficking groups; many leaders have been incarcerated (often after extradition to the US) or killed in shoot-outs with the police or military. Working relationships among gangs are probably based on personal rather than institutional arrangements, so that turn-over increases inter-gang conflict. Second, as already suggested, the dismissal of large numbers of corrupt officials creates uncertainty and hence violence as traffickers search for new sources of protection.

The continuing decline of US expenditures on cocaine and heroin might also play a role. Smaller markets create excess capacity. With a workforce that has few other options with comparable pay, this might trigger an increase in the willingness to use violence to maintain revenues. The violence is different from that in US domestic markets in that a substantial share of the victims are not dealers or customers. The list of victims includes officials, reporters, singers (of narco ballads), and innocent parties (but not merely caught in the cross-fire). Some of the murdered officials are described as corrupt; some are described as zealous opponents of the drug trade. The innocent parties include family members of participants in the trade but others are described as completely unconnected to the trade.

Motivations

The diversity of victims is striking and indicates the variety of motivations for violence in the trade. Remarkably, the gangs often leave notes with the bodies, giving either their own affiliation and/or the motive for the killing. For example, one note left with five bodies in Chihuahua State said, "This is what happens to stupid traitors who take sides with Chapo Guzman." The claims of responsibility are an important data source for the following analysis. That gangs seek reputation enhancement is suggested by the fact that they pay singers to compose ballads about their feats.

I examine here the motivations for killing different kinds of victims. The analysis is necessarily speculative. It assumes that the killings are strategic rather than the result of passion. Undoubtedly some are of the latter kind, given that these are young men, selected for the capacities for violence and in regular contact with a variety of intoxicants. However, the circumstances of many killings, involving elaborate abductions of multiple victims from different places and then killing over a period of time, indicate that some are strategic.

[...]

Honest officials

The killing of zealous prosecutors and police by dealers is most easily explained. These murders serve to remove knowledgeable and effective opponents who might capture high-level traffickers. The killings also have a deterrent effect on other prosecutors and police and perhaps increase the reputation of the gang involved both among enforcement agencies and other gangs. To achieve that deterrent effect among officials, the gang must advertise its connection but may be able to do so in non-public ways, for example, by a phone call to the police; the police may not wish to disseminate that information if they themselves then want to contact the executing gang in order to establish a corrupt relationship.

In some cases, the killings of honest officials are by corrupt officials whose corrupt earnings have been reduced by the honest official. For example, the head of the federal police was killed in May 2008 by an official who was believed to be taking money for protecting shipments at the Mexico City airport and whom the police chief had removed from that post. The distinction between corrupt police officer and gang member is a fine one but important for public policy purposes.

The mass firings of corrupt officials have certainly disturbed existing corrupt arrangements. Some of the killings may be an effort to punish the new and presumably honest officials who replace those who were protecting traffickers, perhaps intimidation as a prelude to offers of bribes for corrupt arrangements.

Corrupt officials

Corrupt officials, primarily but not exclusively police, may be targeted either by those who pay them or those who wish to buy their services. The paying gangs may kill officials who fail to deliver on their promises or who are suspected of betraying their bribers; it may be functional to have an occasional random killing simply to keep others in line. Competing dealers may kill corrupt officials either to persuade other officials to accept payments from them or because they wish to replace one set of officials with another.

Innocent parties

The targeted killings of apparently innocent persons is more difficult to explain. It is hard to see the value of such killings if the gang does not claim credit. If gangs claim credit for these, then presumably the acts are reputation enhancing but that raises the question of the audience for the reputation. At least three are possible:

1 Corrupt officials. Assume that corrupt officials have to choose between competing drug gangs offering bribes. The willingness of a gang to kill even the innocent for reputational purposes may increase its "attractiveness," since refusal to take its offer is now suffused with menace. The fact that so many of the killings are particularly brutal, involving decapitation or torture, is consistent with this; it adds to the sense of dread associated with the gang.

2 Honest officials. Given a choice of gangs to target it is possible that the government, or at least the officials who are at risk, will prefer the less violent since they are less likely to retaliate effectively.

3 Other gangs. Gangs contemplating entering the territory or markets (which may not be geographic) of this gang may be deterred.

[...]

US Crack Market Violence

I turn now to the crack market in the United States, generally viewed as the most violent of modern US retail drug markets. At least four factors may have contributed to this violence:

1 **The youth of participants** Rates for violent crime peak early, at about ages 18–22. The young are particularly likely to lack foresight and thus engage in violence to settle disputes. The crack market was the first mass drug market in which most of the sellers were very young. It is worth noting that the market for bootlegged liquor, which generated great violence in the 1920s, was dominated by very young men; A1 Capone was the dominant gang leader in Chicago by age 22.

2 **The value of the drugs themselves** The cocaine that fills a plastic sandwich bag may be worth thousands of dollars. The return to sudden, situational violence was very high.

3 **The intensity of law enforcement** Transactions are conducted under considerable uncertainty as to whether the other party is an informant. Intensified enforcement increases the incentives for violence by raising the risk that the other person may be attempting to gain reduced penalties by providing information to law enforcement.

4 **The indirect consequence of drug use** More than any other mass market drug, crack use engenders violent behavior, [...]. Users are violent and aggressive and this probably encourages more use of violence by dealers themselves.

It is probably the combination of these factors, rather than any one of them, that accounts for the extraordinary

Table 35.1 Types of illicit drug markets

Dealers	Customers	
	Mostly residents	Mostly outsiders
Mostly residents	Local market	Export market
Mostly outsiders	Import market	Public market

violence associated with crack markets in the late 1980s. That violence seems to have fallen substantially, perhaps reflecting principally the aging of participants in crack markets, though violence itself, as well as enforcement, may also have selected out the most violent participants; Caulkins et al. [1] present a model in which violence declines with more intense enforcement as a consequence of selective incarceration. The sharp decline in the price of drugs that has occurred since the peak of the crack market in the early 1980s may also have reduced violence by reducing the motivation for stealing drugs.

There are, of course, other drug-market characteristics that can also influence the level of violence. Table 35.1 presents a simple classification of retail markets according to whether buyers and sellers come from the neighborhood or elsewhere. This taxonomy, originally created for purposes of analyzing vulnerability to enforcement, may also be useful in the study of violence. Markets characterized by mostly resident dealers and customers are labeled *local markets*. *Export markets* are ones in which residents of the neighborhood sell drugs to non-residents. Markets where mostly non-resident dealers sell to local residents are characterized here as *import markets*. Finally, markets where both sellers and customers are mostly non-residents are labeled here as *public markets* because they tend to occur at large public locations like parks, train or bus stations, and schoolyards.

Each class of market differs in the potential for violence. Local markets, precisely because they involve buyers and sellers who know each other, do not lend themselves to territorial competition. At the other extreme are public markets, in which buyers and sellers cannot readily find each other except at specific locations; the incentives for territoriality are consequently greater.

Transactional violence may also vary in these dimensions. Local markets discourage cheating of buyers, again as a consequence of the ongoing connections between buyers and sellers; a local customer is more likely to effectively spread information about that cheating to other potential customers than is one who has little connection to other buyers. That in turn reduces incentives for violence, this time by buyer against seller.

If this is correct, then the maturation of the crack market will tend to reduce market related violence. This is a consequence of the growing share of all transactions that take place in local markets and thus among participants who are in a continued relationship (indeed web of relationships) that would be imperiled by violence. Moreover, an increasing share of cocaine transactions may, as a result of the dissemination of beepers and cell phones, be occurring in locations (apartments, restaurants, offices) that are agreed upon by the buyer and seller for their mutual convenience. Johnson et al. ([3], p. 191, Table 35.1) report that in New York City in the 1990s, the "seller style" included phone and delivery services as well as freelancers. Poor and incompetent cocaine users still frequently transact in exposed locations, chosen precisely because they facilitate the coming together of buyers and sellers. But the ability to choose locations on the basis of specific situational need not only reduces territorially motivated violence but also reduces the vulnerability of buyers to robbery and other victimization because fewer of them need to congregate at specific locations, which thus become less attractive to predators.

Conclusions

Note again that violence is by no means a common feature of illegal markets, even of markets for illegal drugs. Specific factors are necessary to generate high levels of violence. This essay has discussed the factors that have triggered violence in two markets, the exporting of cocaine, heroin, and other drugs from Mexico in the period 2006–2008, and the retailing of crack in the 1980s in the USA. The two differ a great deal in the factors that triggered the violence and in the nature of the victims. Whereas in Mexico officials

and non-participants have frequently been the targets of killings, people in these categories were hardly ever killed intentionally in the US crack markets. Similarly, whereas enforcement itself has been a major factor in the surge of violence in Mexico, that was not true for the crack markets.

As should be obvious from this account, there is a dearth of both data and well-developed analytic frames for analyzing violence in drug markets. Given the prominence of the Mexican drug market homicides as a national problem, it is striking that there is no evidence of systematic data collection about who is killed by whom for what reasons. For crack markets there are only a few empirical papers on sources of violence [...] which are analyses of closed homicide files in New York City from when the market was at its peak for violence.

Precisely because high drug-market violence is restricted in time and space, it has not been the subject of much policy analysis either. However, the variety of sources and, in the case of Mexico, of victims, suggests that this violence is not easy to suppress once it starts. The failure of the massive crackdown by the Mexican government is indicative of that difficulty. Indeed, for a variety of reasons described above, the crackdown itself is probably one of the principal causes of the upsurge of violence. For both policy and intellectual reasons, the subject is worth further exploration.

References

1   Caulkins, J., Reuter, P., and Taylor, L. (2005). Can supply restrictions lower price?: Illegal drugs, violence and positional advantage. *Contributions to Economic Analysis and Policy*, 5(1), Article 3.

2   Goldstein, P. (1985). The drug/violence nexus: A tripartite conceptual framework. *Journal of Drug Issues*, 14, 493–506.

3   Johnson, B., Golub, A., and Dunlap, E. (2000). The rise and decline of hard drugs, drug markets, and violence in inner-city New York. In A. Blumstein and J. Wallman (eds.), *The crime drop in America* (pp. 164–206). New York: Cambridge University Press.

4   Schelling, T. (1967). Economic analysis of organized crime. In President's Commission on Law Enforcement and the Administration of Justice, *Task Force Report: Organized Crime*, Washington, DC: US Government Printing Office.

Questions

1   What do you think Reuter means by atomistic markets versus markets serviced by larger selling organizations? How might you define the differences between these two markets? What are the factors necessary for violence in illegal drug markets?

2   How do Reuter's assumptions about the likelihood of violence in local markets compare and contrast with the drug violence described by Jacobs? Which portrait seems more accurate? Why? According to Reuter, how are the motivations for violence and/or murder by Mexican cartels different than violence in US domestic drug markets? Why?

3   How might drug-related violence, public fear, and prohibition intersect to create a cycle of continued drug prohibition in the United States? What can be done to end this cycle?

Part IV

Societal Response to Drug Use

In Part IV, we address treatment, education, and policy issues that pertain to the role of drugs in society. This part allows you to think about the kinds of values we, as a society, should bring to the issue of drug use and the problem of drug abuse. We'd like you to think about how you would design American drug policy and practices if you were the President. In so doing, it is very important to educate yourself about what kinds of programs actually work, as opposed to those that are politically expedient or popular. You may want to think about the different value stances and assumptions underlying approaches characterized by interdiction, punishment, demand reduction, harm reduction, and decriminalization.

In shaping your thinking, you may first want to organize your thoughts and strategies around the three sections of this part of the book. Drug education has been part of elementary and high school curricula for several decades now. Still, there is no one agreed-upon way to inculcate knowledge about drugs into the younger population. Many programs, such as DARE, discussed in Chapter 37, began with the seemingly harmless idea that drugs are bad, that children need to know about this, and that adults should inform students about how and why drugs will hurt them. However, these programs have largely used scare tactics, have often not told the whole truth about drugs, and for the most part have been dismal failures because adolescents experiment with drugs and find that their elders have been exaggerating or lying to them about their effects. Drug education, though well-funded for the most part, has not done its job in curtailing the use of drugs or in informing the populace about their pros and cons. Within this context, some drug educators have more recently advocated a harm reduction approach, arguing that people will do drugs no matter what, so that the best educational policy is to provide accurate information so that drug users do not hurt themselves. This approach, outlined in Chapter 38, also known as "Just Say Know," highlights drug education that is honest, straightforward, and nonjudgmental.

As more and more celebrities have found themselves getting into trouble with drugs, a multi-billion dollar treatment industry has emerged that attempts to get people off drugs. There have been many agencies, centers, and rehabilitation facilities that have sprung up

Drugs and the American Dream: An Anthology, First Edition. Edited by Patricia A. Adler, Peter Adler, and Patrick K. O'Brien.
© 2012 John Wiley & Sons, Inc. Published 2012 by John Wiley & Sons, Inc.

to assist these people with their substance abuse problems. However, like education, we have not zeroed in on a single treatment program that works. Whether it is the treatment communities made famous by places such as the Betty Ford Clinic, methadone maintenance programs that are supposed to get people off heroin (but transfer them to another drug addiction), drug courts that deal with meting out punishment and rehabilitation to those who have been arrested, or the many 12-Step programs that have flourished, each modality has its own advantages and disadvantages. These are discussed in the chapters in this book. However, controversially, not all drug researchers agree that these treatments work, or are even necessary. In Chapter 41, we see research on a group of cocaine users that got off drugs through "natural recovery," by simply going "cold turkey" or abstaining from further drug use on their own. Most of us know people who have smoked cigarettes for years, and whether a health scare or other reason motivates them, they quit without the use of treatment counselors, nicotine patches, hypnotism, or any of the other forms of treatment that the industry proffers as the only "real" way to quit. Needless to say, the rehabilitation industry, with its powerful doctors, psychologists, social workers, and other mental health professionals, has balked at the idea of "natural recovery."

Finally, we end this book with a section on Drug Policy and what sociologists and criminologists have offered as ways to deal with drugs in our society. These authors discuss myriad ideas to change our often Draconian drug laws that have filled our prisons with petty crimes related to drugs, cost our society billions of dollars without ever "fixing" the problem, and waged a War on Drugs that has pervaded American culture for much of the past fifty years or more. These policymakers debunk most of the current laws and legislation about drugs, and offer you some new ways we can handle the issues of drug use in a more humane, sensible, and widespread fashion than we have in the past. Rather than locating policy in the hands of law enforcement, public health lies at the bedrock of these authors' concerns.

36

A Decade of DARE
Efficacy, Politics and Drug Education

Earl Wysong and David W. Wright

Most people who read this book will have either taken the DARE curriculum or known others who did. Popular with politicians and law enforcement organizations alike, it sprang out of Nancy Reagan's "Just Say No" initiative and brought policemen into schools to talk to fifth and sixth graders about peer pressure. More than twenty-five years after its inception, these same groups remain bullish about DARE, but educators and scholars have joined together to question its value. They point to a lack of systematic research supporting its claims of effectiveness in diminishing the demand for drugs and turning kids away from the early stages of drug use.

If you think about your personal knowledge of DARE, how would you assess its effectiveness? What did you and your friends think about it at the time? What did you think about it when you got older and started encountering drugs in your peer groups? How do you regard it now? If you think about anti-drug education, how might you design your own program? DARE didn't say much in its curriculum about actual drugs: how they affect people, the physical, psychological, or health dangers they pose, and the issues we have studied here relating to self-control. Based on the curriculum in your course and these readings, what goals would you have for your curriculum? What would you tell young people about drugs? What would you leave out for practical, ideological, or age-related purposes? At what age do you think we most need drug education? If you could administer a drug education agenda that hit young people at two different ages, what ages would you pick, and what would you focus on at each age?

Drugs and the American Dream: An Anthology, First Edition. Edited by Patricia A. Adler, Peter Adler, and Patrick K. O'Brien.
© 2012 John Wiley & Sons, Inc. Published 2012 by John Wiley & Sons, Inc.

The decade following the introduction of the Drug Abuse Resistance Education (DARE) Program in Los Angeles witnessed DARE's transformation into the most widespread drug education program in the United States and perhaps the world. Beginning with 8,000 Los Angeles elementary students in 1983–4, by the mid-1990s DARE had expanded into half of all US local school districts and was reaching 25 million students in all 50 states with total nationwide program expenditures estimated at $750 million. Internationally, DARE programs are operative in several nations including Australia, Canada, Mexico, New Zealand, Norway and Sweden. DARE's international scope reflects, in part, its "adoption for use in US Department of Defense (DOD) schools ... located in the various nations where US military personnel are stationed" (Rogers 1993, p. 151).

DARE's remarkable expansion has been paralleled by the growth of a cottage industry of evaluation research aimed at assessing the program's effectiveness with both DARE and several evaluation projects benefiting, at least in part, from funding associated with the federally-sponsored "War on Drugs." However, despite the extensive evaluation record compiled over the past decade, the issue of DARE's effectiveness has been the subject of recent disputes between program supporters and evaluation researchers and remains unresolved. Even so, DARE remains very popular, continues to expand and appears firmly entrenched as part of the school curriculum in thousands of classrooms nationwide and worldwide.

The unresolved controversies concerning DARE's effectiveness combined with its international scale and expense highlight the importance of inquiring into the efficacy and political dimensions of the program. With these issues as our focus, the purposes of this paper are to: (1) present the findings of our seven-year study on DARE's long-term efficacy; (2) explore the politics of DARE including: (a) DARE's development as a political and organizational phenomenon, (b) the interests of DARE supporters, (c) the tensions between DARE supporters and DARE evaluation research and (d) the implications of DARE as a political force for evaluation research, and for the program's future. To address these goals, we utilize a two-tiered micro/macro assessment and a sociologically-informed narrative format. While the former feature provides a systematic means for considering and linking the two major dimensions of the study, the latter technique permits a relaxation of conventional hypothesis testing, encourages a flexible, multi-faceted inquiry and represents an emerging alternative to traditional positivistic methods. We believe this approach is especially well-suited to our investigation of DARE as a multi-faceted programmatic and political phenomenon.

Evaluating DARE: A Multi-Dimensional Approach

At the micro-prevention level, we explore DARE's long-term effects on high school seniors seven years after their initial exposure to the program through a two-track assessment framework utilizing both impact and process evaluation procedures. The former approach is used as the principal means for assessing, by quantitative measures, whether and/or the extent to which students' exposure to DARE produces lasting effects related to the program's primary and secondary objectives. The latter approach uses qualitative data from focus group interviews with two contrasting senior groups of former DARE participants to explicate program dynamics and interpret outcomes.

At the macro-level, our perspective builds upon the approach taken by Wysong et al. (1994) which views DARE as a socially constructed form of symbolic politics linked to the War on Drugs and supported by powerful, organizationally-based stakeholder groups. [...]

Project DARE

Background, objectives, changes

DARE began in Los Angeles in 1983–84 as a school-based drug prevention program through the joint efforts of the Los Angeles Police Department (LAPD) and the Los Angeles Unified School District (LAUSD). DARE is a standardized, copyrighted anti-drug curriculum taught by uniformed officers who have undergone 80 hours of specialized training. DARE's "major goal ... is to prevent substance abuse among school children" and it seeks to accomplish this objective by teaching students "the skills for recognizing and resisting social pressures to experiment with tobacco, alcohol and drugs" (US Dept. of Justice 1991, p. 3). The DARE lessons also focus on enhancing students' self-esteem, decision-making, coping, assertiveness and communication skills and "teaching positive alternatives to substance use" (ibid.)

The DARE "core" curriculum is designed for fifth and sixth graders and consists of 17 weekly lessons approximately 45 to 60 minutes each in length. All classroom activities are scheduled during the regular school day and encourage active student involvement in exercises such as "question and answer [sessions], group discussions and role-play[ing] activities" (US Dept of Justice 1991, p. 7). The curriculum can also be extended down to earlier grades as well as up to the middle and high school levels. In addition to classroom instruction, several other activities have been developed to enhance the program's effectiveness including the use of selected high school students as DARE "Role Models" in the elementary grades, informal officer/student contacts, teacher orientation, parental education and community presentations.

DARE evaluation research

In the early 1990s, DARE was represented by the US Department of Justice as "a long-term solution" to the problem of drug use (US Dept. of Justice 1991, p. i). Claims for DARE's effectiveness emerged in the late 1980s based on early evaluation studies and have continued into the mid-1990s with some members of Congress recently proclaiming DARE to be the "most effective drug-use prevention education program in the United States" (Congressional Record 1994a). However, as noted earlier, a mixed research record regarding DARE's efficacy began to accumulate in the 1990s with many studies calling DARE's claims of effectiveness into question. Some studies conducted immediately following students' completion of the DARE program found it to be successful in promoting anti-drug attitudes and behaviors. However, a recent "meta-analysis" comparing DARE's short-term results with those of other drug education programs found "that DARE's core curriculum effect on drug use … is slight and … not statistically significant" (Ennett et al. 1994a, p. 1398).

Eight studies have been reported tracking DARE over intermediate periods of time. These include a one-year follow-up study, two two-year studies, a three-year study commissioned by the Los Angeles Board of Police Commissioners, a three- and four-year study and three five-year studies. The findings of the published long-term studies indicate that DARE produces few, if any, measurable anti-drug effects on adolescents' drug-use rates or drug-related attitudes over extended periods of time.

Evaluating DARE: Background and procedures

Kokomo was the first city in Indiana to implement the DARE program. During 1987–88, all Kokomo fifth graders received the full DARE core curriculum while all seventh graders received a shortened eleven-week version. We conducted short-term program assessments for the fifth and seventh grade groups utilizing the "DARE Scale" developed in Los Angeles, which supposedly provides a general measure of DARE's effectiveness in the areas of drug-related attitudes, knowledge and anti-drug coping skills. In a pre- and post-test design, we found significant increases in post-DARE scores for fifth graders, but not for seventh graders. In a later study, following the seventh grade group to graduation, we found that DARE had no long-term effects upon their drug-related behaviors and attitudes as high school seniors. However, unlike the seventh graders, the fifth grade group experienced the full DARE curriculum and responded positively to it. Therefore, the seven-year follow-up results for this group (as 1994 seniors – reported in the "Results" sections) represent an important test of DARE's long-term effectiveness.

Impact evaluation: Objectives, sample, design

The impact dimension of the study uses data from a multi-part questionnaire completed by Kokomo High School (KHS) seniors in 1991 (non-DARE group, no DARE exposure) and in 1994 (DARE group, exposed to DARE as fifth graders). Several comparisons are made to assess whether and/or the extent to which DARE exposure is associated seven years later with effects in four areas. The first two are directly linked to DARE's primary objectives of preventing/reducing/delaying drug use and include measures of: (1) self-reported drug use rates and (2) drug attitudes, drug knowledge and drug-resistant coping skills. If exposure to DARE in the fifth grade produces lasting anti-drug effects, then measures of the DARE group's characteristics in these two areas should be significantly different from the non-DARE group.

[…]

The questionnaire was completed by large samples of 1991 and 1994 KHS seniors nearly evenly divided by gender. Subjects were chosen through a random selection of classes (e.g., English, science, etc.) with students participating on a voluntary basis. Using ballot-box style procedures to ensure confidentiality and anonymity, responses were obtained for 331 of the 1991 seniors (class size = 511) and 238 of the 1994 seniors (class size = 430). Of the latter group, 214 were identified as having completed DARE as fifth graders. This sub-population is referred to as the 1994 "DARE group" in the comparisons presented throughout the study. The questionnaire included four scales: Drug Use Scale, DARE Scale, Self-Esteem Scale and Locus of Control Scale.

Micro-level process evaluation: Objectives and design

The micro-level process portion of the study is based on focus group interviews with two groups of 1994 KHS juniors/seniors who completed the DARE program as fifth graders: (1) The DARE Role Model group and (2) the "At Risk" group. The 21 DARE Role Models interviewed (6 males and 15 females) were part of a program organized by KHS faculty members involving junior and senior volunteers. These students are chosen through a screening process, trained and then serve as DARE peer facilitators. They visit DARE classes in the elementary schools with the DARE officers. By contrast, the seven "At Risk" students interviewed (three males, four females) attend an alternative school at a site removed from the main high school. This program was initiated in 1988 as the "School of Opportunity Program" (SCOOPS). Students are placed in the SCOOPS program based on a variety of considerations, but generally they are considered to have personal, academic and/or social characteristics (e.g., absenteeism problems) that place them "at risk" for remaining in school.

[...]

Results: Impact evaluation

Drug Use Scale

Comparisons of data from the Drug Use Scale for 1991 non-DARE and 1994 DARE seniors reveal that self-reported drug use rates among both groups were very similar for: (1) Lifetime Prevalence, (2) Recency

of Use, (3) Frequency of Use and (4) Grade Level at First Drug Use. Moreover, both groups were also very similar in terms of Perceived Availability of Drugs. Drug use rates were higher for the 1994 DARE group than for the 1991 non-DARE group for some drugs and time periods. However, for other drugs and time periods the rates are reversed.

Grade Level at First Drug Use is the only area where the data suggest a *possible* long-term DARE effect. Compared with the 1991 non-DARE group, the 1994 DARE group recorded significantly higher grade levels at first use for alcohol, marijuana and cocaine. However, for the other five drugs there were no significant differences between the two groups. The mixed results on this measure, the small differences in the means and the absence of a consistent trend for all drugs, make it difficult to know if the observed results are due to a long-term "DARE effect" or to other factors.

Prevalence and Recency data were analyzed in detail comparing Frequency of Use (number of occasions of drug use) among DARE and non-DARE seniors for all drug types/categories and time periods (lifetime, last year, past 30 days). While too lengthy to report in detail here, the results revealed no significant differences in Frequency of Use rates between the two groups for each time period and each drug type/category — with one exception. The results were significant for marijuana use during the last year and the past 30 days because of *higher* use rates by the 1994 DARE group compared with the 1991 non-DARE group.[1] These results, combined with our other statistical analyses, indicate that fifth grade DARE exposure does not produce any long-term prevention effects on adolescent drug use rates.

DARE Scale

DARE exposure appears to produce no significant long-term effects in areas related to the program's primary objectives. [...] [T]he mean percentages of "Appropriate" responses were sharply lower for the 1991 and 1994 senior groups compared with the mean recorded by the 1994 seniors as fifth graders. [...] In addition to the obvious decline in overall mean scores, some interesting differences on individual items were also discovered. For example, consistent with our previous findings, when compared with their fifth grade scores, the scores of the 1994 seniors recorded a sharp decline in positive attitudes towards the police along with a growing unwillingness to condemn peer's consumption of alcohol.[2]

Self-Esteem and Locus of Control Scales

Next, we consider the Self-Esteem Scale and Locus of Control results for the DARE and non-DARE groups. The mean scores on each scale are very similar for both groups. Moreover, the tests indicate no significant differences in the means of the DARE and non-DARE seniors. Since these scales are viewed as measures of DARE's secondary objectives, the results are indicative of two more areas where we see no long-term effects resulting from DARE exposure.

Results: Micro-level Process Evaluation

The focus group interviews reinforced the quantitative findings, with students' subjective views and comments on the issue of DARE's long-term effectiveness also trending in a negative direction. Although several issues were covered in the interviews, due to space limitations, only themes and responses most directly relevant to the DARE recall and long-term effectiveness issues are presented.

All members of the DARE Role Model group recalled their earlier exposure to the DARE program in uniformly positive terms. They also unanimously agreed that DARE was a positive force in the schools, and most expressed the view that their involvement could make it even more effective for younger students. As one student said, "I felt like if, you know, maybe if I was doing my part, you know, maybe something I said will affect them later, you know; [maybe] they [won't] get involved with drugs and alcohol." However, when asked about their assessment of DARE's long-term effectiveness, two convergent response patterns emerged: (1) most of the role models were circumspect or doubtful about DARE's long-term effects; (2) a substantial minority was openly pessimistic. The circumspect theme was expressed by one student who said, "For some people it lasted, but for others it just lasted for a year or two and wore off." Many others reinforced this sentiment as exemplified by the view of another student who

stated, "I still think it has an impact on some of the younger kids, once they reach 8th and 9th grade." By contrast, the more pessimistic view was illustrated by widespread nods of agreement and short verbal remarks such as "that's true" among a sizable minority of the group in response to a student who remarked, "It's true, it doesn't last that long as far as remembering the DARE program. ... It may help just a little bit, but not much."

The "At-Risk" group members had mixed recollections regarding their exposure to the DARE program. Most group members recalled their fifth grade DARE lessons in detail, but a few could not even remember being exposed to DARE. In sharp contrast to students in the DARE Role Model group, the At-Risk students who remembered DARE from the fifth grade recalled the program in negative or derisive terms. For example, a majority recalled the program as boring and echoed the sentiment expressed by one student who said, "They need to bring in movies and stuff like that. It's boring when the cop just sits there and talks all the time." The boredom theme was reinforced by another student who also commented on what she viewed as the "phoniness" of the Dare Role Models: "I was bored with it and a lot of my friends didn't care about it. They [the role models] just sat there and said 'Don't do drugs,' but they didn't talk about it. It was like they was just playing a role and not really sincere."

Among the At-Risk students, DARE was judged as having no long-term drug-prevention effects. These students unanimously agreed that DARE was not effective in promoting anti-drug attitudes or behaviors. When they were asked, "Do you think DARE has any long-term effects on drug-related attitudes or behaviors among students your own age?" the response theme was uniformly negative. Several individuals responded with short answers such as, "Nope," "None at all," and "Not a thing." One student underscored this view emphatically by saying, "Well, for the record, I don't think the DARE program works at all." This statement produced much nodding of agreement among the group and statements such as "Amen!" and "That's for sure!"

It must be recalled that the selection of the two very different student populations represented in the focus groups was deliberate. These groups were not intended to serve as random samples of subjective student opinions on DARE. Instead, the purpose was to afford students with very different academic and personal orientations an opportunity to present and discuss their subjective views and feelings about DARE. The interesting convergence of negative (or at the very least doubtful) views among both groups on the issue of DARE's long-term efficacy provides an interesting commentary on how the program's effectiveness is perceived by the students themselves and strengthens our confidence in the validity of the questionnaire results.

The politics of DARE

We approach the politics of DARE from an organizationally based, social constructionist theoretical tradition that views public policies regarding social problems as grounded in organizations and linked to social, political and cultural processes. According to this view, the formation and implementation of public policies are primarily organizationally driven, political enterprises involving governmental entities, private sector firms and non-profit groups. Since organizational resources and symbolic imagery are viewed as crucial to the politics of policy development, implementation and evaluation, resource dependency theory and dramaturgical analysis serve as key features of the conceptual framework we use to explore the politics of DARE.

Resource dependency theory emphasizes the centrality of resources to organizational growth and survival (Aldrich and Pfeffer 1976) and also recognizes that a wide array of tangible and intangible organizational assets are included in the definition of resources (Scott 1992). Dramaturgical analysis is a technique usually applied to small-group interaction utilizing theater-related imagery such as impression management, performances and front and back regions. It focuses on social actors' efforts to create and sustain positive impressions in the social interaction process (Goffman 1959). We believe this approach can be usefully applied to DARE at an organizational level of analysis because it calls attention to and helps us understand how to create and maintain idealized, positive impressions of their missions, goals and activities (Benford and Hunt 1992; Wysong 1992b).

Since we see public policies as linked to political and cultural processes as well as to organizations and since organizations must accumulate resources (of various sorts) and construct and maintain legitimate identities acceptable to resource-granting organizational constituencies in order to survive, we explore four issues related to the politics of DARE: (1) DARE's development as a political and organizational phenomenon, (2) the interests of DARE stakeholders, (3) tensions between DARE stakeholders and evaluation research and (4) the implications of DARE as a political force for evaluation research and for the future of the program.

DARE: A political and organizational phenomenon

Among members of both political parties, national political interest in the "drug problem" crystallized in 1986 with former President Reagan's televised "War on Drugs" address to the nation and the subsequent passage of the "Anti-Drug Abuse Act of 1986." Once set in motion, the Drug War remained a popular focus of political and media attention through the late 1980s and into the 1990s. It was also transformed into an increasingly complex and multi-faceted political and organizational phenomenon. For example, as a result of the "Anti-Drug Abuse Act of 1988," under the Bush and then the Clinton Administrations the Drug War was systematized into an increasingly refined "National Drug Control Strategy" aimed at controlling both the supply of and the demand for illicit drugs in the US. The latter dimension of this strategy included an emphasis on developing "demand reduction" programs of all types, including drug education. As the Drug War shifted public attitudes in a direction supportive of anti-drug programs, political interest in and federal funding for drug education increased substantially. For example, federal funding for all drug "Educational Prevention Activities" increased from $230 million in 1988 to $660 million in 1995.

In the early phase of the Drug War, DARE was well positioned to take advantage of emerging political and funding support by offering a convenient, individual-level programmatic "solution" to the drug threat. By 1986, DARE had established a positive track record in Los Angeles and was rapidly acquiring an expanding circle of enthusiastic promoters, including LAPD Chief Daryl Gates. Congressional testimony by Gates in favor of DARE, along with political support from powerful members of Congress and former President Bush, led to a 1990 amendment to the 1986 Drug-Free Schools and Communities Act (DFSCA) that mandated federal funding for DARE. As amended, the DFSCA required that 10 percent of DFSCA "Governor's Funds" (30 percent of federal funds made available each fiscal year to states for drug prevention programs) be used to fund programs "such as Project Drug Abuse Resistance Education" (US Code Annotated 1995, p. 337). DARE was the *only* drug education curriculum specifically targeted for federal funding by the DFSCA, giving the program a tremendous boost.

Drug-War-driven public sentiment and substantial federal funding helped create and sustain political and popular support for individuals, officials and organizations directly and indirectly associated with DARE. The result was the creation of an arrangement of mutual support and reinforcement among *direct* DARE stakeholders (individuals and organizations directly linked to supporting and/or implementing the program) and *indirect* stake holders (e.g., political supporters and organizations contributing to the program). Both stakeholder groups benefited from the reflected approval, legitimacy and widespread public support associated with a program linking a popular cause with traditional authority structures symbolized by the involvement of schools and law enforcement agencies.[3]

At the national level, DARE emerged as a bipartisan favorite of political leaders in the late 1980s, with strong political support for the program continuing into the mid-1990s.[...] Funding support and federal resolutions (along with similar actions at the state and local levels) link political leaders to the program as indirect DARE stakeholders who benefit from being identified with a popular program thereby boosting their own popularity. At the same time, their political support further legitimizes the DARE program, and enhances its funding prospects, thereby benefiting individuals and organizations directly involved with its operation and/or expansion.

DARE's direct and indirect stakeholders have also collaborated to embed the program within a complex

organizational support structure that helps ensure a continuing flow of resources necessary to sustain its survival and growth. An important feature of this structure is DARE AMERICA, a nonprofit corporation organized in 1987 as a 501(c)(3) tax-exempt organization. With an annual budget of $1.3 million in 1990, DARE AMERICA has become an effective organizational advocate for DARE with goals that include "the adoption of DARE in all States and communities. ... Support [for] a national DARE instructor training program... [and] Coordinat[ing] national fund-raising for DARE" (US Dept of Justice 1991, p. 11). The organization has actively recruited corporate sponsors as well as numerous corporate, political and entertainment elites, such as TV personality Arsenio Hall and singer Ted Nugent, to serve as DARE spokespersons and fund-raisers. The DARE AMERICA Board of Directors "consists of prominent national business, political, law enforcement and educational leaders" (US Dept of Justice 1991, p. 11) and over the years has included philanthropist Armand Hammer, singer Michael Jackson, Daryl Gates, Diane Disney Miller and former Virginia Governor Gerald L. Baliles.

Another dimension of DARE's organizational support structure consists of a network of ties linking DARE programs to various federal, state and local government agencies as well as to private corporations. For example, the Bureau of Justice Assistance (BJA – an agency within the US Department of Justice) serves as a major organizational link tying DARE programs to the federal government. This connection dates to 1986 when Gates succeeded in arranging a BJA grant of $140,000 to the LAPD "to share [the] unique DARE Program with other communities throughout the United States" (US Congress: Senate 1988b, p. 198). BJA involvement with DARE expanded in the late 1980s and led to agency funding of five regional DARE training centers. The BJA also appoints 5 of the 15 members comprising the DARE Training Center Policy Advisory Board (TCPAB) responsible for overseeing the training of DARE officers (US Dept. of Justice 1991, p. i). Other federal agencies with ties to DARE include the National Institute of Justice (NIJ) and the National Institute on Drug Abuse (NIDA), which have funded DARE evaluation research. Also, the US Department of

Education provides some program funding through the DFSCA and, as previously noted, the DOD has adopted DARE for use in the schools it operates for dependents of US military personnel. Government linkages also extend down to the state and local levels and involve law enforcement agencies, schools and community groups.

Beyond the public sector are numerous links tying DARE to corporate sponsors at the national, state and local levels. DARE AMERICA has been especially instrumental in recruiting national corporate sponsors such as Bayliner, Herbalife, Kentucky Fried Chicken, Kimberly-Clark, McDonald's, Packard Bell, Security Pacific National Bank (SPNB) and Warner Brothers to help fund the program. For example, SPNB contributed $500,000 in 1989 and pledged another $1 million over five years. Corporate support at the state and local levels involves hundreds of large and small firms contributing to the program.

DARE: Stakeholder interests

While direct and indirect DARE stakeholders have different types and levels of interest in the program, the preceding section suggests that both groups share concerns in several areas including political, material and ideological interests. Organizations (and individuals) with direct links to DARE benefit from public and private resources allocated to fund the program and thus have resource-dependency-based political and material interests in maintaining DARE's image as an effective deterrent to drug use. The political and material interests of DARE stakeholders are also closely tied to a related shared interest in maintaining what may be termed "program legitimacy." This term refers to the perception of DARE by relevant public and political constituencies as a sound, rational, effective – and thereby legitimate – program. It is a concept that we believe should be viewed as both an important goal of and an intangible resource for DARE stakeholders.

As noted in the preceding section, DARE stakeholders have succeeded in embedding the program in a network of political and organizational support that has helped establish DARE's reputation as a rational, comprehensive and legitimate program. Stakeholders have also widely disseminated anecdotal information on DARE's effectiveness, but in order to

seal DARE's legitimacy (and win approval from the scientific community), the program needs strong research-based evidence of its effectiveness. Since such evidence has been elusive, this area represents an important weak link in stakeholders' efforts to sustain program legitimacy. As we will see in the next section, it is a continuing problem for DARE stakeholders because negative evaluation results do more than simply call DARE's effectiveness into question; they also represent a challenge to DARE's program legitimacy, thereby threatening a critical resource upon which DARE stakeholders depend for support of their political and material interests.

Some stakeholder groups (especially elite political and corporate supporters/sponsors) can be viewed as having ideologically-based interests in maintaining DARE's legitimacy because the program promotes an individual-level focus upon both drug use and prevention. This orientation helps perpetuate public and political perceptions that the etiology of drug use/abuse is fundamentally a matter of individual attitudes and choice. Thus, public attention and policy discussions regarding drug use and prevention are deflected away from considerations of structural factors related to class or racial inequalities in areas such as income, education or occupational opportunities that may be related to drug use/abuse. In this way, public discourse on the causes of drug use/abuse remains focused at the level of individual attitudes and choices. While it may be argued that any constraining effects DARE may have on public debates regarding the causes of drug use/abuse represent unintended consequences, there is little doubt that DARE's individual-level focus is consistent with an emergent trend of the 1990s. Conservative political leaders, social analysts and "talk radio" have fostered the portrayal of a wide range of social ills from poverty to joblessness to drug use as essentially stemming from "attitude problems" among those groups most affected by such conditions.

The significance and complexity of stakeholder interests in the DARE program make it clear that many groups have strong preferences in seeing the program continue, expand and be defined as effective and "successful." Given this reality, negative findings by evaluation researchers represent potent threats to DARE's program legitimacy, DARE funding and the political and material interests of organizations (and individuals) associated with the program. Thus, we would expect that resource-dependent organizations (e.g., Department of Justice agencies, DARE AMERICA, local police agencies, schools) having political and material interests in defending and perpetuating DARE's image as an effective deterrent to drug use would mount aggressive attacks against negative evaluation studies. [...]

For the future of DARE

The recent evaluation controversies and changes in the political context, including decreases in federal DARE funding as well as President Clinton's recent emphasis on school violence prevention and conflict resolution, illustrate the challenges confronting DARE. However, as we have shown, DARE has numerous political supporters, stakeholder advocates and a formidable organizational support structure – including federal funding in place through 1999. DARE also has a demonstrated ability to adapt to changing circumstances as the core curriculum revision episode illustrates. These realities suggest that despite the emerging negative evaluation record and a changing political context, DARE is likely to survive at least through the end of this decade as America's, and perhaps the world's, largest drug education program. Our prediction of DARE's continued survival derives partly from the program's powerful organizational and political constituencies and partly from the multiple symbolic functions served by drug education generally. For example, as Bangert-Drowns has noted, "It is unlikely that drug education will ever be withdrawn from the schools, even if it is shown to be ineffective. It appears to serve functions other than just the prevention of drug abuse, such as the reassurance that the schools are at least trying to control substance abuse among students" (1988, p. 260).

Conclusions

After tracking DARE for seven years, our quantitative and qualitative data indicate that DARE is not effective over the long term in preventing or reducing adolescent drug use. Of course, we recognize the limitations of our findings given both the local nature of our sample and the complexities associated with conducting longitudinal evaluation research on a popular program addressing the highly charged issue of adolescent drug use. Despite these limitations, we believe our evaluation of DARE represents a fair and accurate assessment of the program's long-term effects *for the group we studied*. We also believe our exploration of the politics of DARE represents an important step towards a more complete understanding of the complex and powerful political and organizational dimensions of this decade-old program. [...] Because this study goes far beyond a one-dimensional impact assessment of DARE, we believe our findings are important and deserve widespread attention.

We think our study will help stimulate a reconsideration of several issues related to the etiology of drug use and assumptions concerning programs aimed at preventing or delaying drug use among young adults. In addition, it should stimulate a greater awareness of DARE's influence as a political force shaping public perceptions of the program and the evaluation process. Regarding the first two issues, we believe there is an especially urgent need to consider whether drug prevention efforts should be expanded to include efforts other than those aimed at changing students' attitudes or improving their social skills through sophisticated persuasive communication programs. Findings from programs such as the Summer Training and Education Program (STEP) that, like DARE, *do not* include provisions or resources for changing young people's social and economic environments in the course of attempting long-term changes in their attitudes and behaviors offer further evidence of the shortcomings of such approaches as well as the complex and difficult problems inherent in such undertakings. The findings regarding DARE's effectiveness (as well as findings from similarly structured and youth-targeted social programs such as STEP and the Job Corps) underscore the need for a more complete consideration of the appropriate balance between prevention approaches that focus primarily on the psychosocial dimension of drug use and policies that address cultural and structural factors related to drug use.

Programs building on the latter approach could include efforts to change structural factors contributing to inequalities, alienation and social isolation among adolescents. For example, programs, even at an experimental or demonstration level, aimed at providing adolescents and young adults with diverse, high-quality educational programs and later meaningful job opportunities that would allow them to be economically self-supporting could be usefully tied to more traditional education-based prevention approaches. However, DARE's formidable organizational and political resources along with DARE stakeholders' interests and impression management activities are likely to pose significant obstacles to policy discussions aimed at framing drug prevention in structural terms and the implementation of such programs. Even so, to the extent that our evaluation results and political analysis of DARE help stimulate public debate on the relative merits of psychosocial and structurally-based drug prevention policies and programs, DARE will have served as a useful point of departure for productive policy discussions on the continuing problem of drug use in American society.

Notes

1   The finding of higher drug use rates for some drugs and time periods among the DARE group raises the *possibility* that drug education programs may increase student curiosity about drugs and lead to higher levels of drug experimentation. However, given the recent increase in national drug use rates among high school seniors, it is difficult to know whether the DARE drug use rate "spikes" are due to increased curiosity, contextual factors or anomalies in the data.

2   Comparisons of results on the DARE Scale with those from the Drug Use Scale call into question the utility of the former scale as a meaningful predictor of drug use. For example, despite approximately two thirds of the respondents in both senior groups giving "Appropriate" responses for 16 of the 19 items on the Dare Scale, substantial majorities in these groups reported using various drugs (especially alcohol and cigarettes). Such results are consistent with a number of findings in the drug education literature showing that while anti-drug information is easily imparted, producing changes in drug-related attitudes and behaviors is much more difficult and problematic. Moreover, the results also suggest that rather than measuring any meaningful attitudinal or behavioral changes, the Dare Scale simply assesses the extent to which DARE encourages students

to uncritically recall and repeat information. In this sense the scale appears to be a very self-serving measure which by the design of its questions and coding procedures elicits the *appearance* of positive results, thereby overstating the impact and efficacy of the DARE program.

3   Despite DARE's widespread popularity, the program also has some opposition among parents and concerned citizens. For example, members of a network known as "Parents Against DARE" as well as other individuals and groups have criticized the program on the grounds that it reduces instructional time for academic subjects, is ineffective, has confused objectives and employs discredited methods from the 1970s. Moreover, DARE has also been criticized by some parents as representing a kind of "Big Brother" spy operation, with DARE students being encouraged by DARE officers to report their drug-using parents to the police. In addition to these developments, investigative journalists have recently published reports on DARE in the popular press with a distinctly negative "spin."

References

Aldrich, Howard E. and Jeffrey Pfeffer. 1976. "Environments of Organizations." Pp. 79–105 in *Annual Review of Sociology*, edited by Alex Inkeles, James Coleman and Neil Smelser. Palo Alto, CA: Annual Reviews, Inc.

Bangert-Drowns, Robert L. 1988. "The Effects Of School-Based Substance Abuse Education – A Meta-Analysis." *Journal of Drug Education* 18: 243–64.

Benford, Robert D. and Scott A. Hunt. 1992. "Dramaturgy and Social Movements: The Social Construction and Communication of Power." *Sociological Inquiry* 62: 36–55.

Congressional Record. 1994a. "Tribute to J. Fletcher Creamer and the DARE program." March 8: E373.

Ennett, Susan T., Nancy S. Tobler, Christopher L. Ringwalt and Robert L. Flewelling. 1994a. "How Effective Is Drug Abuse Resistance Education? A Meta-Analysis of Project DARE Outcome Evaluations." *American Journal of Public Health* 84: 1394–1401.

Goffman, Erving. 1959. *The Presentation of Self in Everyday Life*. NY: Anchor Books.

Rogers, Everett M. 1993. "Diffusion and Re-Invention of Project D.A.R.E." Pp. 139–2 in *Organizational Aspects of Health Communication Campaigns. What Works?*, edited by Thomas E. Backer and Everett M. Rogers. Newbury Park, CA: Sage.

Scott, W. Richard. 1992. *Organizations: Rational, Natural, and Open Systems*. Englewood Cliffs, NJ: Prentice Hall.

US Code Annotated. 1995. 20 USCA section 3192. Amendment to PL 101–647, Cumulative Annual Pocket Part. St Paul, MN: West Publishing.

US Congress: Senate. 1988b. "Drug Abuse, Prevention and Treatment." Committee on Labor and Human Resources. 100th Congress, 2nd session. Washington, DC: US Government Printing Office.

US Department of Justice, Bureau of Justice Assistance. 1991. *PROGRAM BRIEF: An Introduction to DARE:* *Drug Abuse Resistance Education.* 2nd. Washington, DC: Bureau of Justice Assistance.

Wysong, Earl. 1992 "Dramaturgy and Informational Elites: A Backstage Approach to Nonprofits' Policy-Making." *Indiana Academy of the Social Sciences Proceedings* 27: 46–53.

Wysong, Earl, Richard Aniskiewicz and David Wright. 1994. "Truth and DARE: Tracking Drug Education to Graduation and as Symbolic Politics." *Social Problems* 41: 448–72.

Questions

1   Why do you think DARE is so popular in the United States? How would you respond to the claim that DARE simply makes people feel good? How does DARE use impression management to protect its program from criticism?

2   How was the expansion of DARE largely a product of the growth of the War on Drugs? How does DARE provide symbolic and tangible benefits for both direct and indirect stakeholders? Do you think this has anything to do with DARE's continued popularity?

3   Who do you think should be responsible for youth drug education? The parents? The State? The schools? Why? What do you think an effective and honest drug education program might resemble? What would be the key components of the program?

37

Safety First
A Reality-Based Approach to Teens, Drugs, and Drug Education

Marsha Rosenbaum

Marsha Rosenbaum offers us an alternate approach to drug education, one that emphasizes education more than indoctrination. What do you think are the assumptions and values that underlie the program she suggests? What are its strong and its weak points?

Our society had placed a lot of responsibility on the schools to deliver moral education. Courses in elementary and middle school teach kids about puberty, sexually transmitted diseases, drugs, peer pressure, bullying, and a host of other social issues. Do you think the schools are the right place for this? What are the advantages or disadvantages of running these through the schools compared to the family or some other agency such as the church or the media? To what extent is or should drug education focus on moral issues as opposed to practical issues? In these tight economic times, who should pay for them?

Like many parents, when my children entered high school, I wished "the drug thing" would magically disappear and that my kids would simply abstain. Yet as a long-time researcher supported by the National Institute on Drug Abuse, and as a realistic parent, I knew this wish to be a fantasy.

Today's teenagers have been exposed, since elementary school, to the most intensive and expensive anti-drug campaign in history. They've been told, again and again, to "just say no" by school-based programs such as Drug Abuse Resistance Education (DARE) and televised anti-drug media campaigns (remember the "this is your brain on drugs" ads?). Parents, too, have been advised, indeed bombarded, with billboard, newspaper and electronic messages

urging them to become the "anti-drug," to talk to their teens and establish clear limits and consequences for disobeying the rules.

[...]

Let me be clear from the outset. As a mother myself, I do not excuse, encourage or condone teenage drug use, and I believe abstinence is the safest choice. My deepest feelings are expressed in a letter written to my son when he entered high school that was published by the *San Francisco Chronicle* on September 7, 1998.

Dear Johnny,

This fall you will be entering high school and, like most American teenagers, you'll have to navigate drugs.

As most parents, I would prefer that you not use drugs. However, I realize, that despite my wishes, you might experiment.

I will not use scare tactics to deter you. Instead, having spent the past 25 years researching drug use, abuse and policy, I will tell you a little about what I have learned, hoping this will lead you to make wise choices. My only concern is your health and safety.

When people talk about "drugs," they are generally referring to illegal substances such as marijuana, cocaine, methamphetamine (speed), psychedelic drugs (LSD, Ecstasy, "Shrooms") and heroin. These are not the only drugs that make you high. Alcohol, cigarettes and many other substances (like glue) cause intoxication of some sort. The fact that one drug or another is illegal does not mean one is better or worse for you. All of them temporarily change the way you perceive things and the way you think.

Some people will tell you that drugs feel good, and that's why they use them. But drugs are not always fun. Cocaine and methamphetamine speed up your heart; LSD can make you feel disoriented; alcohol intoxication impairs driving; cigarette smoking leads to addiction and sometimes lung cancer; and people sometimes die suddenly from taking heroin. Marijuana does not often lead to physical dependence or overdose, but it does alter the way people think, behave and react.

I have tried to give you a short description of the drugs you might encounter. I choose not to try to scare you by distorting information because I want you to have confidence in what I tell you. Although I won't lie to you about their effects, there are many reasons for a person your age not to use drugs or alcohol. First, being high on marijuana or any other drug often interferes with normal life. It is difficult to retain information while high, so using it, especially daily, affects your ability to learn.

Second, if you think you might try marijuana, please wait until you are older. Adults with drug problems often started using at a very early age.

Finally, your father and I don't want you to get into trouble. Drug and alcohol use is illegal for you, and the consequences of being caught are huge. Here in the United States, the number of arrests for possession of marijuana has more than doubled in the past six years. Adults are serious about "zero tolerance." If caught, you could be arrested, expelled from school, barred from playing sports, lose your driver's license, denied a college loan and/or rejected from college.

Despite my advice to abstain, you may one day choose to experiment. I will say again that this is not a good idea, but if you do, I urge you to learn as much as you can, and use common sense. There are many excellent books and references, including the Internet, that give you credible information about drugs. You can, of course, always talk to me. If I don't know the answers to your questions, I will try to help you find them.

If you are offered drugs, be cautious. Watch how people behave, but understand that everyone responds differently even to the same substance. If you do decide to experiment, be sure you are surrounded by people you can count upon. Plan your transportation and under no circumstances drive or get into a car with anyone else who has been using alcohol or other drugs. Call us or any of our close friends any time, day or night, and we will pick you up, no questions asked and no consequences.

And please, Johnny, use moderation. It is impossible to know what is contained in illegal drugs because they are not regulated. The majority of fatal overdoses occur because young people do not know the strength of the drugs they consume, or how they combine with other drugs. Please do not participate in drinking contests, which have killed too many young people. Whereas marijuana by itself is not fatal, too much can cause you to become disoriented and sometimes paranoid. And of course, smoking can hurt your lungs, later in life and now.

Johnny, as your father and I have always told you about a range of activities (including sex), think about the consequences of your actions before you act. Drugs are no different. Be skeptical and, most of all, be safe.

Love, Mom

Understanding Teenage Drug Use

The 2006 Monitoring the Future survey states that more than 48% of high school seniors have tried illegal drugs at some point in their lifetime; 37% used a drug during the past year; and 22% profess to have used drugs in the past month. The numbers are even higher for alcohol; 73% have tried alcohol (itself a potent drug in every regard); 66% have used it within the year; and 45% (twice the statistic for marijuana) of those surveyed imbibed "once a month or more." The Centers for Disease Control and Prevention's (CDC) 2005 Youth Risk Behavior Survey found that 26% of high school students reported taking "more than a few sips" of alcohol before the age of 13.

In order to understand teenage drug use, it is imperative to recognize the context in which today's teens have grown up. Alcohol, tobacco, caffeine, over-the-counter and prescription drugs are everywhere. Though we urge our young people to be "drug-free,"

Americans are constantly bombarded with messages encouraging us to imbibe and medicate with a variety of substances. We use alcohol to celebrate ("Let's drink to that!"), to recreate ("I can't wait to kick back and have a cold one!") and even to medicate ("I really need a drink!"). We use caffeine to boost our energy, and prescription and over-the-counter drugs to modify our moods, lift us out of depression and help us work, study and sleep.

Drugs are an integral part of American life. In fact, the *Journal of the American Medical Association* reported that 8 out of 10 adults in the US use at least one medication every week, and half take a prescription drug. One in two adults in this country use alcohol regularly; and more than 97 million Americans over the age of 12 have tried marijuana at some time in their lives – a fact not lost on their children.

Today's teenagers have witnessed first-hand the increasing, sometimes forced "Ritalinization" of their fellow (difficult-to-manage) students. Stimulants such as Adderal, an amphetamine product, have become a drug of choice on many college campuses, where "pharm (as in pharmaceutical) parties" are accepted as commonplace. We see prime-time network commercials for drugs to manage such ailments as "Generalized Anxiety Disorder," and teenagers see increasing numbers of their parents using anti-depressants to cope with life's problems.

While "peer pressure" is often blamed for teenage drug use, the 2005 State of Our Nation's Youth survey found that, contrary to popular belief, most are not pressured to use drugs. Instead, teenage drug use seems to mirror modern American drug-taking tendencies. Some psychologists argue that given the nature of our culture, teenage experimentation with legal and illegal mind-altering substances should not be considered abnormal or deviant behavior.

Problems With Current Prevention Strategies

Americans have been trying to prevent teenage drug use for over a century – from the nineteenth-century Temperance campaigns against alcohol to Nancy Reagan's "Just Say No." A variety of methods, from scare tactics to resistance techniques to zero-tolerance policies and random drug testing (not to mention 770,000 arrests in 2005 for marijuana offenses alone),

have been used to try to persuade, coax and force young people to abstain.

The effectiveness of these conventional approaches, however, has been compromised by:

- the unwillingness to distinguish between drug use and abuse by proclaiming "all use is abuse";
- the use of misinformation as a scare tactic; and
- the failure to provide comprehensive information that would help users to reduce the harms that can result from drug use.

Use versus abuse

In the effort to stop teenage experimentation, prevention messages often pretend there is no difference between use and abuse. Some use the terms interchangeably; others emphasize an exaggerated definition that categorizes any use of illegal drugs as abuse.

This hypocritical message is often dismissed by teens who see that adults routinely make distinctions between use and abuse. Young people rapidly learn this difference, too, as most observe their parents and other adults using alcohol without abusing it. They know there is a big difference between having a glass of wine with dinner and having that very same glass of wine with breakfast. Many also know that their parents have tried an illegal drug (likely marijuana) at some point in their lives without abusing it or continuing to use it.

Few things are more frightening to a parent than a teenager whose use of alcohol and/or other drugs gets out of hand. Yet virtually all studies have found that the vast majority of students who try legal and/or illegal drugs do not become drug abusers.

Of course, any substance use involves risk. But we need to talk about alcohol and other drugs in a sophisticated manner and distinguish between *use* and *abuse*. If not, we lose credibility. Furthermore, by acknowledging distinctions, we can more effectively recognize problems if and when they occur.

Scare tactics and misinformation: Marijuana as a case in point

A common belief held by many educators, policy makers and parents is that if young people believe drug use is risky, they will abstain. In this effort, marijuana (the most popular illegal drug among US teens) is consistently mischaracterized by prevention programs, books, ads and websites, including those managed by the federal government. Exaggerated claims of marijuana's dangers are routinely published, and although the old Reefer Madness-style messages have been replaced with assertions of scientific evidence, the most serious of these allegations falter when critically evaluated.

In my workshops parents regularly question claims they have heard about marijuana:

- Is it true that marijuana is significantly more potent and dangerous today than in the past?
- Is today's marijuana really more addictive than ever before?
- Does marijuana really cause users to seek out "harder" drugs?
- Is it true that smoking marijuana causes lung cancer?

To separate myth from fact, (the late) Professor Lynn Zimmer of Queens College of the City University of New York and Dr. John P. Morgan of the City University of New York Medical School carefully examined the published, peer-reviewed scientific evidence relevant to the most popular claims about marijuana in their book, *Marijuana Myths, Marijuana Facts: A Review of the Scientific Evidence.* Professor Mitch Earleywine of the State University of New York at Albany also took a critical look at the research in *Understanding Marijuana: A New Look at the Scientific Evidence.* Each found that claims of marijuana's risks had been exaggerated, even in some instances fabricated. Their findings are not uncommon, as these same conclusions have been reached by numerous official commissions, including the La Guardia Commission in 1944, the National Commission on Marijuana and Drug Abuse in 1972, the National Academy of Sciences in 1982 and the federally chartered Institute of Medicine in 1999.

Using these resources, as well as many others, here's how I've tried, ever so briefly, to answer parents' questions:

Potency

Many people believe that the marijuana available today is significantly more potent than in decades past.

The Drug Czar says so; growers marketing their product say so; and adolescents trying to distinguish themselves from their parents' generation say so.

As marijuana-growing techniques have become more advanced and refined, there has been a corresponding increase in the plant's average psychoactive potency, otherwise known as its THC (delta-9 tetrahydrocannabinol) content level.

As a result, the federally funded University of Mississippi's Marijuana Potency Project estimates that average THC levels have increased since 1988 from approximately 3.7% to over 8%. However, the National Drug Intelligence Center reports that "most of the marijuana available in the domestic drug markets is lower potency, commercial grade marijuana," and the Drug Enforcement Administration affirms that of the thousands of pounds of marijuana seized by law enforcement annually, fewer than 2% of samples test positive for extremely high (above 20%) THC levels.

In short, it appears that marijuana now is, on average, somewhat stronger than in the past, though variation has always been the norm. Does this mean that the marijuana available today is a qualitatively different drug than that smoked by 40- and 50-something-year-olds when they were teenagers? Not really. Essentially, marijuana is the same plant now as it was then, with any increased strength akin to the difference between beer (at 6% alcohol) and wine (at 10–14% alcohol), or between a cup of tea and an espresso.

Furthermore, even with higher potency, no studies demonstrate that increased THC content is associated with greater harm to the user or any risk of fatal overdose. In fact, among those who report experiencing the effects of unusually strong marijuana, many complain of dysphoria and subsequently avoid it altogether. Others adjust their use accordingly, consuming very small amounts to achieve the desired effect.

Addiction

Although marijuana lacks the severe physical dependence associated with drugs such as alcohol and heroin, a minority of users find it psychologically difficult to moderate their use or quit. The vast majority of those who experience difficulty with marijuana also have pre-existing mental health problems that can be exacerbated by cannabis. According to the National Academy of Sciences, 9% of marijuana users exhibit symptoms of dependence, as defined by the American Psychiatric Association's DSM-IV criteria.

Those who argue that marijuana is addictive often point to increasing numbers of individuals entering treatment for cannabis. While some of these individuals are in rehab because they (or their families) believed their marijuana use was adversely impacting their lives, most were arrested for possession and referred to treatment by the courts as a requirement of their probation.

Over the past decade, *voluntary* admissions for cannabis have actually dropped, while criminal justice referrals to drug treatment have risen dramatically. According to current state and national statistics, between 60 and 70% of all individuals in treatment for marijuana are "legally coerced" into treatment.

The gateway theory

The "gateway" theory suggests that marijuana use inevitably leads to the use of harder drugs, such as cocaine and heroin. However, population data compiled by the National Survey on Drug Use and Health and others demonstrate that the vast majority of marijuana users do not progress to more dangerous drugs. The gateway theory has also been refuted by the Institute of Medicine and in a study published in the prestigious *American Journal of Public Health*.

The overwhelming majority of marijuana users never try any other illicit substance. Furthermore, those populations who report using marijuana in early adulthood typically report voluntarily ceasing their cannabis use by the time they reach age 30. Consequently, for most who use it, marijuana is a "terminus" rather than a "gateway."

Today's research also reveals that the vast majority of teens who try marijuana do not go on to become dependent or even use it on a regular basis.

Lung cancer

Although inhaling cannabis can irritate the pulmonary system, research has yet to demonstrate that smoking marijuana, even long term, causes diseases of the lung, upper aero digestive tract, or mouth.

Most recently, in the largest study of its kind ever conducted, National Institute on Drug Abuse researcher Dr. Donald Tashkin and his colleagues at the University of California at Los Angeles compared 1,212 head, lung or neck cancer patients to 1,040 demographically matched individuals without cancer and reported, "Contrary to our expectations, we found no positive associations between marijuana use and lung or [upper aero digestive tract] cancers ... even among subjects who reported smoking more than 22,000 joints over their lifetime."

No drug, including marijuana, is completely safe.

Yet the consistent mischaracterization of marijuana may be the Achilles' heel of current drug prevention approaches because programs and messages too often contain exaggerations and misinformation that contradict young people's own observations and experience. As a result, teens become cynical and lose confidence in what we, as parents and teachers, tell them. We've got to tell the truth, because if we don't, teenagers will not consider us credible sources of information. Although they know we have their best interests at heart, they also know we'll say just about anything – whether or not it's true – to get them to abstain.

Safety First: A Reality-Based Approach

Surveys tell us that despite our admonitions and advice to abstain, large numbers of teenagers will occasionally experiment with intoxicating substances, and some will use alcohol and/or other drugs more regularly. This does not mean they are bad kids or we are neglectful parents. The reality is that drug use is a part of teenage culture in America today. In all likelihood, our young people will come out of this phase unharmed.

Keeping teenagers safe should be our highest priority. To protect them, a reality-based approach enables teenagers to make responsible decisions by:

- providing honest, science-based information;
- encouraging moderation if youthful experimentation persists;
- promoting an understanding of the legal and social consequences of drug use; and
- prioritizing safety through personal responsibility and knowledge.

Honest, science-based education

Young people are capable of rational thinking. Although their decision-making skills will improve as they mature, teenagers are learning responsibility, and do not want to destroy their lives or their health. In fact, in our workshops with students, they consistently request the "real" facts about drugs so they can make responsible decisions – and the vast majority actually do. According to the 2005 National Survey on Drug Use and Health, although experimentation is widespread, 90% of 12- to 17-year-olds choose to refrain from regular use.

Effective drug education should be based on sound science and acknowledge teenagers' ability to understand, analyze and evaluate. The subject of drugs can be integrated into a variety of high school courses and curricula, including physiology and biology (how drugs affect the body), psychology (how drugs affect the mind), chemistry (what's contained in drugs), social studies (who uses which drugs, and why) and history and civics (how drugs have been handled by various governments).

Fortunately, today's educators have a new resource and should consider the innovative approach devised by Rodney Skager, Professor Emeritus, Graduate School of Education & Information Studies at the University of California at Los Angeles and Chair of the California Statewide Task Force for Effective Drug Education. His 2005 booklet, *Beyond Zero Tolerance: A Reality-Based Approach to Drug Education and Student Assistance* (available at www.safety1st.org), takes educators step-by-step through a pragmatic and cost-effective drug education and school discipline program for secondary schools.

As Dr. Skager suggests, through family experience, peer exposure and the media, teenagers often know more about alcohol and other drugs than we assume. Therefore, students should be included in the development of drug education programs, and classes should utilize interaction and student participation rather than rote lecturing. If drug education is to be credible, formal curricula should incorporate the observations and experiences of young people themselves.

Teens clamor for honest, comprehensive drug education, and it is especially apparent when they leave home and go to college. According to Professor Craig Reinarman at the University of California at Santa Cruz,

> Students seem to hunger for information about licit and illicit drugs that doesn't strike them as moralistic propaganda. I've taught a large lecture course called "Drugs and Society" for over twenty years and each year I have to turn away dozens of students because the class fills up so quickly.
>
> I always start by asking them, "How many of you had drug education in high school?" and nearly all of them raise their hands. Then I ask, "How many of you felt it was truthful and valuable?" Out of 120 students, perhaps three hands go up.

The vast majority of teenage drug use (with the exception of nicotine) does not lead to dependence or abusive habits.

Teens who do use alcohol, marijuana and/or other drugs must understand there is a huge difference between use and abuse, and between occasional and daily use.

They should know how to recognize irresponsible behavior when it comes to place, time, dose levels and frequency of use. If young people continue, despite our admonitions, to use alcohol and/or other drugs, they must control their use by practicing moderation and limiting use. It is impossible to do well academically or meet one's responsibilities at work while intoxicated. It is never appropriate to use alcohol and/or other drugs at school, at work, while participating in sports, while driving or engaging in any serious activity.

Understanding consequences

Young people must understand the consequences of violating school rules and local and state laws against the use, possession and sale of alcohol and other drugs – whether or not they agree with such policies.

With increasing methods of detection such as school-based drug testing and zero-tolerance policies, illegality is a risk in and of itself which extends beyond the physical effects of drug use. There are real, lasting consequences of using drugs and being caught, including expulsion from school, a criminal record and social stigma. The Higher Education Act – now being challenged by many organizations, including Students for Sensible Drug Policy (www.ssdp.org) – has resulted in the denial of college loans for 200,000 US students convicted of any drug offense. This law was scaled back in 2006, but the penalty still applies to students who are convicted while they are enrolled in school.

Fortunately, zero-tolerance policies – which have contributed to a high school drop-out rate of 30% in this country – have come under serious attack. The American Psychological Association concluded in 2006 that such policies are "backfiring," making students feel less safe and undermining academic performance. Support is now growing for "restorative practices" that attempt to bring students closer to their communities and schools rather than suspending and expelling those who are troublesome or truant.

Young people need to know that if they are caught in possession of drugs, they will find themselves at the mercy of the juvenile and criminal justice systems.

More than half a million Americans, almost a quarter of our total incarcerated population, are behind bars today for drug violations. As soon as teenagers turn eighteen they are prosecuted as adults and run the risk of serving long mandatory sentences, even for something they believe to be a minor offense. In Illinois, for example, an individual caught in possession of 15 Ecstasy pills (yes, fifteen – this is not a typo) will serve a minimum of four years in state prison.

Put safety first

Alcohol as a case in point

Motor vehicle accidents continue to be the number one cause of untimely death among young people, according to the National Highway Safety Administration. Each year, nearly 2,400 American teenagers die in car accidents involving alcohol and far more are seriously injured.

In suburban communities, where so many young people drive, the teenage practice of having a "designated driver" has become commonplace. In these same communities, there are some parents who have strongly encouraged their teens to abstain, assessed reality and reluctantly provided their homes as safe, non-driving spaces to gather.

Others see these practices as "enabling." They hope to stop alcohol use completely by passing laws that make it a crime to be a teenage designated driver, as well as "social host" ordinances that impose civil or

criminal penalties on parents whose homes are used for parties – with or without their knowledge and/or consent.

What worries me is how young people respond to the proliferation of such ordinances. When asked in particular about social host laws, the response is not, "Okay then, I'm going to stop drinking." Too many teens say they will just move the party to the street, the local park, the beach or some other public place. And they'll drive there.

These are hot-button issues to be sure, with reasonable and well-meaning people coming down on all sides of the debate.

Sober gatherings should, of course, be promoted in every way possible, and parents should devise strategies for minimizing the harm that can result from the use of alcohol. To involve the criminal justice system in parental decisions, however, is not the answer, and will certainly reduce, not improve, teen safety.

Safe sex as a model

A useful model for envisioning safety-oriented drug abuse prevention is the modern, comprehensive sex education approach.

In the mid-1980s, when scientists discovered that the use of condoms could prevent the spread of HIV and other sexually transmitted diseases, as well as teen pregnancies, parents, teachers and policy makers took action. They introduced reality-based sex education curricula throughout the country. This approach strongly encouraged abstinence, and provided the facts along with accurate "safe sex" information.

According to the Centers for Disease Control and Prevention (CDC), this approach has resulted not just in the increased use of condoms among sexually active teenagers, but has also served to decrease overall rates of sexual activity.

This effective, comprehensive prevention strategy presents a strong case and provides a model for restructuring our drug education and abuse prevention efforts.

Epilogue

Shortly before graduating from college in 2006, Dr. Rosenbaum's son, Johnny, read the following letter at an event honoring his mother.

November 15, 2006

Dear Mom,

It has been eight years since I entered high school on the heels of your advice about drugs: "Johnny – be skeptical and, most of all, be safe." Although I'd like to tell you that I never needed your advice because I never encountered drugs, I'd prefer to be as honest with you as you have been with me.

Just as you predicted, I spent high school and college navigating a highly experimental teenage drug culture. While some of the substances that I encountered were illegal, like marijuana, cocaine, and Ecstasy, many were not, like alcohol, cigarettes, and Ritalin. Because you explained that a drug's legality does not mean that it is better or worse for me, I approached every substance with skepticism and common sense.

Our household mantra of "safety first" guided me through a maze of difficult decisions, particularly in college where alcohol use and abuse is widespread.

Because you didn't lie or exaggerate the risks of drug use, I took your warnings seriously. I always made plans for sober transportation; I refused to leave friends alone if they were highly intoxicated; and I was never afraid to call home if I found myself in a dangerous situation.

Of course you advised me not to use drugs, but as an expert in the field, you knew that I was likely to experiment. Most parents panic in response to this likelihood, but you and Dad remained levelheaded: You didn't impose rigid rules that were bound to be broken, and you didn't bombard me with transparent scare tactics. Instead you encouraged me to think critically and carefully about drug use. When I inquired, you armed me with truthful, scientifically based information from which I could make my own decisions. This was excellent practice for adulthood, and we built a loving relationship based on trust and truth.

[…]

Love, Johnny

Questions

1   What do you think about Rosenbaum's letter to her son Johnny? Do you think the letter is effective? Why or why not?

2   If more parents took an honest approach to discussing drugs with their children, do you think youth drug problems might be reduced? What about adult drug abuse? How do most parents already teach moderation through their actions? Why is it so difficult for parents to put actions into words when discussing drug use with their children?

3   Do you think a safety-first approach when discussing drug use with youth is enabling? Why or why not? If young people do experiment with drugs, do you think they should also be taught how to protect their civil rights during police encounters? Why or why not?

Treatment

38

The Therapeutic Community Perspective and Approach

George De Leon

> Therapeutic communities, mostly inpatient, residential treatment programs, are one of the cornerstones of the therapeutic solutions to drug problems. George De Leon traces the development of these programs from their origins in the mid-twentieth century. He discusses the core, foundational elements contained in all of these programs and the kinds of therapies they offer. He then discusses one of the most vital trends in therapeutic communities: specialized treatments for specialized populations.
>
> Thinking about these, what do you think the advantages of such programs are? What are their disadvantages? What underlying assumptions of theirs do you recognize and consider important, and with which might you disagree? How would you contrast these according to their values and effectiveness with non-residential programs such as the Alcoholics Anonymous model? How might you contrast both of these with the proliferation of online cyber support groups? How do these latter two models differ from the therapeutic community model in their leadership, cost, focus, intensity, integration into individuals' lives, expertise, and overall effectiveness?
>
> If you had a drug problem, to which kind of community might you turn? If you had a sister, brother, or friend with a bad drug problem, which kind of community might you prefer for them? Do you see these as better for certain kinds of substances as opposed to certain kinds of populations?

Since the 1960s, the spectrum of drug abusers has widened. Differences among users in drug abuse patterns, lifestyle, and motivation for change are addressed by four major treatment modalities – detoxification, methadone maintenance, drug free outpatient and drug free residential therapeutic communities (TCs). Each modality has its view of substance abuse and each impacts the drug abuser in different ways.

The TC views drug abuse as a deviant behavior, reflecting impeded personality development and/or chronic deficits in social, educational and economic

Drugs and the American Dream: An Anthology, First Edition. Edited by Patricia A. Adler, Peter Adler, and Patrick K. O'Brien.
© 2012 John Wiley & Sons, Inc. Published 2012 by John Wiley & Sons, Inc.

skills. Its antecedents lie in socioeconomic disadvantage, poor family effectiveness and in psychological factors. Thus, the principal aim of the therapeutic community is a global change in lifestyle: abstinence from illicit substances, elimination of antisocial activity, employability, pro-social attitudes and values. The rehabilitative approach requires multi-dimensional influence and training which for most can only occur in a 24-hour residental setting.

The therapeutic community can be distinguished from other major drug treatment modalities in two fundamental ways. *First*, the primary "therapist" and teacher in the TC is the community itself consisting of peers and staff who, as role models of successful personal change, serve as guides in the recovery process. Thus, the community provides a 24-hour learning experience in which individual changes in conduct, attitudes and emotions are monitored and mutually reinforced in the daily regime.

Second, unlike other modalities, TCs offers a systematic approach to achieve its main rehabilitative objective, which is guided by an explicit perspective on the drug abuse disorder, the client and recovery.

This paper outlines the therapeutic community approach to rehabilitation. The initial section provides an overview of the TC, its background and perspective on rehabilitation. The second section draws a picture of the TC approach in terms of its basic elements and the stages of treatment.

Overview

Background
Therapeutic communities for substance abuse appeared a decade later than did therapeutic communities in psychiatric settings pioneered by Jones and others in the United Kingdom.

The two models evolved in parallel independence reflecting differences in their philosophy, social organization, clients served and therapeutic processes. Jones explains that the therapeutic community referred to a movement which originated in psychiatry in the United Kingdom at the end of World War II. It was "an attempt to establish a democratic system in hospitals where the domination of the doctors in a traditional hierarchy system was replaced by open communication, information sharing, decision making by consensus and problem solving sharing, as far as possible, with all patients and staff" (Jones, 1953). The name therapeutic community evolved in these settings.

The therapeutic community for substance abuse emerged in the 1960s as a self-help alternative to existing conventional treatments. Unhelped by the medical and correctional establishments, recovering alcoholics and drug addicts were its first participant-developers. Though its modern antecedents can be traced to Alcoholics Anonymous and Synanon, the TC prototype is ancient, existing in all forms of communal healing and support. Today, the term "therapeutic community" is generic, describing a variety of drug free residential programs. About a quarter of these conform to the traditional long term model. These have made the greatest impact upon rehabilitating substance abusers.

The traditional TC
Traditional therapeutic communities are similar in planned duration of stay (15–24 months), structure, staffing pattern, perspective and in rehabilitative regime, although they differ in size (30–600 beds) and client demographics. Staff are a mixture of TC trained clinicians and human service professionals. Primary clinical staff are usually former substance abusers who themselves were rehabilitated in TC programs. Ancillary staff consist of professionals in mental health vocational, educational, family counseling, fiscal, administration and legal services.

TCs acommodate a broad spectrum of drug abusers. Although they originally attracted narcotic addicts, a majority of their client populations are non-opioid abusers. Thus, this modality has responded to the changing trend in drug use patterns, treating clients with drug problems of varying severity, different lifestyles and various social, economic and ethnic backgrounds.

Clients in traditional programs are usually male (75%) and in their mid-twenties (50%). TCs are almost all racially mixed, and most are age-integrated, with 25 percent of their clients under 21, although a few TCs have separate facilities for adolescents. About half of all admissions are from broken homes or ineffective families, and more than three quarters have been arrested at some time in their lives.

The TC perspective

Full accounts of the TC perspective are described elsewhere. Although expressed in a social psychological idiom, this perspective evolved directly from the experience of recovering participants in therapeutic communities.

Drug abuse is viewed as a disorder of the whole person, affecting some or all areas of functioning. Cognitive and behavioral problems appear, as do mood disturbances. Thinking may be unrealistic or disorganized; values are confused, nonexistent or antisocial. Frequently there are deficits in verbal, reading, writing and marketable skills. And, whether couched in existential or psychological terms, moral or even spiritual issues are apparent.

Abuse of any substance is viewed as over-determined behavior. Physiological dependency is secondary to the wide range of influences which control the individual's drug use behavior. Invariably, problems and situations associated with discomfort become regular signals for resorting to drug use. For some abusers, physiological factors may be important but for most these remain minor relative to the functional deficits which accumulate with continued substance abuse. Physical addiction or dependency must be seen in the wider context of the individual's life.

Thus, the problem is the person, not the drug. Addiction is a symptom, not the essence of the disorder. In the TC, chemical detoxification is a condition of entry, not a goal of treatment. Rehabilitation focuses upon maintaining a drug free existence.

Rather than drug use patterns, individuals are distinguished along dimensions of psychological dysfunction and social deficits. Many clients have never acquired conventional lifestyles. Vocational and educational problems are marked; middle class mainstream values are either missing or unachievable. Usually these clients emerge from a socially disadvantaged sector, where drug abuse is more a social response than a psychological disturbance. Their TC experience is better termed habilitation, the development of a socially productive, conventional lifestyle for the first time in their lives.

Among clients from more advantaged backgrounds, drug abuse is more directly expressive of psychological disorder or existential malaise, and the word

rehabilitation is more suitable, emphasizing a return to a lifestyle previously lived, known and perhaps rejected.

Nevertheless, substance abusers in TCs share important similarities. Either as cause or consequence of their drug abuse, all reveal features of personality disturbance and/or impeded social function. Thus, all residents in the TC follow the same regime. Individual differences are recognized in specific treatment plans that modify the emphasis, not the course, of their experience in the therapeutic community.

In the TC's view of recovery, the aim of rehabilitation is global. The primary psychological goal is to change the negative patterns of behavior, thinking and feeling that predispose drug use; the main social goal is to develop a responsible drug free lifestyle. Stable recovery, however, depends upon a successful integration of these social and psychological goals. For example, healthy behavioral alternatives to drug use are reinforced by commitment to the values of abstinence; acquiring vocational or educational skills and social productivity is motivated by the values of achievement and self-reliance. Behavioral change is unstable without insight, and insight is insufficient without felt experience. Thus, conduct, emotions, skills, attitudes and values must be integrated to insure enduring change.

The rehabilitative regime is shaped by several broad assumptions about recovery.

Motivation

Recovery depends upon positive and negative pressures to change. Some clients seek help, driven by stressful external pressures; others are moved by more intrinsic factors. For all, however, remaining in treatment requires continued motivation to change. Thus, elements of the rehabilitation approach are designed to sustain motivation, or detect early signs of premature termination.

Self help

Although the influence of treatment depends upon the person's motivation and readiness, change does not occur in a vacuum. The individual must permit the impact of treatment or learning to occur. Thus, rehabilitation unfolds as an interaction between the client and the therapeutic environment.

Social learning

A lifestyle change occurs in a social context. Negative patterns, attitudes and roles were not acquired in isolation, nor can they be altered in isolation. Thus, recovery depends not only upon what has been learned, but how and where learning occurs. This assumption is the basis for the community itself serving as teacher. Learning is active, by doing and participating. A socially responsible role is acquired by acting the role. What is learned is identified with the people involved in the learning process, with peer support and staff, as credible role models. Because newly acquired ways of coping are threatened by isolation and its potential for relapse, a perspective on self, society and life must be affirmed by a network of others.

Treatment as an episode

Residency is a relatively brief period in an individual's life, and its influence must compete with the influence of the years before and after treatment. For this reason, unhealthy "outside" influences are minimized until the individuals are better prepared to engage these on their own and the treatment regime is designed for high impact. Thus, life in the TC is necessarily intense, its daily regime demanding, its therapeutic confrontations unmoderated.

The TC Approach

A. TC structure

TCs are stratified communities composed of peer groups that hold memberships in wider aggregates that are led by individual staff. Together they constitute the community, or family, in a residential facility. This peer-to-community structure strengthens the individual's identification with a perceived, ordered network of others. More importantly, it arranges relationships of mutual responsibility to others at various levels of the program.

The operation of the community itself is the task of the residents, working under staff supervision. Work assignments, called job functions, are arranged in a hierarchy, according to seniority, individual progress and productivity. The new client enters a setting of upward mobility. Job assignments begin with the most menial tasks (e.g., mopping the floor) and lead vertically to levels of coordination and management. Indeed, clients come in as patients and can leave as staff. This social organization reflects the fundamental aspects of the rehabilitative approach: mutual self help, work as therapy, peers as role models and staff as rational authorities.

Mutual self help

The essential dynamic in the TC is mutual self help. Thus, the day to day activities of a therapeutic community are conducted by the residents themselves. In their jobs, groups, meetings, recreation, personal and social time, it is residents who continually transmit to each other the main messages and expectations of the community.

The extent of the self help process in the TC is evident in the broad range of resident job assignments. These include conducting all house services (e.g., cooking, cleaning, kitchen service, minor repair), serving as apprentices and running all departments, conducting meetings and peer encounter groups.

The TC is managed as an autocracy, with staff serving as rational authorities. Their psychological relationship with the residents is as role models and parental surrogates, who foster the self help, developmental process through managerial and clinical means. They monitor and evaluate client status, supervise resident groups, assign and supervise resident job functions and oversee house operations. Clinically, staff conduct all therapeutic groups, provide individual counseling, organize social and recreational projects and confer with significant others. They decide matters of resident status, discipline, promotion, transfers, discharges, furloughs and treatment planning.

Work as education and therapy

In the TC, work mediates essential educational and therapeutic effects. Vertical job movements carry the obvious rewards of status and privilege. However, lateral job changes are more frequent, providing exposure to all aspects of the community. Typically, residents experience many lateral job changes that enable them to learn new skills and to negotiate the system. This increased involvement also heightens their sense of belonging and affirms their commitment to the community.

Job changes in the TC are singularly effective therapeutic tools, providing both measures of, and incentives for, behavioral and attitudinal change. In the vertical structure of the TC, ascendency marks how well the client has assimilated what the community teaches and expects, hence, the job promotion is an explicit measure of the resident's improvement and growth.

Conversely, lateral or downward job movements also create situations that require demonstrations of personal growth. A resident may be removed from one job to a lateral position in another department or dropped back to a lower status position for clinical reasons. These movements are designed to teach new ways of coping with reversals and change that appear to be unfair or arbitrary.

Peers as role models

People are the essential ingredient in the therapeutic community. Peers as role models and staff as role models and rational authorities are the primary mediators of the recovery process.

Indeed, the strength of the community as a context for social learning relates to the number and quality of its role models. All members of the community are expected to be role models – roommates, older and younger residents, junior, senior and directorial staff. TCs require these multiple role models to maintain the integrity of the community and assure the spread of social learning effects.

Residents who demonstrate the expected behaviors and reflect the values and teachings of the community are viewed as role models. This is illustrated in two main attributes.

Role models "act as if." They behave as the person they should be, rather than as the person they have been. Despite resistance, perceptions or feelings to the contrary, they engage in the expected behavior and consistently maintain the attitudes and values of the community. These include self motivation, commitment to work and striving, positive regard for staff as authority and an optimistic outlook toward the future.

In the TC's view, "acting as if" has significance beyond conformity. It is an essential mechanism for more complete psychological change. Feelings, insights and altered self-perceptions often follow rather than precede behavior change.

Role models display responsible concern. This concept is closely akin to the notion of, "I am my brother's keeper." Showing responsible concern involves willingness to confront others whose behavior is not in keeping with the rules of the TC, the spirit of the community or the knowledge which is consistent with growth and rehabilitation. Role models are obligated to be aware of the appearance, attitude, moods and performances of their peers, and confront negative signs in these. In particular, role models are aware of their own behavior in the overall community and the process prescribed for personal growth.

Staff as rational authorities

TC clients often have had difficulties with authorities, who have not been trusted or perceived as guides and teachers. Thus, they need a successful experience with a rational authority who is credible (recovered), supportive, correcting and protecting, in order to gain authority over themselves (personal autonomy). Implicit in their role as rational authorities, staff provide the reasons for their decisions and the meaning of consequences. They exercise their powers to train and guide, facilitate and correct, rather than punish, control or exploit.

B.   Daily regime: Basic elements

The daily regime is full and varied. Although designed to facilitate the management of the community, its scope and schedule reflect an understanding of the conditions of drug abuse. It provides an orderly environment for many who customarily have lived in chaotic or disruptive settings; it reduces boredom and distracts from negative preoccupations which have, in the past, been associated with drug use; and it offers opportunity to achieve satisfaction from a busy schedule and the completion of daily chores.

The typical day in a therapeutic community is highly structured, beginning with a 7 AM wakeup and ending at 11 PM in the evening. It includes a variety of meetings, job functions (work therapy), therapeutic groups, recreation and individual counseling. These activities contribute to the TC process and may be grouped into three main elements, community enhancement, therapeutic–educative and community and clinical management.

Community enhancement element

These activities, which facilitate assimilation into the community, include the four main facility-wide meetings: the morning meeting, seminar and house meetings, held each day, and the general meeting, which is called when needed.

Morning meeting: All residents of the facility and the staff on premises assemble after breakfast, usually for 30 to 45 minutes. The purpose is to initiate the daily activities with a positive attitude, motivate residents and strengthen unity. [...]

Seminars convene every afternoon, usually for 1 to 1½ hours. The seminar collects all the residents together at least once during the working day. [...] A clinical aim of the seminar, however, is to balance the individual's emotional and cognitive experience. [...] House meetings convene nightly, after dinner, usually for one hour. [...] In this forum, social pressure is judiciously employed to facilitate individual change through public acknowledgment of positive or negative behaviors among certain individuals or subgroups. General meetings convene only when needed to address negative behavior, attitudes or incidents in the facility. [...]

Therapeutic–educative element

These activities consist of various groups and staff counseling. This element focuses on individual issues. It provides an exclusive setting for expressing feelings for resolution of personal and business issues in the evening. It trains communication and interpersonal relating skills; examines and confronts the behaviors and attitudes displayed in the various roles of the clients; offers instruction in alternate modes of behavior.

There are four main forms of group activity in the TC: encounters, probes, marathons and tutorials. These differ somewhat in format, aims and methods, but all attempt to foster trust and peer solidarity in order to facilitate personal disclosure, insight and therapeutic change.

Peer encounter is the cornerstone of group process in the TC. The term "encounter" is generic, describing a variety of forms which utilize confrontational procedures as their main approach. [...] Probes meet as needed, usually in the early months of residency. These groups, which last 4 to 8 hours, aim to

strengthen trust and identification with others; and to increase the staff's understanding of important background of the person.

Marathons are extended group sessions that meet as needed, usually for 24 to 30 hours, to initiate a process of resolution of life experiences that have impeded the individual's growth or development. Marathons make liberal use of dramatic, visual, auditory and environmental props to facilitate a "working through" of deeper emotional experiences.

Tutorial groups meet regularly and are primarily directed toward training or teaching. Three major themes of tutorials are personal growth concepts (e.g., self reliance, independence, relationships); job skill training (e.g., managing a department or the reception desk); clinical skills training (e.g., use of the encounter tools).
[...]

Counseling

One-to-one counseling further balances the needs of the individual with those of the community. Peer exchange is ongoing, frequent and constitutes the most consistent counseling in TCs. However, staff counseling sessions are conducted on an as needed basis, usually informally. The staff counseling method in the TC is not traditional, evident in its main features: interpersonal sharing, direct support, minimal interpretation, didactic instruction and encounter.

Community–clinical management element

The objective of these activities is to protect the community as a whole and to strengthen it as a context for social learning. The main activities consist of privileges and disciplinary sanctions.

Privilege

In the TC, privileges are explicit rewards that reinforce the value of earned achievement. Privileges are accorded by behavior, attitude change, job performance and overall clinical progress in the program. Displays of inappropriate behavior or negative attitude can result in loss of some or all privileges, offering the resident the opportunity to earn them back by showing improvement.

Privileges acquire their importance because they are **earned**. The earning process requires investment of time, energy, self modification, risk of failure and disappointment. Thus, the earning process establishes the value of privileges and hence their potency as social reinforcements.

The type of privilege is related to clinical progress and time in program, ranging from phone and letter writing in early treatment to overnight furloughs in later treatment. Successful movement through each stage earns privileges that grant wider personal latitude and increased self responsibility.

Discipline and sanctions

Therapeutic communities have their own specific rules and regulations that guide the behavior of residents and the management of facilities. Their explicit purpose is to ensure the safety and health of the community; their implicit aim is to train and teach residents through the use of discipline.

In the TC, social and physical safety are prerequisites for psychological trust. Thus, sanctions are invoked against any behavior which threatens the safety of the therapeutic environment. For example, breaking the TC's cardinal rules – no violence or the threat of violence, verbal or gestural – can bring immediate expulsion. Even minor house rules are addressed, such as stealing mundane sundries (toothbrushes, books, etc.).

The choice of sanction depends upon the severity of the infraction, time in program and history of infractions. For example, verbal reprimands, loss of privileges, speaking bans, may be selected for less severe infractions; job demotions, loss of residential time or expulsion may be invoked for more serious infractions. These measures (contracts) vary in duration from 3 to perhaps 21 days and are re-evaluated by staff and peers in terms of their efficacy.

Though often perceived as punitive, the basic purpose of contracts is to provide a learning experience through compelling residents to attend to their own conduct, to reflect on their own motivation, to feel some consequence of their behavior and to consider alternate forms of acting under stimilar situations.

Contracts also have important community functions. The entire facility is made aware of disciplinary actions that have been taken with any resident. Thus, contracts act as deterrents against violations; they provide vicarious learning experiences in others; and as symbols of safety and integrity, they strengthen community cohesiveness.

C.   The TC process

Rehabilation in the TC unfolds as a developmental process occurring in a social learning context. Values, conducts, emotions and cognitive understanding (insight) must be integrated in the evolution of a socially responsible, personally autonomous individual.

The developmental process itself can be understood as a passage through three main stages of incremental learning; the learning which occurs at each stage facilitates change at the next and each change reflects increased maturity and personal autonomy.

Stage I (induction – 0 to 60 days)

The main goals of this initial phase of residency are assessment of individual needs and orientation to the TC. Important differences among clients generally do not appear until they experience some reduction in the circumstantial stress usually present at entry and have had some interaction with the treatment regime. Thus, observation of the individual continues during the initial residential period to identify special problems in their adaptation to the TC.

The goal of orientation in the initial phase of residency is to assimilate the individual into the community through full participation and involvement in all of its activities. Rapid assimilation is crucial at this point, when clients are most ambivalent about the long tenure of residency. [...]

Stage II (primary treatment – 2 to 12 months)

During this state, main TC objectives of socialization, personal growth and psychological awareness are pursued through all of the therapeutic and community activities. Primary treatment actually consists of three phases separated by natural landmarks in the socialization-developmental process. Phases roughly correlate with time in program (1 to 4 months, 5 to 8 months and 9 to 12 months). These periods are marked by plateaus of stable behavior which signal futher change.

[...]

Stage III (re-entry – 13 to 24 months)

Re-entry is the stage at which the client must strengthen skills for autonomous decision-making and the capacity for self-management with less reliance on rational authorities or a well-formed peer network. There are two phases of the re-entry stage.

Early re-entry (13 to 18 months)

The main goal of this phase, during which clients continue to live in the facility, is preparation for healthy separation from the community.

Emphasis upon rational authority decreases under the assumption that the client has acquired a sufficient degree of self-management. This is reflected in more individual decision-making about privileges, social plans and life design. The group process involves fewer leaders at this stage, fewer encounters and more shared decision-making. Particular emphasis is placed upon life skills seminars, which provide didactic training for life outside the community. Attendance is mandated for sessions on budgeting, job seeking, use of alcohol, sexuality, parenting, use of leisure time, etc.

During this stage, individal plans are a collective task of the client, a key staff member and peers. These plans are actually blue prints of educational and vocational programs, which include goal attainment schedules, methods of improving inter-personal and family relationships, as well as social and sexual behavior. Clients may be attending school or holding full-time jobs either within or outside the TC at this point. Still, they are expected to participate in house activities when possible and carry some community responsibilities (e.g., facility coverage at night).

Late re-entry (18 to 24 months)

The goal of this phase is to complete a successful separation from residency. Clients are on "live-out" status, involved in full-time jobs or education, maintaining their own households, usually with live-out peers. They may attend such aftercare services as AA, NA or take part in family or individual therapy. This phase is viewed as the end of residency, but not of program participation. Contact with the program is frequent at first and only gradually reduced to weekly phone calls and monthly visits with a primary counselor.

Completion marks the end of active program involvement. Graduation itself, however, is an annual event conducted in the facility, for completes at least a year beyond their residency.

Thus, the therapeutic community experience is preparation rather than cure. Residence in the program facilitates a process of change that must continue throughout life, and what is learned in treatment are the tools to guide the individual on a steady path of continued change. Completion, or graduation, therefore, is not an end, but a beginning.

Reference

Jones, M. 1953. *The Therapeutic Community – A New Treatment Method in Psychiatry*. New York: Basic Books.

Questions

1 According to the article, a goal of TCs is to promote a sense of peer-to-community structure. What does this peer-to-community structure provide for those struggling with substance issues? How do you think TCs are different from other recovery programs? How is social learning promoted in the peer-to-community context? Is this important for recovery? Why or why not?

2 According to the article, TCs state that physical addiction or dependency must be seen in the wider context of the individual's life. What larger factors may be impacting the individual's drug use patterns? How might TCs address these larger social factors? Can these factors really be overcome? What do you think about the TC view that the problem is the person, not the drug?

3 For TCs, rehabilitation focuses upon maintaining a drug free existence. Do you think this is a valuable goal? A practical goal? Why or why not? What do you think are the greatest strengths and weaknesses of TCs? How might the TC structure be improved?

Illness Narratives of Recovering on Methadone Maintenance

Lee Garth Vigilant

Lee Garth Vigilant looks at another treatment modality: methadone maintenance. Studying opiate addicts in Boston, he compares the philosophies of the methadone clinic, with its strict standards of abstinence enforced through frequent urinalyses, with the relapse and continuous-recovery model of Narcotics Anonymous. These models rest on very different images of people, of addiction, and of recovery. As you read this you may want to think about which makes more sense to you. Are there any conditions that would make one type of approach seem better than the other, or do you think one is always better? Are there certain kinds of people or personalities (Zinberg and Harding's "set") that are more suited to one approach than another? Do the way we teach kids about drugs and the messages reinforced about them in our culture, especially regarding the possibility of moderation, make one of these approaches more likely to succeed? What kinds of subcultural values are best suited to the methadone maintenance approach versus Narcotics Anonymous? Are these tied to any racial/ethnic, class, gender, or age groups?

Finally, why does Vigilant use the term "ontological" security? What does he mean by it? Can you identify with this feeling?

There is a crisis of interpretation regarding the meaning of recovery, the practice of recovery, and agreements on when exactly recovery takes place in the methadone subculture. In general, there is a meaning lacuna about what recovery actually is and how methadone patients should practice and experience it. Nowhere is this crisis more keenly apparent than in the healing and recovery practices of methadone patients versus the recommendations of the methadone clinic and Alcoholics Anonymous (AA) and Narcotics Anonymous (NA) fellowships. For instance, methadone clinics tend to apply the strictest criterion for recovery to opiate addicts: Recovery is the state where patients break the pattern of self-abuse in opiate consumption. Consequently, not only is recovery defined in this way, but also clinical success. A successful methadone program is one in which the vast majority of its clientele are "clean." Ironically, this definition of recovery appears lacking when compared to the AA/ NA model, which proselytizes absolute sobriety (drugs, alcohol, and in some cases, methadone − a synthetic opiate − itself). Moreover, methadone patients, with their own definitions and practices of recovery, often appear in opposition to both expectations because poly-drug usage is common among this population. It appears that both methadone patients and methadone clinicians come to the healing transaction with vastly different practices of, and expectations for, recovery.

There are two competing recovery paradigms external to methadone patients that have profound sway. The first is the recovery ideal that the clinic itself establishes. The clinical definition of recovery under methadone maintenance treatment is very simple and well known: First and foremost, cessation of opiate consumption. Frequent urinalyses ensure that patients comply with this recovery definition. This narrow meaning of recovery is a contrast, albeit a shallow one, to that of the AA/NA model, which is another frame. For the AA/NA model (and I conflate AA with NA because they share the same proscription for recovery), the core ideal is absolute sobriety. This model sees recovery as a state of complete abstinence from *all* illicit drugs (and some licit ones) that might prevent a return to health, impair personal growth, and hinder recovery. Moreover, recovery under the AA/NA paradigm is always framed in complete or total terms since every aspect of the addict's life is suspect for re-evaluation. In addition to a change in character as the 12-Steps so plainly infer, this recovery encourages attendance at daily or weekly meetings, public testimonials, and maintaining personal contact with a sponsor and with other recovering addicts.

What is interesting and paradoxical about these emotional and time-consuming labors is that "recovery" never takes place: One is perpetually *in recovery*, but never fully *recovered*. Recovery for the AA/NA paradigm, unlike that of the methadone clinic, is not just predicated upon the cessation of heroin use, but is dependent upon a permanent change in how addicts relate to their addictions. Addiction, far from being a temporary illness event, is, for AA/NA, an immutable part of the addict's identity, much like other master statuses like ethnicity, sex, and chronic illness.

Yet, the axial question is this: How do methadone patients understand the meaning of recovery in their own illness careers, and do these conceptualizations conform to, or differ from, the expectations of the methadone clinic and the AA/NA sobriety communes?

Sample and Method

The data in this article come from a qualitative study on the meaning and practice of recovery with 45 methadone patients and were collected during the spring and summer of 2000. The interviews were between one and two hours in length and generally held in the respondents' homes. One-third of the respondent pool came from a classified ad that ran in the *Boston Globe*, and two-thirds by "chain-referral" efforts. There were 21 females and 24 males in this study, with an age range from 21–56 years old. Most respondents were Euro-American ($n = 35$), with the remainder Afro-American ($n = 9$) and Latino ($n = 1$). As an index of social class, 49% ($n = 22$) of the respondents held working class jobs, 27% ($n = 12$) were on state sponsored disability (SSDI), 13% ($n = 6$) were unemployed, and 11% ($n = 5$) had white-collar occupations (two accountants, a nurse, an adjunct professor, and a paralegal). [...]

The Meaning and Practice of Recovery: Ontologically Re-Considered

There were four distinct meaning categories on recovery, and these constructions of recovery were accompanied by distinct practices − actions that at times conformed to the two competing recovery paradigms, but at others, differed markedly from both. These expressions, in their order of frequency, are (1) recovery as being normal and recapturing lost time ($n = 15$), (2) recovery as a perpetual, ongoing process without a "recovered state" ($n = 14$), (3) recovery as self-centered care for the self ($n = 8$), and (4) recovery as associational change ($n = 8$). In addition, a focal theme emerging out of each of these categories was the importance of achieving a sense of ontological security.
[...]

Recovery as Being Normal (or, Ontological Security in Routine, Stability, and the Minimization of Risk)

The most frequently offered meaning category of the concept "recovery" referred to attempts at *being normal* and living in reality. To be normal is to regain a sense of control over heroin addiction with assistance of methadone, ironically, a legal and synthetic opiate. Here, recovery not only implies recapturing lost time with intimate others, but also a state of temporal synchronism where individuals are governed by the constraints of work and family life and not by heroin addiction. To be in recovery is to be "ordinary" – to be like everybody else; and when this state is achieved, one is indeed "recovered." It is natural to assume, however, that to be normal implies sobriety and complete abstinence. It does not.

> Recovery is relative. It's relative. Compared to some of the times in my life, I'm in recovery. I know I'm playing with fire by using [heroin] occasionally. But recovery means maintaining a certain level of living. What I'm recovering from is a lifestyle of craziness where I was running around cashing bad checks, filling prescriptions, and hustling from doctors. Thank God I never had to sell my ass because I can't imagine it. (48-year-old Euro-American female)

For these respondents, recovery is about changing a "lifestyle of craziness" and not necessarily ending the practice of getting high. Moreover, the drug methadone aptly ensures this vision of recovery. Yet, while being normal does not imply sobriety, fully half of the 15 respondents who claimed this meaning category were indeed living up to the mandate of absolute sobriety.

> Recovery is peace of mind. It's not worrying about where your next fix is coming from. It gives you time to think about other things. I mean, heroin pretty much dominates your whole life: It's your job trying to stay high! Right now, I'm working, seeing my counselor, and repairing my family life. I keep my nose clean. I go to AA meetings, and I'm more involved with my family. Before, I didn't have time for anything besides heroin because I was dope-sick all the time. (46-year-old Euro-American male)

Defining recovery as a return to a normal state, [...] "frees" addicts [...] to maintain a routine. Having a routine is crucial because it is through our routines that we are able to order (or re-order) our life-worlds in meaningful ways, [...] to fulfill our interactional obligations. Recovery narratives that emphasize normal-ness are stories on the importance of the ontological security gained from having a life marked by routine and stability.

> With methadone, it's almost like I get a sense of security. I mean, I know I'm safe. I'm not out there getting high and I know I'm not going to be sick. It's like it gives me a sense of security every day; it's like a routine. Like every day, I had to go to the drug dealer, but now I just go to the clinic and get my medication. And I like a routine. I like to know what's going to go down. I do the same thing every day at the same time. I go to the clinic. I come here [to a café] and have my breakfast. I go to the YMCA. And then I go have lunch. It's the same thing every day. (38-year-old Euro-American male)

[...]

Finally, there is a corollary source of ontological security in the narratives of respondents who define recovery in terms of regaining a sense of normality *but* without the requisite of complete abstinence: the ontological security that methadone offers in enabling some addicts to more "safely" manage the risk of poly-drug usage, including heroin. The ontological security of managing risk in a perilous milieu is especially important for those who view methadone in pragmatic terms, namely as a drug that abates withdrawal pain, so-called dope-sickness, and alleviates the craziness of the heroin lifestyle.

> Methadone is a safety valve for me right now. It works for some people, but unfortunately, all it is right now is a safety valve. I have to get it through my head that I cannot use heroin every day. It has to be a special occasion type of thing. (48-year-old Euro-American male)

Yet, it would be a mistake to posit that methadone allows these respondents to manage the risk of using without also noting that it brought many to acknowledge that the stakes of heroin addiction were far too high.

> My biggest fear is that I don't have another run left with it. I'm getting old. I'm 42 years old, and I don't see

myself being on the streets at 50 or 60. I don't see it. When I'm 50, I want to have some kind of career. I want to have a fucking life, man, at 50! Not trying to buy dope off some fucking 20-year-old kid. (42-year-old Afro-American male)

[...] For many, the risk of using heroin, even with the relative security a methadone recovery offers, is too high when weighed against other important factors such as the possibility of relapsing into the same non-productive hustling patterns.

Perpetual Recovery (or, Ontological Security in Biographical Work)

The second meaning of recovery, found among 14 respondents, was the belief that a "recovered state" was not possible. A perpetual recovery differed from the "being normal" meaning in one major way: Under the being normal category, there is a definitive sense that a state of recovery is possible even with the persistence of the addiction disease, a position anathema to AA/NA. For those respondents, recovery meant the resumption of ordinary patterns without the persistent worry of dope-sickness, and having to hustle to abate this condition. Recovery was to be *ordinary* again. This view sharply contrasts that of respondents in the perpetual recovery category who had a more nuanced view of the healing ideal. These respondents accepted Alcoholics Anonymous' 12-Steps program that views recovery as a life-long process, but where they differed was on the possibility of ever halting the disease's progress. [...] These individuals defined recovery as a continual process with no end – a process that includes both periods of heroin use and prolonged sobriety.

In a sense, I think "recovered" is a term used at an end phase. Probably ten years from now if you asked me if I were recovered, I would still be in recovery. Just because I haven't answered to drugs today doesn't mean my recovery is over. I'm in constant recovery. I don't think I will ever be able to sit here and tell you with a 100% guarantee that there will never be any drugs in my life again. (56-year-old Euro-American male)

These informants are keenly cognizant of the fragility of the recovery ideal and the frangibility of claiming to be a "recovered heroin addict." [...] They reject, as farcical, the supposition of a supposed recovered state, preferring instead to see heroin addiction as a chronic condition, and recovery as a perpetual process with no end. [...]

[C]onceptualizing recovery in perpetual terms, as a process with no discernible end, offers some methadone patients the opportunity to remain constantly vigilant about their addiction disease. Seeing one's self in a state of perpetual recovery demands a host of re-integrative strategies to match the constant vacillations between periods of sobriety and periods of heroin abuse, or the shifts between the self as heroin addict and the self as recovering addict. [...] A methadone recovery affords many heroin addicts an opportunity to remake their biographies by engaging in [...] counseling sessions and group therapies that the clinic provides. Consequently, it was counseling at the methadone clinic that brought many respondents face-to-face with their denials.

There was a lot of denial in the early years of my addiction despite going in and out of detoxes. I remember once this black woman in one of the detoxes telling me, "You better get down on your hands and knees and pray to God that you are still alive today." And I said to her, "I'm not an addict." I reasoned that since I took percocets at home and I didn't use a needle, I wasn't an addict. Four or five years later, I went into the same detox and the same woman was there, and this time she said to me, "I bet if I threw a rock of cocaine on the floor you would get down on your hands and knees." That was my wake-up call. I knew I was no different. (46-year-old Euro-American female)

If recovery is truly "the process of discovery," as one respondent so resolutely affirmed, then methadone maintenance offers patients the time and resources to confront the existential and biographical questions that are the very foundations of ontological security. Moreover, the re-integrative strategies that biographical re-ordering entails, such as seeing your recovery as a perpetual process with no end, accepting the "once an addict, always an addict" mantra, and being omni-vigilant about your addiction disease, fortifies ontological security.

Recovery as Care for the Self (or, Ontological Security in Strategic Life Planning)

This category, reported by eight respondents, is perhaps one of the most intriguing, although not surprising, meanings of the recovery ideal. By care for the self, these respondents are referring to two things in particular. They frame recovery as a time to reflect upon and resolve the emotional or corporeal crises that catalyzed their entrances into the heroin subculture. Recovery also stands for a literal period of self-care for a body neglected during the months, years, or decades of heroin addiction.

[...]

Recovery, as a period of self-care, is a time to recapture health, to heal the body, and resolve emotional and corporeal issues that led to heroin addiction. This recovery is also a time to envision, and plan for, future possibilities of action and actualization.

> Recovery means going to meetings, talking to my therapist, learning more about me, and why I put myself in the position I did. Recovery means dealing with the issues that I seemed to have camouflaged. Just to backtrack a little, the reason why I became an addict is I was raped by my brother-in-law for seven years from the time I was 14. And I came to drugs and alcohol to cover-up the pain. (43-year-old Euro-American female)

Recovery, as a period of self-care, also speaks volumes to what happens to the body during heroin addiction. The body, and this thought is easily overlooked, is both an active and a passive object during the hustling period. The body is active because the very pains of dope-sickness fuel the need to hustle, ensuring a free-following supply of heroin. Yet, it also is a passive object because concern for the body – its care and maintenance, appearance, and health – disappears when withdrawal symptoms take precedence over self-care. Thus, recovery for these respondents is a time to recapture and to revitalize a body that fell apart during the hustling period. Consequently, this period of self-care is essential to creating future possibilities of actions and choices. [...]

Methadone, by giving respondents time to engage in strategic life planning, reduces the existential anxieties that come from the unknowable future. Yet, efforts to colonize the future often double back upon the risk of thinking that because one's future is strategically outlined, then one is therefore "recovered." These attempts are rarely unyoked from the continued vigilance of maintaining sobriety:

> These people that raise their hands in meetings and say they have 15 years clean, do you know how far away from using they are? They are no farther away from using as I am right now. In fact, it is easier. The longer time you have under your belt, the more secure you get in your head and the more comfortable and relaxed. And like I said, the addiction doesn't stop. It still grows. (36-year-old Euro-American male)

The colonization of, and the strategic planning for, a future without heroin is a means of strengthening recovery efforts and maintaining ontological security for methadone patients. However, the pervasive threat of relapse – a threat that can potentially destroy determined efforts at recovering a semblance of ontological assuredness – is never far off.

Recovery as Associational Change (or, Ontological Security of Care Networks)

The final meaning category, observed among eight respondents, was the view of recovery as a period of associational change. Eight respondents defined recovery as a time to sever those associational ties that were reminders of the heroin lifestyle. [...] This recovery enjoins the pursuit of new support relationships concomitant with ardent efforts at avoiding the old places and peoples of the subculture.

> I had to cut my best friend off. He was the one that introduced me to percodan and heroin, and he will die with a needle in his arm. He has been in and out of jail for the past ten years. It's crucial to break away from the old friends. (39-year-old Euro-American male)

Each of these respondents made explicit the ideal of "loving from a distance" or severing completely their dope-fiend associations when undertaking recovery. Sometimes, recovery even necessitates a break from friends at the methadone clinic, or, in other cases, going to another clinic to get away from illicit drug use. [...] For many patients, recovery concerns avoiding not only the dope influences outside the halls of recovery, but also the pitfalls of associating with individuals who continue to use illicit drugs while on methadone. Beyond this, it is important to underscore that change, like self-care in recovery, necessarily implies a degree of self-centeredness.

> Everybody in my life right now, right down to my kids, is part of my support group. That's the only people allowed in my life right now. My kids will ask me right off the bat, "Dad, how was your day? Did you do a meeting?" I don't have time for anybody who isn't going to give me support. I really don't have time for them. My vision of the world has been narrowed down to this little tunnel, and it has to be focused. Although heroin addiction is a very self-centered addiction, I need to apply that same self-centeredness to my recovery. I have to be very self-centered because if I don't focus on myself right now in the early stages of my recovery, there will be nothing there to share with anybody that is any good later on – and I know that. (39-year-old Euro-American male)

Recovery change, severing ties with lifelong friends and acquaintances, is not easy to accomplish, and many respondents lamented this as especially difficult. Nonetheless, breaking with the old is essential to remaking one's identity as a person in recovery. [...]

In severing drug friendships and hustling ties, respondents must rely on their recovery community (i.e., methadone clinic or AA or NA group) as a crucial source of meaningful social interactions – contacts that buttress the new recovery identity. The methadone clinic provides a support system to addicts through frequent urinalyses to monitor compliance, and individual and group therapies to support sobriety. These monitors act as a care-apparatus, albeit a form of micro-surveillance, to remind addicts they belong to a community that is concerned about their well-being. [...] The encouragement, education, counseling, and medication that the clinic provides to heroin-addicted individuals are also crucial steps in rebuilding an addict's ego, self-concept, and power to resist the lure to use. This constitutes a primordial

form of ontological security, one grounded upon mutual care and empathy.

Summary and Implication

The focal expression of recovery for the 45 respondents in this study concerns the achievement of a sense of ontological security. [...] Although many strive for, and some achieve, total abstinence, full sobriety from all illicit substances is not [the] raison d'etre of recovery for most respondents; this is certainly anathema to the policies of the clinic and of the ideology of the AA/NA commune. What methadone patients want, and this may seem counterintuitive, is to have order, safety, security, a little discipline, and a daily routine in their lives without the requisite of absolute sobriety. But first, they want ontological security.

The implication of this vision of recovery, whose primary emphasis is ontological security, is that it speaks to the need for a greater emphasis on harm reduction public policies that stress the reduction of the most harmful outcomes of illicit and illegal behaviors over policies that enjoin stigma, punishment, or incarceration. In the case of heroin addiction, a harm reduction approach would emphasize treatment over punishment in reducing the most problematic outcomes of heroin consumption. For instance, a harm reduction approach to heroin addiction might focus on reducing Hepatitis C and HIV infections through needle exchange programs for active users, while removing both legal and moral sanctions from methadone patients who continue to use while in treatment. What the 45 respondents in this study envision is a state of affairs where methadone can assist them in recapturing lost time, regaining a sense of normality, and dealing with their biographies in reflexive ways in order to colonize a future without the craziness of addiction. Perhaps what methadone patients need – now more than at any other time in recent memory with cheaper and more potent opiates in circulation – are programs in the vein of harm reduction that can listen to their visions of recovery and respond in ways that assist them in achieving their recovery goals, rather than programs steeped in ideological inducements to total abstinence or punishment.

Questions

1   What other factors involved in the recovery process are neglected by a sole focus on complete sobriety? How might sobriety be only a minor factor in living a "normal" life for those struggling with drug dependence? Do you think heroin use was the cause of the craziness in the lives of the addicts in the article? Or was heroin use a symptom of their crazy lives?

2   How might seeing oneself in a perpetual state of recovery benefit the recovery process? How might it hinder the quest for "normalcy?" How do the strategies of self-care and/or associational change relate to the strategies of TCs? What do you think is more important for the recovery process, personal sobriety or changes in environmental factors?

3   Do you think the goal of AA and/or NA of absolute sobriety is effective? Do you think responsible and/or moderate use would be a more reasonable and/or attainable goal? Do you find any irony with a recovery process that preached abstinence but prescribes methadone? Why or why not?

The Elephant that No One Sees
Natural Recovery among Middle-Class Addicts

Robert Granfield and William Cloud

The multi-billion dollar treatment industry in America is huge and powerful. Narratives communicated by doctors, psychiatrists, and counselors tend to suggest that people with drug problems need to subject themselves to some form of psycho-medical treatment in order to recover. Robert Granfield and William Cloud challenge this notion by presenting data on people who overcame their struggles with alcohol and drugs without such assistance.

As you read this article, think about how reasonable their points sound to you. Researchers have suggested that an inadvertent by-product of people associating with organizations and institutions designed to treat deviance is that their deviance may be reinforced. Do you think that might be the case for some of the treatment modalities already discussed? Thinking about some of the selections in this book, what kinds of sociological factors do you think make some approaches work better for different kinds of people?

A smoking cessation hypnotherapist once told us that the best predictor of success in quitting smoking is for someone to have previously tried and failed. What do you think of this idea? Why might that be? How would this image of people and addiction fit with some of the assumptions underlying the various treatment modalities discussed here?

Introduction

Social deviance literature typically portrays drug and alcohol addicted individuals as possessing distinct subcultural characteristics that marginalize them from the nonaddicted world. Whether this marginalization occurs because of a personality profile which predisposes an individual to addiction or whether it follows from being labeled and stigmatized as "an addict," the outcome is thought to be the same. Such individuals are considered to be distinctly different from the majority of the population. Indeed, the social deviance literature has played a role in classifying addicts as "other" thereby contributing to the production of an outsider status. However, as Waterston (1993: 14) has recently argued, such portrayals have

Drugs and the American Dream: An Anthology, First Edition. Edited by Patricia A. Adler, Peter Adler, and Patrick K. O'Brien.
© 2012 John Wiley & Sons, Inc. Published 2012 by John Wiley & Sons, Inc.

contributed to the "ghettoization" of drug users and to the "construction of a false separation between 'them and us.'"

While the social deviance paradigm of addiction has produced insightful material documenting the lifestyle, experiences, and world views of drug and alcohol addicted persons, this literature has excluded groups not conforming to the image of social disparagement. [...]

Often absent from the research on hidden populations are those drug addicts and alcoholics who fail to fit into the previously constructed categories that are consistent with current models of deviance. [...] One population that remains hidden due to the fact that they deviate from socially constructed categories regarding addiction are middle-class drug addicts and alcoholics who terminate their addictive use of substances without treatment. Research exploring the phenomena of natural recovery has found that significant numbers of people discontinue their excessive intake of addictive substances without formal or lay treatment. While it is difficult to estimate the actual size of this hidden population because they are largely invisible, researchers agree that their numbers are large and some even contend that they are substantially larger than those choosing to enter treatment facilities or self-help groups. Some have estimated that as many as 90% of problem drinkers never enter treatment and many suspend problematic use without it. Research in Canada has shown that 82% of alcoholics who terminated their addiction reported using natural recovery.

Research on natural recovery has focused on a variety of substances including heroin and other opiates, cocaine, and alcohol. Much of this literature challenges the dominant view that addiction relates primarily to the substance being consumed. The dominant addiction paradigm maintains that individuals possess an illness that requires intensive therapeutic intervention. Failure to acquire treatment is considered a sign of denial that will eventually lead to more advanced stages of addiction and possibly death. Given the firm convictions of addictionists as well as their vested interests in marketing this concept, their rejection of the natural recovery research is of little surprise.

Research on natural recovery has offered great insight into how people successfully transform their lives without turning to professionals or self-help groups. The fact that people accomplish such transformations naturally is by no means a revelation. Most ex-smokers discontinue their tobacco use without treatment while many "mature-out" of a variety of behaviors including heavy drinking and narcotics use. Some researchers examining such transformations frequently point to factors within the individual's social context that promote change. Not only are patterns of alcohol and drug use influenced by social contexts as Zinberg (1986) illustrated, but the experience of quitting as well can be understood from this perspective. Others have attributed natural recovery to a cognitive appraisal process in which the costs and benefits of continued drinking are assessed by alcoholics.

Perhaps one of the most detailed investigations of natural recovery is Biernacki's (1986) detailed description of former heroin addicts. Emphasizing the importance of social contexts, Biernacki demonstrates how heroin addicts terminated their addictions and successfully transformed their lives. Most of the addicts in that study as well as others initiated self-recovery after experiencing an assortment of problems that led to a resolve to change. Additionally, Biernacki found that addicts who arrest addictions naturally utilize a variety of strategies. Such strategies involve breaking off relationships with drug users, removing oneself from a drug-using environment, building new structures in one's life, and using social networks of friends and family that help provide support for this newly emerging status. Although it is unclear whether the social context of those who terminate naturally is uniquely different from those who undergo treatment, it is certain that environmental factors significantly influence the strategies employed in the decision to stop.

While this literature has been highly instructive, much of this research has focused on respondents' circumvention of formal treatment such as therapeutic communities, methadone maintenance, psychotherapy, or regular counseling in outpatient clinics. Many of those not seeking professional intervention may nevertheless participate in self-help groups. Self-help groups have been one of the most popular avenues for people experiencing alcohol and drug problems. This may be due in large part to the fact that groups such as Alcoholics Anonymous (AA), Narcotics Anonymous (NA), or Cocaine Anonymous (CA) medicalize substance abuse in such a way as to alleviate personal responsibility and related guilt. Moreover, these groups contribute to the cultivation of a support community which helps facilitate behavioral change.

Despite these attractions and the popularity of these groups, many in the field remain skeptical about their effectiveness. Research has demonstrated that addicts who affiliate with self-help groups relapse at a significantly greater rate than do those who undergo hospitalization only. Some have raised concerns about the appropriateness of self-help groups in all instances of addiction. In one of the most turgid critiques of self-help groups, Peele (1989) estimates that nearly half of all those who affiliate with such groups relapse within the first year. Peele contends that these groups are not very effective in stopping addictive behaviors since such groups subscribe to the ideology of lifelong addiction. Adopting the addict-for-life ideology, as many members do, has numerous implications for a person's identity as well as ways of relating to the world around them.

[...]

Given the emerging challenges to the dominant views of recovery, research on recovery will be advanced through an examination of those who terminated their addictive use of alcohol and drugs without the benefit of either formal or informal treatment modalities. While research has provided insight into those who reject formal treatment modalities, we know little about the population who additionally reject self-help groups, particularly those from middle-class backgrounds. This paper examines the process of natural recovery among middle-class drug addicts and alcoholics. [...]

Method

Data for the present study were collected from a two-stage research design involving 46 former drug addicts and alcoholics. [...] Lengthy, semistructured interviews with respondents were conducted to elicit thickly descriptive responses.

Strict criteria were established for respondent selection. First, respondents had to have been drug or alcohol dependent for a period of at least 1 year. On average, our respondents were dependent for a period of 9.14 years. [...] Second, to be eligible, individuals had to have terminated their addictive consumption for a period of at least 1 year prior to the interview. The mean length of time of termination from addiction for the entire sample was 5.5 years. Finally, the sample includes only individuals who had no, or only minimal, exposure to formal treatment. [...]

All of our respondents in the present study report having stable middle-class backgrounds. Each of the respondents had completed high school, the majority possessed college degrees, and several respondents held graduate degrees. Most were employed in professional occupations, including law, engineering, and health-related fields, held managerial positions, or operated their own businesses during their addiction. Of the respondents participating in this study, 30 were males and 16 were females. The age range in the sample was 25 to 60 with a mean age of 38.4 years.

Forming a Postaddict Identity

[...]

The perspective of symbolic interaction has frequently been used when analyzing the adoption of deviant identities. For instance, the societal reaction model of deviance views the formation of a spoiled identity as a consequence of labeling. Reactions against untoward behavior in the form of degradation ceremonies often give rise to deviant identities. In addition, organizations that seek to reform deviant behavior encourage the adoption of a "sick role" for the purposes of reintegration. AA, for instance, teaches its members that they possess a disease and a lifelong addiction to alcohol. Such organizations provide a new symbolic framework through which members undergo dramatic personal transformation.

Consequently, members adopt an addict role and identity, an identity that for many becomes salient (Brown 1991). One respondent in Brown's study, for instance, indicated the degree of engulfment in the addict identity.

> Sobriety is my life's priority. I can't have my life, my health, my family, my job, or anything else unless I'm

sober. My program [participation in AA] has to come
first ... Now I've come to realize that this is the nature
of the disease. I need to remind myself daily that I'm an
alcoholic. As long as I work my program, I am granted a
daily reprieve from returning to drinking.

Brown's (1991:169) analysis of self-help programs and
the identity transformation process that is fostered in
those settings demonstrates that members learn "that
they must constantly practice the principles of
recovery in all their daily affairs." Thus, it is within
such programs that the addict identity and role is
acquired and reinforced (Peele 1989).

If the addict identity is acquired within such
organizational contexts, it is logical to hypothesize
that former addicts with minimal contact with such
organizations will possess different self-concepts. In
the interviews, a striking pattern emerged in relation
to their present self-concept and their past drug and
alcohol involvement. They were asked, "How do you
see yourself now in relation to your past?" and, "Do
you see yourself as a former addict, recovering addict,
recovered addict, or in some other way?" A large
majority, nearly two-thirds, refused to identify
themselves as presently addicted or as recovering or
even recovered. Most reported that they saw
themselves in "some other way." While all identified
themselves as being addicted earlier in their lives, most
did not continue to define themselves as addicts. In
several cases, these respondents reacted strongly against
the addiction-as-disease ideology, believing that such
a permanent identity would impede their continued
social development. As one respondent explained:

I'm a father, a husband and a worker. This is how I see
myself today. Being a drug addict was someone I was in
the past. I'm over that and I don't think about it anymore.

These respondents saw themselves neither as addicts
nor ex-addicts; rather, most references to their past
addictions were not central to their immediate self-
concepts.

Unlike the alcoholics and drug addicts described
by Brown (1991) and others, they did not adopt this
identity as a "master status" nor did this identity
become salient in the role identity hierarchy. Instead,
the "addict" identity was marginalized by our

respondents. Alcoholics and addicts who have
participated extensively in self-help groups often
engage in a long-term, self-labeling process which
involves continuous reference to their addiction.
While many have succeeded in terminating addiction
through participation in such programs and by
adopting the master status of an addict, researchers
have raised concern over the deleterious nature of
such self-labeling. Peele (1989), for instance, believes
that continuous reference to addiction and reliance
on the sick role may be at variance with successful
and enduring termination of addictive behaviors.
Respondents, by contrast, did not reference their
previous addictions as being presently central in their
lives. Their comments suggest that they had
transcended their addict identity and had adopted
self-concepts congruent with contemporary roles.

[...]

The fact that our respondents did not adopt addict
identities is of great importance since it contradicts
the common assumptions of treatment programs. The
belief that alcoholics and drug addicts can overcome
their addictions and not see themselves in an indefinite
state of recovery is incongruous with treatment
predicated on the disease concept which pervades
most treatment programs. Such programs subscribe to
the view that addiction is incurable; programmatic
principles may then commit addicts to a life of
ongoing recovery, often with minimal success. [...]

Circumventing Treatment

Given the pervasiveness of treatment programs and
self-help groups such as AA and NA, the decision to
embark upon a method of natural recovery is curious.
Some of our respondents in the first stage of the study
reported having had direct exposure to such groups
by having attended one or two AA, NA, or CA
meetings. Others in this sample, although never
having attended, reported being indirectly familiar
with such groups. Only two of them claimed to have
no knowledge of these groups or the principles they
advocate. Consequently, the respondents, as a group,
expressed the decision not to enter treatment, which
represented a conscious effort to circumvent treatment
rather than a lack of familiarity with such programs.

[...] They credited treatment programs and self-help groups with helping friends or family members overcome alcohol or drug addictions. Overall, however, our respondents in the first sample disagreed with the ideological basis of such programs and felt that they were inappropriate for them.

Responses included a wide range of criticisms of these programs. In most cases, rejection of treatment programs and self-help groups reflected a perceived contradiction between these respondents' world views and the core principles of such programs. Overcoming resistance to core principles which include the views that addiction is a disease (once an addict always an addict), or that individuals are powerless over their addiction, is imperative by those who affiliate with such programs. Indeed, individuals who subscribe to alternative views of addiction are identified as "in denial" (Brissett 1988). Not unlike other institutions such as the military, law school, or mental health hospitals, self-help groups socialize recruits away from their previously held world views (Granfield 1992; Goffman 1961). It is the task of such programs to shape its members' views to make them compatible with organizational ideology (Brown 1991; Peele 1989). Socialization within treatment programs and self-help groups enables a person to reconstruct a biography that corresponds to a new reference point.

Respondents in this sample, however, typically rejected specific characteristics of the treatment ideology. First, many expressed strong opposition to the suggestion that they were powerless over their addictions. Such an ideology, they explained, not only was counterproductive but was also extremely demeaning. These respondents saw themselves as efficacious people who often prided themselves on their past accomplishments. They viewed themselves as being individualists and strong-willed. One respondent, for instance, explained that "such programs encourage powerlessness" and that she would rather "trust her own instincts than the instincts of others." Another respondent commented that:

> I read a lot of their literature and the very first thing they say is that you're powerless. I think that's bullshit. I believe that people have power inside themselves to make what they want happen. I think I have choices and can do anything I set my mind to.

Consequently, these respondents found the suggestion that they were powerless incompatible with their own self-image. While treatment programs and self-help groups would define such attitudes as a manifestation of denial that would only result in perpetuating addiction, they saw overcoming their addictions as a challenge they could effectively surmount. Interestingly, and in contrast to conventional wisdom in the treatment field, the overwhelming majority of our respondents in the first sample reported successful termination of their addictions after only one attempt.

They also reported that they disliked the culture associated with such self-help programs. In addition to finding the ideological components of such programs offensive, most rejected the lifestyle encouraged by such programs. For instance, several of them felt that these programs bred dependency and subsequently rejected the notion that going to meetings with other addicts was essential for successful termination. In fact, some actually thought it to be dangerous to spend so much time with addicts who continue to focus on their addictions. Most of our respondents in this first sample sought to avoid all contact with drug addicts once they decided to terminate their own drug use. Consequently, they believed that contact with addicts, even those who are not actively using, would possibly undermine their termination efforts. Finally, some of these respondents reported that they found self-help groups "cliquish" and "unhealthy." One respondent explained that, "all they do is stand around smoking cigarettes and drinking coffee while they talk about their addiction. I never felt comfortable with these people." This sense of discomfort with the cultural aspects of these programs was often keenly felt by the women in our sample. Most women in this group believed that self-help groups were male-oriented and did not include the needs of women. [...]

The Elements of Cessation

The fact that our respondents were able to terminate their addictions without the benefit of treatment raises an important question about recovery. Research that has examined this process has found that individuals who have a "stake in conventional life" are better able to alter their drug-taking practices than those who experience a sense of hopelessness (Waldorf et al. 1991). In their longitudinal research of cocaine users, these authors found that many people with structural supports in their lives such as a job, family, and other involvements were simply able to "walk away" from their heavy use of cocaine. According to these authors, this fact suggests that the social context of a drug user's life may significantly influence the ability to overcome drug problems.

The social contexts of our respondents served to protect many of them from total involvement with an addict subculture. Literature on the sociocultural correlates of heavy drinking has found that some groups possess cultural protection against developing alcoholism. In addition, Peele (1989) has argued that individuals with greater resources in their lives are well equipped to overcome drug problems. Such resources include education and other credentials, job skills, meaningful family attachments, and support mechanisms. In the case of our respondents, most [...] reported coming from stable home environments that valued education, family, and economic security, and for the most part held conventional beliefs. All of our respondents in the first group had completed high school, nine were college graduates, and one held a master's degree in engineering. Most were employed in professional occupations or operated their own businesses. Additionally, most continued to be employed throughout their period of heavy drug and alcohol use and none of our respondents came from disadvantaged backgrounds.

It might be concluded that the social contexts of these respondent's lives protected them from further decline into alcohol and drug addiction. They frequently reported that there were people in their lives to whom they were able to turn when they decided to quit. Some explained that their families provided support; others described how their nondrug-using friends assisted them in their efforts to stop using. One respondent explained how an old college friend helped him get over his addiction to crack cocaine:

> My best friend from college made a surprise visit. I hadn't seen him in years. He walked in and I was all cracked out. It's like he walked into the twilight zone or something. He couldn't believe it. He smoked dope in college but he had never seen anything like this. When I

saw him, I knew that my life was really screwed up and I needed to do something about it. He stayed with me for the next two weeks and helped me through it.

Typically, respondents in our sample had not yet "burned their social bridges" and were able to rely upon communities of friends, family, and other associates in their lives. The existence of such communities made it less of a necessity for these individuals to search out alternative communities such as those found within self-help groups. Such groups may be of considerable importance when a person's natural communities break down. Indeed, the fragmentation of communities within postmodern society may account for the popularity of self-help groups. In the absence of resources and communities, such programs allow individuals to construct a sense of purpose and meaning in their lives. Respondents in our sample all explained that the resources, communities, and individuals in their lives were instrumental in supporting their efforts to change.

In some cases, these respondents abandoned their using communities entirely to search for nonusing groups. This decision to do so was often triggered by the realization that their immediate social networks consisted mostly of heavy drug and alcohol users. Any attempt to discontinue use, they reasoned, would require complete separation. Several from this group moved to different parts of the country in order to distance themselves from their using networks. This finding is consistent with Biernacki's (1986) study of heroin addicts who relocated in order to remove any temptations to use in the future. For some women, the decision to abandon using communities, particularly cocaine, was often preceded by becoming pregnant. These women left boyfriends and husbands because they felt a greater sense of responsibility and greater meaning in their new maternal status. In all these cases, respondents fled using communities in search of more conventional networks.

In addition to relying on their natural communities and abandoning using communities, these respondents also built new support structures to assist them in their termination efforts. They frequently reported becoming involved in various social groups such as choirs, health clubs, religious organizations, reading clubs, and dance companies. Others reported that they returned to school, became active in civic organizations, or simply developed new hobbies that brought them in touch with nonusers. Thus, respondents built new lives for themselves by cultivating social ties with meaningful and emotionally satisfying alternative communities. In each of these cases where respondents formed attachments to new communities, they typically hid their addictive past, fearing that exposure would jeopardize their newly acquired status.

[...]

Given the apparent roles that severing ties with using networks and having resources play in the natural recovery process, one might draw the compelling conclusion that those individuals from the most disadvantaged segments of our society are also least likely to be in a position to overcome severe addiction problems naturally. Unfortunately, these individuals are also at greatest risk for severe drug and alcohol problems, least likely to be able to afford private treatment, and least likely to voluntarily seek public treatment.

Discussion and Implications

While the [...] present study is small, there is considerable evidence from additional research to suggest that the population of self-healers is quite substantial. Despite empirical evidence, many in the treatment field continue to deny the existence of such a population. The therapeutic "field" possesses considerable power to construct reality in ways that exclude alternative and perhaps challenging paradigms. [...] The power of the therapeutic field lies in its ability to not only medicalize behavior, but also in the ability to exclude the experiences and world views of those who do not fit into conventional models of addiction and treatment.

Finding empirical support for natural recovery does not imply that we devalue the importance of treatment programs or even self-help groups. Such programs have proven beneficial to addicts, particularly those in advanced stages. However, the experiences of our respondents have important implications for the way in which addiction and recovery are typically conceptualized. First, denying the existence of this population, as many do, discounts the version of reality held by those who terminate their addictions naturally. Natural recovery is simply not recognized as a viable option. This is increasingly the case as the media has reified dominant notions of addiction and recovery. Similarly, there is an industry of self-help literature that unquestionably accepts and reproduces these views. Denying the experience of natural recovery allows treatment agencies and self-help groups to continue to impose their particular view of reality on society.

Related to this is the possibility that many of those experiencing addictions may be extremely reluctant to enter treatment or attend self-help meetings. Their resistance may stem from a variety of factors such as the stigma associated with these programs, discomfort with the therapeutic process, or lack of support from significant others. Whatever the reason, such programs do not appeal to everyone. For such people, natural recovery may be a viable option. Since natural recovery demystifies the addiction and recovery experience, it may offer a way for people to take control of their own lives without needing to rely exclusively on experts. Such an alternative approach offers a low-cost supplement to an lareary costly system of formal addiction treatment.

A third implication concerns the consequences of adopting an addict identity. While the disease metaphor is thought to be a humanistic one in that it allows for the successful social reintegration of deviant drinkers or drug users, it nevertheless constitutes a deviant identity. Basing one's identity on past addiction experiences may actually limit social reintegration. The respondents in our sample placed a great deal of emphasis on their immediate social roles as opposed to constantly referring to their drug-addict pasts. Although there is no way of knowing, such present-centeredness may, in the long run, prove more beneficial than a continual focusing on the past.

Fourth, for drug and alcohol treatment professionals, as well as those who are likely to refer individuals to drug and alcohol treatment programs, this research raises several important considerations. It reaffirms the necessity for individual treatment matching. It also suggests that individuals whose profiles are similar to these middle-class respondents are likely to be receptive to and benefit from less intrusive, short-term types of interventions. Given the extent of the various concerns expressed by these respondents around some of the possible long-term negative consequences of undergoing traditional treatment and related participation in self-help programs, the decision to specifically recommend drug and alcohol treatment is a profoundly serious one. It should not be made capriciously or simply because it is expected and available. A careful assessment of the person's entire life is warranted, including whether or not the condition is so severe and the absence of supportive resources so great that the possible lifelong identity of addict or related internalized beliefs are reasonable risks to take in pursuing recovery. Overall, the findings of this study as well as previous research on natural recovery could be instructive in designing more effective treatment programs.

Finally, the experiences of our respondents may have important social policy implications. If our respondents are any guide, the following hypothesis might be considered: those with the greatest number of resources and who consequently have a great deal to lose by their addiction are the ones most likely to terminate their addictions naturally. While addiction is not reducible to social class alone, it is certainly related to it. [...] Having much to lose gave our respondents incentives to transform their lives. However, when there is little to lose from heavy alcohol or drug use, there may be little to gain by

quitting. Social policies that attempt to increase a person's stake in conventional life could not only act to prevent future alcohol and drug addiction, they could also provide an anchor for those who become dependent on these substances.

[...]

References

Biernacki, P. 1986. *Pathways from heroin addiction: Recovery without treatment*. Philadelphia: Temple University Press.

Brissett, D. 1988. Denial in alcoholism: A sociological interpretation. *Journal of Drug Issues* 18(3): 385–402.

Brown, J.D. 1991. Preprofessional socialization and identity transformation: The case of the professional ex. *Journal of Contemporary Ethnography* 20(2): 157–78.

Goffman, E. 1961. *Asylums*. Garden City: Anchor Books.

Granfield, Robert 1992. *Making elite lawyers: Visions of law at Harvard and beyond*. New York: Routledge, Chapman and Hall.

Peele, S. 1989. *The diseasing of America: Addiction treatment out of control*. Lexington: Lexington Books.

Waldorf, D., C. Reinarman, and S. Murphy 1991. *Cocaine changes: The experience of using and quitting*. Philadelphia: Temple University Press.

Waterston, A. 1993. *Street addicts in the political economy*. Philadelphia: Temple University Press.

Zinberg, N. 1986. *Drug, set and setting: The basis for controlled intoxicant use*. New Haven: Yale University Press.

Questions

1 Why are middle-class addicts considered a hidden population? How does natural recovery conflict with the dominant addiction paradigm?

2 According to the article, what were the main factors that contributed to a natural recovery? How did the social contexts of the respondents impact their recovery process? How did you think the recovery experience of these middle-class addicts compare and contrast to an addict in a TC?

3 Why do you think the engulfment of an addict identity might hinder the recovery process? How might the presence of other roles and/or identities impact the recovery process? How did the respondents respond to the notion that they were powerless to their addiction? How might their social status and/or social power have impacted their ability and/or resources to respond to their addiction?

Drug Treatment Courts and the Disease Paradigm

James L. Nolan, Jr

One of the major shifts in law enforcement over the last couple of decades has been the rise of drug courts. James Nolan offers us a history of the rise and spread of this movement along with the philosophy underlying it. He discusses the difference between the traditional criminogenic approach to dealing with drug offenders and the medical model of treatment embodied in the drug court.

As you read this, think about what kinds of assumptions underlie these competing approaches. How does the traditional model view drug offenders' decision-making processes compared to this new view? With which one do you agree? Can you see benefits for the offenders in the new approach? In what ways might society benefit as well? What are the downsides? In what way do drug courts fall under the rubric of treatment?

Are there different kinds of populations, by age, race/ethnicity, gender, socioeconomic status, and particular drug, that make some kinds of people more suited for processing through a drug court than a traditional one? Might the effectiveness of the drug court model be in any way affected by people's locations in their careers in drugs? Finally, if drugs are, indeed, the glue that binds most crime and criminals together, what do you think about the morality and effectiveness of extending this approach to broader areas of crime?

Drugs and the American Dream: An Anthology, First Edition. Edited by Patricia A. Adler, Peter Adler, and Patrick K. O'Brien.

As opposed to using the traditional criminal justice paradigm, in which drug abuse is understood as a willful choice made by an offender capable of choosing between right and wrong, DTCs shift the paradigm in order to treat drug abuse as a "biopsychosocial disease." (Judge Peggy Hora, Judge William Schma, and John Rosenthal)

Introduction

The first US drug treatment court was started in 1989 in Florida's populous Dade County. Miami is well known as a heavily trafficked drug area. With jails, prisons, and court dockets overcrowded with new and repeat drug offenders, officials became convinced something new had to be tried in criminal justice efforts to handle drug crimes. Under the leadership of Janet Reno, Florida's State Attorney at the time, Dade County launched America's first drug treatment court. Judge Stanley Goldstein, a former police officer and prosecutor, would preside over what would become a model for more than 700 similar drug treatment courts established throughout the United States since.

The drug treatment court introduces into the courtroom drama a conspicuously therapeutic orientation. The judge in many instances behaves as a therapist. Some judges unapologetically describe themselves as "therapeutic judges" or social workers. Instead of being dispassionate, detached judicial officers, they directly engage the defendant, showing personal care and concern. Defendants or "clients" as they are referred to in the drug treatment courts regularly return to court to face a judge who oversees their entire treatment program – which may include participation in individual and group counseling sessions, acupuncture treatment, and regular urinalysis testing. The level of judicial oversight and personal involvement is much more extensive in the drug treatment court than in the normal traditional criminal court.

Lawyers who traditionally relate to one another in an adversarial manner act cooperatively in the drug treatment court, working together to see their clients progress toward recovery. When clients finish the drug treatment court program, which is typically projected to last one year (though often it lasts much longer), they participate in graduation ceremonies, where they are given prizes, certificates, and words of encouragement from the judge. At these ceremonies the defendants often give public testimony about their "recovery" to an applauding audience, an audience which includes not only their families and friends, but the judge, attorneys, treatment counselors, and court clerks.

In short, the drug treatment court offers the drug offender a therapeutic alternative to the traditional adjudication process. With the promise that successful completion will result in the dismissal of a charge or the expungement of an arrest, offenders are offered court-monitored-therapy instead of incarceration. Responses to the drug treatment court by the media and from both US political parties have been largely celebratory. Conservatives support it because of its tough intrusive nature, liberals because of its ostensibly more humane and compassionate approach toward offenders. In many important ways the style and scope of the drug treatment court transcend conventional political categories. Without getting into a discussion of the efficacy or political viability of the drug treatment courts, in this article I wish to bring the sociological lens to bear on one of the important unintended consequences of the drug treatment court movement, namely, the manner in which the drug treatment court opens the door for a possible reinterpretation of criminal behaviors according to pathological rather than traditional legal categories.

Curiously, the expansion of the drug treatment court movement – and the therapeutic idiom which informs it – comes on the heels of a several decades-long retreat of the so-called "rehabilitative ideal" in American criminal law. In the 1970s such central rehabilitative practices as indeterminate sentences, the discretionary exercises of judicial, parole, and probation officers, and the individualized orientation of juvenile courts came under severe criticism. At the same time, however, such scholars as Philip Rieff, Christopher Lasch, and Peter Berger began to discuss the emergence, even the triumph, of a dominant therapeutic sensibility in American culture. Though clearly related to the discredited legacy of rehabilitative practices in certain respects, the drug treatment court movement more fully personifies the institutionalization of the cultural impulses first detected by Rieff and others, and as such represents a qualitatively distinct development.

Even Francis Allen, who at the end of the 1970s offered what is arguably the most comprehensive analysis of the "*decline of the rehabilitative ideal*," recognized this paradox. "*Accompanying ... the decline of the rehabilitative ideal in penal justice has been the rise of a new psychologism, a phenomenon of such magnitude that it can fairly be identified as one of the principal characteristics of contemporary American society.*"[1] And Allen is very clear in understanding this "*new psychologism*" as something "*sharply distinguishable*" from the rehabilitative ideal. As he puts it, "*the dominant assumptions of much of the new psychologism are radically different from those manifested in traditional applications of the rehabilitative ideal.*"[2]

[...]

The door was opened for greater cooperation between the criminal justice system and the treatment community when Congress passed the 1966 Treatment and Rehabilitation Act. The act, which gave the courts statutory authority to commit drug-user offenders to residential and outpatient treatment programs, paved the way for the initiation of such diversion programs as TASC (Treatment Alternatives to Street Crime). TASC programs, which began around 1973, divert offenders out of the normal adjudication process for the purposes of drug user treatment. Upon completing a treatment program, offenders return to court where they receive some kind of disposition. With TASC, then, treatment and criminal justice are linked, but they still remain separate institutions serving distinct functions. With the drug treatment courts, however, the treatment approach is introduced into the very center of the adjudicative process; law and therapy become a fully collaborative enterprise. A defining feature of this new arrangement is the *legal* reinterpretation of drug use as a disease rather than simply a criminal offense deserving a specified legal sanction. This article considers the extent to which criminal justice approaches to drug-user crimes, that historically did

not involve ascertaining conditions of "wellness," much less helping criminal "clients" recover from these illnesses, have adopted the disease or pathological reinterpretation of behavior. It also looks at how the disease model endemic to the drug treatment courts has expanded to inform the adjudication of other types of criminal behavior, and portends to transform the very meaning of criminal justice.

A Note on Method

The findings reported here are just one part of a larger research project, which involved ethnographic observation of drug treatment courts throughout the United States. In the four-year period between August 1994 and August 1998, I visited 21 different drug treatment courts in a total of 11 different states and the District of Columbia. The drug user treatment courts I visited varied by region. Seven were in the Northeast, six on the West Coast, five in the Mid Atlantic region (i.e., Maryland, Delaware, Virginia, and the District of Columbia), and three in the South. The courts also varied with respect to the size of the locations in which they were situated. Twelve of the courts were in large urban areas. Five were in rural regions. Three were in midsize cities of around 100,000 residents, and one was in an outlying suburban area of a Northeastern city. The courts also varied with respect to how long they had been in existence, varying from first-generation drug treatment courts to courts that were still in the planning stages. Eleven of the courts I visited had been in existence for more than a year. Eight had been in existence for less than a year, and two were still in the planning stages.

I conducted a face-to-face open-ended interview with the judge at each of the drug treatment courts. I also formally interviewed or had informal discussions with dozens of other drug treatment court officials, including district attorneys, public defenders, treatment counselors, private attorneys, program coordinators, evaluators, and acupuncturists. On occasion, I also had informal conversations with drug treatment court clients and visited outside-of-the-court treatment sites serving the drug treatment court. The treatment modalities that I observed included acupuncture sessions, AA/NA meetings, group counseling sessions, and a probationary/treatment introductory meeting. I was invited to sit in on the preliminary meetings preceding the drug treatment court session at five of the courts. At these meetings the judge and other drug treatment court officials discussed each of the clients who would be appearing in the drug treatment court that day.

[...]

The Illness Model

Drug treatment court officials adopting the disease view of drug addiction fundamentally depart from the justice system's historical position. It is not so much that the legal world was openly hostile to the treatment approach to drug-user crimes, though there was some of this. Rather, treatment was simply seen as something in which the judicial system was not involved. Judges were trained in the law, not in providing treatment. Since drug use was regarded as illegal it was the justice system's duty to determine guilt, and when found, to impose a "just" punishment for the offense. The initiation and remarkable growth of the drug treatment court movement changed this. The treatment perspective, like previous understandings of criminal behavior, is not neutral. It profoundly shapes the way judges view and treat defendants. Some are fully cognizant of the profundity of this change and are openly dismissive of traditional judicial interpretations of criminal activity.

For example, Peggy Hora, a drug treatment court judge in Hayward, California, avers a pronounced distinction between therapeutic justice and traditional understandings of criminal adjudication in her advocacy of the disease view.

> There was a time when we used religion to try to deal with drug abuse by saying "nice people don't do this." The drunkards were put in the stocks. In Puritan times religion dealt in different ways with addiction. ... But it is not a moral failing. It used to be treated as that, but that, in fact, is not what it is. The "just say no" to drugs business. You might as well tell a clinically depressed person, you know, "just cheer up." It has about as much effect. It is a ridiculous way to approach the problem ... and I don't think a moral failure model was ever the right place to be.

The treatment perspective recasts the traditional view of human behavior as antiquated and irrelevant. It also fundamentally alters the manner in which drug-user offenders are handled in the criminal justice system. In other words, the new orthodoxy demands a new praxis. Judge Robert Fogan explains this new perspective and corresponding courtroom process to the clients who come into his Broward County drug treatment court. Fogan asks one defendant how long he had been in jail. "Since Friday," the client responds. Judge Fogan empathizes, "Long enough to last a lifetime? You don't ever need to see the inside of a jail again, do you?" The defendant shakes his head in agreement. Fogan then explains to this client and to the others present in the courtroom that the drug treatment court is a different kind of court. "One of the reasons we started this program was so that people — young men and women like yourselves — wouldn't have to spend a lot of time in jail or prison simply because you've got a drug problem. We recognize that a drug problem may be part of an addiction, that it is a treatable disease." According to Fogan, then, jail is not the appropriate remedy. As Fogan explains, "We are not in the business of punishing people because they have a drug problem. We are going to give you help. It's called treatment."

In a subsequent interview Judge Fogan elaborated on this point, comparing drug addiction to cancer, then later to diabetes. "A better example than cancer would be diabetes," Fogan argued, "You can control it by various means, watching your diet and all that type of thing. But you are still a diabetic even though you may not be going into a coma or having problems like that. But you are still a diabetic. And you have to watch what you eat, watch your insulin, and all that stuff. It is the same thing with an alcoholic or a drug addict. It's the exact same thing." Suggested here is the view common in the AA and NA subcultures that one never fully recovers from alcoholism or drug addiction, that one always remains in recovery, even if sober for over 20 years. [...]

Based on this belief, drug treatment court clients should be dealt with patiently. Recovering from an illness can take a long time and, like the patient fighting cancer, the drug addict can be expected to relapse. [...]

Judges, who have not typically worked within a treatment paradigm, sometimes go through a cognitive reorientation or period of "consciousness raising" in order to understand the full implications of the treatment view of behavior and the kind of patience that it requires. In other words, a judge's traditional training prepared him or her to see a "dirty" urinalysis test as something like a probation violation, which most often required the imposition of some form of incarceration. According to the new treatment paradigm, a "dirty urine" instead represents something more like the recurrence of a temporarily latent flu. The treatment response requires patience, compassion, and understanding. This reorientation or "consciousness raising thing" according to Judge Langston McKinney of the Syracuse, New York drug treatment court, *"makes judges like myself and my colleagues come to grips with the notion that substance abuse is a disease."* Once realized, judges can then understand that drug abuse *"has to be treated and that there are ways in which it can be treated."* They also come to recognize that *"we traditionally have punished people who we really shouldn't have punished."* [...]

For Judge Anthony Violante of the Niagara Falls, New York drug treatment court, having his consciousness raised in this way was *"extremely difficult."* Violante accurately notes that the criminal justice system historically rejected the treatment perspective. The criminal justice community, according to Violante, essentially told the treatment community to make itself scarce, a position that the judge himself shared. His previous attitude toward the treatment community was: *"Don't tell me how I'm going to sentence. Don't tell me how I'm going to accept a plea. Don't tell me he's sick. Nobody forced him on the ground and forced this alcohol or these drugs down his throat."* After coming to terms with the anemic results such a position yielded, Violante converted to the treatment perspective and discovered the necessity of patience with relapses. *"What I don't think I ever really realized was that to facilitate the handling of these people I must understand what dependency is all about, and more important than that, from the point of view of treatment, what recovery is all about. I had no idea that recovery involved an aspect of relapse and relapse prevention."* Now Violante realizes that relapse is *"what it's all about."*

[...]

Equipped with the disease view of behavior, drug treatment court judges involve themselves directly in the recovery process. Doing this means getting at what they understand to be the root of the addictive behavior or illness. But what is at the root of this behavior? Why do these people need to use drugs? According to many of the judges and drug treatment court officials with whom I spoke, the fundamental problem is a low self-esteem. That is, people use drugs because they don't feel good about themselves. It is held that many drug treatment court clients come from backgrounds where they received little affirmation or encouragement. They were not, it is argued, helped to feel good about themselves. Consequently they have a low self-esteem and are more inclined to use drugs and participate in other "unhealthy" behaviors. The questionable validity of this view notwithstanding,[3] it is a common perspective among drug treatment court officials. Correspondingly, judges and treatment providers devote much energy to helping clients build their self-esteem. Tim Smith, a counselor at the San Bernidino, California drug treatment court, speaks for many when he says, *"Drugs are just a symptom of our disease. Drugs are not the problem of the recovering addict."* Rather, according to Smith, the root problem is a *"low self-esteem."* Therefore, the focus of treatment is to help clients *"start building their self-esteem."*

The Centrality of Self-Esteem

To follow the physiological metaphor offered by the judges, then, one could say that drug addiction is a symptom of a low self-esteem in the same way that fatigue is a symptom of diabetes. The judge must work to raise the self-esteem level of clients in the same way that the physician works to medically raise a patient's insulin level. Based on this understanding, the raising of self-esteem is a central component of the drug treatment court judge's role. Judge William Schma, of the Kalamazoo, Michigan drug treatment court, certainly sees this as part of his job. Consider the following discussion regarding the place of self-esteem in his court. *"One of the chronic character traits of addicts is that they lack self-esteem. They've had so many negative influences in their lives, had so many negative experiences, that their sense of self-worth is almost zero."* Given this fundamental problem it is the judge's role *"to build up that self-esteem. And you can imagine what it does for someone's self-esteem to have a judge come down off the bench and shake their hand; talk to them in their first name instead of 'hey you'; treat them with some respect and obvious affection to the extent that they spend time with them, talk to them, listen to them, talk about their families, treat them like human beings. You know, they just haven't been treated that way."*

[...]

Guiltless Justice

Self-esteem, of course, has for several decades been a taken for granted value in American society, especially in the area of education. When applied to the criminal justice system, however, self-esteem essentially offers itself as a replacement to that which previously defined the essence of the adjudicative process, namely the determination of guilt. Inasmuch as the therapeutically-defined ideals of illness and of self-esteem assume a more central place in the adjudicative process, the notion of guilt is made increasingly less relevant. As the judges argue, the drug-using defendant has not done something morally wrong, but has a sickness. Guilt, therefore, is philosophically nongermane (as legal practitioners might say) to such a process.

[...]

Such a philosophical reorientation has, in the drug treatment courts, taken on structural form. For example, many of the courts are preadjudicative. That is, in the context of the drug treatment court, the defendant is not faced with having to enter a plea of guilty or not guilty. A 1997 Justice Department survey of 93 operational drug treatment courts found that 30% of the courts surveyed were preplea only. That is, these courts are made up only of clients who have not entered any kind of plea. An additional 33% of the drug treatment courts include at least some clients (usually the majority) who have not entered a plea. Therefore, 66% of the drug treatment courts have clients who have not even faced the predicament of having to state a disposition of guilt or innocence. In a very concrete and practical manner, then, the notion of guilt for many drug treatment court clients is irrelevant.

[...]

Judge William Schma also agrees that in the drug treatment court the admittance of guilt is "*pretty much*

immaterial." More important to him is that defendants "*admit that they are addicts. That's what I want them to do.*" Schma thus makes a distinction between admitting guilt and admitting addiction. "*It is more useful*" he believes "*to get someone to admit addiction, because people will admit guilt, but not addiction, and then you don't cure the addiction.*" The right story in this setting is to admit one's illness. To see one's behavior in terms of guilt/innocence, right/wrong, moral/immoral is "*immaterial.*" The drug treatment court demands a therapeutically revised form of confession: "*I am sick*" instead of "*I am guilty.*" Of greater importance is the therapeutically correct view that one recognize, come to terms with, and confess one's addiction. To simply admit guilt and not addiction is to remain in denial. Guilt, in the context of therapeutic jurisprudence, is increasingly untenable.

This undermining of guilt, as such, should not be interpreted to suggest a mitigation of legal responsibility, as some might mistakenly conclude. As Judge Henry Weber of Louisville, Kentucky explains, drug treatment court "*is a combination of taking responsibility and also recognizing that some things are beyond the control of the individual. Addiction to drugs is a health problem.*" Thus, while guilt may be disregarded, "*taking responsibility*" and the disease view can work together. Judge Weber, for example, prefers to use the term "*responsibility rather than guilt.*" As drug treatment court judges readily concede, drug treatment courts (and their so-called emphasis on responsibility) are often more demanding and intrusive than normal criminal courts. [...] Thus, just as therapeutic justice is not synonymous with a "soft on crime" approach, so a central judicial emphasis on guilt is not the practical concomitant to highly punitive penal practices. The jettisoning of guilt may well represent the most important, albeit rarely reflected upon, consequence of the drug treatment court. If, as Philip Rieff argued, culture is not possible without guilt, one wonders what will become of a criminal justice system bereft of the same quality that once defined its very existence.

Expansion to Other Crimes

The notion of guiltlessness (and therapeutic justice more generally) is not limited to drug offenses. Indeed, only a few years after launching the first drug treatment court, movement activists began talking about and implementing the drug treatment court model to other types of crime. As early as 1994 the Justice Department reported that "*in a number of locations the innovative and collaborative methods characterizing the first generation of treatment drug treatment courts were being adapted to other justice system populations.*" Commending "*remarkable local innovation*" in 1993 the Justice Department reported on the initiation of new juvenile, domestic violence, family, and community courts based upon the drug treatment court treatment model. By June of 1998 the Justice Department reported that "*50 juvenile and/or family drug treatment courts have been implemented and another 50 are being planned.*"[4]

Even existing drug treatment court programs have expanded eligibility criteria to include non-drug-related offenses. The 1997 Justice Department survey found that many drug treatment courts include offenders with non-drug-related charges. According to the survey, 22% of the drug treatment courts include clients with theft/property charges, 4% with check and credit card forgery crimes, and another 4% with prostitution offenses. Included among these are clients with charges of grand theft, breaking and entering, possession of a firearm, knowingly concealing stolen property, burglary, fraud, assault, forgery, shoplifting, prostitution, and child neglect. [...] In the Pensacola, Florida drug treatment court, the overwhelming *majority* of the clients were in for non-drug-related charges. A full 68% of the Pensacola drug treatment court clients were arrested for property crimes, while only 10% were in the program because of drug possession charges.

Some drug treatment court judges now publicly advocate the expansion of the drug treatment court to include violent crimes. To an applauding audience of some 2000 drug treatment court practitioners at a June 1998 conference in Washington, DC, Judge Dierdre Hair of the Cincinnati, Ohio drug treatment court asserted, "*I will confess that it seems to me we are fairly idiotic in our policy of not accepting people with violent histories.*" Judge Hair speculated that most drug treatment courts do take violent offenders and even confessed to "*having taken a murderer*" into her court. This particular client, according to Hair, was "*one of our most successful drug user treatment court people.*"

For some, understanding drug addiction as an illness is one matter, but expanding the disease concept to include other types of criminal behavior is more problematic. That the justice system would move in the direction of interpreting an increasing number of behaviors through the lens of the illness model, however, makes sense for two reasons. First, the overwhelming majority of arrests, court cases, and prison spaces in today's criminal justice system are made up of offenders who have had some kind of involvement with illicit drugs. Many of the offenses, though they may not be sale or possession charges, stem from involvement with drugs. Offenders commit robbery, larceny, forgery, and prostitution in order to support their drug habit. Moreover, many domestic violence cases, manslaughter, and other violent offenses result from the lack of self-control and sober reasoning that drug use may effect. If drug use is a disease, and this disease is believed to cause other criminal behaviors, then these other behaviors are themselves symptoms of the disease. This anyway is the conclusion to which many in the drug treatment court have come, and it is the reason offered for including in drug treatment court offenses other than charges for sale and possession of narcotics.

A second and related reason for the plausibility of the shift is the larger cultural context. As noted above, the very meaning of guilt is called into question in a highly therapeutic culture. When antisocial behavior, criminal or otherwise, can be explained by low self-esteem and other psychological categories, labeling a person guilty for any crime becomes less plausible. This essentially is what many have concluded in interpreting the behavior of individuals like Ted Kazinski (aka the Unabomber), even against his protests to the contrary; Lorena Bobbit, who in a "fit of rage" severed her husband's penis with a kitchen knife; Susan Smith, the South Carolina woman who in 1994 drowned her two boys; and Michael Carneal, the Kentucky boy who in December of 1997 shot and killed three classmates and wounded five others while they participated in a high school prayer meeting.

Typical of the commentary surrounding the prosecution of these individuals, including that offered by legal counsel, was the expressed belief that to have committed the acts these individuals committed, they must have been mentally ill, even if only temporarily.

It is almost as though the criminal act itself is proof either of a pathology, a disorder, or a low self-esteem. If, as Rieff argues, our ideas about guilt and punishment are "*meaningless legacies*" then how can we justifiably interpret any behavior as though someone were wrong, immoral, bad, or guilty? That individuals have difficulty interpreting even such heinous acts as those committed by Kazinski according to traditional categories suggests, at the least, that the cultural saliency of traditional meaning systems is waning. To be sure, many Americans are not comfortable extending the disease model so comprehensively. However, given the codes of moral understanding that define the contemporary zeitgeist, this is a plausible end to which the current rationales lead.

[...]

Other judges, without acknowledging political currents, were not sure in their own minds whether it was right to extend the model to non-drug-related crimes. However, even judges with personal reservations were not definite in their opposition. Judge Stephanie Duncan-Peters of Washington, DC, for example, did not think she could give "*a definite opinion*" about expanding the disease model, and thought it prudent to "*be a little careful about this domestic violence stuff.*" Still, according to Duncan-Peters, there were some cases where it might be justifiable.

> I think that it probably wouldn't hurt to have domestic violence cases dealt with where you are treating the entire problem that the person has. They may have a drug or alcohol problem and the victim says he gets violent when he drinks, or when he uses drugs. In those cases it probably would make sense to have some sort of a system set up to deal with the drug problems. But in other cases when drugs are not the cause of the violence, I wouldn't think there would be any need to treat those people's cases in the same way.

[...] For many drug treatment court officials this is the critical issue. As long as the crime is somehow related to drug use, then the drug treatment court model is fully warranted. These other behaviors are a symptom of a deeper problem – the disease of drug addiction. The additional criminal behaviors, therefore, like drug addiction, can be addressed through therapy. For this reason individuals with non-drug-related offenses are allowed into drug treatment courts. On this issue,

many with whom I spoke were much less equivocal, both on the matter of expanding drug treatment court eligibility criteria and on the issue of starting new courts geared toward particular criminal populations, e.g., domestic violence courts.

Regarding the latter, Judge Robert Ziemian of the Boston drug treatment court thinks it makes perfect sense. "*In probably 80% of domestic violence cases*" according to Ziemian, "*substance abuse is a contributing factor.*" Until "*you get to the substance abuse problems and clean up that ... you can't even deal with those other problems.*" Cathy Delaney, the former director of treatment in Ziemian's program, agrees. She holds that "*89% of the batterers are under the influence of something when they batter.*" If you deal with the drug issue, "*a percentage of them will never ever hit another human being in a battering situation again. I think the model can work.*" For the same reason, Judge Robert Russell of the Buffalo, New York drug treatment court justifies taking prostitution and theft offenses in his court (which together make up 35% of the total drug treatment court clientele in Buffalo). "*If it's drug driven and a person is stealing in order to support that addiction, or a man or woman, if they are out prostituting and the motivating factor is their addiction, then yes we would entertain having them go through the drug treatment court model.*" Judge Gerald Bakarich, of Sacramento, California agrees. "*If you are really going to open this up to the real drug addict ... you've got to expand it to the second degree burglaries, auto thefts, petty thefts, and grand thefts.*"

[...]

Courtroom Therapy for Non-Drug-Related Crimes

Judge Diane Strickland of Roanoke, Virginia also believes treatment is appropriate for crime when no drug use is involved. Consider her reflections on its applicability to domestic violence.

> You are dealing with someone with an abusive personality. This is something that they don't have control over anymore just like someone with a drug problem ... in both cases you are approaching an illness, if you will, and you need to treat that illness before you can expect behavior to be changed. If you have an offender who has grown up in a household where violence was the mode then you have a whole childhood

of learned behavior that needs to be broken down and unlearned and a new way of learning and dealing with stress and anger that needs to be taught to these people in much the same way as dealing with the addicted offender where you are teaching them that this dependence on drugs is not what is appropriate for their lives and they need to find a new way to approach their personal problems which does not involve the reliance on drugs. So I see them as being pretty analogous.

Here Judge Strickland makes an important leap. Not only should domestic violence cases receive treatment when drug use is involved, but domestic violence constitutes a disease in its own right. Some of the drug treatment court officials with whom I spoke, particularly the treatment people, share this position. That is, they believe that the illness model should be extended to include other criminal activities, even those that are not directly related to drug use. This is Cathy Delaney's position on the matter. "*All this model is is investing time in people, and giving them the tools to do their life differently. And if you want to put it in its simplest form, it doesn't matter whether it's drugs or battering or shoplifting. Basically what you are going to look at is investing time to find out why the people do what they do, and give them the tools to show them how there is a different way.*"

A treatment provider at the Fort Lauderdale drug treatment court argued the same as it relates to the issue of prostitution.

I don't think that most women wake up in the morning and think, "gosh, what a great thing to go out and prostitute myself." To have reached that point they have some major life issues to deal with. My own experience with the bulk of our clients who have come in here who are prostitutes is that the incident of incest is extraordinarily high. I mean incredibly high. So, again, I think that these are people who have real problems. I don't think anybody with a healthy sense of self is going to go out and sell themselves on the street. So, if all we do is basically warehouse them and don't help them address this problem, then what is going to change when they come out? I do think that there are a lot of people who probably need help.

Therefore, a treatment process that helps a person deal with their low sense of self is justifiable, even when drug use is not a part of the problem.

Judge Tauber also holds to this position. For him it is commonsensical. "*You know, once again, this stuff ain't rocket science. It is common sense. If you put people in a system and make it real clear that they are not going to escape or fall through cracks — forgive the pun — and you are going to be on top of them, you are going to provide services, you are going to do better. There is no mystery there. It is a good model. You know, it just makes sense to deal with people in a caring way, but in a very direct and intense way as well.*" Given the "obvious" utility of the model, then, Tauber could see it applied to domestic violence and to prostitution. "*Obviously there are already domestic violence courts. Prostitution also makes a lot of sense, in fact probably even more than any of this other stuff. You know, prostitutes generally get right back out on the streets, and if there were directed and immediate intervention I bet you would have significant success with that particular population. … It is a model that makes sense.*"

[…]

Judge Schma offers the most strident defense for the expansion of the drug treatment court model, first as it is connected to drug related crimes: "*It's the breaking and enterings, it's the larcenies, it's the malicious destruction of property, there's a whole bunch of addicts running around out there committing a whole bunch of crimes that are not drug crimes but they are drug related, because they are doing that — passing bad paper, prostitution, stuff like that — all that because they are addicts and they need the money.*" But he also saw the treatment model relevant to behaviors not stemming from drugs. "*Therapeutically, from a therapeutic jurisprudence standpoint, it's not just the addict who can be dealt with. There is no question about that. It's anybody who is amenable to a rather intensive program of treatment. It could apply conceivably to a sex offender. It could apply to a habitual thief, you know, the chronic thief. It could apply to a lot of other deviant behaviors.*"

Discussion

As illustrated by the various drug treatment court judges' comments, the applicability of the disease model can logically be (and in some cases already has been) extended to include any number of criminal behaviors. [...] The drug treatment court opens the door for the inclusion of therapeutic concepts into the central processes of criminal adjudication. Once let into the judicial process in this way, therapeutic ideals are bound to expand. [...] If drug addiction is a disease, then so are behaviors aimed to support drug addiction.

Once the therapeutic categories, e.g. the negative effects of low self-esteem, are accepted in the legal context it becomes increasingly difficult to object to similar interpretations of other behaviors, even when drug use is not involved. Whether drug-related or non-drug-related, violent or non-violent crimes, the same categories are used to make sense of the behaviors.

The effects of this judicial reorientation are significant. In addition to advancing the reinterpretation of behaviors according to pathological categories, it offers to redefine what constitutes a successful judicial program. Acceptance of the disease view of criminal behavior also calls into question the saliency of concepts that once more profoundly defined the substance and scope of criminal law. Not only does it challenge the central significance of guilt and confession, but it also portends to alter the meaning and practice of such civil rights as due process, trial by jury, and the right to a speedy trial.[5] The therapeutic outlook is not a neutral one, and evidence considered here suggests that it may expand.

[...]

Providing judges with new categories for interpreting the behavior of the offenders/clients/patients that come before them, the drug treatment court movement opens the door for the further "judicial pathologization" of behavior, and potentially the transformation of American criminal justice. It is a development that some drug treatment court advocates celebrate. As one judge put it, "*What we are doing here, I think, is no less than a complete revolution in jurisprudence.*" Politicians, legal practitioners, and social scientists alike do well to look beyond questions of efficacy regarding developments like the drug treatment court, because there may well be something of even greater significance going on here.

Notes

1   Allen, F. *The Decline of the Rehabilitative Ideal: Penal Policy and Social Purpose*; Yale University Press: New Haven, 1981.
2   Allen goes so far as to argue that new psychologism was in fact an "important factor" in the decline of the rehabilitative ideal. The distinction made by Allen between the new psychologism and the rehabilitative ideal is very similar to that made by John Steadman Rice between earlier "therapies of adaptation" and the newer "therapies of liberation." Both authors see such themes as the preoccupation with self-esteem, self-realization, and self-actualization as clearly more pronounced in the newer forms of therapy/psychologism – an emphasis that, as demonstrated in this article, is prominent in the drug court movement.
3   Recent studies not only reveal that self-esteem isn't positively correlated with healthy social behavior but that high self-esteem may in fact be positively related to violent behavior.
4   *Looking at a Decade of Drug Courts;* Prepared by the Drug Court Clearinghouse and Technical Assistance Project, US Department of Justice, Office of Justice Programs, American University, Washington, DC, June 1998.
5   In many courts clients actually sign documents waiving their rights to a speedy trial and to a trial by jury.

Questions

1   According to the article, how does the atmosphere in a drug court differ from the traditional atmosphere in a court of law? How might this environmental factor impact the identity and/or recovery process of the drug offender? Why might drug courts persuade offenders to complete their treatment?

2   How would you compare the social stigma individuals face when they are viewed as having a moral failing compared to a sickness or illness? How do you think the drug treatment court's adopting a disease model is beneficial? How is it problematic?

3   According to the article, many judges considered low self-esteem to be at the root of addictive behavior or illness. Do you agree with this? Why or why not? What other sociocultural factors might the judges be ignoring? Do you think drug courts should be extended to any drug related crime? Why or why not? What modes of treatment and crime/violence models do you think drug courts identify with?

Policy

Reducing Harms from Youth Drinking

Stanton Peele

Stanton Peele takes on the most widespread issue for the youth of America today: binge drinking. In this selection he discusses some of the social correlates associated with different styles of youth drinking and reviews many of the existing approaches to dealing with this social problem.

As a college student yourself, what do you think of the portrait he presents? Do you think that the correlates he describes are still accurate? Do you think youth drinking is a problem? Why do you think America has one of the highest rates of binge drinking in the world? How and why do you think youth in other countries drink in more moderate ways? Is this something that youth just naturally grow out of, or are interventions necessary to modify these patterns?

Thinking about the demographic factors we've presented in this book, how might you think that youth drinking trends vary by race/ethnicity, gender, socioeconomic status, and/or location? Are enforcement policies different for members of these different groups? What do you think of the morality and effectiveness of the harm reduction as opposed to the prohibitionist approach?

Introduction

Youthful drinking is of tremendous concern in the United States and elsewhere. Alcohol is the psychoactive substance used the most often by adolescents and college students and is associated with more youthful dysfunction and morbidity than any other drug. Alcohol use by youth contributes significantly to academic and social problems, risky sexual behavior, and traffic and other accidents, and is a risk factor for the development of alcohol-related problems during adulthood. As a result, youthful drinking – and particularly binge drinking – has been a target for public health interventions. It is thus highly troubling that these efforts have produced few benefits; high-risk drinking by both adolescents and college students has not declined over the past decade. According to the Monitoring the Future (MTF) survey, the percentage of high school seniors who have been drunk in the past month has gone below 30 percent one year in the last

Drugs and the American Dream: An Anthology, First Edition. Edited by Patricia A. Adler, Peter Adler, and Patrick K. O'Brien.
© 2012 John Wiley & Sons, Inc. Published 2012 by John Wiley & Sons, Inc.

decade and a half (in 1993 the figure was 29%; in 2005 it was 30%). Some data show startling increases in binge drinking by young people: the National Survey on Drug Use and Health (NSDUH) reported for 1997 that 27 percent of Americans aged 18 to 25 had consumed five or more drinks at one time in the prior month; in 2004, the figure was 41 percent.

Although research has found that American adolescents who begin drinking earlier in life are more likely to display adult alcohol dependence, another body of research has found that drinking varies tremendously among religious, ethnic, and national groups. In particular, those groups that are less proscriptive towards alcohol and in fact permit and even teach drinking in childhood, and in which drinking is a regular integrated part of social life, display fewer alcohol problems. This work has usually been the province of sociology and anthropology. As such, it has not had a firm status in epidemiology and public health. The thrust in the public health field has been towards labeling alcohol an addictive drug and towards reducing and even eliminating youthful drinking.

[...]

Religious/ethnic differences in drinking styles and problems

Differences in drinking have frequently been noted among religious groups in the US and elsewhere, including among youth and college students. Drinking by Jews has been one special object of attention due to their apparently low level of drinking problems. Weiss (2001) indicated that, although drinking problems in Israel have increased in recent decades, absolute rates of problem drinking and alcoholism in Israel remain low compared with Western and Eastern European countries, North America, and Australia. The HBSC study found that Israel, among 35 Western nations, had the second lowest rates of drunkenness among 15-year-olds: 5% of girls and 10% of boys have been drunk two or more times, compared with 23% and 30% for the US.

Studies of drinking by Jews compared with other groups have included a study of male Jewish and Christian students at an American university by Monteiro and Schuckit (1989), in which Jewish

students were less likely to have 2 or more alcohol problems (13% v. 22%), or to have more than five drinks on a single occasion (36% v. 47%). Weiss (1997) compared drinking by Jewish and Arab youths, and found Arab drinking is far more frequently excessive, despite the Moslem prohibition on drinking. Weiss (2001) explained such differences as follows: "The early socialization of Jewish children to a ritual, ceremonial and family use of alcoholic beverages provides a comprehensive orientation to the when, where, and how of drinking" (p. 111).

The nonproscriptive approach to alcohol characterizes not only Jewish drinking. Some American Protestant sects are highly proscriptive towards alcohol (e.g., Baptists); others (e.g., Unitarians) not at all. Kutter and McDermott (1997) studied drinking by adolescents of various Protestant affiliations. More proscriptive denominations were more likely to produce abstinent youth, but at the same time to produce youth who binged, and who binged frequently. That is, while 90 percent of youth in nonproscriptive sects had consumed alcohol, only 7 percent overall (or 8% of drinkers) had binged 5 or more times in their lives, compared with 66 percent of those in proscriptive sects who had ever consumed alcohol, while 22 percent overall in these sects (33% of drinkers) had binged 5 or more times.

At the same time that youth in proscriptive groups have less exposure to controlled drinking, these groups set up a "forbidden fruit" scenario. According to Weiss (2001), "Forbidding drinking and conveying negative attitudes toward alcohol may prevent some members from experimenting with alcohol, but when members violate that prohibition by using alcohol, they have no guidelines by which to control their behavior and are at increased risk of heavy use" (p. 116).

NSDUH presents abstinence and binge-drinking rates (defined as 5 or more drinks at a single sitting in the past month) for racial-ethnic groups. Examining drinkers 18 and older, ethnic-racial groups with higher abstinence rates are more prone to binge. Among whites, the only group among whom a majority drink, 42 percent of drinkers binge. Fewer than half of all other racial/ethnic groups listed have drunk in the past month, but more of these binge. Among African Americans, 49 percent of drinkers binge; Hispanics, 55 percent; and Native Americans, 71 percent. The exception to this pattern is Asians, among whom a low percentage drink and a low percentage of these (33 percent) binge. This is true as well for collegiate Asian-American and Pacific Islanders (APIs): "rates of drinking and heavy drinking have been found to be lower among API college students than among other ethnic groups" (Makimoto, 1998, p. 270)…

National differences in binge drinking and alcohol problems

Although differences in cross-cultural drinking have long been noted, such differences have not been quantified. Recent international epidemiological research has filled in this gap. For example, Ramstedt and Hope compared Irish drinking with drinking in six European nations measured in the ECAS (Ramstedt and Hope, 2003).

[…]

These European data show regular drinking is inversely related to binge drinking. Countries in which people are unlikely to drink daily (Ireland, UK, Sweden, and Finland) have high binge drinking rates, while countries with higher rates of daily drinking (e.g., France, Italy) have lower levels of binge drinking. Germany is intermediate. Ireland combines the highest level of abstinence, the lowest level of daily drinking, and by far the highest rate of binge drinking. Furthermore, according to the ECAS study, the countries with greater binge-drinking occasions tend to have more negative consequences (including fights, accidents, problems on the job or at home, etc.), while those countries with the highest frequency of drinking have fewer adverse consequences.

Boback et al. (2004) compared Russian, Polish, and Czech rates of problem drinking and the negative consequences of drinking. Both were much higher in Russian men (35% and 18%, respectively) than in Czechs (19% and 10%) or Poles (14% and 8%). Although the Russian men had a substantially lower average annual intake (4.6 liters) than Czech men (8.5 liters) and drank far less frequently (67 drinking sessions per year, compared with 179 sessions among Czech men), they consumed the highest dose of alcohol per drinking session (means = 71 g for Russians, 46 g for Czechs, and 45 g for Poles) and had the highest prevalence of binge drinking.

Adolescent drinking cross-culturally

The claim is frequently made now that adolescent intoxication is becoming homogenized across cultures – that is, traditional differences are diminishing, or have in fact already disappeared. "Increased binge drinking and intoxication in young people – the pattern of consumption associated with Northern Europe – is now reported even in countries such as France and Spain in which drunkenness was traditionally alien to the drinking cultures.…" (McNeil, 2000, p. 16).

WHO's HBSC which measures drinking and drunkenness among 15-year-olds, and ESPAD data about 15–16-year-olds from 35 countries, do not support these contentions. The results of these studies show large, continuing discrepancies between Northern and Southern European countries, differences that in some regards are increasing.

[…]

The HBSC results were summarized by the authors of the alcohol chapter as follows:

> Countries and regions can be clustered according to their traditions in alcohol use. One cluster comprises countries on the Mediterranean sea. … (such as France, Greece, Italy, and Spain). Here, 15-year-olds have a relatively late onset and a low proportion of drunkenness.
>
> Another cluster of countries (such as Denmark, Finland, Norway and Sweden) may be defined as representative of the Nordic drinking tradition… On some of these, drunkenness has a rather early onset (Denmark, Finland and Sweden) and is widespread in young people (Denmark in particular). (Schmid and Nic Gabhainn, 2004, pp. 79, 82)

Thus, we see that cross-cultural differences in drinking patterns persist with remarkable vitality among the young. These cultural drinking styles express underlying views of alcohol that are passed across generations. As expressed by one ECAS scientist:

> In the northern countries, alcohol is described as a psychotropic agent. It helps one to perform, maintains a Bacchic and heroic approach, and elates the self. It is used as an instrument to overcome obstacles, or to prove one's manliness. It has to do with the issue of control and with its opposite – "discontrol" or transgression.

In the southern countries, alcoholic beverages – mainly wine – are drunk for their taste and smell, and are perceived as intimately related to food, thus as an integral part of meals and family life. … It is traditionally consumed daily, at meals, in the family and other social contexts. (Allamani, 2002, p. 197)

Abstinence versus reality: are our current policies counterproductive?

Alcohol education programs are prevalent in secondary schools and earlier in the United States. Their emphasis is typically abstinence. Indeed, since drinking is illegal for virtually every American high school student, as well as most college students (which is not true in Europe), it might seem abstinence is the only possible alcohol education goal for minors. In 2006, the US Surgeon General issued a "call to action on *preventing* underage drinking" (emphasis added).

There are nonetheless obvious deficiencies in a solely, or primarily, abstinence approach. According to NSDUH, in 2004 a majority (51%) of 15-year-olds, three quarters (76%) of 18-year-olds, and 85 percent of 20-year-olds have consumed alcohol. Among 20-year-olds, 56 percent have done so – and 40 percent have binged – in the past month. According to the 2005 MTF, three quarters of high school seniors have consumed alcohol, and well over half (58%) have been drunk. What would be a realist goal of a program to eliminate underage drinking, particularly considering this age group has been bombarded with no-drinking messages already? Seemingly, large numbers of underage drinkers will remain given even the most optimistic scenario.

Moreover, at age 21, young Americans are legally able to drink alcohol, and 90 percent have done so – 70 percent in the last month. They have not drunk well. More than 40 percent of those in every age group between 20 and 25 have binge drunk in the past month. The highest figure is for 21-year-olds, 48 percent of whom have binge drunk in the past month, or nearly 7 in 10 drinkers (69%). Moreover, 17 percent of those aged 18 to 25 were abusing, or dependent on, alcohol. How exactly are young people to be prepared for what will shortly be their legal introduction to drinking? The danger from failing to learn the value

of moderation is that under-age drinkers will continue to binge drink, even after they achieve legal drinking age.

Although there is a strong tendency for alcohol problems to diminish with age, recent American epidemiological research has found this maturation pattern to have slowed – that is, youthful binge and excessive drinking is continuing until later ages than previously noted. NSDUH indicates binge drinking is frequent for adults – while 54 percent of Americans over 21 have consumed alcohol in the past month, 23 percent (43% of drinkers) have binged in the past month. Among college students, binge drinking is extremely frequent, as revealed by the College Alcohol Study (CAS), which found the overall rate for such drinking over the past two weeks to be 44 percent of all college students.

Moreover, the collegiate binge-drinking figure remained the same from 1993 to 2001, despite a host of efforts to cut the rate. A funded program to reduce such intensive drinking did show higher rates of abstainers (19 percent in 1999 compared with 15 percent in 1993), but also an increase in frequent bingers (from 19 percent in 1993 to 23 percent in 1999). Other research combining several data bases has shown that collegiate risk-drinking persists; indeed, driving under the influence of alcohol increased from 26 to 31 percent between 1998 and 2001.

Data also show that recent age cohorts are more likely to become and remain alcohol dependent. Examining the National Longitudinal Alcohol Epidemiologic Survey (NLAES) conducted in 1992, Grant (1997) found the youngest cohort (those born between 1968 and 1974) was most likely to become, and remain, alcohol dependent even though this cohort overall was less likely as a group to drink than the cohort just before it. The follow-up National Epidemiologic Survey on Alcohol and Related Conditions (NESARC), conducted in 2001–2002, found that alcohol dependence (median age of incidence = 21) was slower to show remission than in the 1992 NLAES study.

Finally, as even those groups seeking to reduce alcohol consumption acknowledge, "medical epidemiology has generally accepted as established. … the protective effects of light drinking for general mortality." Likewise, the *Dietary Guidelines for Americans* reports, "The lowest all-cause mortality occurs at an intake of one to two drinks per day." And binge drinking, as this paper has shown, is associated with more adverse consequences. Yet young people do not believe regular moderate drinking is better than binge drinking. MTF finds that more high school seniors disapprove of people 18 and older having "one or two drinks nearly every day" (78%) than disapprove of having "five or more drinks once or twice each weekend" (69%).

Is a Reorientation of American Alcohol Policy and Education Advisable?

The data we have reviewed show that the current (and, in terms of the Surgeon General's initiative, intensifying) efforts to encourage abstinence have not reduced binge drinking and alcohol dependence. Indeed, major American surveys have shown clinical problems from drinking, for young people and beyond, to be increasing, even though overall drinking rates have declined. The combination of high abstinence and high binge drinking is typical in many contexts, as this paper has shown.

Comparisons of two primary cultural patterns of drinking – one in which alcohol is consumed regularly and moderately versus one in which alcohol is consumed sporadically but drinking occasions often involve high levels of consumption – show that the regular, moderate style leads to fewer adverse social consequences. Cultures where moderate drinking is socially accepted and supported also have less youthful binge drinking and drunkenness.

Conveying the advantages of one cultural style to those in other cultures, however, remains problematic. It is possible that drinking styles are so rooted in a given cultural upbringing that it is impossible to extirpate the binge drinking style in cultures where it is indigenous in order to teach moderate drinking on a broad cultural level. Nonetheless, there may still be benefits to educating youth to drink moderately in cultures where binge drinking is commonplace.

The approach propagated by many international policy groups (and many epidemiologists and other researchers) favors reducing overall drinking in a society and zero-tolerance (no-drinking) policies for the young. Yet, as indicated by variations in legal drinking ages, most Western nations continue to follow a different model. For example, the United States is the only Western country that restricts drinking to those 21 years of age or older. The typical age of majority for drinking in Europe is 18; but some Southern countries have lower age limits. Age limits may also be lower (for example, in the UK) when drinking occurs in a restaurant when a youth is accompanied by adults.

The United States, by restricting drinking to those 21 years of age and older, has adopted a model of alcohol problems that assumes drinking per se raises the risk of problems. Evidence supports that raising the drinking age lowers drinking rates and accidents among the young – primarily in precollegiate populations. Nonetheless, most Western nations continue to accept the concept that encouraging youthful drinking in socially governed public environments is a positive societal goal. By learning to drink in such settings, it is hoped, youth will develop moderate drinking patterns from an early age.

Indeed, the policy of the National Institute on Alcohol Abuse and Alcoholism (NIAAA) when it was initially created in 1970 under its first director, Morris Chafetz, included the creation of moderate drinking contexts for young people. But this approach was never widely adopted in the United States and declined in popularity when youthful drinking accelerated in the late 1970s. One contemporary alternative to a zero-tolerance or decreased-overall-consumption model is the "social norms" model. The social norms approach informs students that many more students abstain, or drink moderately, than they are aware, assuming this will lead students to drink less themselves. However, CAS investigators found that colleges adopting the social norms approach showed no reduction in drinking levels and harms.

A new paradigm: harm reduction

At this point, it is obviously easier to point to failures in alcohol education and prevention programs for youths than to identify successes. As a result, leading researchers continue to uncover a growth in risk drinking among college students and to advocate stricter enforcement of zero-tolerance:

Among college students ages 18-24 from 1998 to 2001, alcohol-related unintentional injury deaths increased from nearly 1600 to more than 1700, an increase of 6% per college population. The proportion of 18–24-year-old college students who reported driving under the influence of alcohol increased from 26.5% to 31.4%, an increase from 2.3 million students to 2.8 million. During both years more than 500,000 students were unintentionally injured because of drinking and more than 600,000 were hit/assaulted by another drinking student. *Greater enforcement of the legal drinking age of 21 and zero tolerance laws*, increases in alcohol taxes, and wider implementation of screening and counseling programs and comprehensive community interventions can reduce college drinking and associated harm to students and others. (Hingson et al., 2005, p. 259, emphasis added)

However, Hingson et al. in their recommendations also adumbrate a newer approach to youthful alcohol-related problems (and other substance abuse). Called "harm reduction," this approach does not insist on abstinence and instead focuses on reducing identifiable harms that result from overimbibing. Two examples of harm reduction in the substance abuse field are clean needle programs for injecting drug users and safe driver programs for drinking youths. Teaching moderate drinking is another example of harm reduction. Any policy that recognizes drug use and underage drinking occur, while seeking to reduce their negative consequences, represents harm reduction.

CAS has tested a program that focuses on reducing harms rather than on abstinence per se. The program, "A Matter of Degree" (AMOD), is funded by the Robert Wood Johnson Foundation and supported by the American Medical Association. AMOD entails a wide panoply of techniques, including advertising restrictions, enforcement of underage drinking violations, opening hours for alcohol sales, community norms against excessive drinking, and other environmental and local cultural factors. Many of these techniques, for instance enforcement of age restrictions on drinking, are part of existing zero-tolerance programs. Nonetheless, AMOD explicitly aims to forestall "heavy alcohol consumption" and acknowledges youthful drinking while attempting to reduce binge drinking. A test of AMOD at ten sites found no significant changes in actual drinking or harm associated with drinking. Nonetheless, the investigators conducted an internal analysis – based on those schools that implemented the most specific elements of AMOD – and found reduction of both alcohol

consumption and alcohol-related harm due to adoption of AMOD policies.

Is harm reduction a viable policy for American collegiate drinking?

The AMOD goal of "reducing drinking" (like the phrase "reducing underage drinking") is actually ambiguous, in a significant way. It can mean either (a) reducing the number of people under 21 who drink at all with a goal of having few or no underage drinkers, or (b) reducing the amount of alcohol that underage drinkers typically consume. Both would reduce the overall levels of alcohol consumed by young people. The first is a zero-tolerance approach; the second is harm reduction. Of course, the goal could be to increase both phenomena. An important question is whether it is possible to combine these policies – the question involves both political and technical, programmatic considerations.

AMOD does not explicitly endorse teaching students how to drink moderately, at the same time that the program aims to reduce excessive drinking. AMOD thus incorporates harm reduction without accepting underage drinking as a natural passage into adulthood, as is customary in cultures which inculcate moderate drinking patterns. Socializing children into drinking remains outside the pale of harm reduction programs like those represented by AMOD. It may be that exclusion of moderate-drinking concepts is necessary in the mixed cultural environment presented in the United States, at least in terms of gaining popular acceptance for harm reduction ideas.

Hope and Byrne (2002), ECAS researchers working in the Irish context, analyzed the policy implications of ECAS results. These investigators recommend importing into Irish and other binge-drinking cultures what might be called the Mediterranean approach to youthful drinking:

The experience of the southern countries suggests that it is important to avoid both demonizing alcohol and promoting abstinence as key elements of alcohol control. In order to emulate the success of the alcohol control policies of the southern countries, the EU should consider a strategy that includes the following elements:

Encourage moderate drinking among those who choose to drink with moderate drinking and abstinence being presented as equally acceptable choices.

Clarify and promote the distinction between acceptable and unacceptable drinking.

Firmly penalize unacceptable drinking, both legally and socially. Intoxication must never be humoured or accepted as an excuse for bad behavior. *Avoid stigmatizing alcohol as inherently harmful, as such stigmatization can create emotionalism and ambivalence.* (pp. 211–12, emphasis added)

In fact, Hope and Byrne themselves fall short of fully adopting harm reduction approaches, just as AMOD does, by failing to understand that a certain amount of drunkenness will inevitably occur, and that even intoxicated young people should also be protected from irreversible harmful consequences of their own actions – like accidents or alcohol poisoning.

Finally, the goal of achieving moderate drinking is most controversial in the United States in the case of alcoholism treatment. Although research continues to point to the value of such approaches, Alcoholics Anonymous and virtually all American treatment programs emphasize abstinence as the only way to resolve an alcohol problem. Moderation training for problem drinkers is one form of harm reduction. Research on training heavy or problematic collegiate drinkers to moderate their usage has proven highly successful, although this approach is still extremely limited in its utilization across the United States.

There is no single optimal policy for youth drinking – there are dangers and drawbacks to both zero-tolerance and moderate-drinking approaches. Nonetheless, especially given the current policy imbalance that strongly favors the former, collegiate officials and health professionals should consider the following in developing harm reduction policies:

- Epidemiologic research has established advantages to moderate drinking, particularly when compared with binge drinking, advantages that should be acknowledged and encouraged as a model for alcohol use on campuses.
- Insisting on abstinence does not guarantee the absence of drinking on campus, and harm-reduction

techniques for reducing the extent and impact of binge or other excessive collegiate drinking should be developed and implemented (e.g., safe rides, providing protected settings for intoxicated students).
- Alternative treatment/prevention approaches – approaches that recognize and encourage moderation – are particularly appropriate for younger drinkers for whom moderation is more achievable than it is for long-term alcoholics and for whom lifelong abstinence is very unlikely.

Unhealthy (or at least less than optimal) American attitudes towards alcohol are regularly promoted by governmental and public health officials, researchers, clinicians, and college administrators. Indeed, even when such individuals adopt moderate drinking practices in their personal lives, they are reluctant to consider them in formulating public policy. This disconnect between sensible drinking practices, identified both individually and epidemiologically, and policy implementation is not a healthy state of affairs for American alcohol policy towards young people.

References

Allamani A. Policy implications of the ECAS results: A southern European perspective. (2002). In T. Norström (ed.), *Alcohol in postwar Europe: Consumption, drinking patterns, consequences and policy responses in 15 European countries* (pp. 196–205). Stockholm: National Institute of Public Health.

Bobak, M., Room, R., Pikhart, H., Kubinova, R., Malyutina, S., and Pajak, A., et al. (2004). Contribution of drinking patterns to differences in rates of alcohol related problems between three urban populations. *Journal of Epidemiology and Community Health, 58*, 238–42.

Grant, B. F. (1997). Prevalence and correlates of alcohol use and DSM-IV alcohol dependence in the United States: Results of the National Longitudinal Alcohol Epidemiologic Survey. *Journal of Studies on Alcohol, 58*, 464–73.

Hingson, R., Heeren, T., Winter, M., and Wechsler, H. (2005). Magnitude of alcohol-related mortality and morbidity among U.S. college students ages 18–24: Changes from 1998 to 2001. *Annual Review of Public Health, 26*, 259–79.

Hope, A., and Byrne, S. (2002). ECAS findings: Policy implications from an EU perspective. In T. Norström (ed.), *Alcohol in postwar Europe: Consumption, drinking* patterns, consequences and policy responses in 15 European Countries (pp. 206–12). Stockholm: National Institute of Public Health.

Kutter, C., and McDermott, D. S. (1997). The role of church in adolescent drug education. *Journal of Drug Education, 27*, 293–305.

Makimoto, K. (1998). Drinking patterns and drinking problems among Asian-Americans and Pacific Islanders. *Alcohol Health & Research World, 22*, 270–5.

McNeil, A. (2000). Alcohol and young people in Europe. In A. Varley (ed.). *Towards a global alcohol policy: Proceedings of the Global Alcohol Policy Advocacy Conference* (pp. 13–20). Syracuse, NY.

Monteiro, M. G., and Schuckit, M. A. (1989). Alcohol, drug and mental health problems among Jewish and Christian men at a university. *American Journal of Drug and Alcohol Abuse, 15*, 403–12.

Ramstedt, M., and Hope, A. (2003). *The Irish drinking culture: Drinking and drinking-related harm, a European comparison.* Retrieved May 24, 2006, from http://www.healthpromotion.ie/uploaded_docs/Irish_Drinking_Culture.PDF.

Schmid, H., and Nic Gabhainn, S. (2004). Alcohol use. In C. Currie, et al. (eds.), *Young people's health in context. Health Behaviour in School-Aged Children (HBSC) study: International report from the 2001/2002 survey* (pp. 73–83). Geneva: World Health Organization Regional Office for Europe.

Weiss, S. (1997). Urgent need for prevention among Arab youth in 1996 (in Herbew). *Harefuah, 132*, 229–31.

Weiss, S. (2001). Religious influences on drinking: Influences from select groups. In E. Houghton and A. M. Roche (eds.), *Learning about Drinking* (pp. 109–27) Philadelphia: Brunner-Routledge.

Questions

1 According to the article, what type of drinking is more healthy, moderate daily drinking or heavier episodic drinking? Why do young people think otherwise? Which form of alcohol consumption does the US culture promote? Why? How might our temperance culture and mass consumption culture (e.g., Reinarman) contribute to a culture of binge drinking?

2 Do you think teaching moderate drinking to youth would lower rates of alcoholism in the United States? Why or why not? If alcohol appeared today as new on the drug scene, do you think it would be legal? Why or why not? Would it be Schedule I? Schedule II?

3 How would you design a treatment program for American youth that would promote moderate drinking? Do you think lowering the legal drinking age to 18 years of age would promote more moderate drinking? Why or why not?

Reflections on Drug Policy

Duane C. McBride, Yvonne Terry-McElrath, Henrick Harwood, James A. Inciardi, and Carl Leukefeld

Duane McBride, Yvonne Terry McElrath, Henrick Harwood, James Inciardi, and Carl Leukefeld offer a review of American drug policies ranging from laissez-faire to strict prohibitionism. In recent years, there has been little federal interest in drug policy reform and a continuing focus on a prohibitionist deterrence approach. During this period, state initiatives have been in the forefront of drug policy experimentation via ballot initiatives, legislative actions, or judicial administrative policy decisions. The resulting state-level drug policy landscape includes continued prohibition as well as harm reduction, medicalization, and decriminalization.

As you read this selection, you may want to think about the value of the various approaches described here. Should we have a more unified national drug policy? Is there a universal morality that should be driving our national drug policy? Do you think our drug policies are effective? Are we still best off aiming for total prohibitionism and settling for whatever we get? Or should we reduce our costs, move parts of drug enforcement policy into other social realms, and aim for improvements in public health and safety? How might this affect us? Which segments of society might benefit, and which might suffer, if any? How is this issue affected by some of the moral campaigning and the status politics we read about earlier in this book?

The Origins of Drug Policy

In any era people tend to believe that they encounter issues unique in human history. Those involved in today's drug policy debate are no different. However, scholars such as Musto (1999) and Inciardi (2008) have documented that drug policies in the United States have historically varied dramatically and have sparked public discourse, debate, and hysteria in each era. From the colonial era through the late 1800s, drug policy focused on light regulation and has been characterized as laissez faire. Addictive substances were a major part of global trade in this highly entrepreneurial era, and many powerful drugs were sold over-the-counter, through itinerant medicine shows and major store catalogs. The *Sears Catalog* of

Drugs and the American Dream: An Anthology, First Edition. Edited by Patricia A. Adler, Peter Adler, and Patrick K. O'Brien.

1897 advertised Peruvian Wine of Coca, guaranteeing that the product would provide energy, reduce fatigue, and enable workers to be productive under any conditions. Social reformers increasingly recognized the broad consequences of addiction. During the early twentieth century, drug policy was debated vigorously, mirroring in many ways our own current debate.

The Reaction to a Laissez Faire Drug Policy

Drug policy changes in the twentieth century should be viewed within the context of major social reforms. Society began to realize individuals were consuming highly addictive substances they did not realize were in over-the-counter medicines. The broad social reforms of the period included safe foods and drugs, and two major drug policies resulted from these reforms: (a) the Pure Food and Drug Act of 1906, which introduced labeling of ingredients and prescription requirements for many drugs, and (b) the Harrison Act of 1914. Although the Harrison Act only regulated and taxed production, importation, distribution, and use of drugs such as opium and coca leaf derivatives, it was interpreted as de facto prohibition. From a policy development perspective, it is important to note that these federal acts followed years of state policy development that served as a model for federal action.

America went from a relatively open market approach to drugs to one that was strongly moralistically prohibitionist. Those who previously had access to cocaine, opium, and injection paraphernalia suddenly found themselves experiencing the pain of withdrawal or engaging in illegal behavior to access the drugs on which they were now dependent. From the 1930s on, largely through Harry Anslinger, Commissioner of the US Bureau of Narcotics from 1930 to 1962, illicit drug use was defined as a foreign threat destroying America's soul. The media focused on drug-maddened foreign or minority-group rapists. Classic examples of these efforts were the movies *Reefer Madness* (originally titled *Tell Your Children*), and *The Man with the Golden Arm*. While this film was considered ground breaking in its stark portrayal of the life of a heroin user, it also supported the view of the inevitable destruction of a life of illicit drug use and provide continued dramatic

support for a strong prohibitionist policy position. Such prohibitionist policy remained largely unchallenged until the 1960s.

The Generational Revolution

During the 1960s and 1970s, the US underwent a generational revolution when the Baby Boomers (those born between 1946–64) became adolescents. The socialization mechanisms of American society struggled to integrate the millions of baby boomers into conventional social norms. Sufficient numbers existed to create an alternative culture that questioned conventional wisdom about race, parental and institutional authority, and traditional values about sexual behavior and substance use. Data show an increase in the use of a variety of substances from the late 1960s through about 1980. By 1980, the Monitoring the Future study showed that 60 percent of twelfth graders had used marijuana in their lifetime; in fact, lifetime marijuana prevalence rates (60%) were approaching those for tobacco use (71%). Many policy makers and media figures called for the legalization of marijuana. They argued that marijuana was not as addictive as tobacco or alcohol and had less dangerous consequences. Some of the authors of this paper participated in high-level discussions about legalizing marijuana through regulation during this era.

Policy Reactions to the Drug Revolution

The election of Ronald Reagan in 1980 strongly affected drug policy reform. President Reagan took a strong stance against the legalization of marijuana or any type of drug policy reform. The public was alarmed at the rapid increase in drug use among youth. Other issues, such as the growing recognition of the relationship between drug use and crime, resulted in many calls for a "war on drugs" to prevent illicit drug use among youth. Government disbursements for law enforcement and drug interdiction increased significantly. The mantra for national drug policy during the 1980s was "Just Say No." Prohibitionist policy was strengthened at federal and state levels with mandatory minimums for drug law violations and border patrols were increased. Such prohibitionist policies may have reflected a shift in public disapproval of drug use. Drug trend data show a fairly steady decrease in the lifetime use of marijuana and other illicit drugs over the next 10 years through 1992.

Consequences of the "War on Drugs"

Drug policy in the 1980s had major consequences for American society in general and for members of minority groups in particular. As a result of mandatory minimum sentences, a significant percentage of those incarcerated were completing sentences for drug law violations. The US had the highest proportion of 18- to 25-year-olds in prison of any industrial society, considerable prison overcrowding, and deteriorating conditions. In some states, a higher proportion of young men were under criminal justice supervision than were in college. The rate of imprisonment was not equally distributed among the ethnic groups. While neither the National Survey on Drug Use and Health nor the Monitoring the Future study shows significant differences in rates of illicit drug use among youth by race or ethnic group, data from the criminal justice system show major differences in imprisonment. African-American males are considerably overrepresented among incarcerated populations. A wide variety of evidence suggests that major problems continue to exist in unequal application of drug policy law enforcement. Many observers have also argued that the war on drugs has undermined civil rights, affecting issues such as police rights to enter a dwelling, search and seizure, and punishments that meet the proportionality of the offense.

The Continuum of the Current Drug Policy Debate

Today's vigorous drug policy debate has emerged from observing the successes and consequences of current drug policy and can be described as a continuum of often overlapping positions. Each of the points along this continuum represent positions that at times provide important alternatives, at times seem to add to the confusion of the policy debate, and at times seem internally contradictory. Essentially, the history of drug policy (and debates about the future of drug policy) can be broken down into five main approaches: prohibition, harm reduction, medicalization, legalization and regulation, and decriminalization.

Prohibition

Prohibition emphasizes severe penalties for illicit drug possession, distribution, or production. This position rests on the philosophical position of deterrence. It argues that if penalties are sufficiently high, certain, and swift, the targeted behavior will be reduced. This position is the underlying rationale for mandatory minimum sentencing. Deterrence, in many ways, underlies society's basic approach to violations of criminal law, and some research supports its effectiveness. Deterrence drug policy does show some evidence of relating to lower levels of drug use. However, the consequences of a strong deterrence policy have been high, resulting in a dramatic increase in the number of individuals held in jail for drug related offences and concerns that drug law enforcement appears to be differentially applied to minorities.

Harm reduction

Harm reduction uses a public health approach to reduce the risks and harms associated with illicit drug use. This approach includes drug prevention education, safer drug use practices that reduce the harm caused by those who continue to use, and treatment in lieu of incarceration. These types of policies have been shown to be effective in many cases, but some see this position as a screen for drug legalization, often preventing a full discussion of harm reduction as a policy alternative. In recent years, federal officials were not permitted to participate in public discussions of harm reduction as a drug policy alternative. However, harm reduction is not necessarily equivalent to legalization and can be incorporated in a public health approach to drug policy that emphasizes prevention education and diversion to treatment in lieu of incarceration.

Medicalization

Medicalization calls for a medical approach to dealing with those who use or are addicted to illicit drugs.

From this perspective, substance abuse is primarily a medical issue that should be managed by physicians. It is argued that since the medical profession is entrusted with the management of a wide variety of very powerful addictive substances, they are most able to successfully select and manage the drugs that address patient needs. Policy advocates for medicalization have focused primarily on marijuana. They argue that marijuana has been shown to have positive medical benefits for a variety of medical conditions including glaucoma and the consequences of chemotherapy. Medical marijuana initiatives are a major emphasis of many drug policy change advocates, and such efforts are gaining ground. [...]

Legalization and regulation

A legalization and regulation policy supports access to drugs through governmental regulation of distribution, legal age of use, and other regulatory components. It is argued that such a policy approach would reduce the crimes inherent to the illicit drug trade and would provide tax revenue. Although this position has many advocates, extensive data indicate that the regulation of tobacco and alcohol is hardly a shining success. Cigarette smoking accounts for one in every five deaths in the US each year, adding up to more mortality than that caused by HIV, illicit drug or alcohol use, traffic accidents, suicides, and murders combined. Drinking among high school students is statistically normative, with nearly half of all high school seniors engaging in heavy episodic drinking. Alcohol is strongly related to violent crime and traffic accidents – the leading cause of death in people aged 4 to 34. These data suggest that regulation may not be a particularly effective policy in preventing the use and consequences of addictive substances.

Decriminalization

As a policy, decriminalization calls for an end to the use of criminal law to address individual drug use. Generally, this policy is particularly advocated for marijuana possession. The National Commission on Marihuana and Drug Abuse (often called the Shafer Commission) issued a report in 1972 that called for the decriminalization of marijuana possession.

Decriminalization was defined in this report as the removal of criminal penalties for the possession of marijuana for personal use or for amounts to be shared with others without any remuneration of any type. A report by Pacula and her colleagues (2003) noted that twelve states are often classified as having decriminalized marijuana. However, as these researchers noted, the definition of decriminalization at times just refers to reduced penalties or no penalties for first time offenders. The decriminalization of marijuana is a major effort of the National Organization for the Reform of Marijuana Laws. This approach has also been characterized as libertarian, a position that argues the government has no right to regulate individual behavior, even if such behavior is harmful to the individual practicing it. This approach is often based on the late nineteenth century work of John Stuart Mill. The advocates of decriminalization argue that the removal of penalties for small amounts of marijuana possession has not had a significant effect on youth marijuana use. However, the evidence here is mixed. While Pacula and her colleagues note that removal of penalties for small quantity marijuana possession has not shown relationships with youth marijuana use, they also document a positive association between penalties for marijuana possession and lower use rates (Pacula et al. 2003).

A Complex Range of Policy and Substance Specific Positions

This brief discussion of the points along the drug policy continuum debate provides an overview of the discussion that has been occurring in the United States and the World in a formal way for well over a century. These issues are debated in state legislatures, the US Congress, and in the halls of the United Nations. Each of these positions has strong proponents and often generous governmental, philanthropic, or foundation support. Many of these positions have ended up as state ballot initiatives. While prohibition has remained the official national position and the position of many states, evidence shows considerable variation in state policy overall and for specific substances. Throughout the history of the United States, there has been a dynamic tension between state policy and national policy. As was noted earlier, the prohibition movement at the beginning of the twentieth century began at the state level. Now we are seeing an increased willingness of states to reform drug policy.

The Complexity of State-Level Drug Policy Implementation

While the Reagan years brought mandatory minimum sentencing to the forefront, they also reversed the trend toward the federalization of social policies. During the 1960s and 1970s, the federal government and the U.S. Supreme Court tended to define national to local social policy. Under Reagan, authority moved from the federal to state governments. Research has shown that most prosecutions for drug law violations take place at the state level. As a result, major policy experiments have been possible at state levels. The drug policy debate increasingly takes place on the floor of state legislatures or through state ballot initiatives rather than on the federal level, and is increasingly – and awkwardly – at odds with federal policy.

Current Modifications to a Deterrence/Prohibitionist Approach

Today's drug policy is undergoing rapid change involving increased sentencing flexibility, continued attempts to discourage emerging drug use through severe deterrence, and the use of a harm reduction or public health approach.

The End of, or Modifications to, Mandatory Minimum Sentences

By 1990, prison officials were reporting that mandatory minimum sentencing was resulting in significant prison overcrowding. Facing such overcrowding, many states have modified their mandatory minimum sentencing laws. At the state level, the late 1990s and the first decade of the twenty-first century have seen considerable state willingness to try different policy approaches for substance use.

For some substances, state policy is moving toward increased deterrence and/or regulation. One group of drugs experiencing increased policy severity includes ecstasy and substances known as "date rape drugs": Rohypnol®, GHB, and ketamine. Media stories about deaths associated with ecstasy and sexual assaults associated with the date rape drugs resulted in many states increasing penalties for their distribution and possession. More recently, penalties have increased for the manufacturing of methamphetamine, and severe restrictions exist for obtaining the precursor chemicals needed to make methamphetamine. Methamphetamine precursor laws probably represent the most significant variance in state policies that exist today. Oregon has the most restrictive policy, with a physician's prescription needed to purchase cold medications containing methamphetamine precursors. However, many northeastern states have minimal regulation. These emerging policies show that states are willing to take a highly regulatory and deterrent approach to specific drugs that appear to cause high levels of community harm. Such policies exist within a general environment of decreased use of deterrence, with a co-occurring increase in willingness to use harm reduction or medicalization approaches for specific drugs.

State Implementation of a Harm Reduction Approach: The Possibilities of Public Health

Of all the various policy positions currently used or debated, the one we feel holds the most promise for society is that of harm reduction and a public health approach. This link between harm reduction and a public health approach involving a wide range of risk behaviors has been described in a book edited by Marlatt (1998). A 2000 editorial by Des Jarlais in the *American Journal of Public Health* called for a public health approach to drug policy that included an emphasis on prevention, treatment in lieu of incarceration, and programs to reduce health consequences. Acknowledging that views of what constitutes a harm reduction drug policy approach may differ, the following provides a brief description of key components that we believe deserve serious policy consideration.

Prevention

One of the key emphases of a harm reduction/public health approach is prevention. Regardless of the illness or societal condition under discussion, public health places a very high priority on prevention. Public health has also had a history of understanding the broader social nature of health problems, including socioeconomic factors. A public health approach to drug use would include consistent primary and secondary prevention efforts. Accurate information and relevant messages would be emphasized with a focus on messages that would be effective with high-risk individuals. Research suggests that about one-third of the nation's youth reside in communities where the local public health agency is actively involved in drug abuse prevention. Considerable research over the last decade documents effective prevention programming. Within a public health framework, economic opportunity and social structure would become priorities in attempts to prevent individuals from turning to drug use, as research indicates that the initiation of substance use is lower when the economy is stronger. A prevention approach would also need to recognize the importance of supply reduction (but not at the cost of de-emphasizing other critical efforts or undermining civil rights). Harm reduction/public health approaches to drug use recognize that primary and secondary prevention will not always succeed. Steps to prevent the harms associated with drug use also play key roles. Such steps include efforts to protect the public from drug-related crime and the spread of disease related to drug use through programs such as needle exchange and treatment for those dealing with drug addiction.

Treatment Instead of Incarceration

While the exact nature of the relationship between drugs and crime may be debated, the preponderance of research substantiates the co-occurrence of drug use and criminal behavior. The public has a legitimate need to be protected from drug-related crime, but in a manner that neither exacerbates criminality nor precludes treatment and rehabilitation for offenders. Drug-related crime exists along a continuum of severity ranging from index crimes (e.g., murder, armed robbery, etc.) to more minor offenses, such as nonviolent drug possession. For drug-involved offenders who have committed serious violent crimes, the public and offender might best be served by providing drug treatment services in a more restrictive prison setting. In contrast, nonviolent offenders might receive treatment and ongoing supervision through drug court proceedings. For either type of offender, ongoing supervision and monitoring that incorporate rewards for success and increased penalties for noncompliance are critical; such an approach often involves graduated sanctions.

State and/or local policy initiatives related to diversion to treatment have been among the most active areas of drug policy in recent years. Such policies support the diversion of arrested drug users to treatment in lieu of incarceration. The Nixon administration initiated this policy at the federal level in the early 1970s, and it has been accepted widely at the state level. A wide range of political groups has supported diversion to treatment. The lower costs of treatment in comparison to incarceration, with the use of graduated sanctions and criminal justice supervision to protect the public, appeal to conservatives. From a moderate to liberal perspective, diversion limits the impact of labeling and the consequences of incarceration, and it also provides needed treatment that has a significantly greater chance at reducing drug use than the implementation of severe punishment. In addition, a variety of research shows that treatment is generally more cost-effective than incarceration.

While diversion is often supported by a variety of policy positions, willingness to use such programming appears to have significant local variation. Research by Terry-McElrath and McBride (2004) found that the majority of prosecutors in a national sample reported the availability of diversion programming for juvenile substance offenders (especially for drug possession offenses). However, the likelihood of receiving diversion varied dramatically by substance as well as by community socio-demographics (Terry-McElrath et al., 2005). Prosecutors reported that they were much more willing to divert juveniles for marijuana possession than possession of other drugs or sales of marijuana or other drugs. The Des Jarlais

2000 editorial calling for a public health approach to drug policy may be feasible. Recent research by McBride and his colleagues (2008) suggests that many local public health agencies are already advocating for treatment in lieu of incarceration and providing treatment services, particularly in urban areas and areas with a higher proportion of minorities.

[...]

The Future of Policy

United States drug policy will never be a simple process. It is often contradictory: focused on specific drugs and widely diverse, with state and local-level policy often at odds with national policy. Some policy movements are encouraging, however. Diversion to quality treatment appears to have a wide base of support across the political spectrum. The increasing dissemination of best practice knowledge and the implementation of best practice requirements in state policy may give some encouragement to drug policy advocates. National policy development also includes some discouraging elements. Basic drug policy reform or social reforms that address the underlying causes of substance abuse did not receive support from the Bush administration. In addition, drug research policy appears to have been more focused on understanding the neuromechanisms of addiction rather than a broader-based approach that would include underlying social conditions and practices that are integrally connected with the initiation and continuation of use as well as the disproportionate incarceration of and consequences for minority groups.

Given the recent policy climate at the federal level, significant discussions of drug policy change are occurring within and between states. While this can lead to a patchwork of policies, it does provide the opportunity to use varying state drug policies as a kind of natural laboratory to examine the effect of different drug policies. Although opportunities for cross-state policy evaluation exist, changes in funding priorities have hampered the ability to conduct this research. The federal government appears reluctant to conduct policy research. One of the major funding agencies for drug policy research has been the Robert Wood Johnson Foundation (RWJF) in general and their Substance Abuse Policy Research Program (SAPRP) in particular. RWJF and SAPRP have played a major role in developing and testing best-practice research, examining best-practice diffusion, and evaluating state-based policy initiatives. However, over time, the priorities of all funding agencies change. In the last few years, RWJF has focused on a different major national public health issue: youth obesity. This has left drug policy researchers without one of the major sources of funding outside government control. If we are going to take advantage of the opportunities that are, in many ways, available to us for the first time, other foundations will be needed to support this important work. This is particularly true with a new administration in the White House that may be more amenable to drug policy research and change within the framework of health care reform. The Marijuana Policy Project argues that the Obama administration is at least modifying federal efforts to enforce federal marijuana laws in states that have medical marijuana in such a way as to not interfere with state law.

References

Des Jarlais, D.C. 2000. Research, politics and needle exchange. *American Journal of Public Health, 90*(9), 1392–4.

Inciardi, J.A. 2008. *War on drugs IV: The continuing saga of the mysteries and miseries of intoxication, addiction, crime and public policy.* Boston, MA: Allyn and Bacon.

Marlatt, G.A. (Ed.). 1998. *Harm reduction.* New York: Guilford Press.

McBride, D. C., Terry-McElrath, Y. M., VanderWaal, C. J., Chriqui, J. F., and Myllyluoma, J. 2008. United States public health agency involvement in illicit drug policy, planning, and prevention at the local level, 1999–2003. *American Journal of Public Health, 98*, 270–7.

Musto, D. F. 1999. *The American disease.* New York: Oxford University Press.

Pacula, R. L., Chriqui, J. F., Reichmann, D. A., and Terry-McElrath, Y. M. 2002. State medical marijuana laws: Understanding the laws and their limitations. *Journal of Public Health Policy, 23*(4), 413–39.

Questions

1   If drugs were legalized and regulated, how might a policy similar to the Pure Food and Drug Act of 1906 reduce drug-related harm to users? Why? How do you think the legalization and control/regulation of drugs would impact rates of use and/or abuse? Would regulation and control reduce the problems created by prohibition?

2   Given the slow rate of change in our society with regard to drug policy, how do you think harm reduction strategies could be introduced into our current prohibitionist framework? What harm reduction strategies could be introduced? How would these strategies reduce harm caused by the prohibition and criminalization of drugs? What other policy models in the article could be introduced into the prohibition framework to reduce drug related harm?

3   Why do you think the US federal government is reluctant to conduct policy research to develop and test best-policy drug research? Do you think there might be tangible and/or symbolic benefits for federal government agencies to continue the War on Drugs? Why or why not?

44

Think Again: Drugs

Ethan Nadelmann

In this upbeat and readable selection, Ethan Nadelmann challenges some of the common assumptions underlying American drug policy and debunks them. In so doing, he raises and examines issues that may be considered heretical to some groups in society. Is this a liberal agenda, a conservative agenda, a libertarian agenda, or a radical agenda? What are the characteristics of each of these approaches? Could it be a practical agenda? What about it seems practical or impractical? What do you see as the impediments to implementing some of the policy suggestions Nadelmann proposes?

Thinking about some of the sociological factors we have considered in this book, are there some racial/ethnic, age, socioeconomic, or gender groups that would respond better or worse to a harm reduction approach? Might it be more effective or realistic if applied to some kinds of drugs and not others? Finally, how might all of this impact on the international drug trade?

"The Global War on Drugs Can Be Won"

No, it can't. A "drug-free world," which the United Nations describes as a realistic goal, is no more attainable than an "alcohol-free world" – and no one has talked about that with a straight face since the repeal of Prohibition in the United States in 1933. Yet futile rhetoric about winning a "war on drugs" persists, despite mountains of evidence documenting its moral and ideological bankruptcy. When the UN General Assembly Special Session on drugs convened in 1998, it committed to "eliminating or significantly reducing the illicit cultivation of the coca bush, the cannabis plant and the opium poppy by the year 2008" and to "achieving significant and measurable results in the field of demand reduction." But today, global production and consumption of those drugs are roughly the same as they were a decade ago; meanwhile, many producers have become more efficient, and cocaine and heroin have become purer and cheaper.

It's always dangerous when rhetoric drives policy – and especially so when "war on drugs" rhetoric leads

Drugs and the American Dream: An Anthology, First Edition. Edited by Patricia A. Adler, Peter Adler, and Patrick K. O'Brien.
© 2012 John Wiley & Sons, Inc. Published 2012 by John Wiley & Sons, Inc.

the public to accept collateral casualties that would never be permissible in civilian law enforcement, much less public health. Politicians still talk of eliminating drugs from the Earth as though their use is a plague on humanity. But drug control is not like disease control, for the simple reason that there's no popular demand for smallpox or polio. Cannabis and opium have been grown throughout much of the world for millennia. The same is true for coca in Latin America. Methamphetamine and other synthetic drugs can be produced anywhere. Demand for particular illicit drugs waxes and wanes, depending not just on availability but also fads, fashion, culture, and competition from alternative means of stimulation and distraction. The relative harshness of drug laws and the intensity of enforcement matter surprisingly little, except in totalitarian states. After all, rates of illegal drug use in the United States are the same as, or higher than, Europe, despite America's much more punitive policies.

"We Can Reduce the Demand for Drugs"

Good luck

Reducing the demand for illegal drugs seems to make sense. But the desire to alter one's state of consciousness, and to use psychoactive drugs to do so, is nearly universal – and mostly not a problem. There's virtually never been a drug-free society, and more drugs are discovered and devised every year. Demand-reduction efforts that rely on honest education and positive alternatives to drug use are helpful, but not when they devolve into unrealistic, "zero tolerance" policies.

As with sex, abstinence from drugs is the best way to avoid trouble, but one always needs a fallback strategy for those who can't or won't refrain. "Zero tolerance" policies deter some people, but they also dramatically increase the harms and costs for those who don't resist. Drugs become more potent, drug use becomes more hazardous, and people who use drugs are marginalized in ways that serve no one.

The better approach is not demand reduction but "harm reduction." Reducing drug use is fine, but it's not nearly as important as reducing the death, disease, crime, and suffering associated with both drug misuse

and failed prohibitionist policies. With respect to legal drugs, such as alcohol and cigarettes, harm reduction means promoting responsible drinking and designated drivers, or persuading people to switch to nicotine patches, chewing gums, and smokeless tobacco. With respect to illegal drugs, it means reducing the transmission of infectious disease through syringe-exchange programs, reducing overdose fatalities by making antidotes readily available, and allowing people addicted to heroin and other illegal opiates to obtain methadone from doctors and even pharmaceutical heroin from clinics. Britain, Canada, Germany, the Netherlands, and Switzerland have already embraced this last option. There's no longer any question that these strategies decrease drug-related harms without increasing drug use. What blocks expansion of such programs is not cost; they typically save taxpayers' money that would otherwise go to criminal justice and healthcare. No, the roadblocks are abstinence-only ideologues and a cruel indifference to the lives and well-being of people who use drugs.

"Reducing the Supply of Drugs Is the Answer"

Not if history is any guide

Reducing supply makes as much sense as reducing demand; after all, if no one were planting cannabis, coca, and opium, there wouldn't be any heroin, cocaine, or marijuana to sell or consume. But the carrot and stick of crop eradication and substitution have been tried and failed, with rare exceptions, for half a century. These methods may succeed in targeted locales, but they usually simply shift production from one region to another: Opium production moves from Pakistan to Afghanistan, coca from Peru to Colombia, and cannabis from Mexico to the United States, while overall global production remains relatively constant or even increases.

The carrot, in the form of economic development and assistance in switching to legal crops, is typically both late and inadequate. The stick, often in the form of forced eradication, including aerial spraying, wipes out illegal and legal crops alike and can be hazardous to both people and local environments. The best thing to be said for emphasizing supply reduction is that it provides a rationale for wealthier nations to spend a little money on economic development in poorer countries. But, for the most part, crop eradication and substitution wreak havoc among impoverished farmers without diminishing overall global supply.

The global markets in cannabis, coca, and opium products operate essentially the same way that other global commodity markets do: If one source is compromised due to bad weather, rising production costs, or political difficulties, another emerges. If international drug control circles wanted to think strategically, the key question would no longer be how to reduce global supply, but rather: Where does illicit production cause the fewest problems (and the greatest benefits)? Think of it as a global vice control challenge. No one expects to eradicate vice, but it must be effectively zoned and regulated – even if it's illegal.

"US Drug Policy Is the World's Drug Policy"

Sad, but true

Looking to the United States as a role model for drug control is like looking to apartheid-era South Africa for how to deal with race. The United States ranks first in the world in per capita incarceration – with less than 5 percent of the world's population, but almost 25 percent of the world's prisoners. The number of people locked up for US drug-law violations has increased from roughly 50,000 in 1980 to almost 500,000 today; that's more than the number of people Western Europe locks up for everything. Even more deadly is US resistance to syringe-exchange programs to reduce HIV/AIDS both at home and abroad. Who knows how many people might not have contracted HIV if the United States had implemented at home, and supported abroad, the sorts of syringe-exchange and other harm-reduction programs that have kept HIV/AIDS rates so low in Australia, Britain, the Netherlands, and elsewhere. Perhaps millions.

And yet, despite this dismal record, the United States has succeeded in constructing an international drug prohibition regime modeled after its own highly

punitive and moralistic approach. It has dominated the drug control agencies of the United Nations and other international organizations, and its federal drug enforcement agency was the first national police organization to go global. Rarely has one nation so successfully promoted its own failed policies to the rest of the world.

But now, for the first time, US hegemony in drug control is being challenged. The European Union is demanding rigorous assessment of drug control strategies. Exhausted by decades of service to the US-led war on drugs, Latin Americans are far less inclined to collaborate closely with US drug enforcement efforts. Finally waking up to the deadly threat of HIV/AIDS, China, Indonesia, Vietnam, and even Malaysia and Iran are increasingly accepting of syringe-exchange and other harm-reduction programs. In 2005, the ayatollah in charge of Iran's Ministry of Justice issued a *fatwa* declaring methadone maintenance and syringe-exchange programs compatible with *sharia* (Islamic) law. One only wishes his American counterpart were comparably enlightened.

"Afghan Opium Production Must Be Curbed"

Be careful what you wish for

It's easy to believe that eliminating record-high opium production in Afghanistan – which today accounts for roughly 90 percent of global supply, up from 50 percent 10 years ago – would solve everything from heroin abuse in Europe and Asia to the resurgence of the Taliban.

But assume for a moment that the United States, NATO, and Hamid Karzai's government were somehow able to cut opium production in Afghanistan. Who would benefit? Only the Taliban, warlords, and other black-market entrepreneurs whose stockpiles of opium would skyrocket in value. Hundreds of thousands of Afghan peasants would flock to cities, ill-prepared to find work. And many Afghans would return to their farms the following year to plant another illegal harvest, utilizing guerrilla farming methods to escape intensified eradication efforts. Except now, they'd soon be competing with poor farmers elsewhere in

Central Asia, Latin America, or even Africa. This is, after all, a global commodities market.

And outside Afghanistan? Higher heroin prices typically translate into higher crime rates by addicts. They also invite cheaper but more dangerous means of consumption, such as switching from smoking to injecting heroin, which results in higher HIV and hepatitis C rates. All things considered, wiping out opium in Afghanistan would yield far fewer benefits than is commonly assumed.

So what's the solution? Some recommend buying up all the opium in Afghanistan, which would cost a lot less than is now being spent trying to eradicate it. But, given that farmers somewhere will produce opium so long as the demand for heroin persists, maybe the world is better off, all things considered, with 90 percent of it coming from just one country. And if that heresy becomes the new gospel, it opens up all sorts of possibilities for pursuing a new policy in Afghanistan that reconciles the interests of the United States, NATO, and millions of Afghan citizens.

"Legalization Is the Best Approach"

It might be

Global drug prohibition is clearly a costly disaster. The United Nations has estimated the value of the global market in illicit drugs at $400 billion, or 6 percent of global trade. The extraordinary profits available to those willing to assume the risks enrich criminals, terrorists, violent political insurgents, and corrupt politicians and governments. Many cities, states, and even countries in Latin America, the Caribbean, and Asia are reminiscent of Chicago under Al Capone – times 50. By bringing the market for drugs out into the open, legalization would radically change all that for the better.

More importantly, legalization would strip addiction down to what it really is: a health issue. Most people who use drugs are like the responsible alcohol consumer, causing no harm to themselves or anyone else. They would no longer be the state's business. But legalization would also benefit those who struggle with drugs by reducing the risks of overdose and disease associated with unregulated products, eliminating the need to obtain drugs from dangerous criminal markets, and allowing addiction problems to be treated as medical rather than criminal problems.

No one knows how much governments spend collectively on failing drug war policies, but it's probably at least $100 billion a year, with federal, state, and local governments in the United States accounting for almost half the total. Add to that the tens of billions of dollars to be gained annually in tax revenues from the sale of legalized drugs. Now imagine if just a third of that total were committed to reducing drug-related disease and addiction. Virtually everyone, except those who profit or gain politically from the current system, would benefit.

Some say legalization is immoral. That's nonsense, unless one believes there is some principled basis for discriminating against people based solely on what they put into their bodies, absent harm to others. Others say legalization would open the flood-gates to huge increases in drug abuse. They forget that we already live in a world in which psychoactive drugs of all sorts are readily available – and in which people too poor to buy drugs resort to sniffing gasoline, glue, and other industrial products, which can be more harmful than any drug. No, the greatest downside to legalization may well be the fact that the legal markets would fall into the hands of the powerful alcohol, tobacco, and pharmaceutical companies. Still, legalization is a far more pragmatic option than living with the corruption, violence, and organized crime of the current system.

"Legalization Will Never Happen"

Never say never

Wholesale legalization may be a long way off – but partial legalization is not. If any drug stands a chance of being legalized, it's cannabis. Hundreds of millions of people have used it, the vast majority without suffering any harm or going on to use "harder" drugs. In Switzerland, for example, cannabis legalization was twice approved by one chamber of its parliament, but narrowly rejected by the other.

Elsewhere in Europe, support for the criminalization of cannabis is waning. In the United States, where roughly 40 percent of the country's 1.8 million annual drug arrests are for cannabis possession, typically of tiny amounts, 40 percent of Americans say that the drug should be taxed, controlled, and regulated like alcohol. Encouraged by Bolivian President Evo Morales, support is also growing in Latin America and Europe for removing coca from international antidrug conventions, given the absence of any credible health reason for keeping it there. Traditional growers would benefit economically, and there's some possibility that such products might compete favorably with more problematic substances, including alcohol.

The global war on drugs persists in part because so many people fail to distinguish between the harms of drug abuse and the harms of prohibition. Legalization forces that distinction to the forefront. The opium problem in Afghanistan is primarily a prohibition problem, not a drug problem. The same is true of the narcoviolence and corruption that has afflicted Latin America and the Caribbean for almost three decades – and that now threatens Africa. Governments can arrest and kill drug lord after drug lord, but the ultimate solution is a structural one, not a prosecutorial one. Few people doubt any longer that the war on drugs is lost, but courage and vision are needed to transcend the ignorance, fear, and vested interests that sustain it.

[...]

References

Terry-McElrath, Y. M., and McBride, D. C. 2004. Local implementation of drug policy and access to treatment services for juveniles. *Crime and Delinquency*, *50*(1), 60–87.

Terry-McElrath, Y. M., McBride, D. C., Ruel, E. E., Harwood, E. M., Vander Waal, C. J., and Chaloupka, F. J. 2005. Which substance and what community? Differences in juvenile disposition severity. *Crime and Delinquency*, *51*(4), 548–72.

Questions

1　Why do you think a "drug-free world" is unattainable in our society? Do you think a "drug-free world" would be better or worse for our society and its citizens? Why?

2　Why is reducing the demand for drugs problematic? Why do you think the interdiction of a drug transaction is such a difficult endeavor? Why is the interdiction of drugs coming in through the United States border such a difficult endeavor?

3　Do you think if drugs were legalized and regulated, it would decrease the prevalence of homemade drugs/drug use such as methamphetamine? Why or why not? Furthermore, who would control and regulate drugs? According to Nadelmann, it's the alcohol, tobacco, and pharmaceutical companies. Do you agree? If the pharmaceutical companies gained control of drugs after legalization, do you think they would spend more money on recreational or medicinal research and development? Why?

45

The Secret of Global Drug Prohibition
Its Uses and Crises

Harry G. Levine

Harry Levine interjects several under-recognized factors influencing global drug policy in this clear and comprehensible selection. He reviews the history of international drug policy and reveals the content of mostly unknown international drug treaties and alliances. He then points out the benefits governments all over the world secretly accrue from their participation in the global war on drugs. He concludes by discussing the rising opposition to this global anti-drug cabal.

As you read it, you may want to think about whether this kind of international drug policy is, indeed, a temporally and geographically universal requisite. To what extent does this parallel the kinds of moral entrepreneurial anti-drug crusades presented in Part I being played out on the international level? Are there status politics at play here that benefit some countries to the detriment of others? Are there connections between drug policies or drug enforcement and other kinds of international political negotiations and alliances? What role do drugs play in international politics? Finally, do the benefits countries gain from global drug prohibition and the commitments they have to it preclude the possibility of meaningful drug policy reform?

The Invisible System

What percentage of countries in the world have drug prohibition? Is it 100%, 75%, 50%, or 25%? I recently asked many people I know to guess the answer. Most people in the United States, especially avid readers and the politically aware, guess 25 or 50%. More suspicious individuals guess 75%. The correct answer is 100%, but *almost no one* guesses that figure. Most readers of this paragraph will not have heard that every country in the world has drug prohibition. Surprising as it seems, almost nobody knows about the existence of global drug prohibition.

Global drug prohibition is a world-wide system structured by a series of international treaties that are supervised by the United Nations. Every country in the world is either a signatory to one or more of the treaties, or it has laws in accord with them. As a result, every country has drug prohibition enforced by its police and military. Every country criminalizes the production

Drugs and the American Dream: An Anthology, First Edition. Edited by Patricia A. Adler, Peter Adler, and Patrick K. O'Brien.
© 2012 John Wiley & Sons, Inc. Published 2012 by John Wiley & Sons, Inc.

and sale of cannabis, cocaine, and opiates (except for limited medical use). Most countries criminalize the production and sale of some other psychoactive substances. Most countries also criminalize simple possession of small amounts of the prohibited substances.

Until recently, the term "drug prohibition" was rarely used by governments, the news media, or academics. This non-use of the phrase drug prohibition occurred even though, and perhaps because, alcohol prohibition was always called "prohibition," especially by the people in favor of it. Government publications and other writings have instead used the terms "narcotics control" and "drug control." The UN agency that supervises world-wide drug prohibition is still called the International Narcotics Control Board.

In the last decade of the twentieth century, men and women in many countries became aware of *national* drug prohibition. They came to understand that the narcotic or drug policies of the United States and some other countries are properly termed *drug prohibition*. Even as this understanding spread, the fact that drug prohibition covers the entire world remained a kind of hidden-in-plain-view secret.

Now, in the twenty-first century, that too is changing. As global drug prohibition becomes more visible and easier to see, it loses some of its ideological and political powers.

The drug prohibition continuum

In *Crack in America: Demon Drugs and Social Justice* (1997), Reinarman and Levine suggested that the varieties of drug prohibition can be seen as a long continuum. At one end of the continuum are the most criminalized and punitive forms of drug prohibition; at the other end are the most decriminalized and regulated forms of drug prohibition.

The drug policy of the United States of America is the best known example of criminalized drug prohibition. It uses police and imprisonment to punish people who use specific psychoactive substances, even in minute quantities. US federal drug laws prohibit supervised medical use of cannabis by terminally ill cancer and AIDS patients. US drug prohibition gives long prison sentences for repeated possession, use, and small-scale distribution of forbidden drugs. Many US drug laws explicitly remove sentencing discretion from judges and do not allow for probation or parole. The United States now has nearly half a million men and women in prison for violating its drug laws. Most are poor, from racial minorities, and are imprisoned for possessing an illicit drug, or "intending" to sell small amounts of it. From 1988 to 2010, the mandatory federal penalty for possessing 5 grams of crack cocaine, for a first offense, has been 5 years in prison with no parole.

The cannabis policy of the Netherlands is the best known example of the other end of the drug prohibition continuum – of a decriminalized and regulated form of drug prohibition. Several UN drug treaties – especially the Single Convention on Narcotic Drugs of 1961 – require the Netherlands and other governments to have laws criminalizing the production and distribution of cannabis and other drugs. However, since the early 1980s, national legislation and policy in the Netherlands also limit the prosecution of over 800 cafes and snack bars that are licenced to sell small quantities of cannabis for personal use on premises and off. These "coffee shops" are permitted to operate as long as they are orderly and stay within well-defined limits that are monitored and enforced by the police. Like other formal illegal activities, cannabis sales are not taxed; the coffee shops cannot advertise cannabis, and they may sell only small amounts to adults.

Even as cannabis sales in the Netherlands are open, routine, and appear to be completely legal, importing and commercially producing this cannabis remain illegal. As a result, the coffee shops have always been supplied, as the Dutch say, through the "back door." This is still formal drug prohibition and the Netherlands prosecutes importers (smugglers), dealers, and commercial growers who handle large quantities of cannabis – as required by the UN anti-drug treaties. In short, for over two decades, the Netherlands has sustained a unique system of regulated, open, quasi-legal cannabis sales supplied by illegal importers and growers. This is as far as any country has been able to go within the current structures of global drug prohibition. However, beginning on January 1, 2012, The Netherlands banned entrance to "coffee shops" to anyone but Dutch citizens. This, no doubt, will have a profound effect on their tourism industry.

The prohibition policies of other Western countries fall between the heavily criminalized crack cocaine policies of the United States and the regulated cannabis prohibition of the Netherlands. No Western or democratic country has ever had forms of drug prohibition as criminalized and punitive as the United States, though some undemocratic governments have drug laws even harsher than the United States. Further, since at least the early 1990s, drug policy in Europe, Canada, Australia, and elsewhere has been shifting away from the criminalized end of the prohibition continuum. But all these countries are required by international treaties to have – and still do have – formal, legal, national drug prohibition.

The spread of drug prohibition throughout the world

Drug prohibition is a world-wide system of state power. Global drug prohibition is a "thing," a "social fact" (to use sociologist Emile Durkheim's term). Drug prohibition exists whether or not we recognize it, and it has real consequences.

National criminalized drug prohibition began in the 1920s in the United States as a subset of constitutional alcohol prohibition. In 1930 the US Congress separated drug prohibition from the increasingly disreputable alcohol prohibition and created a new federal drug prohibition agency, the Federal Bureau of Narcotics, headed by the committed alcohol prohibitionist Harry J. Anslinger. By that time there was massive, open violation of constitutional prohibition in most US cities. Then the enormous impoverishment, dislocation, and despair caused by the Great Depression further delegitimized alcohol prohibition. In 1933, a combination of majority votes in some state legislatures, and unprecedented state-wide public referendums in other states, ended national alcohol prohibition. The question of alcohol policy was turned back to state and local governments to do with as they wished. A few states retained alcohol prohibition for years, and many US counties today still have forms of alcohol prohibition.

The story of drug prohibition took an entirely different course. Since the early twentieth century, the United States found European governments far more willing to consider anti-narcotics legislation than anti-alcohol laws. The founding Covenant of the League of Nations explicitly mentioned the control of "dangerous drugs" as one of the organization's concerns. In the 1930s, with Anslinger's guidance, the United States helped write and gain acceptance for two international anti-drug conventions or treaties

aimed at "suppressing" narcotics and "dangerous drugs." In 1948 the new UN made drug prohibition one of its priorities. The UN Single Convention of 1961, as amended in 1972 supplemented by UN anti-drug treaties in 1971 and 1988, established the current system of global drug prohibition.

Since the early twentieth century, nearly every political persuasion and type of government has endorsed drug prohibition. Capitalist democracies took up drug prohibition, and so did authoritarian governments. German Nazis and Italian Fascists embraced drug prohibition, just as American politicians had. Various Soviet regimes enforced drug prohibition, as have their successors. In China, mandarins, militarists, capitalists, and communists all enforced drug prohibition regimes. Populist generals in Latin American and anti-colonialist intellectuals in Africa backed drug prohibition. Over the course of the twentieth century, drug prohibition was supported by liberal prime ministers, moderate monarchs, military strongmen, and Maoists. It was supported by prominent archbishops and radical priests, by nationalist heroes and imperialist puppets, by labor union leaders and sweat shop owners, by socialists, social workers, social scientists, and socialites – by all varieties of politicians, practicing all brands of politics, in all political systems. National drug prohibition was one of the most widely accepted, reputable, legitimate government policies of the entire twentieth century. Why should this be so?

The Usefulness of Drug Prohibition

There is no doubt that governments throughout the world have accepted drug prohibition because of enormous pressure from the US government and some powerful allies. But US power alone cannot explain the global acceptance of drug prohibition. Governments of all types, all over the world, have also found drug prohibition useful for their own purposes. There are several reasons for this.

The police and military powers of drug prohibition

Drug prohibition has given governments additional police and military powers. Anti-narcotics police and military units can legitimately do undercover investigations almost anywhere because almost anybody could be in the drug business. In the United States, more undercover police are in narcotics squads than in any other branch of police work. Police anti-drug squads can make secret recordings and photographs; they have cash for buying drugs and information. In the United States, anti-drug police often receive substantial federal subsidies; sometimes they are allowed to keep money, cars, houses, and other property that they seize. Top politicians and government officials in many countries may have believed deeply in the war on drugs and drug use. But other health-oriented causes could not have produced for them so much police, coast guard, and military power.

Government officials have used anti-drug squads to conduct surveillance operations and military raids that they would not otherwise have been able to justify. Many times anti-drug forces have been deployed against targets other than drug dealers and users – as was the case with US President Richard Nixon's own special White House anti-drug team, led by former CIA agents, which later became famous as the Watergate burglars. Nixon was brought down by his squad's mistakes. But over the years, government anti-drug forces have carried out numerous successful non-drug operations.

The uses of anti-drug messages and of drug demonization

Drug prohibition has been useful for governments and politicians because it has required at least some anti-drug crusades and what is properly called *drug demonization*. Anti-drug crusades articulate a moral ideology that depicts "drugs" as extremely dangerous and destructive substances. Under drug prohibition, the police, the media, and religious and health authorities tend to describe the risks and problems of drug use in extreme and exaggerated terms. "Drugs" are dangerous enemies. "Drugs" are called evil, vile, threatening, and powerfully addicting. Politicians and governments crusade against "drugs," declare war on them, and blame them for many unhappy conditions and events. Anti-drug crusades and drug scares popularize images of "drugs" as highly contagious invading evils. Words like plague, epidemic, scourge, and pestilence are used to describe psychoactive substances, drug use, and moderate, recreational drug users.

Government officials, the media, and other authorities have found that drug addiction, abuse, and even use can be blamed by almost anyone for long-standing problems, recent problems, and the worsening of almost anything. Theft, robbery, rape, malingering, fraud, corruption, physical violence, shoplifting, juvenile delinquency, sloth, sloppiness, sexual promiscuity, low productivity, and all around irresponsibility – nearly any social problem at all – can be said to be made worse by "drugs."

In a war on "drugs," defining the enemy necessarily involves defining and teaching about morality, ethics, and the good things to be defended. Since the temperance or anti-alcohol campaigns of the nineteenth century, anti-drug messages, especially those aimed at children and their parents, have had recognizable themes. Currently these anti-drug messages stress: individual responsibility for health and economic success, respect for police, resisting peer-group pressure, the value of God or a higher power in recovering from drug abuse, parents knowing where their children are, sports and exercise as alternatives to drug use, why sports heroes should be drug tested, low grades as evidence of drug use, abstinence as the cause of good grades, and parents setting good examples for their children. Many people – police, politicians, educators, medical authorities, religious leaders – can find some value that can be defended or taught while attacking "drugs."

Newspapers, magazines, and other media have long found that supporting anti-drug campaigns can be good for public relations and good for business. The media regularly editorially endorse government anti-drug efforts and favorably cover them as a "public service." For doing so, they are praised by government officials and prominent organizations. Further, since the 1920s, top editors in the news media have clearly recognized, as an economic fact of their business, that an alarming anti-drug story can increase sales of magazines and newspapers. This is especially so when the story is about drugs that threaten middle-class teenagers and their families. News editors and TV producers understand that a front page or "top of the news" story about a tempting, dangerous, illegal drug can attract readers and TV viewers. There is no doubt that many publishers, editors, and broadcasters have believed deeply in fighting drugs. But few of the causes that people in the media believe in can so easily be turned into stories that are simultaneously good for business and for public relations. As a result, it has not been difficult to get anti-drug messages to the public.

All forms of drug prohibition, from the most criminalized to the most decriminalized, have probably involved at least some explicit drug demonizing. In general, drug demonization and drug prohibition reinforce each other. But drug demonization existed before drug prohibition, and can certainly survive without it.

Drug prohibition unites political opponents

In the eighteenth and nineteenth centuries, many political movements and thinkers tended to distrust the police powers of the centralized state; they tended to favor greater liberty from state power and to believe that "power corrupts." In the twentieth century, however, liberals, conservatives, fascists, communists, socialists, populists, left-wingers, and right-wingers shared a more optimistic view of the benevolent effects of using state power to police morality and regulate daily life for the "common good." In the twentieth century, politicians, voters, and political movements were often willing to use state police power against public and private behavior they did not like. Drug prohibition benefited from this.

Because politicians in many countries from one end of the political spectrum to the other shared an overwhelmingly negative view of psychoactive "drugs," a largely positive view of government police power, and because drug prohibition was so useful, they could all agree on drug prohibition as good non-partisan policy. In the United States during the 1980s and the 1990s, Democrats feared and detested Presidents Reagan and both President Bushes, and Republicans feared and detested President Clinton. But the parties united to wage the "War on Drugs." They even competed to enact more punitive anti-drug laws, build more prisons, hire more drug police, expand antidrug military forces, and fund many more government sponsored anti-drug messages and "drug-free" crusades. Opposing political parties around the world have disagreed about many things, but until recently they have often joined together to fight "drugs."

The influence of the United Nations

Drug prohibition has also enjoyed widespread support and legitimacy because the United States has used the UN as the international agency to create, spread, and supervise world-wide prohibition. Other than the government of the United States, the UN has done more to defend and extend drug prohibition than any other organization in the world. The UN currently identifies the goal of its anti-drug efforts as "a drug-free world."

The spread of drug prohibition in the twentieth century

To summarize: In the twentieth century, drug prohibition spread from the United States to every country in the world, for a number of reasons. First, drug prohibition spread so successfully because of the enormous economic, political, and military power of the United States. Second, many different kinds of governments throughout the world supported drug prohibition because they found that police and military resources marshaled on behalf of drug prohibition could be used for many nondrug-related activities. Third, drug prohibition also gained substantial popular support in many countries because drug demonization crusades and anti-drug ideology were rhetorically, politically, and even financially useful to many politicians, the media, schools, the police, the military, religious institutions, and some elements of the medical profession. Fourth, the spread of drug prohibition was aided by the twentieth century's ideologies about the benefits of coercive state power, making the fight against "drugs" the one topic on which politicians of all stripes could usually agree. Finally, drug prohibition gained great legitimacy throughout the world because it was seen as a UN project.

The growing crises of global drug prohibition

Since the early 1980s, global drug prohibition has had to face ever growing challenges to its authority and legitimacy. Two of these crises stand out: First, the continued growth of a serious, reputable opposition to criminalized and punitive drug policies. And second, the inability of drug prohibition to stop the cultivation and use of cannabis throughout the world.

The rising opposition to punitive drug policies

In many countries increasing numbers of people – physicians, lawyers, judges, police, journalists, scientists, public health officials, teachers, religious leaders, social workers, drug users, and drug addicts – now openly criticize the more extreme, punitive, and criminalized forms of drug prohibition. These critics, from across the political spectrum, have pointed out that punitive drug policies are expensive, ineffective at reducing drug use, take scarce resources away from other health and policing activities, and are often racially and ethnically discriminatory. Criminalized drug prohibition violates civil liberties, imprisons many nonviolent offenders, builds huge criminal and DNA databases, ruins the lives of many petty offenders, and worsens serious health problems such as the AIDS epidemic. The international harm reduction movement is a major part of the critical opposition to punitive drug policies. Indeed, harm reduction is the first popular, international movement to develop within drug prohibition to openly challenge drug demonization and the more criminalized forms of drug prohibition.

The harm reduction and drug policy reformers have changed the debate. For example the British business magazine, *The Economist,* has endorsed decriminalization, harm reduction, and even consideration of drug legalization. *The Economist* also reported that US government anti-drug publications "are full of patently false claims" and that US drug policy "has proved a dismal rerun of America's attempt, in 1920–33, to prohibit the sale of alcohol."

As drug policy reform movements have grown, supporters of drug prohibition have been discovering that they cannot make the critics of criminalized prohibition go away. In the reports of the International Narcotics Control Board and other publications, the most knowledgeable defenders of drug prohibition warn regularly about the increasing growth of cannabis cultivation and use on every continent, and about the increasing legitimacy given to the critics of drug prohibition. These defenders of global drug prohibition recognize that the advocates of decriminalized drug

prohibition – and the political, economic, and cultural forces driving that opposition – are gaining strength and legitimacy.

All of this opposition is fairly recent. For much of its history, global drug prohibition has had very few critics. Even today, despite the impressive growth in many countries of the harm reduction movement and of drug policy reform activities, world-wide drug prohibition still has very few explicit opponents. One reason for the lack of organized opposition to the drug treaties is that until recently the global drug prohibition system has been so invisible and undiscussed. In effect, global drug prohibition has operated for many years as a kind of official secret. Its existence was on a "need to know basis," and most people, it seems, did not need to know.

Further, even fewer people currently understand that by ending or even modifying the Single Convention on Narcotic Drugs of 1961, the question of national drug policy could be returned to individual countries and local governments to handle as they wished. Defenders of global drug prohibition like to evoke an international conspiracy of what they call "drug legalizers." But nobody thus far has tried to launch even a half-baked international campaign with slogans like "Repeal the Single Convention" or "End Global Drug Prohibition."

Yet it may well be that the Single Convention stands in much the same relationship to world-wide drug prohibition that the 18th Amendment to the Constitution and the Volstead Act stood in relation to US alcohol prohibition. Once the 18th Amendment was gone, state and local governments were free to create alcohol policy at the local level. If the Single Convention was repealed, or even modified, national governments around the world would be freer to create drug laws and policies geared to their own conditions – including prohibition if they should so desire.

At present, many nations, and many more regional and local governments, are reforming their drug policies, expanding harm reduction, and adopting less criminalized forms of drug prohibition. But no national government is even discussing withdrawing from the Single Convention and global drug prohibition. In addition to the domestic political obstacles to such a move, a potential "rogue" nation confronts international barriers in the form of economic and political sanctions from the United States and its allies. Therefore, no single country can now formally end its national prohibition regime and completely "defect" from the world-wide prohibitionist system.

The crisis of cannabis prohibition

Global drug prohibition's most glaring weakness and greatest vulnerability is cannabis. As UN experts point out, cannabis is by far the most widely used illegal drug in the world. Cannabis grows wild throughout the world, and is commercially cultivated in remote areas, in backyard gardens, and in technologically sophisticated indoor farms. Just as it was impossible for prohibitionists to prevent alcohol from being produced and used in the United States in the 1920s, so too it is now impossible to prevent cannabis from being produced and widely used, especially in democratic countries. As a result of this enormous and unstoppable production and use, global cannabis prohibition faces a growing crisis of legitimacy.

Since the 1980s, the Netherlands has successfully administered its system of regulated, decriminalized cannabis sales. A generation of Europeans, Australians, North Americans, and others have learned from the Dutch experience. Politicians, policy makers, police officials, journalists, and ordinary tourists from many countries have seen that decriminalizing drug use and regulating cannabis sales have substantial advantages and benefits – especially when compared with the disadvantages and costs of punitive US drug policies. The continued success of the Netherlands' strikingly different and less punitive cannabis policy alternative – within drug prohibition – has undermined the US anti-drug crusade and contributed to the spread of de facto and formal cannabis decriminalization.

Further, since the 1960s recreational cannabis use has been steadily normalized in many parts of the world, especially among young adults. Prominent middle-aged politicians admit they have used cannabis without deleterious effects. As a result, it has become much harder for drug war advocates to persuasively portray cannabis as one of the dangerous, evil "drugs." Punitive drug prohibition still requires drug demonization. But defenders of cannabis prohibition find it increasingly difficult to offer plausible

justifications for harsh anti-cannabis laws, or even for the Single Convention's cannabis policies. Growing numbers of prominent, influential individuals and organizations are concluding that criminalized cannabis prohibition causes more problems than cannabis use.

In recent years, some veteran drug policy reformers have confronted the problem of the currently invincible drug treaties. Like Professor Peter Cohen of the University of Amsterdam and Dr Alex Wodak of St Vincents Hospital in Sydney, they have suggested that the Single Convention and other narcotics treaties are an unenforceable "paper tiger" or even a "paper corpse." In private conversations and public meetings, these critics recommend that policy makers disregard the anti-drug treaties when considering drug policy reforms within their own countries. Public officials in a number of countries seem increasingly open to such arguments, at least for cannabis. In Europe, political support for harm reduction programs and drug policy reform has become so strong that some government officials have discussed systems for licencing cannabis production.

Openly licencing, regulating, and taxing cannabis production moves well beyond what the Netherlands has ever done. Licencing production as well as sales creates cannabis legalization within one country. At some point, Switzerland, the Netherlands, and other countries could choose to licence cannabis farms for domestic consumption. In so doing they would build upon the Dutch experience, but would completely bypass the Netherlands' complicated problems of "backdoor" and illegal cannabis supply. When officials have substantial domestic public support, they will be freer to ignore international pressure and define their own nation's situation as a permissible exception to the anti-drug treaties. And countries that may decide for various reasons to allow open sales may also decide to grow their own supply. In short, sooner or later some Western country is likely to be the first to create a system of licenced, regulated, and taxed cannabis sale and production, despite the narcotics treaties.

And before that happens, some state, regional, or local government may do so first. The referendum process in California put Proposition 19 on the ballot for the 2010 election. Prop 19, as it was called, would have legalized possession of less than an ounce of marijuana. It also would have permitted people to grow a small plot of cannabis plants at home. And it would have permitted local governments to licence and tax the sale of small amounts of marijuana. This is completely legal for a state to do. States do not need to have marijuana prohibition laws just because the federal government does. Prop 19 lost in 2010, but similar measures will be on the ballot of other states in the coming years, perhaps Washington, Oregon, Nevada, and Colorado (western states with strong referendum systems). And eventually one of these will win. If it should be in the state of California, the largest in the country, with forty million inhabitants, it would have a huge impact on the rest of America.

In political democracies, when laws and policies are unenforceable and unpopular, over time *de facto* changes usually become *de jure* (in law). This process occurs with international laws as well. For opiates, stimulants, and other drugs, the ongoing trend of increasing decriminalization, harm reduction, and medical use could continue for decades within global drug prohibition. But cannabis is a different story. In some countries, cannabis use and cultivation already threatens to burst the bounds of the international drug treaties. Even drug prohibitionists who study global trends openly worry about their capacity to make world-wide cannabis prohibition a workable system.

Recently, some students of global drug policies have begun urging serious attention to modifying the drug treaties to bring them more in line with current practice and proposed changes. The Dutch researcher Martin Jelsma has likened defenders of punitive drug policies and the UN treaties to a *Monty Python* sketch where a pet shop clerk cheerfully tries to sell a dead parrot. "It's not dead," the salesman tells the incredulous customer, "it's just resting." Jelsma suggests rejecting such arguments and points out that policy makers in a number of countries have urged international discussions about modifying the drug treaties.

Calls and pressure for modifying the treaties are likely to increase in coming years. And whatever happens with efforts to reform the Single Convention and other drug treaties, some Western democracies, and local governments within them, are likely to continue moving toward creating their own new internal policies for cannabis sales, distribution, and even production.

The End of Global Drug Prohibition?

Global drug prohibition is in crisis. The fact that it is becoming visible is one symptom of that crisis. In the short run, that crisis seems certain to deepen, especially for cannabis prohibition and the more punitive and criminalized drug policies. In the long run, for a variety of practical and ideological reasons – especially the spread of information, democracy, and trade – democratic governments in Europe and elsewhere are likely to transform and eventually dismantle world-wide drug prohibition.

If and when this happens, it would not mean the end of all local or national drug prohibition. Rather, ending global drug prohibition, like ending constitutional alcohol prohibition in the United States, would clear the path for hundreds of local experiments in drug policy. Many communities and some nations would likely retain forms of drug prohibition and continue to support vigorous anti-drug crusades. But most democratic and open societies probably would not choose to retain full-scale criminalized drug prohibition. Over time democratic societies will gradually develop their own varied local forms of regulated personal cultivation, production, and use of the once prohibited plants and substances. Many places will also allow some forms of commercial growing, production, and sale – first of all of cannabis.

All of this could take a long time. Drug prohibitionists in every country, especially prosecutors and police departments, can be expected to fight tenaciously to maintain their local regimes. And it is likely that enormous power will be employed to prevent the Single Convention of 1961 and its related treaties from being repealed or modified.

As a result, in coming years there will be even more public discussion and debate about the varieties of drug prohibition and about the alternatives to it. As part of that conversation, many more people will discover – often with considerable astonishment – that they have lived for decades within the invisible system of global drug prohibition. That growing understanding will itself push global drug prohibition closer to its end.

Questions

1 Why do you think the US government has put enormous pressure on other countries across the world to accept and support drug prohibition? How might this international prohibition contribute to the globalization of the illegal drug market? According to the article, why is the global drug prohibition system so useful? How might legalization and control be useful in a similar manner?

2 Do you think the goal of a "drug-free world" identified by the United Nations may shift as the economic and political power of the United States changes? Why or why not? Do you think the current changes in marijuana policy in the United States will pave the way for international changes? Why or why not?

3 Do you agree that until recently the global drug prohibition system has been invisible? Do you think there are currently any organizations/countries with the power to challenge world drug prohibition? Why do countries across the world adhere to the "Single Convention?"

Index

abuse: by adolescents, 329; alcohol and, 8; club drugs and, 238; mothers and drug, 162, 163; pharmacists and drug, 123, 128; prescriptions and, 20; recognition of, 14; recovery from, 344; therapeutic communities and drug, 336; violence and, 280

Adams, Samuel Hopkins: as reformer, 14

addiction, 127, 129, 159–72, 330–1; alcohol and, 96; circumventing treatment and, 354–5; controlled use phase of, 205–7, 233–5; definition of, 81; disease model of, 211; elements of cessation, 355–7; employment and, 99; frequency of, 10; heroin and, 70–1, 75, 83–4, 109; identity and, 353; infrequency of, 10; initiation, 91, 109; junkie phase of, 210–11; losing control over, 207–8, 235–7; medicalization of, 380–1; methadone maintenance and, 344–50; methamphetamine and, 235–7; morphine and, 10, 11; opium, 11; pharmaceuticals and, 190; quitting, 70–1, 99–100, 190–1, 200, 237–8; race and, 70; rates of, 12; size of habit, 83, 117, 164, 167, 209, 253; steroids and, 115; stigmatization of, 351–2; tolerance and, 126–7, 244; treatment and, 336–43; veterans and, 10, 28–9

adolescents and young adults, 72–9, 131–9, 141–51, 152–60, 184–92, 199, 215–23, 240–8, 266–76; 237–334, 370–7; arrest and, 328; binge drinking and, 370–7; drug abuse by, 329; rates of drug consumption, 328–9

adults, 64–71, 72–9, 120–30, 159–72, 205–12, 224–30, 231–9, 249–55, 336–43; drug courts and, 359–68; drug treatment for, 336–43, 344–50; methadone maintenance and, 344–50

African Americans: cocaine use and, 12–13, 102–11, 193–202, 224–30; crack use and, 266–76; drug robbery and 285–93; heroin use and, 80–6, 193–202, 205–12, 224–30, 266–76; jail and, 105, 380; marijuana and, 42; methamphetamine and, 205–12; percentage of population as new inmates in, 73; war on drugs and, 380; women, 257–65

age: adolescents and young adults, 72–9, 131–9, 141–51, 152–60, 184–92, 199, 215–23, 240–8, 266–76, 327–34, 370–7; adults, 64–71, 72–9, 120–30, 159–72, 205–12, 224–30, 231–9, 249–55, 285–93, 336–43, 351–8, 359–68; children, 174–83, 316–26; older, 80–6, 193–202

alcohol: absorption of, 6; abuse of, 8, 370–7; American Indians and, 94–100; antidote for, 6; aqua vitae, 5; binge drinking, xiv, xv, 96, 144, 155–8, 370–7; blood alcohol content (BAC), 7; consumption with food, 26–7; consumption rates, 56; costs of abuse, 8; cross-cultural differences in use of, 372–3; discovery of, 5; effects of, 6, 7;

ethnic differences and, 371–2; femininity and use of, 155–6, 158–9; history of, 5, 25–6; learning consumption limits of, 27; malnutrition and, 6; masculinity and, 152–60; metabolization, 6–7, 8; moderate use of, 26; motherhood health and, 7–8; national differences in use of, 372; natural recovery from, 352; nutritional value of, 7; oral ingestion of, 152–60; pervasiveness of, 4; policies of abstinence versus reality, 373–4; religious differences and, 371–2; social connectedness and, 96–9; socialization to, 27, 28; strength (proof) of, 6; tolerance to, 8; underage use of, 370–7; violence and, 8

Alcoholics Anonymous, 344–50; circumventing treatment and, 354–5; disease model and, 347, 353–7; meetings of, 361–2; skepticism toward, 353–5

American Indians: alcohol use and, 94–100

Amethyst Initiative, xiv

Anslinger, Harry J., 42, 379, 393

arrest: adolescents and, 328; corruption and, 299; dealing and, 109, 110; domestic violence and, 108; drug abuse monitoring (ADAM), 286; drug courts and, 360, 385; drug testing and, 309; drug use and, 208, 286; effects on children, 168; family and, 109; fear of, 196; gang membership and, 267, 269, 270, 273–4; history of, 28; marijuana possession and, 76, 175, 390;